IET COMPUTING SERIES 33

Edge Computing

Models, technologies and applications

Other volumes in this series:

Edge Computing
Models, technologies and applications

Edited by
Javid Taheri and Shuiguang Deng

The Institution of Engineering and Technology

Published by The Institution of Engineering and Technology, London, United Kingdom

The Institution of Engineering and Technology is registered as a Charity in England & Wales (no. 211014) and Scotland (no. SC038698).

© The Institution of Engineering and Technology 2020

First published 2020

The Institution of Engineering and Technology
Michael Faraday House
Six Hills Way, Stevenage
Herts, SG1 2AY, United Kingdom

www.theiet.org

British Library Cataloguing in Publication Data
A catalogue record for this product is available from the British Library

ISBN 978-1-78561-940-3 (hardback)
ISBN 978-1-78561-941-0 (PDF)

Typeset in India by MPS Limited
Printed in the UK by CPI Group (UK) Ltd, Croydon

Javid:

To my beloved Hadis and precious Lyanna

Shuiguang:

To all my family members for their love and support

Contents

Editors' biographies

Javid Taheri is a full professor at the Department of Computer Science of Karlstad University, Sweden. His areas of interest include profiling, modelling and optimization techniques for private and public cloud infrastructures and software-defined networks, and network-aware scheduling algorithms for edge, cloud and green computing. He is the recipient of the prestigious IEEE TSCS-MCR award in 2019. He is the editor of the IET book *Big Data and Software Defined Networks* in 2018 (ISBN: 978-1-78561-304-3).

Shuiguang Deng is a full professor in the College of Computer Science and Technology, Zhejiang University, China, where he received a PhD degree in Computer Science. His research interests include edge computing, service computing, mobile computing and business process management. He serves as associate editor for the journals *IEEE Access* and *IET Cyber-Physical Systems: Theory & Applications*. He has published three monographs. In 2018, he was granted the Rising Star Award by IEEE TCSVC.

Preface

The past ten years have witnessed the rapid developments and applications of cloud computing, which has evolved as a cost-effective, easy-to-use, elastic and scalable computing paradigm to transform today's business models. Recent technological trends such as Industry 4.0 and China-2050, however, have introduced new challenges that cannot be solved using current cloud architectures. Such ambitions demand the connection of thousands, if not millions, of sensors and actuators coupled with optimized operations to automate various operations inside factories, cities or even countries. This led to a new era where lightweight devices are envisaged to send vital information to computing platforms for further processing and decision-making.

Despite being large-scaled and powerful, current cloud computing architectures are not able to efficiently digest and process collected information from such vast number of devices and actuators, especially for those with strict requirements such as communication delay or processing deadlines. To address these issues, the new computing paradigm of 'Edge Computing' is proposed and has rapidly attracted great attention from both academia and industry. Edge Computing aims to push the frontier of computing applications, data and services away from centralized nodes to the very edge network where analytics and knowledge generation can occur at the source of the data.

This book aims to focus only on the 'Edge Computing' paradigm – as opposed to other similar disciplines such as Fog Computing – due to its unique characteristics where heterogeneous devices can be equipped with decision-making processes and automation procedures to carry out applications (mostly) across widely geographically distributed areas.

The book is sectioned into three parts (Models, Technologies and Applications) to reflect complementary viewpoints and shed light onto various aspect of Edge Computing platforms. The first part (Models) serves as an introductory section to differentiate Edge Computing from its fairly close/similar paradigms such as Fog Computing, Multi-access Edge Computing and Mobile Cloud Computing. It then highlights various theoretical models through which Edge Computing systems could be mathematically expressed and their relevant technological problems could be systematically solved or optimized. The second part (Technologies) focuses on different technologies (virtualization, networking, orchestration, etc.) where Edge Computing systems could be realized. And finally, the third part (Applications) focuses on various application domains (e.g., smart cities) where Edge Computing systems could, or already did, help in providing novel services beyond the reach of pure/typical cloud computing solutions.

Prof. Javid Taheri
Karlstad University, Sweden

Prof. Shuiguang Deng
Zhejiang University, China

Acknowledgements

First and foremost, we would like to thank and acknowledge the contributors to this book for their support and patient, and the reviewers for their useful comments and suggestions that helped in improving earlier outlines of the book. We would also like to thank the IET (Institution of Engineering and Technology) editorial and production teams for their extensive efforts during many phases of this project and the timely manner in which the book was produced.

Part I

Models

Chapter 1

Introduction to edge computing

Auday Al-Dulaimy[1], Yogesh Sharma[1],
Michel Gokan Khan[1] and Javid Taheri[1]

Edge computing is the model that extends cloud computing services to the edge of the network. This model aims to move decision-making operations as close as possible to data sources since it acts as an intermediate layer connecting cloud data centres to edge devices/sensors. Transferring all the data from the network edge to the cloud data centres for processing may create a latency problem and outstrip the network's bandwidth capacity. To resolve this issue, it might be best to process data closer to the devices/sensors. This chapter will take a deep dive into edge computing, its applications, and the existing challenges related to this model.

1.1 Evolution of computing systems

Computing has come a long way from where it started. At the very beginning, a computer could only perform one task at a time. Several distributed computers had to run in parallel when performing multiple tasks, and distributed systems were formed by connecting those computers, which usually communicated and coordinated their actions through message exchange. Then, personal computers and multitasking operating systems emerged and made it possible to run multiple tasks on the same computer. This enabled the systems' developers to build and run an entire system within one or more connected computers. As the price of computing power and storage fell, organisations all over the world started using distributed systems. The breakthrough time of distributed systems came when Internet-based companies became so large that they needed to build distributed systems that spanned across the World as data centres. The standardisation of the concept of distributed computing led to the development of other models, including cluster computing, autonomic computing, utility computing, and grid computing. Engineers and developers then started to think about a way to create multiple virtual computers within the same machine. This led to the concept of virtualisation by which the same computer could act as multiple computers all running at the same time. On top of these predecessor models, the

[1] Department of Mathematics and Computer Science, Karlstad University, Karlstad, Sweden

construction of the cloud computing model was a natural step forward from grid computing [1]. Cloud computing leveraged the existing models and used the virtualisation concept to provide users with new services including new features and characteristics [2].

That was a good idea, but it was not the best option when it came to the utilisation of the resource of the host computer. Running multiple operating systems required using additional resources that were not needed when running one operating system. This led to the invention of containers in which multiple programs required separate runtime when using the same host operating system kernel. Containers act as virtual machines without the need for a separate overhead operating system. Due to its innovative characteristics and services, the cloud computing model has captured significant attention among individual users, academia, industries, and even governments. Cloud computing services are offered by providing access to a wide range of infrastructures hosted on cloud data centres [3]. Despite the increasing usage of cloud computing, its inherent issues remain unresolved. These include unreliable latency, lack of mobility support, location-awareness, as well as privacy and security issues. Other models have emerged in an attempt to solve these problems, but edge computing is still the most promising state-of-the-art computing system that continues to evolve.

1.2   An overview of edge computing

The idea of having computational resources near the data sources might not be something new [4]. The term 'edge computing' first appeared in 2002, to state that from a business perspective, applications should be served and moved from the cloud data centre to the network edge [5]. The term was then used in 2004 to describe a system that distributed program methods and the corresponding data to the edge of the network in order to enhance the system's performance [6]. Edge computing continued to advance until it was able to resolve many of the problems associated with cloud computing, as it provided elastic resources to end users at the edge of the network, at a time when cloud computing could only provide resources distributed and hosted on cloud data centres in the core network.

This section defines edge computing, discusses its concept, introduces representative application scenarios, and identifies various aspects of issues that may arise when designing and implementing edge computing systems. It also highlights some opportunities and challenges and serves as a guidance for potential future work in related techniques.

1.2.1   Motivation

As stated in Section 1.1, computing systems evolved from using one computer to perform one or more tasks to providing centralised and consolidated services and applications in the cloud data centres that emerged in the last decade. Recent technological developments such as powerful domestic connection boxes, high-capacity mobile end-user devices, wireless networks, and the increasing user concerns about reliability, privacy, and autonomy all call for controlling computing applications, data, and services from the logical extreme (the 'edge') of the Internet rather than from the central nodes (the 'core') [7]. The centralised nature of remote computing resources hinders their ability to handle huge data traffic originating from geographically dispersed edge devices. Thus, it is necessary to push the servers to the edge of the network, and it is actually an unavoidable trend as shifting towards (the 'edge') becomes indispensable. Several factors make edge computing an essential necessity, and such factors must be examined independently from the end users' and operators' perspective. The following requirements propel computing to move to the edge and they explain why edge computing is an essential model [8,9].

Push from cloud services: Placing all computing tasks on the cloud has proved to be an effective method for data processing, because the computing power on the cloud surpasses the capacity of the things on the edge. However, the network suffers a deadlock compared to the speed of the rapidly developing data processing. As the amount of data generated at the edge continues to increase, the speed of data transportation impedes the traffic flow in the cloud-based computing model. Two examples can be given here: The first example, in [10], states that a Boeing 787 generates about 5 gigabytes of data every second, but the bandwidth between the aircraft and either the satellite or the base station on the ground is insufficient for data transmission. The second example in [11] states that a vehicle generates 1 gigabyte of data every second, and that the vehicle needs real-time processing in order to make correct decisions. Sending all data to the cloud for processing would ineffectively prolong the response time. It would also pose a challenge on the reliability of the current network bandwidth and its ability to support a large number of vehicles in one area. Thus, processing data at the edge ensures less response time and network pressure as well as better processing.

Pull from Internet of things (IoT): In the near future, most electric devices will be included in the IoT, and they will play the roles of both data producers and consumers alike, such as air quality sensors, light-emitting diode (LED) bars, streetlights, and even an Internet-connected microwave oven [8]. We can conclude that, in a few years, the number of things on the edge will exceed billions. Thus, they will produce massive raw data that the standard cloud computing model will not be able to handle. This leads to the fact that most IoT data will not make its way to the cloud, and will rather be consumed at the network edge. The classical structure of the cloud computing model is inadequate for IoT for many reasons: First, the amount of data at the edge is too large and it utilises a lot of unnecessary bandwidth and computing resources. Second, the requirement for privacy protection hinders cloud computing in IoT. Third, energy constraints restrict most of the IoT end nodes, and the wireless communication module usually consumes a lot of energy, so it might be more energy efficient to discharge some computing tasks to the edge.

Change from data consumer to producer: The front-end devices at the edge usually act as a data consumer in the cloud computing model, such as watching a YouTube video on your smart phone, but nowadays people are also generating data via their mobile devices. Switching from data consumer to data producer/consumer requires more peripheral placement. For instance, people nowadays normally take pictures or record videos and then share the data via a cloud service such as Twitter, Snapchat, and Instagram. Twitter users sent around 473,400 tweets per minute in 2018; Snapchat users shared 2,038,333 snaps; and Instagram users posted 49,380 new photos in that year [12]. However, uploading a large image or a video clip would occupy a lot of bandwidth, and this requires adjusting the video clip to an appropriate resolution before uploading it on the cloud. Wearable health devices can also be an example. As physical data collected by the things at the edge of the network are often privately owned, users privacy could be better protected by processing data at the edge rather than uploading them on the cloud.

Decentralised cloud and low-latency computing: Centralised cloud computing is not always the ideal strategy for geographically distributed applications. To enhance the service provided, the computing must be done closer to the data source. For any web-based application, this benefit can be generalised [13]. Recently, users have become more interested in using location-aware applications, and this entices application providers to improve their service by computing on edge nodes that are closer to users. Edge devices generate many data streams, and performing the analytics on a distant cloud obstructs real-time decision-making. Using current cloud infrastructures in real-time applications causes serious latency issues between an edge device and the cloud, and any potential delay would not be in line with the requirements of latency-sensitive applications. Video streaming generates most of the mobile traffic, and it is still difficult to maintain users' satisfaction when the majority of the network traffic flows to the same source. In the same way, gamers face similar latency obstacles when using multimedia applications [9]. In this case, employing edge nodes closer to users can minimise network latency to enhance the computations performed on the cloud.

Surmounting resource limitations of front-end devices: User devices have somewhat restrained hardware resources when compared to compute and/or storage resources of the servers hosted within a cloud data centre. Front-end devices can be mainly divided into two types [14]: devices carried by people and others placed in the environment. The main role of the two front-end device types is to obtain real-time data by capturing sensory input in the form of text, audio, video, touch, or motion, and then cloud services process the transferred data. These devices, however, are unable to perform complex analytics due to their hardware limitations. Therefore, data often needs to be transmitted to the cloud to meet computational processing requirements and to send back useful information to the front-end device. However, the service does not have to use all the data it receives from the front-end device in order to build analytical cloud workloads. Data can possibly be filtered or even analysed at edge nodes, which may have spare computer resources for managing data [9].

Sustainable energy consumption: Numerous energy-consuming data centres have been recently established worldwide. However, the financial and environmental impact of the high energy consumption at these data centres is a major issue that needs to be tackled, and enhancing the energy efficiency of such data centres is a main challenge in the cloud computing model. As the number of applications moving on to the cloud is increasing, the growing energy demand may become unsustainable.

For this purpose, it is highly important to develop energy-efficiency strategies and to propose new approaches to enhance energy efficiency in cloud data centre [3,15]. To some extent, integration of practical power management strategies could contribute to a reduction in energy consumption. Some analytical tasks could be done on edge nodes, such as base stations or routers, that are closer to the data source, rather than overloading data centres with minor tasks that could be carried out at edge notes with minimal energy consumption [9].

Dealing with data explosion and network traffic: Cloud providers expand their infrastructure to include IoT devices/sensors at the edge of the network, so as to meet the rapidly growing demands for cloud services, and the number of these devices/sensors has significantly increased. Cisco Internet Business Solutions Group predicts that 50 billion devices will be connected to the Internet by 2020 [16], and according to the International Data Corporation (IDC), approximately 80 billion devices will be connected to the internet by 2025 [17]. Data generating from those IoT devices/sensors continues to increase rapidly. The work in [9] states that 43 trillion gigabytes of data are expected to be produced by 2020. The architecture of the cloud computing model is not designed to work with the volume, variety, and speed of data generated by edge devices/sensors. Thus, data centres have to expand to carry out monitoring tasks and analytical workloads. However, this raises further concerns about sustainable energy consumption at data centres, because resource limitations on the edge devices make it difficult to perform analytics on the edge device. Collective analytics (of multi-edge devices) cannot be performed on edge devices either. The volume of network traffic to and from clouds data centres is another concern with increasing data generation, as it causes delays edge devices and depletes the network bandwidth capacity. In this case, using very close nodes in the network to complement the device computations or those of the data centre would solve the issue of handling data growth and the distribution of traffic in a network.

Smart computation techniques: In order to reduce latency and minimise the impact of energy consumption of data generated by end users to and from cloud data centres, there is a need to adopt a collaborative approach in the manipulation of network resources and the distribution of computation among these sources. The work in [9] identifies two cases of computation distribution. In the first case, the generated data are filtered on the front-end device by the application pipeline, and then edge nodes carry out the workload analysis, while the more complex tasks are done at the cloud nodes. The second case allows data centres to offload computations requiring limited resources on to edge nodes, or it allows the edge nodes to use volunteer devices to enhance computational capacities. Edge nodes have the ability to facilitate computations closer to the source, and they can also incorporate strategies to remotely enhance front-end device capabilities.

1.2.2 Definition

Many definitions for edge computing have been proposed over the past years. However, no standard definition exists. The most widely adopted definitions are as follows.

As defined by the authors in [8] and [18], '*Edge Computing refers to the enabling technologies allowing computation to be performed at the edge of the network, on downstream data on behalf of cloud services and upstream data on behalf of IoT services*'. In [19], '*Edge Computing is the model that pushes localised processing in the advanced manner, i.e., closer to the data source*'. As defined in [20], '*Edge Computing is an umbrella term covering the latest trend of bringing the computational resources to the proximity of the end devices*'. The author in [21] stated that '*Edge Computing is moving processing close to where data is being generated*'. Another work [22] defined edge computing as follows: '*Edge Computing is a new paradigm in which substantial computing and storage resources (variously referred to as cloudlets, micro data centers, or fog nodes) are placed at the Internet's edge in close proximity to mobile devices or sensors.*' In [23], '*Edge Computing refers to applications, services, and processing performed outside of a central data center and closer to end users. The definition of "closer" falls along a spectrum and depends highly on networking technologies used, the application characteristics, and the desired end user experience*'.

Edge computing can, therefore, be defined as the model that optimises cloud computing systems by processing data close to its source at the edge of the network. It enables technologies to place computing/storage resources at a close proximity to the data source, mainly to the edge of the network.

1.2.3   Architecture

The philosophy of edge computing is primarily based on performing computation at the edge that is in the proximity of a data source. Edge computing resources can be a network or a computing resource run among end users on the one side, and fog nodes and cloud data centres on the other. The interconnected sensors/devices at the IoT layer generate and transfer data among each other using a modern communication network infrastructure. Generated data are processed at other layers determined by specific application requirements. Edge computing architecture can be explained in four layers: IoT layer, edge layer, fog layer, and cloud layer. Figure 1.1 illustrates the architecture of edge computing.

In this architecture, IoT layer includes millions of devices/sensors which constantly produce data, exchange important information amongst themselves through a modern communication network infrastructure, and monitor and control critical smart-world infrastructures. All these IoT devices/sensors are end users for edge computing.

IoT and edge computing are rapidly evolving in an independent manner. However, the edge computing platform can assist IoT in resolving a number of key issues and improving performance. In general, IoT devices/sensors can benefit from the high computational capacity and large storage of the edge, fog, and cloud computing layers. However, edge computing has further advantages over fog and cloud computing for IoT, even though its occupational capacity and storage are more limited. IoT specifically requires fast response time rather than high computational capacity and large storage. Edge computing offers a tolerable computational capacity, enough

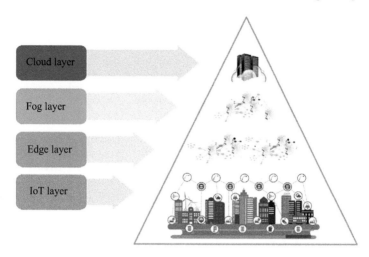

Figure 1.1   Edge computing architecture

storage space, and fast response time to satisfy IoT application requirements. Edge computing can benefit from IoT by extending the edge computing structure so that it can handle the distributed edge computing nodes. IoT devices can be used as edge nodes to provide services. As the number of IoT devices continues to grow, IoT and edge computing are likely to become inseparable. Edge computing can also benefit from the fog computing layer, as the resources capabilities on the fog layer are relatively stronger than those on the edge layer.

In the literature, edge computing and fog computing are sometimes used interchangeably, or considered as one layer. However, edge computing focuses more on the side of the things, while fog computing focuses on the side of infrastructure. The cloud computing layer consists of multiple high-performance servers and storage devices. Among all layers, the cloud computing layer has the highest computation power and storage capacity.

1.2.4   Characteristics

In general, IoT and edge computing have similar characteristics with regard to the IoT layer. On the other hand, edge computing has a lot of common characteristics with fog computing.

The prime objectives of edge computing and fog computing are similar. Both models bring cloud computing capabilities to the edge of the network. They enable the computation and storage capacities located within a close proximity to end users to reduce service latency and to save network bandwidth for delay-sensitive applications [24]. Both edge and fog computing models have distributed, hierarchical, and decentralised architectures which are different from the centralised cloud computing architecture. Their service locations are also at a close proximity to end users. Edge computing is located on edge devices, while fog computing takes place in network

Table 1.1　Characteristics of IoT, edge, fog, and cloud computing

Characteristic	IoT	Edge	Fog	Cloud
Deployment	Distributed	Distributed	Distributed	Centralised
Components	Physical devices	Edge nodes	Fog nodes	Virtual resources
Location awareness	Aware	Aware	Aware	Not aware
Computational	Limited	Limited	Limited	Unlimited
Storage	Very limited	Limited	Limited	Unlimited
Data	Source	Process	Process	Process
Distance to data source	The source	The nearest	Near	Far
Response time	No response time	The fastest	Fast	Slow
Nodes count	The largest	Very large	Large	Small

edge devices that are one or a few network hops away from the edge. When compared to cloud computing resources, those of the edge and fog computing models (e.g. computing, communication, and storage resources) are quite limited. Network edge devices also have a relatively higher resource and service capability than those of edge devices.

In some works, the edge and fog computing models are considered to be one layer. However, there are still some fundamental differences between the two, even if they share the same goals [25]. Edge devices are unable to implement several IoT applications in the edge computing layer, as the limited sources would cause resource contention and would also increase processing latency. In contrast, fog computing can successfully overcome these limitations and prevent resource contention at the edge by smoothly incorporating edge devices with cloud resources. Fog computing coordinates, balances, and improves the utilisation of geographically distributed network edge devices, and it exploits the cloud resources for that purpose. In addition, edge computing is focused on the things, while fog computing is more focused on the infrastructure. Table 1.1 further demonstrates a comparison of the characteristics of all layers.

1.3　Applications

Edge computing has many applications, as described in the following subsections [8,26].

1.3.1　Smart systems

In smart systems, which can be called '*SmartX*', network communication technologies are interlinked with sensors and actuators that are meant to send signals to the system to take action. Smart systems are viewed as an extension of IoT technologies. The integration of sensors offers countless opportunities for data collection, physical system management, as well as allocation and optimisation of resources. The utilisation of smart systems enables edge computing to reduce latency to the lowest level possible and to increase storage capacity in devices lacking computational efficiency. In the same way, edge data analysis can ensure a high degree of resilience in compromised systems. Smart systems have several significant areas, including smart homes, smart grids, smart cities, smart farms, smart transportation, smart healthcare, and others.

Smart home: IoT can be very beneficial in a home environment. Some products, such as smart lights, smart TVs, and robot vacuums, have already been developed and sold in the market. However, smart homes are not created by just adding a Wi-Fi module to the current electrical device and connecting it to the cloud. In addition to the connected device, cheap wireless sensors and controllers must be deployed in the rooms, pipes, floors, and even walls of a smart home. Such devices would report a substantial amount of data, which should primarily be consumed in the smart home if we take into account data transportation pressure and privacy protection issues. Regardless, edge computing is considered to be a perfect model for smart home establishment. Things can be easily connected and controlled in the smart home by using an edge gateway that runs a specialised edge operating system (EdgeOS). The generated data can be locally processed to reduce Internet bandwidth usage, and the EdgeOS also offers a better service in terms of management and delivery [27].

Smart city: The edge computing model can feasibly extend from a single home to an entire community or even a city. In this model, computing should be done as close as possible to the data source. This design allows the generation of a request at the top of the computing paradigm and processing it at the edge. A smart city utilises distributed IoT devices supported by various sensors. These devices improve transportation and traffic management, air quality monitoring (e.g. pollution, temperature, and humidity), smart parking, smart lighting, and smart garden irrigation systems [28]. Edge computing can be a perfect platform for a smart city due to the following characteristics [8]:

- Large data quantity: Due to the traffic overload, it is not possible to establish centralised cloud data centres that can handle vast amounts of data (generated from public safety, health, utility, transportation systems, etc.). In this case, edge computing may become an effective solution, as data would be processed at the edge of the network.
- Low latency: Edge computing also works well with applications that require low, predictable latency, such as those used for healthcare emergency or public safety purposes, as this model can save data transmission time and facilitate the network structure. It is more efficient to make decisions and diagnostics on the edge of the network than to collect information and make decisions at a central cloud.
- Location awareness: Given its location awareness, edge computing works better than cloud computing when used for geographic-based applications, such as transportation and utility management applications. In this model, data can be collected and processed in its geographical location without being transported to the cloud.

Smart healthcare: Healthcare systems would extremely benefit from IoT. In general, cloud computing frees IoT devices/sensors battery-draining computing tasks and provides virtually unlimited sources. Large-scale data sets can be collected from various sensors to carry out the analytical tasks mentioned above. However, such a simple sensor-to-cloud architecture is not feasible in many applications operating within healthcare information systems. Regulations sometimes prevent the storage of patients' data outside the hospital premises. Moreover, some applications cannot entirely rely on remote data centres, as network and data centre failure would jeopardise patient safety. Edge computing is one possible solution to narrow the gap between sensors and analytics in healthcare information systems.

Healthcare has recently undergone some of its most profound transformations, and the introduction of wireless sensor technology was one of the main factors behind this change. In addition to providing further access to biometric parameters, sensors are getting smaller in size and can be worn without interfering with everyday life. This is essential for ongoing data collection. Such technologies allow patients to use many sensors and fitness trackers, and in the future, these sensors will serve as a tool to monitor the health condition of any human being regardless of their health status.

Sensory data can be more useful in healthcare systems when adopting other driving factors, such as big data analysis and machine learning. In addition to providing computer-assisted analysis of medical images, large data analysis can be used to investigate treatment effectiveness, identify patients who are at risk of developing chronic diseases, ensure patients' adherence to treatment plans, optimise processes, and develop personalised care plans. At this point, sensors used to monitor patients must be wireless and wearable. However, this limits the sensors' size and affects their energy quality memory and processing capacity. Moreover, data can only be valued in context, and it must be accumulated from various sensors. Thus, sensors send data to other more capable computing devices for accumulation, storage, and analysis. However, in a broader environment, it is not possible to adopt such vertical approaches. Their specific infrastructure is expensive and difficult to maintain when several patients need to be equipped with many sensors individually. In this case, the IoT offers an alternative approach. Using a common infrastructure allows sensor devices to transmit their data to more comprehensive applications. This added flexibility in computing offers new opportunities to meeting current healthcare challenges. Improving mobility and the integration of patients will ensure ongoing monitoring, as mentioned above, and will enable the utilisation of new applications. In many countries, healthcare systems face great challenges because chronic diseases increase with age.

There is also a growing shortage of nursing staff in many countries. At the same time, there is a high demand for cost reduction while maintaining high-quality patient care. As a result, the healthcare industry is promoting a model that focuses on information delivery. A part of this model that delivers medical services enables remote monitoring of patients, as this increases accessibility to the patients and improves healthcare quality, efficiency, and sustainability. It also reduces the overall healthcare cost. Today, the manual measuring of biometric parameters and transfer of data between systems in hospitals is extremely time-consuming. Remote monitoring would be time saving for caregivers, and automated monitoring would replace manual monitoring. Processes taking place within the hospital would also improve, as remote monitoring would enable effective utilisation of resources. Many processes are planned manually, and therefore done in a sequence, rather than using resources effectively. Moreover, sensors would make it easier to obtain correct information about current health conditions, equipment location, caregivers, and patients. Sensors can also provide a more accurate image of patients by continuously capturing data and providing insights into a wide range of biometric parameters. Medical treatment and diagnostics will be revolutionised. Data would not be processed in isolated silos; it would be combined with other sources and viewed within context. The healthcare industry is moving towards preventive medicine. Reactive healthcare involves treating patients only when they face health issues, while preventive care monitors individuals to keep them healthy and out of hospitals. Moreover, patients can be discharged from hospitals earlier and monitored at home. It primarily means removing boundaries between hospitals, homes, and any other healthcare facilities, so healthcare becomes an ongoing process [29].

Smart grid: When monitoring devices are deployed, the smart grid collects huge amounts of energy-related data at an unprecedented speed. The smart grid becomes data-driven, and this requires extracting important data from a large data set. The traditional data extraction approach enhances computing efficiency in a temporal dimension, but it only works for one task in the smart grid. Furthermore, current solutions do not take into account the geographical distribution of computing capacity within a large-scale smart grid [30].

In the field of grid technology and implementation, the smart grid is considered to be the next generation. To reap the benefits of the smart grid (e.g. safety, security, and self-healing), many smart meters, sensors, and actuators must be used to collect and share measured data in the smart grid. Thus, edge computing can potentially meet the requirements of the smart grid deployment.

Smart transportation: The deployment of a cloud-based vehicle control system is necessary to ensure safety and efficiency in self-driving vehicles because it can collect data from sensors via a vehicle-to-vehicle network. This system can control and coordinate a large number of vehicles. A real-time vehicle management system certainly entails strict requirements, such as low latency, which can be provided by edge computing [26].

Smart surveillance: Smart surveillance systems monitor, screen, and track activities to provide security in public places like airports. Several aspects, such as the screening of objects and people, maintaining a database of potential threats, biometric identification, and video surveillance, work in tandem to monitor activities. The scope of the surveillance applications' work includes the control of access to specific areas, human identification, and event detection. This is added to monitoring traffic, hospitalised patients, and activities in public places, including shopping malls, industries, banks, and government institutions. Any surveillance system should be able to compress large video recordings effectively and thus facilitate subsequent processing [31]. Smart surveillance applications that are based on cloud computing face major challenges. These applications require real time for object detection and tracking by processing video streams collected from broadly distributed data sources, such as networked cameras and smart mobile devices. However, the transfer of large amounts of raw data to cloud centres has an uncertain time frame and it overloads communication networks. Moreover, the remote transfer of data can jeopardise data protection and privacy, as it would be more exposed to attackers. Surveillance video streams are often viewed as a tool for forensic analysis, rather than as a proactive tool to help thwart suspicious activities before the damage is actually done. Therefore, new technologies are needed to handle critical and security-sensitive tasks locally. IoT technology is paving the way for a new post-cloud era. Thousands of the smart 'things' we use in our daily life generate and process a lot of data on the edge of the network [32]. However, edge computing can provide the real-time management that surveillance systems require.

Smart farm: To meet future demands of food production, the agricultural sector has to integrate IoT in various production, management, and analysis processes. Smart farms can use edge computing to operate autonomous vehicles (tractors) and to perform remote monitoring and real-time analytics. IoT devices/sensors can provide data on crop production, rainfall, pest infection, and soil nutrition. Such information is helpful for production and can also help improve farming techniques in the long run [33].

1.3.2   Video analytics

The rapid spread of mobile phones and network cameras is giving rise to video analytics technology. Cloud computing does not work for applications requiring video analytics, as it entails data transmission latency and privacy issues. An example of this is finding a lost child in a city. Today, various types of cameras are deployed in urban areas and vehicles. A camera somewhere might capture an image of the child. However, the camera data might not be uploaded on the cloud for privacy issues or traffic cost. This makes it extremely hard to leverage the data of cameras in a vast area. The data might already be available on the cloud, but it would take too long to upload and analyse large amounts of data to find the missing child. In this case, the edge computing model can be used to generate a search request for the child from the cloud and transmit it to all the things in the target area. For example, a smartphone can receive the request, search its local camera data, and only report the results to the cloud. This model makes it possible to leverage data and computing power to get faster results than those obtained through the cloud computing model [8].

1.3.3   Collaborative edge

Cloud computing has certainly become a platform for processing large amounts of data in academics and industries. In cloud computing, data should be held or transmitted to the cloud for processing. However, stakeholders rarely share data due to privacy issues and the very high cost of data transfer, and thus, collaboration among several stakeholders can be limited. The edge may be part of the logical concept, as it is a small physical data centre with data processing capabilities that connects end users to the cloud. It proposes a collaborative edge that connects the edges of many geographically distributed stakeholders regardless of their location and network structure [34]. These instantly connected edges give stakeholders the chance to share and coordinate data.

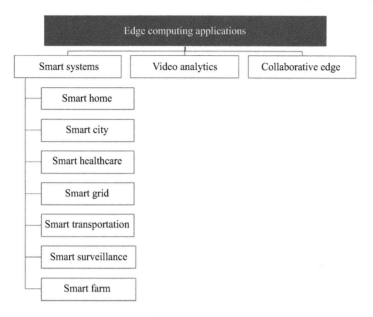

Figure 1.2   Edge computing applications

Applications that process geographically distributed data (e.g. healthcare data) require companies in several domains to collaborate and share data. Edge computing can meet this challenge through merging geographically distributed data and creating virtually shared data views. The virtual data are then shared with end users via a predefined service interface terminal, and an application will use this public interface to deliver complex end-user services. Collaborative edge participants deliver these services, and the computation only occurs at the participants' data centre to ensure data privacy and integrity [8].

Edge computing applications can be summarised in Figure 1.2.

1.4   Open challenges

Edge computing open challenges can be summarised in the following subsections [8,9,26,35].

1.4.1   Naming

It is safe to assume that there are a lot of things in edge computing. Many applications run at the top of the edge, and each has its own structure and service method. Like any other computer system, the naming scheme in edge computing is very significant for programming, identification of things, and data communication. However, there is no standardised naming mechanism for the edge computing model yet. Edge practitioners often need to learn various communication and network protocols so they can interact with a variety of things in the system. The naming scheme for edge computing has to tackle the portable nature of things, the highly dynamic network geographical distribution, privacy and safety, and the scalability of an enormous number of unreliable things [8].

1.4.2   System integration

Supporting different types of devices and meeting various service demands are a huge challenge in the edge computing environment. Edge computing integrates the combination of different platforms, network typologies, and servers. Therefore, the heterogeneous nature of this system makes it difficult to program and manage data and resources for many applications that run on various platforms in different locations. From a programming perspective, all applications and user programs are deployed and operated on cloud servers in cloud computing. Cloud providers, such as Google and Amazon, place these applications and programs in the appropriate locations and hardware to ensure their smooth operation. Most users do not know how these applications function or where the data and resources are located. Cloud computing offers manageable, centralised cloud service as one of its advantages. Furthermore, developers need to use just one programming language to develop applications for a specific platform because the cloud application is deployed on just one particular cloud service provider. Edge computing is, by contrast, very different from cloud computing. While there are many advantages to distributed topology, edge nodes are usually divergent platforms. Thus, developers would face serious challenges when developing an application that might be deployed and run on an edge computing platform. Certain schemes have been designed to address the challenges of programming in edge computing, but none of these schemes is designed for specific IoT purposes. The first step in IoT is finding the edge nodes. Before that, IoT devices cannot identify the type of platforms deployed in their vicinity. Moreover, many programs on the server side need to be deployed on the edge nodes, and this poses another challenge for edge node providers who need to deploy and manage those programs. As for data management, different storage servers are run by various operating systems. This represents another challenge for file naming, resource allocation, file reliability management, etc. As many IoT devices are simultaneously generating and uploading data, naming data resources becomes a difficult task [26].

1.4.3   Programmability

Users in the cloud computing model program and deploy their code on the cloud. The cloud provider then decides where cloud computing tasks are executed. Users do not usually know how the application is served. However, cloud computing is known for its transparent infrastructure. The program is usually written in a certain programming language and compiled in the cloud for a specific target platform, because the program only runs on the cloud. In contrast, computation is done from the cloud in edge computing, and the edge nodes are probably heterogeneous platforms. Thus, these nodes have different runtimes, and it is hard for the programmer to write an application that can be deployed in the edge computing model [8].

1.4.4 General-purpose computing on edge nodes

Hypothetically speaking, edge computing can run on several nodes located between the edge device and the cloud, including access points, base stations, gateways, traffic aggregation points, routers, switches, etc. For instance, base stations include Digital Signal Processors (DSPs) that are tailored to handle their workload. However, in practice, base stations may not be able to handle analytical workloads because DSPs are not designed to carry out general-purpose computing tasks. Furthermore, whether these nodes can perform additional computing tasks remains unknown. It might be useful to use such base stations at an off-rush time to leverage the computational capabilities of several available computing cores. Many business suppliers have made the first step towards software solutions that use edge computing. For instance, Nokia developed a software solution for mobile edge computing (MEC) that is meant to establish base station sites for the edge computing model. Likewise, Cisco's IOx16 provides an implementation environment for its incorporated service routers. As these solutions are hardware specific, they might not work in a heterogeneous environment. It would be challenging to develop portable software solutions that can function in different environments. Currently, research is underway to upgrade edge node resources that would support general-purpose computing. General-purpose CPUs can replace specialised DSPs as an alternative solution, but this would be a large investment [9].

1.4.5 Resource management

The integration of IoT and edge computing requires a thorough, comprehensive understanding and reinforcement of resource management. Network traffic and latency have a major impact on IoT devices and often result in computation deficiency and resource shortage because it requires utilising more power to re-transfer data in jammed settings. Edge computing can help reduce latency in devices, and decentralised resources will be instrumental in motivating and sharing these assets. These resources can be managed by various means, provided that it involves inexpensive computation. However, the disparity between service providers, devices, and applications causes a lot of complexities, and such interactions should be taken into consideration. In particular, the motivating factors of Edge/IoT resource management are synchronised with those of smart systems. The direct service of a system – which has multiple resource providers and a huge variety of applications and user needs – can be allocated, shared, and priced by optimisation global welfare or some other metric through competitive bidding or any other strategy [26].

1.4.6 Service management

To ensure the system's reliability, service management at the network edge requires supporting the following four essential features: differentiation, extensibility, isolation, and reliability [8].

Differentiation: The rapid development of IoT deployment will lead to the deployment of many services at the edge of the network, such as smart homes.

The priorities of these services will vary. For instance, critical services, such as diagnostics of things and failure alarm should be delivered faster than other services. Another example is health-related services, such as fall detection or heart failure detection, which should have a higher priority over other services like entertainment ones.

Extensibility: Extensibility presents a major challenge at the edge of the network. The things in the IoT are very dynamic. A versatile service management layer can resolve some of the current issues. When a user purchases a new thing, they need to add the current service with ease. Moreover, when a thing wears out and gets replaced, the previous service should easily adopt a new node.

Isolation: Isolation is another issue on the network's edge. When an application fails or crashes in a mobile OS, the whole system usually crashes or reboots. In a distributed system, various synchronisation mechanisms, such as a lock or a token ring, can be used to manage the shared resource. This problem, however, is more complicated in a smart EdgeOS. Many applications could share the same data resource, light control, for example. If one application crashes or does not respond, the user can still control their lights as this would not make the entire EdgeOS crash. Another example is when a user eliminates the only application that controls lights from the system, and the lights still work without losing connection to the EdgeOS. The introduction of a deployment framework may resolve this issue. If the OS detects the issue before the application is deployed, it will alert the user to avoid any access issues. Another aspect of this challenge is isolating a user's private data from third-party applications. For instance, your activity tracking application should not have access to your electricity usage data. To resolve this issue, the EdgeOS service management layer must be equipped with a reliable control access mechanism.

Reliability: Reliability is also another major challenge at the edge of the network, and it is viewed from various service, system, and data aspects. From a service aspect, it is sometimes difficult to identify the cause of a service failure in an accurate manner. For example, an air conditioning system stops working because the cable is cut, the compressor is broken, or even the battery of a temperature controller is dead. A sensor node might have lost connection to the system as a result of a battery outage, bad connection, component failure, etc. Thus, when some nodes lose connection at the network's edge, it is not enough to just maintain the current service; it would be more useful to provide the action after the node fails. From a system aspect, maintaining the network topology of the entire system is truly essential for the EdgeOS. All system components can send status/diagnosis data to the edge. This feature allows simple system deployment of services, such as failure detection, replacement of things, and data quality detection. From a data aspect, data sensing and communication are mainly responsible for reliability issues. Things at the network's edge fail for various reasons, and they report inaccurate data under uncertain conditions, such as low battery level. There have been various proposals for new communication protocols for data collection. Such protocols can support a large number of sensor nodes and the highly dynamic network condition. However, the connection is not as reliable as the one in Bluetooth or Wi-Fi. It remains a challenge for a system to provide a reliable service by leveraging many reference data sources and data history records, even when the sensing data and communication are not so reliable.

1.4.7 Discovering edge nodes

The literature thoroughly examines the resources and services provided in a distributed computing setting. Various techniques are used in monitoring tools and service brokerages to facilitate such examination in both closely integrated environments as well as separate ones. To enhance performance, using a technique like benchmarking supports the mapping of tasks by setting up decision-making onto the most suitable resources. However, using the network's edge requires exploring mechanisms to help identify suitable nodes for a decentralised cloud configuration. Due to the large number of devices at this layer, such mechanisms cannot be manual. Furthermore, the mechanisms have to work well with heterogeneous devices from several generations as well as modern ones. The benchmarking techniques need to determine the resources availability and efficiency in a very rapid manner. These mechanisms should facilitate smooth nodes' integration and elimination at various hierarchical levels in the computational workflow without increasing latency or compromising the user's experience. Users appreciate the system's ability to tackle faults and to enable automatic recovery on the node in a reliable and proactive manner. In this context, current cloud approaches do not practically discover edge nodes [9].

1.4.8 Partitioning and offloading tasks

The evolution of computing environments has brought forth many techniques that facilitate the distribution of tasks over multiple geographic locations. Workloads are distributed and executed across various locations, and the distribution of tasks is usually carried out via a language or management tool. However, if we use edge nodes to offload computations, it will be challenging to partition computations in an effective manner. This should be done automatically, regardless of the edge nodes' storage and computing capacities, by developing schedulers that deploy tasks onto edge nodes [9].

1.4.9 Uncompromising QoS and QoE

Edge nodes ensure that quality of service (QoS) and quality of experience (QoE) are effectively delivered to users. One of the edge computing principles is to avoid overloading nodes with intensive computing workloads. In this case, it is difficult to ensure the nodes' high performance and reliability when delivering the intended workloads as well as workloads received from a data centre or edge devices. The user of an edge device or a data centre still expects some service even when the edge node is fully exploited. For instance, overloading a base station might affect the service provided to the connected edge devices. This requires realisation of rush hours of edge nodes' usage in order to partition and schedule tasks in a flexible manner. A management framework can be very useful in this sense, but it causes issues in terms of monitoring, scheduling, and rescheduling at infrastructure and platform levels [9].

1.4.10 Smart system support

Smart systems essentially interlink network communication technologies with sensors and actuators to achieve system awareness and actuators that are meant to send signals to the system to take action. Smart systems are viewed as an extension of IoT technologies. The integration of sensing devices offers countless opportunities for data collection, system management, and resource allocation and optimisation. Smart systems are mainly utilised in areas such as smart grids, smart cities, smart transportation, smart healthcare, and others. The increasing utilisation of smart systems enables edge computing to reduce latency to the lowest level possible and to increase storage capacity in devices that are computationally deficient. In the same way, edge data analysis can also ensure a high degree of resilience in compromised systems [26].

1.4.11 Advanced communication

Edge computing has currently changed remote computation and storage as it has removed barriers to offer fast, low-latency, and high-computation applications. In the same way, future 5G cellular network technologies, including ultra-dense networks (UDNs), massive MIMO (multiple-input and multiple-output), and millimetre-wave, are improving as they move towards reducing latency, increasing throughput, and providing support for interconnected groups in dense networks. This will inevitably develop communication technology. 5G is considered to be the next generation in communication technology. It aims to provide users with pervasive network connectivity and access to data. In this regard, 5G, IoT, and edge computing can be integrated to achieve flexible and efficient communication. 5G technology can also help make many IoT applications more efficient [26].

1.4.12 Privacy and security

Privacy and security are important issues that require careful consideration. Cloud and edge computing paradigms both have numerous security issues and challenges. Edge computing specifically involves connecting various multiple technologies (e.g. peer-to-peer systems, wireless networks, and virtualisation), and this requires a comprehensive integrated model to safeguard and manage each technology platform and the system as a whole. However, the advancement of edge computing may result in some unpredicted issues. Certain situations that remain unexamined, such as the interplay of various edge nodes and the local and global migration of services, all create the potential for malicious behaviour. Moreover, the built-in features of edge computing further determine the viability of privacy and security measures.

Although the distributed framework offers many advantages to IoT, it is difficult to maintain privacy and security in such distributed structures. In terms of privacy, edge computing can provide an efficient platform to future IoT. Processing data at the edge enables the edge computing model to utilise privacy-sensitive data belonging to end users. Sensing data from IoT systems is stored at edge nodes, which are more susceptible than cloud servers. Thus, edge computing should utilise efficient data protection mechanisms to protect data privacy. As for security issues, authenticating gateways on different levels is a main problem in edge computing.

For example, smart meters used at residential homes have their own IP address [26]. Offloading an application from the end user's device to the edge server requires transferring data from the mobile device to the edge server. It allows intruders to access data by committing security violations. End users' devices are battery powered, and therefore require applying lightweight security and safety mechanisms. Security and privacy solutions should also be flexible so they can promote the edge computing goal of reducing execution time. However, it is difficult to find a reliable lightweight solution for a complex security problem in a diverse environment [35]. We can conclude here that security and safety are the main issues preventing advances in edge computing.

1.4.13 Using edge nodes publicly and securely

Hardware resources at data centres, supercomputing centres, and private organisations can be converted into computing services using virtualisation. As providers identify associated risks for users, they provide computing on a pay-as-you-go basis. The computing marketplace has, therefore, become highly competitive as it offers numerous options that meet the standards of the service-level agreements (SLAs). However, using alternative devices, such as switches, routers, or base stations, as publicly available edge nodes would create some issues. First, there is a need to identify the risk associated with the devices owned by public and private organisations as well as the entities that employ them. Second, the device's intended purpose cannot be compromised when it serves as an edge computing node, such as when using a router to manage Internet traffic. Third, multi-tenancy on edge nodes requires using a security-oriented technology. For instance, containers represent a lightweight technology used on edge nodes, but they need to demonstrate potent security features. Fourth, the edge node user must be guaranteed a minimum level of service. In addition, to develop appropriate pricing models for accessible edge nodes, the workload, computation, data location, data transmission, and cost of maintenance and energy bills all need to be addressed [9].

1.4.14 Monitoring, accounting, and billing

It is important to manage edge computing resources, accounting, and billing to ensure QoS and to set the appropriate charge for the offered edge computing service, and this requires service providers to apply a sustainable business model. However, it is difficult to design such a model given the customer's mobile nature and the limited services range. A user usually uses an edge node service for a limited time, such as students who use the service at a university cafeteria during lunch hours. This short-time use makes it difficult to maintain a business model. In addition, when a user moves and execution is transferred from one edge platform to another, it becomes difficult to divide charges between the involved service providers and to maintain a business model for monitoring, accounting, and billing. This requires a business model that includes multiple levels of granular charging [35].

1.4.15 Social collaboration

It is difficult for various service providers to collaborate and accomplish a common goal. Standardisation and competition are the main obstacles that hinder such social

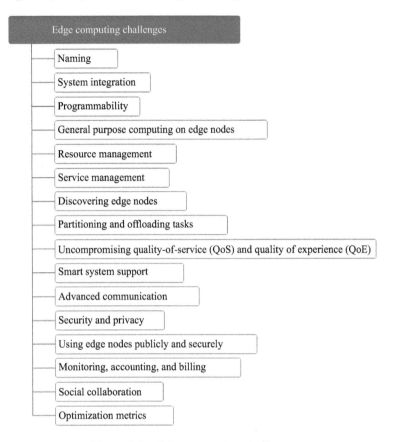

Figure 1.3   Edge computing challenges

collaboration. Various companies offer different edge services. However, it is difficult to achieve social collaboration among them given the competitive marketplace. The heterogeneous nature of the devices provided by different companies also presents an obstacle for achieving such collaboration. Overcoming the collaboration challenge would enhance data analytics efficiency [35].

1.4.16   Optimisation metrics

Edge computing involves several layers with different computing capacities. The workload distribution can be problematic because we need to choose the layer that would handle the workload or the number of tasks to assign for each part. Many allocation strategies can be applied to complete a workload. For example, the workload can be evenly distributed on each layer or completed at each layer as much as possible. In extreme cases, the workload would be fully processed on the cloud. When choosing an optimal allocation strategy, some measures must be taken into consideration, such as latency, bandwidth, energy, and cost [8].

Edge computing challenges can be summarised in Figure 1.3.

1.5   Conclusions

Edge computing extends cloud computing by bringing the services closer to the end user at the network edge. This chapter aims to explore the edge computing model. Although this model offers numerous benefits, it presents many new challenges. The chapter highlights the significance of edge computing as it provides an insight into its definition, architecture, and distinguishing characteristics as compared to fog and cloud computing characteristics. It also demonstrates the applications the edge computing enables. There is a need to address the challenges of adopting the edge computing model, as this model will become the core component of the future computing landscape. The chapter serves as a guideline for related future directions.

References

[1]   Shawish A, and Salama M. Cloud computing: paradigms and technologies. In: Xhafa F, and Bessis N, editors. Inter-cooperative Collective Intelligence: Techniques and Applications. Studies in Computational Intelligence, Vol. 495. Berlin, Heidelberg: Springer Berlin Heidelberg; 2014.

[2]   Al-Dulaimy A, Zantout R, Itani W, and Zekri A. Job submission in the cloud: energy aware approaches. The 24th World Congress on Engineering and Computer Science (WCECS 2016), Vol. 1, International Association of Engineers (IAENG), San Francisco, USA, 2016.

[3]   Al-Dulaimy A, Itani W, Zantout R, and Zekri A. Type-aware virtual machine management for energy efficient cloud data centers. Journal of Sustainable Computing: Informatics and Systems (SUSCOM), Elsevier, Vol. 19, pp: 185-203, 2018.

[4]   Chang C, Srirama S, and Buyya R. Internet of things (IoT) and new computing paradigms In: Buyya R, Srirama S, editors. Fog and Edge Computing: Principles and Paradigms. Wiley. 2019. pp. 1–23.

[5]   Margulius D. Apps on the edge, InfoWorld. Last accessed July 2019. https://www.infoworld.com/article/2677229/apps-on-the-edge.html.

[6]   Pang HH, and Tan K. Authenticating query results in edge computing. In: Proceedings. 20th International Conference on Data Engineering; 2004. pp. 560–571.

[7]   Garcia Lopez P, Montresor A, Epema D, *et al.* Edge-centric computing: vision and challenges. ACMSIGCOMM Comput Commun Rev. 2015;45(5):37–42.

[8]   Shi W, Cao J, Zhang Q, Youhuizi L, and Lanyu X. Edge computing: vision and challenges. IEEE Internet of Things Journal. 2016;3(5):637–646.

[9]   Varghese B, Wang N, Barbhuiya S, Kilpatrick P, and Nikolopoulos D. Challenges and opportunities in edge computing. In: 2016 IEEE International Conference on Smart Cloud (SmartCloud); 2016. pp. 20–26.

[10] Finnegan M. Boeing 787s to create half a terabyte of data per flight, says Virgin Atlantic, Computer World, UK. Last accessed July 2019. https://www.computerworlduk.com/data/boeing-787s-create-half-terabyte-of-data-per-flight-says-virgin-atlantic%2D3433595/.

[11]   van Rijmenam M. Self-driving cars will create 2 petabytes of data: what are the big data opportunities for the car industry? DataFloq. Last accessed July 2019. https://datafloq.com/read/self-driving-cars-create-2-petabytes-data-annually/172.

[12]   Data Never Sleeps 6.0, DOMO. Last accessed July 2019. https://www.domo.com/learn/data-never-sleeps-6.

[13]   Zhu J, Chan DS, Prabhu MS, Natarajan P, Hu H, and Bonomi F. Improving web sites performance using edge servers in fog computing architecture. In: 2013 IEEE Seventh International Symposium on Service-Oriented System Engineering; 2013. pp. 320–323.

[14]   Sawasaki N, Ishihara T, Mouri M, Murase Y, Masui S, and Nakamoto H. Front-end device technology for human centric IoT. Fujitsu Scientific & Technical Journal. 2016 10;52:61–67.

[15]   Al-Dulaimy A, Itani W, Zekri A, and Zantout R. Power management in virtualized data centers: state of the art. Journal of Cloud Computing. Advances, Systems and Applications (JoCCASA), Springer. 2016;5(1):6.

[16]   Evans D. The Internet of things: how the next evolution of the Internet is changing everything. Cisco Internet Business Solutions Group (IBSG); 2011. https://www.cisco.com/c/dam/en_us/about/ac79/docs/innov/IoT_IBSG_0411FINAL.pdf.

[17]   International Data Corporation (IDC). In: IDC Directions Conference; 2016.

[18]   Cao J, Zhang Q, and Shi W. Introduction. In: Cao J, Zhang Q, Shi W, editors. Edge Computing: A Primer. Springer; 2018. pp. 1–9.

[19]   Singh SP, Nayyar A, Kumar R, and Sharma A. Fog computing: from architecture to edge computing and big data processing. The Journal of Supercomputing. 2019;75:2070–2105.

[20]   Baktir AC, Ozgovde A, and Ersoy C. How can edge computing benefit from software-defined networking: a survey, use cases, and future directions. IEEE Communications Surveys Tutorials. 2017 Fourthquarter;19(4):2359–2391.

[21]   Lea P (editor). Cloud and fog topologies, in Internet of Things for Architects. Packt Publishing; 2018. pp. 338–371.

[22]   Satyanarayanan M. The emergence of edge computing. Computer. 2017; 50(1):30–39.

[23]   SNIPS. Last accessed 2019. https://snips.ai/content/intro-to-edge-computing/?utm_campaign=2019_Edge\&gclid=Cj0KCQjwjYHpBRC4ARIsAI%2D3G kFHj9hwwA6upDLKCk3oTsg8sFJnGfXKYHux8U6aliFqhyFBG9yh_x4aAi XhEALw_wcB#what-is-edge-computing.

[24]   Khan SU. The curious case of distributed systems and continuous computing. IT Professional. 2016;18(2):4–7.

[25]   Hu P, Dhelim S, Ning H, and Qiu T. Survey on fog computing: architecture, key technologies, applications and open issues. J Network and Computer Applications. 2017;98:27–42.

[26]   Yu W, Liang F, He X, *et al.* A survey on the edge computing for the Internet of things. IEEE Access. 2018;6:6900–6919.

[27]   Cao J. SOFIE: Smart operating system for Internet of everything, PhD Thesis, Graduate School of Wayne State University. 2018.

[28]   Samie F, Bauer L, and Henkel J. IoT technologies for embedded computing: a survey. In: 2016 International Conference on Hardware/Software Codesign and System Synthesis (CODES+ISSS); 2016. pp. 1–10.

[29]   Kraemer F, Brten A, Tamkittikhun N, and Palma D. Fog computing in healthcare: a review and discussion. IEEE Access. 2017;9206–9222.

[30]   Hou W, Ning Z, Guo L, and Zhang X. Temporal, functional and spatial big data computing framework for large-scale smart grid. IEEE Transactions on Emerging Topics in Computing. 2019;7(3):369–379.

[31]   Babu RV, and Makur A. Object-based surveillance video compression using foreground motion compensation. In: 2006 9th International Conference on Control, Automation, Robotics and Vision; 2006. pp. 1–6.

[32]   Xu R, Nikouei SY, Chen Y, *et al.* Real-time human objects tracking for smart surveillance at the edge. In: 2018 IEEE International Conference on Communications (ICC); 2018. pp. 1–6.

[33]   Porambage P, Okwuibe J, Liyanage M, Ylianttila M, and Taleb T. Survey on multi-access edge computing for Internet of things realization. IEEE Communications Surveys Tutorials. 2018 Fourthquarter;20(4):2961–2991.

[34]   Bonomi F, Milito R, Zhu J, and Addepalli S. Fog computing and its role in the Internet of things. In: Proceedings of the First Edition of the MCC Workshop on Mobile Cloud Computing. MCC'12. New York, NY, USA: ACM; 2012. pp. 13–16. Available from: http://doi.acm.org/10.1145/2342509.2342513.

[35]   Ahmed E, Ahmed A, Yaqoob I, *et al.* Bringing computation closer toward the user network: is edge computing the solution? IEEE Communications Magazine. 2017;55(11):138–144.

Chapter 2
Edge computing architectures
Nhu-Ngoc Dao[1], Quang Dieu Tran[2], Ngoc-Thanh Dinh[3], Sungrae Cho[4] and Torsten Braun[1]

By considering an edge computing platform as one of the main computing tiers in a fully comprehensive cloudisation model, this chapter first discusses the distinguished features of edge computing compared to other platforms from the perspectives of service, operation and control. In addition, a local view of the intrinsic architecture of an edge computing host is analysed. Subsequently, a standard reference architecture of the edge computing platform is presented, which defines the internal and external interfaces among components at the computing host and system levels. The reference architecture is matched to the network function virtualisation management and orchestration (NFV MANO) model for consideration as a virtualised network function (VNF). In particular, the position and roles of VNF edge computing in the standard mobile network reference model are demonstrated. Finally, the open issues and challenges are presented by way of conclusion.

2.1 Introduction

In recent years, (multi-access) edge computing, network softwarisation and Internet of Things (IoT) have been trending for the realisation of the fifth generation (5G) mobile networks [1,2]. IoT applications have increasingly generated large amounts of heterogeneous data into the networks. In addition, IoT devices are considered everyday objects which are low-performance and lightweight hardware with transceivers powered by diverse access technologies for Internet connectivity. Therefore, IoT vitally requires an in-network computational platform with tailored services and standard interfaces to handle such heterogeneous data. To this end, 5G networks

[1]Institute of Computer Science, University of Bern, Bern, Switzerland
[2]Center for Information Technology and Applications, Ho Chi Minh Academy of Politics, Hanoi, Vietnam
[3]School of Electrical and Telecommunication, Soongsil University, Seoul, Republic of Korea
[4]School of Computer Science and Engineering, Chung-Ang University, Seoul, Republic of Korea

are the most promising sources for IoT satisfaction [3]; 5G network softwarisation and its associated core technologies, i.e. software-defined networking (SDN) and NFV, enable flexible architectures to create, distribute and operate networking services [4,5].

Advances in 5G network softwarisation expand the cloudisation capability from the cloud at the core to the edge of the network. As a result, a new concept, namely multi-access edge computing (MEC), is derived from this development [6]. The most common definition and framework of MEC are proposed by the European Telecommunications Standardisation Institute (ETSI). The standardisation for MEC has been developed and managed by the MEC industry specification group (ISG) since December 2014. As defined by ETSI in its White paper No. 28 on the MEC in 5G [7], '*MEC offers application developers and content providers cloud-computing capabilities and an IT service environment at the edge of the network. This environment is characterized by ultra-low latency and high bandwidth as well as real-time access to radio network information that can be leveraged by applications*'. The applications benefited by the power of MEC are spread over a wide range of business segments such as video analytics, location services, IoT, augmented reality, content distribution and data caching.

When participating in MEC ecosystems, user terminals are the key agents operate on and consume most of the data in the network. These data are further handled, processed, archived and distributed by in-network applications and service providers as central points of contact for content acquisition. In this context, mobile telecom operators provide transportation infrastructure for data delivery as well as IT resources for intermediate data processing and application/service implementation. Operational harmonisation among these participants decides the success of the MEC ecosystems.

For optimal exploitation and development of the MEC, it is necessary to fully understand the MEC models along with their components, positions, features, connections and interfaces from an architectural perspective. In particular, this chapter aims to address the following research questions:

- **(Q1)** How to position MEC among related terms in comprehensive cloudisation? – Discussed in Section 2.2.
- **(Q2)** What concepts are included in the standard reference architecture of MEC? – Discussed in Section 2.3.
- **(Q3)** What are the distinguishing features of MEC as a VNF? – Discussed in Section 2.4.
- **(Q4)** How to integrate MEC into a standard mobile reference architecture? – Discussed in Section 2.5.
- **(Q5)** What are the open issues and challenges of MEC from an architectural perspective? – Discussed in Section 2.6.

Finally, a summary of the present study and future directions are presented by way of conclusion in Section 2.7.

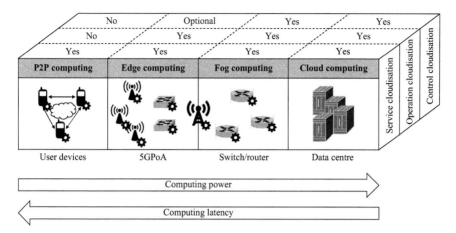

Figure 2.1 Edge computing in a cloudisation model

2.2 Edge computing in a cloudisation model

2.2.1 Cloudisation definition

Cloudisation is a method that provides in-network computational ability spanning the entire network in both vertical and horizontal directions. The vertical approach integrates storage and computational resources into network devices from the core to the edge of the network for various capabilities and performances (e.g. memory space and computational power). On the contrary, the horizontal approach defines the granularity of computational services that accommodate complex requirements of users and/or operator applications (e.g. virtualisation, infrastructure as a service (IaaS), platform as a service (PaaS) and anything as a service (XaaS)). In particular, network cloudisation not only upgrades the existing infrastructure to be open, flexible, intelligent, efficient and costly but also supports service-oriented optimisation. Therefore, cloudisation has been identified as an irreversible trend towards next generation mobile networks.

2.2.2 Computing tier comparison

From a computational perspective, a cloudisation model consists of four tiers namely cloud, fog, edge and peer-to-peer (P2P) computing levels; see Figure 2.1. Derived from an original definition introduced in [8], cloud computing systems provide remote computing and storage resources with very high performance to users in an on-demand fashion without direct physical deployment and management. Generally, the term 'cloud computing' is coupled with services at central data centres that are available to a large number of users and accessed through the Internet. At the next tier, fog computing systems are defined as an intermediate infrastructure to alleviate the burden of the cloud to handle a substantial amount of workload inside each local area [9].

Table 2.1   Computing tier comparison

Characteristics	Cloud computing	Fog computing	Edge computing	P2P computing
Implementation location	Core network	Distribution network	Access network	Peer-aware network
Physical devices	Dedicated and high-power servers	Medium-power servers located at macro base stations	Low-power servers located at small-cell base stations	Computing-shareable user devices
Deployment model	Highly centralised	Centralised	Distributed	Clusterised
Virtualisation	Supported	Supported	Partial	No (mostly)
Resource management	Network controller and hypervisor	Network controller and hypervisor	Network controller and (possible) hypervisor	Resource manager in device's OS
Capability	Very high	High	Medium	Low
Latency	High	Medium	Low	Ultralow
Localisation	Low	Medium	High	Very high
Stability	Very high	High	High	Low

To this end, fog computing systems are implemented on network switches/routers equipped with medium-power servers [10–12]. Further, edge computing systems aim to utilise free pieces of computing and storage resources in mobile points of attachment (5GPoA) at the access network for serving local users in the vicinity [6,7]. To complete the cloudisation model, P2P computing systems establish temporal computing platforms in groups among user devices for their specific purposes. Ideally, the P2P computing systems operate in an infrastructureless manner with fully distributed coordination [13,14]. Table 2.1 shows the detailed comparison between the edge computing and remaining systems in terms of implementation location, physical devices, deployment model, virtualisation ability, resource management, capability, latency, localisation and stability. Two main observations derived from the above analysis are increase of computing power from the P2P to the cloud and vice versa for computing latency characteristics.

As demonstrated in Figure 2.1, all the computing tiers are able to accommodate user applications' requirements at different satisfaction levels in the service cloudisation plane. In particular, the cloud and fog computing systems have sufficient resources for highly virtualised computing services such as PaaS and XaaS efficiently while the edge and P2P computing systems may provide at most IaaS and virtualised computing infrastructure, respectively. As a result, the cloud and fog computing systems target serving large-scale applications with complex functions and features that consume high computing and storage resources. By contrast, individual applications significantly benefit from the edge and P2P computing systems with prompt responses and high localisation.

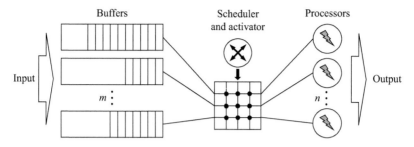

Figure 2.2   Intrinsic architecture of a queuing theoretic edge computing host

In an operation cloudisation plane, the operation software that defines physical resource utilisation and virtualised resource allocation policies establishes the operating environment for deploying third-party applications in order to provide computing services to users. Openness and flexibility of the operation software significantly impact the supportive categories of the computing services. From this view, the cloud, fog and edge computing systems possess sufficient characteristics to enable operation cloudisation while the P2P computing systems mainly work with the built-in resource management functions in the user devices' operating systems (OSs).

For control purpose, the cloud and fog computing systems are deeply integrated into the network as a mandatory VNF. In other words, these systems operate under managements and controls that are centrally supervised by the network orchestrator. A well-known control model standardised for 5G mobile network is the ETSI NFV MANO [15] scheme, which may be implemented using the SDN technology. On the other hand, although the edge computing systems definitely adapt well to SDN utilisation, it is optional to deploy control cloudisation for these systems because of two reasons. The first is that the edge computing system generally has a small scale; therefore, control cloudisation is unnecessary and inappropriate. The latter is that the devices implementing edge computing can be either in-network devices (e.g. eNodeB and femtocells) or premier devices (e.g. home hub and Wi-Fi access point), such that users may have the right to select the control solution. Lastly, no control cloudisation is assumed in the P2P computing systems because of their temporary operation, privacy and limited performance in user devices.

2.2.3   Intrinsic edge computing architecture

This section introduces a queuing theoretic edge computing model from an intrinsic computing architecture perspective. Although incoming/outgoing traffic is handled by the data plane, without loss of generality, the data processing operation of a queuing theoretic edge computing host considers the input data as a stochastic process, and the output data may either be stored in local storage or be forwarded to external entities [16–18]. With these assumptions, a queuing theoretic edge computing model consists of three main components: buffers for temporal input data storage, processors for data execution and a central scheduler and activator for task assignment and processor activation; see Figure 2.2.

Since data arrival at the buffers is random, the edge computing host self-optimises its operation by scheduling the input tasks to appropriate processors and/or activating/deactivating processors depending on the workload. Typically, the central scheduler and activator perform this optimisation. As most edge computing hosts have commercial off-the-shelf (COTS) designs, the processors can be controlled at the core level of processing chip architecture.

(Q1) How to position MEC among related terms in comprehensive cloudisation?
Among computing tiers in the cloudisation model, the edge computing systems distinguish themselves from the remaining systems by proposing stable services at the in-network level for local users in the vicinity while retaining responses with low latency.

2.3   Standard reference architecture

Although similar concepts have been introduced in literature since the past decade [19,20] such as micro datacentre [21] and cloudlet [22], lack of support from a standardisation organisation has caused these studies to be diverse and undirectional. On the contrary, edge computing technology has been defined, standardised and managed by the ETSI to popularise MEC* as a global standard for vendors, service providers and third parties to refer. The MEC ISG group released a set of specifications that provide guidelines and recommendations for MEC development and implementation. Table 2.2 shows a selected list of MEC architecture-related specifications derived from the ETSI standard repository.

A standard reference architecture for MEC is described in the ETSI GS MEC 003 V2.1.1 (2019-01) specification titled *Multi-access Edge Computing (MEC); Framework and Reference Architecture* [23]. Derived from this specification, Figure 2.3 illustrates the functional elements that comprise the MEC and the reference points between them in the operation and management/control domains.

2.3.1   Operation domain

In the operation domain, the internal architecture of MEC host is analysed. An MEC host is a network entity that contains computing environmental software and (virtualised) hardware infrastructure for providing MEC applications with networking resources. MEC host can be specific network devices dedicated for mobile service functions (e.g. switches and routers) or supplemented components (e.g. servers and storage) that are attached. The computing environmental software is referred to as

---

*Without a specific note, the terms edge computing, mobile edge computing and multi-access edge computing are used interchangeably and abbreviated by MEC in this chapter.

Table 2.2   ETSI MEC specifications

Specification	Description
GS MEC-IEG 005 V1.1.1	MEC; Proof of Concept Framework
GR MEC 022 V2.1.1	MEC; Study on MEC support for V2X use cases
GR MEC 017 V1.1.1	MEC; Deployment of MEC in an NFV environment
GS MEC 016 V2.1.1	MEC; UE application interface
GS MEC 015 V1.1.1	MEC; Bandwidth Management API
GS MEC 014 V1.1.1	MEC; UE Identity API
GS MEC 013 V1.1.1	MEC; Location API
GS MEC 012 V1.1.1	MEC; Radio Network Information API
GS MEC 011 V1.1.1	MEC; Mobile Edge Platform Application Enablement
GS MEC 010-2 V1.1.1	MEC; Mobile Edge Management; Part 2: Application life cycle, rules and requirements management
GS MEC 010-1 V1.1.1	MEC; Mobile Edge Management; Part 1: System, host and platform management
GS MEC 003 V2.1.1	MEC; Framework and Reference Architecture
GS MEC 001 V2.1.1	MEC; Terminology

Selected specifications related to MEC architecture. Available: https://www.etsi.org/standards-search. Updated 20 July 2019.

the MEC platform that offers MEC services, service registry, traffic rules control and domain name system (DNS) handling.

• MEC services are either predefined services provided by the MEC platform or additional services registered by MEC applications. Prime examples of the predefined MEC services include radio network information, location parameters and bandwidth management. To support additional MEC services, the service registry provides methods and authorisation for MEC applications.
• Traffic rule control drives the data plane for traffic routing among MEC applications and services according to the observed traffic rules dispatched by the MEC platform manager (MEPM), applications and services.
• DNS handling configures the DNS proxy functions based on records received from the MEC platform.

In addition, the (virtualised) hardware infrastructure is abstracted as the data plane. The data plane provides environment for traffic transfer as per requests from MEC applications and services. MEC applications are considered to be virtual machines running on top of the hardware infrastructure. The requirements of MEC applications in terms of (computing, storage and networking) resources, response time and supportive services are handled by the MEC system-level management through the MEC platform of the MEC host.

In brief, Mp1 and Mp2 reference points are defined for the MEC platform interfaces with the MEC applications and the data plane, respectively, while the Mp3 reference point is used for collaboration between two MEC hosts.

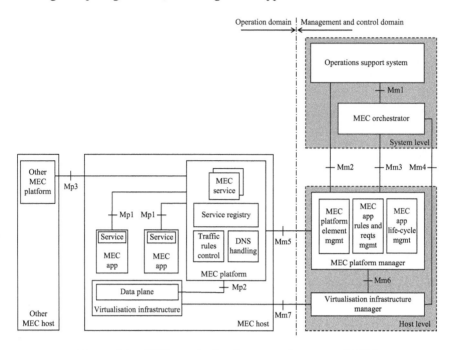

Figure 2.3   ETSI standard reference architecture of MEC

2.3.2   Management and control domain

Hierarchical architecture is utilised for management and control purposes in MEC systems; see right-hand side in Figure 2.3. A central MEC system manager harmonises operations of the MEC hosts via several MEC host managers located at each service cluster. At the MEC system level, the MEC orchestrator (MEO) plays a key role while operations support system (OSS) refers to the OSS of the mobile network for user applications interaction. The MEO is responsible for the following functions:

- Developing and maintaining a complete topology of the MEC system, including resource states and available MEC services in every managed MEC host. The system topology is based on information reported from representative MEC host managers.
- Handling third-party applications that (possible) utilise services in the MEC system in terms of application package verification and authentication, application requirements authorisation and rules validation, management and resource preparation for running the applications.
- Orchestrating available resources among appropriate MEC hosts in the service cluster(s) via MEC host manager(s) for application instantiation according to recent constraints of response time and application priority.
- Triggering application relocation and termination.

At the MEC host level, each MEC host manager consists of two components, namely MEPM and virtualisation infrastructure manager (VIM):

- The MEPM offers three main functions. The first is a function related to MEC platform elements such as availability and states of MEC services. The second is MEC application-related function, e.g. life-cycle management, event report and rule and request adjustments. The last is a state collection that listens to resource faults and performance measurement reports from the VIM for further processing.
- The VIM provides virtualised (computing, storage and networking) resources management in terms of configuration, allocation, release and performance reports following requirements from the MEO as well as sharing the performance report with the MEPM.

Internal reference points used in the management and control domains include Mm1 (OSS–MEO), Mm2 (OSS–MEPM), Mm3 (MEO–MEPM) and Mm4 (MEO–VIM). On the contrary, Mm5 and Mm6 reference points are for MEMP–in-host MEC platform and VIM–in-host virtualisation infrastructure interactions, respectively.

(Q2) What concepts are included in the standard reference architecture of MEC?

According to the ETSI specifications, a standard reference architecture of the MEC system defines functional elements at MEC hosts and managers as well as their reference points in both the operation and management/control domains. In this architecture, management and control domains adopt hierarchical topologies with two levels of MEC system and host while the operation domain follows a flat topology to provide equal roles to the MEC hosts.

2.4   Edge computing as a VNF

To be considered one of key features in the next generation mobile network, the MEC system, as a VNF, should be integrated into the network as a native function. This section first introduces an overview of the NFV architecture. Consequently, an integration of the MEC system into the NFV architecture is discussed.

2.4.1   Overview of NFV architecture

Network functions virtualisation is an approach that utilises IT virtualisation technologies to virtualise network functions that traditionally run on proprietary and dedicated hardware, thus allowing the network functions to be installed, manipulated and controlled by software running on standardised servers. In order to make an open reference point for vendor, operators and manufacturers, the ETSI has standardised a complete reference architectural framework of NFV consisting of three main components: VNF, NFV infrastructure (NFVI) and NFV MANO that is divided into two domains – execution and management/orchestration; see Figure 2.4. The framework is described in

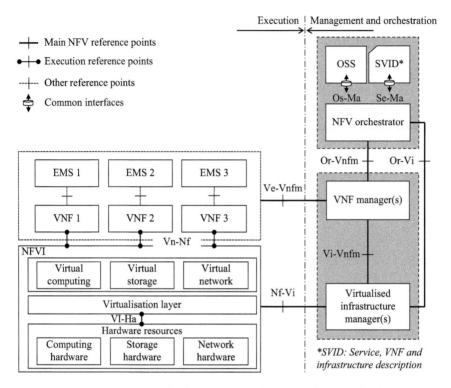

Figure 2.4   ETSI standard reference architectural framework of NFV

the ETSI GS NFV-MAN 001 V1.1.1 (2014-12) specification titled *Network Functions Virtualisation (NFV); Management and Orchestration* [15].

The execution domain comprises VNF and NFVI. A VNF is a software virtualisation of a network function that has functional behaviour, states, operational roles and responsibilities similar to the legacy network function. Targeted VNFs include Evolved Packet Core (EPC) network elements (e.g. Mobility Management Entity (MME), Serving Gateway (SGW) and Packet Data Network Gateway (PGW)), elements in a home network (e.g. Residential Gateway (RGW)) and conventional network functions (e.g. Dynamic Host Configuration Protocol (DHCP) servers and firewalls) [24,25]. Depending on the scale and specific requirements, a VNF can be implemented on one or several virtual machines along with different (virtualised) capacities. In order to flexibly tailor an appropriate operational environment for the VNFs, NFVI manages and controls hardware resources through a virtualisation layer (e.g. hypervisor) that is responsible for abstracting and partitioning the underlying hardware components to provide virtual resources for processing, storage and connectivity. The NFV framework defines execution reference points such as Vn-Nf for VNF–NFVI interface and VI-Ha for the virtualisation layer to manage hardware resources.

In the MANO domain, there are five elements positioned at two management levels: NFV orchestrator (NFVO), OSS and service, VNF and infrastructure description

(SVID) at the system level; VNF manager (VNFM) and virtualised infrastructure manager (VIM) at the host level. Among these elements, the NFVO plays a central role and connects with VNFMs and VIMs in all NFV groups for internal management purposes. In particular, the NFVO is in charge of orchestrating NFVI resources across the VIMs and life-cycle-managing VNFs via VNFMs in the entire system. In addition, the NFVO performs external management via interactions with the OSS and SVID, which are considered the network operators' elements. At the NFV host level, from a life-cycle management perspective, the VNFM has responsibilities of instantiating, scaling, updating/upgrading and terminating VNFs as commanded by the NFVO or react to operational states reported by traditional management functions. On the contrary, the VIMs possess functionalities of interaction management between the VNFs and their required resources such as allocation, modification, termination as well as usage reports. The NFVO interfaces the VNFMs and VIMs through reference points Or-Vnfm and Or-Vi, respectively, while the VNFMs and VIMs interact with each other through the Vi-Vnfm reference point. For external interconnection, Os-Ma and Se-Ma reference points are used for the OSS and SVID, respectively. Between the execution and management/orchestration domains, Ve-Vnfm and Nf-Vi reference points are defined for VNF–VNFM and NFVI–VIM, respectively.

2.4.2 MEC integration into the NFV architecture

From a network function management perspective, MEC is considered a VNF in the NFV reference framework [23]. Integration of the MEC into the NFV architecture is illustrated in Figure 2.5. Note that several elements are removed since there is no change on them. Moreover, reference points without updates in operation are blurred using grey colour and are omitted from discussion.

In addition to the original MEC reference architecture as mentioned in Section 2.3, there are several remarkable modifications follows:

- MEC platform and applications are considered as VNFs from the NFV MANO management perspective, i.e. life-cycle management for network function services such as initiation, update and termination.
- Virtualisation architecture of the data plane is considered as a component of the NFVI; therefore, it is managed directly by the VIM in NFV MANO architecture.
- The MEPM is replaced by an MEPM-NFV (MEPM-V) that delegates MEC operational management to VNFM.
- The MEO is replaced by an MEC application orchestrator (MEAO) that relies on the NFVO for virtualised resource orchestration. On the other hand, MEC service orchestration is retained and managed via Mm3* reference point between the MEAO and MEPM-V.
- Accordingly, sets of new reference points are defined, including (i) NFV reference set: Ve-Vnfm-em (MEPM-V–VNFM for MEC platform management), Ve-Vnfm-vnf (MEC platform VNF–VNFM for MEC platform management) and Nf-Vn (MEC platform VNF and MEC application VNF–NFVI); (ii) MEC reference set: Mm3* for specific MEC function management excluding resource management; and (iii) MEC-NFV reference set: Mv1 (MEAO–NFVO), Mv2

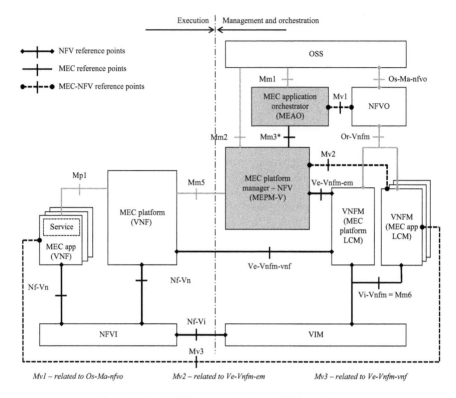

Figure 2.5　MEC integration into NFV architecture

(MEPM-V–VNFM for MEC application management) and Mv3 (MEC application VNF–VNFM for MEC application management).

(Q3) What are the distinguishing features of MEC as a VNF?

From the NFV management perspective, MEC platform and applications are considered as VNFs. Therefore, all virtualised resource MANO are handled by appropriate NFV elements in the NFV MANO architecture through the Mv1 and Mv2 reference points at the system and host levels in the management/ orchestration domain as well as Mv3 reference points in the execution domain. Other specific MEC service orchestration functions remain as in the standard MEC architecture.

2.5　Edge computing in a standard mobile reference model

Recently, MEC has been deployed in the fourth generation (4G) mobile networks as an optional service supplemented by the existing architecture [26,27]. Interactions

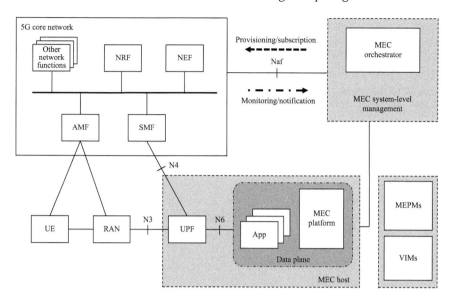

Figure 2.6   MEC in the 3GPP service-based architecture of 5G mobile network

between the MEC and the core network are performed through the OSS element, as introduced in the previous sections. In 5G mobile network, the MEC is promoted as an integrated function that is mapped onto the application function (AF) in the network architecture designed by the third generation partnership project (3GPP) standardisation organisation [7]. An MEC can interact directly with other network functions for their offered services and information, which are specified by the configuration policies. Figure 2.6 shows integration of the MEC into the 5G service-based architecture.

In particular, MEC, as an AF, introduces its services via the network exposure function (NEF). In addition, the NEF plays a key role for authorisation against all requests arriving from the MEC to access internal 5G network functions. On the other hand, services produced by 5G network functions are registered in the network resource function that acts as a central point of available service exposure. The 5G network functions and services are accessed directly when authenticated and authorised. At the system-level management, MEO (or MEAO if NFV is available), seen as an AF, interacts with the 5G network functions via the Naf reference point. Typically, operational procedures supported over the Naf point include provisioning and subscription from the MEO to the 5G core network and monitoring and notification in the inverse direction. Logically, the MEPMs and VIMs at the host management level can interact with the 5G network functions in the core network. However, these elements are generally deployed in the distribution network for cluster-based MEC host management. Therefore, an instance of the NEF can be established at the same networking level to provide high serviceability to the MEC host managers.

In the operation domain, the user plane function (UPF) is an interconnection point between the MEC and 5G network. The UPF performs traffic routing/switching to handle data coming in/out MEC applications and services using programmable rules. In case the MEC is deployed as an external component located at a 5G network device, the UPF is considered to be an additional and configurable data plane from the MEC point of view on the N6 reference point; see Figure 2.6. On the contrary, when the MEC is an advanced service provided by a 5G network device, the UPF is a local data plane of the MEC host.

From an operational perspective, services offered by the MEC can be considered to be the same as MEC applications. The 5G network manages accesses to/from the MEC applications using the session management function (SMF), which supports service continuity at the session level and provides reported data if requested from authorised network elements and systems. Session management includes initiation, maintenance, record and termination. Note that the management of the SMF is for external applications from the 5G network point of view; therefore, it does not conflict with the functional operations of the MEC platform inside the MEC host.

As to ensure service continuity, application mobility must be stringently addressed by the MEC system. Fortunately, since the MEC system collaborates with networking elements to provide low latency and high bandwidth services at the edge of the network, data handover is naturally handled by the networking device. In this circumstance, application service must be maintained according to the data handover that may be informed by the access and mobility management function (AMF). To this end, there are two main strategies applied in the MEC system from a software design perspective. First, an instance of the application is deployed in multiple neighbouring MEC hosts. These instances may run concurrently to provide load sharing. Second, service states of stateful applications are synchronised between the current and relocated MEC hosts.

(Q4) How to integrate MEC into the standard mobile reference architecture?

In the management domain, MEC system is considered as an AF in the 5G mobile architecture where the MEC (application) orchestrator interacts with the 5G network functions at core network while MEC host managers interact with an instance of the NEF at distribution network. In the operation domain, the MEC applications and services are managed by the SMF as external applications from the 5G point of view. The UPF of the 5G network device plays the role of data plane for traffic transfer to/from the MEC host.

2.6 Open issues and challenges

Despite great endeavours by the ETSI to standardise MEC technology, there are several issues and challenges against MEC popularisation. From an architectural perspective, five problems should be addressed as follows.

First, a standardisation of direct interoperation interfaces and protocols among MEC systems in multiple networks is necessary. Based on the ETSI specifications for

MEC, open-source communities in various industry segments are working on developing MEC software projects. Prime examples include Akraino Edge Stack, EdgeX Foundry, Edge Virtualization Engine, Open Glossary of edge computing and Home Edge, which are supported by the LF Edge organisation of the Linux Foundation, StarlingX supported by the OpenStack Foundation and OpenVolcano as a part of Europe's Horizon 2020 5G Infrastructure Public Private Partnership (5G-PPP) projects. Since the targeted business segments are different from each other, their system features and system designs do not adopt a common model. This leads to a diversity of MEC implementation even inside a local network, resulting in inefficiency of resource utilisation as well as MEC service quality.

Second, MEC technology has a close relationship with 5G network. On the other hand, MEC system is deployed at the edge of the network where 5GPoA devices are heterogeneous not only with different access technologies but also with a wide range of hardware capabilities. In this context, MEC architecture has to adapt to its running environment. Therefore, a variant of a customised MEC architecture for each environment should be developed and modified accordingly. This problem burdens MEC development and issues delay for system architecture update whenever each version of access technology is released. To mitigate this negative impact, self-adaptation and self-organisation should be featured on the MEC architecture.

Third, MEC application mobility, currently, partly depends on handover mechanisms supported by the networking elements at the edge of the network. This is an effective approach in a homogeneous environment of access network. However, a seamless connectivity among different access networks (e.g. Wi-Fi hotspots and cellular eNodeB) is not always guaranteed. Hence, a transparent application mobility that is independent of the networking infrastructure is necessary. A soft handover from the software design perspective should be addressed to provide service redundancy and migration among neighbouring MEC hosts.

Fourth, MEC system, by default, considers task arrival offloaded from user devices on the uplink through access network as a stochastic process and is uncontrollable. The distribution of task arrival mostly depends on the association scheme implemented among 5GPoA devices in order to optimise specific metrics on the radio interface such as spectrum efficiency, throughput maximisation and energy minimisation owing to resource limitation. However, a variety of MEC application scenarios exist, where service availability and response latency are the most important compared to these resource constraints. Smart manufacturing, precise farming and autonomous driving are some prime examples. In these situations, a close collaboration between MEC service orchestration and radio access association scheme in architectural design of MEC system and the 5GPoA can support task arrival control and distribution. As a result, offloaded tasks are directly assigned to appropriate MEC hosts efficiently.

Fifth, current MEC architecture does not consider security and privacy integration into the design. For external thread protection, at least an internal agent set-up for these purposes is mandatory although the security and privacy protection may be outsourced to an external system. Moreover, reference points and protocols for the external systems have to be defined and recommended. To countermeasure against internal attacks, authentication and authorisation procedure development as well as corresponding functions/components must be supplemented in the architecture design.

(Q5) What are the open issues and challenges of MEC from an architectural perspective?
From an architectural perspective, there are five main challenges that the MEC system faces, namely (i) standardisation of interoperation interfaces and protocols among MEC systems, (ii) heterogeneity of access networks where MEC systems are deployed, (iii) MEC application mobility dependence on the networking elements, (iv) MEC service aware association scheme in the access network and (v) security and privacy protection as an internal feature.

2.7 Summary

This chapter presents a detailed description of edge computing architectures that are developed and standardised by the ETSI organisation. The edge computing architectures are analysed from different points of view, including stand-alone architecture, VNF in the NFV architecture and an integration into the 5G mobile network. In each theoretical architecture, position and roles of elements are clarified which may help to validate mathematical system objective expressions and suggest feasible relevant systematical solutions as a solver or optimiser. Furthermore, open issues and challenges of the current edge computing systems are derived from the theoretical analysis which indicates five main problems from an architectural perspective in terms of scale, collaboration, integration, availability and security.

References

[1] Ge X, Tu S, Mao G, Wang CX, and Han T. 5G ultra-dense cellular networks. IEEE Wireless Communications. 2016;23(1):72–79.

[2] Farris I, Orsino A, Militano L, Iera A, and Araniti G. Federated IoT services leveraging 5G technologies at the edge. Ad Hoc Networks. 2018;68: 58–69.

[3] Na W, Jang S, Lee Y, Park L, Dao NN, and Cho S. Frequency resource allocation and interference management in mobile edge computing for an Internet of things system. IEEE Internet of Things Journal. 2019;6(3):4910–4920.

[4] Ordonez-Lucena J, Ameigeiras P, Lopez D, Ramos-Munoz JJ, Lorca J, and Folgueira, J. Network slicing for 5G with SDN/NFV: Concepts, architectures, and challenges. IEEE Communications Magazine. 2017;55(5): 80–87.

[5] Dao NN, Sa'ad U, Vu VC, Tran QD, Ryu ES, and Cho S. A softwarized paradigm for mobile virtual networks: Overcoming a lack of access infrastructure. IEEE Vehicular Technology Magazine. 2018;13(4):106–115.

[6] Dao NN, Lee Y, Cho S, Kim E, Chung KS, and Keum C. Multi-tier multi-access edge computing: The role for the fourth industrial revolution. In: Proceedings of the 8th International conference on information and communication technology convergence (ICTC); 18–20 October 2017; Jeju, South Korea. IEEE; 2017. pp. 1280–1282.

[7] Kekki S, Featherstone W, Fang Y, *et al*. ETSI White paper No. 28 – MEC in 5G networks. Sophia Antipolis CEDEX, France: European Telecommunications Standards Institute; 2018.

[8] Zhang Q, Cheng L, and Boutaba R. Cloud computing: State-of-the-art and research challenges. Journal of Internet Services and Applications. 2010;1(1):7–18.

[9] Bonomi F, Milito R, Zhu J, and Addepalli S. Fog computing and its role in the Internet of things. In: Proceedings of the 1st MCC workshop on mobile cloud computing; 17 August 2012; Helsinki, Finland. ACM; 2012. pp. 13–16.

[10] Dao NN, Lee J, Vu DN, *et al*. Adaptive resource balancing for serviceability maximization in fog radio access networks. IEEE Access. 2017;5:14548–14559.

[11] Mai L, Dao NN, and Park M. Real-time task assignment approach leveraging reinforcement learning with evolution strategies for long-term latency minimization in fog computing. Sensors. 2018;18(9):2830.

[12] Vu DN, Dao NN, Jang Y, *et al*. Joint energy and latency optimization for upstream IoT offloading services in fog radio access networks. Transactions on Emerging Telecommunications Technologies. 2019;30(4):e3497.

[13] Chung K, and Park RC. P2P cloud network services for IoT based disaster situations information. Peer-to-Peer Networking and Applications. 2016;9(3): 566–577.

[14] Cesario E, Mastroianni C, and Talia D. Distributed volunteer computing for solving ensemble learning problems. Future Generation Computer Systems. 2016;54:68–78.

[15] ETSI GS NFV-MAN 001 V1.1.1 – Network functions virtualisation (NFV); Management and orchestration. Sophia Antipolis CEDEX, France: European Telecommunications Standards Institute; 2014.

[16] Mao Y, Zhang J, and Letaief KB. Dynamic computation offloading for mobile-edge computing with energy harvesting devices. IEEE Journal on Selected Areas in Communications. 2016;34(12):3590–3605.

[17] Dao NN, Vu DN, Na W, Kim W, and Cho S. SGCO: Stabilized green crosshaul orchestration for dense IoT offloading services. IEEE Journal on Selected Areas in Communications. 2018;36(11):2538–2548.

[18] Dao NN, Vu DN, Lee Y, Cho S, Cho C, and Kim H. Pattern-identified online task scheduling in multitier edge computing for industrial IoT services. Mobile Information Systems. 2018;2018:9 pp.

[19] Shi W, Cao J, Zhang Q, Li Y, and Xu L. Edge computing: Vision and challenges. IEEE Internet of Things Journal. 2016;3(5):637–646.

[20] Mach P, and Becvar Z. Mobile edge computing: A survey on architecture and computation offloading. IEEE Communications Surveys & Tutorials. 2017;19(3):1628–1656.

[21]   Greenberg A, Hamilton J, Maltz DA, and Patel P. The cost of a cloud: Research problems in data center networks. ACM SIGCOMM Computer Communication Review. 2008;39(1):68–73.

[22]   Satyanarayanan M, Bahl V, Caceres R, and Davies N. The case for VM-based cloudlets in mobile computing. IEEE Pervasive Computing. 2009;8(4):14–23.

[23]   ETSI GS MEC 003 V2.1.1 – Multi-access edge computing (MEC); Framework and reference architecture. Sophia Antipolis CEDEX, France: European Telecommunications Standards Institute; 2019.

[24]   ETSI GS NFV 002 V1.2.1 – Network functions virtualisation (NFV); Architectural framework. Sophia Antipolis CEDEX, France: European Telecommunications Standards Institute; 2014.

[25]   Chatras B. On the standardization of NFV management and orchestration APIs. IEEE Communications Standards Magazine. 2018;2(4):66–71.

[26]   Giust F, Verin G, Antevski K, *et al.* ETSI White paper No. 24 – MEC deployments in 4G and evolution towards 5G. Sophia Antipolis CEDEX, France: European Telecommunications Standards Institute; 2018.

[27]   Tran TX, Hajisami A, Pandey P, and Pompili D. Collaborative mobile edge computing in 5G networks: New paradigms, scenarios, and challenges. IEEE Communications Magazine. 2017;55(4):54–61.

Chapter 3

Big data analytical models for/on edge computing

Narasimha Kamath Ardi[1] and Nikhil Joshi[1]

3.1 Introduction

Edge computing is a new paradigm for a plethora of mission-critical systems. With its variety of features, including low operational cost, high scalability, and real-time data analysis, edge computing has revolutionized various domains, including healthcare and e-commerce. With its seamless integration with different forms of wireless networks, edge computing applications are undoubtedly the best option to manage data trafficking and avoid delays related to packet transportation during dynamic routing. With the advent of big data analytics in today's digital era, edge computing applications can be incorporated with Internet of things to make it more intelligible and mitigate related computational problems. Figure 3.1 depicts the architecture of edge computing.

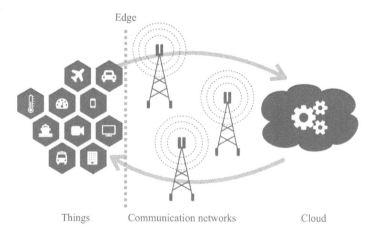

Edge

Things   Communication networks   Cloud

Figure 3.1   Architecture of edge computing

[1] Department of Analytics, The University of Chicago, Illinois, USA

Data management has undoubtedly become a critical challenge in any environment, be it cloud or on-premise. As edge computing is primarily based on the computation performed on the edge devices, as opposed to the centralized system, data management can be quite tricky as the devices at the edge are typically not high powered. Also, the fundamental challenges associated with big data applications to explore or retrieve the large volume of data might pose issues during the integration of edge computing applications. With that in mind, the chapter proposes an application model 5GHealthNet—to seamlessly manage medical data through higher generation networks via a cloud-based framework.

The chapter is organized as follows. Section 2 presents a brief introduction of analytical modeling concepts for edge computing. Section 3 discusses the advent of the in-memory database in edge computing. Section 4 highlights the privacy and security challenges within the big data-based edge applications. Finally, the chapter is concluded in Section 5.

3.2   Concept of analytical modeling for edge computing

With the advent of edge, there has been a considerable rise in the usage of edge-based applications that will undoubtedly utilize data from diverse sources to perform computations. Hence, the sharply increasing data deluge in the significant data era brings about enormous challenges on data acquisition, storage, management, and analysis [1]. With this in mind, there is a need for specific methods or algorithms to manage this significant boom in the data. Before this, there is a need to analyze some of the critical challenges about the field of big data analytics that might impact edge applications as well in some way or the other. Listed are some of the essential problems that exist in the field of big data analytics.

1. *Data storage/retrieval.* This is a significant hurdle in data analytics and is directly proportional to the volume of the incoming/outgoing data. With the advent of big data, large business enterprises are navigating towards favorite data storage techniques, including cloud/warehouses. Irrespective of the vast storage space, the extensive incoming data, when combined with other forms of inconsistent data from diverse sources, result in data conflicts and redundancy, and thus, it becomes quite tedious to retrieve the relevant data.
2. *Insufficient knowledge of big data analytics.* With the vast usage and production of data, there has always been a significant demand for data professionals. But there are very few professionals out there who understand the foundations of data, which is certainly not confined to the optimization of structured and unstructured data.
3. *Database type, data migration, and affordability.* With the rise of in-memory, column-oriented, relational database example SAP HANA, access to real-time data has become faster than ever before. SAP HANA (SAP High-Performance Analytic Appliance) combines OLAP (Online Analytical Processing) and OLTP (Online Transaction Processing), processing into a single in-memory database

eliminating disk bottlenecks. But many of the traditional enterprises are either stuck or currently migrating the data from the legacy database to the in-memory database. The cost of licensing is enormous for any cloud-based ERP (enterprise resource planning) system. This makes smaller enterprises with limited financial support, trying to bear the licensing cost. In a client-service model, mainly smaller enterprises are at risk as the clients are navigating towards large enterprises and are currently migrating the data to the in-memory database.

4. *Privacy and security*. We are literally producing voluminous data per minute. In a cloud-integration model, mainly SAP Cloud Platform Integration (data services), there will be approximately 10,000 to 50,000 data sets per full run. The clients are primarily concerned with the security of the data that are being sent to the third-party vendor system. However, are the data systems connected to the third-party systems secure? An increase in the data volume is directly proportional to the rise in its vulnerability. Data leaks in the production environment can lead to substantial financial losses as it can contain payroll data of an employee or much other similarly sensitive data. Although there is a considerable rise in the use of security algorithms to encrypt/decrypt incoming/outgoing data, the process is still in progress. It must be implemented in every possible stream dealing with data.

While these attributes are typically achieved by designing a robust architecture, the data generated by the devices with which edge applications can be integrated with would be in the order of zettabytes shortly [2]. This is evident as per the latest statistics shared by Gartner in its annual report [3]. It advocates that nearly 50 billion devices would be connected to the internet by 2020. Hence, relaying of such massive data to the existing cloud infrastructure may create network bottlenecks in the future [3]. With that in mind, latency might affect the overall system productivity, which is of primary concern to the enterprises marketing edge applications.

To understand a suitable approach where an existing design can be altered with the addition of a new pattern to manage the incoming load of data, a current application has to be taken into account. Through a case study, a suitable approach can be thought through to fine-tune the architecture. Figure 3.2 depicts the architecture of 5GHealthNet—a cloud-based framework for faster and authorized access to private medical records through 5G networks [4].

A load balancer initiates the data stream transfer; SEMS (security and edge management system) is implemented using the double encryption algorithm to ensure secure data access. DTB (data transport broker), DIP (data integration and processing), and PC (persistence and concurrency) modules provide data flow within the cloud [3]. A backup copy of the data to be accessed is created every time the access request is raised. The control flow of the entire operation is monitored in API Library and API (Application Programming Interface) management, which have the functionalities to ensure the access of private data [4]. However, having a large segment of data managed by one single-tier architecture has its drawbacks, too. One clear example is the impact of cycle-wise data uploads and downloads, where data ingestion and processing component within the architecture has to manage the entire volume. This

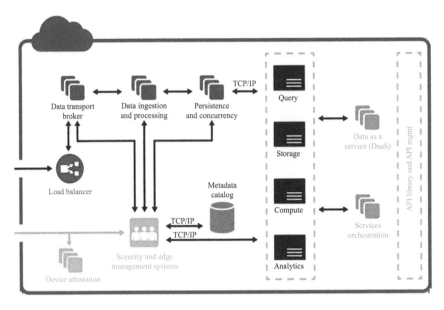

Figure 3.2   Architecture of 5GHealthNet

might cause issues regarding performance. To nullify the impact due to huge data volume, is it wise to choose a multi-tier architecture with multiple data integration components? Well, the entire scenario for considering the pattern change has to be thought through considering few scenarios like user count, batch size, number of cycles of data load and offload, network latency, and so forth.

Typically for edge-based applications, ultralow latency services in 5G network technology are used, which is the prime solution to tackle problems related to network latency. Ultralow latency services can be either push based (initiated by the content provider) or request based (started by the user) [5]. At the application layer, when the data volume is injected, the data transport broker transmits the message chunks to other subordinate controllers at all levels. The problem arises when the cycle of data load and offload exceeds the average threshold that poses issues related to data processing at the edge level. As devices connected to the edge are low-powered devices, processing huge data volume requires a component to break the essential data into smaller chunks that will typically eliminate the usage of multi-tier architecture for data modeling.

As discussed in one of the critical challenges, combining data from multiple sources will surely drive the need for an approach to avoid redundancy and conflicts related to the message structure. A cloud-based middleware can be one of the solutions to handle massive data volumes retrieved from the HealthNet platform. With this in mind, in this section, we discuss an approach of using cloud-based middleware to nullify the requirement for implementing a multi-tier architecture, which is obviously not a cost-effective option to go with. To sum up, meeting the needs of the edge applications and services with low end-to-end latency requires unified allocation and treatment of the communication, storage, and computing resources [5]. This yields a comprehensive arrangement of resources across the architecture level. With the help of middleware, we can surely lower the burden of data management and integration at the architecture level, which is discussed in the next subsection.

3.3 Advent of in-memory database in edge computing

An in-memory database is a data store that primarily uses the main memory of a computer. Since this main memory (a.k.a. RAM) has the fastest access time, data stored in the main memory affords the most speed for database applications. Primary stream databases mostly store data in a permanent store (such as a hard disk or network storage) which increases its access time and is thus not as fast when compared to in-memory databases.

Mission-critical applications, which need swift response times, such as medical and telecom applications, always relied on in-memory databases. However, the recent development of memory devices that can fit large amounts of data for a meager price has made in-memory databases very attractive to commercial applications as well.

In-memory databases generally store data in proprietary forms. Several open-source in-memory databases store data in a "key-value" format. So, in that sense, these databases are not similar to traditional relational databases that use SQL. However, there are a few in-memory databases that support SQL as well.

With the well-known in-memory database like SAP HANA, computation speed within the cloud environment has significantly improved with vast improvements in the storage of bulk data. In-memory databases can be quite useful for edge devices, which are often prone to low-power data computation and thus can be designed within the 5GHealthNet application to process more massive data sets successfully, without network latency. As discussed in the previous section, incorporating a cloud middleware was the solution presented to tackle the challenge of data and resource management within the network. However, cloud middleware supporting or having in-memory computation speed is the prime choice that can be considered while designing the architecture for the 5GHealthNet application.

However, there are only two downsides to in-memory database systems, and these are the following: (1) the cost of memory (DRAM (dynamic random access memory)) is higher than persistent memory (SSD or HDD) and (2) despite the higher cost, it is not possible to configure a server with as much DRAM as persistent storage, which limits the size of an in-memory database on a single server. An in-memory database can be distributed (shared) across many servers to overcome the size limitation (but, then, magnifies the cost discrepancy between in-memory and persistent DBMS).

Concerning "very few workloads" requiring an all-in-memory solution, this is subjective. No doubt, as a percentage of all DBMS workloads, those requiring an in-memory database system are a minority. But, on an absolute basis, there are ample cases. However, a right in-memory database system that is written and optimized to use memory as the storage media from the get-go will use far less "storage" (memory) to store any given amount of raw data ingested. For example, a disk-based database system might need between 2 MB and 10 MB of storage space to ingest 1 MB of raw data, whereas a simple in-memory database system might need only 1.15–1.5 MB to store the same 1 MB of raw data. The wide range is somewhat arbitrary and largely depends on the number, type, and complexity of the indexes defined. The more indexes defined, the more significant is the gap in storage space requirements between in-memory and persistent storage.

For losing all the data, most in-memory database systems have measures to mitigate or eliminate this risk (albeit, at the cost of some of the performance advantage of an IMDS (in-memory database systems)); there are three examples to illustrate this: (1) An in-memory database can be created in shared memory so that an application software failure does not cause the loss of any data (but does not protect against a kernel panic or hardware failure). (2) An in-memory database can be replicated to a hot-standby instance (i.e., high availability). (3) A transaction logging mechanism can be employed to be able to recover an in-memory database after a kernel panic or hardware crash (while relying on persistent media, and IMDS transaction logging is still substantially faster than a database stored on persistent media).

3.4   Privacy and security challenges in the edge-based modeling

"We just lost 50 million dollars!"—A dreadful statement even the world's largest companies would never want to hear. With the growing demand for data in multinational companies, the issue of data remaining private is always at stake. Besides, data and information are soft targets for malicious attackers, adding to the problem. Although the cloud is becoming the prime source for data storage, big data and cloud storage integration have caused a challenge to privacy and security threats as these security technologies are inefficient to manage dynamic data and are limited to static data. Therefore, information storage and retrieval require the best information security measures.

With the edge paradigm communicating with the various devices, it becomes imperative to examine the sources or assets posing threats at the edge-based networks to potentially identify and block them from attacking the resources [6]. With that in mind, risk-causing sources at edge paradigm are described in detail as follows:

- *Network infrastructure.* Edge paradigms make use of various communication networks to interconnect their instances: from wireless networks to core mobile networks [6]. An adversary can try to target any of this communication infrastructure by injecting duplicate packets within the system, taking control over the host network, and get access to the network resources and disrupt the edge network functionality entirely by disabling them.
- *Network data centers.* The network data center hosts the virtualization servers and several management services, amongst others. However, for an external adversary, the attack surface of an edge data center is quite considerable: from multiple public APIs that provide services to all actors (e.g., users, virtual machines, and other data centers) to other access points such as web applications [6]. The primary

threat due to this asset can be of physical network damage where the attacker has complete control of all the services provided in an intended location and can manipulate all interactions with external systems [6].

- *Communicating devices.* Communicating devices connected to the edge paradigm are also the essential elements of the entire ecosystem. They are the active participants in sharing the net sources and communicating with other neighbor devices across various levels to use the system service. Concerning this asset, an adversary can try to gain control over any of these devices and manipulate the service outcome to disrupt the functioning of the system.

- *Edge cloudlets.* Cloud system being the major operational hub in the edge devices, native cloud applications used to access the data from the target infrastructure can serve as a primary threat, especially during the data transfer. With the edge network connected by various cloud platforms, an adversary can potentially hack the cloud system, and control the functioning of the target devices.

To create an active layer of defense for multiple threats, it is essential to integrate various security mechanisms during the architecture design to avoid aggressive and passive attacks from the attacker. Different security mechanisms can be taken into account while designing the edge-based big data applications that are primarily concerned with the management of enormous data loads during the load and offload of information. In this section, a few underlying security mechanisms are being discussed as follows:

- *Identity and authentication management.* In a typical edge-based big data application, there are multiple users or actors (administrator, developer, tester, and user) that are interacting in an ecosystem where numerous trust domains coexist. This situation brings innumerable challenges as we have to assign an identity to every entity, but also all entities should mutually authenticate each other. Without this, it will be straightforward for an adversary to target the service infrastructure with impunity. To avoid this, it is necessary to design an authentication management system that provides substantial evidence of the users who have used the system.

- *Monitoring network traffic.* In case of unusual network traffic within the system, there are chances that the intruder has started to control the network system to manipulate the system resources. Due to the low computation power of the edge paradigm, there are considerable chances of the network data to be altered by the intruder if the favorable traffic rates are not monitored. To resolve issues like this, periodic system audits and network performance reports are necessary to identify the weak spots that can be attacked by the adversary. Therefore, it is essential to assign a unique id to the network packets, and the same has to be provided to the destination queue/receiver. Once the packet ids are matched, they are decrypted to fetch the information. This is by far the most straightforward and suitable approach for small-scale networks connected to edge applications. For large-scale systems, more layers of security mechanisms should be introduced to reject the duplicate packets ultimately.

It is absolutely necessary to focus on specific research areas such as secure software engineering, fault tolerance, and resilience by considering the particular features of edge paradigms during the development of security-aware software systems, due to which the vulnerabilities specific to our context will be significantly reduced. Lastly, malicious adversaries can be detected and prosecuted if the right steps are taken before the design of the security system.

3.5 Conclusion

In this chapter, we have presented a holistic approach to the concept of big data modeling towards edge computing. In the first part of our analysis, we have introduced a detailed introduction, critical challenges in the field of big data analytics, and how those challenges can impact edge applications deployed on the cloud. In the third section, we have presented the technical aspects of in-memory databases that can speed up the data computation for the low-power edge devices. In the fourth part, we have highlighted a few of the security challenges and mechanisms to overcome the problems during the system design phase. Nevertheless, many open issues and challenges can arrive in the field of edge computing as it's an advanced stream that has started to flourish across the various domains.

References

[1] Hesham El-Shayed, Sharmi Shankar, Mukesh Prasad, *et al.*, "Edge of Things: The Big Picture on the Integration of Edge, IoT and the Cloud in a Distributed Computing Environment," IEEE Access, vol. 6, 2017.

[2] Kuljeet Kaur, Sahil Garg, Gagangeet Singh Ahujla, Neeraj Kumar, Joel J.P.C. Rodrigues, and Mohsen Guizani, "Edge Computing in the Industrial Internet of Things Environment: Software-Defined-Networks-based Edge-cloud Interplay," IEEE Communication Magazine, vol. 56, no. 2, 2018.

[3] Narasimha Kamath Ardi and Nikhil Joshi, "5GHealthNet—A Cloud Based Framework for Faster and Authorized Access to the Medical Records through 5G Wireless Networks," First IEEE/ACM Symposium on Edge Computing, 2016.

[4] Kan Zheng, Zhe Yang, Kuan Zhang, and Periklis Chatzimisios, "Big Data-driven Optimization for Mobile Networks Toward 5G," IEEE Network, vol. 30, no. 1, 2016.

[5] Min Chen, Shiwen Mao, and Yunhao Liu, "Big Data—A Survey," ACM Mobile Network Applications, vol. 19, no. 2, 2014.

[6] Rodrigo Roman, Javier Lopez, and Mashahiro Mambo, "Mobile Edge Computing, Fog *et al.*: A Survey and Analysis of Security Threats and Challenges," Elsevier, vol. 78, part 2, pp. 680–698, 2018.

Chapter 4

Data security and privacy models for/on edge computing

Lichuan Ma[1,2], Qingqi Pei[1,2], Huizi Xiao[1] and Weisong Shi[3]

As a new computing paradigm, edge computing (EC) has gained much popularity in various delay-sensitive application scenarios (like vehicular networks and autonomous driving). With the prevalence of EC, its security and privacy issues become more and more significant for its further development. When referring to the security and privacy issues in EC, its meaning is twofold: the first is the inherent security issues of EC architectures and the other is how we can strengthen the security of current systems by introducing the paradigm of EC. Thus in this chapter, after analyzing the unique properties of EC, intrusion, lightweight authentication, access control and private information leakage are chosen to be four typical threats and challenges for the security or privacy issues of EC. Then, some practical security and privacy solutions prompted by EC in existing research works are present. After that, several open research issues are given to draw more attentions from academia and industry to guarantee the security of this new paradigm.

4.1 Introduction

Nowadays, with the popularity of Internet of Things (IoT) gadgets, it will be possible to seamlessly connect all things in the physical world through the network. In addition, the data collected from the "things" have built a concrete foundation for machine learning technologies to infer more useful information. Industries such as manufacturing, autonomous driving, smart grid and mobile crowdsensing have benefited from the IoT.

As is shown in Figure 4.1(a), traditional IoT architectures rely on a cloud server to collect and process data for different applications. Here, all the data should be transmitted to the cloud server and these data are then processed in a centralized way. However, according to a Cisco report, the volume of the data generated by

[1]The State Key Laboratory of Integrated Services Networks, Xidian University, Xi'an, China
[2]Shaanxi Key Laboratory of Blockchain and Security Computing, Xi'an, China
[3]Department of Computer Science, Wayne State University, Detroit, MI, USA

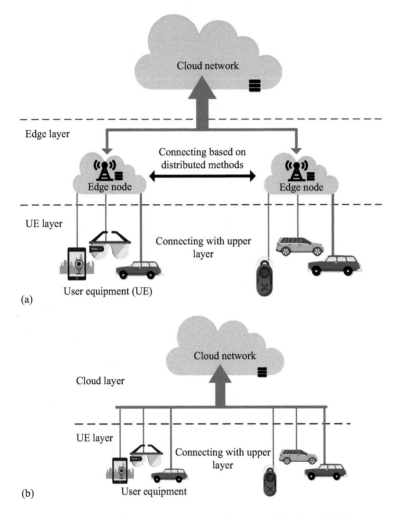

Figure 4.1   (a) The cloud computing architecture; (b) the EC architecture

the things would reach 507.9 ZB by 2019 [1]. If all the data were transmitted to the cloud server, the cost and transmission delay cannot be tolerated. As more and more services or applications become delay-sensitive, the traditional cloud-centralized IoT architecture is not suitable nowadays.

Since moving computation is much cheaper than moving data when the volume of data is dramatically vast, a new computing paradigm, EC, comes out. In EC, it is capable of bringing on-demand services and applications much closer to devices to improve user experience and redundancy in case of failure. Comparing with the traditional two-layer cloud-centralized architecture, there are three layers in the EC architecture, namely the device layer, the edge layer and the cloud layer (refer to

Figure 4.1(b)). Here, the edge layer is formed by geographically distributed devices equipped with computation, communication and storage capabilities. These devices can be smartphones, personal computers, smart gateways and even small data centers. Obviously, there still exists a centralized cloud server which is responsible for orchestrating the geographically distributed edge nodes (ENs) to fulfill different tasks and applications. From this perspective, EC is the extension of cloud computing.

Via EC, various services can be responded faster and more flexible. But without proper data security and privacy protection, the benefits of EC would be diminished [2]. In addition, with the popularity of this new paradigm, the data security and privacy issues may hinder EC from going further. As one computing paradigm of information systems, EC confronts some general security threats like external intrusion, denial of services (DoS), data forgery and private information leakage. In the meanwhile, several security and privacy threats that are typical in EC due to its unique properties are summarized in Section 4.2. Since many applications benefit from EC for the lower latency and more stable access, existing solutions for guaranteeing security and preserving privacy may benefit from EC. From this meaning, four typical security and privacy solutions prompted by EC are present in Section 4.3. Then, some open research issues related to data security and privacy models for EC are given in Section 4.4. In the end, this chapter is concluded in Section 4.5.

4.2 Threats and challenges for security and privacy in EC

As is known, the appearance of EC makes it possible to process data at the edge of the networks. According to [3], the ENs are responsible for computations on "downstream data on behalf of cloud services and upstream data on behalf of IoT services." In this sense, EC holds the following three main properties:

1. *ENs are usually equipped with limited computation, communication and storage capabilities.* This is compared with the centralized cloud centers which are considered with infinite computing powers. Usually, each EN manages the data from a small part of the whole network. Due to different applications, the EN can be smartphones, gateways or small data centers running cloudlets.
2. *ENs are geographically distributed and orchestrated by the cloud.* To respond requests instantaneously, the ENs should be in proximity to the users and thus exchange data with the users via short-range communication technologies. By this way, the requests from different users can be responded in a distributed manner. For some complicated tasks, like online training for behavior pattern recognition of the users, the ENs should be orchestrated by the cloud to cooperate with each other to fulfill these tasks.
3. *Large amount of original data circulates through the three-layer EC architecture.* Since the ENs are closer to the data source, they can be "the first entry" of data for processing. Then, data are preprocessed by the ENs and the results are sent to the cloud server for further analysis. During the whole process, data circulate through the three-layer EC architectures.

For general information systems, there can be many security threats and challenges. But related to the properties of EC, external/internal intrusion, lightweight authentication, access control and private information leakage are considered as the most typical ones. In the following, we will illustrate why these threats and challenges are catastrophic in EC and some possible solutions are also given.

4.2.1 Intrusion

Intrusion is usually considered as behaviors to evade computer security policy or standard and it is also known as attack [4]. As stated by [5], traditional intrusion techniques include asymmetric routing, buffer overflow attacks, protocol-specific attacks, traffic flooding, trojans, worms, etc. Among them, the traffic flooding attack is the most famous one and it is also referred as the DoS attack or the distributed DoS (DDoS) attack. The DoS or DDoS attack aims to run out the resources of bandwidth, storage and computation via leveraging a large number of devices to send requests to the target simultaneously. In this manner, the resources of the target can be exhausted and the requests from normal users would be congested. The methods to launch DoS or DDoS attack can be classified into three categories [6]: (1) to send data packets to the target at the same time to congest the bandwidth; (2) to send particular packets to make the TCP/IP module exhaust the resources of CPU; and (3) to send packets of particular formats to make the network service software to exhaust the resources of CPU.

When moving to the scenarios of EC, the intrusion attack can be more severe as the ENs are equipped with limited storage, computation and communication capabilities. To defend against this kind attack, intrusion detection systems (IDSs) are usually utilized. An IDS is to discover unauthorized network behaviors or anomalies in the system, collect behaviors that violate security policies and perform statistical aggregation to support audit analysis and unified security management decisions [4]. It usually includes a series of functions such as detection, analysis, response and collaboration.

The intrusion detection devices in the traditional network are connected to the mirror port of the enterprise switch. It is responsible for detecting and analyzing the mirrored traffic forwarded by the switch. If an abnormal event is detected, the dynamic policy configuration would be implemented through the linkage mechanism between the intrusion detection device and the firewall, and the active response behavior such as real-time blocking of the attack behavior can be implemented. Intrusion detection technology can be divided into two typical categories:

1. *Misuse detection-based techniques.* Misuse detection techniques are also known as knowledge-based detection or pattern-matching detection techniques. It assumes that all network attack behaviors and methods have certain patterns or characteristics. If the characteristics of all previously discovered network attacks are summarized based on which an intrusion information database can be constructed, an IDS is to capture the current network behavior characteristics. After comparing these characteristics with the attack feature information in the constructed data base, whether the current is considered as an intrusion can be

determined. This comparison process can be very simple (such as a string match to find a simple entry or instruction). Also, it can be rather complex (such as using regular mathematical expressions to express changes in security state).

2. *Anomaly detection-based techniques.* Anomaly detection techniques, also known as behavior-based detection techniques, refer to determining whether there is a network attack based on the users' behavior and the usage of system resources. The anomaly detection techniques first assume that the network attack behavior is abnormal and is different from all the normal behaviors. If the behavioral rules can be extracted from all the normal behaviors of the users and systems, the behavioral model can be established. Then, an IDS can compare the captured network behavior with the behavioral model. If it deviates from the normal behavioral trajectory, the current behavior would be considered as an intrusion. Specifically, an IDS based on anomaly detection techniques first defines a set of thresholds for normal system activities, such as CPU utilization, memory utilization and file checksum. Then it compares the current values corresponding to the dimensions required to be monitored with the predefined "normal" thresholds to determine whether there is a sign of attack. The core of this detection method is how to analyze and extract the normal behavior patterns of different system operations.

At present, most intrusion detection techniques are designated for cloud computing application scenarios. Since the ENs provide users with parts of the cloud computing functions, they can be considered as "small cloud centers." In this sense, the implementation of IDSs in EC can refer to those in cloud computing. In [4], the authors propose a framework in which mobile devices using 5G networks can delegate intrusion detection tasks to centralized services located in the cloud. Even though this framework is for centralized cloud services, it might be expanded to deploy the IDSs in ENs to defend against malicious attacks. The authors of [7] present a distributed IDS deployed in a cloud mesh architecture. Here, the cloud servers can collaborate with external entities to detect malware, malicious attacks, etc. This decentralization design of the proposed IDS is very possible to be directly implemented by EC architectures. As a result, many malicious attacks and suspicious activities can be accurately detected via the collaboration of the geographically distributed ENs. However, how to motivate the owners of these devices to work together for the detection of intrusions remains to be questionable.

4.2.2 Lightweight authentication

In EC, there exist three kinds of entities, namely the cloud server, the ENs and the users. Here, there can be different trust domains where different entities offer and access real-time services. This makes it difficult to ensure all the involved entities trusted. As a result, a malicious attacker is able to forge his identity and profile to make himself look like a legitimate user in the network. In this manner, the other entities might be misguided by the fake information generated by such attackers. Also, attackers can stand between two legal parties to launch the man-in-the-middle attack. To be worse, attackers can be enabled to pretend to be service providers to offer fake or phishing services [8]. All these malicious activities can ruin any network. In order to conquer this problem, different authentication mechanisms have been proposed to guarantee the trust of entities involved in various services.

In the traditional two-layer cloud architecture, it only requires the mutual authentication between the cloud server and the users. But when considering the three-layer EC architecture, it is compulsory to guarantee the mutual authentications between the cloud server and the ENs, the ENs and the cloud servers, the cloud server and the users, and any two different ENs. Aiming to ensure the security of the whole process for EC architectures to provide services, it is never a simple task to design a thorough authentication scheme. Since many capability-constrained IoT gargets are enrolled by EC and their mobility can be extremely high (such as automobiles or unmanned aerial vehicles), this makes the authentication in EC a much more challenging task.

4.2.2.1 Public key infrastructures

Generally, public key infrastructures (PKIs) are well-accepted choices for authentication. The PKI is a system or platform that provides public key cryptography and digital signature services for the purpose of managing keys and digital certificates. An organization can establish a secure network environment by managing keys and certificates using the PKI framework.

PKI is a system that uses public key technology to realize network service security. It is an infrastructure that can guarantee the security of network communication and online transactions. A PKI system mainly includes the following contents:

1. *Certification authority.* The certificate authority is the core of the PKI infrastructure, which is an authoritative, trustworthy and impartial third-party organization.
2. *X.500 directory server.* It is utilized to publish user's certificate and certificate revocation list information. Users can query their own or others' certificates and download certificate revocation lists through the standard Lightweight Directory Access Protocol.
3. *Key backup and recovery system.* This is responsible for backing up the user's decryption key and restoring this key when lost. However, the signature key cannot be backed up and restored.
4. *Certificate revocation processing system.* This system manages a certificate revocation list. If the certificate needs to be invalidated or terminated for some reason, such a list helps to achieve this.
5. *PKI application interface system.* It provides a secure, consistent and trusted way to interact with PKI for a wide variety of applications to ensure the security and reliability of the network environment while reducing management overhead.

A complete PKI architecture also includes the formulation of certification policies, like technical standards to be followed, subordinate relationship between central authorities (CAs), security policies, security levels, client management principles and frameworks, etc. In summary, PKI is based on public key cryptography and establishes trust relationships through digital certificates.

To implement PKIs, any entity in the EC architecture needs to store many certificates to achieve authentication with others. It is feasible for ENs or cloud server to manage these certificates due to the adequate storage spaces and computation ability of these devices. But for the users, many of them are equipped with very limited storage and computation capabilities. Also, many applications in EC are rigorously delay-sensitive. This makes it very inefficient and unsuitable to deploy PKIs in real application scenarios. As a result, it is impossible to rely on PKIs to satisfy the complex and heterogeneous authentication requirements for EC.

4.2.2.2 Identity-based encryptions

To deal with the performance issues of PKI-based schemes, the identity-based encryption (IBE) scheme is proposed by Boneh in [9]. In the IBE scheme, the keys for authentication can be computed by the users' identities. As the identity of any user is unique, the certificates are not needed to bind pubic keys to entities in a network.

In order to explain the basic idea for the IBE scheme, we borrow the simple scheme, called BasicIdent, from [9]. BasicIdent includes four algorithms: Setup, Extract, Encrypt and Decrypt. Let k be the security parameter given to the Setup algorithm. These algorithms are the following:

Setup: The Setup algorithm is to generate the parameters utilized in the scheme. It works as follows:

1. Choose a large k-bit prime p such that $p = 2 \bmod 3$ and $p = 6q - 1$ for some prime $q > 3$. Let E be the elliptic curve defined by $y^2 = x^3 + 1$ over $\mathbb{F}_p$. Choose an arbitrary $P \in E/\mathbb{F}_p$ of order q.
2. Pick a random $s \in Z_q^*$ and set $P_{pub} = sP$.
3. Choose a cryptographic hash function $H : \mathbb{F}_{p^2} \to \{0, 1\}^n$ for some n. Choose a cryptographic hash function $G : \{0, 1\}^* \to \mathbb{F}_p$. The security analysis will view H and G as random oracles.

The message space is $\mathcal{M} = \{0, 1\}^n$. The ciphertext space is $\mathcal{C} = E/\mathbb{F}_p \times \{0, 1\}^n$. The system parameters are params $= \{p, n, P, P_{pub}, G, H\}$. The master-key is $s \in \mathbb{Z}_q$.

Extract: For a given string ID $\in \{0, 1\}^n$, the algorithm builds a private key d_{ID} as follows:

1. Use MapToPoint$_G$ to map ID to a point $\mathcal{Q}_{ID} \in E/\mathbb{F}_p$ of order q.
2. Set the private key d_{ID} to be $d_{ID} = s\mathcal{Q}_{ID}$ where s is the master key.

Encrypt: To encrypt $M \in \mathcal{M}$ under the public key ID do the following: (1) use MapToPoint$_G$ to map ID into a point $\mathcal{Q}_{ID} \in E/\mathbb{F}_p$ of order q; (2) choose a random $r \in Z_q^*$; and (3) set the ciphertext to be

$$C = \langle rP, M \oplus H(g_{ID}^r) \rangle \text{ where } g_{ID}^r = \hat{e}(\mathcal{Q}_{ID}, P_{pub}) \in \mathbb{F}_{p^2}$$

Decrypt: Let $C = \langle U, V \rangle \in \mathcal{C}$ be a ciphertext encrypted using the public key ID. If $U \in E/\mathbb{F}_p$ is not a point of order q reject the ciphertext. Otherwise, to decrypt C using the private key d_{ID} compute:

$$V \oplus H\left(\hat{e}\left(d_{ID}, U\right)\right) = M$$

This completes the description of BasicIdent. When everything is computed as above, it derives:

1. During encryption M is Xored with the hash of g_{ID}^r.
2. During decryption V is Xored with the hash of $\hat{e}(d_{ID}, U)$.

Here, the function MapToPoint is to map the ID to a point on an elliptic curve and we refer the readers to [9] for further details.

4.2.3   Access control

In EC, geographically distributed ENs are in charge of different groups users, and for some particular scenarios (like vehicular networks), a user can move from the cover range of an EN to that of another EN. When taking the cloud server into consideration, the situation becomes more complicated. Thus, for different services and applications, different entities enrolled in the three-layer EC architecture can have very distinctive rights to access data or utilize resources of storage, communications and computations. Without proper authorization mechanisms, external intruders, or internal malicious users are able to arbitrarily access personal accounts and tamper normal services [10]. From this perspective, designing appropriate access control is of far-reaching significance to ensure the security of EC.

Access control mechanisms are responsible for restricting entities' access to critical resources of applications, and prevent illegal ones from entering the system and illegal use of system resources by legitimate users. Generally, discretionary access control (DAC), mandatory access control (MAC) and role-based access control (RBAC) technologies are generally used in traditional access control. With the advent of distributed application environments, a variety of access control technologies such as attribute-based access control (ABBC), task-based access control (TBAC) and object-based access control (OBAC) have been developed.

4.2.3.1   Role-based access control

In the RBAC model, roles are the basic semantic terms that implement access control policies and access permissions are related to roles. The core idea of RBAC is to associate permissions with roles, and the user's authorization is done by assigning the corresponding roles. Whether a user is permitted to get access to the data is determined by the union of all the roles owned by this user. Roles have logical relationships such as inheritance and restriction, and influence the actual correspondence between users and permissions through these relationships.

The entire access control process is divided into two parts; that is, the access rights are associated with the roles, and the roles are associated with the users, thereby realizing the logical separation between the user and the access rights. The role can be regarded as a semantic structure expressing the access control policy that indicates eligibility for a specific job.

4.2.3.2   Attribute-based access control

The emergence of service-oriented architectures and network environments has broken the traditional closed information system. This makes the whole platform include several independent systems interconnected by various interfaces. In this environment, it is required to be able to establish an access control policy based on the context of the access, and to handle the heterogeneity and variability of the subjects and objects. Traditional user RBAC models are not suitable for such environments. Nevertheless, ABBC utilizes attribute expressions to describe the access policies. By this way, it does not directly define authorization between the subject and the object, but uses their associated attributes as the basis for authorization decisions. As a result, access control decisions can be updated in a timely manner according to the dynamic changes of related entity attributes, thus providing a more granular and flexible access control policies.

4.2.3.3 Task-based access control

TBAC is a task-focused, active security model that utilizes dynamic authorization. When authorizing a user, the permission to access, it depends not only on the subject and the object, but also on the task and the state of the task being executed by the subject currently. When the task is active, the subject has access rights. Once the task is suspended, the access rights owned by the subject are frozen. If the task resumes execution, the principal will regain access. When the task is in the terminated state, the permissions owned by the subject are immediately revoked. From the perspective of tasks, TBAC dynamically manages permissions, which is suitable for distributed computing environments and multi-access control information processing. However, such a model significantly increases the complexity to achieve access control.

4.2.3.4 Object-based access control

OBAC associates access control lists with controlled objects and designs access control options as a collection of users, groups or roles and their corresponding permissions. It also allows policies and rules to be reused, inherited and derived. This is extremely useful for an application system with a large amount of data and frequent state changes in information. The main advantage is to alleviate the workload for distributing and assigning role rights caused by derivation, evolution and reorganization of resources.

Up to now, there have already existed some access control mechanisms deployed in the context of EC. For instance, the so-called OPENi framework is proposed by [11] on the basis of OAuth2.0. The owner of the cloud defines the access permission of each resource by creating and storing access control lists in the NoSQL database. This access control mechanism is more suitable for private clouds. In terms of policy execution component deployment and security policy management, the authors of [12] design a fog computing policy management framework. Here, the choreography layer of fog architecture is supported by the policy management module, and the policy management module defines various components, including rule base, attribute database and session management, which can be executed on edge data centers and IoT devices. A RBAC strategy demonstrated in [13] develops a distributed access control framework for the cloud environment. Also, inter-domain role mapping and constraint verification are provided by this framework. In this manner, various entities from different trust domains can be seamlessly linked.

4.2.4　Private information leakage

With the prevalence of EC, more and more services and applications are provisioned. When utilizing the services or applications, lots of data would be generated. Even for some cases (like crowdsensing), users are required to provide data to the ENs nearby for preprocessing. All these data might contain sensitive information like locations, preferences or behavior patterns. If such sensitive information is disclosed, the privacy of the users would be violated and this is rigorously forbidden by the General Data Protection Regulation [14].

In most existing research works, both the ENs and the cloud server are assumed to follow the semi-honest model. This means that these entities would act properly to realize their predefined functions but are curious about what they have received. Hence, it requires that no private information would be leaked to unauthorized entities and the privacy of the users should be preserved.

Contemporarily, privacy preserving is a hot topic in both academia and industry. It plays an important role in theoretical research and practical application. Without loss of generality, the methods for privacy preserving can be classified into three categories: distortion based, encryption based, and restricted-publishing based.

4.2.4.1　Distortion-based privacy-preserving methods

Data distortion technology implements privacy protection by perturbing raw data. It is necessary to make the disturbed data satisfy the following requirements at the same time: (a) the attacker cannot reconstruct the real original data through the released distortion data; (b) the distorted data still retain certain characteristics, meaning that some statistical properties derived from the distorted data are equivalent to the information derived from the original data.

Distortion-based privacy-preserving methods can maintain certain statistical properties by adding noise and other methods to distort sensitive data while maintaining certain data or data attributes. To achieve this, the first method is to add random noise to the original data and then release the data after the disturbance. The second one is blocking and condensing. Here, blocking refers to the method of not releasing certain specific data and condensing refers to replacing the original data with its statistical information. The third is differential privacy protection. Generally, when classifier construction and association rule mining are performed, and the data owner does not want to publish real data, the original data may be disturbed before being released.

4.2.4.2　Encryption-based privacy-preserving methods

Encryption-based privacy-preserving methods utilize cryptographic tools to keep the sensitive data secret during the data mining process. Mostly, they are used in distributed application scenarios, like achieving secret query, geometric computing and scientific computing in a distributed manner.

A typical example is to realize encrypted keyword search in the ciphertexts. The data owner uploads the ciphertexts of original data and related encrypted indexes to the cloud service provider. Here, the data are usually encrypted by a general cryptographic algorithm (such as AES) while the indexes are generated via a specific searchable encryption mechanism. The searchable encryption mechanisms can be divided into asymmetric key searchable encryption-based and symmetric key searchable encryption-based ones. When a data consumer wants to search for encrypted data in a cloud server, he would create a trapdoor (when using asymmetric searchable encryption) or request a trapdoor from the data owner (when using symmetric searchable encryption). Then, the trapdoor is sent to the cloud service provider. After receiving the trapdoor, the cloud service provider executes the search algorithm and returns the results to the data consumer. This kind of search can return the top n most suitable results based on a specific sorting criterion. During the whole process, the service provider cannot know the original data or what the consumer has requested for.

4.2.4.3 Restricted-publishing-based privacy-preserving methods

Restricted publishing means to selectively publish raw data. This means not to publish or publish sensitive data with low precision for privacy protection. Current research on such technologies focuses on "data anonymization." It aims to find the trade-off between privacy disclosure risk and data accuracy when selectively publishing sensitive data. Here, the risk of disclosing sensitive data should be kept at an acceptable level. Data anonymization research mainly focuses on two aspects: the design of better anonymization principle and the design of more "efficient" anonymization algorithms following specific anonymization principles. Currently, how to realize the practical application of anonymization technology has become the focus of current researchers.

Most current privacy protection schemes do not require a centralized infrastructure and only require a trusted platform module, so they can be implemented on the EC platform. And there have already existed some privacy-preserving mechanisms for EC. In [15], the authors propose a privacy protection mechanism for privacy protection in EC. The problem to be addressed is how to implement privacy policies when migrating code and data between mobile devices. Since eavesdroppers can locate users to a fairly small range by observing the service migration among ENs, a chaff control policy based on heuristic strategies in [16] is proposed to preserve the location privacy of the users. Here, the tracking accuracy of the eavesdropper can be minimized. For some other specific privacy mechanisms, such as data encryption and secure data sharing, the complex operations on ciphertexts can be offloaded to the ENs nearby and the computational requirements on users' devices are much lower than before. This builds solid foundations for the future design of privacy mechanisms for EC scenarios.

4.3 EC-based security and privacy solutions

The previous section presents the inherent threats and challenges for security and privacy in EC. Once these issues are addressed, the EC paradigm can strengthen the security of different applications. Thus, in this section, several examples are given to illustrate how we can benefit from EC when designing different security solutions.

4.3.1   EC-based solutions for DDoS

As stated before, the DDoS attack refers to combining a great number of devices as an attack platform to launch DoS attack toward a target server of network. In order to shut down the services provided by the target, this attack fully exploits the flaws of the target network service functions or just consumes its system resources directly.

From this perspective, DDoS attacks can be roughly divided into two categories. The first is spoofing. Hackers spoof the server by sending fake packets. Specifically, the source IP address in the packet is masqueraded to a value that does not exist or is illegal. Once the server accepts the packet, it will return a response packet, but in fact the package will never return to the bogus source IP address. This method requires the target to open its own monitor port to wait. As these requests are from attackers, the system resources are wasted during the waiting period. The other is non-spoofing. Many DDoS attacks do not involve any spoofing techniques. These attacks can by botnets to generate a large amount of malicious burst traffic. Specifically, the attackers use these "broiler chickens" to launch a large number of requests to the target in a short period of time. Via this way, the bandwidth resource of the target can be exhausted and the availability of its online services is corrupted.

To defend against the DDoS attack, [17] proposes a DDoS attack defense architecture in mobile networks, namely MECPASS, by leveraging flexible implementation and resource allocation in EC environments. As is shown in Figure 4.2, the architecture of MECPASS involves two hierarchical levels of nodes: local nodes and central nodes. The local nodes are located at the edges of local area networks to execute DDoS defense detection whereas the central nodes are in the centralized cloud to execute global defense detection with the help of geographically distributed local nodes.

In detail, a local node consists of two core modules: the anti-spoofing module and the detection engine. The anti-spoofing module reads a copy of the data from the MEC (mobile edge computing) raw packet stream and verifies the availability of the source IP addresses of received packet. If any spoofed packets are found, discard them immediately. The anti-spoofing function is realized by implementing a source IP and tunnel end point identifier (TEID) matching mechanism. In fact, a hash table is created to mapping uplink TEID and user equipment IP. Then, the source IP address of user equipment can be extracted. Finally, check whether this IP address match with the same TEID in the hash table. If there is a match, the packet passes the anti-spoofing module and is forwarded to the next procedure, otherwise, it is abandoned. Then, unfiltered traffic packets (non-spoofing and legitimate ones) are sent to the detection engine. The feature information of these packets is obtained by the extraction module and then acts as input to the detection algorithm in the local detection engine. It can be determined whether it is an abnormal traffic through a specifically designed threshold and score system.

Due to the dynamic nature of mobile networks, it is very possible for the users to frequently move between the coverages of adjacent local nodes. In this sense, the central nodes located in the centralized cloud are responsible for performing abnormal behavior monitoring as they can receive aggregated data streams from the local nodes periodically. As a result, the detection algorithm in central detection engine can use

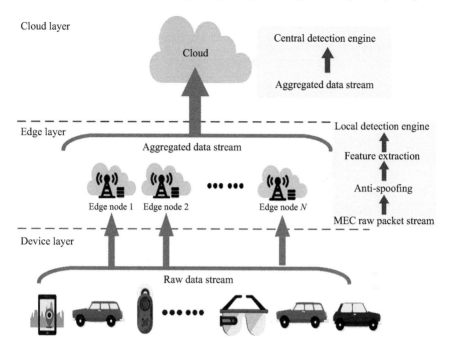

Figure 4.2   The MECPASS architecture in [17]

aggregated feature information to identify abnormal traffic comprehensively. This can significantly improve the detection rate of whole framework.

By implementing such a framework, the traffic to the cloud is obviously reduced than sending all the raw packets to the central nodes in cloud. Moreover, additional bandwidth and required computation resources are also decreased for DDoS defense.

From the experimental evaluation in [17], it shows that the higher the handover frequency is, the more effective the MECPASS architecture is. Most of the spoofing traffic and high-volume attacks can be filtered successfully at the local nodes. In this architecture, the capabilities of ENs and the cloud server are fully utilized for effective defense of DDoS attacks. Even though the practical implementation of such a defending architecture remains to be discussed, this presents a clear idea to design EC-enhanced defending strategies for DDoS attacks.

4.3.2   EC-based solutions for mutual authentication

Authentication is of great significance to guarantee the security of EC because data can securely flow across different trust domains. In [18], the authors propose Octopus, which is an IoT security authentication scheme based on EC.

Octopus is the first security mutual authentication between end points and edge servers in edge networks for the three-layer EC architecture. In this solution, each end

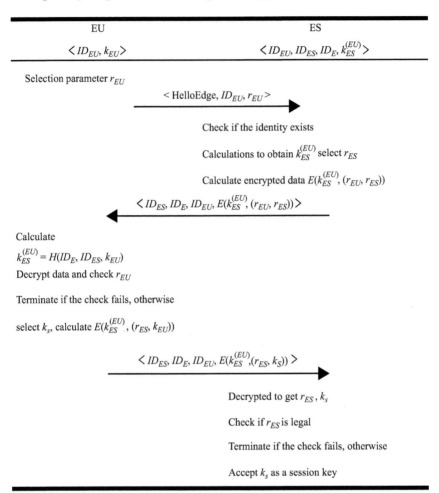

Figure 4.3   The authentication phase of Octopus [18]

user EU (edge user) needs to save a long-term master key (with a sufficiently long bit length). There are three phases in Octopus:

1. *Initialization phase.* Registration authority (RA) and ESs (edge servers) save their own public and private key pairs, respectively. In the meanwhile, RA stores the public key of each edge server and assigns an identity ID to each EU which is signed by RA with its signature key.
2. *Registration phase.* Each EU needs to obtain and store the master key from RA. Then, RA calculates the authentication keys for EU and ES that are returned via a secure communication channel (e.g. secure sockets layer (SSL)). ES is responsible for storing an ID-key table for all the EUs.
3. *Authentication phase.* The mutual authentication occurs between the terminal and the edge server and Figure 4.3 presents the detailed process.

Due to the large number of IoT devices, it is difficult to implement large-scale PKI on the edge of the network. Octopus is an IBE-based scheme and allows each end user to authenticate with any edge server with the authorization of the cloud service provider. By doing this, multiple types of attacks, like replay and middleman, can be effectively resisted. The solution does not require the terminal to be included in any PKI system, but only the primary key needs to be stored once during the registration phase. This setting offers a countermeasure against the situation where one or more servers are compromised by attackers. Even if all the edge servers are destroyed, the security of the master key can be ensured without reinitialization or registration of the master key. Octopus adopts symmetric key encryption/decryption in the authentication process and thus it can be effectively implemented for the resource-constrained IoT devices. This solution provides a good direction for guaranteeing the authentication process in EC.

4.3.3   EC-based solutions for cryptographic implementations

Since in EC ENs are equipped with considerable storage, communication and computation capabilities, some complex computations can be offloaded to the ENs nearby for some resource-constrained devices. This is one of the main advantages of EC. With the help of EC architecture, it becomes possible to implement complicated cryptographic security solutions on resource-constrained IoT devices by offloading complex ciphertext operations to the ENs. From this perspective, ensuring security for IoTs benefits much from the appearance of EC.

In [19], the authors propose a secure outsourced computation framework in the scenario of connected vehicular cloud computing (CVCC). By introducing the EC paradigm, the computing resources among the cloud, roadside infrastructure and vehicles are efficiently exploited. In this scheme, the complex pairing-based cryptographic primitives are outsourced to the ENs to ease the computation burden of the users. As is shown in Figure 4.4, there are two major kinds of pairing outsourcing services in CVCC, that is, outsourcing to the cloud and outsourcing to ENs which include road-side units (RSUs) and other vehicles in this scene. Regarding the pairing outsourcing service to the edge, the authors further classified it into two subclasses. One is that the client vehicle can outsource the pairing computations to an EN as an agent who is responsible for decomposing, delegating and distributing tasks to other vehicles. Another is that any client vehicle directly outsources pairing computations to an EN who execute the computation tasks.

In details, the pairing-based cryptography primitive is built on bilinear groups. Let the groups G_1 and G_2 be additive cyclic groups and G_T be a multiplicative cyclic group. All of them have order q, and they are equipped with an admissible pairing $e : G_1 \times G_2 \to G_T$, such that for all $a, b \in Z_q^*, p \in G_1, Q \in G_2, e(aP, bQ) = e(P, Q)^{ab}$ holds.

Since it is necessary to protect the input and output of the outsourced pairing, the inputs P and Q are required to be kept secret. However, it is still possible that the result of outsourced pairing $e(P, Q)$ would reveal the secret information of the client vehicle. As different vehicles must belong to different individuals, vehicles cannot

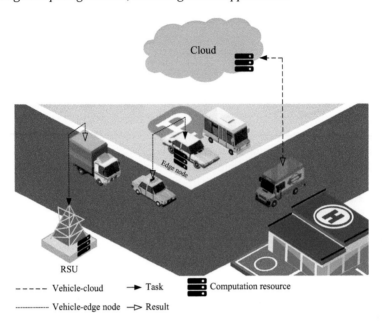

Figure 4.4   The secure outsourced computation framework for CVCC [19]

be considered to be trustworthy. This leads to the necessity to verify the results from other vehicles.

In the proposed framework, any user is permitted to outsource a series of pairing computations to other vehicles that are idle. Here, these idle vehicles act as the EN. As the pairing and scalar operations are quite time-consuming, the preprocessed version of these operations should be applied. Given $A_i \in G_1$, $i = 1, 2, \ldots, n$, and $B \in G_2$, P is a generator of G_1, the client vehicle wants the result of outsourced pairing $e(A_i, B)$ from server vehicle to be used for complex cryptographic implementation, they assumed A_is are secret variables and B is a public constant. The specific process is as follows:

Step 1: The client vehicle chooses random numbers a_i and α_i from Z_q^* for every i, then computes $P_i = a_i P$ by using the preprocessed scalar multiplication in G_1 for $i = 1, 2, \ldots, n$ and computes $A_i' = \alpha_i A_i$ by using the normal scalar multiplication in G_1. As P is known in advance, it can be computed in the preprocessed version of scalar multiplication operation. To protect the confidentiality of the input A_i, the client vehicle sets $U_i = A_i + P_i$ and $V = \sum_{i=1}^{n} A_i'$ to mask A_i. Then, a cryptographically secure hash function H is used to compute $h = H(U_1 || \cdots || U_1 || V || B)$, which is used as a label to identify the computation task. The client vehicle should record the tuple $(\{a_i, \alpha_i\}_{i=1}^{n}, h)$ as a task with a series of paring outsourcing computations. In this tuple, $\{a_i, \alpha_i\}_{i=1}^{n}$ are applied to verify the validity of results from server client.

Step 2: Upon receiving $(\{U_i\}_{i=1}^{n}, V, B, h)$ from client vehicle, the server vehicle computes $S_i = e(U_i, B) = e(A_i + P_i, B) = e(A_i, B)e(P, B)^{a_i}$ and

$T = e(V, B) = e\left(\sum_{i=1}^{n} A'_i, B\right) = e(A, B)^{\alpha_1} e(A, B)^{\alpha_2} \cdots e(A, B)^{\alpha_n}$ for $i = 1, 2, \ldots,$ n by the normal pairing computation and then sends the computed results to the client vehicle.

Step 3: Since P is known in advance and B is a public constant, $X = e(P, B)$ can be pre-computed by using preprocessed pairing computation to save time and resources. After receiving paring result tuple $(\{S_i\}_{i=1}^{n}, T, h)$ from the server vehicle, the client vehicle can find the corresponding $\{a_i, \alpha_i\}_{i=1}^{n}$ according to h and compute $W_i = X^{a_i} = e(P, B)^{a_i}$ for $i = 1, 2, \ldots, n$ by using the preprocessed exponentiation computation in G_T, as well as $E_i = S_i / W_i$ can be computed. Consequently, if $\prod_{i=1}^{n} E_i^{\alpha_i} = T$ holds, the validity of result from server vehicle can be verified and the client vehicle apparently gets $E_i = e(A_i, B)$ for $i = 1, 2, \ldots, n$. Otherwise, the received results are false.

From the performance evaluation results of [19], it is obvious to find that the bandwidth and computation cost of the proposed pairing outsourcing protocol can be reduced by large margin if outsourcing pairing computations to other vehicles for all curves.

Due to the capability limitation, most IoT devices cannot perform too many cryptographic computations. Meanwhile, it is verified to be not effective to send all the original data to the cloud server for processing. Since "moving computation is much cheaper than moving data," the appearance of EC paradigm permits the data to be processed near its source, and complex computations can be offloaded to the ENs nearby. In this sense, security for IoTs can be strengthened by EC as it is possible to implement complex cryptographic scheme on IoT devices with the help of ENs nearby.

4.3.4 EC-based solutions for privacy preserving

EC is proposed as a feasible solution to mitigate the delay issues. The core idea is to geographically distribute a number of ENs with efficient storage spaces and computational capabilities. In this manner, the data from end users can be first preprocessed by the ENs and only the preprocessed results are transmitted to the cloud server. As the ENs and the cloud server are assumed to be honest but curious, how to protect the original data is the key problem when designing privacy-preserving mechanisms for EC.

As stated in Section 4.2.4, there are three types of privacy-preserving methods: distortion based, encryption based and restricted-publishing based. Among them, both distortion-based and restricted-publishing-based methods introduce changes in the original data to different levels. More or less, they would influence the accuracy of the preprocessed or final results. One interesting way to protect the original data without sacrificing the accuracy is to introduce homomorphic encryption (HE) schemes. In HE, it allows a certain number of operations (i.e. additions and multiplications) over ciphertexts without the need to decrypt them at first. This scheme is consistent with the EC paradigm as the complex operations on ciphertexts can be offloaded to the EN. Moreover, if the ENs and the cloud server are from different parties, these two kinds of entities form a two-server model to help implement different secure multiparty computation schemes.

In [20], the authors propose a privacy-preserving reputation management scheme to preserve privacy and deal with malicious participants simultaneously in the scenario of mobile crowdsensing. Here, all the sensing data are encrypted and only the participant who invokes the sensing task can decrypt the final aggregating result. To tackle malicious participants, a new rule to update the reputation values based on the deviations of the encrypted sensing data to the final aggregating result are designed without exposing the original sensing data.

In the scheme, there are a central manager (CM), a reputation manager (RM), a CA, multiple ENs and a number of participants. Here, CM, RM and CA are located in the cloud and in charge of distributing sensing tasks, updating reputation values and generating keys, respectively. ENs are spatially distributed in different regions.

As is shown in Figure 4.5(a) and (b), there are two phases to achieve the aforementioned goal. The first is to fulfill the sensing task and the other is to update reputation values.

1. Fulfilling the sensing task (Figure 4.5(a) presents the detailed process)

    Step 1: Before sending the request τ to EN_q, the requester q first asks the CA to generate the public and private key pair (sk_τ, pk_τ) for preserving privacy of the participants when fulfilling the sensing task.

    Step 2: The CA outputs the public-secret key pair (sk_τ, pk_τ) for the current task request.

    Step 3: q keeps sk_τ private and sends the request for τ together with pk_τ to EN_q.

    Steps 4–6: After EN_q receives the request from q, it forwards this request to CM. Then, CM distributes τ and pk_τ to EN_τ, which is the EN in the area where τ should be performed. After that EN_τ broadcasts τ and pk_τ to the participants nearby.

    Step 7: By receiving the broadcast, a set of participants, denoted by P_τ, would like to perform τ. For the ith participant in P_τ, let s_i denote the participant's sensing data. Assume that s_i is an m-dimension vector and thus $s_i = \{s_{i,j}, j = 1, 2, \ldots, m\}$. To preserve privacy, the ith participant encrypts each element in s_i to derive $[[s_i]]$, where $[[s_i]] = \{[[s_{i,j}]], j = 1, 2, \ldots, m\}$. Then, s_i is sent to EN_τ.

    Step 8: After receiving the sensing data from the participants in P_τ, EN_τ requests the reputation values of these participants from RM.

    Step 9: Once receiving the reputation values of the participants in P_τ, EN_τ aims to aggregate all the sensing data to derive the encrypted final sensing result $[[s_\tau]]$. To guarantee the correctness of the final result, the aggregating rule is defined as computing the weighted mean of all the sensing data where the weights are the reputation values of the participants in P_τ. When all the sensing data are not encrypted, s_τ can be computed by

$$s_\tau = \left(\sum_{i \in P_\tau} r_i \cdot s_i\right) \Big/ \sum_{i \in P_\tau} r_i$$

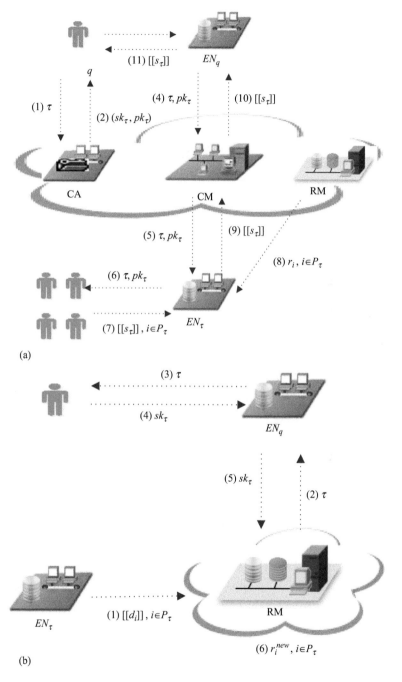

Figure 4.5   (a) The process to fulfill sensing task [20]. (b) The process to update reputation values [20]

As the somewhat homomorphic encryption (SHE) scheme is utilized here, it holds that $[[r_i \cdot s_i]] = [[r_i]] \cdot [[s_i]]$ for any $i \in P_\tau$. Note that r_i is included in RC_i and EN_τ can extract the reputation values after each reputation certificate is validated. To compile $[[s_\tau]]$, EN_τ first computes $[[r_i]]$ (for all $i \in P_\tau$) and $[[1/\sum_{i \in P_\tau} r_i]]$. It is easy to complete these computations since all the reputation values are known to EN_τ. According to the weighted sensing data aggregation rule, $[[s_\tau]]$ can be computed by

$$[[s_\tau]] = \left[\left[\frac{\sum_{i \in P_\tau} r_i \cdot s_i}{\sum_{i \in P_\tau} r_i} \right]\right] = \left[\left[1 \bigg/ \sum_{i \in P_\tau} r_i \right]\right] \cdot \sum_{i \in P_\tau} [[r_i]] \cdot [[s_i]]$$

After obtaining $[[s_\tau]]$, EN_τ sends it to the CM.

Steps 10–11: $[[s_\tau]]$ is returned to the querier q by the CM via EN_τ. Using sk_τ, q can decrypt s_τ to get the plaintext of $[[s_\tau]]$.

2. Updating reputation values (the detailed process in Figure 4.5(b))

   Step 1: Given $[[s_i]]$ ($i \in P_\tau$) and $[[s_\tau]]$, EN_τ computes $[[d_i]]$

$$[[d_i]] = \left[\left[\sum_{j=1}^{m} \frac{1}{(ub_j - lb_j)^2} \left(s_{i,j} - s_{\tau,j} \right)^2 \right]\right]$$

$$= \sum_{j=1}^{m} \left(\left[\left[\frac{1}{(ub_j - lb_j)^2} \right]\right] \cdot [[s_{i,j}]] + [[-s_{\tau,j}]] \right) \cdot ([[s_{i,j}]] + [[-s_{\tau,j}]])$$

ub_j and lb_j are the upper and lower bounds of the j-th attribute values, respectively. Then, EN_τ sends $[[d_i]]$ ($i \in P_\tau$) to the RM.

Steps 2–3: After receiving the encrypted deviations, the RM needs to decrypt them with the secret key sk_τ owned by the querier q. Thus, the RM sends the request for sharing sk_τ to q via EN_q.

Steps 4–5: When q gets this request and completes the sensing task τ, sk_τ is sent to the RM via EN_q utilizing the secure communication channel between q and the RM.

Step 6: Once the RM obtains sk_τ, all the deviations can be decrypted and the reputation values of the participants in P_τ are updated.

During the whole process, the users just need to encrypt their sensing data and send them to the EN nearby. The aggregation of encrypted sensing data and the update of reputation values are achieved via the collaboration of ENs with the RM located in the cloud.

4.4 Open research issues

In this section, several open research issues related to security and privacy in EC are discussed. We hope these issues can draw more attentions and efforts from researchers and engineers to corporately guarantee the security of EC.

4.4.1 Uniform authentication scheme for cloud–edge–user architecture

In the three-layer architecture of EC, there are three types of entities: the cloud, ENs and users. All of them have heterogeneous formations. Different users can have different devices to request various services from ENs and cloud servers. To fulfill some complicated tasks, ENs and cloud servers from different service providers are required to cooperate with each other. During this process, the mutual authentication among the enrolled parties becomes much more sophisticated than ever. In addition, the owner–member relationships between users and ENs are ambiguous. For the smart home scenario, the EN can be a smart gateway owned by user but it would be managed by T-mobile or China Unicom when the basic communication infrastructures introduce the EC paradigm. Also, the users can move in a high speed and the ENs to provide services can be switched frequently. How to achieve efficient mutual authentications with different ENs becomes rather difficult. Even though authentication is an old and classic research topic in information security, no existing work can propose an efficient solution to address the above issues. From this perspective, a uniform authentication scheme for EC is necessary. Under such a scheme, the heterogeneity of each layer in EC architecture and the lightweight requirement on the user side should be thoroughly considered.

4.4.2 Practical zero knowledge proof for offloaded computations

In EC, the core concept is offloading. There have been a great number of works aiming to work out optimal offloading strategies via different manners for different applications. In some privacy-preserving works, the ENs are assumed to be honest but curious. All these works assume that the ENs would honestly undertake tasks as predefined. Actually, this is not always the case because ENs are fragile to different intrusion attacks and much easier to be compromised than cloud servers. As a result, the correctness of the results offered by ENs should be verified in a lightweight manner by the users. Otherwise, the consequences caused by false results of offloaded computations cannot be imagined. Taking autonomous driving as an example, severe traffic accidents can occur if the vehicles make wrong decisions due to these false results. Moreover, since the results might reveal some sensitive information about other users, zero knowledge proof for offloaded computations is of great potential to tackle the above problem. However, most existing methods for zero knowledge proof are very complex and time-consuming. This makes them impractical to be implemented in actual applications. Hence, it is of great importance to customize different practical zero knowledge proof methods for different applications in EC.

4.4.3 Privacy preserving for edge intelligence

Recently, artificial intelligence (AI) applications based on machine learning (especially deep learning algorithms) have gained popularity in a wide range of fields due to its capability to obtain knowledge from huge volumes of data. Pushed by EC techniques and pulled by AI applications, edge intelligence has been pushed to horizon

[21]. In edge intelligence scenarios, the ENs are responsible for both training and inference. Since the volume of data possessed by one EN is limited, collaborations among different ENs are compulsory to derive a more accurate global model. As intermediate parameters in a learning model can reveal a lot of sensitive information of original sensing data and the model should be also kept secret to the users in the inference phase, how to address the privacy-preserving problem is one of the key factors that determine the prevalence of edge intelligence. As the applications enhanced by edge intelligence can be very different, we should design different methods based on proper privacy-preserving tools corresponding to different requirements of the practical applications.

4.5   Conclusion

Along with the popularity of EC, its security and privacy problems become more and more severe currently. Considering the unique properties of EC, we illustrate the security and privacy threats/challenges from four aspects: intrusion, lightweight authentication, access control and private information leakage. Even though there exist some other security issues, these four aspects highlighted above are much more typical in such a new computing paradigm. Then, the security and privacy issues in EC are discussed in a different viewpoint, referred as how we can benefit from EC when designing security and privacy solutions for current systems. To enroll more researchers and engineers to work together for guaranteeing the security of EC, several related open research issues are given. We hope this chapter can help the readers to build the basic understanding on the security and privacy issues in EC.

References

[1]   Hassan N, Gillani S, Ahmed E, Yaqoob, I, and Imran M. The role of edge computing in Internet of things. IEEE Communications Magazine, 2018, 56(11): 110–115.

[2]   Lin F, Zhou Y, An X, You I, and Choo KKR. Fair resource allocation in an intrusion-detection system for edge computing: Ensuring the security of Internet of Things devices. IEEE Consumer Electronics Magazine, 2018, 7(6): 45–50.

[3]   Shi W, Cao J, Zhang Q, Li Y, and Xu L. Edge computing: Vision and challenges. IEEE Internet of Things Journal, 2016, 3(5): 637–646.

[4]   Gai K, Qiu M, Tao L, and Zhu Y. Intrusion detection techniques for mobile cloud computing in heterogeneous 5G. Security and Communication Networks, 2016, 9(16): 3049–3058.

[5]   Hoque N, Bhuyan MH, Baishya RC, Bhattacharyya DK, and Kalita JK. Network attacks: Taxonomy, tools and systems. Journal of Network and Computer Applications, 2014, 40: 307–324.

[6]   Mirkovic J, and Reiher P. A taxonomy of DDoS attack and DDoS defense mechanisms. ACM SIGCOMM Computer Communication Review, 2004, 34(2): 39–53.

[7] Shi Y, Abhilash S, and Hwang K. Cloudlet mesh for securing mobile clouds from intrusions and network attacks. 2015 3rd IEEE International Conference on Mobile Cloud Computing, Services, and Engineering. IEEE, 2015: 109–118.

[8] Ni J, Zhang K, Lin X, and Shen X. Securing fog computing for Internet of things applications: Challenges and solutions. IEEE Communications Surveys & Tutorials, 2017, 20(1): 601–628.

[9] Boneh D, and Franklin M. Identity-based encryption from the Weil pairing. In: Advances in Cryptology – CRYPTO 2001, pp. 213–229. Springer (2001).

[10] Goyal V, Pandey O, Sahai A, and Waters B. Attribute-based encryption for fine-grained access control of encrypted data. Proceedings of the 13th ACM Conference on Computer and Communications Security. ACM, 2006: 89–98.

[11] McCarthy D, Malone P, Hange J, *et al.* Personal cloudlets: Implementing a user-centric datastore with privacy-aware access control for cloud-based data platforms. Proceedings of the First International Workshop on Technical and Legal Aspects of Data Privacy. IEEE Press, 2015: 38–43.

[12] Dsouza C, Ahn GJ, and Taguinod M. Policy-driven security management for fog computing: Preliminary framework and a case study. Proceedings of the 2014 IEEE 15th International Conference on Information Reuse and Integration (IEEE IRI 2014). IEEE, 2014: 16–23.

[13] Almutairi A, Sarfraz M, Basalamah S, Aref W, and Ghafoor A. A distributed access control architecture for cloud computing. IEEE Software, 2011, 29(2): 36–44.

[14] GDPR, https://eugdpr.org/.

[15] Ravichandran K, Gavrilovska A, and Pande S. PiMiCo: Privacy preservation via migration in collaborative mobile clouds. 2015 48th Hawaii International Conference on System Sciences. IEEE, 2015: 5341–5351.

[16] He T, Ciftcioglu EN, Wang S, and Chan KS. Location privacy in mobile edge clouds: A chaff-based approach. IEEE Journal on Selected Areas in Communications, 2017, 35(11): 2625–2636.

[17] Nguyen VL, Lin PC, and Hwang RH. MECPASS: Distributed denial of service defense architecture for mobile networks. IEEE Network, 2018, 32(1): 118–124.

[18] Ibrahim MH. Octopus: An edge-fog mutual authentication scheme. International Journal of Network Security, 2016, 18(6): 1089–1101.

[19] Shao J, and Wei G. Secure outsourced computation in connected vehicular cloud computing. IEEE Network, 2018, 32(3): 36–41.

[20] Ma L, Liu X, Pei Q, and Xiang Y. Privacy-preserving reputation management for edge computing enhanced mobile crowdsensing. IEEE Transactions on Services Computing, 2019, 12(5): 786–799.

[21] Zhang X, Wang Y, Lu S, Liu L, Xu L, and Shi W. OpenEI: An open framework for edge intelligence. In Proceedings of the 39th IEEE International Conference on Distributed Computing Systems (ICDCS), Vision/Blue Sky Track, July 7–10, 2019, Dallas, USA.

Chapter 5

Networking models and protocols for/on edge computing

Yogesh Sharma[1], Mohammad Ali Khoshkholghi[1] and Javid Taheri[1]

Edge computing is a distributed computing paradigm which brings the computing infrastructure at the edge of the network and close to the users in order to reduce the latency and improve the user experience. It is the realisation of a concept of an intermediate layer between the users and cloud computing infrastructure to accommodate explosive growth of data generated by underlying user devices and to process it with lesser response time than cloud computing systems. Mobile network operators are the potential providers of edge computing as a service by using the infrastructure of their service networks existing in close proximity to users. In order to establish the synergy between the devices or resources of user end, edge layer and cloud layer, a thorough understanding of networking models and communication protocols is required. This will help the researchers and system designers to design optimised and efficient edge computing systems, which will improve the user experience with minimum incurred costs. This chapter provides an overview of networking/reference models and the corresponding communication protocols for edge computing systems. First, the chapter starts with a layered system architecture representing interaction between the user devices with cloud computing infrastructure via fog layer followed by reference models corresponding to each layer. Description of communication protocols corresponding to each reference model is also provided besides a taxonomy classifying all the discussed communication protocols on the basis of their characteristics.

5.1 Introduction

Edge computing is recognised as a key technology for future 5G era. It has been emerged as a quick fix for end-user-related problems by bringing the far located data processing resources closer to the data originating points such as mobile devices and sensors. Such relocation of computing resources let the end users to process the data in real time locally with negligible response time and at the fraction of cost of cloud services, while maintaining the advantage provided by cloud services

[1]Department of Mathematics and Computer Science, Karlstad University, Karlstad, Sweden

such as unlimited computing and storage. Figure 5.1 shows an end-to-end layered solution representing synergy between data collection devices from edge to the cloud resources. In order to realise such edge computing systems, a substantial amount of knowledge about the networking models/stacks and corresponding protocols is required. As shown in Figure 5.1, there are three levels of networking in an edge

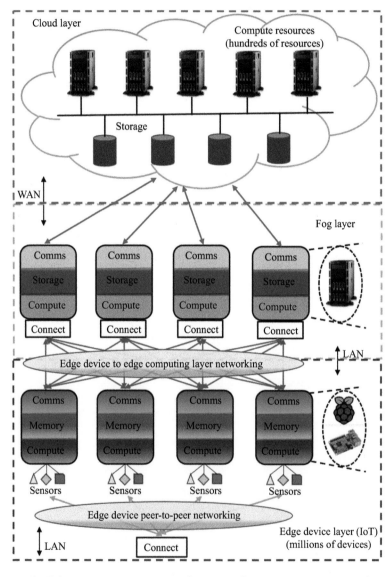

Figure 5.1   Edge computing system architecture showing interconnection between various computing layers, type of devices and networking models

computing system, i.e. edge device peer-to-peer networking, edge device to fog layer and fog layer to cloud layer. For every level, there are specific set of protocols and reference models proposed in the literature with respect to the type of communicating devices and requirements of end-user applications. In this chapter, we highlighted the layered networking models and corresponding communication protocols (Figure 5.2)

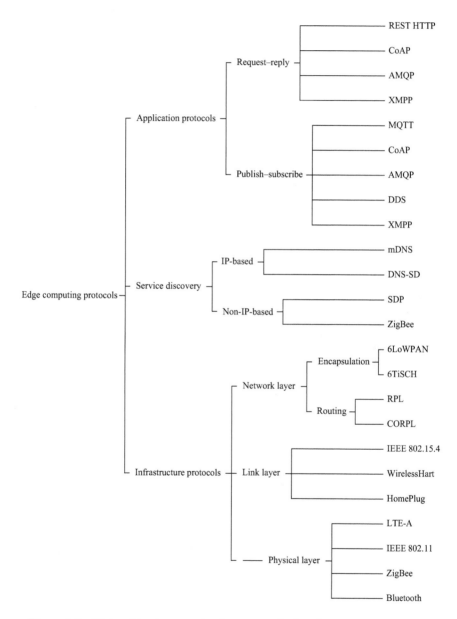

Figure 5.2   Networking/communication protocols for edge computing systems

proposed by International Telecommunication Unit (ITU), Institute of Electrical and Electronics Engineers (IEEE), Internet Engineering Task Force (IETF) and many other standardising organisations for each aforementioned level of edge computing system.

5.2   Networking models for edge computing

A networking model is a set of protocols in a specific order which is used to standardise the interoperability of heterogeneous or homogeneous entities/devices of a network. In an edge computing system, a huge number of different types of devices are connected to each other. So there is a critical need of a layered networking/reference model. However, none of the networking model proposed in the literature has converged to generic reference model for edge computing systems because of different types of devices involved at different levels [1,2]. In this section, networking models or a reference models corresponding to each level of networking in an edge computing system in Figure 5.1 are shown and discussed. The reference models are built on the basis of the type of devices covered in a layer, such that for edge device layer, the reference model has lesser number of layers and lightweight protocols in comparison to fog layer reference model because of relatively constrained resources. Discussion about the reference models and the corresponding communication protocols for cloud layer and fog layer to cloud networking model is out of scope of this chapter because of the unconstrained resources and their use of conventional protocol stack (Transmission Control (TCP)/Internet Protocol (IP) stack).

5.2.1   Edge device peer-to-peer networking

This networking model exists at edge device layer, which consists of resource-constraint edge devices (also known as single-board computers). These edge devices are usually integrated with a set of sensors and are further divided into two categories: devices supporting TCP/IP suite and other security-related modules (Raspberry PI, Beaglebone Black and Intel Galileo) and devices that do not support TCP/IP stack and work on non-IP-based proprietary protocol suits. Devices without the support of TCP/IP suite are generally used only for data acquisition where as other type of edge devices plays a crucial role in data processing despite of their limited data processing capability besides the data aggregation. A reference model corresponding to edge device peer-to-peer communication is shown in Figure 5.3. The reference model consists of four different layers ranges from physical layer to application layer. Devices that belong to edge device layer collect, analyse and act on the collected data within milliseconds using protocols present at physical layer. Such data collection and processing is very crucial for certain time-constrained-based operations such as fire alarms and video surveillance systems. Only aggregated data are sent to fog layer (Figure 5.1) using protocols present in machine access code (MAC) layer and low-weight IP for intense data analytic operations, which reduces the bandwidth usage, response time and operational expenses. For local communication, devices of edge device layer establish a peer-to-peer communication with each other to share and

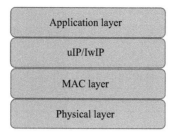

Figure 5.3   Edge computing network model with resource-constraint devices

retrieve the objects within their scope. For such arrangement, understanding of dedicated communication protocols with low resource usage corresponding to each layer of the reference model is important and discussed further in this section. We considered the protocols only for the devices without TCP/IP suite support because of an assumption that the devices that belong to edge device layer (Internet of things (IoT)) do not have direct Internet connectivity and communicate with each other within a local area network (LAN). For Internet connectivity, they have to rely on edge device to fog layer networking model which is discussed later on in the chapter.

5.2.1.1   Application layer protocols

In order to support the messaging services for the users and machine-to-machine (M2M) communication for automation systems, application layer protocols play a crucial role. However, due to the limited capability of edge device layer computing resources (IoT resources), the native application protocols such as Hyper Text Transport Protocol (HTTP), Domain Name System (DNS) and Simple Network Management Protocol (SNMP) do not provide an optimised solution because of their verbose nature and large parsing overheads [3,4]. This raised the requirement of designing of lightweight application protocols while considering the computing capabilities of resource-constrained devices that belong to edge device layer or IoT devices. In this section, we surveyed some promising application protocols designed specifically for resource-constrained devices.

Constrained Application Protocol (CoAP):   This application protocol is created by IETF Constrained RESTful Environments (CoRE) working group [5] and supports both request–reply and publish–subscribe interaction model. It is a User Datagram Protocol (UDP)-based web transfer protocol using REpresentational State Transfer (REST) architecture [6] which enables it to use request/response paradigm similar to HTTP. This protocol is best suitable for resource-constraint devices such as IoT devices because it uses less complex UDP transport protocol and binary encoded headers, methods and status codes, thus reducing the protocol overheads. The functionality of CoAP is divided into two sub-layers: request/response layer and message layer. Request/response layer handles the RESTful communication and allows CoAP clients to use HTTP methods such as GET, PUT, POST and DELETE for sending requests to server in order to achieve corresponding Create, Retrieve, Update and Delete

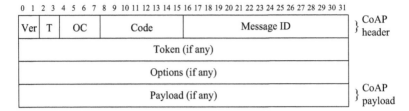

Figure 5.4   CoAP message format

(CRUD) operations. For each CoAP message (Figure 5.4), the first and fixed four bytes represent a binary encoded header consisting of information about version (Ver), type of message or transaction type (T), option count (OC) field, CoAP request/response code (Code) and message ID. The OC field represents availability of option header. If it set to 0, the payload immediately follows the token field (if available). Code field represents the code of request method (GET, PUT, POST and DELETE) ranges from 1 to 10 and response message (40–255). Message ID is used to match the request and response messages; value of message ID in a response message for an operation (GET, PUT, POST and DELETE) has to be similar to the one defined in corresponding request message. Although use of UDP instead of TCP makes the protocol less complex and lightweight, it also reduces the reliability. In order to compensate the reliability up to some extent, functions defined in message layer come into play which are designed to detect duplicate messages and to re-transmit the lost packets. This layer has four types of messages: confirmable (CON), non-confirmable (NON), reset (RST) and acknowledgment (ACK). The CON messages are used to provide reliable communication by pairing them with ACK messages, such that sender of each CON message demands an ACK message from receiver end to ensure the successful reception.

Data Distribution Service (DDS):   It is a UDP-based publish–subscribe interaction model-based protocol designed by Object Management Group (OMG) to support resource-constraint M2M communication [7]. Unlike other publish–subscribe protocols (discussed in later sections), DDS follows a decentralized peer-to-peer approach for communication and does not depend on any broker component enabling asynchronous message exchange between interested parties. Absence of broker also reduces the probability of a single point failure of the system which increases the reliability of the system. Similar to CoAP protocol, DDS also has a two-layer architecture: Data-Centric Publish Subscribe (DCPS) layer and Data-Local Reconstruction Layer (DLRL). Methods defined in DCPS are responsible to deliver information to the users. However, DLRL is an optional layer consisting of methods to facilitate the sharing of distributed data among distributed objects [8]. DDS architecture has a few main entities: Domain, Domain Participant, Topic, Publisher, Subscriber, Data Writer and Data Reader [9]. A domain consists of publisher and subscriber nodes as participants which share common interests. Publisher is an entity that spreads the data and subscriber is a data-consuming entity that forwards the consumed/received data to the applications. Data reader is an entity employed by the subscriber to access the received data. Data writer is used by the publisher to interact with the applications to publish the data of a given type.

5.2.1.2   Service discovery protocols

With the enormous growth in the number of sensing devices because of the emergence of IoT, it is required to have efficient and automated resource registration and discovery services. Currently, DNS is the most accepted service architecture the Internet has. However, the use of standard DNS for the environments with constrained computing resources is questionable [10] because of its host-based design and not taking constraints of sensing devices or smart objects in to account. In order to have an automated naming system for constrained computing resources with low memory and computing power at different levels of an edge computing system, the lightweight resource discovery and registration protocols are required. In this section, various such protocols are discussed. Although, the trend of IP-based Internet connectivity for resource-constraint devices is increasing, we considered only non-IP-based service discovery protocols (SDPs) in this section. This is on the basis of an assumption that edge devices will be limited to a LAN. In order to have an Internet connectivity, edge devices use fog-computing layer resources.

Bluetooth SDP: Designed specifically for Bluetooth environment providing service discovery for the low-profile devices such as mobile phones and smart watches based on their radio-frequency (RF) proximity [11]. The resource discovery mechanism of SDP triggers discovery broadcasts periodically and scans for the enquiries. Once the address of a service provider is known, the connection gets established and information about the available services on the connected devices is provided. The biggest disadvantage for SDP is its limited use only to Bluetooth environments.

ZigBee: ZigBee is an IEEE 802.15.4-based protocol suite for personal area networks consisting of small and low-power devices. ZigBee device discovery mechanism provides a facility to find node-wide information in a network such as addresses, power source, type of running applications and many more. The service discovery messages can be unicasted to a specific node, multicasted to a group of nodes or broadcasted to all the nodes in a network. If the address of a device is not known, a node sends a broadcast requesting a certain services and addresses of the nodes in a network offering the desired service are received as reply. After receiving the information, node establishes a direct connection with the service-providing node. The device and service discovery is usually performed during the device configuration and integration into a ZigBee network [12].

5.2.1.3   Infrastructure protocols

This section covers all the protocols that belong to physical, MAC and network layers (Figure 5.2). All the covered protocols are responsible for physical connectivity of devices (physical layer), moving data packets within the LAN or between different networks (link layer), packet forwarding and routing and encapsulation (network layer). Although the resource-constraint devices can use the combination of protocols performing all the functions in the case of having Internet connectivity, we assumed that the resource-constrained devices taking part in edge device peer-to-peer networking model are limited to LAN and have no direct Internet connectivity. So only protocols corresponding to link layer and physical layer are considered in this section. A thorough survey of such protocols can be found in [13].

IEEE 802.15.4: This is a standard protocol designed to define MAC and physical layer for low-rate wireless private area networks (LR-WPANs) and has been successfully adopted in environments with sensing devices (IoT) for M2M communication [14]. Besides its low power consumption and high message throughput, it provides a reliable communication, encryption and decryption services but does not provide quality of services (QoS) guarantees and can handle a large number of nodes, i.e. around 65,000 nodes. This protocol is the basis of ZigBee protocol discussed above. For physical layer functions, IEEE 802.15.4 supports star, peer-to-peer and cluster-tree arrangement of devices and operates on three frequency bands (2.4 GHz, 915 MHz and 868 MHz) and uses direct-sequence spread spectrum (DSSS) method for data transmission. At MAC level, the protocol performs channel hopping for time-slotted access to wireless medium and also controls the activity of devices such that when to activate them or when to put them in sleep mode in order to save the battery power. It also handles the network formation by sending the join command to the advertising devices. In the distributed systems, the join request is processed locally whereas in centralised formation, it is routed to a manager or coordinator node for processing.

WirelessHart: WirelessHart is a data link protocol that works on top of IEEE 802.15.4 physical layer. While operating on 2.4 GHz band as transfer medium, it uses time-division multiple access (TDMA) to share the transmission medium among different devices and synchronise the participants within 10 ms time frames. This reduces the time lag to activate the station or device, which makes the network collision free and reliable. WirelessHart uses flat mesh network where every device act as a signal source and repeater. A transmitter sends a message to its nearest neighbour which further forwards (if required) it until the message reaches the actual receiver. During the set-up phase of a mesh network, routes get created besides the alternative routes. In case, the primary route fails, messages will be sent through the alternative routes. Such route redundancy further adds to the reliability provided by the WirelessHart protocol.

HomePlug: This is a protocol suite that covers both physical and MAC layer and is used mainly for home automation. This protocol enables resource-constrained devices to communicate with each other and over the Internet using existing home electrical wiring by increasing the communication frequencies to avoid interference from electrical noise. HomePlug has three versions: HomePlug AV (Audio-Video), HomePlug Green Phy and HomePlug AV2. HomePlug AV was released in 2005 and it uses TDMA and Carrier Sense Multiple Access/Collision Avoidance (CSMA/CA) as MAC layer protocol and offers a peak data rate of

200 Mbits/s at physical layer and 80 Mbits/s at MAC layer. For HomePlug AV2, the data rate for physical layer has been increased to gigabit class and support for multiple-input and multiple-output (MIMO) radio transmission is added. HomePlug Green Phy is designed specifically for IoT devices. The main objective of this version is to reduce the power consumption and operational cost in comparison to HomePlug AV while keeping the same reliability, coverage and interoperability level. Green Phy uses 75% less energy than AV and uses both CSMA and TDMA channel access methods.

Bluetooth: It is a communication standard designed for a short-range communication between mobile or fixed devices [15]. Physical layer of Bluetooth standard consists of IEEE 802.15.1-based radio and baseband specifications. It uses TDMA as channel access method and supports the data rate of 1 Mbit/s. Whereas the MAC layer consists of Link Manager Protocol (LMP) and Logical Link Control and Adaptation Protocol (L2CAP). LMP is used to establish and control the link whereas L2CAP provides reliability to LMP by providing flow control and error control services. In order to make it more compatible with resource-constraint devices of edge device layer (IoT), a low power consuming version Low-power Bluetooth or Bluetooth Smart or Bluetooth 4.0 is introduced [16]. Its operational transmission power is between 0.01 and 10 mW. This makes Bluetooth 4.0 version to consume 10 times lesser power than the standard Bluetooth and makes it a good candidate for IoT applications. It uses a master–slave architecture and two types of frames to establish connections: advertising and data frames. Advertising frames are sent by slave nodes to discover and connect to a master node. After establishing the connection, master node tells the slave about their waking cycles and scheduling sequence.

ZigBee: In Section 5.2.1.2, ZigBee protocol suite has been explored as a device discovery mechanism. However, it also provides a physical and data link layer connectivity between the devices of personal area networks. It provides a low-power and lost-cost connectivity for devices that need battery life as long as for months to several years with lesser data transfer rate than Bluetooth. ZigBee-based devices can transmit the messages within the range of 10–75 metres and use mesh network to transmit messages to longer distances using neighbour nodes. It supports three data rates with three operating frequencies, i.e. 250 kbps at 2.4 GHz, 40 kbps at 915 MHz and 20 kbps at 868 MHz [17]. ZigBee Smart Energy is a version designed specifically for the resource-constrained devices of edge device layer (IoT) running applications including smart homes, remote controls and healthcare systems [13].

5.2.2 *Edge device to fog layer networking*

In order to avail the services of core cloud and fog servers to perform data and compute intensive operations, an intermediate or interconnection networking model between the edge device layer and fog layer is required. This networking model allows data gathered by the sensing devices of edge device layer to be communicated to the computing devices that belong to fog layer. Unlike the previous networking model,

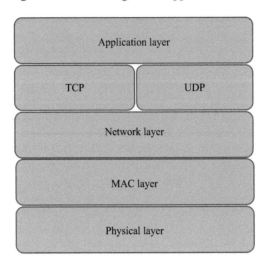

Figure 5.5   Edge computing network model with resource-rich devices

the networking model existing between edge device layer and fog layer has a set of protocols with higher complexity. Although the resource-constraint devices are present at one end, because of the presence of resource-rich devices at the other end, this networking model has more services to offer such that encryption/decryption, routing and packet reliability services. Similar to the aforementioned networking model, a layered references model (Figure 5.5) is explained for edge device and fog layer networking. However, the given reference has five layers covering extra services in comparison to a reference model explained in Figure 5.3. Each layer has its corresponding set of protocols which are covered in the following sections.

5.2.2.1   Application protocols

Similar to the application layer discussed in Section 5.2.1.1, this layer also consists of a set of protocols providing communication interfaces between the users and system. However, protocols defined in the application layer of edge device to fog layer networking model use more features of their predecessor protocols such as DNS and HTTP. Unlike edge device peer-to-peer networking model where only UDP-based application protocols were considered due to the resource-constraint device, in this reference models, we considered the TCP-based application protocols, although UDP-based protocols can also be used.

Message Queuing Telemetry Transport Protocol (MQTT):   Known as the most prominent application layer protocol for M2M communication, MQTT is a TCP-based protocol which follows publish–subscribe interaction model. MQTT is designed by IBM and adopted by Organisation for the Advancement of Structured Information Standards (OASIS) [18]. Being built on top of TCP protocol, MQTT provides great reliability and delivers messages using three levels of QoS.

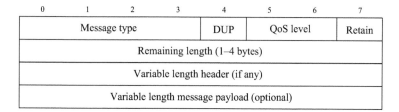

Figure 5.6   MQTT message format

Each MQTT message exchange process consists of three entities: subscriber, publisher and broker. Each interested user registers with the broker as subscriber to get information about a specific topic. Whenever a publisher publish a data corresponding to the topic a subscriber interested in, broker informs the subscriber. Broker also provides the service of authorisation to ensure the rightness of publishers and subscribers. MQTT appears as an ideal application layer protocol for IoT and M2M communication because of its use by a number of applications such as healthcare, monitoring, energy meter and Facebook notifications [8]. Figure 5.6 shows the message format for MQTT which consists of a fixed 2 byte header plus optional variable header and payload. The fixed header consists of control information and packet length field. The control information field is further divided into four sub-fields: Message type shows the type of packet in a coded format such as Reserved (0), CONNECT (1), CONNACK (2), PUBLISH (3) and many more. Duplicate flag (DUP) represents the control flags responsible for managing the duplicated attempts to deliver the control packets. DUP = 0 represents the clients first attempt to send MQTT control packet, otherwise DUP = 1. QoS-level field assures the message delivery by using three levels of QoS. Retain field informs the broker or server to keep the last received message for future subscribers. Remaining length shows the length of optional parts, if they are available. Based on TCP, the use of MQTT in resource-constraint devices such as devices in Layer 3 of Figure 1.1 can be critical due to large overheads. In order to overcome such overheads, MQTT for Sensor Networks (MQTT-SN) version that uses UDP has also been proposed [19]. Although, MQTT-SN is considered as an improved version of MQTT, its use is limited because of being supported by few platforms and the availability of only one broker implementation known as Really Small Message Broker [4].

Advanced Message Queuing Protocol (AMQP):   AMQP is an open standard TCP-based application layer protocol for message-oriented environments standardised by OASIS [20]. The given protocol has two versions AMQP 0.9.1 and AMQP 1.0 and are completely different from each other in terms of working paradigm. Version AMQP 0.9.1 uses publish–subscribe interaction model with publisher, subscriber and broker entities. In this version, the communication is handled by two main queues that belong to broker: exchange and message queues. The exchange queues are a part of a broker used to route the messages received from publishers and message queues are used to store the messages and then be sent to subscribers/receivers. This routing process of linking exchange and message queues is called binding which is based on predefined rules and conditions. However, the newer version AMQP 1.0 uses a peer-to-peer (request–reply) interaction model with different communication patterns such as client-to-client, client-to-broker and broker-to-broker. Broker is used only in the cases where a store-and-forward mechanism is required to forward messages otherwise direct messaging between sender and receiver takes place. While using TCP as transport protocol, AMQP uses three QoS levels to ensure the reliable delivery of packets. QoS 0 is the best effort policy without any confirmation/acknowledgement, QoS 1 assures the delivery of a message by using confirmation and QoS 2 also handles the message duplication besides being supported by message delivery confirmation.

Extensible Messaging and Presence Protocol (XMPP): It is an application layer protocol initially designed for instant messaging applications and is standardised by IETF. XMPP uses both request–reply and publish–subscribe interaction models and TCP as transport protocol [21]. In the set-ups consisting of resource-constraint devices such as IoT systems, this protocol can be useful to send messages in real time. Clients and servers use a stream of XML stanzas to communicate with each other. Each stanza represents a piece of code consisting of three components: message, presence and info/query (iq). Message part of stanzas consists of source and destination addresses, types and IDs, which are required to push the information to another entity. Presence stanza represents the network availability of an entity (online/offline) and is also used to negotiate and manage the subscription between entities. Iq represents a structured request–response message between sender and receiver [22]. Methods provided by XMPP seem to be important and are useful for resource-constrained systems (IoT) of Layer 3 of Figure 1.1. However, its use of TCP to provide reliability in addition to the mechanisms for authentication, access control, privacy measurement, hop-by-hop and end-to-end encryption makes it more feasible for resource-rich devices of Layer 2 because of large overheads.

RESTful HTTP (REST HTTP): HTTP is a fundamental and widely accepted application protocol because of its compatibility with existing computing infrastructure. It is based on request–reply interaction system where a client sends a request for a content and after receiving the request, server replies with requested resource. Conjunction of HTTP with RESTful web services made it efficient for IoT-based systems with constrained computing resources by establishing the mapping between create, read, update and delete operations (CURD operations) of REST and HTTP POST, GET, PUT and DELETE methods. This facilitates the developers to build REST model for IoT-based systems more efficiently and easily [4]. For transport protocols, REST HTTP uses TCP and ensures the reliable delivery of data between the clients and servers. However, the use of TCP creates a challenge for the resource-constraint devices used in Layer 1 of Figure 1.1. This is because of the high frequency of sensing devices of sending small amount of data. For each attempt, establishing a TCP connection brings a lot of overheads, which adds to the latency in the network and makes the devices less energy efficient. So rather than using it for edge device peer-to-peer communication, REST HTTP is more compatible for the communication between edge device layer and edge computing (fog computing) layer.

5.2.2.2 Service discovery protocols

Utilisation of non-IP-based service discovery mechanisms has a drawback that service discovery remains limited to a network domain or LAN. However, with the emerging need to connect sensing or edge devices or M2M systems to the Internet in order to discover the services at back end computing systems (fog computing or cloud computing systems), IP-based SDPs for resource-constrained devices are required and discussed in this section.

Multicast DNS (mDNS): It is a protocol designed to resolve host names to IP addresses within small networks without local name server. It provides a zero configuration service because it uses the packet format and programming interfaces of unicast DNS system and does not need any extra configuration and infrastructure. This gives the protocol a great flexibility without having any extra configuration and makes it suitable for embedded Internet-based devices. mDNS enquires by multicasting a request message within a domain asking for an IP address corresponding to a name. After receiving the request, the device with the asked name multicasts its IP address as a reply. After receiving the multicasted IP address, all the receiver nodes within the domain update their local DNS cache with the given name and IP address for future reference. This mechanism helps to provide Internet connectivity between the low-power nodes in the edge device layer and relatively resource-rich nodes of edge/fog computing layer.

DNS Service Discovery (DNS-SD): This protocol defines the pairing functions for mDNS to discover the services by clients. It is a UDP-based protocol which can use either multicast DNS or unicast DNS to send queries to specific addresses. There are two essential steps of service discovery in DNS-SD: finding host names of required services and pairing host names with found IP address using mDNS [23].

5.2.2.3 Infrastructure protocols

Most of the infrastructure protocols covered in Section 5.2.1.3 can also work in edge device to fog layer networking as well. However, because of the presence of relatively resource-richer devices, some of the extra protocols performing certain functions such as routing and encapsulation besides link layer and physical layer functions are considered in this section.

Routing Protocol for Low-power and Lossy Networks (RPL): It is an Internet Protocol version 6 (IPv6)-based proactive distance vector routing protocol designed for power-limited battery-operated devices [24]. It operates on top of IEEE 802.15.4 standard. RPL organises a topology as direct acyclic graph (DAG) and partitions it into one or more destination-oriented DAGs (DODAG) such that for each DODAG, one root node will be available for each leaf node through which the whole data will be routed. Every node in DODAG will have a rank which increases as nodes move away from the root. During communication, a node sends a Destination Advertisement Object (DAO) to its parents which further gets propagated to the root and then root decides where to send it depending on the destination. Whenever a new node wants to join a network, it sends DODAG Information Solicitation (DIS) request to the root and root replies with acknowledgement confirming the addition.

Cognitive Routing Protocol for Low-power and Lossy Networks: This protocol also known as CORPL is a non-standardised extension of RPL protocol for cognitive networks [25]. It uses the same mechanism to create DODAG-oriented topology but has different packet forwarding method. CORPL uses opportunistic packet-forwarding method where a set of packet-forwarding nodes is created and it coordinates between nodes to choose the best next hope to forward the packets. Similar to RPL, CORPL employees DODAG Information Object (DIO) messages to update the information about a node's neighbours. On the basis of the updated neighbours information, each node prepares its forwarder set according to the priorities of neighbouring nodes.

IPv6 over Low-power Wireless Personal Area Networks (6LoWPAN): It is a standard which provides an abstraction layer to encapsulate the IPv6 packets to be sent or received over IEEE 802.15.4-based networks [26]. The standard provides fragmentation to meet IPv6 maximum transmission unit (MTU), overhead reduction by header compression and multi-hop delivery support by forwarding the data packets to link layer. Each 6LoWPAN-encapsulated datagram is followed by combination of headers which can be any among four types: No LoWPAN header, dispatch header, mesh addressing and fragmentation. In No 6LoWPAN header case, any frame which is not in accordance with 6LoWPAN specifications gets discarded. Dispatch headers are used for IPv6 header compression and multicasting. Mesh headers are used for broadcasting where as fragmentation headers are used to break long IPv6 headers to fit into fragments of maximum 128-byte length.

IPv6 over Time-slotted Channel Hopping (6TiSCH): This is a newly formed working group of IETF designing the standards to allow the passing of IPv6 packets through Time-slotted Channel Hopping (TSCH) mode of IEEE 802.15.4e datalinks [27]. 6TiSCH defines a new channel distribution/usage (CDU) matrix formed of cells to form the communication schedules with neighbour nodes similar to TSCH. Each matrix is divided into chucks containing time slots and operating frequency information. Each chuck is known to all the nodes in a network to support the negotiation between the nodes of an interference domain such that transmission scheduling between the nodes is decided during negotiation process. The scheduling can be centralised or distributed depends upon the type of application and the topology at MAC layer.

Long-term Evolution-Advanced (LTE-A): It is a mobile communication standard defining set of protocols that enables the M2M communication in cellular networks with high scalability and low service cost [28]. At physical layer, it uses orthogonal frequency-division multiple access (OFDMA) where the bandwidth is partitioned into smaller bands called physical resource blocks (PRBs). An

LTE-A network architecture consists of a core network (CN), a radio access network (RAN) and nodes. CN controls the nodes and IP packet flows between them whereas RAN handles the radio communication and access. Both CN and RAN entities communicate with each other using S1 connections. Though LTE-A is a suitable protocol for communication between resource-constrained and resource-rich devices of edge device layer and fog layer, respectively, it has a problem of network congestion as the number of devices/nodes accessing the network increase. Some of the solutions the given QoS problems are provided in [28] and [29].

IEEE 802.11ah: This is the lightweight version of IEEE 802.11, which is the most widely used wireless communication standard defining protocols for physical and MAC layers. IEEE 802.11ah is specifically designed for resource-constrained devices with low overheads and high power efficiency. In comparison to 30-byte MAC frame of IEEE 802.11, IEEE 802.11ah has it only of 12 bytes and supports data rate up to 347 Mbits/s. Because of its low power-consumption feature required for resource-constrained devices, IEEE 802.11ah supports longer sleep time period and short activation period to exchange data [13].

5.3   Open issues and challenges

In order to realise the vision of edge computing, various open issues and challenges corresponding to networking protocols and reference models need to be addressed. Addressing these challenges will make the edge computing technology more profitable for providers and accessible to users. Some of the important challenges in the area of edge computing networking are highlighted in this section.

Performance evaluation: Performance evaluation of networking protocols is a major challenge because of heterogeneous types of workloads and edge devices and their interoperability. It is not necessary that a protocol suite working for an end-to-end edge computing solution will perform the same for other similar types of edge computing scenarios. In order to provide edge computing solutions with high reliability and availability, performance evaluation of networking protocols at all the networking levels using various metrics such as communication speed, cost and other networking KPIs is required. Despite some work in the literature [30–33] reporting the results of individual protocols, a thorough performance evaluation still remains an open challenge and needs a careful attention.

Security and privacy: Due to the lack of generic reference networking models and protocols, security and privacy in edge computing present a significant challenge. The data exchange between the devices of different layers in an edge computing paradigm makes the security and privacy issues to be addressed at every layer. Such multi-layer architecture of edge computing systems demonstrated the feasibility of rough node or identity forgery attacks such as man-in-the-middle attack [34]. In such attacks, the fake gateway devices between different layers pretend to be legitimate and coaxes the end users to connect to them. Once connected, the adversaries can manipulate the requests between the users or edge devices, and collect the sensitive information which can be used to launch further attacks. Many measurement- [35], encryption- [36] and authorisation-based [37] solutions have been provided to avoid such kind of attacks. However, dynamic nature of the paradigm, complex trust management schemes and device heterogeneity make the adoption of proposed solutions challenging in a generic manner. This leaves an open issue and a future direction for the researchers to come up with naive network security protocols to thwart such system jeopardising attempts.

Interoperability and integration: Because of the processing delays due to the distance from the data sources and centralised architecture, the cloud computing-based solutions entail limitations for time-sensitive and data-insensitive applications. This gives a surge to solutions using edge computing which brings computing resources next to the data sources and reduces the turn-around time for requests made by end users. However, cloud computing being the backbone for edge computing paradigm, the integration and interoperability of edge computing-based solutions with cloud computing systems is emerged as another challenge [38]. In order to have the best use of close proximity of edge computing resources to the users and compute intensive resources of cloud computing systems, smart network communication models and protocols are required to be developed. Such attempts are needed to handle the complex coordination between the applications running at different levels and for smart service orchestration. This will help to use the resources optimally while maintaining the quality of services and security.

5.4   Conclusions and future works

With the aim of reducing the bandwidth usage, response time and improving the user experience, edge computing is rapidly getting adopted by service providers. Efforts to standardise the edge computing frameworks/architectures and communication protocols have been done by various standardising organisations across the world. This chapter presents an overview of such standardised or non-standardised reference models and corresponding communication protocols which enables the realisation of optimised edge computing systems. This chapter provides a good insight to researchers about edge computing networking models, communication protocols and corresponding challenges at a single venue. An layered architecture of an edge computing system showing the interaction between all the components and networking models is presented. This chapter also provides a comprehensive survey and taxonomy for edge computing communication protocols to facilitate the researchers to understand the concepts easily. In future, the proposed taxonomy will be expanded by adding realised edge computing systems using covered protocols. Also new taxonomies will be proposed highlighting various challenges, and performance parameters need to be considered before selecting the communication protocols.

References

[1]   Zhao Y, Wang W, Li Y, Meixner CC, Tornatore M, and Zhang J. Edge computing and networking: a survey on infrastructures and applications. IEEE Access. 2019;7:101213–101230.

[2]   Hu P, Dhelim S, Ning H, and Qiu T. Survey on fog computing: architecture, key technologies, applications and open issues. Journal of Network and Computer Applications. 2017;98:27–42.

[3]   Sethi P, and Sarangi SR. Internet of things: architectures, protocols, and applications. Journal of Electrical and Computer Engineering. 2017:1–25.

[4]   Dizdarević J, Carpio F, Jukan A, and Masip-Bruin X. A survey of communication protocols for Internet of things and related challenges of fog and cloud computing integration. ACM Computing Surveys (CSUR). 2019;51(6):1–29.

[5]   Shelby Z, Hartke K, and Bormann. The Constrained Application Protocol (CoAP). The Internet Engineering Task Force – IETF. 2014:1–112.

[6]   Richardson L, and Ruby S. RESTful web services. O'Reilly Media, Inc.; 2008.

[7]   Data Distribution Service (DDS) [homepage on the Internet]. Object Management Group; 2015. Available from: https://www.omg.org/spec/DDS/1.4/PDF.

[8]   Al-Fuqaha A, Guizani M, Mohammadi M, Aledhari M, and Ayyash M. Internet of things: a survey on enabling technologies, protocols, and applications. IEEE Communications Surveys & Tutorials. 2015;17(4):2347–2376.

[9]   Pardo-Castellote G, Farabaugh B, and Warren R. An introduction to DDS and data-centric communications. Real-Time Innovations (RTI). 2005;1–15.

[10] Jara AJ, Martinez-Julia P, and Skarmeta A. Light-weight multicast DNS and DNS-SD (lmDNS-SD): IPv6-based resource and service discovery for the Web of Things. In: 2012 Sixth International Conference on Innovative Mobile and Internet Services in Ubiquitous Computing. IEEE; 2012. pp. 731–738.

[11] Service Discovery Protocol (SDP) [homepage on the Internet]. Available from: https://www.amd.e-technik.uni-rostock.de/ma/gol/lectures/wirlec/bluetooth_info/sdp.html.

[12] Villaverde BC, Alberola RDP, Jara AJ, Fedor S, Das SK, and Pesch D. Service discovery protocols for constrained machine-to-machine communications. IEEE Communications Surveys & Tutorials. 2013;16(1):41–60.

[13] Salman T. Internet of Things protocols and standards. Available from: https://www.cse.wustl.edu/~jain/cse570-15/ftp/iot_prot.pdf. 2015:1–28.

[14] Callaway E, Gorday P, Hester L, et al. Home networking with IEEE 802.15.4: a developing standard for low-rate wireless personal area networks. IEEE Communications Magazine. 2002;40(8):70–77.

[15] Haartsen JC. The Bluetooth radio system. IEEE personal communications. 2000;7(1):28–36.

[16] Gomez C, Oller J, and Paradells J. Overview and evaluation of Bluetooth low energy: an emerging low-power wireless technology. Sensors. 2012;12(9):11734–11753.

[17] Ergen SC. ZigBee/IEEE 802.15. 4 Summary. UC Berkeley, September. 2004;10:17.

[18]   Standard O. MQTT version 3.1.1. URL http://docs.oasis-open.org/mqtt/mqtt/v3.2014;1.

[19]   Hunkeler U, Truong HL, and Stanford-Clark A. MQTT-SA publish/subscribe protocol for wireless sensor networks. In: 2008 3rd International Conference on Communication Systems Software and Middleware and Workshops (COMSWARE'08). IEEE; 2008. pp. 791–798.

[20]   OASIS Advanced Message Queuing Protocol (AMQP) Version 1.0 [homepage on the Internet]; 2012. Available from: http://docs.oasis-open.org/amqp/core/v1.0/os/amqp-core-complete-v1.0-os.pdf; 2013.

[21]   Saint-Andre P. Extensible messaging and presence protocol (XMPP): Core. RFC 6120, March 2011.

[22]   Extensible Messaging and Presence Protocol (XMPP): Instant Messaging and Presence [homepage on the Internet]. Network Working Group; 2004. Available from: https://xmpp.org/rfcs/rfc3921.html.

[23]   DNS Service Discovery (DNS-SD) [homepage on the Internet]; 2013. Available from: http://www.dns-sd.org/.

[24]   Winter T, Thubert P, Brandt A, *et al.* IPv6 routing protocol for low-power and lossy networks. RFC6550 of IETF. 2012:1–157.

[25]   Aijaz A, and Aghvami AH. Cognitive machine-to-machine communications for Internet-of-Things: a protocol stack perspective. IEEE Internet of Things Journal. 2015;2(2):103–112.

[26]   Palattella MR, Accettura N, Vilajosana X, *et al.* Standardized protocol stack for the Internet of (important) Things. IEEE communications Surveys & Tutorials. 2012;15(3):1389–1406.

[27]   Dujovne D, Watteyne T, Vilajosana X, and Thubert P. 6TiSCH: deterministic IP-enabled industrial Internet (of Things). IEEE Communications Magazine. 2014;52(12):36–41.

[28]   Hasan M, Hossain E, and Niyato D. Random access for machine-to-machine communication in LTE-advanced networks: issues and approaches. IEEE Communications Magazine. 2013;51(6):86–93.

[29]   Niyato D, Wang P, and Kim DI. Performance modeling and analysis of heterogeneous machine type communications. IEEE Transactions on Wireless Communications. 2014;13(5):2836–2849.

[30]   Colitti W, Steenhaut K, De Caro N, Buta B, and Dobrota V. Evaluation of constrained application protocol for wireless sensor networks. In: 2011 18th IEEE Workshop on Local & Metropolitan Area Networks (LANMAN). IEEE; 2011. pp. 1–6.

[31]   Thangavel D, Ma X, Valera A, Tan HX, and Tan CKY. Performance evaluation of MQTT and CoAP via a common middleware. In: 2014 IEEE Ninth International Conference on Intelligent Sensors, Sensor Networks and Information Processing (ISSNIP). IEEE; 2014. pp. 1–6.

[32]   Siekkinen M, Hiienkari M, Nurminen JK, and Nieminen J. How low energy is Bluetooth low energy? Comparative measurements with zigbee/802.15. 4. In: 2012 IEEE Wireless Communications and Networking Conference Workshops (WCNCW). IEEE; 2012. pp. 232–237.

[33] Cody-Kenny B, Guerin D, Ennis D, Simon Carbajo R, Huggard M, and Mc Goldrick C. Performance evaluation of the 6LoWPAN protocol on MICAz and TelosB motes. In: Proceedings of the 4th ACM Workshop on Performance Monitoring and Measurement of Heterogeneous Wireless and Wired Networks. ACM; 2009. pp. 25–30.

[34] Stojmenovic I, and Wen S. The fog computing paradigm: scenarios and security issues. In: 2014 Federated Conference on Computer Science and Information Systems. IEEE; 2014. pp. 1–8.

[35] Li C, Qin Z, Novak E, and Li Q. Securing SDN infrastructure of IoT–fog networks from MitM attacks. IEEE Internet of Things Journal. 2017;4(5):1156–1164.

[36] Diro AA, Chilamkurti N, and Kumar N. Lightweight cybersecurity schemes using elliptic curve cryptography in publish–subscribe fog computing. Mobile Networks and Applications. 2017;22(5):848–858.

[37] Kaur K, Garg S, Kaddoum G, Guizani M, and Jayakody DNK. A lightweight and privacy-preserving authentication protocol for mobile edge computing. arXiv preprint arXiv:190708896. 2019.

[38] Mahmud R, Koch FL, and Buyya R. Cloud–fog interoperability in IoT-enabled healthcare solutions. In: Proceedings of the 19th International Conference on Distributed Computing and Networking. ACM; 2018. pp. 32.

Chapter 6

Computing and storage models for edge computing

Yogesh Simmhan[1], Aakash Khochare[1]
and Sheshadri K. Ramachandra[1]

6.1 Introduction

Edge computing is an emerging computing paradigm, driven by the growth of computing devices deployed at the edge of the Internetwork. While smart phones and personal
wearables are the common manifestation of edge devices, an emerging domain, whose
device count is expected to dwarf these, is Internet of Things (IoT). In IoT, devices
are deployed as part of the physical infrastructure to help sense the environment and
actuate controls. Examples include smart city services such as utility meters and traffic cameras, building management solutions for cooling and energy controls, and
even autonomous vehicles like self-driving cars and drones [1]. The edge computing
devices may range from embedded platforms like Arduino to low-end computers like
Raspberry Pi. These devices themselves are connected to the Internet through local or
wide area networks (LAN/WAN), and using various wireless or wired communication
links like 2–5G, LoRa, Bluetooth, and mesh networks.

Making effective use of such a distributed computing fabric requires the ability to
store, manage and access data generated at the edge, and to deploy, run, and orchestrate
applications on the edge. Application and storage *platforms* designed for clusters of
servers or cloud virtual machines (VMs), or for individual edge devices such as smart
phone SDK and apps, are inadequate for distributed edge devices. The former tend to
be heavyweight for the low compute and memory footprint of the edge, while the later
do not make use of the access to cumulative resources. On the other hand, existing
abstractions and models for distributed storage and application composition can be
leveraged and extended to support edge computing. These should ease the design,
development, and execution of edge applications.

In this chapter, we discuss *conceptual models for computing and storage* relevant
to the edge computing paradigm, and offer case studies of their *runtime instantiations*.
We discuss models where computing and storage are predominantly performed *on the*

[1]Department of Computational and Data Sciences, Indian Institute of Science, Bangalore, India

edge devices, as well as models *for* supporting edge computing which use additional computing abstractions such as fog and cloud computing.

6.2   Edge, fog, and cloud computing resources

Edge computing devices have lower-end computing capacity, typically an ARM-based processor with 4 cores, 1 GHz clock speed, and 1 GB of RAM, and are connected using wireless protocols. These tend to be at the edge of the Internetwork. Many edge devices may be part of the same LAN. These devices are less reliable, given their commodity hardware that cost <US$50 and their use in outdoor environments.

Individual edge devices by themselves have limited use without some manner of coordination across them and back-end computing and persistence support that may be more reliable and with higher-end resources. To this end, edge devices are often complemented by two additional computing layers, *fog* and *cloud* [2]. Cloud computing offers elastic and virtualized computing and storage resources at large scales, hosted at centralized data centers accessed across the WAN. They have high availability and reliability. Fog computing tends to be closer to the edge on the network, within a metropolitan area network (MAN), and may consist of a workstation or server-class resource with optional accelerators, and broad-band connectivity. They are also more reliable than the edge devices.

Often, these computing abstractions work in concert to support applications, complementing their capabilities. As shown in Figure 6.1, edge devices are low-cost captive resources, with low latency to the IoT sensor data source, but are unreliable and have lower computing power. Clouds have unlimited resources but use a pay-as-you-go pricing model and have higher latency and potentially lower bandwidth from the edge. Fogs fall in-between on latency and computing power and have better reliability than the edge, but may be costlier as they have lower economies of scale than clouds.

The boundary between the edge and the fog can be fuzzy. An alternative design considers the sensor or actuation device, with its embedded computing platform, itself to be a first-class entity, and the edge and fog abstractions are combined into a single edge computing abstraction to complement the cloud. Here, the embedded devices tend to have static computing logic in their firmware that is specialized for their domain, local storage for data buffering, and use proprietary or industry standard protocols such as BACnet [3] and Extensible Messaging and Presence Protocol (XMPP) [4] for external interfacing. However, they typically do not allow dynamic application logic or service-based APIs to be exposed to leverage them as a general-purpose computing and storage platform. Hence, we do not emphasize such an architecture in this chapter. However, the devices can serve as clients to the compute and storage platform exposed at the edge.

6.3   Reference architecture

A typical architecture having edge, fog, and cloud resources is illustrated in Figure 6.1 [5]. Edge devices are geographically distributed across a city or a region,

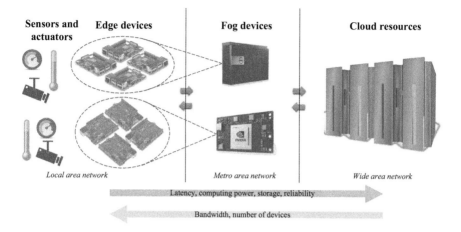

Figure 6.1 Edge, fog, and cloud computing layers

co-located with field devices such as smart utility meters, pollution monitors, traffic cameras, etc., and 100–10,000 of these may be present citywide. Multiple edge devices may be proximate within a LAN or even part of the same *ad hoc* mesh network. Typically, fog devices are used to help manage a collection of edge devices, such as in a *spatial neighborhood*, in an *organization* like a campus, or for a particular *network segment* like a border gateway for a mesh network. They are typically within a couple of network hops of the edge devices. There may be 10–100s of such devices in a city. Lastly, cloud data centers may be present at the regional or national level, several network hops away and connected through the WAN and Internet with the edge and fog. These public clouds are shared across a multitude of tenants.

There are typically two key sources of data within such an architecture: from the sensors near the edge and at the cloud. Sensors may generate a continuous stream of data that needs to be acquired, processed, analyzed, and archived by applications. Clouds may be repositories of historic data from the sensors, or data from other sources that may need to be combined and processed by applications. These applications may operate in real time to control physical systems, such as the power grid or send alerts to users, or they may need to work over accumulated data, such as billing of utilities or training of models. As we shall discuss, the data used for processing may be stored at any or all of these layers, and the applications processing them may be present at various resources as well. These reflect the storage and computing models for edge, fog, and cloud computing.

6.4 Characteristics of the ecosystem

Distributed programming models offer a higher-level abstraction for composing applications. Subsequently, *platforms and runtimes* can deploy and execute these composed applications across the distributed resources. For example, *MapReduce* is a programming model while *Hadoop* or *Spark* are platforms for executing applications designed using MapReduce primitives. Similarly, *storage models* offer different means to access data, such as files, blocks, or streams, while *distributed storage platforms* help store, manage, and access them by applications. For example, *Hadoop Distributed File System (HDFS)* lets Hadoop or Spark applications access input and write output data as files or blocks within a cluster [6].

Designing applications for execution across multiple edge devices, or across edge, fog, and cloud resources poses unique challenges, as does storing and accessing data required by them. These are distinct from operating on a single edge device or using application or storage platforms designed exclusively within a cloud data center. At the same time, applications operating on the edge also pose novel requirements compared to traditional desktop or web applications. We highlight some of these challenges here. These influence both the compute and the storage models that we discuss later.

6.4.1 Application and data characteristics

Applications designed for edge computing are typically motivated by the need for *low-latency* processing and/or to *reduce the bandwidth* consumed in accessing the input data. Applications that process data sourced from sensors near the edge may perform analysis and decisions to send control signals to actuators near the edge. Such closed-loop applications tend to be latency sensitive, and the network delay in moving the data stream to the cloud may exceed the time budget to take a decision. Processing at the edge reduces the network costs, albeit at the expense of higher compute latency.

Edge applications may also operate on large volumes of data sourced from field equipment such as surveillance cameras within transit networks and Phasor Measurement Units in smart grids. These data may be accumulated over time and processed in-batch. Here, the monetary and resource cost of moving data from these devices to the cloud can be punitive. This forces the application to be deployed at the edge to mitigate this resource constraint. There may be cases of both these features intersecting, such as taking low-latency decisions based on analytics over bandwidth-hungry video feeds, as we discuss later in our case study. At the same time, edge applications may also need to operate on data present at the fog or cloud layers.

Applications may also be modular or monolithic, and have hardware, library, and license dependencies. These affect their ability to be decomposed for distributed execution. It also restricts the resources on which they may be deployed. Metrics used for describing the quality of service (QoS) required by these applications include the *latency* between data generation and decision enactment, the *throughput* of event rates that can be supported, and even the *quality or accuracy* of the application as a consequence of the various resource constraints.

6.4.2 Resource characteristics

Edge devices tend to have a high degree of heterogeneity when it comes to their architecture, operating system, and software stack available. This becomes even more acute when we include fog and cloud resources as well [5]. Applications need to run across ×86, ARM and GPU architectures, 32 bit and 64 bit, and a variety of OS distributions. These devices have diverse computing capacities as well, from server-grade many-core processors with possibly hundreds of GB RAM in the cloud to mobile processors with 1 GB RAM on the edge. GPU accelerators also come in disparate form factors for low- and high-end computing. The number of edge devices may be in the thousands and more unreliable that fog or cloud resources, making coordination among them challenging. This limits the use of Big Data platforms, which are resource-heavy or that are tightly coupled, on edge devices. It may also be necessary to have multiple flavors of the application for different target architectures and resource limitations, which may affect the QoS that is achievable.

The available bandwidth also varies from a few hundred Mbps to tens of Gbps, and this also varies between intra- and inter-abstraction performance. For example, clouds may have high bandwidth within the data center but have a lower bandwidth between the edge and the cloud across the WAN. The expected latency varies as well, and the latency values may also be more dynamic across MAN and WAN. As a consequence, making efficient and effective use of such hybrid resources to meet the application requirements while meeting its QoS is challenging for edge application platforms.

6.4.3 Security, privacy, and trust

This crosscutting dimension affects applications, data, and the edge, fog, and cloud resources they are hosted on. Enterprise or regulatory policies or users' choice may limit the geographical, organizational, or device boundaries within which applications must run, or where data may be moved and stored. These can also vary by the content or their longevity. For example, aggregated, de-identified, or transient data may have fewer restrictions [7]. There can also be security requirements such as encrypting the data when crossing certain boundaries or when persisted at certain locations [8].

There are divergent views on the security and trust in the resources themselves. Storing and processing data from sensors at the co-located edge may offer higher privacy on a trusted device. These may work for wearables and smart phones. But if the edge is deployed on the field and inadequately secured, it may be physically compromised. All edges may not be equal either, and *ad hoc* edge peers that are not part of an infrastructure deployment may be less trusted.

Public cloud data centers are physically well secured and industry best practices are followed to digitally secure them as well. However, there have been incidents of data present on the cloud being leaked or lost due to faulty system configuration. Also, keeping data centrally or with a single entity makes them more susceptible to access by state actors, and more attractive for non-state actors to try opportunistic attacks. So a number of factors influence both the application and data needs, as well as the capabilities of the resource. While we highlight this as a challenge, we do not discuss it further as it is highly domain dependent and no one size fits all.

6.5 Computing models and platforms

In this section, we discuss application models and runtime systems that help design, deploy, and orchestrate applications for edge computing, with the complementary use of fog and cloud computing. Our focus is on applications that will execute on distributed resources and not just a single edge. Some of these are generic to non-edge computing applications as well, but are equally relevant for the edge.

6.5.1 Programming models

6.5.1.1 Dataflow model

The dataflow programming model captures units of computation as *nodes* in a directed acyclic graph (DAG), with *edges* indicating input data dependencies of sink tasks on the output from source tasks. This is a classic model popular with stream and Big Data processing systems, and allows for the composition of complex applications from modular and reusable building-block tasks.

Many edge computing platforms adopt the dataflow programming model [9–12]. Such a decomposition of tasks and their interdependencies also allows individual tasks to be placed on different edge resources, or even on fog and cloud resources, for task-parallel distributed execution. Users can also design platform-aware tasks to address hardware heterogeneity. The same logical task with different implementations to capture compute vs. quality trade-off can also be developed. This model can exploit pipeline parallelism too. Finally, tasks can also serve as units of fine-grained control over privacy and security policies.

The dataflow model works equally well with *batch or streaming* data sources. In a batch or a file-based execution model, the application is triggered once for a given input file/batch, while for a stream-based execution model, the dataflow and its constituent tasks are triggered for each input event that arrives on the input stream. Processing data in a batch helps improve the throughput by amortizing the static application or task cost across the whole data. A stream-based model reduces the latency for processing a single event as it does not have to wait for all events that are part of a batch to complete execution. Batching can also be performed on a stream of events before their execution, and this is also called a *micro-batch* execution model and been adopted by Big Data platforms like Apache Spark Streaming. This can help get higher throughput while not sacrificing latency a lot. However, determining the number of events in the batch can be a challenge.

6.5.1.2 Publish–subscribe model

Unlike a dataflow model where the tasks are tightly coupled to each other as part of the composition, the publish–subscribe model allows users to define tasks that will consume data from certain *input topic(s)* and send their response to other *output topic(s)*. Tasks can be *publishers* and/or *subscribers* to topics, sending or receiving events from them. An *event broker* is typically used to implement the topics, and for routing events between the publishers and the subscribers.

Tasks dependencies can be coupled together by having dependent tasks set their input topic to be the same as the output topic of an upstream task. As a result, the tasks in the application need not be aware of each others' presence, enabling *loose coupling*. This also simplifies adding new tasks at runtime as it can simply subscribe to an existing topic. It can also handle intermittent failures more gracefully; the broker can buffer messages for the subscriber task which can be relayed once it comes online after a failure. The other benefits of dataflow models such as modular composition, placement, hardware-specific implementations, and security domains hold here as well. However, this loose coupling also means that tasks scheduling for an application is done independently, and meeting the performance QoS becomes more challenging. There is also an overhead of in directing all messages through a broker service. *AWS Greengrass* [13] is an example of an edge platform that uses the publish–subscribe model, and *Message Queuing Telemetry Transport (MQTT)* [14] is a popular publish–subscribe protocol for IoT.

6.5.1.3   Domain-specific languages

While dataflow and publish–subscribe are general-purpose programming models, there are also domain-specific languages (DSLs) that simplify the development of a narrower and well-defined class of applications. They typically offer a fixed set of patterns that are common in the domain, and an application is composed of these primitives. There are well-defined semantics on their execution model, which is optimized for these patterns. The goal is to reduce the design complexity and enhance the performance for this application class. This particularly lowers the barrier to entry for the developer and is beneficial for well-defined and specialized IoT applications. DSL must provide a certain level of automation to justify the restrictions on the application expressibility [15]. These patterns can also be used to encompass QoS trade-offs and security requirements, and help in decomposing the application for scheduling.

For example, *DSL-4-IoT* [16] is designed to abstract away the complexity of programming IoT applications that span across the edge, fog, and cloud. To deal with the heterogeneity of resources and tasks, the design of the network of devices is divided into hierarchical clustering of system, subsystem, device, and physical or virtual channel. *Stratum* [17] manages the life cycle of machine learning (ML) models on edge computing resources to allow rapid deployment [18]. Its DSL lets users provide just an abstract ML model, and then automates the selection of model instances and their validation for deployment using a constraint checker. Finally, the code is generated and run on GPU/CPU containers. Later in our case study, we will discuss *Anveshak* [19] as a DSL for tracking objects of interest across a network of camera video streams using edge computing.

6.5.1.4   Event-driven model

An event-driven model lets the developer define their application through a set of composable primitives (or operators) that operate on a *stream of events* with well-defined structure. A primitive consumes and produces a stream of events. In that sense, it has flavors of both the publish–subscribe model, where streams are like topics, and a DSL since there are well-defined patterns to operate on event streams.

The primitives themselves may be composed as a dataflow, with the arrival of an event on a stream triggering that primitive.

Complex event processing (CEP) is a popular manifestation of such a model [20]. Users can define SQL-like queries over the stream of tuples with filters, projection, and user-defined logic for performing transformation of events. It also offers specific support for temporal operators such as detecting a *sequence* of events that match some pattern, and aggregation over a *window* of events. The primitives can also be stateful, allowing them to operate across events. Given that sensor event streams are commonplace in IoT and edge computing and finding patterns is a popular requirement, event-driven models allow rapid composition of such applications. *WSO2's Siddhi CEP* [21] and *Apache Edgent* [11] are CEP systems, with the latter having specific support for edge computing.

6.5.1.5   Micro-services model

A micro-service is a lightweight service that encapsulates a well-defined function or task, typically in a stateless manner, and has a request–response pattern of operation. This allows each micro-service to be easily and rapidly scaled using a multiple instances to meet the current demand. Applications are designed using a service-oriented architecture (SOA), where the core functions are decomposed into micro-services that are then composed together based on their dependencies. The application composition itself can be manifested as a separate composite service that invokes and orchestrates the interactions between multiple micro-services in a specific order, or a generic workflow or dataflow service that uses a dependency graph to invoke the micro-services based on the given definition.

The stateless nature of micro-services simplifies the fault tolerance, since the failing micro-services can simply be restarted on other devices. Application developers can manage platform diversity by developing independent micro-services for the various platforms with the same request–response signature. Performance disparity can also be managed by designing specific micro-services that can benefit from accelerators available on the devices. Micro-services can also be deployed across different devices thus allowing developers to meet any privacy requirements specific to the application. Linux Foundation's *EdgeX Foundry* [22] is a micro-service-based architecture for edge computing.

6.5.2   Runtime environment

6.5.2.1   Edge computing platforms

Runtime platforms translate the programming model and application definition to their actual deployment, execution, and orchestration on top of edge, fog, and cloud resources. Besides the examples offered above as part of specific programming models, there are several other runtime platforms in the research and open-source domains that are worth discussing.

Node-Red [11] is a open source platform that lets users wire dataflows spanning across edge devices using Node.js. It uses an event-based execution model. The platform provides an intuitive browser-based interface, an admin API to remotely manage the runtime, and a storage API that configures the storage location for the runtime. *Apache Edgent* [10] is another open source platform designed to run analytics on the edge. It offers a DSL based on CEP. Users can compose CEP primitives such as a range *filter* or identify a *sequence* or matching events as a dataflow that operates on a stream of events. Edgent itself is a library that can be embedded in memory as part of a single Java application. The user is responsible for deployment and coordination across multiple devices.

ECHO [12] is a research platform designed to support dataflow applications that span edge, fog, and cloud. It allows users to write applications with either event-driven or file-based execution model. Thus, developers can select the right model based on their latency and throughput needs. ECHO allows different tasks in a dataflow to be written in different programming languages by providing wrappers. Finally, ECHO provides a rebalance feature that enables easy rescheduling of the application to dynamically meet QoS needs. This changes the scheduling of tasks to devices at runtime with minimal disruption.

Some edge platforms also extend Big Data platforms such as *Apache Storm* [23]. However, these tend to be heavyweight for edge devices. *EdgeWise* [24] is a stream processing engine that adopts a dataflow programming model to process a stream of events. The authors mitigate context switches between threads on constrained edge devices using a thread pool managed by an application-level scheduler. EdgeWise achieves a lower latency than Storm on edge devices. Platforms like *F-Storm* [25] allow tasks to run on edge devices accelerated using field-programmable gate arrays (FPGAs) [26]. F-Storm uses a dataflow programming model along with a micro-batch-based execution model. F-Storm abstracts away the hardware details from the application developer thereby simplifying development of applications using accelerators.

6.5.2.2   Scheduling aspects

Scheduling is the process of *allocating* computing resources to an application, and *placing* its decomposed tasks onto specific resources, while meeting a QoS goal for the application. With edge computing, scheduling becomes more challenging since tasks must be executed on devices with a compatible platform, privacy constraints must not be violated, and energy conservation may be required on constrained devices. The scheduling goal may also vary over time based on the application's needs, and the edge resource behavior may change also, say, when it goes into low-power mode due to low battery [27]. Trade-offs between quality/accuracy and performance can also be exploited by the scheduler. While the scheduling problem definition across edge, fog, and cloud has more constraints, different objectives, and a much larger solution space, existing scheduling algorithms designed for clouds [2] or mobile clouds [28] can be adopted here.

Further, the intrinsic characteristics of the different resource layers can be used to guide the resource selection and task placement schedule at the high level. Figure 6.2 captures the intuitive *placement matrix* of a single (monolithic) application (or task) on either the edge, fog, or cloud layer, depending on the location of its input data and the consumer of its output data within these layers, the size of the input data (i.e.,

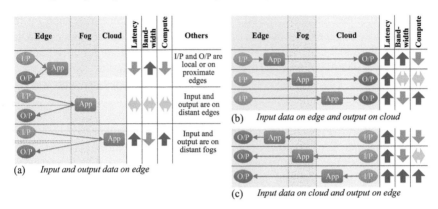

Figure 6.2   Data and application placement matrix

bandwidth required), and the latency required by the application. If the input and output data are on the edge, the bandwidth requirements of the input are high, there is a low-latency requirement, and the application is not compute-intensive, then the edge would be the natural choice of the computing layer to schedule this application. Relaxing these three constraints modestly while keeping the input and output data on the edge would place the application at the fog. If the compute needs are high, a higher latency can be tolerated, and the input data size is small, then cloud can be the best fit even if the input and output data are on the edge. Other such natural schedules are also illustrated in the matrix.

6.6   Storage models and systems

6.6.1   Motivation

Cloud data centers have been immensely popular to store and access data for many enterprise and web applications. This holds true for IoT and edge computing applications as well. The key benefits are lower storage costs due to economies of scale, low or no bandwidth charges for data ingress into the cloud, high reliability and availability, and co-location of applications that access the data within the cloud. However, IoT data and applications have unique characteristics that can be coupled with the availability of edge and fog resources to consider alternative storage strategies. We discuss these in this section.

As the number of IoT and edge devices grows and applications start running on the edge, the ability of the cloud storage to scale and perform becomes doubtful. The exponential trend in the volume of data being moved from the edge to the cloud will increase the storage costs, and the bandwidth available into the data center will be constrained. For applications running on the edge, moving data from/to the cloud will incur additional latency and charges for bandwidth. The network performance is also more variable on the WAN, and highly time-sensitive applications will not be able to guarantee QoS. At the same time, not all data generated by IoT devices need to be persisted long term. So it is possible that a lot of edge data moved to the cloud may never be used. While strategies like data aggregation and sampling have been used to reduce this quanta of data moved to the cloud [29], they require prior knowledge of the usefulness of data to decide on what to retain and what to aggregate.

Traditionally, edge devices have not been considered as a primary resource for data storage. At best, they are used to cache data or fetch and retain them transiently while an application is executing on them. A key challenge to using the edge devices for persistent storage is their lower reliability compared to cloud storage. This affects data persistence and availability. Individual edge devices also have much lower capacity, typically hosted on SD cards with $\approx$100 GB size. Lastly, the lower compute power of the edge means that it will not be able to serve a large number of concurrent clients.

But such a view may be a wasted opportunity when we consider the set of all edges collectively to host the storage layer. The number of edges is likely to grow proportionally with the number of data sources. So there is a natural growth in cumulative capacity. Data generated in the short-to-medium timescales could be retained within this capacity. Hosting applications that consume these data on the edge enhances co-location of data and compute, and reduces the latency for data access for real-time applications. Retaining data at the edge or fog layer also utilizes the higher bandwidth within the LAN or MAN, rather than be limited by the WAN bandwidth. The key to edge-based storage is to ensure that the reliability and availability challenges are addressed through the intelligent use of the fog and the cloud layers.

Besides storing data, we also need to consider the need to store *metadata* about these data and use these to discover relevant IoT data at scale. This is all the more so given the thousands of data sources and their unique characteristics. Maintaining the provenance of data also becomes important.

6.6.2 Data storage and access models

It is worth examining *what* we store, and *how* we store and access data, before we examine *where* we store it. Some of the well-known storage models treat data as files and directories, as a stream of events, or as a collection of blocks.

Files and directories are the most common data model for storage. Files are a sequence of bytes and they may be logically organized into a directory hierarchy. Files are stored in a local or distributed file system. Each file is uniquely identified by its path in the file system. They can be accessed as a sequential stream of bytes, or by requesting bytes at a random offset from the start. Files may also store minimal metadata as part of the file system.

Event streams are a popular data model when it is generated continuously by sensors. Streams may be transient, in which only the "current" data are available, or they can be persisted, where older events in the stream can be replayed for specific time durations. The latter can also be seen as a time-series data model. It may also be possible to buffer a transient stream until all its consumers have received it. Streams may be accessible from an end point or a topic, and searching and discovery of streams is done out of bands. An event broker using a topic-based publish–subscribe access model is a common manifestation of this data model.

A *block-based storage model* allows data to be stored as a collection of blocks, possibly grouped into containers or buckets. It is a form of object storage. Blocks are typically managed and accessed independently. This can enhance parallel performance and reliability. Each block can also have its own metadata. Such block-based storage can have a logical overlay on top of them, such as a file system, where each file is modeled as an ordered sequence of blocks in a container.

6.6.3   Storage location for edge computing

6.6.3.1   Only on the fog or the cloud

Public cloud providers natively provide file, block, and stream-based services for data storage and access. These are designed to be highly reliable and available, and scale with the number of clients and number of data items. Stream-based services are typically supported by scalable publish–subscribe brokers such as *Kafka*. For block and file storage services, there are distributed Big Data platforms such as *HDFS* [30] or *Ceph* [31]. Here, the data are split into blocks or objects and stored on a cluster of machines in the data center. Blocks are replicated to ensure durability even if one machine holding the replicas is lost (see Figure 6.3(a)). There is also work to dynamically increase or decrease the replication factor based on the access characteristics of certain data [32]. Some of these systems also make use of erasure coding to ensure reliability with sublinear increases in storage costs [33,34]. Finally, data can be persisted for years together, the only limit being the amount of available storage in the system and the cost.

Similar storage systems have also been tried with a cluster of fog servers, using Big Data storage platforms like *Cassandra* [35,36]. Here, the fog servers are assumed to be co-located in a micro data center. Others have also considered the heterogeneity of fogs to place data based on the resource capacity [37]. For a stream-based model, specific protocols like *MQTT* [14] are designed to support edge and IoT application requirements.

As we observed before, the limitations of cloud-only placement are the cost of storage, and the resource usage and the latency in moving the data to the cloud and back for edge-based applications. Storing data at the fog mitigates the latter but requires more reliable fog resources to be available and many of them clustered together to make use of existing Big Data storage platforms. This may not always be feasible or may be cost-prohibitive.

6.6.3.2   Only on the edge

Peer-to-peer (P2P) systems for file sharing is an edge-based storage architecture that has been successful [38]. Here, the edge devices form an overlay network and the data being stored are hashed to specific edges based on their key to form a distributed hash table (DHT) or a key-value store (see Figure 6.3(b)). Both inserts and lookups can be done in $\log(n)$ hops with n devices. The reliability of the data can be enhanced by inserting the same data with different key suffixes as a form of replication [39].

P2P systems are also designed for device churn, with robust means for device additions and removals. For stream-based data, a federated publish–subscribe broker design has also been proposed [40].

In the past, systems like *Chord*, *Pastry*, and *Tapestry* [39,41,42] have been proposed. Protocols like *BitTorrent* and *Kademlia* for P2P file sharing have also been popular [43]. More recently, the *InterPlanetary File System (IPFS)* uses P2P principles for content-based addressing and data replication on the WWW [44].

However, there are some downsides to the traditional P2P edge-only storage approach. Reliability and durability are not directly a focus of such systems, but rather opportunistic storage. The default approach is of replication, but this has storage overheads that may be addressed using erasure coding. There is also a lack of awareness on the computing that could happen on the edge, and storage adapting to it. The assumption that all resources are unreliable and equal also means that the membership protocol to maintain the DHT can be costly. There may also be limitations on the cumulative storage capacity on the edge. However, depending on the available storage and the volume of content generated, we can host the data for hours, weeks, or months with a gradual phasing out and possible archival at the cloud for longer periods of persistence.

6.6.3.3 On the edge, fog, and cloud, cooperatively

Given the availability of all three resource abstractions, we can also make use of them collectively for the storage layer. One approach is to use the cloud and/or the fog as the storage layer using existing distributed storage services, and the edge as an intelligent cache for the data [45,46] (see Figure 6.3(c)). Here, data that are frequently read but infrequently modified can be cached on one or more edge devices that are accessing it [13]. The authoritative and durable data will remain on reliable fog or cloud resources. This has the benefits of reducing the latency for access from the edge while reusing mature storage services. But these benefits do not accrue if the access pattern for files are at random. The cost of storage is still exclusively paid on the cloud or fog.

Alternatively, we can consider a storage service that actively spans these tiers. Their roles can be distinguished by the *control and data separation* or *data-tiering strategies* used. In the former, data may be exclusively stored on unreliable edges, using replication to ensure durability, but the reliable fog or cloud resource may coordinate the management of the edges, plan the replica placement, and ensure recoverability in case of failures (see Figure 6.3(d)). This is similar to *HDFS* [6], where the edge devices are the data nodes and the fog or cloud the name node [47]. The fogs themselves may coordinate among each other and reflect a super-peer model. *ElfStore*, discussed later as a case study, takes this approach [48].

The three tiers can also be responsible for different types of data, depending on the workload and reliability needs (see Figure 6.3(e)). Various data placement strategies can be examined. One could place recent data that are expected to be used often at the edge and move them to the fog or cloud over time, keep one copy of the data at each layer to enhance reliability and latency, place data used by several edges at the fog, etc. [49,50].

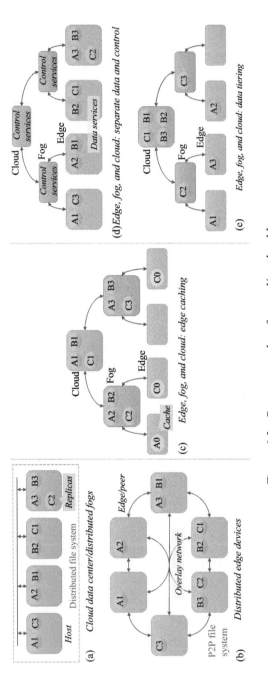

Figure 6.3 Storage on edge, fog, and/or cloud layers

6.6.4 Storage techniques and features

There are several techniques used by distributed storage systems which explore facets of performance, reliability, and context. We discuss how such generic concepts are applicable to edge storage, and aspects that are unique to such storage.

6.6.4.1 Replication

Replication is a widely used technique for providing reliability on top of unreliable storage devices [30,31]. It uses the concept that the failure probability of different devices is independent, and keeping multiple copies of the data on these devices geometrically increases the reliability of the data. This is particularly useful when storing data on the edge devices which are unreliable and have heterogeneous reliability. It is also used to increase the reliability of data stored in the fog or cloud. Replication has the added benefit of offering multiple devices on which applications consuming the data replica can be deployed, and this can be dynamically changed for "hot" data [32]. However, it has the downside of linearly increasing the storage requirement, which can be challenging on edge devices with constrained capacity.

6.6.4.2 Data compression

Compression techniques can be used to reduce the space required for storage, and it is natively supported by many storage platforms [6]. This is useful when the storage space is limited, such as for edge resources, and particularly beneficial for time-series and observational data, as is common from IoT sensors, which can be compressed significantly. However, this can involve compute overheads both at the time of compression and decompression, and associated latency for accessing the original data. This is also done each time the data are accessed and are not well suited when applications require low latency.

6.6.4.3 Erasure coding

Erasure coding uses coding theory to generated parity blocks from the data blocks such that having access to a subset of the blocks is adequate to reconstruct the original data. This provides fault-tolerant storage at a much lesser space compared to replication. At the same time, retaining the original data blocks means that no additional processing is required to access the data in the absence of any failure. There is an additional overhead to create the parity blocks. While it has been used in distributed storage systems [51], it is also a good fit for reliable storage on the edge.

6.6.4.4 Encryption

Edge and fog devices are deployed in the field and hence may be vulnerable to unauthorized physical access and potentially compromise data stored on them. As a result, data may need to be kept encrypted on disk to enhance its security and privacy. However, traditional encryption techniques like AES may not have instruction-level support on the low-power processors running on the edge, unlike consumer- and server-grade processors. This makes them compute-intensive to encrypt and decrypt.

Alternative lightweight encryption algorithms used for securing Wireless Sensor Networks (WSNs) [52] can possibly be used. Alternatively, there are systems that offload the costly encryption to the cloud but retain the encrypted data on the edge [53].

6.6.4.5   Energy efficiency

The edge devices in an IoT setup may be transient and have relatively high failure rates compared to fog and cloud. These devices are often powered by battery and can have a limited uptime. We need to efficiently make use of the resources of the edge devices to maximize their availability. To this end, we need to look at the placement of data at optimal locations in the edge which minimizes the energy needed to retrieve data. Chen *et al.* [54] propose a model for retrieving data from a set of edge nodes in a energy-efficient manner. They associate a cost to each edge device based on the amount of battery that is remaining in the device, and account for parameters such as transmission cost to propose a function which optimizes energy usage and retrieves the data. Fault tolerance is provided by using k-of-n erasure coding, and files are fragmented and placed at different locations in an energy-efficient manner.

6.6.4.6   Data provenance and trust

Data provenance is a form of metadata that provides information about the derivation history of data [55]. Edge and fog devices may not always be part of an infrastructure deployment, but are made available by volunteers or in an *ad hoc* manner by retail businesses. When data are stored on such third-party devices, it becomes necessary to ensure the integrity and trust in the data. As a result, having knowledge on the provenance of the data in a reliable and non-repudiable manner is important [56]. Provenance may be as simple as an audit trail of operations on a particular file or a dependency graph of all processes that accessed the data, and their input data as well. Such provenance data itself may need to be secured to ensure privacy and could grow large over time.

6.6.4.7   Location and context awareness

Edge devices may be mobile and also run applications on behalf of the end users. In such cases, the data storage and access patterns are sensitive to the context and location of the device and applications/users accessing it. Quality of user Experience (QoE) is a measure of this responsiveness. In location-aware storage, the system anticipates the data that will be needed by the edge application and will pre-fetch it so that when the actual request for the data arrives, the data already are cached or replicated in that edge device, thus reducing the latency for access [57]. The key insight is to correlate the location with the access pattern by a user or an application, and use its past actions to predict the future information needs. Location is one of the broader classes of context metadata, where a combination of network strength, location, file requested, etc., is used to decide where the data are stored to enhance the QoE [58].

6.7 Edge computing case study: *Anveshak*

In this section, we offer a case study of an edge computing platform that highlights the dimensions we have discussed above. *Anveshak* (Sanskrit for *explorer*) is a programming platform for scheduling and coordinating analytics over video streams generated from edge devices, within a network of surveillance cameras deployed in smart cities [19,59]. For example, London is estimated to have about 500,000 cameras by 2020 [60,61], and manual examination of such feeds is intractable. Deep and ML algorithms have been effective in automating this analysis to identify specific objects or situations. Besides public safety, such cameras serve as a *versatile proxy sensor* for other environmental observations such as the traffic flow, free parking spots, or pollution levels, when coupled with the appropriately trained deep neural network (DNN) [62]. However, such model inferencing tends to be compute-intensive. For example, *Yolo*, a fast DNN that classifies object in an image, would require hundreds of GPU cards for a citywide network of thousands of cameras [63].

At the same time, such cameras are often co-located with edge resources that can perform low-end computer vision operations. Thousands of such edge resources can be complemented by fog resources within neighborhoods having on-board accelerators. Given the high bandwidth required for moving cumulative video feeds to the cloud, it is essential that such analytics be performed close to the stream source rather than at a remote data center.

However, composing, deploying, and managing such analytics across edge, fog, and cloud resources, with good performance, required accuracy, and at large scales, is challenging. Anveshak addresses this. It is specifically designed to support the class of *tracking applications*, where given a query image of an object or a person, we should detect and track this mobile entity across the camera network. This is also called Object Reidentification [64]. Such a capability can be used to detect stolen vehicles, missing persons, or even to detect emergency vehicles and control traffic signals based on their route [59]. We discuss the design of this platform next.

6.7.1 Architecture

Anveshak operates over edge, fog, and cloud resources. The edge and fog are part of the citywide MAN while the cloud is accessed over the WAN. Each camera has a co-located edge device that can acquire data from it and also control it. There may be additional edge and accelerated fogs present. The end user accesses the system through a cloud-based interface. For simplicity, Anveshak assumes that all devices are reliable and not mobile.

Anveshak offers a *DSL* to design tracking applications. This is expressed as a static dataflow composition, as shown in Figure 6.4. Here, the semantics of tasks at each layer of the dataflow, their wiring, and execution semantics are well defined by Anveshak. It also uses stream-based data channels between tasks in the dataflow.

A developer must implement the following modules to compose an application.

Filter control (FC): This controls the flow of images into the dataflow. It may entirely stop the images coming from a camera, thereby deactivating it. This helps

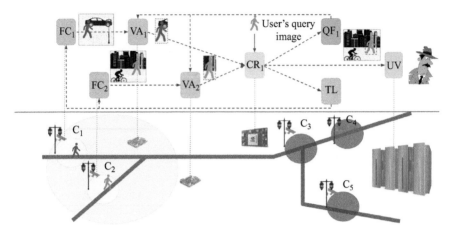

Figure 6.4   Anveshak architecture. DSL dataflow, modules, and their placement are shown on top. A sample tracking scenario shown in the bottom

leverage the user-defined *tracking logic*, described next, that helps control the relevant cameras whose stream should be processed.

Video analytics (VA): This implements a computer vision or a low-end DNN model required to recognize the object of interest from a *single camera*. A single instance of VA may independently process streams from multiple cameras. This typically runs on an edge.

Contention resolution (CR): VA may report false positives about the queried entity. The CR uses a higher-end DNN model to resolve such errors and give an accurate detection. CR is often deployed at an accelerated fog and operates on the output of multiple VA instances to enhance the throughput.

Tracking logic (TL): The compute requirements of the DNNs makes it infeasible to process the video streams from all cameras in the city concurrently. This module addresses this constraint by limiting the search scope to the most relevant cameras. If the object of interest is present within the current feed of a camera (i.e., found), then only cameras in its vicinity are of interest. If the object went missing from a camera, the search space of cameras gradually expands over time till the object is found again. TL is defined based on the domain over which tracking occurs, e.g., a road or a transit network with knowledge of the camera location and the object speed, and it informs the FC about the cameras to activate and deactivate.

Query fusion (QF): As the object of interest crosses the field of view of multiple cameras, several angles of the object get captured. ML algorithms can fuse these multiple views to improve the quality of the query image, thus increasing the accuracy of the model on the fly. The application developer may provide logic that updates the parameters of the model based on the different views detected, and this is sent back to the VA and the CR modules.

User visualization (UV): This acts as the front end for the application, where the object query can be submitted and the results of the tracking viewed. This typically runs on the cloud.

6.7.2   Runtime features

The Anveshak runtime deploys and runs the module instances of a application across the edge, fog, and cloud. At the same time, it must be able to cater to the performance needs of the application. Specifically, the runtime addresses three dimensions of QoS: (1) a bounded end-to-end latency for processing a video frame, from being generated at the FC to being reported at the UV, to support the real-time searching needs; (2) the number of active cameras that can be supported within the given resource capacity, which enables a larger search space and improves the chances of finding the object of interest; and (3) the accuracy of the application, without any loss of detections of the object of interest.

These QoS requirements offer a trade-off space, e.g., having more active cameras processed within the same set of resources may cause the latency to increase, but also increase the chances of finding the entity. Anveshak offers three *tuning knobs* to help the user explore this solution space.

First, the runtime can be configured to *batch* frames and events for processing by a module. This can increase the throughput and support more cameras by amortizing the static costs of the model inferencing, but can also increase the end-to-end latency due to the buffering and batch execution overheads. While a fixed batch size can be provided, Anveshak is intelligent enough to dynamically select the largest batch size while meeting the maximum tolerable latency specified by the user. Second, we allow *dropping* of events that exceed the maximum latency. Here, the drops are performed early on in the dataflow so that events that are highly unlikely to be fully processed within the latency deadline are discarded. This avoids wasting resources on them and can help other events meet their latency goals. However, this can reduce the accuracy of the application. Lastly, *resource scaling* allows more instances of the resources to be configured to run the module instances. This can increase the number of streams supported, but will also increase the cost for the application. Importantly, these mechanisms are automated, reducing the burden on the application developer.

Thus, Anveshak exemplifies an edge computing platform to support applications for a specific domain. It eases composition of the application along with runtime techniques that are tuned to the domain, as well as the resource abstractions of edge, fog, and cloud.

6.8   Edge storage case study: *ElfStore*

Here, we present a case study of a edge storage system that reflects some of the characteristics and techniques that we have introduced above. Edge local federated Store or *ElfStore* [48] is a distributed data store for persisting stream of block data at the edge layer, with coordination performed by the fog layer (Figure 6.3(d)). ElfStore assumes that the edge devices are unreliable and are prone to failure, but with a well-specified reliability level. The fog devices are expected to be reliable, but they are limited to management and not data storage. Given this, the storage system guarantees the reliability of blocks in a stream at a required level by the user. In addition, it supports indexing and querying for blocks and streams based on their metadata, and recovery from edge failures.

6.8.1   Architecture

ElfStore uses a P2P architecture with a two-tier overlay network. Fogs act as super-peers while edges are peers within each parent fog. The fog devices form the control plane and edge devices form the data plane of the system.

Each fog has a set of edges that are connected to it, and these form a *fog family*. All fogs are partitioned into *buddy groups*. Fogs that are not part of a buddy group are further partitioned and each partition assigned as *neighbors* to a fog in the buddy group. So each fog will be part of one buddy group and occur once as part of the neighbors in every other buddy group. Such an overlap allows any fog to reach any edge in the P2P system within a maximum of three hops, fog–buddy–neighbor–edge, and bounds the search time. For example, Figure 6.5 shows (F1,F2) as a buddy group with edges (E1,E2) and (E3,E4) as part of their family, respectively. Similarly, (F3,F4) are part of a buddy group. F3 is a neighbor of F2 while F2 is a neighbor of F4.

Each edge periodically sends lightweight *heartbeats* to its parent fog, along with statistics on its storage capacity and reliability as payload. If the heartbeats from an edge are missed for multiple times, the parent fog treats the edge as failed and recovers blocks present on it. Each fog locally maintains the *statistics* of edges in its family. It also shares these statistics with fogs for which it is a neighbor. Periodically, each fog shares consolidated statistics of its edges and its neighbors with other fogs in its buddy group. In this way, a fog can aggregate statistics from all its buddies and their neighbors to get global and approximate information on the reliability and storage capacity of all the edges in the system.

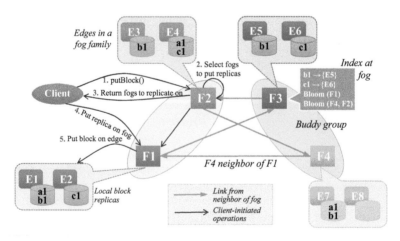

Figure 6.5   ElfStore architecture. P2P overlay, storage, indexing, and operations

6.8.2 Data management

Clients can contact any fog to *put* and *get* blocks. These are in the namespace of a particular *stream*. They can also search for blocks or streams that have certain metadata properties. ElfStore uses *asymmetric replication* to ensure the reliability of blocks. When putting a block to a stream, the fog receiving the request needs to decide how many replicas to create and the edge devices to place them on, in order to meet the reliability goals. These two decisions are inter-related—the reliability of the edges chosen to place a replica determines the number of additional replicas required to meet the reliability for that block.

As part of its statistics, each fog maintains a ten-tuple for every other fog: the minimum, median, and maximum storage and reliability of all its edges, and the number of edges falling into each quadrant of these division, i.e., high storage–high reliability (HH), high storage, low reliability (HL), etc. These are globally aggregated for all the fogs. When selecting the replica locations, a fog prioritizes fogs having edges with higher cumulative storage capacity. It alternates between selecting fogs with HH and HL, and uses their median or minimum reliability as the incremental reliability for the replica. This selection continues until the requested reliability for a block is met and gives us the replica count. The fog receiving the request then sends a copy of the input block to these selected fogs, and each of these fogs locally select an appropriate edge to place the block on. The block can also be optionally compressed before storage. All block operations are also logged, offering an audit trail of clients that performed the operations.

This strategy ends up selecting edges with high capacity that are near the median global reliability, and as their capacity gets exhausted, other edges with higher and lower reliabilities will move toward the median. This ensures a uniform distribution of edge reliabilities for selection, over time.

6.8.3 Data discovery

ElfStore allows metadata about the streams and the blocks to be stored as part of a *put* operation, and allows querying for blocks or streams based on these key–value pairs. To support the *find* operation, each fog maintains several indexes over the metadata. Specifically, it maintains an *exact inverted index* of the metadata properties to the block IDs and edge devices, for blocks replicas that are present within edges in its family. This is updated when new streams are registered or new blocks are *put* within the fog family.

Each fog also folds the name–value pairs of its local index into a *Bloom filter*. This is a compact and approximate structure that can test if an item is present in it or not, and return a response with a small false positive rate. This is shared with all fogs which it is a neighbor of, and each fog maintains a Bloom filter of block metadata from all its *neighbors*. Lastly, a fog folds the Bloom filter from its local metadata and the Bloom filter from its neighbors into a *consolidated Bloom filter*, and shares it with the fogs in its buddy group. So each fog also maintains a consolidated Bloom filter from all its *buddies*. These Bloom filters, each 20 bytes long, are exchanged as part of the heartbeat messages.

Given this, when a *find* query is received by a fog, it checks for the presence of the query metadata in its local index, its neighbors' Bloom filters, and its buddies' consolidated Bloom filters. A hit with the local index will return the block IDs and their edge device locations in the local family. A hit with a neighbor will cause this fog to forward the query to the neighbor, which will check and return the block ID and edge devices from its local index (assuming it was not a false positive). A hit with a buddy will cause the request to be forwarded to the buddy, and possibly its neighbors, to return a response. So the query completes within 0–2 hops, with another hop to retrieve the block.

In summary, ElfStore is an edge-centric distributed storage service that provides guaranteed reliability of data blocks and discovery of blocks. It also enhances data locality for edge applications. Edge computing platforms can use knowledge of ElfStore and its data replicas to plan their application scheduling on a co-located edge device.

6.9   Open issues

There are several open problems to consider in edge computing and storage models. One key dimension is of *dynamism*. Edge resources tend to operate in highly variable environments. There can be network changes, resource failures, and device mobility. Algorithms and strategies are needed to characterize the resource behavior and proactively respond to variability in order to meet the application and data needs. Actively using the relative features of edge, fog, and cloud will be important, rather than pin-specific tasks or data to specific layers. This will also require the ability to migrate (stateful) tasks from one resource to another. Data storage on the edge that responds to application workloads, by caching or replicating data on demand, will also help reduce access latency. The reliability of edge devices may also deteriorate over time, say, when they are placed outdoors or as their battery levels vary. So adapting the application and storage to such situations will be necessary.

Another key challenge is one of *monitoring and managing* the edge platforms and infrastructure. Here, we need to have mechanisms for patching the OS, updating the platform version, and installing different application environments over time. Doing this seamlessly for thousands of devices while ensuring consistent operations and minimal downtimes is challenging. Lightweight *containers* offer a possible solution for defining application environments and dependencies. Likewise, monitoring the health of these devices and responding to these, as discussed above, is a challenge.

Leveraging the *Tensor Processing Units (heterogeneity)* of the resources is another key aspect. In particular, as *accelerators* such as Tensor Processing Units (TPUs), GPUs, and FPGAs become commoditized for the edge, and Artificial Intelligence (AI) and ML applications grow popular, these asymmetric resources will need to be efficiently used for both training and inferencing. We will also need to investigate issues such as the accuracy of the results from the applications, e.g., when using quantization in DNNs, against the QoS performance of these. Federated learning is already a key challenge for ML, and this will be key for data sourced from the edge as well. These may require new computing models and DSLs to be defined for the edge. Storing and managing the life cycle of models on the edge will also be a concern.

Lastly, defining the requirements of *security*, *privacy*, and *trust* for applications and data and enforcing them unambiguously will be important. Data and applications running in the wild, rather than in secure data centers, will put additional onus on the platforms to offer guarantees on the correctness of results, protection against data leaks and manipulation, and auditing of operations. The growing rise of cybersecurity threats on IoT infrastructure such as smart grids is also a concern as these can affect life and property. Hijacking of unsecured edge devices for mounting distributed denial-of-service attacks have also been reported. This requires concerted effort that balances performance on constrained devices against the needs of the application domains using the edge resources.

6.10 Conclusions

Edge devices are poised to be first-class resources for computing and storage. In this chapter, we have examined the value proposition of such an approach, and the complementary benefits of edge, fog, and cloud resources. We have explored different computing and storage models to support application composition and data storage on edge resources, alongside fog and cloud. There are also existing techniques and runtime strategies from cloud computing, Big Data platforms, distributed storage systems, and P2P systems that can be suitably extended and adapted to meet these unique needs. We have offered two case studies of an edge-based video analytics platform for tracking, and an edge-centric storage system, which highlight these design elements. Lastly, we have highlighted open problems in the context of computing and storage models for the edge.

References

[1] Simmhan Y, Ravindra P, Chaturvedi S, Hegde M and Ballamajalu R. Towards a data-driven IoT software architecture for smart city utilities. Softw Pract Exper. 2018;48(7):1390–1416.

[2] Varshney P, and Simmhan Y. Characterizing application scheduling on edge, fog, and cloud computing resources. Softw Pract Exper. 2019.

[3] BACnet—A Data Communication Protocol for Building Automation and Control Networks (ANSI Approved). American Society of Heating, Refrigerating and Air-Conditioning Engineers; 2016. Standard 135–2016.

[4] Saint-Andre P. Extensible Messaging and Presence Protocol: Core. Internet Engineering Task Force; 2011. RFC 6120. https://xmpp.org.

[5] Varshney P, and Simmhan Y. Demystifying fog computing: Characterizing architectures, applications and abstractions. In: IEEE International Conference on Fog and Edge Computing; 2017. pp. 1–10.

[6]   Shvachko K, Kuang H, Radia S, *et al.* The Hadoop Distributed File System. In: IEEE Symposium on Mass Storage Systems and Technologies; 2010. pp. 1–10.

[7]   Simoens P, Xiao Y, Pillai P, *et al.* Scalable crowd-sourcing of video from mobile devices. In: International Conference on Mobile systems, applications, and services. ACM; 2013. pp. 139–152.

[8]   Acar A, Aksu H, Uluagac AS, *et al.* A survey on homomorphic encryption schemes: Theory and implementation. ACM Comput Surv. 2018;51(4): 79:1–79:35.

[9]   Vogler M, Schleicher JM, Inzinger C, *et al.* DIANE-dynamic IoT application deployment. In: IEEE International Conference on Mobile Services. IEEE; 2015. pp. 298–305.

[10] Apache. Node-Red; 2019. Accessed: 2019/07/28. https://nodered.org/.

[11] Apache. Edgent, v1.2.0; 2019. http://edgent.apache.org/.

[12] Ravindra P, Khochare A, Reddy SP, *et al.* ECHO: An adaptive orchestration platform for hybrid dataflows across cloud and edge. In: International Conference on Service-oriented Computing. vol. 10601 of LNCS. Springer, Cham; 2017. pp. 395–410.

[13] Amazon. AWS GreenGrass; 2019. Accessed: 2019-07-31. https://docs.aws. amazon.com/greengrass/latest/developerguide/what-is-gg.html.

[14] Coppen R. MQTT Version 5.0. OASIS; 2019.

[15] Ranabahu AH, Maximilien EM, Sheth AP, *et al.* A domain-specific language for enterprise grade cloud-mobile hybrid applications. In: ACM Conference on Systems, Programming, Languages, and Applications: Software for Humanity (SPLASH) workshops. ACM; 2011. pp. 77–84.

[16] Salihbegovic A, Eterovic T, Kaljic E, *et al.* Design of a domain-specific language and IDE for Internet of things applications. In: International Convention on Information and Communication Technology, Electronics and Microelectronics. IEEE; 2015. pp. 996–1001.

[17] Bhattacharjee A, Barve Y, Khare S, *et al.* Stratum: A serverless framework for the lifecycle management of machine learning-based data analytics tasks. In: USENIX Conference on Operational Machine Learning; 2019. pp. 59–61.

[18] Hofmann M, and Klinkenberg R. RapidMiner: Data Mining Use Cases and Business Analytics Applications. CRC Press, Taylor & Francis Group, Boca Raton, FL, USA; 2013.

[19] Khochare A, Aravindhan K, and Simmhan Y. A Scalable Framework for Distributed Object Tracking across a Many-camera Network. CoRR. 2019;abs/ 1902.05577. Available from: http://arxiv.org/abs/1902.05577.

[20] Dayarathna M, and Perera S. Recent advancements in event processing. ACM Comput Surv. 2018;51(2):1–36.

[21] WSO2. Complex Event Processor; 2019. https://wso2.com/products/complex-event-processor/.

[22] Foundation L. EdgeX Foundry; 2019. https://www.edgexfoundry.org.

[23] Toshniwal A, Taneja S, Shukla A, *et al.* Storm@ twitter. In: ACM SIGMOD International Conference on Management of Data. ACM; 2014. pp. 147–156.

[24] Fu X, Ghaffar T, Davis JC, *et al.* Edgewise: A better stream processing engine for the edge. In: USENIX Annual Technical Conference; 2019. pp. 929–946.

[25] Wu S, Hu D, Ibrahim S, *et al.* When FPGA-accelerator meets stream data processing in the edge. In: IEEE International Conference on Distributed Computing Systems; 2019.

[26] Biookaghazadeh S, Zhao M, and Ren F. Are FPGAs suitable for edge computing? In: USENIX Workshop on Hot Topics in Edge Computing; 2018.

[27] Ghosh R, and Simmhan Y. Distributed scheduling of event analytics across edge and cloud. ACM Trans Cyber-Phys Syst. 2018;2(4):1–28.

[28] Wang Y, Chen IR, and Wang DC. A survey of mobile cloud computing applications: Perspectives and challenges. Wirel Pers Commun. 2015;80(4):1607–1623.

[29] Yousefpour A, Fung C, Nguyen T, *et al.* All one needs to know about fog computing and related edge computing paradigms: A complete survey. Journal of Systems Architecture. 2019;98:289–330.

[30] Ghemawat S, Gobioff H, and Leung ST. The Google File System. SIGOPS Oper Syst Rev. 2003;37(5):29–43. Available from: http://doi.acm.org/10.1145/1165389.945450.

[31] Weil SA, Brandt SA, Miller EL, *et al.* Ceph: A scalable, high-performance distributed file system. In: USENIX Symposium on Operating Systems Design and Implementation; 2006. pp. 307–320.

[32] Abad CL, Lu Y, and Campbell RH. DARE: Adaptive data replication for efficient cluster scheduling. In: IEEE International Conference on Cluster Computing. IEEE; 2011. pp. 159–168.

[33] Sathiamoorthy M, Asteris M, Papailiopoulos D, *et al.* XORing elephants: Novel erasure codes for big data. In: Proceedings of the VLDB Endowment (PVLDB); 2013.

[34] Plank JS. Erasure codes for storage systems: A brief primer. login: the Usenix Magazine. 2013 December;38(6):44–50.

[35] Lakshman A, and Malik P. Cassandra: A decentralized structured storage system. SIGOPS Oper Syst Rev. 2010;44(2):35–40. Available from: http://doi.acm.org/10.1145/1773912.1773922.

[36] Confais B, Lebre A, and Parrein B. Performance analysis of object store systems in a fog and edge computing infrastructure. Transactions on Large-Scale Data-and Knowledge-Centered Systems XXXIII. 2017.

[37] Lee CW, Hsieh KY, Hsieh SY, *et al.* A dynamic data placement strategy for Hadoop in heterogeneous environments. Big Data Research. 2014;1: 14–22.

[38] Balakrishnan H, Kaashoek MF, Karger D, *et al.* Looking up data in P2P systems. Commun ACM. 2003;46(2):43–48.

[39] Stoica I, Morris R, Karger D, *et al.* Chord: A scalable peer-to-peer lookup service for Internet applications. In: Conference on Applications, Technologies, Architectures, and Protocols for Computer Communications (SIGCOMM). ACM; 2001. pp. 149–160.

[40] Fox G, and Pallickara S. The Narada event brokering system: Overview and extensions. In: International Conference on Parallel and Distributed Processing Techniques and Applications; 2002.

[41] Rowstron A, and Druschel P. Pastry: Scalable, decentralized object location, and routing for large-scale peer-to-peer systems. In: Guerraoui R, editor. Middleware. Berlin, Heidelberg: Springer Berlin Heidelberg; 2001. pp. 329–350.

[42] Zhao BY, Ling H., Stribling J, *et al.* Tapestry: A resilient global-scale overlay for service deployment. IEEE Journal on Selected Areas in Communications. 2004;22(1):41–53.

[43] Maymounkov P, and Mazières D. Kademlia: A peer-to-peer information system based on the XOR metric. In: Druschel P, Kaashoek F, and Rowstron A, editors. Peer-to-peer Systems. Berlin, Heidelberg: Springer Berlin Heidelberg; 2002. pp. 53–65.

[44] Benet J. IPFS—Content Addressed, Versioned, P2P File System. CoRR. 2014;abs/1407.3561. Available from: http://arxiv.org/abs/1407.3561.

[45] Tran TX, Hajisami A, Pandey P, *et al.* Collaborative mobile edge computing in 5G networks: New paradigms, scenarios, and challenges. IEEE Communications Magazine. 2017;55(4):54–61.

[46] Wang S, Zhang X, Zhang Y, *et al.* A survey on mobile edge networks: Convergence of computing, caching and communications. IEEE Access. 2017;5:6757–6779.

[47] Yang BB, and Garcia-Molina H. Designing a super-peer network. In: International Conference on Data Engineering. IEEE; 2003. pp. 49–60.

[48] Monga SK, Ramachandra SK, and Simmhan Y. ElfStore: A resilient data storage service for federated edge and fog resources. In: IEEE International Conference on Web Services; 2019. pp. 336–345.

[49] Mortazavi SH, Salehe M, Gomes CS, *et al.* Cloudpath: A multi-tier cloud computing framework. In: ACM/IEEE Symposium on Edge Computing; 2017.

[50] Mayer R, Gupta H, Saurez E, *et al.* Fogstore: Toward a distributed data store for fog computing. In: IEEE Fog World Congress. IEEE; 2017. pp. 1–6.

[51] Xia M, Saxena M, Blaum M, *et al.* A tale of two erasure codes in HDFS. In: USENIX Conference on File and Storage Technologies; 2015. pp. 213–226.

[52] Hayouni H, Hamdi M, and Kim TH. A survey on encryption schemes in wireless sensor networks. In: International Conference on Advanced Software Engineering and Its Applications. IEEE; 2014. pp. 39–43.

[53] Zhou Z, and Huang D. Efficient and secure data storage operations for mobile cloud computing. In: International Conference on Network and Service Management and Workshop on Systems Virtualization Management. IEEE; 2012. pp. 37–45.

[54] Chen CA, Won M, Stoleru R, *et al.* Energy-efficient fault-tolerant data storage and processing in mobile cloud. IEEE Transactions on Cloud Computing. 2015;3(1):28–41.

[55] Simmhan YL, Plale B, and Gannon D. A survey of data provenance in e-Science. SIGMOD Rec. 2005;34(3):31–36.

[56]   Bauer S, and Schreckling D. Data provenance in the Internet of things. In: EU Project COMPOSE, Conference Seminar; 2013:1–15.

[57]   Stuedi P, Mohomed I, and Terry D. WhereStore: Location-based data storage for mobile devices interacting with the cloud. In: ACM Workshop on Mobile Cloud Computing & Services: Social Networks and Beyond; 2010.

[58]   Gedeon J, Himmelmann N, Felka P, *et al.* vStore: A context-aware framework for mobile micro-storage at the edge. In: International Conference on Mobile Computing, Applications, and Services. Springer, Cham; 2018. pp. 165–182.

[59]   Khochare A, Sheshadri KR, Shriram R, and Simmhan Y. Dynamic scaling of video analytics for wide-area tracking in urban spaces. In: IEEE/ACM International Symposium on Cluster, Cloud and Grid Computing; 2019.

[60]   Ananthanarayanan G, Bahl P, Bodík P, *et al.* Real-time video analytics: The Killer App for edge computing. Computer. 2017;50(10):58–67.

[61]   caughtoncamera. How Many CCTV Cameras in London; 2019. Accessed: 2019-07-29.   https://www.caughtoncamera.net/news/how-many-cctv-cameras-in-london/.

[62]   Nafi NS, and Khan JY. A VANET-based intelligent road traffic signalling system. In: Australasian Telecommunication Networks and Applications Conference; 2012. pp. 1–6.

[63]   Redmon J, and Farhadi A. YOLO9000: Better, Faster, Stronger. CoRR. 2016;abs/1612.08242. Available from: http://arxiv.org/abs/1612.08242.

[64]   Shiva Kumar KA, Ramakrishnan KR, and Rathna GN. Distributed person of interest tracking in camera networks. In: ACM International Conference on Distributed Smart Cameras; 2017.

Chapter 7
Resource allocation models in/for edge computing

*Mohammad Ali Khoshkholghi[1], Michel Gokan Khan[1],
Yogesh Sharma[1] and Javid Taheri[1]*

During last decades, cloud computing enabled centralization of computing, storage and network management through cloud data centres, cellular core networks and backbone IP networks. Unlimited computing resources and storage can be used to provide elastic cloud services to a vast range of customers from organizations encompassing hundreds of servers to resource-constrained end users. Despite numerous advantages, Cloud computing is facing increasing limitations such as remarkable communication delay, jitter and network traffic caused due to far located data centres from end users. Edge computing has emerged in order to shift the traditional cloud model towards a decentralized paradigm to deal with strict requirements of latency, mobility and localization of new systems and applications (e.g. Internet of Things (IoT)). Edge computing places the content and resources near to end users to ensure a better user experience.

Edge computing is still at the stage of development and encounters many challenges such as network architecture design, fault-tolerance and distributed service management, cloud-edge interoperability and resource allocation. In this chapter, we present an overview on existing resource allocation models proposed for and leveraged in edge computing. Specifically, we explore the key concepts of resource allocation in edge computing, and investigate recent researches have been conducted in this domain along with their optimization models. Finally, we discuss challenges and open issues.

7.1 Introduction

Edge computing is a model that extends cloud computing and services to the edge of the network. Edge systems provide application, storage, data and compute services to end users similar to cloud, but closer to users with dense geographically distribution, and support for mobility [1]. Edge computing does not exclusively rely on clouds, as it can store, process and make decision individually, but it needs clouds for complex

[1]Department of Mathematics and Computer Science, Karlstad University, Karlstad, Sweden

tasks with more resource requirements. In the latter case, it acts as an intermediate layer between cloud and end users upon which the amount of data transferred to cloud significantly is decreased. For example, intelligent transportation systems in the edge are able to compress and extract necessary GPS data before sending to the cloud [2]. As an extension of edge computing, mobile edge computing (MEC) refers to the cloud resources and services at the edge of the mobile networks within the radio access network and in vicinity of mobile devices. MEC allows cellular operators to add edge computing functionality to existing base stations [3]. Micro data centres with virtualization capability can be used in MEC as well.

Contrary to the cloud where resources are elastic by nature, edge devices cause notable processing delay due to their limited resources. However, edge devices potentially provide lower network delay due to their proximity to users. Another distinguishing characteristic of the edge is that numerous edge nodes spread into an enormous number of locations, in opposition to the cloud composed of several huge data centres.

An edge computing infrastructure consists of various nodes in terms of type, size and configuration. They range from mobile devices, smart access points (APs), base stations to the edge clouds composed of many servers located in a variety of networks with different service delay. In addition, various types of services need different properties, requirements and priorities and may only be served by specific edge nodes satisfying certain criteria. While the capacity of edge nodes is limited, edge services intend to be provided by the closest nodes to obtain low latency and at the same time, they desire to achieve as much resource as possible. On the other hand, due to the diverse demands for services, some nodes may become over-demanded while others are under-demanded [4].

Due to the reasons mentioned above, resource allocation is a crucial challenge in edge computing. Resource allocation refers to the efficient allocation of constrained resources to competing services with various features and requirements, in a way that edge system obtains maximum resource utilization and also satisfies the services. There is a variety of resource allocation models proposed for edge computing which aim to optimize resource utilization, profit, power efficiency, quality of service (QoS) (e.g. response time) or a combination of these objectives as we discuss in more detail in the next section.

7.2   Taxonomy of resource allocation in/for edge computing

In this section, we propose a taxonomy of research topics related to resource allocation in/for edge computing, and then, we present some latest researches conducted in each topic and demonstrate the allocation model for each work. Literature in this domain can be categorized as follows.

7.2.1   Task offloading and resource allocation

Task offloading refers to the transfer of intensive computational tasks to the nearby edge servers in order to provide computing agility, low latency and high bandwidth.

Table 7.1 Description of parameters and variables used in Section 7.1

Symbol	Description	Symbol	Description
α	Offloading decision variable	T	Time slots
E_l^i	Energy consumed by local execution	U	Set of users
E_t^i	Energy consumed by offloaded tasks	K	Set of APs
q	Computation power parameter	M	Number of users
$f_i(t)$	CPU-cycle frequency	c	Type of services
$w_i^c t_i^c$	Weighted sum of users' delay	P_i^M	Power budget
P_i^T	Computation power	f_{ik}	Resource demands
F_m	Computation capability	S	Storage capability
b	Size of computing tasks	P_i^C	Transmit power

End users, mobile or smart devices have to decide whether tasks can be done locally on its own resources or have to be migrated to edge servers. In the case that tasks would be sent, then each destination edge server will decide if the tasks can be accomplished by itself or have to be redirected to the cloud. Therefore, the question is which tasks and when are needed to be offloaded and what resources should be devoted to them according to the resource constraints and given QoS. In the rest of this section, we investigate some recent task offloading and resource allocation studies. The parameters and variables used in this section are shown in Table 7.1.

Zhou *et al.* [5] proposed a resource allocation algorithm for task offloading in MEC environment. Optimizing allocation of either radio or compute resources separately may lead to suboptimality, since congestion of one resource causes the waste of another resource. For this reason, authors in this study address resource allocation problem for both radio and compute resources coordinately. The proposed allocation model aims to optimize resource utilization and consequently decrease energy consumption of mobile devices to enhance their battery life. The objective function is modelled as mixed-integer non-liner programming problem (MINLP) as follows:

$$minimize \sum_{i=1}^{M} (1 - \alpha_i) \times E_l^i + \alpha_i \times E_t^i \qquad (7.1)$$

Here (7.1) denotes that total energy consumption of mobile users should be minimized. M denotes the number of users, α is an indicator which shows if tasks are offloaded, E_l^i is the amount of energy consumed for local execution of tasks and E_t^i is the energy consumption for offloading. Authors have addressed the allocation problem in two scenarios:

1. Computational capabilities are unlimited: For the first case, users including heavy workload should get high priority to be offloaded, since few subcarriers are needed for satisfying the deadline requirements. To find such users, an algorithm are proposed in a way that allocates subcarriers in a minimum set for each user.

Then, the tasks with minimum energy consumption and minimum subcarriers will be selected to offload to the edge. This algorithm can be also used as the performance upper bound for the second case.

2. Computational capabilities are limited: In the second case, congestion can cause the violation of the QoS requirements since queuing delay and execution time are also considered in the system. A joint subcarrier and energy allocation algorithm are proposed so that it obtains the minimum subcarrier set and most energy saving for each CPU cycle. The proposed algorithm consequently optimizes both CPU and radio resource allocation.

Liu *et al.* [6] proposed a dynamic task offloading and resource allocation for reliable and low-latency edge environments used for mission-critical applications. The objective of allocation is minimizing the amount of energy consumed by users while satisfying latency requirements. Since end users leverage dynamic voltage and frequency scaling (DVFS) technique in order to minimize energy consumption, the following constraints have been imposed to each user:

$$\begin{cases} q[f_i(t)]^3 + P_i(t) \le P_i^M \\ f_i(t) \ge 0 \\ P_i(t) \ge 0 \end{cases} \tag{7.2}$$

Here $q[f_i(t)]^3$ refers to the amount of power consumed by the user i, f_i denotes the CPU-cycle frequency and P_i refers to the transmit power.

In this work, the end-to-end delay for the locally computed tasks is defined as queuing delay and users' computing delay. In the case of offloading, the end-to-end delay is considered as queuing delay and computing delay at the edge server, along with queuing delay and transmission delay caused by offloading. Optimization model is formulated as follows:

$$\text{minimize} \sum_{i \in U} P_i^C + P_i^T \tag{7.3}$$

where

$$P_i^C = \lim_{T \to \infty} \frac{1}{T} \sum_{t=0}^{T-1} q[f_i(t)]^3 \tag{7.4}$$

$$P_i^T = \lim_{T \to \infty} \frac{1}{T} \sum_{t=0}^{T-1} P_i(t) \tag{7.5}$$

where P_i^C denotes the computation power, P_i^T denotes the transmission power, T denotes the time slot index and U refers to the set of users. To solve this problem, a two-timescale framework has been proposed using Lyapunov stochastic optimization and match theory.

Another study [7] investigated the problem of delay-aware resource allocation for multi-access edge computing considering heterogeneous services. To enhance fairness and network efficiency, a user association mechanism has been proposed along with the resource allocation algorithm. Given a multi-cell network, two heterogeneous services (content delivery service and computing service) are considered in this work, and the edge cluster is deployed in all network cells. High computational tasks can be offloaded to the edge servers, and also contents can be cached in order to minimize the download delay. The objective of the proposed allocation model is to minimize the weighted sum of users' delay. The optimization model is formulated as an MINLP problem as follows:

$$minimize \sum_{c=0}^{1} \sum_{i \in U} w_i^c t_i^c \tag{7.6}$$

subject to

$$\sum_{k \in K} \alpha_{ik}^c \leq 1 \tag{7.7}$$

$$\sum_{i \in U} \alpha_{ik}^0 f_{ik} \leq F_m \tag{7.8}$$

$$\sum_{c=0}^{1} \sum_{i \in U} \alpha_{ik}^c b_i^c \leq S \tag{7.9}$$

where K refers to the APs, U refers to the users, $c = \{0, 1\}$ refers to the types of services, f_{ik} is resource demands, F_m is the computation capability of MEC, S is the storage capability and b is the size of computing task. If $\alpha_i^c = 0$, it means user's task will be served locally, and 1 otherwise. Constraint (7.7) guarantees that one user can be associated to only one AP. Constraints (7.8) and (7.9) ensure the resource limitations of the edge servers. A coalition-game-based algorithm has been proposed to solve allocation and user association problem. The coalition-game algorithm refers to a game-theory-based algorithm in which a groups of players (coalitions) compete to earn the resources. The proposed algorithm tries to form partitions covering end users in such a way that overall game utility is improved and consequently the users' delay is minimized.

7.2.2 Server placement

The location of edge servers could significantly influence on the efficient deployment of edge environments such as mobile edge computing and smart cities. A proper placement of edge servers across large-scale networks leads to reducing access delays and improving resource utilization of edge servers. In server placement, the challenge is how to select the best location for each edge server, and how to assign base stations to edge servers. Most existing studies conducted in the area of edge resource allocation overlooked the necessity of efficient placement of edge servers. They assumed edge servers have been appropriately deployed in the edge environment, and they solely determined how to allocate the available resources to the incoming workloads. A few studies considered the server placement in edge computing as we discuss in the rest of this section. The parameters and variables used in this section are shown in Table 7.2.

Table 7.2   Description of parameters and variables used in Section 7.2

Symbol	Description	Symbol	Description
B	Set of base stations	T_i	Workload of edge server i
E	Set of links	t_b	Workload of base station b
En_i	Energy consumed by edge server i	E_x	Set of base stations allocated
$P_i(t)$	Power consumed by server i at time t		to the edge server x
$d(s_i, b_j)$	Distance between a base station and	x_i	Number of edge servers
	corresponding edge server		assigned to AP i
$w(s_i)$	Workload of server i	$l(s_i)$	Location of server i
$d(l_b, l_s)$	Access delay between base stations	$l(b_j)$	Location of base station j
	and servers	s	Edge servers
S	Set of potential server places	$u_i(t)$	Server utilization at time t
ws_{max}	Upper bound of workload	n	Number of servers

Authors in [8] investigate the problem of server placement in mobile edge environments for smart cities. They formulated the server placement as a multi-objective optimization problem in order to locate edge servers in strategic locations for the sake of reducing access delay and obtaining a more harmonious load balancing between edge servers. The network system model is introduced as an undirected graph $G = (V, E)$ including a set of potential edge server places, a plenty of mobile users, and many base stations. E denotes the set of links connecting a base station to a mobile user. $V = (B, S)$, in which B refers to the set of base stations and S is the set of potential server places. The mobile users send their requests to the base stations. Each base station has a fixed radio coverage and is able to process the users' requests and send them to the edge servers. The users receive required services provided by edge severs through base stations. The specific problem is how to optimally place a set of $\{s_1, s_2, ..., s_n\}$ edge servers to k potential server locations. Optimization model is formulated as follows:

$$minimize\ Max(T_i - T_j) \tag{7.10}$$

$$minimize\ Max\ d(l_b, l_s) \tag{7.11}$$

where T_i refers to the workloads of edge server i and $d(l_b, l_s)$ denotes the distance between a base station and the corresponding edge server. Equation (7.10) denotes that the workload difference between any pair of edge servers should be minimized, and (7.11) ensures that access delay between base stations and edge servers should be minimized.
    Subject to

$$E_i \cap E_j = \varnothing \tag{7.12}$$

$$\cup_{s \in S} E_s = B \tag{7.13}$$

$$T_s = \sum_{b \in E_s} t_b \tag{7.14}$$

where t_b denotes the workload of the base station b, and E_s is the set of base stations allocated to the edge server s. Constraints (7.12) and (7.13) guarantee that each server has a different set of base stations and all base stations will be allocated to the edge servers. Constraint (7.14) ensures that for all base stations devoted to a given edge server, all user requests will be processed by the edge server.

Mixed-integer programming is adopted to achieve the optimal server placement. The number of potential server locations is equal to the number of base stations since each edge server can be placed along with a base station. Fitness value of the solutions is measured based on both distance and workload. The smaller distance between assigned servers to their base stations, and more balanced workload of servers are more desired.

Another study [9] addresses the problem of cost-effective edge server placement in wireless metropolitan area networks. The proposed placement algorithm aims to minimize the number of deployed edge server while guaranteeing QoS requirements. The capacity of edge servers has been considered in two ways. First, the capacity can be configured on demand and second, all edge servers will have the same capacity.

The introduced system model comprises remote cloud, APs and edge servers. Wireless network is divided into several clusters, each of which consists of some APs and an edge server as the head of cluster. The size of clusters varies. In the case of offloading, tasks from all the APs located in a cluster will be sent to the head of cluster, but if the relevant edge server is overloaded, another cluster head will be selected as the host. Another option is sending the tasks to the remote cloud.

The server placement problem is formulated as an integer linear programming (ILP). The objective is minimizing the number of edge servers assigned for all APs in the network.

$$minimize \sum_{i \in V} x_i \tag{7.15}$$

There are several constraints defined for the problem such as follows: (1) The edge servers must have enough capacity for the offloading tasks. (2) The distance between APs and the cluster head must be shorter than the upper bound for the sake of satisfying edge access delay. (3) The number of APs in each cluster must not be more than cluster size limitation.

In the case of on-demand edge server capacity condition, a greedy algorithm is proposed to find the optimal solution. The algorithm selects the nodes that have highest degree among all other nodes, under the cluster size and delay constraints. In addition, a simulated annealing algorithm is proposed for the global optimization since the greedy algorithm may get stuck to the local optimization. For the second condition (fixed edge server capacity), another greedy-based algorithm is proposed to solve the optimization problem. The major difference between these two greedy algorithms is that the second algorithm adjusts some constraints on the capacities of the edge servers.

Authors in [10] proposed an energy-aware edge server placement algorithm in mobile edge computing. The objective of this study is to find the optimal edge server placement in order to minimize total energy consumption of the edge servers while satisfying latency constraints. In this study, the network architecture consists of three levels as mobile users, edge servers and cloud data centres, but the focus is on the placement of edge servers. The access delay between edge server s_i and b_j is formulated as follows:

$$d(s_i, b_j) = \sqrt{(l(s_i) - l(b_j))^2} \tag{7.16}$$

where $l(s_i)$ refers to the server location and $l(b_j)$ denotes the base station location. The energy consumption model is also modelled as follows:

$$En_i = \int_{t_1}^{t_2} P_i(t)dt \tag{7.17}$$

$$P_i(t) = P_{idle} + (P_{max} - P_{idle}) \times u_i(t) \tag{7.18}$$

where En_i is the amount of energy consumed by edge server s_i, $P_i(t)$ is the power usage of server at time t and $u_i(t)$ is server utilization. Based on the above formulation, optimization function is formulated as follows:

$$minimize \sum_{i=1}^{n} En_i \tag{7.19}$$

subject to

$$d(s_i, b_j) \leq lim \tag{7.20}$$

$$w(s_i) \leq ws_{max} \tag{7.21}$$

Constraints (7.20) and (7.21) guarantee that the distance between a base station and corresponding edge server should be shorter than the limit, and the workload of each server should not exceed the upper bound, respectively. The multi-objective optimization problem is solved by particle swarm optimization heuristic.

7.2.3 Service caching

Service caching refers to maintaining various sets of cloud services on the edge servers to accelerate short-distance connections and faster access to the services requested by users/devices. Therefore, service caching speeds up the cloud services using computation capacity and short-distance connections of edge servers. A variety of services are maintained on the edge servers, so that mobile users can communicate with the edge servers to receive the required services.

A proper selection of cached services may significantly influence on the efficiency of the resource allocation mechanism. Hence, the problem is how to optimally select the most qualified services among all cloud services to be cached on each edge server in order to decrease the latency and consequently improve the user experience with respect to the resource constraints.

Although existing researches conducted on cache policy mostly focus only on data caching, several researches have been done on the service caching in edge computing.

Table 7.3   Description of parameters and variables used in Section 7.3

Symbol	Description	Symbol	Description
f_i	Popularity of service i	$t_i(y)$	Response time of service i
R	Resource capacity of a given server	r_i	Resource consumed by service i
y	The vector that describes cache policy	α	Skewness factor
		K	Set of contents
R	Total number of content requests	M	Number of mobile users
R_k	Number of requests for content k	$x_{i,j}^k, y_j^k$	Boolean variables
J	Number of base stations	C_{CP}	Average processing cost paid by CP
P	Profit		
CP	Content provider	C_n	Average processing cost paid by the node n
C_l	Transmission cost		
C_{ca}	Cache cost	C_0	Bandwidth cost
C_{re}	Retrieval cost	H	Average hop between CP and base station
S	Size of contents		

We investigate the recent studies on service caching in the rest of this section. The parameters and variables are shown in Table 7.3.

Deng *et al.* [11] have investigated the problem of IoT service caching in MEC. In this study, only the cost of service caching from cloud data centres to edge servers has been considered, and the cost of transmitting data has been neglected. In addition, the microservices technology allows the services cooperate together to provide a composite service.

The optimization model is formulated in order to minimize the average service response time as follows:

$$minimize \sum_{i=1}^{m} f_i t_i(y) \tag{7.22}$$

subject to

$$\sum_{i=1}^{n} y_i r_i \leq R, y_i \in \{0, 1\} \tag{7.23}$$

where f_i is popularity of service s_i, $t_i(y)$ is the service response time, R is the resource capacity of the edge server i and r_i is resource consumption of service s_i.

Authors proposed a brute-force method to find the optimal solution along with a genetic algorithm (GA)-based algorithm to reach to a near optimal but more practical and faster. The fitness function used in the proposed GA algorithm is formulated as follows:

$$F(y) = \begin{cases} 1/ \sum_{i=1}^{n} f_i \cdot t_i(y), & R \geq \sum_{i=1}^{n} r_i \cdot y_i \\ 0, & otherwise \end{cases} \tag{7.24}$$

where y is the vector that describes cache policy. If $y_i = 1$, the service i is cached, and 0 otherwise. Another study [12] investigated edge cached-based collaboration between Internet service providers (ISPs) and content providers (CPs) for content delivery networks, in order to decrease network delay and enhance the efficiency of content transmission. The collaboration scheme is proposed both online and offline with the intent of maximizing the network profit. The model is taken the benefits of edge cache and content popularity simultaneously. Content popularity is leveraged based on Zipf distribution as follows:

$$R_k = R \left(K^{-\alpha} \Big/ \sum_{k=1}^{K} K^{-\alpha} \right), \quad k = 1, 2, ..., K \tag{7.25}$$

where k denotes content, R denotes the number of content requests and α is the skewness factor. The objective is increasing the network profit which is defined as network revenue minus its cost. The revenue consists of the membership fees paid to CPs, and traffic fees paid to ISPs by customers. The cost includes both expenses of CPs and ISPs defined as the retrieval cost, bandwidth cost and processing cost, and it depends on network links and users' requests. The optimization model is formulated as a non-linear programming problem as shown in (7.26).

$$maximize \quad M \cdot P_{cp} + R \cdot S \cdot (P_{ISP} - C_0) - (B \cdot N \cdot S \cdot C_{ca})$$

$$- (R \cdot C_{re}) \cdot \left(1 + \sum_{k=N+1}^{K} K^{-\alpha} \right) \Big/ \sum_{k=1}^{K} K^{-\alpha}$$

$$- [C_0 + C_{CP} + (H - 1)(C_n + C_l)]S \cdot r \cdot \sum_{k=N+1}^{K} K^{-\alpha} \Big/ \sum_{k=1}^{K} K^{-\alpha}$$

$$\tag{7.26}$$

subject to

$$\sum_{j \in J} x_{i,j}^k \leq 1 \tag{7.27}$$

$$\sum_{k \in K} y_j^k \leq N \tag{7.28}$$

where M is the number of mobile clients, J is the number of base stations, P denotes profit, C_{CP} denotes average processing cost paid by CP, C_n refers to average processing cost paid by the nodes, C_l is transmission cost, C_0 is bandwidth cost, C_{ca} is cache cost, C_{re} is retrieval cost, S is size of content, H is the average hop between the CP and a base station $x_{i,j}^k$ and y_j^k are Boolean variables.

7.2.4　Service placement

In most cases, edge servers cooperate together to provide required services for different applications. Service providers can provide service chains from distinct microservices in a specific order each of which responsible for a part of a given service. These microservices can be placed on different edge servers while they need to communicate with each other. For instance, in Network Function Virtualization Infrastructures (NFVIs), service function chains composed of virtualized network functions (VNFs), can be deployed on various edge/cloud nodes.

Due to the resource constraints of network links and servers, application heterogeneity, varying of demanded service performance and also the budget limitation to rent edge nodes, an optimal service placement is critical to satisfy both users and service providers. It is because the location of microservices in the edge environment can increase or reduce the system metrics such as latency, deployment cost and energy consumption. The service placement is an NP-hard optimization problem which has been solved by exact solutions or near-optimal heuristic solutions in the literature. We review some recent researches conducted on service placement. The parameters and variables used in this section are shown in Table 7.4.

The authors in [13] have investigated the problem of service placement in edge computing. The objective of this research is minimizing the end-to-end (overall) delay of IoT devices. To this end, authors have proposed an ILP optimization model and solved it using an optimization solver considering the number of instances for each service chain and the number of replicas for each microservice. The placement of microservices are determined based on traffic flows, users' Service Level Agreement (SLA), network topology, capacity of computing resources and latency of the links. Service chains are placed in two phases. In the first phase, n number of configurations are selected and then optimal route with the minimum end-to-end-delay is selected based on some specific constraints. Objective function is proposed as follows:

$$minimize \sum_{c \in C} \sum_{y \in Y} \sum_{sd \in SD} \sum_{l \in L} \sum_{i=1}^{n_c-1} b\alpha_{sd}^y d_l + \sum_{c \in C} \sum_{l \in L} \sum_{sd \in SD} d_l(y_l^{f_1(c),sd} + y_l^{f_n(c),sd})$$

(7.29)

where C denotes the set of service chains, Y denotes different configurations of service chains, SD denotes the set of source–destination pairs, L denotes the set of links, n_c denotes number of microservices in a service chain, d_l denotes link delay, B denotes binary link variable for path between microservices, α refers to binary user assignment variable, z refers to binary configuration variable, $y_l^{f_1(c)}$ refers to the binary path variable from the source to first microservice and $y_l^{f_n(c)}$ refers to the binary path variable between the last microservice and destination.

A latency-aware service chain placement is proposed for 5G mobile networks using edge computing in [14]. In this study, three ILP models are proposed as (7.30), (7.31) and (7.32) to obtain the optimal placement in order to minimize the end-to-end latency (ILP-Lat) and deployment cost of service chain requests (ILP-Co), and number of VNF migrations (ILP-Mig).

$$minimize \sum_{u \in U} \sum_{c \in C} (L_{uc})$$

(7.30)

Table 7.4   Description of parameters and variables used in Section 7.4

Symbol	Description	Symbol	Description
C	Set of service chains	P_{sc_x}	Power consumed by SC to being
SD	Set of source–destination pairs		switched on for service s
n_c	Number of microservices in a	d_s	Service delay
	service chain	Y	Configuration set of service chains
B	Binary link variable for path	L	Set of links
	between microservices	d_l	Link delay
z	Binary configuration variable	α	Binary user assignment variable
x_{ns}	Binary variable for the service s	$y_l^{f_i(c)}$	Binary path variable from source
	and base station n		to first microservice
y_{nu}	Binary variable for the routing	B_n	Bandwidth capacity of node n
	decision to base station n	b_{s_u}	Bandwidth demand
y_{lu}	Binary variable for the routing	L	Latency
	decision to cloud	U	Set of users
$y_l^{f_n(c)}$	Binary path variable between last	r_s	Storage space occupied by service s
	microservice and destination	Com_N	Computation capacity of node n
M	Number of VNF migrations	t	Time slot
R_N	Storage capacity of node n	I_r^f	Binary variable for path allocation
Com_{s_u}	Computation demand	k	Number of switches
Co	Deployment cost	Bu	Service budget
F	Sets of flows	S	Number of services
$P_r(t)$	Fault probability of path r	$a_{i,j}$	Amount of resource allocated
Re_i	Revenue function of service i		to service i
N	Number of edge nodes	V	Set of VNFs
$s_{i,j}$	Revenue of service i from resource j	net	Cost of network links
com	Cost of computation resources	cap	Capacity of nodes
dem	Resource demands	Y	Set of VMs
X_{vn}	Binary variable to show if v is	P_{switch}	Switch power consumption
	placed on the node n	Sc	Cluster of small cells
P_{cpu}	CPU power consumption	D_{max_s}	Maximum accepted service delay

$$minimize \sum_{u \in U} \sum_{c \in C} (Co_{uc}) \tag{7.31}$$

$$minimize \sum_{u \in U} \sum_{c \in C} (M_{uc}) \tag{7.32}$$

where U denotes users, C denotes the set of service chains, L refers to latency, Co refers to deployment cost and M denotes the number of VNF migrations. In addition, a heuristic is proposed to find a near-to-optimal solution and compared to the exact solutions. Figure 7.1 shows the network topology, service chain request and service chain placement considered in this study. As we can see in Figure 7.1(a), the mobile network consists of the 5G core, centralized and decentralized units connected via backhaul and fronthaul links. Figure 7.1(b) shows two samples of requested service chains by two different users, and Figure 7.1(c) indicates the optimized placement of service functions regarding three optimization models mentioned previously.

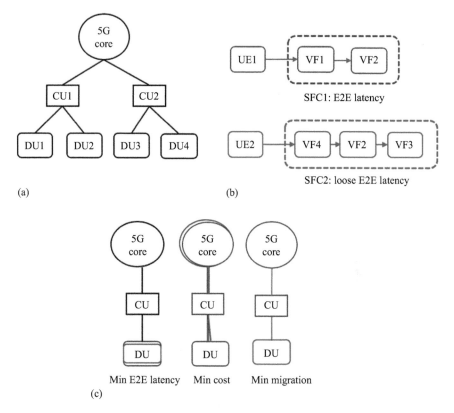

Figure 7.1   A sample of network topology, service chain request and service chain placement [14]. SFC, service function chain; VF, virtual function; E2E, end-to-end; DU, decentralized unit; CU, centralized unit; UE, user equipment

The problem of service placement and request routing in multi-cell mobile edge computing is addressed in [15]. This work aims to maximize the resource utilization so that more service requests can be served by the base stations and consequently aims to minimize the load of the cloud. The optimization model is proposed as follows:

$$minimize \sum_{u \in U} (y_{lu}) \tag{7.33}$$

subject to

$$\sum_{s \in S} x_{ns} r_s \leq R_n, \quad n \in N \tag{7.34}$$

$$\sum_{u \in U} y_{nu} com_{s_u} \leq Com_n, \quad n \in N \tag{7.35}$$

$$\sum_{u \in U} y_{nu} b_{s_u} \leq B_n, \quad n \in N \tag{7.36}$$

where U denotes users, y_{lu} denotes the binary variable for the routing decision to cloud, y_{nu} denotes the binary variable for the routing decision to base station n, x_{ns} denotes the binary variable for the service s and base station n , r_s denotes the storage space occupied by s, R_N denotes the storage capacity of node n, Com_N denotes the computation capacity of node n, Com_{s_u} denotes the computation demand by s, b_{s_u} denotes the bandwidth required by s and B_n denotes the bandwidth capacity of n. To solve the optimization problem, authors have proposed an approximation algorithm using randomized rounding technique.

In [16], the service placement and path allocation problem in edge computing is formulated in the form of ILP. The aim is to minimize failure probability of the paths allocated to the flows, and network congestion:

$$minimize \sum_{f \in F} \sum_{r=1}^{2^k} (I_r^f(t) \times P_r(t)) \tag{7.37}$$

where I_r^f denotes a binary variable for path allocation, $P_r(t)$ refers to fault probability of path r, t refers to time slot, and F and k are the sets of flows and number of switches, respectively. An software defined network (SDN)-based failure recovery architecture is proposed along with a heuristic failure recovery algorithm to find an approximated solution compared with the exact solution obtained by ILP solvers.

Since the edge node resources are limited, unlike the huge amount of resources in cloud data centres, there is a need for an efficient allocation of geographically distributed edge resources to competing services regarding the fairness and service priorities. A market equilibrium approach is proposed in [4] for edge computing. In this study, the services hire the edge resources in a way that the resource utilization and consequently either revenue or net profit are maximized. Authors formulated two optimization models to maximize the (1) revenue and (2) net profit.

1. Revenue: The allocation approach aims to maximize revenue regardless of the cost paid for hiring resources as long as the revenue is more than budget constraints. The optimization model is formulated as follows:

$$maximize \sum_{i=1}^{S} Bu_i \ln Re_i \tag{7.38}$$

subject to

$$Ru_i = \sum_{j=1}^{N} a_{i,j} x_{i,j} \tag{7.39}$$

$$\sum_{i=1}^{S} x_{i,j} \leq 1, \quad x_{i,j} \geq 0 \tag{7.40}$$

where Bu_i is the budget of service i, Re_i is the revenue function of service i, S is the number of services, N is the number of edge nodes and $a_{i,j}$ and $s_{i,j}$ are amount of resource allocated to service i and the revenue of service i from resource j, respectively.

2. Net profit: The services aim to maximize their net profits (revenue minus cost):

$$minimize \sum_{j=1}^{N} p_j - \sum_{j=1}^{N} Bu_i \ln(Re_i) \tag{7.41}$$

subject to

$$p_j \geq a_{i,j} Re_i, \quad p_j \geq 0 \tag{7.42}$$

where p_j denotes price of computing resource j.

Another study [17] addressed the service chain placement problem in order to minimize deployment cost of services. The placement strategy intends to place the VNFs onto physical nodes in a way that the total cost caused by computation (CPU, memory and storage) and network resources are minimized. The optimization model is formulated as follows:

$$minimize \sum_{n \in N} \sum_{c \in C} \sum_{v \in V} cost_{cv}^n = \sum_{n \in N} \sum_{c \in C} \sum_{v \in V} com_{cv}^n + \sum_{n \in V} \sum_{c \in C} \sum_{v \in V} net_{cv_i v_j}^{n_i n_j} \tag{7.43}$$

subject to

$$\sum_{c \in C} \sum_{v \in V} dem_{com}^{cv} X_{vn} \leq cap_{com}^n \tag{7.44}$$

$$\sum_{c \in C} \sum_{v \in V} dem_{bw}^{cv_i v_j} X_{v_i n_i} X_{v_j n_j} \leq cap_{bw}^{n_i n_j} \tag{7.45}$$

where V denotes the set of VNFs, com_{cv}^n denotes the cost of computation resources of node n allocated to function v from service chain c, $net_{cv_i v_j}^{n_i n_j}$ refers to the cost of network links between physical nodes, dem denotes resource demands, cap denotes nodes' capacity, bw denotes bandwidth and X_{vn} is a binary variable to show if v is placed on the node n or not. Constraints (7.44) and (7.45) guarantee that the resource demands of the services are less than or equal to the capacity of the physical nodes.

Two self-healing genetic algorithms are proposed to solve the placement problem using roulette wheel and tournament selection techniques. The authors considered two service placement strategies as simultaneous and one-at-a-time. In the first strategy, all the service chains are placed onto physical nodes at the same time while in the second strategy, service chains are sent to the nodes one by one. The results show that although placing services at the same time can minimize cost rather than the second strategy, it needs more time to find optimized solution. However, one-at-a-time strategy can make a balance between running time and cost reduction.

A robust energy-aware service placement is proposed in [18] for the multitenant 5G networks that provide mobile edge computing services. To integrate the microservices for virtualization execution, the cloud-enabled small cells are employed. The goal of the optimization model is to minimize the power consumption regarding to the service latency constraints under service demand uncertainty. Figure 7.2 shows the placement process proposed in this study. Network Service (NS) refers to a set of VNFs needed for a 5G service. Network tenants send the requests for new services to

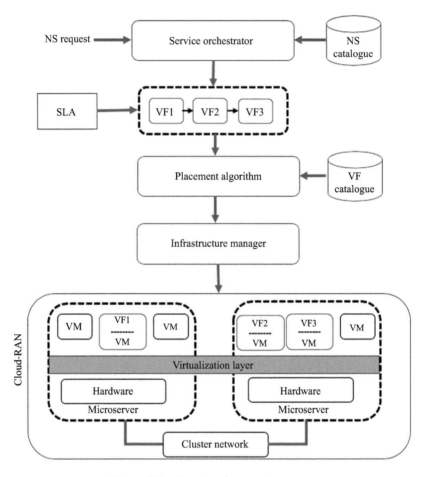

Figure 7.2   Service placement process

the service orchestrator by which the requests are analysed and correspondent service chains are extracted. Then, a placement decision will be made based on the SLA and available resources.

The power consumption is calculated based on the amount of power consumed by CPUs and switches. The optimization problem is formulated as

$$minimize\ P = \sum_{s \in S} \sum_{n \in N} \sum_{y \in Y} P_{cpu}^{s,n,y} + \sum_{i \in V} \sum_{j \in V} P_{switch_{i,j}} + \sum_{s \in S} P_{Sc_s} \qquad (7.46)$$

subject to

$$d_s < D_{max_s} \qquad (7.47)$$

where $P_{cpu}^{s,n,y}$ denotes the amount of power consumed by a CPU for the virtual machine (VM) y running the service s on node n, $P_{switch_{i,j}}$ denotes the amount of power consumed by a switch to send the VNFs' traffic, Sc denotes the cluster of small cells and P_{Sc_x} denotes power consumption of SC to being switched on for service s. Constraint (7.47) guarantees that the delay of the service s must be smaller than the maximum accepted delay (D_{max_s}) for that service.

7.2.5   Service migration

Due to dynamically moving the users in MEC (e.g. connected vehicles and smart-phones), seamless service migration has become a crucial issue to ensure service continuity and better user experience. Limited coverage of physical servers and mobility of users can lead to dramatic performance degradation and, consequently, result in edge service interruption. Service migration is a major solution to cope with this problem. The main challenge of service migration is to realize when and where an edge service allocated to a mobile user should be migrated from current edge server to another with respect to the changes in demand and user mobility [19]. In the following part of this section, we investigate the recent studies on service migration mechanisms. The parameters and variables are shown in Table 7.5.

Brandherm *et al.* [20] proposed a learning-based framework for optimizing service migration in MEC. Using the proposed general framework and in terms of different optimization goals, a reinforcement learning technique aims to provide efficient service migration strategies. The proposed framework is not bounded to a particular underlying architecture.

Another study [21] has proposed a cognitive-based edge computing architecture along with a mobility-aware and dynamic service migration mechanism for edge cognitive computing (ECC). ECC brings the cognitive computing services to the edge of the network and is able to improve energy efficiency and quality of experience compared to edge computing. The services are migrated based on both user behaviour and network conditions.

As we can see in Figure 7.3, the service manager deploys the functionalities needed for the edge services. Decision engine decides when and which services should

Table 7.5   Description of parameters and variables used in Section 7.5

Symbol	Description	Symbol	Description
$delay(x_t, p)$	Acquisition time of service request x for the strategy p	$R(x_t)$ x_t	Type of the service request x Service request at time t
$E(x_t)$	Expectation of service request x	$U_{km}(t)$	Request queues
$r_{knm}(t)$	Routing decision in time slot t	$u_{km}(t)$	Number of requests sent
$Z_{km}(t)$	Delay-aware queues		from $U_{km}(t)$ to the cloud
$G_{km}(t_f, l)$	Queue-length weighted service rate	VM	Reconfiguration cost
$V_{c_{knm}}, V_{e_{km}}$	Control parameters for back-end transmission costs	k m	Index of applications Index of edge-cloud servers
T_f	Frame length	n	Index of users

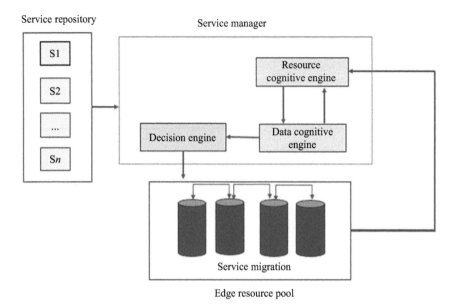

Figure 7.3   Framework of service migration in MEC [21]

be deployed or migrated regarding the information provided by resource cognitive engine, such as user mobility, service resolution and resource demands.

The service migration can be formulated as an optimization problem as shown in (7.49). The optimization goal is to maximize QoE, meanwhile minimizing the migration cost which depends on available bandwidth and server size.

$$\text{maximize } F(x_t,p) = Score(x_t,p) - Cost(x_t,p) \tag{7.48}$$

where

$$Score(x_t,p) = \frac{R(x_t) - E(x_t)}{delay(x_t,p)} \tag{7.49}$$

where x_t refers to the a request at time t, $R(x_t)$ denotes the service request type (e.g. service resolution), $E(x_t)$ denotes the expectation of a service request and $delay(x_t,p)$ refers to the acquisition time of the service for the strategy p. A reinforcement learning solution is proposed to obtain the optimized migration scenario for each individual service request.

Another study [22] has addressed the problem of live service migration in MEC. The problem is divided into two sub-problems as reconfiguration and request routing. An online control algorithm is proposed for joint application configuration decisions and request routing. The optimization models aim to minimize the time-average overall transmission and reconfiguration costs while serving all the service requests in a maximum expected delay. The proposed algorithm includes three components as user-to-edge-cloud (UEC) request routing and edge-cloud to back-end (EB) cloud request routing and service reconfiguration. The optimal solution for each component is obtained by solving following optimization models as follows:

1. UEC request routing optimization model:

$$minimize \sum_{k,m} \sum_{n} (U_{km}(t) + Vc_{knm}(t))r_{knm}(t) \tag{7.50}$$

2. EB request routing optimization model:

$$minimize \sum_{k,m} (Ve_{km} - U_{km}(t) - Z_{km}(t))u_{km}(t) \tag{7.51}$$

3. Application reconfiguration:

$$minimize \; 1/T_f \sum_{t=0}^{T_f-1} (Jt + VM(t_f + t) - \sum_{km} G_{km}(t_f, l)) \tag{7.52}$$

where $r_{knm}(t)$ refers to the routing decision in time slot t, $U_{km}(t)$ denotes the request queues, $Z_{km}(t)$ denotes delay-aware queues, $u_{km}(t)$ denotes the number of requests sent from $U_{km}(t)$ to the cloud, $G_{km}(t_f, l)$ refers to the queue-length weighted service rate, $VM(t_f + t)$ denotes the reconfiguration costs in time slot $(t_f + t)$, $V_{e_{km}}$ and $V_{c_{knm}}$ denotes the control parameters for back-end transmission costs. T_f is the frame length, and m, n and k refer to edge-cloud servers, users and applications, respectively.

7.3 Open issues and challenges

In this section, we identify and introduce some open issues and challenges of resource allocation in edge computing.

7.3.1 SLA-aware server placement and service migration

Most focus in the previous studies on the resource allocation problem in edge computing has been on task offloading, service caching and service placement, and a few works have been done on server placement and service migration. However, optimally locating of a wide range of heterogeneous edge servers across the edge network with different domains and features becomes a big challenge of resource allocation in edge computing. In addition, service migration strategies are needed to cope with the high mobility of dynamic edge environments in order to satisfy the user expectations and also guarantee the required SLA. For this end, more studies can be conducted in this area.

7.3.2 Resilient and dynamic resource allocation

Reliability and availability are two critical challenges that edge computing faces with. The movement ability of users, limited resources of nodes and the need for cooperation between cloud data centres and edge servers may cause a high risk of fault and failure in the edge infrastructure. Therefore, design and implementing a failure-aware and multi-holistic provisioning and allocation mechanism is an open issue which is neglected in the literature yet. Moreover, static bandwidth allocation is mostly considered in the previous works, which leads to unfairness in resource sharing and allocation. Therefore, proposing dynamic bandwidth allocation approaches provide more effective techniques for the edge environments.

7.3.3   Edge federation framework

There is still a lack of comprehensive federation framework (similar to hybrid cloud federation) to monitor and control the resources across the edge network by which resource sharing and allocation can be performed more effective. To gain more benefits from task offloading and resource allocation in edge networks, there is a need to conduct a variety of large-scale experiments on the real-edge services along with cooperation between edge servers.

7.3.4   Optimization criteria

To find an optimal solution for resource allocation problem, optimization metrics may influence on each other. For example, increasing utilization of resources in order to reduce energy consumption may lead to increasing latency, failure and unavailability of the edge networks. Because of that, optimization criteria should be prioritized based on different workloads and required QoS.

7.4   Conclusions

Resource allocation models used in edge computing have been discussed in this chapter. We divided previous researches conducted on resource allocation in five categories as task offloading and resource allocation, server placement, service caching, service placement and service migration. Task offloading refers to sending intensive computation tasks to the edge of network in order to decrease latency and cope with resource constraints of user devices. Server placement implies locating the edge servers across the edge network, and server caching indicates caching a set of cloud services on the edge servers to accelerate short-distance connection and faster access to the required services by users. Service placement models try to optimize locating of edge services into the physical nodes regarding optimization criteria and constraints, and service migration aims to transfer services among servers across the edge network in order to manage the users' mobility.

   We introduced and explained some recent studies for each resource allocation category and then highlighted some challenges and open issues in edge computing as SLA-aware server placement and service migration, resilient and dynamic resource allocation, edge federation framework, and optimization criteria.

References

[1]   Fog computing and the Internet of Things: Extend the cloud to where the things are. Cisco Systems; 2016. Cisco White Paper. Available from: https://www. cisco.com/c/dam/en_us/solutions/trends/iot/docs/computing-overview.pdf.

[2] Acharya J, and Gaur S. Edge compression of GPS data for mobile IoT. In: 2017 IEEE Fog World Congress (FWC). IEEE; 2017. pp. 1–6.

[3] Hu YC, Patel M, Sabella D, Sprecher N, and Young V. Mobile edge computing: A key technology towards 5G. ETSI White Paper. 2015;11(11):1–16.

[4] Nguyen DT, Le LB, and Bhargava V. Price-based resource allocation for edge computing: A market equilibrium approach. IEEE Transactions on Cloud Computing. 2018.

[5] Yu Y, Zhang J, and Letaief KB. Joint subcarrier and CPU time allocation for mobile edge computing. In: 2016 IEEE Global Communications Conference (GLOBECOM). IEEE; 2016. pp. 1–6.

[6] Liu CF, Bennis M, Debbah M, and Poor HV. Dynamic task offloading and resource allocation for ultra-reliable low-latency edge computing. IEEE Transactions on Communications. 2019;67(6):4132–4150.

[7] Zhou J, Zhang X, and Wang W. Joint resource allocation and user association for heterogeneous services in multi-access edge computing networks. IEEE Access. 2019;7:12272–12282.

[8] Wang S, Zhao Y, Xu J, Yuan J, and Hsu CH. Edge server placement in mobile edge computing. Journal of Parallel and Distributed Computing. 2019;127:160–168.

[9] Zeng F, Ren Y, Deng X, and Li W. Cost-effective edge server placement in wireless metropolitan area networks. Sensors. 2019;19(1):32.

[10] Li Y, and Wang S. An energy-aware edge server placement algorithm in mobile edge computing. In: 2018 IEEE International Conference on Edge Computing (EDGE); 2018. pp. 66–73.

[11] Deng S, Xiang Z, Yin J, Taheri J, and Zomaya AY. Composition-driven IoT service provisioning in distributed edges. IEEE Access. 2018;6:54258–54269.

[12] Fang C, Yao H, Wang Z, *et al.* Edge cache-based ISP-CP collaboration scheme for content delivery services. IEEE Access. 2019;7:5277–5284.

[13] Zamani A, and Sharifian S. A novel approach for service function chain (SFC) mapping with multiple SFC instances in a fog-to-cloud computing system. In: 2018 4th Iranian Conference on Signal Processing and Intelligent Systems (ICSPIS). IEEE; 2018. pp. 48–52.

[14] Harutyunyan D, Shahriar N, Boutaba R, and Riggio R. Latency-aware service function chain placement in 5G mobile networks. In: IEEE Conference on Network Softwarization (NetSoft 2019); June 24 2019, pp. 133–141.

[15] Poularakis K, Llorca J, Tulino AM, Taylor I, and Tassiulas L. Joint service placement and request routing in multi-cell mobile edge computing networks. In: IEEE INFOCOM 2019-IEEE Conference on Computer Communications. IEEE; April 29 2019. pp. 10–18.

[16] Tajiki MM, Shojafar M, Akbari B, Salsano S, and Conti M. Software defined service function chaining with failure consideration for fog computing. Concurrency and Computation: Practice and Experience. 2019;31(8):e4953.

[17] Khoshkholghi MA, Taheri J, Bhamare D, and Kassler A. Optimized service chain placement using genetic algorithm. In: 2019 IEEE Conference on Network Softwarization (NetSoft). IEEE; 2019. pp. 472–479.

[18]   Blanco B, Taboada I, Fajardo JO, and Liberal F. A robust optimization based energy-aware virtual network function placement proposal for small cell 5G networks with mobile edge computing capabilities. Mobile Information Systems. 2017;2017.

[19]   Wang S, Xu J, Zhang N, and Liu Y. A survey on service migration in mobile edge computing. IEEE Access. 2018;6:23511–23528.

[20]   Brandherm F, Wang L, and Mühlhäuser M. A learning-based framework for optimizing service migration in mobile edge clouds. In: Proceedings of the 2nd International Workshop on Edge Systems, Analytics and Networking. ACM; 2019. pp. 12–17.

[21]   Chen M, Li W, Fortino G, Hao Y, Hu L, and Humar I. A dynamic service migration mechanism in edge cognitive computing. ACM Transactions on Internet Technology (TOIT). 2019;19(2):1–5.

[22]   Urgaonkar R, Wang S, He T, Zafer M, Chan K, and Leung KK. Dynamic service migration and workload scheduling in edge-clouds. Performance Evaluation. 2015;91:205–228.

Chapter 8

Human-in-the-loop models for multi-access edge computing

Amin Ebrahimzadeh[1] and Martin Maier[1]

8.1 Introduction

Mobile edge computing has been recognized by the European 5G Infrastructure Public Private Partnership (5G PPP) as a promising solution to move cloud capabilities to the edge of communication networks in close proximity to the end users [1]. More recently, the European Telecommunications Standards Institute (ETSI) has dropped the word "mobile" and introduced the term *multi-access edge computing* (MEC) in order to broaden its applicability to heterogeneous networks (HetNets), including Wi-Fi and fixed access technologies (e.g., fiber) [2]. MEC is known to be one of the key enablers of a variety of emerging concepts such as the Tactile Internet [3,4]. The Tactile Internet combines a tactile device with a nearby cloudlet (i.e., local cloud) to provide an end user with step-by-step cognitive guidance through a complex task [5]. To cope with the latency and reliability issues that conventional cloud computing may suffer from, the Tactile Internet is expected to rely on advanced MEC capabilities [6].

With the wide deployment of passive optical networks (PONs) providing high capacity and reliability and wireless networks offering ubiquitous and flexible connectivity, interest has been growing in bimodal fiber-wireless (FiWi) networks that leverage the complementary benefits of optical fiber and wireless technologies [7]. FiWi-enhanced LTE-Advanced (LTE-A) HetNets represent a compelling solution to enable 4G cellular networks to meet the quality-of-service requirements of low-latency and mission-critical applications. Recently, we have evaluated the maximum aggregate throughput, offloading efficiency, and delay performance of FiWi-enhanced LTE-A HetNets and have shown that via Wi-Fi offloading and fiber backhaul sharing, an ultralow latency of $<10\,\mathrm{ms}$ and highly reliable network connectivity can be achieved for a wide range of traffic loads [8]. Both high reliability and ultralow latency are key design goals of the Tactile Internet. Note, however, that the authors of [8] did not investigate the merits and limitations of MEC and, in particular, its role in enabling teleoperation in the emerging Tactile Internet based on FiWi-enhanced mobile networks.

[1]Optical Zeitgeist Laboratory, INRS, Montréal, QC, Canada

8.1.1   Teleoperation over FiWi networks

Despite significant progress over the last years, teleoperation in a highly dynamic remote environment has not yet been fully realized due to the following reasons. First, it is well known that communication-induced artifacts such as latency and packet loss have a detrimental impact on the performance and stability of haptic communication systems. Second, an immersive teleoperation system may not provide sufficient transparency to the human operator (HO), whereby the mechanical impedance (i.e., mapping of velocity to force) perceived by the HO has to match with that of the remote environment. Third, at the heart of the aforementioned issues is the fact that since the physical interaction between the HO and remote environment takes place in real time, there is an upper limit to the tolerable round-trip delay imposed by the underlying communication network. This delay constraint, which can be either tight or partially relaxed, largely depends on the type of the task and dynamic nature of the remote environment.

A bilateral teleoperation system provides the HO with an impression of being present in the remote task environment, thereby enabling her to manipulate remote objects via a teleoperator robot (TOR). To achieve full immersion in the remote task environment, the HO has to be provided with comprehensive sensory, i.e., auditory, visual, and haptic feedback [9]. Latency is known to be the major restricting factor in realizing teleoperation systems. Even a minor delay may destabilize the system and reduce the immersion as well as transparency in the remote task environment. The strict latency requirements of haptic communications generally range from 3 to 60 ms [10]. This renders the delay constraint of haptic traffic much more stringent compared to conventional audiovisual traffic and thus poses a significant challenge to realizing haptics-involved teleoperation over communication networks. In addition to latency, packet loss is also of high importance in teleoperation systems. Typically, the maximum tolerable packet loss of haptic communications varies between 0.01% and 10% [10]. The stability and performance of teleoperation systems is largely affected by the communication-induced artifacts, e.g., delay and packet loss, which are usually direct consequence of occurring congestion in the underlying networking infrastructure. Packet loss and/or excessive latency may result in the so-called *buffer under-run*, for which a variety of common compensating methods are used. For a more detailed study of the impact of packet loss in teleoperations systems, the interested reader is referred to [11] and the references therein.

To achieve the aforementioned latency and reliability requirements of the Tactile Internet, it is of high importance to design proper resource allocation mechanisms tailored to the unique characteristics of the haptic traffic. We note, however, that although the Tactile Internet has gained some attention recently, there is not an adequate amount of understanding of the haptic traffic characteristics, especially at the packet level. For simplicity and analytical tractability, Tactile Internet traffic has been assumed to be Pareto or Poisson distributed in recent studies, which might be at least inaccurate, if not incorrect.

8.1.2 *Artificial intelligence*

Our envisioned MEC servers incorporate artificial intelligence (AI) capabilities in addition to storage and computation resources of cloudlets placed at the network edge. In order to alleviate the negative impact of latency on teleoperation systems, AI represents a promising solution. AI, as the concept of emulating intelligent behavior in machines, has been receiving a great amount of attention from both industry and academia. Toward realizing intelligent machines, the notion of artificial neural networks (ANNs) picked up momentum. ANNs offer advantages over classical AI methods in a way that they learn from data without requiring an expert to provide rules [12]. Today, ANNs are part of a broader category referred to as machine learning which includes a variety of other mathematical and statistical approaches.

In this chapter, we state our considered problem as a time series forecasting problem. More precisely, MEC servers are used to provide the HO with forecast samples based on the past recorded observations. To address the problem, ANNs are well known to be capable of providing nonparametric nonlinear data-driven time series models which have considerable advantages over alternate approaches as they are able to adaptively capture the nonlinear dynamics of input data, allowing them to remain virtually accurate and robust, yet less susceptible to model mis-specifications [12]. In the past, deep learning has successfully addressed many real-world problems, including image classification, language translation, and e-mail spam identification. Representation learning comprises a set of methods that allow a machine to automatically discover the representations needed for detection after being fed with raw data. Note that deep learning methods are actually representation learning methods with multiple levels of representation obtained from composing simple but nonlinear modules, each transforming the representation at a separate level. Thus, a deep neural network may be viewed as an ANN with multiple hidden layers between input and output layers. More specifically, deep learning allows computational models that are composed of multiple processing layers to learn the representation of data with multiple levels of abstractions [13].

8.1.3 *Chapter outline*

In this chapter, we address teleoperation over FiWi networks using AI-enhanced MEC servers that bring not only computation and storage resources but also intelligence to the edge of access networks. To provide insights into the usefulness of AI, we first demonstrate via a trace-driven haptic traffic analysis that there exist useful temporal patterns in haptic signals for forecasting upcoming samples and providing the HO with forecast packets in a timely manner, resulting in an improved latency and reliability performance in terms of packet loss probability. The contributions of this chapter are threefold: (i) trace-driven haptic traffic analysis and modeling, (ii) performance evaluation of teleoperation over FiWi networks in terms of round-trip delay, and (iii) use of AI and, in particular, time series forecasting to help realize MEC-based Tactile Internet teleoperation over FiWi networks.

The rest of the chapter is structured as follows. Section 8.2 discusses the human-centric aspect of the Tactile Internet and briefly reviews the related work on human-in-the-loop (HITL)-centric networks. In Section 8.3, after presenting a detailed traffic modeling and characterization of both packet arrival and sample auto-correlation of haptic traffic, we explore how AI may be leveraged to help realize HITL-centric teleoperation over MEC-enabled FiWi-enhanced HetNets. Section 8.4 briefly discusses open issues and remaining challenges in realizing HITL-centric networks. Finally, Section 8.5 concludes the chapter.

8.2 HITL-centric networks

The term Tactile Internet was first coined by Fettweis in 2014. In his seminal paper [3], the Tactile Internet was defined as a breakthrough enabling unprecedented mobile applications for tactile steering and control of real and virtual objects by requiring a round-trip latency of <10 ms. Later in 2014, International Telecommunication Union-Telecommunication (ITU-T) published a Technology Watch Report on the Tactile Internet, which emphasized that scaling up research in the area of wired and wireless access networks will be essential, ushering in new ideas and concepts to boost access networks' redundancy and diversity to meet the stringent latency as well as carrier-grade reliability requirements of Tactile Internet applications [14].

Clearly, the Tactile Internet opens up a plethora of exciting research directions toward adding a new dimension to the human-to-machine (H2M) interaction via the Internet. According to the aforementioned ITU-T Technology Watch Report, the Tactile Internet is supposed to be the next leap in the evolution of today's Internet of things (IoT), though there is a significant overlap among 5G, IoT, and the Tactile Internet, as illustrated in Figure 8.1. Despite their differences, all three converge toward a common set of design goals:

- very low latency on the order of 1 ms;
- ultrahigh reliability with an almost guaranteed availability of 99.999%;
- human-to-human (H2H)/machine-to-machine (M2M) coexistence;
- integration of data-centric technologies with a particular focus on Wi-Fi.

In [4], we elaborated on the subtle differences between the Tactile Internet and the IoT and 5G vision, which may be best expressed in terms of underlying communications paradigms and enabling end devices. Importantly, the Tactile Internet involves the inherent HITL nature of H2M interaction, as opposed to the emerging IoT without any human involvement in its underlying M2M communications. While M2M communications is useful for the automation of industrial and other machine-centric processes, the Tactile Internet will be centered around human-to-machine/robot (H2M/R) communications and thus allows for a human-centric design approach toward creating novel immersive experiences and extending the capabilities of the human through the Internet, i.e., augmentation rather than automation of the human [15].

For a comprehensive survey and a general overview of the enabling technologies, existing solutions, projects, and taxonomic analysis of HITL cyber-physical systems (CPSs), the interested reader is referred to [16]. According to [16], depending on the level of human intervention, existing HITL-based applications can be categorized

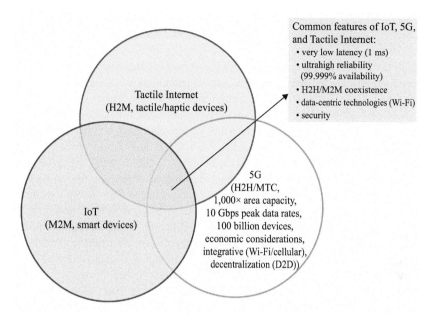

Figure 8.1   The three lenses of 5G, IoT, and the Tactile Internet: commonalities and differences [4]

into three different types: (i) human-controlled systems which are overseen by HOs (e.g., HITL control of a wheelchair-mounted robotic arm [17]), (ii) human-monitored systems, also known as *people-centric sensing*, where humans passively monitor the system and take necessary actions if needed, and (iii) a hybrid of the aforementioned approaches. A human-monitored CPS can be either an open- or closed-loop system. Despite the human being in the loop, open-loop systems usually do not take any proactive actions and simply gather and relay the context information. On the other hand, closed-loop systems use their sensory data and processing capabilities to actively intervene and take actions toward a defined objective. An example of such a system can be seen in a smartshirt, which can consistently monitor a human's exercise level in a gym. The HITL control may use such information, along with the current temperature information coming from the mounted sensors, as a feedback to signal the heating, ventilation, and air conditioning (HVAC) system to adjust the room temperature to the human's liking. Different from human-controlled and human-monitored systems, hybrid systems take people-centric sensing information as feedback to their control loops while taking into account direct human inputs. The aforementioned smartshirt example can further be equipped with a smartphone application to allow for the human to monitor her activity level and the current room temperature to further adjust the room temperature to her desired level.

In [6], we have focused on the emerging Tactile Internet as one of the most interesting 5G low-latency applications enabling novel immersive experiences. After describing the Tactile Internet's HITL-centric design principles and haptic communications models, we have elaborated on the development of decentralized cooperative dynamic bandwidth allocation algorithms for the end-to-end resource coordination in FiWi access networks. We have then used machine learning in the context of FiWi-enhanced HetNets to decouple haptic feedback from the impact of extensive propagation delays. This enables humans to perceive remote task environments in real time at a 1-ms granularity. In [15], we have shown that the 5G ultra-reliable low-latency communications requirements can be achieved by enhancing coverage-centric 4G LTE-A HetNets with capacity-centric FiWi access networks based on low-cost, data-centric Ethernet PON (EPON) and wireless local area network (WLAN) technologies in the backhaul and front end, respectively. We investigated the beneficial gains of considering the human as a "member" of a team of intelligent machines instead of keeping him as a conventional "user" in the loop. In addition, we have emphasized the role of AI-enhanced agents (e.g., MEC servers) may play in supporting humans in their task coordination between humans and machines. Toward achieving advanced human–machine coordination, we developed a distributed allocation algorithm of computational and physical tasks for fluidly orchestrating hybrid human–agent–robot teamwork (HART) coactivities. More specifically, all HART members established through communication a collective self-awareness to minimize the task completion time based on the shared use of robots that may be either user- or network-owned. We were particularly interested in the impact of spreading ownership of robots across people whose work they may replace. From a task execution time viewpoint, our results indicate that no degradation happens if the ownership of robots is shifted entirely from network operators to mobile users (MUs), though spreading ownership across end users makes a huge difference in who reaps the benefits from new technologies such as robots. More recently in [18], we have introduced our proposed architecture of MEC-enabled FiWi LTE-enhanced HetNets, enabling the coexistence and cooperation between conventional (remote) cloud and MEC servers. After presenting our analytical framework to evaluate the energy-delay performance, we have proposed our distributed cooperative offloading strategy with the objective of minimizing the average response time of MUs.

In the following, we pay our attention to bilateral teleoperation as an interesting example of HITL applications and present an in-depth study of haptic traffic characterization and modeling in terms of packet arrival and sample autocorrelation. We develop new models of describing packet interarrival times as well as three-dimensional (3D) sample autocorrelation. We then explore how MEC in general and edge intelligence in particular may be leveraged to help realize an immersive, reliable teleoperation experience over FiWi-based networking infrastructures.

8.3   HITL teleoperation over MEC-enabled FiWi networks

8.3.1   Network architecture

Figure 8.2 illustrates the generic architecture of our considered FiWi network with AI-enhanced MEC capabilities. The optical backhaul consists of an IEEE 802.3ah EPON with a typical fiber length of 20 km between the central optical line terminal (OLT) and remote optical network units (ONUs). Note that the fiber reach might be extended up to 100 km to incorporate long-reach PON scenarios as well. The PON may comprise multiple stages, each stage separated by a wavelength-broadcasting splitter/combiner (or alternatively a wavelength multiplexer/demultiplexer). We consider two types of PON: (i) time-division multiplexing (TDM) PON and (ii) wavelength-division multiplexing (WDM) PON. The TDM PON uses a single time-shared upstream wavelength channel λ_{up} and a separate single time-shared downstream wavelength channel λ_{down}, which is broadcast to all ONUs. Unlike the TDM PON, the WDM PON uses a set of multiple wavelength channels $\Lambda = \{w_1, w_2, \ldots, w_{|\Lambda|}\}$. Each of these $|\Lambda|$ wavelengths allow for bidirectional transmission.

We consider three different subsets of ONUs, as depicted in Figure 8.2. An ONU of the first subset serves residential/business subscribers, referred to as fixed wired users (FWUs) henceforth. An ONU of the second subset connects to a cellular network base station (BS). All BSs together provide ubiquitous service to MUs. Hence, MUs are assumed to be always connected to the cellular network, i.e., being covered by any of the BSs at any given time. The third subset of ONUs is equipped with an IEEE 802.11s WLAN-based mesh portal point (MPP) to interface with the wireless mesh network (WMN), which consists of mesh points (MPs) acting as relay nodes and mesh access points (MAPs) serving wireless end users that are located within their coverage area. Typically, the coverage area of MAPs is smaller than that of BSs. Note that MPP-ONUs and BSs may be connected to our considered MEC servers.

For convenience, we refer to end users as *wireless subscribers*, which are either MUs or teleoperation Wi-Fi-only users. Furthermore, we note that local teleoperation

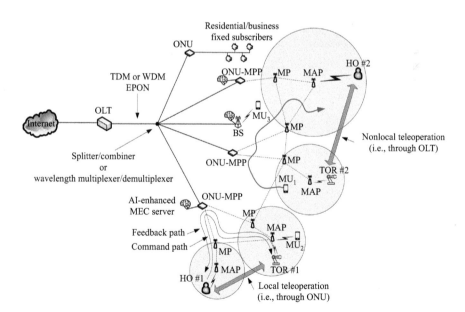

Figure 8.2   Generic architecture of FiWi network with AI-enhanced MEC capabilities

takes places in a single Wi-Fi zone, where both HO and TOR are associated with the same MAP. Conversely, nonlocal teleoperation involves an HO–TOR pair, where the HO and TOR are located in different Wi-Fi zones and associated by two different MAPs. Note that in the nonlocal teleoperation scenario, the HO and TOR are connected via the OLT. As opposed to MUs, we assume that HOs and TORs are stationary.

8.3.2   ANN model

In our edge-computing paradigm, sample forecast will be key in compensating for the end-to-end delay in the feedback path, as shown in Figure 8.3. Toward this end, we need a family of parameterized ANNs, referred to as multilayer perceptrons (MLPs), that are flexible enough to perform a mapping between the observed input and forecast output. More specifically, one-hidden layer MLPs are proved to be universal estimators in the sense that they are well capable of approximating any linear/nonlinear function to an arbitrary degree of accuracy [19]. An MLP with N_h hidden neurons is viewed as a linear combination of N_h parameterized nonlinear functions called neurons (see Figure 8.4). A neuron is a nonlinear function $g(\cdot)$ of a linear combination of its input variables. Our considered ANN is an MLP with L input variables and one output variable. Let Ξ denote the set of $L \times N_h + N_h + 1$ weights of the model, i.e., $\Xi = \{c_{i,j} : i = 1, \ldots, N_h, j = 1, \ldots, L\} \cup \{c'_j : j = 0, 1, \ldots, N_h\}$, that are estimated during the training phase. The output of the MLP is then given by

$$\Psi(\mathcal{A}, \Xi) = \sum_{j=1}^{N_h} c'_j g \left(\sum_{i=1}^{L} c_{i,j} \mathcal{A}(i) \right) + c'_0 \tag{8.1}$$

where $\mathcal{A} \in \mathbb{R}^L$ denotes the input vector. Note that our proposed edge sample forecast (ESF) module is responsible for providing the HO with forecast samples by means of multi-sample-ahead-of-time forecasting of delayed and/or lost samples. Note that

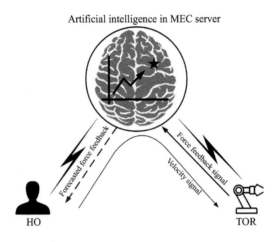

Figure 8.3   A high-level illustration of the role of AI-enhanced MEC servers

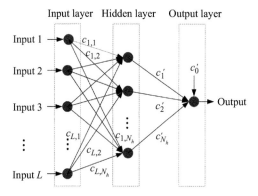

Figure 8.4   Generic architecture of MLP-ANN deployed at ESF modules at HO side

the weights Ξ of the ANN are calculated in the associated MEC server and then are transmitted to the corresponding HO.

8.3.3   Teleoperation traffic modeling

To better understand the characteristics of the real Tactile Internet traffic, we reached out to several robotic teleoperation research groups across the globe, the results of which are two recent state-of-the-art sets of teleoperation experiment traces. In the following, after explaining the experiment setups, we explore through our available traces the best models to capture the features of Tactile Internet traffic. A thorough understanding of the best possible stochastic model of packet arrival is key to evaluate the performance of the network in terms of round-trip latency. Further, in order to compensate for the excessive delay by means of sample forecasting, we also analyze the traces in terms of sample autocorrelation, to be discussed in technically greater details later on. Note that the human perception of haptics can be exploited to reduce the haptic packet rate. Specifically, the well-known Weber's law determines the just noticeable difference (JND), i.e., the minimum change in the magnitude of a stimulus that can be detected by humans. Weber's law of the JND gives rise to the so-called deadband coding (DC) technique, whereby a haptic sample is transmitted only if its change with respect to the previously transmitted haptic sample exceeds a given deadband parameter $d > 0$ (given in percent).

The first set of our traces are from an evaluation of haptic-enabled telesurgery demonstrated by the authors of [20], in the *Centre National de la Recherche Scientifique* (CNRS) at Institut de Recherche en Informatique et Systèmes Aléatoires (IRISA). The system is composed of a six-degree-of-freedom (6-DoF) haptic interface at the HO side, a 6-DoF manipulator, and a six-axis force/torque sensor at the TOR side. The system enables the HO to control the motion of the TOR end effector while providing her with the haptic feedback associated with the task/remote environment (see [20] for details). The 6-DoF haptic interface measures the position of the HO end effector to set the position of the TOR end effector. Note that at refresh time instants, an update sample, which consists of the position and orientation of the HO end effector, is transmitted. Further, through the same master end effector, the HO is provided with haptic force/torque feedback.

We note that our available traces of "6-DoF telesurgery" include only the sensor readings from the HO side, needle/indenter position, and 6-DoF feedback perceived by the HO while teleoperating without using DC. The HO and task environment were put back-to-back during the experiments—i.e., there was no communication-induced artifacts such as latency. The traces that we analyze were recorded during a 373.699-s experiment, including 372,857 and 372,694 samples, in the command and feedback paths, respectively, which is sufficient to ensure statistical stability.

The authors of [21] at the Technical University of Munich provided us with the second set of traces which are associated with experiments performed during roughly 16 s with different deadband parameter values set to $d = d_c = d_f = 20\%$, 15%, 10%, 5%, 0, where d_c and d_f denote the deadband parameter in the command and feedback paths, respectively. Two Phantom Omni devices were used as master (i.e., HO) and slave (i.e., TOR) devices to create a 1-DoF bilateral teleoperation scenario. The communication channel between HO and TOR was emulated using a queue architecture to generate constant or time-varying delays. The velocity signal at the HO side was sampled before being transmitted to the TOR, which in turn fed the force signal back to the HO (see [21] for details).

In the following, we explain the packetization process of the traces, which were sensor readings. Note that N_{DoF} haptic samples coming from the application layer are encapsulated in a single segment with a prepended RTP/UDP/IP header. Define $\lambda^{c,d}$ and $\lambda^{f,d}$ as the rate at which the packets arrive at the medium access control (MAC) layer in the command and feedback paths of a teleoperation system with deadband parameter d, respectively. Each DoF haptic sample typically consists of 8 bytes, thus translating into a total $8N_{\text{DoF}}$ bytes of payload. The haptic samples are packetized using the real-time transport protocol (RTP), user datagram protocol (UDP), and Internet protocol (IP) with a typical header size of 12, 8, and 20 bytes, respectively. Hence, the size of the resultant packet at the MAC layer service access point (SAP) is equal to $8N_{\text{DoF}} + 40$ bytes. Therefore, the haptic packet size is fixed for a given N_{DoF}.

8.3.4   Packet interarrival times

We begin by investigating the packet interarrival times of both teleoperation traces. For a given deadband parameter d, let $\lambda^c(d_c)$ and $\lambda^f(d_f)$ denote the mean packet rate at which packets arrive at the MAC layer of the wireless interface in the command and feedback paths, respectively. In the following, we discuss both teleoperation traces separately, first without DC ($d = 0$) and then with DC ($d > 0$).

8.3.4.1   Teleoperation without DC

Note that in our 1-DoF teleoperation traces without DC, packet interarrival times are deterministic with a constant packet arrival rate of $\lambda^c(d_c)|_{d_c=0} = \lambda^f(d_f)|_{d_f=0} = 1{,}000$ packets/s in both command and feedback paths due to the fixed haptic sampling rate of 1 kHz. Conversely, in our 6-DoF teleoperation traces without any DC, haptic samples are immediately packetized and transmitted at varying (i.e., nondeterministic) refresh time instants. In the following, we examine the command and feedback paths of our 6-DoF teleoperation traces separately and try to find the best fitting distribution for the respective packet interarrival times.

First, let us focus on the position and orientation samples in the command path, which are measured as a triplet and quaternion (i.e., quadruple) at each refresh time instant, respectively. As discussed in Section 8.1, let **COMD**$_i$ denote the resultant position-orientation sample i, which is transmitted as packet in the command path at time instant $T_i^{(c)}$. Thus, the corresponding packet interarrival times $I_i^{(c)} = T_i^{(c)} - T_{i-1}^{(c)}$, $i = 2, 3, \ldots$, represent realizations of the random variable $I^{(c)}$. In an effort to find a probability distribution function (PDF) that best fits the experimental packet interarrival times, we considered a variety of well-known distributions. Our preliminary evaluations narrowed down our choice to three candidate PDFs, namely, exponential, generalized Pareto (GP), and gamma distributions. Our method of selecting the best fitting PDF comprised the following three steps. First, we used the maximum likelihood estimation method to estimate the parameters of each PDF. Second, the estimates of the first step were verified by computing the complementary cumulative distribution function (CCDF) $F_{I^{(c)}}(\zeta) = P(I^{(c)} > \zeta)$. Third, to compare the relative goodness of fit among the three PDFs under consideration, we used the maximum difference D^* between the fitted and experimental CCDFs, which is given by $D^* = \sup_\zeta |\hat{F}_{I^{(c)}}(\zeta) - F_{I^{(c)}}(\zeta)|$, whereby $\hat{F}_{I^{(c)}}(\zeta)$ denotes the experimental CCDF. Figure 8.5(a) and (b) shows the CCDF of the three fitted PDFs and experimental 6-DoF teleoperation packet interarrival times without DC in the command path. We observe from the figure that the gamma distribution matches the experimental data reasonably well, as opposed to the exponential and GP distributions. This observation was further verified by the fact that the gamma distribution achieved the smallest value of D^*. Next, we proceed by fitting the best PDF to the 6-DoF experimental packet

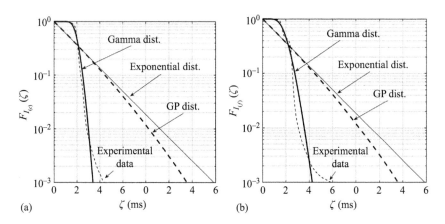

Figure 8.5   CCDF of fitted PDFs and experimental 6-DoF teleoperation packet interarrival times without DC

interarrival times in the feedback path. Similar to the command path, we observe from Figure 8.5(b) that for the CCDF in the feedback path, $F_{I^{(f)}}(\zeta) = P(I^{(f)} > \zeta)$, the gamma distribution again fits the experimental data best.

8.3.4.2   Teleoperation with DC

Next, we study teleoperation with DC. Recall that in our original haptic traces DC was applied only in the 1-DoF teleoperation scenario. For fair comparison of the two sets of haptic traces, we proceed by applying DC in the original 6-DoF traces. Figure 8.6(a) and (b) illustrates the beneficial impact of DC on reducing the haptic packet rate in the feedback path and in particular the command path. More specifically, note that in the command path a deadband parameter of only $d_c = 0.01\%$ decreases the mean packet rate $\lambda^{c,d}$ to roughly 400 packets/s, translating into a haptic packet rate reduction of 58.12% compared to the case without DC (i.e., $d_c = 0$). As shown in Figure 8.6(a), $\lambda^{c,d}$ further decreases for increasing d_c and levels off for $d_c > 0.1\%$. We observe from Figure 8.6(b) that DC is less effective in the feedback path, where a deadband parameter of as high as $d_f = 20\%$ (compared to $d_c = 0.01\%$ above) is needed to reduce the mean packet rate $\lambda^{f,d}$ to roughly 400 packets/s. The observed difference between command and feedback paths is due to the fact that the position-orientation samples are much smoother than their force/torque counterparts.

Next, we determine the best-fitting PDFs for the packet interarrival times with different deadband parameter values by following the same approach as described previously. Figure 8.7 comprehensively summarizes our findings on the different best-fitting packet interarrival time distributions for command and feedback paths with and without DC in both teleoperation scenarios under consideration. We observe that in general command and feedback paths can be jointly modeled by the GP, gamma, or deterministic packet interarrival time distribution, depending on the given value of deadband parameters d_c and d_f, as shown in Figure 8.7. Note that Poisson traffic

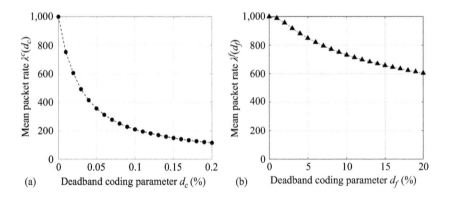

Figure 8.6   Mean packet rate (in packets/s) vs. deadband parameter d for 6-DoF teleoperation in (a) command path and (b) feedback path

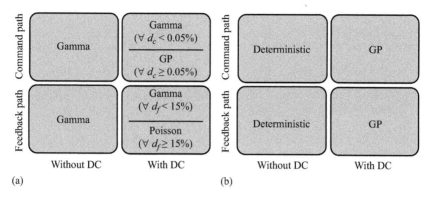

Figure 8.7   Summary of best fitting packet interarrival time distributions for command and feedback paths with and without DC: (a) 6-DoF teleoperation and (b) 1-DoF teleoperation

with exponentially distributed packet interarrival times is found valid only for 6-DoF teleoperation in the feedback path with deadband parameter values of $d_f \geq 15\%$.

8.3.5   Sample autocorrelation

Future 5G networks will rely on edge intelligence to provide ultra-reliable low latency networking infrastructures for Tactile Internet applications, e.g., augmented/virtual reality. Toward this end, we take a closer look at our available traces in the feedback path to identify possible correlation patterns in haptic samples. Such correlation patterns can be useful in developing sample forecasting techniques, leveraging AI capabilities at the network edge to compensate for delayed feedback samples by making accurate forecasts [6]. In the following, we are going to answer the following questions: (i) How deep are the feedback samples correlated with their own lagged samples? (ii) What is the impact of DC on the autocorrelation of the feedback samples?

To answer these questions, we devise the autocorrelation function. We note, however, that haptic packets transmitted in a typical teleoperation system contain the samples taken from continuous signals, which are either 1D (i.e., force signal in 1-DoF teleoperation) or 3D (i.e., force/torque signal in 6-DoF teleoperation) vector-valued functions of time. Unlike 1D signals, estimating the autocorrelation function of a multidimensional vector-valued function is not straightforward. We thus present our method of estimating autocorrelation function of a given multidimensional discrete vector-valued function. For the sake of argument, let us consider $\mathbf{x}(t)$ as a 3D vector-valued function evaluated at time t, which is characterized by $\mathbf{x}(t) = x_1(t)\mathbf{i} + x_2(t)\mathbf{j} + x_3(t)\mathbf{k}$, where $x_1(t)$, $x_2(t)$, and $x_3(t)$ are the corresponding x-, y-, and z-coordinates of $\mathbf{x}(t)$, respectively. Note that $\mathbf{i}$, $\mathbf{j}$, and $\mathbf{k}$ are unit vectors representing the axes of the Cartesian coordinate system. We estimate the sample mean $\bar{\mathbf{x}} \in \mathbb{R}^3$ of a given vector-valued function $\mathbf{x}(t)$ by $\frac{1}{N_s} \sum_{i=1}^{N_s} \mathbf{x}(i\bar{T}_s)$, where N_s and $\bar{T}_s$ denote the total number of samples and inter-sample time, respectively. We then estimate the sample variance

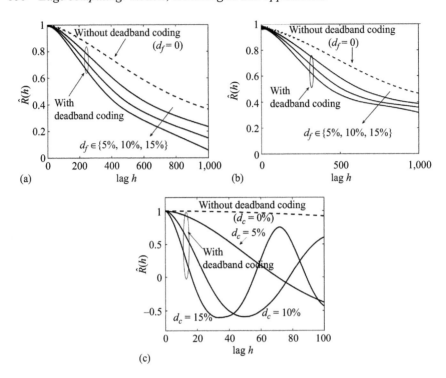

*Figure 8.8   Autocorrelation function of (a) force samples in 6-DoF teleoperation,
(b) torque samples in 6-DoF teleoperation, and (c) force samples in
1-DoF teleoperation*

$\sigma_\mathbf{x}^2 \in \mathbb{R}^+ \cup \{0\}$ by $\frac{1}{N_s - 1} \sum_{i=1}^{N_s} \left\| \mathbf{x}(i\bar{T}_s) - \bar{\mathbf{x}} \right\|^2$, which can be generalized to estimate the
autocorrelation function $\hat{R}_\mathbf{x}(h)$ by $C(h)/\sigma_\mathbf{x}^2$, where $C(h)$ is given by

$$C(h) = \frac{1}{N_s - 1} \sum_{i=1}^{N_s - h} \ll (\mathbf{x}(i\bar{T}_s) - \bar{\mathbf{x}}) \cdot (\mathbf{x}((i + h)\bar{T}_s) - \bar{\mathbf{x}}) \gg \tag{8.2}$$

where $\ll \cdot \gg$ denotes the inner product.*

Figure 8.8 depicts the autocorrelation function of the force/torque feedback samples of both available sets of traces for different teleoperation scenarios with and without DC. We observe that the force/torque samples represent a quite deep correlation with their own lagged samples. Let correlation depth $h^*_{\alpha_{\mathrm{corr}}}$ denote the maximum time lag such that, for $h < h^*_{\alpha_{\mathrm{corr}}}$, force/torque sample autocorrelation $\hat{R}(h)$ is greater than $\alpha_{\mathrm{corr}}\%$. Note that DC, in general, decreases the amount of autocorrelation of

---

*Note that our defined autocorrelation function is based on the notion of the inner product of vectors $\mathbf{x}_1$ and $\mathbf{x}_2$, which is given by $\|\mathbf{x}_1\| \cdot \|\mathbf{x}_2\| \cdot \cos\theta$, where θ is the angle between $\mathbf{x}_1$ and $\mathbf{x}_2$ in a multidimensional space. As θ deviates from zero, the two vectors are less correlated and vice versa.

Table 8.1 FiWi network parameters and default values

Parameter	Value
Minimum contention window W_0	16
Maximum back-off stage H	6
Empty slot duration ε	9 μs
DIFS	34 μs
SIFS	16 μs
PHY header	20 μs
MAC header	36 bytes
RTS	20 bytes
CTS	14 bytes
ACK	14 bytes
Line rate r in wireless fronthaul	600 Mbps
Uplink and downlink data rate r_{PON} in PON	1 Gbps
Propagation delay δ_p in WMN	3.33 μs
l_{BKGD}	1,500 bytes
p_b	10^{-6}
N_{DoF}	6
l_{PON}	20 km

DIFS, Distributed coordination function interframe space; SIFS, short interframe space; PHY, physical layer header; RTS, request to send; CTS, clear to send; ACK, acknowledgement

feedback samples for a given time lag h, thus decreasing the correlation depth. For instance, the force feedback signal in 6-DoF teleoperation without DC exhibits a correlation depth $h_{90\%}^*$ of 202. DC, in turn, reduces the correlation depth to 142, 116, and 98 for $d = 5\%$, $d = 10\%$, and $d = 15\%$, respectively. Further, we find that the torque samples show a slightly higher autocorrelation compared with that of the force samples in 6-DoF teleoperation.

8.3.6 Results

In this section, we present trace-driven simulation results along with numerical results derived from the analysis. Note that the obtained simulation results include confidence intervals at a 95% confidence level. The following results were obtained by using the FiWi network parameter settings listed in Table 8.1. We consider a FiWi network architecture consisting of four FWUs and four ONU-APs. First, we start by evaluating the performance of the FiWi network in the presence of only H2H traffic, i.e., no Tactile Internet traffic is considered. Toward this end, we set the traffic of MUs and FWUs to λ_{BKGD} and $\alpha_{PON}\lambda_{BKGD}$, respectively. In the coverage area of each ONU-AP, we consider four MUs, two of which communicate with each other via the associated ONU-AP, i.e., local H2H communication, whereas the other two MUs use the backhaul EPON to realize nonlocal H2H communication. The average end-to-end delay vs. background traffic λ_{BKGD} for different values of the backhaul traffic scale α_{PON} is illustrated in Figure 8.9, where we observe that an average end-to-end delay of

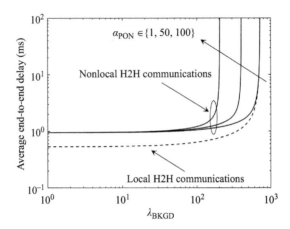

Figure 8.9   Average end-to-end delay vs. background traffic λ_{BKGD} (value of traffic scale α_{PON} increases along the direction of solid arrow)

533 and 945 μs can be achieved for local and nonlocal H2H communication, respectively. Further, we observe the impact of backhaul traffic on the delay performance of nonlocal traffic as well as the maximum achievable packet rate, at which the MAC queues are stable. To be more specific, the maximum achievable λ_{BKGD} is 204, 400, and 717 packets/s for α_{PON} equal to 100, 50, and 1, respectively.

Next, we include teleoperation subscribers in our simulation scenario as follows. We consider the same scenario as explained above except that within the coverage area of each ONU-AP reside two MUs, one HO and one TOR. The following results include scenarios with and without DC in the command path, whereas no DC is performed in the feedback path. For this scenario, we ran trace-driven simulations, where the packet arrival times of Tactile Internet traffic are those of the traces, whereas for the remaining nodes, we generate the arrival times based on our considered (fitted) distributions. Note that the number of samples (arrivals) in our traces is large enough to ensure statistical stability. The results of the average end-to-end teleoperation delay of the trace-driven simulations along with those of the numerical results achieved from the analysis are illustrated in Figure 8.10, where three different traffic arrival models, i.e., Gamma, GP, and deterministic, are considered. First, we note that the minimum achievable average end-to-end delay is 4.62 ms for $d_c = 0$, i.e., an 8.6 times increase with respect to H2H communications without Tactile Internet traffic. In addition, we recognize the beneficial impact of DC not only for reducing the average end-to-end delay, but also for increasing the MUs' throughput. As for the packet delay, we note that using DC with $d_c = 0.01\%$ results in a 67% decrease of the average end-to-end teleoperation delay from 4.62 to 1.53 ms.

In order to investigate the impact of DC on the average throughput of MUs, let us define the coding gain G_{coding} as the difference between the maximum throughput that is achieved in coded and uncoded teleoperation to meet the same level of average end-to-end delay. Figure 8.10 demonstrates that DC results in a coding gain

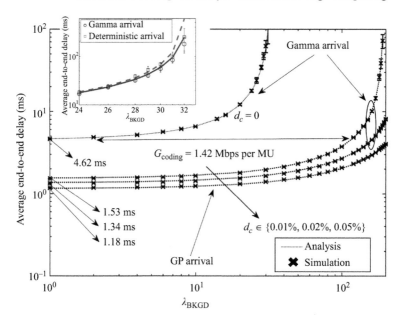

Figure 8.10 Average end-to-end local teleoperation delay vs. background traffic λ_{BKGD} (value of deadband parameter d_c increases along the direction of solid arrow)

G_{coding} of 1.42 Mbps per MU, given that the average end-to-end delay is limited to 4.8 ms. Recall from Section 8.3.3 that in 6-DoF teleoperation with no DC, the packet interarrival time distribution well-fits a Gamma distribution, whereas in 1-DoF teleoperation, the packet interarrival times are deterministic. Interestingly, according to our simulation/analysis, the average packet delay of both arrival models exhibit similar results except for large values of λ_{BKGD}, where we observe that the packet delay for Gamma arrival is slightly lower compared to deterministic packet arrival. The average packet delay in nonlocal teleoperation is depicted in Figure 8.11, where different values of backhaul fiber length l_{PON} are considered. Similar to local teleoperation, the beneficial impact of DC in nonlocal teleoperation is further highlighted by increasing the throughput of FWUs. Specifically, for $l_{PON} = 20$ km and $d_c = 0.01\%$, a coding gain G_{coding} of 141.6 Mbps per FWU is achieved, given that the average nonlocal teleoperation delay is below 5.2 ms.

Next, we measure the performance of our proposed ANN-based sample forecasting scheme against a naive forecaster, where a forecast sample is simply set to the last received sample. In order to quantitatively measure the forecasting accuracy, we use the mean absolute error (MAE), mean squared error (MSE), and mean absolute percentage error (MAPE) [22]. In our simulations, we used our available 6-DoF teleoperation feedback samples. We used MATLAB® to build and train a one-hidden-layer ANN using 59,710 feedback samples of the z-coordinate force f_z. We then ran the simulation for the next 1,000 samples.

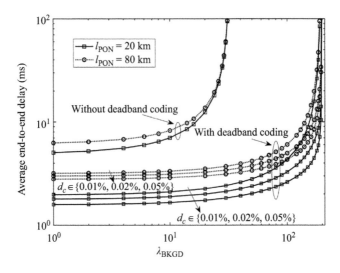

Figure 8.11   Average end-to-end nonlocal teleoperation delay vs. background traffic λ_{BKGD} (value of deadband parameter d_c increases along the direction of solid arrow)

In the following, we present the results of a scenario, where no DC is used in the command path and T_{thr} is set to 1 ms, i.e., the ESF scheme calculates and delivers a forecast sample if the real packet does not arrive within T_{thr}. The results of the forecasting accuracy in terms of MAE, MSE, and MAPE are illustrated in Figure 8.12. First, we observe that the obtained results of our ANN-based ESF scheme exhibit a better performance compared with the naive sample forecaster. This is due to the relatively high autocorrelation in the haptic samples that allows an accurate forecast beyond what can be achieved by a naive forecaster. Second, the forecast accuracy remains approximately constant in both ANN-based and naive sample forecaster for a wide range of λ_{BKGD} up to 25 packets/s, above which we observe a linear increase in ANN-based ESF in terms of MAE and MSE. On the other hand, in the naive forecaster, the forecast error is exponentially increased. Third, and more importantly, Figure 8.12(c) links the forecasting accuracy to the human JND. To be more specific, in local teleoperation, for increasing λ_{BKGD} up to 25 packets/s, MAPE remains below 8.20%, which is less than the human JND threshold. Further, the maximum MAPE equals 68.29%, which is achieved at $\lambda_{BKGD} = 33$, where the average end-to-end delay in the feedback path equals 62.37 ms. In comparison, the naive forecaster achieves a forecast error of up to 81.32%.

For nonlocal teleoperation, the obtained values of MAE and MSE remain quite constant for a wide range of λ_{BKGD}. The results confirm the fact that a more accurate forecast is done by our ANN-based sample forecaster in comparison with the naive ESF. With our ANN-based ESF, MAPE does not exceed 14.58% for increasing λ_{BKGD} up to 25 packets/s, as opposed to 24.21% with naive ESF. We note that by using the ESF scheme, the end-to-end delay in the feedback path is adequately compensated,

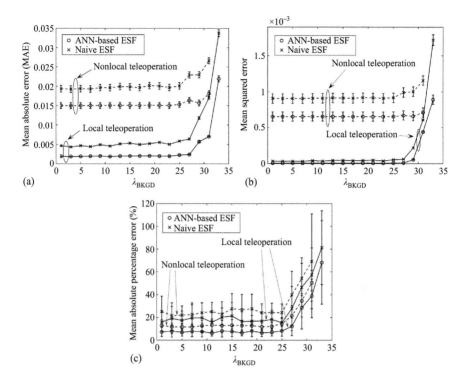

Figure 8.12 Forecasting accuracy of the proposed ESF module in terms of (a) MAE, (b) MSE, and (c) MAPE

thus delivering a prompt haptic feedback to the HO. This, however, is achieved at the expense of an increased forecast error, which is shown to remain below the human JND threshold for a wide range of background traffic intensity.

Our obtained results exhibit the potential of the proposed ESF scheme to deliver real-time feedback samples with a reliability of almost 100%. Nevertheless, in order to further verify the feasibility of our proposed scheme, additional experiments with different types of teleoperation systems should be performed. To be more specific, we have shown by means of simulation that the average forecast error remains below the human JND. Nevertheless, we still need to explore the user experience (i.e., quality of experience) of HOs at time instants, when the forecast error exceeds the JND threshold. This can be evaluated only in subjective experiments.

8.4 Open issues and challenges

Clearly, in order for an HO to experience an immersive teleoperation experience, our proposed ESF module has to provide accurate multi-step-ahead-of-time forecast samples according to the past observations. In this study, we showed that a simple

MLP-ANN is capable of providing an HO with accurate forecast samples provided that the average end-to-end delay is below a certain threshold. Despite the achievements accomplished in this chapter, it should be noted that in this work all involved teleoperation peers were connected through a shared fiber backhaul, whose fiber reach did not exceed the typical 20 km of EPONs. Clearly, an interesting research problem to address is to what extent the demonstrated low latency and jitter performance on the order of 1–10 ms can be also achieved for significantly larger geographical distances, e.g., connecting the US and Europe. Toward this end, it may be interesting to explore the role of deep learning in rendering a more accurate forecasting performance compared to that of an MLP-ANN.

The Internet has been constantly evolving from the mobile Internet to the emerging IoT and future Tactile Internet. Similarly, the capabilities of future 5G networks will extend far beyond those of previous generations of mobile communication. In [23], we recently outlined some research ideas that help tap into the full potential of the Tactile Internet. More specifically, we shed some light on various concepts that will be instrumental in creating new ideas to facilitate local human–machine coactivity clusters by completely decentralizing edge computing via emerging Ethereum blockchain technologies. The next-generation Internet powered by decentralized blockchain technology is ushering in a new era. A blockchain of particular interest is Ethereum which enables the development of decentralized applications that are not limited to cryptocurrencies, a capability that Bitcoin lacked. A salient feature of Ethereum that cannot be found in the Bitcoin blockchain is the decentralized autonomous organization (DAO). Unlike AI-based agents that are completely autonomous, a DAO still requires heavy involvement from humans. Despite recent progress on realizing the blockchain IoT (B-IoT), at present it is yet unclear in many ways how Ethereum blockchain technologies, in particular the DAO, may be leveraged to realize future techno-social systems such as the Tactile Internet that by design still require heavy involvement from humans at the network edge instead of automating them away.

We note that our available traces are restricted to only 1-DoF teleoperation and 6-DoF telesurgery systems under consideration, thus posing limitations to our reported results above due to being application- and/or device-specific, especially given that the emerging advanced robotic teleoperation systems with relatively larger number of DoF may rely on the exchange of a wider variety of haptic feedback samples, rather than simply 6-DoF force/torque samples. This, in turn, mandates the need to come up with a simple yet descriptive model with the capability of generalizing to a wide variety of teleoperation systems. Our study may be considered as a starting point to suggest methods of overcoming the aforementioned challenges of investigating the haptic traffic characteristics.

8.5 Conclusions

In this chapter, we studied the role of HITL-centric networks based on the concept of MEC-enabled FiWi-enhanced LTE-A HetNets in realizing the Tactile Internet's

$<$10-ms delay challenge, thereby paying particular attention to coexistent local/nonlocal teleoperation and inquiring into the specific characteristics of haptic traces at the packet level. Our Tactile Internet traffic analysis reveals that the teleoperation command and feedback paths can be jointly modeled by the GP, gamma, or deterministic packet interarrival time distribution, depending on the value of DC parameter d. DC was shown to be particularly effective in the command path. Alternatively, in the feedback path, our proposed AI-based sample forecasting module embedded in MEC servers is instrumental in achieving a very high haptic sample forecasting accuracy with an MSE of zero in case of local teleoperation.

Acknowledgments

The authors would like to thank the authors of [20] and [21] for providing the teleoperation experiment traces. This work was supported by NSERC Discovery Grant 2016-04521 and the FRQNT B2X doctoral scholarship program.

References

[1]   ETSI Industry Specification Group (ISG). Mobile Edge Computing—A Key Technology Towards 5G. White Paper. 2015;11:1–16.

[2]   Taleb T, Samdanis K, Mada B, Flinck H, Dutta S and Sabella D. On Multi-access Edge Computing: A Survey of the Emerging 5G Network Edge Cloud Architecture and Orchestration. IEEE Communications Surveys Tutorials. 2017;19(3):1657–1681.

[3]   Fettweis GP. The Tactile Internet: Applications and Challenges. IEEE Vehicular Technology Magazine. 2014;9(1):64–70.

[4]   Maier M, Chowdhury M, Rimal BP, and Van DP. The Tactile Internet: Vision, Recent Progress, and Open Challenges. IEEE Communications Magazine. 2016;54(5):138–145.

[5]   Chen Z, Jiang L, Hu W, *et al.* Early Implementation Experience with Wearable Cognitive Assistance Applications. In: Proceedings of the 2015 Workshop on Wearable Systems and Applications. New York, NY, USA: ACM; 2015. pp. 33–38.

[6]   Maier M, and Ebrahimzadeh A. Towards Immersive Tactile Internet Experiences: Low-latency FiWi Enhanced Mobile Networks with Edge Intelligence [Invited]. IEEE/OSA Journal of Optical Communications and Networking, Special Issue on Latency in Edge Optical Networks. 2019;11(4):B10–B25.

[7]   Liu J, Guo H, Nishiyama H, Ujikawa H, Suzuki K, and Kato N. New Perspectives on Future Smart FiWi Networks: Scalability, Reliability, and Energy Efficiency. IEEE Communications Surveys Tutorials. 2016;18(2):1045–1072.

[8]   Beyranvand H, Lévesque M, Maier M, *et al.* Toward 5G: FiWi Enhanced LTE-A HetNets with Reliable Low-latency Fiber Backhaul Sharing and WiFi Offloading. IEEE/ACM Transactions on Networking. 2017;25(2):690–707.

[9]   Steinbach E, Hirche S, Ernst M, *et al.* Haptic Communications. Proceedings of the IEEE. 2012;100(4):937–956.

[10]   Eid M, Cha J, and Saddik AE. Admux: An Adaptive Multiplexer for Haptic-Audio-Visual Data Communication. IEEE Transactions on Instrumentation and Measurement. 2011;60(1):21–31.

[11]   Hirche S, and Buss M. Packet Loss Effects in Passive Telepresence Systems. In: Proc. IEEE Conference on Decision and Control (CDC). Vol. 4; 2004. pp. 4010–4015.

[12]   Prieto A, Prieto B, Ortigosa EM, *et al.* Neural Networks: An Overview of Early Research, Current Frameworks and New Challenges. Neurocomputing. 2016;214:242–268.

[13]   LeCun Y, Bengio Y, and Hinton G. Deep Learning. Nature. 2015;521(7553): 436–444.

[14]   *ITU-T Technology Watch Report.* The Tactile Internet. 2014 Aug.

[15]   Maier M, Ebrahimzadeh A, and Chowdhury M. The Tactile Internet: Automation or Augmentation of the Human? IEEE Access. 2018;6:41607–41618.

[16]   Nunes DS, Zhang P, and Sá Silva J. A Survey on Human-in-the-loop Applications Towards an Internet of All. IEEE Communications Surveys Tutorials. 2015;17(2):944–965.

[17]   Tsui KM, Kim DJ, Behal A, Kontak D, and Yanco HA. I Want That: Human-in-the-loop Control of a Wheelchair-mounted Robotic Arm. Journal of Applied Bionics and Biomechanics. 2011;8(1):127–147.

[18]   Ebrahimzadeh A, and Maier M. Distributed Cooperative Computation Offloading in Multi-access Edge Computing Fiber-wireless Networks (Invited Paper). Optics Communications. 2019;452:130–139.

[19]   Hornik K, Stinchcombe M, and White H. Multilayer Feedforward Networks Are Universal Approximators. Neural Networks. 1989;2(5):359–366.

[20]   Meli L, Pacchierotti C, and Prattichizzo D. Experimental Evaluation of Magnified Haptic Feedback for Robot-assisted Needle Insertion and Palpation. International Journal of Medical Robotics and Computer Assisted Surgery. 2017;13(4):e1809.

[21]   Xu X, Schuwerk C, Cizmeci B, and Steinbach E. Energy Prediction for Teleoperation Systems That Combine the Time Domain Passivity Approach with Perceptual Deadband-based Haptic Data Reduction. IEEE Transactions on Haptics. 2016;9(4):560–573.

[22]   Lv Y, Duan Y, Kang W, Li Z, and Wang F. Traffic Flow Prediction with Big Data: A Deep Learning Approach. IEEE Transactions on Intelligent Transportation Systems. 2015;16(2):865–873.

[23]   Maier M. The Tactile Internet: Where Do We Go from Here? (Invited Paper). In: Proc. IEEE/OSA/SPIE Asia Communications and Photonics Conference (ACP); 2018. pp. 1–3.

Part II

Technologies

Chapter 9
Distributed big data computing platforms for edge computing

Dumitrel Loghin[1], Lavanya Ramapantulu[2] and Yong Meng Teo[1]

9.1 Introduction

The surge in the number of devices and gadgets connected to the Internet is crystallizing two trends in the modern computing landscape. First is the rise of *big data*, due to the vast amount of data produced by these devices, which needs to be processed and stored. Big data is often described using three *V*s, namely, volume, velocity and variety. The large *volume* of data requires distributed computing and storage platforms because a single machine is no longer sufficient for these tasks. The high data *velocity* requires new stream processing platforms that need to abide by certain latency requirements. Data *variety* requires multiple processing platforms suitable for different tasks. For example, a modern application may need platforms for batch data analytics, stream processing and machine learning (ML).

Second, we are witnessing the advent of *edge computing*. Traditionally, Internet-based applications adopt the client-server computing model. In the past, most companies used their own, on-premise data centers to host servers, but currently, they prefer to use cloud computing due to ease of management and reduced cost. Both on-premise and cloud computing require the data to be uploaded from edge devices. The increasing amount of data exerts high pressure on networking connections. One solution is to off-load the processing to the edge of the network, closer to the devices, giving rise to edge processing.

The proliferation of 5G telecommunication technologies is going to accelerate the development of big data analytics at the edge [1]. The high bandwidth, low latency and high device densities within 5G cells represent an ideal environment for big data analytics. Conversely, big data analytics are needed at the edge for better security analytics, Internet of things (IoT) preprocessing and industrial process optimization, smart city, among other scenarios.

[1]Department of Computer Science, National University of Singapore, Singapore
[2]School of Electrical and Electronic Engineering, Nanyang Technological University, Singapore

In this chapter, we present and analyze some popular platforms for big data processing, with a focus on edge computing. We start with a review of edge computing, followed by a classification of frameworks and models for big data processing. In the next section, we describe some well-known platforms for big data processing, such as MapReduce, Spark, Flink and Google Cloud Dataflow with its open-source version under Apache Beam. In Section 9.3, we present big data frameworks specific to edge computing, including hybrid MapReduce and Apache Edgent. Finally, we summarize the chapter by presenting challenges and opportunities for research in this area.

9.1.1   Edge computing

In contrast to cloud computing, where the storage and processing is done in a centralized facility, far from the devices that produce data or request services, edge computing implies that storage and processing happens at the edge of the network, close to the devices. Edge computing is usually classified into (i) multi-access edge computing (MEC), (ii) cloudlets and (iii) fog computing [1–3].

MEC is a newer name for mobile edge computing, introduced in 2016 by the European Telecommunications Standards Institute (ETSI) [1]. It represents a set of standards that are supposed to accelerate the adoption of edge computing, given the multitude of providers in terms of cloud-like services, applications and mobile infrastructure, as well as the multitude of hardware platforms, communication protocols and processing frameworks. The adoption of 5G mobile communication technologies is predicted to accelerate the development and adoption of MEC [1], because 5G supports (i) higher bandwidths, hence, more data can be uploaded, at least to the base stations, (ii) higher device densities and (iii) virtualized networking stack. Virtualization will play a key role in edge computing because it allows operators to elastically scale resources based on demand, thus helping in meeting quality of service and reducing costs.

A cloudlet [4] is a mini-data center located at the edge of the network, typically one hop away from the devices. The cloudlet provides hardware resources for compute- and storage-intensive applications, while leveraging on virtualization technology to run cloud-like services in isolation. In addition, virtualization technology provides a way to migrate personalized services in mobility-dependent scenarios. For example, consider the case of a mobile game that requires intensive computations that cannot be run on a smartphone. To offer a good user experience, the communication between the smartphone and the service provider needs to be fast. In this case, the cloud is not a suitable option. However, running these computations at the edge introduces a new challenge, because the results need to be personalized. Moreover, the user is playing the game while on board a moving vehicle. In this case, the smartphone will connect to successive base stations, thus, losing the connection to the initial cloudlet. The edge service needs to transfer the state of the computations among successive cloudlets. By using virtual machines, this transfer can be done faster and safer. As an optimization, only the differences compared to a base virtual machine image are transferred among cloudlets [5].

The definition of fog computing is not standardized. Many researchers use the terms edge and fog interchangeably [3]. In this chapter, we consider fog computing distinct from edge. The fog is placed between cloud and edge, and includes devices along the way from the edge to the cloud, such as routers, base stations and backbone connections. This definition is closer to the original Cisco proposal [6]. While fog computing introduces interesting challenges and opportunities, in this chapter we focus on edge computing, where the services and data processing happen on the devices or one hop away, in the base station.

9.1.2 Big data processing

Big data processing refers to processing large volumes of data in a distributed computing environment. Based on the hardware resources utilized, big data processing can be classified into (i) *compute-intensive*, where the central processing unit (CPU) or accelerators, such as the graphics processing unit (GPU) or digital signal processor (DSP), do most of the work, or (ii) *data-intensive* where the application uses large amounts of memory and incurs a high number of input/output (I/O) operations. The line between compute- and data-intensiveness is blurred because there are applications with mix resource demands. For example, matrix multiplication would be a compute-intensive application at a first glance, but fetching the data from the main memory or the disk may overshadow the arithmetic operations done by the CPU, both in terms of time and power [7]. In particular, MapReduce implementation of big data matrix multiplication is data-intensive due to the particularities of both MapReduce programming model and Hadoop platform [7]. More details about MapReduce and Hadoop are presented in Section 9.2.

Based on the exposed parallelism, we distinguish (i) *data-parallel* and (ii) *task-parallel* big data applications and platforms. The former represents applications where the same processing is applied to multiple batches of data, in parallel, while the later represents applications consisting of multiple tasks with different functionality, operating on the same or on different sets of data. Drawing a parallel with Fynn's taxonomy [8], data-parallelism corresponds to *Single Instruction, Multiple Data (SIMD)*, while task-parallelism corresponds to *Multiple Instruction, Single Data (MISD)* or *Multiple Instruction, Multiple Data (MIMD)*.

Data-parallel applications can be classified into (i) *batch processing* where an entire set of data, or batch, is processed at a time, and (ii) *stream processing* where data items arrive periodically in the system and are processed on-the-fly. In batch processing, developers are focused on achieving high processing throughput, while in stream processing the focus in on achieving low latency. In the next section, we shall analyze both batch processing, represented by MapReduce/Hadoop [9,10] and Spark [11], and stream processing, represented by Storm [12], Flink [13], Spark Streaming [14], Google Cloud Dataflow [15] and Beam [16]. In Section 9.3, we shall present batch and stream processing for edge computing.

The explosion of big data and the developments in hardware accelerators, especially GPUs, gave rise to *deep learning*, where ML algorithms are applied to huge amounts of data to build neural networks of unprecedented depth. Since most of the data used by ML is produced at the edge, and given data privacy concerns, it makes sense to run ML training at the edge. However, edge devices have both limited computational capacity and limited view of the entire data set. *Federated learning* [17–19] is proposed to address these issues by allowing multiple devices to work on model training, while a coordinator aggregates the final model. Although not a classical example of big data processing, deep learning at the edge is presented in Section 9.3.5.

9.1.3   Running example: temperature sensors

Throughout this chapter, a real use case is selected to illustrate the programming models and frameworks for big data processing at the edge or in the cloud. This use case is represented by computing the average temperature across a region, as measured by a set of sensors deployed at the edge of the network, in different locations covering the region. Each sensor has an *id*, and outputs a real value representing air temperature, with an associated time stamp. In our experiments, we use real data provided by the Government of Singapore through its data hub for developers*. The data downloaded in JavaScript Object Notation (JSON) format include the time stamp, location id, coordinates and temperature values for each sensor, as shown in Listing 9.1. This JSON record is parsed to extract sensor data consisting of *sensor.id* and *sensor.value*. Since the majority of big data platforms are written in Java, we present the Java code used to parse sensors JSON in Listing 9.2. The method `parseSensors()` is used by other algorithms throughout this chapter[†].

The objective of our big data analytics task is to compute the average temperature across the entire region, as well as for each sensor. In addition to getting the average across the region using the entire data set, developers may want to compute an average for a certain period, and issue an alert in case the temperature is beyond a threshold.

```
{
"metadata":
    {
    "stations": [
        {
        "id": "S109",
        "device_id": "S109",
        "name": "Ang Mo Kio Avenue 5",
        "location": {
            "latitude": 1.3764,
            "longitude": 103.8492
            }
        },
        ...
    },
"items": [
    {
    "timestamp": "2019-06-11T12:05:00",
    "readings": [
        {
        "station_id": "S109",
        "value": 32.2
        },
        {
        "station_id": "S117",
        "value": 31.6
        },
        ...
}
```

```
/**
 * Parse a JSON with sensors information
 * and return a list of pairs,
 * where each pair cosists of a sensor's id and its value.
 */
public static List<Pair<String,Double>> parseSensors(String record) {
    List<Pair<String,Double>> sensors = new LinkedList<>();
    try {
        JsonObject jobject =
            new JsonParser().parse(record).getAsJsonObject();
        if (jobject.has("items")) {
            jobject = jobject.get("items").getAsJsonArray()
                .get(0).getAsJsonObject();
            if (jobject.has("readings")) {
                JsonArray jarray = jobject.getAsJsonArray("readings");
                for (JsonElement reading : jarray) {
                    sensors.add(Pair.of(
                        reading.getAsJsonObject().get("station_id").getAsString(),
                        reading.getAsJsonObject().get("value").getAsDouble()));
                }
            }
        }
    }
    catch (Exception e) {
        System.err.println(e.getMessage());
    }

    return sensors;
}
```

Listing 9.1   Sensors JSON   *Listing 9.2   Parse sensors JSON in Java*

---

*Air temperature data is taken from https://data.gov.sg/dataset/realtime-weather-readings
[†]The source code for these examples is at https://github.com/dloghin/edge-temperature-analytics

The average for a certain period can be computed using a *window* over the entire data, a method used in stream processing. In summary, this sensors analytics use case covers both batch and stream processing, and it is representative of both edge and cloud computing.

9.2   Big data processing platforms

In this section, we present classical big data processing platforms, covering both batch and stream processing. These platforms can be used at the edge, but they are designed for traditional high-performance server clusters, with reliable networking and power supply, typically found in data centers.

9.2.1   Batch processing

MapReduce [9] is a well-known batch-processing platform introduced by Google in 2004. MapReduce is both a programming model and a distributed data processing platform, used extensively by Google. Its open-source version is Hadoop [10], a widely studied distributed platform [20] written in Java. From the programming perspective, MapReduce exposes two key functions to developers, namely `map()` and `reduce()`. From the processing perspective, MapReduce executes a batch job in four phases, as shown in Figure 9.1. In the first phase, the input is split into multiple chunks, and each chunk is processed by a Map task. In the second phase, the `map()` function provided by the developer is applied sequentially on each input record. While record processing is done sequentially in a Map task, the tasks run in parallel on different CPU cores and on different cluster nodes. The Map phase produces a set of <*key, value*> pairs which are, then, grouped based on their *key* by the Shuffle and Sort phase. Finally, each list of values associated with a key is processed by the `reduce()` function provided by the developer, which runs inside Reduce tasks. The <*key, value*> results of the Reduce phase are written to the output.

For our temperature sensor example, the input files contain on each line a JSON record with multiple sensor data. The `map()` function parses this JSON record and outputs the id and temperature reading for each sensor individually, as key and value, respectively. In the background, Shuffle phase groups all readings based on their

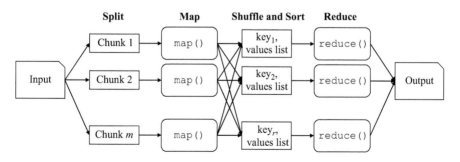

Figure 9.1   Execution phases in MapReduce

Algorithm 9.1: Temperature analytics in MapReduce

 1: **procedure** MAP(*key, value*)
 2:    *sensors* ← parseSensors(*value*)
 3:    **for all** *sensor* ∈ *sensors* **do**
 4:       emit(*sensor.id, sensor.value*)
 5:    **end for**
 6: **end procedure**
 7: **procedure** REDUCE(*key, values*)
 8:    *avg* ← computeAverage(values)
 9:    emit(*key, avg*)
10: **end procedure**

---

sensor id and sends them to a Reduce task. The reduce() function computes the average of the values in the list associated with a sensor id and outputs the result. In Hadoop's terminology, the emit() method is used to perform the outputting after each phase. The pseudocode for this MapReduce processing is presented in Algorithm 9.1.

If the application has to compute the average air temperature across all sensors, we define a new key, different from any sensor id, and emit each sensor reading associated with this key. A Reduce task will compute the average associated with this new key. From another perspective, if the application has to compute the average for a certain time span, also called *window* in stream processing terminology, the map() function filters sensor readings based on their time stamps. We leave the pseudocode design for these two variations as an exercise for the reader.

Traditionally, MapReduce has been used in cloud computing. But with the emergence of edge computing and the performance improvements in low-power nodes, MapReduce is increasingly used at the edge. For example, there are works that adapt and optimize MapReduce on low-power devices with ARM big.LITTLE architecture [21], GPUs [22,23] and field-programmable gate arrays (FPGAs) [24,25]. We shall discuss both MapReduce on low-power, wimpy edge devices and hybrid edge–cloud MapReduce, in Section 9.3.

Spark [11] is a newer platform for batch big data processing, offering significant performance and usability improvements over Hadoop. Spark was developed by Zaharia *et al.* [26] at the University of California, Berkeley, and released as open-source within the Apache Foundation in 2013. This platform is based on the resilient distributed data sets (RDDs) abstraction [27]. An RDD is an immutable collection of records kept in the main memory (RAM) such that it can be reused by multiple computations, in case of iterative or interactive query processing. This in-memory computation, together with the support for iterative computations and generic operators, can improve the performance by several orders of magnitude compared to a pipeline of MapReduce jobs.

Spark is written in Scala, a functional programming language that is compiled to bytecode and run on Java virtual machine (JVM). Besides Scala, Spark provides

---

Algorithm 9.2: Temperature analytics in Spark

1: **procedure** PIPELINE(*input*, *output*)
2:     sc.textFile(*input*)
3:     .flatMap(*line* => parseSensors(*line*))
4:     .reduceByKey((*a*, *b*) => (*a*._1 + *b*._1, *a*._2 + *b*._2))
5:     .map(*rec* => (*rec*._1, *rec*._2._1/*rec*._2._2))
6:     .save(*output*)
7: **end procedure**

---

application programming interface (API) in Java and Python. We present the Scala-like pseudocode for our temperature analytics application in Algorithm 9.2. We observe that the application is a chain of transformations and that Spark requires explicit input and output operations, in contrast to Hadoop. In our example, the JSON input file is loaded into an RDD where each line is a record. A `flatMap()` operator creates a new RDD of *(sensor.id,(sensor.value,1))* records by parsing input JSON lines. For ease of development, we append a value of one to each tuple to represent its uniqueness. This value is used during the reduce phase to count how many tuples are associated with a certain *sensor.id*. Next, a `reduceByKey()`[‡] operator computes the temperature sum for each sensor and counts how many values are contained in that sum. These values are used by a `map()` operator to compute the average temperature. Finally, the results are explicitly written to the output.

In comparison to MapReduce, we observe that Spark code has some particularities, especially due to its functional nature. First, a `flatMap()` operator is used to produce multiple *(sensor.id,(sensor.value,1))* per input JSON record and to create a linear list of tuples. In contrast, a `map()` Spark operator produces a single output per input record. Hence, `map()` is suitable to compute the final average, which has a 1:1 mapping to each sensor id. From this perspective, Spark's `flatMap()` is closer to the Map functionality in MapReduce. Second, we do not use the same method as in MapReduce to compute the average because of the functional nature of Scala, which does not allow stateful methods.

In hybrid edge–cloud applications, Spark is mostly used on the cloud to perform big data processing, including ML model training [28,29]. In such a setup, Spark is used to parallelize ML training on powerful cloud servers, while edge devices download the model to run inference on local data. But there are recent projects using Spark on edge-class devices. For example, Spark is used to run ML applications on Zynq, a low-power device integrating ARM CPU cores and Xilinx FPGA [30].

Hadoop Distributed File System (HDFS) is a key component of many big data analytics platforms, including Hadoop and Spark. In HDFS, big files are split into chunks, typically of 128 MB size, and each chunk is stored in DataNodes. To ensure fault tolerance, a chunk is replicated in multiple, typically three, DataNodes.

[‡] *a*._1 and *a*._2 represent the first and second members of a tuple, in this case *(sensor.value, 1)*.

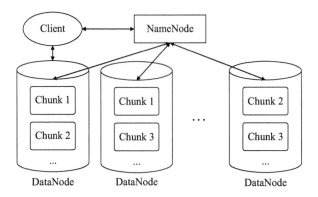

Figure 9.2   The architecture of HDFS

A NameNode keeps track of the metadata, such as file paths and DataNodes where chunks are replicated. The HDFS architecture, highlighted in Figure 9.2, was influenced by Google File System (GFS) [31]. A performance summary of HDFS on low-power edge devices is presented in Section 9.3.1.

9.2.2   Stream processing platforms

In contrast to batch-processing platforms, stream processing aims to achieve low latency by processing each element or record as soon as possible. In stream platforms, data access is push based [32] such that data are flowing through the system, starting from the sources. The flows of data in such a system are called *streams*. In batch processing, data access is pull based, since the tasks need to explicitly fetch the data. In batch-processing terminology, data are grouped in *collections* [32], and each collection comprises multiple records. In batch and stream processing, a record is usually represented as a *<key, value>* and as a *(key, value, timestamp)* tuple, respectively.

A tuple may be delivered once, multiple times or may be lost. In a stream platform that offers *at-most-once* delivery, a tuple may be lost. On the other hand, in a platform that offers *at-least-once* delivery, there may be duplicated tuples, since the platform tries to re-deliver the message upon failure or timeout. There are also stream platforms that offer *exactly-once* delivery. Consequently, this last type of stream platform has lower performance since it has to ensure that a tuple is delivered exactly once. The complex code implementing this mechanism leads to higher latency.

Data streams can be *bounded* or *unbounded*. A bounded stream is similar to a collection in batch processing, having a finite set of records. In contrast, an unbounded stream is infinite and requires a different approach to processing. For aggregated analytics, such as those using reduce operators, unbounded streams need to be split into finite *windows*. We note that windowing can also be applied to bounded streams. We shall use this technique in our temperature analytics example.

Before presenting the temperature analytics, we describe some popular stream processing platforms, which are widely used in both academia and industry. These platforms are designed for data centers, but they can run at the edge when sufficient

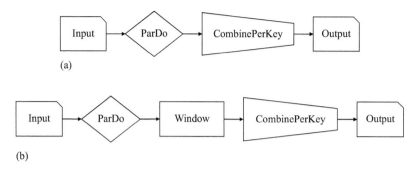

Figure 9.3   Average temperature stream processing (a) On bounded streams (b) On unbounded streams, using windowing

resources are available. We discuss edge-native stream processing platforms in Section 9.3.4. For a comprehensive list of distributed data stream platforms, we direct the reader to the surveys in [32,33].

Storm [12] was released as open-source by Twitter in 2011 and became a top-level Apache project in 2014. In Storm, a data source is called *spout* and an operator processing the data is called *bolt*. Storm can operate in both *at-most-one* and *at-least-one* mode.

Flink [13] is another Apache project that started in the academia, under the name Stratosphere [34]. The project was specifically designed for cloud computing; however, there exist edge platforms that use Flink as the underlying stream processing framework, such as MEC-ConPaaS [35].

Spark Streaming [14,36] is an extension of Spark to support stream processing. However, the underlying engine is still handling RDDs and applies *micro-batching* to keep the latency low [36]. Micro-batching is a technique that unifies stream and batch processing, trying to achieve both low latency and high throughput. Spark Streaming offers an *exactly-one* delivery guarantee.

Google Cloud Dataflow [15] represents an effort to unify batch and stream processing at the programming interface level. It offers a high-level API for developers, which is decoupled from the execution engine. In Google Cloud, the engine that runs Dataflow is based on FlumeJava [37] and MillWheel [38]. FlumeJava is a platform for defining data processing pipelines. We note that the underlying execution in Flume-Java consists of MapReduce jobs [37]. On the other hand, MillWheel is a native stream processing engine that can process a dataflow graph with very low latency.

Beam [16] is the open-source version of Google Cloud Dataflow, incubating in Apache since 2016. Beam can run Dataflow code on different execution engines, such as Spark, Flink or on Google Cloud. For quick development, Beam can run directly on a single node. The developer defines a pipeline of operators that are applied to data sets, as depicted in Figure 9.3. These data sets are called *PCollections*, in an effort to unify batch and stream processing. New PCollections are obtained through

---

Algorithm 9.3: Temperature analytics in Cloud Dataflow/Beam

1: **procedure** PIPELINE(*input, output*)
2:     output.write(
3:     input.read()
4:     .apply(ParDo(parseSensors))
5:     .apply(CombinePerKey(computeAverage))
6:     )
7: **end procedure**

---

transformations applied to existing PCollections. In the following, we present the basic operators, also called *transforms* in Beam:

- *ParDo* can be applied in parallel to each record of the input data set. It is similar to the Map task in the MapReduce platform. The developer can define her custom code inside the ParDo operator.
- *GroupByKey* can group *<key, value>* into separate collections, based on their key. It is similar to the Shuffle phase of MapReduce, but in Beam, this can be used explicitly by the developer.
- *CoGroupByKey* can be used to perform a join of multiple data sets.
- *Combine* can be used to combine collections or some records in collections, for example, per key. The Reduce task in MapReduce is an example of Combine, where multiple values with the same key are processed.
- *Flatten* can be used to merge multiple collections of the same type.
- *Partition* is the opposite of Flatten. It splits a collection into smaller partitions.

Returning to our running example, the pseudocode of its implementation in Beam is presented in Algorithm 9.3 and its visual representation in Figure 9.3(a). Similar to Spark, Beam requires explicit input/output operations. The processing starts with parsing all JSON records in parallel, using a `ParDo` operator. This creates a *PCollection* of *<sensor.id, sensor.value>* key-value pairs. A `CombinePerKey` operator is used to compute the average for each sensor.

Stream processing in Beam supports the windowing technique mentioned above. This technique is used especially on unbounded streams. Our temperature sensor readings represent such an infinite data stream, producing data continuously. If we want to compute the average temperature over a certain period, we need to define a window. For example, the code in Algorithm 9.4 and its representation in Figure 9.3(b) use one-day windows.

9.3 Big data processing at the edge

While the previous section described generic big data processing platforms, in this section we focus on edge processing, where there are limitations in terms of computing, storage and networking resources. We start by describing MapReduce on

---

Algorithm 9.4: Temperature analytics in Cloud Dataflow/Beam with window

---

```
1: procedure PIPELINE(input, output)
2:     output.write(
3:         input.read()
4:         .apply(ParDo(parseSensorsWithTimestamps))
5:         .apply(Window.into(FixedWindows.of(OneDay)))
6:         .apply(CombinePerKey(computeAverage))
7:     )
8: end procedure
```

---

low-power devices typically found at the edge. Then, we analyze big data processing on hybrid edge–cloud setups. We end with stream processing using Apache Edgent and with a brief presentation of big data ML at the edge.

9.3.1 MapReduce on low-power edge devices

With the increasing compute capabilities of the devices at the edge and the communication bottleneck with respect to latency and bandwidth, it is useful to filter, pre-process and aggregate geo-distributed data to ease these bottlenecks and make efficient use of the computational capacities of edge devices. To achieve this, MapReduce framework needs to be augmented to utilize geo-distributed edge nodes in an efficient manner and mitigate reliability issues when the edge nodes are used on a volunteer basis. This challenge has been addressed by Nebula [39] which enables efficient utilization of edge devices for both compute and storage by using node allocation strategies based on both proximity and location awareness, in addition to data availability and high resilience despite transient network failures and node down-times especially in a volunteer environment.

Nebula's [39] system architecture consists of a front end called Central, which is used for nodes to join as computer and/or storage on a volunteer basis and a user interface to create the metadata for the application in terms of the number of component jobs and the set of tasks. The Central interacts with the DataStore and ComputePool architecture components of Nebula which manage the location-aware data storage and the per-application computations resource allocation, respectively. In addition, the Nebula system architecture has a Monitor to log the resource utilization of network bandwidth as well as memory and storage capacities that aid the DataStore and ComputePool to allocate data and compute nodes in an efficient manner. Lastly, the resource manager component of Nebula is used for sharing multiple edge devices across applications by matching the current requirements of resources per application and available resource capacities.

With the majority of edge devices being low-power, wimpy [40] nodes, it is useful to summarize the works addressing performance issues in MapReduce running on both wimpy-only and heterogeneous brawny–wimpy clusters. In a performance study of MapReduce on low-power ARM-based nodes, Loghin *et al.* [21] show that low-power nodes are struggling to run big data analytics due to their small memory size, and low main memory bandwidth. Hence, it is expected that in-memory data analytics platforms, such as Spark, would perform even worse on this type of devices, unless the processing is done on small data sets. On the other hand, low-power nodes are more energy-efficient and may lead to better data center cost, if the user is willing to trade-off throughput and speed.

Interestingly, the study shows that Hadoop's implementation in Java is inefficient on some ARM low-power nodes due to the software emulation of integer division [21]. Re-implementing the benchmark in C++, while still using the Hadoop framework, renders a five times improvement in execution time. Since the majority of big data processing platforms are implemented in Java, or are compiled to Java bytecode and run on JVM, application developers need to pay attention when deploying their applications at the edge, on ARM-based devices.

In the same study [21], the authors analyze the performance of HDFS on six low-power nodes, in comparison with six Xeon servers. The results show that traditional servers exhibit two and three times higher throughput compared to low-power ARM nodes. On the other hand, the study finds that the throughput significantly decreases with more nodes due to the replication mechanism. While this analysis is done on a local, on-premise cluster, it would be useful to evaluate the performance of a distributed file system on edge nodes deployed across a region, with heterogeneous connection protocols.

Targeting brawny–wimpy heterogeneous clusters, Yigitbasi *et al.* [41] and Faraz *et al.* [42] propose methods to achieve higher time and energy efficiency compared to Hadoop. Similar to [21], Yigitbasi *et al.* [41] show that wimpy nodes are more efficient at running I/O tasks, while brawny nodes are better at running compute-intensive jobs. Based on this observation, a task is placed on the most energy-efficient node given the task's resource demands. This heuristic achieves up to 27% energy savings compared to Hadoop.

The work behind Tarazu [42] is motivated by Hadoop applications that, compared to the homogeneous clusters, run slower on a heterogeneous cluster with 10 brawny nodes based on Intel Xeon CPU and 80 wimpy nodes based on Intel Atom CPU. The authors show that the issues are (i) significant network usage during the Map phase because Hadoop's load balancer transfers work from slower wimpy nodes to faster brawny nodes, and (ii) the imbalance in the Reduce phase because the work is equally distributed among nodes with different capacity. To solve these issues, Tarazu includes three optimizations, namely, (i) a Communication-Aware Load Balancer (CALB) for the Map phase, (ii) a Communication-Aware Scheduler (CAS) for the same Map phase and (iii) a Predictive Load Balancer (PLB) for the Reduce phase. With these optimizations, Tarazu is around 70% faster than Hadoop on the heterogeneous cluster.

In the end, we discuss another important aspect of big data edge computing, namely handling failures. Edge computing introduces new challenges in handling failures, due to the remoteness and geographical distribution of the nodes. Mandrake [43] is an approach to automatically tackle failures in remote edge devices. When a physical edge node fails, Mandrake redistributes its virtual machines to other available nodes. Conversely, when a node comes back to live, the system can start virtual machines on it. Mandrake's architecture comprises two main services, namely, a Coordinator Service and an Application Orchestrator Service. While the authors claim that their approach is generic, the evaluation is done on Hadoop and shows a small overhead over the default version.

9.3.2 MapReduce on heterogeneous edge devices

With the fast adoption of mobile devices based on low-power architectures and with the end of Dennard scaling [44], many systems on chip integrate CPU, GPU and DSP cores on the same die. In addition, with the rise of deep learning and its efficient computation on GPUs, many low-power systems integrate powerful GPUs. For example, Nvidia has a family of low-power development kits with ARM CPU cores and hundreds of low-power Nvidia GPU cores.

Starting with Jetson TK1 [45], with 2 GB of RAM, four 32-bit ARM cores and 192 Kepler GPU cores, the series continues with Jetson TX1 [46], with 4 GB of RAM, four 64-bit ARM cores and 256 Maxwell GPU cores. Jetson TX2 [47] exhibits significant improvements over TX1, with 8 GB of RAM, a heterogeneous 4+2 64-bit ARM CPU and 256 Pascal GPU cores. The newest device in the series is Jetson Nano [48], which is supposed to be more power-efficient, at the cost of downgrading hardware specifications. Jetson Nano has 4 GB of RAM, four 64-bit ARM cores and 128 Maxwell GPU cores.

Given this hardware landscape, some researchers aimed to answer the question of whether MapReduce is able to utilize the computational resources of these low-power devices. Loghin *et al.* [23] propose a *lazy processing* technique to process multiple records in parallel on GPU cores. This technique is similar to micro-batching in Spark [36]. Besides utilizing the GPU, lazy processing requires minimal code modifications since each GPU thread is processing an input record, similarly to the CPU. The minimal code modifications involve the replacement of some CPU API calls with their GPU equivalents.

The performance evaluation of lazy processing implemented in CUDA (Compute Unified Device Architecture) and integrated into Hadoop shows that multiple Jetson TK1 nodes can achieve the same performance as one single traditional x86/64 Intel server, while saving significant energy. For example, three TK1 nodes achieve the same throughput as one Intel server, while saving 68% of the energy when running KMeans [23].

Using the same Hadoop-CUDA platform with lazy processing, Loghin *et al.* [7] compared the cost of cloud and edge computing while running MapReduce applications. The cost of cloud computing can be derived directly, based on the execution time. In contrast, a cost model is used for edge computing. The assumption is that edge nodes are self-hosted, hence the model includes hardware, electricity, maintenance and manpower costs. A second assumption is that 12 edge nodes achieve the same performance as a single cloud node, based on the measurements performed on Amazon EC2, Jetson TK1 and Jetson TX1. This ratio is very relaxed, since some applications may need only two edge nodes to match the performance of a cloud instance. A more efficient approach is to dynamically configure the edge nodes based on application requirements.

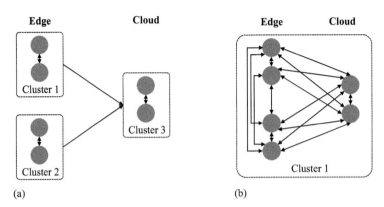

*Figure 9.4   Types of hybrid edge–cloud setups (from [49]) (a) Separate clusters
(b) Single hybrid cluster*

While hardware and manpower costs are fixed, the cost of electricity is dynamic and depends on the system's utilization. The authors propose a simple energy model based on the average active power when the system is utilized, and idle power when the system is not running any job. The results show that the on-demand cloud may be cheaper than edge computing. The efficiency threshold depends on the type of edge device used. For example, edge computing is more expensive than cloud when the utilization is below 27% and 55% on Jetson TK1 and Jetson TX1, respectively.

To amortize the cost of manpower, there needs to be a large number of edge devices under the administration of a single person. For example, an edge cluster with 1,200 nodes is much cheaper than a cloud cluster with 100 instances, even if the salary of a single technician is relatively high [7].

9.3.3   Hybrid MapReduce

With many businesses moving their compute and storage capabilities to the cloud, and given the dispersed geographical distribution of edge devices, many applications embrace a hybrid edge–cloud architecture. A typical hybrid application collects data and does some preliminary processing at the edge. Next, it transfers data to the cloud where advanced data processing takes place, followed by post-processing in the form of storage or visualization.

In hybrid edge–cloud computing, we distinguish three possible setups, namely, (i) *edge-only*, (ii) *cloud-only* and (iii) *hybrid edge–cloud* processing. In edge- and cloud-only setups, the entire processing is done at the edge or on the cloud, respectively. In contrast, a hybrid edge–cloud setup distributes the processing among edge and cloud nodes. In this section, we present hybrid edge–cloud processing from a MapReduce perspective [49].

In a hybrid MapReduce setup, Map and Reduce tasks are distributed among edge and cloud nodes. We distinguish two possible hybrid MapReduce setups represented by (i) a single cluster that encompasses edge and cloud nodes and (ii) separate edge and cloud clusters that require an explicit communication step to share intermediate data, as shown in Figure 9.4. In a typical single-cluster setup, Map tasks are processed at

---

Algorithm 9.5: Temperature analytics in hybrid MapReduce, phase 1

1: **procedure** MAP(*key*, *value*)
2:      *sensors* ← parseSensors(*value*)
3:      **for all** *sensor* ∈ *sensors* **do**
4:          emit(*sensor.id*, *sensor.value*)
5:      **end for**
6: **end procedure**
7: **procedure** REDUCE(*key*, *values*)
8:      *sum* ← 0
9:      *n* ← 0
10:      **for all** *value* ∈ *values* **do**
11:          *sum* ← *sum* + *value*
12:          *n* ← *n* + 1
13:      **end for**
14:      **if** *n*! = 0 **then**
15:          emit(*key*+"_*sum*", *sum*)
16:          emit(*key*+"_*no*", *n*)
17:      **end if**
18: **end procedure**

---

the edge, while the Reduce tasks are handled by the cloud. In such a setup, the Hadoop MapReduce framework handles data shuffling and communication between edge and cloud nodes, transparent to application developers. In contrast, having separate clusters at the edge and on the cloud requires laborious data transfers. Nonetheless, these transfers can be automated, but the application developer needs to consider it. While a setup with multiple clusters may require more work, it is useful in cases where there is no consistent link between the edge and the cloud. In this case, the MapReduce job would fail due to timeouts. Nonetheless, even when the edge–cloud bandwidth is sufficient, some applications exhibit better performance on separated clusters.

The performance of hybrid MapReduce data processing depends on the application [49]. For applications with large intermediate data, such as WordCount and KMeans, a single hybrid cluster achieves higher performance compared to separate clusters. This is due to the powerful Shuffle mechanism in Hadoop, where peer-to-peer connections are established among edge and cloud nodes. In contrast, applications that produce small intermediate data sets, such as Pi estimation or Grep, are faster on separate clusters, by avoiding the unnecessary overhead of a single edge–cloud setup.

From the application development perspective, Algorithms 9.5 and 9.6 show how our temperature sensors analytics can be adapted to work on a hybrid setup with separate clusters. In the first phase, at the edge, the functions is the same as in the original application presented in Algorithm 9.1. The `reduce()` function at the edge does a partial reduction, by computing the sum, counting the values and sending them to the next phase that is handled in the cloud. The `map()` function on the cloud

---

Algorithm 9.6: Temperature analytics in hybrid MapReduce, phase 2

 1: **procedure** MAP(*key, value*)
 2:     *sensorKey* ← parseSensorKey(*value*)
 3:     emit(*sensorKey, value*)
 4: **end procedure**
 5: **procedure** REDUCE(*key, values*)
 6:     *sum* ← 0
 7:     *n* ← 0
 8:     **for all** *value* ∈ *values* **do**
 9:         **if** *value*.contains("*_sum*") **then**
10:             *sum* ← *sum*+ parseSumValue(*value*)
11:         **else**
12:             *sum* ← *n*+ parseNumberValue(*value*)
13:         **end if**
14:     **end for**
15:     **if** *n* = 0 **then**
16:         *avg* ← 0
17:     **else**
18:         *avg* ← *sum/n*
19:     **end if**
20:     emit(*key, avg*)
21: **end procedure**

---

just forwards the sums and the counts, such that the Reduce phase computes the average by summing all the partial sums and dividing them to the total count, for a given sensor id.

9.3.4 *Stream processing at the edge*

With the emergence of edge computing, there is growing interest in stream processing platforms at the edge of the network. Classic stream platforms, as those presented in Section 9.2.2, are too heavy for edge computing where both hardware resources and energy are limited. In this section, we review some stream platforms for edge computing, and focus on Apache Edgent [50] for which we provide an example application. For a detailed survey of big data stream processing at the edge, we direct the reader to the surveys in [51,52].

Similar to hybrid MapReduce, there are solutions that consider a hybrid edge–cloud setup for stream processing. SpanEdge [53] considers both centralized, cloud-based facilities and *near-the-edge* facilities, while splitting them into smaller, micro data centers. To avoid expensive data transfers to the cloud, streams are processed at the edge, based on a placement algorithm where developers can provide hints on where their task should be processed. SpanEdge is implemented on top of Apache

---

Algorithm 9.7: Temperature analytics in Edgent

1: **procedure** AVERAGETEMPERATURETOPOLOGY()
2:    Topology tp = newTopology(*"AverageTemperature"*);
3:    TStream<JsonObject> sensors = getEdgeSensors();
4:    TWindow<JsonObject,JsonElement> sensorWindow = sensors.last(1, TimeUnit.HOURS, j -> j.get(*"id"*));
5:    sensors = JsonAnalytics.aggregate(sensorWindow, *"id"*, *"value"*, MIN, MAX, MEAN, STDDEV);
6:    sensors.print();
7:    submit(topology);
8: **end procedure**

Storm [12], which is a classic stream processing platform used in centralized cloud data centers.

In another implementation [54] based on Apache Storm [12], the authors address the issue of high latency by reducing edge–cloud data transfers. A novelty of this work is that users and software components, such as databases, are assimilated to edge entities, in addition to hardware nodes. This leads to higher development flexibility and better code organization.

Apache Edgent [50] is a stream data analytics platform for edge computing. Edgent, previously known as Quarks, is more lightweight compared to the full-fledged stream engines presented in Section 9.2.2. In the Edgent programming model, a topology is a graph that represents streams of data and transformations on these data. The idea behind this platform is that not all data need to be sent to the cloud or a centralized facility. Instead, only useful or critical data should be sent, and Edgent helps in filtering these data at the edge.

Algorithm 9.7 presents our temperature sensors example in Edgent, based on the *SensorsAggregates* sample topology that comes with Edgent examples. Our sensors are grouped in a unified stream inside `getEdgeSensors()` method. For example, this method can get the data using HTTP requests. Next, a window is applied to the stream, since it is an unbounded data collection. In our example, the window is one hour and is applied per sensor id. Using this window, we compute the minimum, maximum, average and standard deviation for the temperature. The last line of Algorithm 9.7 submits the topology to be executed.

9.3.5 *ML at the edge*

In the last decade, we have witnessed the explosion of ML, which was fuelled by similar factors involved in the rise of edge computing. First, the explosion of data produced at the edge, by smart devices, allows ML models to be trained extensively, in order to achieve high accuracy. Second, the improvements in hardware devices, especially accelerators such as GPUs, made possible the training of very deep neural networks in an acceptable time spans, in the order of days or weeks. At the crossing of big data, edge computing, 5G technology and ML, we provide a brief review of ML platforms for edge computing in this section.

ML development consists of two steps, training and inference. During training, parameters are tuned such that the ML model achieves high accuracy. A trained model is then used to predict based on new inputs, in a phase called inference. Traditionally, ML at the edge involves only inference, while training is done on very powerful machines on the cloud. Even if the inference is less resource-intensive compared to training, the large depth of modern deep learning models leads to high latency on low-power devices. Hence, multiple techniques need to be employed to better utilize low-power edge nodes. Among them, we distinguish model pruning and quantization [55].

ML edge hardware accelerators. ML involves massive amounts of arithmetic operations, especially in the form of matrix multiplications. Hence, hardware accelerators, such as GPUs, are well suited to run ML training and inference due to their highly parallel computing capacity. With the observation that inference is less compute-intensive compared to training, edge nodes can be equipped with low-power, low-performance ML accelerators.

As mentioned in Section 9.3.2, Nvidia developed a series of low-power devices with integrated GPU targeting ML at the edge. Jetson systems integrate ARM CPU cores with Nvidia GPU cores, suitable for processing ML workloads. However, to run full-fledged deep learning models on these low-power devices requires optimizations such as pruning and quantization [55]. To address this, Nvidia had open-sourced its software for increasing the performance of inferences at the edge, called TensorRT [56].

With the observation that GPUs are not efficiently utilized during the inference step, Google designed a chip called tensor processing unit (TPU) [57]. This chip is connected through the PCI Exprex link to a host CPU, similarly to a discrete GPU. A TPU has a big matrix multiplication unit capable of computing 65,536 multiply-and-add (MAC) of 8-bit integers in every cycle. In addition, there is a local buffer of 28 MB that pumps data to the matrix multiply unit. To reduce memory access, the TPU chains multiple MAC units. This chaining leads to significant power savings. The authors report that a TPU exhibits a performance-to-power ratio which is 80 times and 30 times better compared to an x86/64 CPU and a GPU, respectively [57].

While GPUs and TPUs have proprietary design and architecture, the increasing attention given to RISC-V [58] open-source architecture brings new opportunities to develop energy-efficient chips for inference at the edge. RISC-V instruction set architecture (ISA) is extensible, allowing hardware designers to add domain-specific instructions. For example, different widths of integer and floating-point representations can be implemented in hardware to achieve high time-energy performance at the edge.

ML edge software platforms. With the increasing interest in deep learning, both the academia and industry developed software platforms for training deep learning models. Among others, we distinguish Tensorflow [59] developed at Google, PyThorch [60] developed at Facebook, Caffe [61] developed at University of California, Berkeley and Apache Singa [62] started by the Database Systems group at the National University of Singapore and incubating under Apache.

One of the challenges while performing inference at the edge is represented by the high diversity and heterogeneity of edge devices, as shown in a study done at Facebook [63]. To address this, developers tend to provide a generic implementation that can run on all platforms, while trading off efficiency. Another approach consists of providing optimized libraries that are used on devices equipped with higher-performance GPUs or DSPs. For example, Caffe2/PyThorch used (i) NNPACK for fast 32-bit floating-point convolutions and (ii) QNNPACK for 8-bit integer convolutions with small kernels [63].

Federated learning. Until recently, edge devices were used only for inference. But with the increasing integration of powerful GPUs and DSPs, as well as the adoption of fast interconnection networks, such as 5G, we are witnessing the rise of *federated learning* [17,18], where multiple devices work together to train a model. Instead of training the model in the cloud, on a few powerful systems, federated learning proposes the usage of countless edge devices to share the task of training a large model. While there is a need for a coordinator to assign the tasks and monitor the progress, device-to-device (D2D) connections in the emerging 5G networks will further increase the power of federated learning. On the other hand, researchers need to pay attention to the aspects of privacy and security in such a data-sharing approach.

9.4 Challenges and opportunities

Edge computing is considered the next big phase in computing, following after cloud in a succession of alternations between centralized and decentralized computing. While being a very promising field of research, there are important challenges facing edge computing. In this section, we highlight three such challenges that we consider of the most importance:

1. **Lack of standards and edge environments.** A significant issue in the area of edge and fog computing is the limited number of setups for developers to test and evaluate their applications [64]. This is a serious limitation for the development of big data processing platforms targeting the edge, given the scale of processing. In contrast, cloud computing is represented by a few important players, among which Amazon has set the scene and imposed a series of practices followed by other players.

2. **Heterogeneity.** The high device heterogeneity at the edge [63] renders complex code to handle all variations and corner cases. For example, the significant difference in performance between low-end, low-power devices, such as Raspberry Pi, and higher-end devices, such as low-power Intel NUC, leads to imbalances in data-parallel platforms. Low-end devices are becoming stragglers and the research question that needs to be answered is whether these devices should be mixed with higher-performance nodes, or segregated. The problem of stragglers is well studied in cloud environments for MapReduce [65] running in virtual machines, but the edge brings new challenges. Among these challenges, we distinguish hardware diversity and heterogeneity, intermittent network connections, geographical distribution and energy budget constraints.

3. **Connectivity.** Another key challenge in edge computing, in general, and in big data edge processing, in particular, is represented by networking connections that exhibit high variability in a heterogeneous geographically distributed environment. Current wireless protocols, such as WiFi, Bluetooth, 4G and LoRA, among others, exhibit a series of limitations. With the adoption of 5G, there is a promising communication platform that addresses some of the limitations found in the aforementioned protocols. More opportunities brought by 5G are discussed in the next paragraph. For a survey on 5G and edge computing, we direct the reader to [1].

In addition to the above challenges, researchers have identified a series of other challenges facing edge computing, such as reduced physical security [64], significant administrative and maintenance costs [64]. However, these challenges, coupled with the rise and adoption of new technologies, bring exciting research opportunities. We highlight three such opportunities as follows:

1. **RISC-V.** This open-source, extensible RISC ISA [58] is supposed to bring hardware development to new heights. Due to its versatility and extensibility, RISC-V will be adopted by IoT and edge devices in an attempt to further reduce energy usage. Having modularized ISA allows parts of the silicon to be powered off when the system is running certain applications. For example, the matrix multiplication module can be powered off while caches and advanced branch predictors could be switched on during big data analytics. Conversely, the advanced matrix multiplication module is powered on during the execution of ML or high-performance computing (HPC) tasks.
2. **Increasing performance of low-power systems.** This motivates developers and designers to consider edge computing as an alternative to the cloud. First, cheap low-power development kits with impressive performance-to-power ratio [7] allow developers to quickly prototype and test their solutions. Second, low-power wimpy nodes are a real option for edge nodes and cloudlets due to their small form-factor which allows increased device densities.
3. **5G communications.** The adoption of 5G technologies, especially network virtualization and D2D communications [1], is expected to accelerate the development of edge computing. Network virtualization is enabling efficient resource utilization and isolation between development and production environments. Hence, we expect that more edge environments will be available for developers and enthusiasts once 5G networks become pervasive. On the other hand, D2D communications will speed up data sharing in edge environments while reducing the pressure on base stations and other centralized facilities.

9.5 Summary

In this chapter, we presented contemporary big data software platforms, with focus on edge computing. We started with classic big data analytics platforms, such as MapReduce, Hadoop, Spark, Cloud Dataflow and Beam, and discussed how these platforms can be used at the edge and what special techniques are employed to adapt them for edge computing. In particular, we analyzed how MapReduce can run on low-power, wimpy devices, we presented a micro-batching technique called lazy processing which allows MapReduce to run efficiently on heterogeneous devices with GPU, and we analyzed hybrid edge–cloud MapReduce. With the adoption of stream processing due to the increasing real-time requirements of modern applications, we presented Apache Edgent and other platforms for stream processing at the edge.

To combine the theory with hands-on experience, we used a real-world example consisting of temperature analytics to present the application development in different platforms, including MapReduce, Spark, Beam and Edgent. In this chapter, the applications are presented at pseudocode level, but the source code is available on Github [66].

We believe that edge computing is an area with vast potential, but we identify some challenges that need to be addressed to accelerate the development and adoption of edge computing, in general, and big data edge processing, in particular. Among the challenges, we highlight the lack of edge setups and test beds that make the evaluation of new ideas slow, the heterogeneity of edge devices and communication protocols that affect the *write once, run everywhere* principle, and the high cost of maintenance for remotely distributed nodes. On the other hand, the adoption of 5G technologies is going to bring a fresh breeze to edge computing.

References

[1] T. Taleb, K. Samdanis, B. Mada, H. Flinck, S. Dutta, and D. Sabella, On Multi-access Edge Computing: A Survey of the Emerging 5G Network Edge Cloud Architecture and Orchestration, *IEEE Communications Surveys Tutorials*, 19(3):1657–1681, 2017.

[2] C. Mouradian, D. Naboulsi, S. Yangui, R.H. Glitho, M.J. Morrow, and P.A. Polakos, A Comprehensive Survey on Fog Computing: State-of-the-art and Research Challenges, *IEEE Communications Surveys Tutorials*, 20(1):416–464, 2018.

[3] W. Shi, J. Cao, Q. Zhang, Y. Li, and L. Xu, Edge Computing: Vision and Challenges, *IEEE Internet of Things Journal*, 3(5):637–646, 2016.

[4] M. Satyanarayanan, P. Bahl, R. Caceres, and N. Davies, The Case for VM-based Cloudlets in Mobile Computing, *IEEE Pervasive Computing*, 8(4):14–23, 2009.

[5] K. Ha, Y. Abe, T. Eiszler, *et al.*, You Can Teach Elephants to Dance: Agile VM Handoff for Edge Computing, *Proc. of 2nd ACM/IEEE Symposium on Edge Computing*, pages 12:1–12:14, 2017.

[6] Cisco, Fog Computing and the Internet of Things: Extend the Cloud to Where the Things Are, https://bit.ly/2eYXUxj, 2015.

[7] D. Loghin, L. Ramapantulu, Y.M. Teo, On Understanding Time, Energy and Cost Performance of Wimpy Heterogeneous Systems for Edge Computing,

Proc. of 1st IEEE International Conference on Edge Computing (EDGE), pages 1–8, 2017.

[8]   M. J. Flynn, Some Computer Organizations and Their Effectiveness, *IEEE Transactions on Computers*, C-21(9):948–960, 1972.

[9]   J. Dean and S. Ghemawat, MapReduce: Simplified Data Processing on Large Clusters, *Proc. of 6th Conference on Symposium on Operating Systems Design and Implementation*, pages 137–150, 2004.

[10]   Apache, Hadoop, http://hadoop.apache.org/.

[11]   Apache, Spark, https://spark.apache.org/.

[12]   Apache, Storm, https://storm.apache.org/.

[13]   Apache, Flink, https://flink.apache.org/.

[14]   Apache, Spark Streaming, https://spark.apache.org/streaming/.

[15]   T. Akidau, R. Bradshaw, and C. Chambers, The Dataflow Model: A Practical Approach to Balancing Correctness, Latency, and Cost in Massive-scale, Unbounded, Out-of-order Data Processing, *VLDB Endowment*, 8(12):1792–1803, 2015.

[16]   Apache, Beam, https://beam.apache.org/.

[17]   J. Konečný, H.B. McMahan, F.X. Yu, P. Richtárik, A.T. Suresh, D. Bacon. Federated Learning: Strategies for Improving Communication Efficiency, CoRR, 2016, abs/1610.05492

[18]   B. McMahan, E. Moore, D. Ramage, S. Hampson, and B.A. y Arcas, Communication-efficient Learning of Deep Networks from Decentralized Data, *Proc. of 20th International Conference on Artificial Intelligence and Statistics, AISTATS 2017*, 20–22 April 2017, Fort Lauderdale, FL, USA, pages 1273–1282, 2017.

[19]   S. Wang, T. Tuor, and T. Salonidis, *et al.*, Adaptive Federated Learning in Resource Constrained Edge Computing Systems, *IEEE Journal on Selected Areas in Communications*, 37(6):1205–1221, 2019.

[20]   F. Li, B.C. Ooi, M.T. Özsu, and S. Wu, Distributed Data Management Using MapReduce, *ACM Computing Surveys*, 46(3):31:1–31:42, 2014.

[21]   D. Loghin, B.M. Tudor, H. Zhang, B.C. Ooi, and Y.M. Teo, A Performance Study of Big Data on Small Nodes, *Proc. VLDB Endow.*, 8(7):762–773, 2015.

[22]   L. Chen, X. Huo, and G. Agrawal, Accelerating MapReduce on a Coupled CPU-GPU Architecture, *Proc. of International Conference on High Performance Computing, Networking, Storage and Analysis*, pages 25:1–25:11, 2012.

[23]   D. Loghin, L. Ramapantulu, O. Barbu, and Y.M. Teo, A Time-energy Performance Analysis of MapReduce on Heterogeneous Systems with GPUs, *Perform. Eval.*, 91(C):255–269, 2015.

[24]   Y. Shan, B. Wang, J. Yan, Y. Wang, N. Xu, and H. Yang, FPMR: MapReduce Framework on FPGA, *Proc. of 18th Annual ACM/SIGDA International Symposium on Field Programmable Gate Arrays*, pages 93–102, 2010.

[25]   Z. Wang, S. Zhang, B. He, and W. Zhang, Melia: A MapReduce Framework on OpenCL-based FPGAs, *IEEE Transactions on Parallel and Distributed Systems*, 27(12):3547–3560, 2016.

[26]   M. Zaharia, M. Chowdhury, M.J. Franklin, S. Shenker, and I. Stoica, Spark: Cluster Computing with Working Sets, *Proc. of 2nd USENIX Conference on Hot Topics in Cloud Computing*, pages 10–10, Berkeley, CA, USA, 2010. USENIX Association.

[27]   M. Zaharia, M. Chowdhury, and T. Das, *et al.*, Resilient Distributed Datasets: A Fault-tolerant Abstraction for In-memory Cluster Computing, *Proc. of 9th USENIX Conference on Networked Systems Design and Implementation*, pages 2–2, Berkeley, CA, USA, 2012. USENIX Association.

[28]   M. A. Alsheikh, D. Niyato, S. Lin, H. Tan, and Z. Han, Mobile Big Data Analytics Using Deep Learning and Apache Spark, *IEEE Network*, 30(3):22–29, 2016.

[29]   Y. Huang, X. Ma, X. Fan, J. Liu, and W. Gong, When Deep Learning Meets Edge Computing, *Proc. of 25th IEEE International Conference on Network Protocols (ICNP)*, pages 1–2, 2017.

[30]   E. Koromilas, I. Stamelos, C. Kachris, and D. Soudris, Spark Acceleration on FPGAs: A Use Case on Machine Learning in Pynq, *Proc. of 6th International Conference on Modern Circuits and Systems Technologies (MOCAST)*, pages 1–4, 2017.

[31]   S. Ghemawat, H. Gobioff, and S.T. Leung, The Google File System, *Proc. of 19th ACM Symposium on Operating Systems Principles*, pages 20–43, Bolton Landing, NY, 2003.

[32]   W. Wingerath, N. Ritter, and F. Gessert, *Real-time and Stream Data Management Push-based Data in Research and Practice*, Springer, Cham, 2018.

[33]   M. D. de Assunção, A. da Silva.Veith, and R. Buyya, Distributed Data Stream Processing and Edge Computing: A Survey on Resource Elasticity and Future Directions, *Journal of Network and Computer Applications*, 103:1–17, 2018.

[34]   A. Alexandrov, R. Bergmann, S. Ewen, *et al.*, The Stratosphere Platform for Big Data Analytics, *VLDB Endowment*, 23(6):939–964, 2014.

[35]   A. van Kempen, T. Crivat, B. Trubert, D. Roy and G. Pierre, MEC-ConPaaS: An Experimental Single-board Based Mobile Edge Cloud, *Proc. of 5th IEEE International Conference on Mobile Cloud Computing, Services, and Engineering (MobileCloud)*, pages 17–24, 2017.

[36]   M. Zaharia, T. Das, H. Li, T. Hunter, S. Shenker, and I. Stoica, Discretized Streams: Fault-tolerant Streaming Computation at Scale, *Proc. of 24th ACM Symposium on Operating Systems Principles*, pages 423–438, 2013.

[37]   C. Chambers, A. Raniwala, F. Perry, *et al.*, FlumeJava: Easy, Efficient Data-parallel Pipelines, *Proc. of ACM SIGPLAN Conference on Programming Language Design and Implementation*, pages 363–375, 2010.

[38]   T. Akidau, A. Balikov, K. Bekiroglu, *et al.*, MillWheel: Fault-tolerant Stream Processing at Internet Scale, *Proc. of Very Large Data Bases*, pages 734–746, 2013.

[39]   M. Ryden, K. Oh, A. Chandra, J. Weissman, Nebula: Distributed Edge Cloud for Data Intensive Computing, *Proc. of IEEE International Conference on Cloud Engineering*, pages 57–66, 2014.

[40]   V. Gupta and K. Schwan, Brawny vs. Wimpy: Evaluation and Analysis of Modern Workloads on Heterogeneous Processors, *Proc. of 27th International Symposium on Parallel and Distributed Processing Workshops and PhD Forum*, pages 74–83, 2013.

[41]   N. Yigitbasi, K. Datta, N. Jain, and T. Willke, Energy Efficient Scheduling of MapReduce Workloads on Heterogeneous Clusters, *Proc. of 2nd International Workshop on Green Computing Middleware*, pages 1:1–1:6, 2011.

[42]   F. Ahmad, S.T. Chakradhar, A. Raghunathan, and T.N. Vijaykumar, Tarazu: Optimizing MapReduce on Heterogeneous Clusters, *Proc. of 17th International Conference on Architectural Support for Programming Languages and Operating Systems*, pages 61–74, 2012.

[43]   K. Carson, J. Thomason, R. Wolski, C. Krintz, and M. Mock, Mandrake: Implementing Durability for Edge Clouds, *Proc. of 3rd IEEE International Conference on Edge Computing (EDGE)*, pages 95–101, 2019.

[44]   H. Esmaeilzadeh, E. Blem, R.S. Amant, K. Sankaralingam, and D. Burger, Dark Silicon and the End of Multicore Scaling, *Proc. of 38th Annual International Symposium on Computer Architecture (ISCA)*, pages 365–376, 2011.

[45]   Nvidia, Nvidia Unveils First Mobile Supercomputer for Embedded Systems, http://www.webcitation.org/6VdkUISQn, 2014.

[46]   D. Franklin, Nvidia Jetson TX1 Supercomputer-on-module Drives Next Wave of Autonomous Machines, http://www.webcitation.org/6qK3fusRx, 2015.

[47]   D. Franklin, NVIDIA Jetson TX2 Delivers Twice the Intelligence to the Edge, http://www.webcitation.org/73M0i1pIf, 2017.

[48]   Nvidia, Big Performance in a Pocket-size Module, http://archive.today/FdAo3.

[49]   D. Loghin, L. Ramapantulu, and Y.M. Teo, Towards Analyzing the Performance of Hybrid Edge-Cloud Processing, *Proc. of 3rd IEEE International Conference on Edge Computing (EDGE)*, pages 87–94, 2019.

[50]   Apache, Edgent, https://edgent.apache.org/.

[51]   M. Dias de Assuno, A. da Silva.Veith, and R. Buyya, Distributed Data Stream Processing and Edge Computing, *J. Netw. Comput. Appl.*, 103(C):1–17, 2018.

[52]   W. Yu, F. Liang, and X. He *et al.*, A Survey on the Edge Computing for the Internet of Things, *IEEE Access*, 6:6900–6919, 2018.

[53]   H. P. Sajjad, K. Danniswara, A. Al-Shishtawy, and V. Vlassov, SpanEdge: Towards Unifying Stream Processing over Central and Near-the-edge Data Centers, *Proc. of IEEE/ACM Symposium on Edge Computing (SEC)*, pages 168–178, 2016.

[54]   A. Papageorgiou, E. Poormohammady, and B. Cheng, Edge-computing-aware Deployment of Stream Processing Tasks Based on Topology-external Information: Model, Algorithms, and a Storm-based Prototype, *Proc. of IEEE International Congress on Big Data*, pages 259–266, 2016.

[55]   S. Han, H. Mao, and W.J. Dally, Deep Compression: Compressing Deep Neural Network with Pruning, Trained Quantization and Huffman Coding, *Proc. of 4th International Conference on Learning Representations*, 2016.

[56] Nvidia, NVIDIA TensorRT—Programmable Inference Accelerator, https:// developer.nvidia.com/tensorrt, 2019.

[57] N. P. Jouppi, C. Young, and N. Patil, *et al.*, In-datacenter Performance Analysis of a Tensor Processing Unit, *Proc. of 44th ACM/IEEE Annual International Symposium on Computer Architecture (ISCA)*, pages 1–12, 2017.

[58] A. Waterman, Y. Lee, and D.A. Patterson, *et al.*, The RISC-V Instruction Set Manual, 2014.

[59] M. Abadi, P. Barham, J. Chen, *et al.*, TensorFlow: A System for Large-scale Machine Learning, *Proc. of 12th USENIX Conference on Operating Systems Design and Implementation*, pages 265–283, 2016.

[60] A. Paszke, S. Gross, S. Chintala, *et al.*, Automatic Differentiation in PyTorch, *NIPS-W*, 2017.

[61] Y. Jia, E. Shelhamer, J. Donahue, *et al.*, Caffe: Convolutional Architecture for Fast Feature Embedding, *arXiv preprint arXiv:1408.5093*, 2014.

[62] W. Wang, G. Chen, A.T.T. Dinh, *et al.*, SINGA: Putting Deep Learning in the Hands of Multimedia Users, *Proc. of 23rd ACM International Conference on Multimedia*, pages 25–34, New York, NY, USA, 2015.

[63] C. Wu, D. Brooks, K. Chen, *et al.*, Machine Learning at Facebook: Understanding Inference at the Edge, *Proc. of IEEE International Symposium on High Performance Computer Architecture (HPCA)*, pages 331–344, 2019.

[64] D. Bermbach, F. Pallas, D.G. Pérez, *et al.*, A Research Perspective on Fog Computing, L. Braubach *et al.*, editors, *Proc. of Service-oriented Computing and Workshops*, pages 198–210, 2018.

[65] M. Zaharia, A. Konwinski, A.D. Joseph, R. Katz, and I. Stoica, Improving MapReduce Performance in Heterogeneous Environments, *Proc. of 8th USENIX Conference on Operating Systems Design and Implementation*, pages 29–42, Berkeley, CA, USA, 2008.

[66] D. Loghin, L. Ramapantulu, and Y.M. Teo, Source Code for Chapter 9— Distributed Big Data Computing Platforms for Edge Computing, https:// github.com/dloghin/edge-temperature-analytics, 2019.

Chapter 10

Distributed execution platforms for edge computing

Ahmed Salem[1], Tamer Nadeem[2], Theodoros Salonidis[3] and Nirmit Desai[3]

10.1 Introduction

Edge computing emerges as a natural evolution for the community adoption of smart devices. Edge computing is a new paradigm that addresses the explosive mobile data growth through pushing computation to the network's edge close to the data sources. Compared to cloud computing which transports all mobile data to cloud servers for processing, edge computing reduces delay, network bandwidth usage, and mobile device energy consumption. Most existing edge computing approaches use compute resources on the static edge network infrastructure, e.g., smart access points (APs), instead of mobile devices. On the edge, however, the network infrastructure will not keep up with the explosive edge data growth and real-time application requirements [1–3].

The collective compute, storage, connectivity, and sensing resources of network edge smart devices such as smartphones, wearables, and vehicles, offer a new opportunity to extend the boundaries of the network edge closer to the data sources, not only for computation but also for other capabilities such as sensing, storage, and connectivity. The Internet of things (IoT) phenomenon amplifies the untapped potential that fuels rapid proliferation of edge devices in multiple forms.

In this chapter, we present an edge computing framework to harvest and orchestrate distributed edge resources for executing complex applications, e.g., video analytics, that overwhelms the back end, while infeasible on a single smart device. This aims at maximizing the gain from edge data and enabling a new set of applications. For example, recruit a set of microphones and CPUs on restaurant patron phones in Manhattan, NY, and re-purpose them to find the least noisy or crowded restaurant. In this scenario, and many others, edge computing enables decisions based

---

[1]Amazon Web Services (AWS), Seattle, WA, USA. All the work was done while Ahmed was affiliated with Old Dominion University.
[2]Virginia Commonwealth University, Richmond, VA, USA
[3]IBM Research, Yorktown Heights, NY, USA

on live data, unlike static current offerings based on address, pictures, and customer reviews.

10.2   Three-tier architecture

In this section, we present *LAMEN**, an edge computing architecture for orchestrating edge devices and using their resources in executing an application [4,5]. We define an *application* as a code routine ready to run on edge devices. In order to allocate resources to applications, e.g., sensors and CPU, *LAMEN* needs to provide four main features: resource lookup, resource orchestration, application delivery, and a rewards model—*Resource Lookup* to discover and allocate resources required by the application, *Resource Orchestration* to synchronize the performance of heterogeneous resources and present themselves to the application as a virtually single homogeneous resource, and *Application Delivery* that requires an efficient way to deliver applications for end devices, monitor their performance, and return their results. Finally, a *Rewards Model* to compensate for resource usage. In short, *LAMEN* prepares edge devices to host applications, whose resources requirements exceed what a single device could offer, in a way that is more efficient than going to the cloud.

Unlike centralized solutions, e.g., Micro-Blog [6], *LAMEN* proposes a layered architecture where devices are clustered based on their proximity. Each cluster has a head node, i.e., mediator, acting as the cluster coordinator and contact to other layers. In *LAMEN*, we design mediators to keep track of devices and their resources within a cluster, organize them according to their resource similarity, and then recruit a group to execute incoming services. This design enables optimized discovery for a group of resources as they will be close to each other. Also, users can keep their data locally for privacy concerns. Moreover, resource owners maintain their identity anonymous at the mediator level, such that incoming services from different clusters have no clue who executed them, only the mediator keeps the record to be used for rewards estimation.

10.2.1   *LAMEN overview*

LAMEN, a three-tier architecture, consists of (1) cloud server, (2) mediators, and (3) edge devices as shown in Figure 10.1. *LAMEN* users interact using a mobile App to authenticate, grant access to their device resources at their convenient time slots, and issue resource requests.

Cloud server is a repository for sensing and compute applications. It deploys them on proximal clusters and acts as a communication channel between proximal clusters. Also, it receives user requests for executing applications with known resource requirements. During resource discovery, it probes mediators for resources in their clusters. After resource discovery, it notifies the mediators to reserve resources and send them the application code for execution.

---

*A magical pendent to fulfill the wishes of its owner.

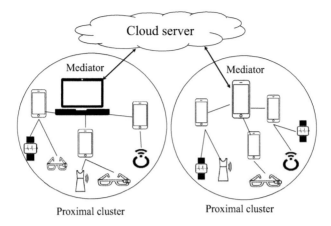

Figure 10.1   LAMEN: a three-tier edge computing architecture

Mediators are proximal cluster managers playing a key role in orchestrating the cluster resources without the need for a cloud. Mediators have the following responsibilities: (a) to establish a communication channel to the cloud server as well as other mediators, (b) to aggregate and expose cluster resources to cloud and other mediators while protecting the identities of edge devices and their owners, (c) to discover and register new devices and their resources in clusters as well as detect their departure, and (d) to respond to requests for resources. A mediator is a logical entity, it can be physically hosted on any of the edge devices, e.g., laptop, AP, wireless local area network (WLAN) controller, or smartphone. Although a mediator can sit in an AP, its area of operation, i.e., cluster, spans beyond the AP limits. For example, in an enterprise, e.g., mall, covered by multiple APs a single mediator brings together all resources using inter-AP communication, e.g., AllJoyn [7]. Further, mediator-to-mediator interactions offer a wider variety of resources for edge applications.

In case a mediator device leaves the cluster, a leader election algorithm elects a new mediator. Since mediator election is expensive, the election algorithm takes into account the expected mobility of a candidate mediator and elects a device having the least expected mobility. These algorithms are well known, hence this chapter does not provide details beyond using a k-leader election algorithm [8].

Edge devices and proximal clusters. At the lowest layer are *edge devices* that opt-in to *LAMEN* to share their compute and sensing resources. Each *LAMEN* edge device may advertise local or non-IP connected resources. For example, a smartphone may advertise a gyroscope either as an on-board sensor or a wearable sensor connected via Bluetooth. We say that devices sharing a certain context and a degree of trust among them form a *proximal cluster*, where devices communicate with each other either in a peer-to-peer (P2P) fashion or via a gateway. For example, devices in a retail store, a restaurant, or a home would form proximal clusters.

LAMEN supports multiple flavors of proximal clusters. The simplest proximal cluster can be a single WLAN where devices communicate using wireless AP(s),

Wi-Fi Direct, or Bluetooth. This is common for IoT scenarios and is currently being standardized. Further, *LAMEN* envisions proximal clusters wherein devices across multiple locations need to collaborate. For example, video surveillance cameras over a larger area may collaborate to infer that a theft is taking place, although such a conclusion cannot be drawn from a single video stream.

Users. *LAMEN* targets three kinds of users: (a) application developers, (b) device owners, and (c) application users. Application developers submit resource requests to the cloud service, allowing them to develop and deploy applications without having direct access to the sensing and computing resources. The device owners opt-in to *LAMEN* by registering their devices and specifying expected incentives. Smart contracts and Blockchain [9] can be readily applied for this purpose. Application users put their request on the app, which triggers discovery and sending the corresponding apps to device owners.

10.2.1.1 Cloud server

Cloud Server, the first *LAMEN* module shown in Figure 10.2, facilitates communication between multiple proximal clusters shown in Figure 10.1. Also, it is an open layer for developers to upload their applications and offer them to *LAMEN* users. To post an application in *LAMEN*, a developer has to register and upload his application in the *Application Repository*.

Similar to Google and Apple App stores, we coin the term *LAMEN store* to hold edge applications. Located over the cloud, *LAMEN store* requires developer's registration before posting their applications. Then, *LAMEN* users can select an

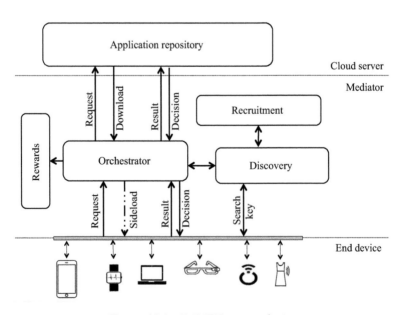

Figure 10.2   LAMEN system design

application to be executed at their preferred location and time. The *store* carries the following features: track service usage, maintain user rating per service, recommend services to users, estimate the price per service, and calculate the developer's reward.

Edge applications run on multiple heterogeneous devices and generate results in a different form. Therefore, each needs different aggregation towards a unified decision or information—e.g., is it a quiet restaurant? Thus, every developer has to include the corresponding aggregation service within his application.

10.2.1.2 Mediator

Mediator, the second layer, consists of the following modules: *Resource Discovery* locates a set of devices holding the required resources; *Recruitment* selects suitable ones out of the previous set based on the service requirements; *Orchestrator* establishes communication between devices within a proximal cluster, sends apps to recruited devices, monitors their performance, receives results from devices, aggregates them, and if needed reports back final results to the cloud; and *Rewards* receives resource utilization from the previous module and uses it to estimate a reward to be used within the proximal cluster.

Resource Discovery, *LAMEN*'s initial step in executing applications on the edge, is locating resource requirements. Resources are scattered across multiple smart devices, e.g., smartphones, IoTs, or TVs. Thus, a resource discovery approach has to find devices holding the proper resource, and make sure they are available at the requested execution time. Moreover, resources of a kind have different quality-of-service features. For example, two devices have cameras, but each has different frame rate, zoom level, resolution, etc. Hence, the discovery approach has to provide a device with the right resource and availability to execute an app. To carry such discovery, first we have to identify a procedure to compose a detailed resource request, post it on devices in the target proximity, and identify available ones to be used in the next module *Recruitment*.

Recruitment is extracting a subset of discovered devices to fulfill the request. In this section, we present the fundamentals of the *recruiter* module. Once a group of resources are discovered, *mediator* should decide which nodes to appoint. This chapter will address the mediator's job in detail using another algorithm, *Kinaara*, on top of *LAMEN*.

Orchestrator is the point of contact between end devices and their mediator. It is responsible for passing services to devices and receiving their results as shown in Figure 10.2. Moreover, it receives a request from proximal users, and sees if it can be fulfilled within the current cluster using available services. If not the request and its service are forwarded to the corresponding *mediator* through *cloud server*, then *orchestrator* can initiate discovery and distribute the service among the recruited candidates.

Rewards is the module responsible for estimating the correct incentive for device owners to participate. No one is expected to offer his resources for free. However, details of this module are out of the scope of this chapter.

10.2.2 How LAMEN works

LAMEN consists of a collection of applications available over the cloud for registered users to request as shown in Figure 10.2. Alice needs to (a) select an application, e.g., *noise level* detection, (b) identify the target region, and (c) submit a *request* to the *cloud server*, which *downloads* the application to *mediators* in region.

Mediators parse the request and generate a *search key* for devices with microphone, accelerometer, and CPU available for sharing, and then trigger *device discovery* module to match the *search key* with available devices and locate good matches. The *recruitment* selects a subset of them through checking their availability and features. Then the *service middleware* transmits apps to the recruited devices for execution. Each app operates on a user's device to analyze the noise levels. *Results* are averaged per mediator to express the proximity and sent back to the *cloud*. Upon sorting them, Alice receives feedback in the form of list containing restaurants sorted by their noise levels in Manhattan to pick accordingly. Meanwhile devices in the selected restaurant will receive their compensation through a point system.

10.3 Resource discovery

In the remainder of the chapter, we will focus on resource discovery and its modules shown in Figure 10.3. We will elaborate on *Kinaara*[†], an algorithm to discover resources at the network's edge based on their availability and readiness to execute an application [10]. As shown in Figure 10.3, the discovery process has two phases: resource representation and resource allocation. *Resource Representation* (Section 10.3.1) names and indexes devices within a proximal cluster; *Resource Allocation* (Section 10.3.2) analyzes resource requirements per incoming request and discovers devices matching these requirements.

Throughout both phases, *Kinaara* uses the following components: a *key* to represent resources and their attributes for each edge device; a *Similarity Table* wherein each device holds pointers to other devices with similar resources; and a *Similarity Function* used to identify how similar two or more keys are to each other, e.g., via Hamming distance.

10.3.1 Resource representation

Devices consist of a set of computing, memory, and sensing resources, each characterized by a set of features. For example, (a) a camera resource has frame rate and resolution features, and (b) an accelerometer resource has sampling frequency and accuracy features. A key challenge in representing such resources is the sheer heterogeneity of the types of device resources and features. Another challenge is in enabling scalable search for suitable resources across all proximal clusters. In this section, we

[†]Edge in Hindi.

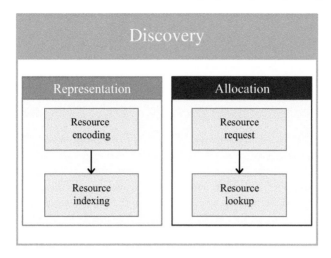

Figure 10.3 Kinaara phases of resource discovery

describe the novel techniques of resource encoding and resource indexing that enable *Kinaara*.

10.3.1.1 Resource encoding

Discovery Encoder (Dicoder), pronounced as "Die Coder," is the module responsible for mapping resources on a device to a name, which will be called *key* from now on.

The main novelty of *Kinaara* resource encoding scheme is to enable each *mediator* to encode a small subset of all resource types and features. The cloud service maintains a dictionary of all resource types and features recognized by *Kinaara*. The dictionary maps each resource type, feature types, and feature values to a unique binary code, e.g., {*camera* → 1011000110011111}. When a *mediator* opts-in to *Kinaara*, the cloud service shares the current dictionary. Each *mediator* chooses the maximum number of resource types it encodes, for scalability, and comes up with its own local dictionary. For example, if a *mediator* chooses to support a maximum of eight resource types, it allocates 3 bits for the mapping of first eight resources it encounters in the proximal cluster. Thus, the domain of the local dictionary is a much smaller subset of the global dictionary, which is dynamically constructed as *Kinaara* discovers edge devices. For example, assume the first resource witnessed by the *mediator* is a camera, the local dictionary would be {*camera* → 000}. When the *mediator* communicates its aggregated resources to cloud service or other *mediators*, it maps the local codes to the global ones. In case of expanding the cluster supported resources, mediator informs all devices to modify their keys by padding 0s to the most significant bit (MSB) per resource. The padded 0s double the resource bits to minimize the repetition of such low-performance operation.

Similar to the resource encoding described above, each feature associated with a resource type is also encoded via a dictionary mapping. For simplicity, without

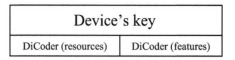

Figure 10.4 Kinaara device key

loss of generality, we assume two feature types: *binary* and *range*. *Binary* features indicate whether or not the corresponding feature is available on the resource or not, e.g., camera flash. *Range* features discretize a domain of values to a small number of categories wherein the domain itself can be discrete or continuous. For example, discretize a range of camera resolution features into "high," "medium," or "low."

The codes for a resource and its associated features are combined into a *chunk* via their concatenation in a predefined order. Similarly, chunks corresponding to all resources offered by a device in the ascending order of resource codes are combined to form a *key* in the format shown in Figure 10.4. Note that *Kinaara* does not require the *key* to be unique, i.e., devices with identical resources will have identical *keys*. For example, device A with key "**001**0111**101**111" consists of two resources camera (code = "001") and accelerometer (code = "011") shown in bold. The camera supports a resolution of 8 Mpixel images (code = "0111") and frame rate of 10 fps (code = "1"), while the accelerometer reads with frequency 10 Hz (code = "11"). Table 10.1 shows the encoding function we used in *Kinaara*.

Finally, resource similarity plays a major role in their indexing strategy, as described later. *Kinaara* employs hamming distance between *keys* estimate similarity of the resources offered by two devices. If the *keys* correspond to devices with no common resources, their distance is deemed infinite.

10.3.1.2 Resource indexing

Kinaara indexes resources in a distributed fashion to avoid maintaining replicas for centralized indexing and cope with *mediator*'s mobility. In this component, we explain how devices join and leave *Kinaara* using their keys. *Kinaara* creates a link between resource similar devices through a structure we call *ring* to enable easy resource lookup. For example, a request for a camera from a device whose camera is currently busy is forwarded to another device with a similar camera instead of denying the request. In this work, similarity expresses how close resource features are between devices and is measured by the sum of Hamming distances between keys.

In *Kinaara*, resources are dynamic in *Magnitude* and *Availability*. *Magnitude* represents the number of resources that an edge device selects to share at any time. *Availability* shows whether a resource is currently busy. Modifying the magnitude requires new key generation, and then joining the ring as a new device. *Kinaara* detects availability during resource discovery. Our experiments showed that representing the magnitude only in the key yields better performance. *Kinaara* indexes clusters through a ring supporting device join and leave operations.

Table 10.1 Resource/feature encoding guide in Kinaara

Resource		Feature		
Name	Value	Name	Value	
Camera	001	Size	4 bits to express minimum of 14 common picture sizes [11]	
			0 = not supported, 1 = supported	
		Orientation	4 bits flag, with 4-megapixel increment, up to 64 megapixels	
		Bit per pixel	2 bits, with an increment of 10 fps to support up to 40 fps	
		Frame rate	0 = not supported, 1 = supported	
		Focus	0 = not supported, 1 = supported	
		Flash	0 = picture, 1 = video	
		Snapshot		
Network Status	010	Interface	00 = Bluetooth, 01 = Wi-Fi, 11 = Cellular, 10 = Wi-Fi Direct	
Audio [12]	011	Frequency	2 bits, each increment supports 3 of the 9 common rates	
		Channel	3 bits to map the 6 channels of 5.1 sound system	
		Sampling rate	2 bits, each increment supports 3 of the 9 common rates	
GPS	100	–		
Sensor	101	Frequency	2 bits, with an increment of 10 Hz to support up to 40 Hz	
	110	Range	2 bits, each increment represents 5 rad/s	
	111	Direction	2 bits to express the three axes	

Magnetometer (101), Accelerometer (110), Gyroscope (111)

Kinaara's ring

Inside a proximal cluster, *Kinaara* sorts devices on a logical ring by their resource similarity. In order to maintain the ring structure each device carries a direct link to its successor and predecessor. Moreover, each device carries a data structure called *Similarity Table*, whose entries are the most resource similar devices on the ring. This structure creates a link between similar resources on the ring enhancing the lookup operation. To mitigate an oversized *similarity table*, *mediators* limit similarity entries to $\log N$ of cluster devices.

During the initiation of the ring, *Kinaara* will have similarity gaps, where non-similar devices are placed next to each other on the ring. The reason is that initially devices with different resources may be joining the ring. Our assumption is that the number of device will be much larger than the number of distinct resources within each device. After multiple devices join, the distance gaps between devices will be smoothed out as more devices with similar resources join.

Device join

An edge device joining the ring sends the *mediator* resources he is offering with time slots. The mediator generates a *key* and forwards the join request to the closest device in its *similarity table*. This is repeated till finding the closest device, placing the new device after creating links to predecessor and successor, and building the *similarity table*.

Throughout our search for the right location on the ring, *Kinaara* maintains a variable called *"nearestNode"* that is updated every hop between two edge devices if the current device is more similar than the previous one. When the similarity function could not find closer entries, we use *nearestNode* as the new location. In case of duplicate keys, we place them as successors and the lookup could fetch their resources.

Figure 10.5 depicts the details of device join algorithm. After *Kinaara* finds the location for the new device on the ring (lines 2–9), it creates a two-way pointer with successor and predecessor (lines 15–19), and then builds its *Similarity table*—the first entry is always the mediator to maintain a direct link, i.e., "0000" (line 20). Then device's spatial locality in terms of resources enables borrowing the similarity table entries from the successor to save the effort looking through the whole cluster. *Kinaara* applies Hamming distance similarity check on the borrowed table entries, the new device selects candidates for its similarity entries by iterating between predecessors and successor repeatedly till filling its table entries (lines 21–26).

Moreover, the new device announces its presence to cluster devices (line 27) by reaching out to its similarity entries and their entries.

Device leave

Detected by successor and predecessor once, their direct link with the device drops. They establish a link together to mend the broken ring using a knowledge every device keeps, i.e., successor of successor and predecessor of predecessor. Since the device who left is still in other similarity tables, we remove these links individually whenever any results in a communication failure. We chose this approach over broadcasting a

```
 1: Function deviceJoin(Node n, Key k, Node nearestNode){
 2:   IF (simFunction(n.key, k) <= 1)
 3:     appendNode(n, k)
 4:   else
 5:     IF (isEmpty(n.successor))
 6:       appendNode(nearestNode, k)
 7:     else
 8:       nearestNode = nearestNode.closer(n)
 9:       deviceJoin(n.successor, k, nearestNode)
10:     end IF
11:   end IF
12: end Function
13:
14: Function appendNode(Node n, Key k)
15:   Node newN = new Node(k)
16:   newN.successor = n.successor
17:   newN.predecessor = n
18:   n.successor = newN
19:   (newN.successor).predecessor = newN
20:   newN.similarityTable.add("0000")
21:   Loop (count(newN.simTable) < length(k))
22:     newN.simTable.add(newN.successor.simTable)
23:     IF (count(newN.simTable) < length(k))
24:       newN.simTable.add(newN.predecessor.simTable)
25:     end IF
26:   end Loop
27:   announcePresence(newNode)
28: end Function
29:
30: Function announcePresence(Node n)
31:   Loop i = 1:length(n.similarityTable)
32:     Node p = n.similarityTable(i)
33:     IF (simFunction(p.simEntriess, n.key) < simFunction(p.key, n.key))
34:       p.similarityEntry.updateSimTable(n.key)
35:     ELSE
36:       p.updateSimilarityTable(n.key)
37:     END IF
38:   END LOOP
39: END Function
```

Figure 10.5   Kinaara device join algorithm

device leaving event to eliminate the overhead imposed by reaching out to the whole cluster.

Indexing scenario

Figure 10.6 shows a sample ring in *Kinaara*. For simplicity, each device holds a single resource represented by 4 bits chunk (resource and features), and this can be extrapolated on the application's need. When new device "1010" joins, the *mediator* searches his similarity table for the most similar device and forwards its control to its similarity table, i.e., "0011," which has a closer device, i.e., "1011." Hence, the new device request is forwarded to new ring location and after checking its *similarity*

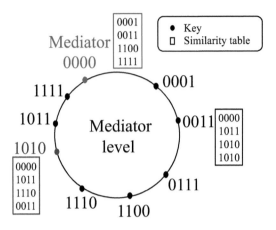

Figure 10.6   Kinaara sample ring

table and the two following hops, it finds his location prior to 1011. Therefore, the new device is placed on the ring and readjust pointers of "1110" and "1011" such that it is the successor of the former and predecessor of the latter. Meanwhile, it points to "1110" and "1011" as predecessor and successors, respectively. Building a four-entry similarity table, mediator comes first and the rest is borrowed from neighbors. Now, the ring is ready to for resource requests.

Mediator-to-mediator interaction

In an effort to incorporate the largest possible resources per application, *Kinaara* employs direct mediator interaction. This enables applications to fetch resources from surrounding mediators either because of resource shortage or expanding the geographical area of operation.

Similar to devices in *Kinaara*, mediators follow the same procedures in establishing a ring, except for key generation and similarity table. In a mediator ring, *Kinaara* uses only available resources in the key generation excluding features. Our experiments showed mobility to cause high feature variation compared to resources, hence ignored to generate a mediator key that is less susceptible to changes. In the mediators' ring, similarity tables hold two extra columns, *location* and *least recently used (LRU)*. The location holds geographical location (i.e., latitude, longitude, and elevation) enabling applications to expand their operations in specific locations. The LRU field holds the latest time of calling the corresponding mediator. Eliminating features from mediator keys generates higher redundancy, hence LRU ensures fair distribution of resources on applications.

The mediator's life cycle on the ring has three phases: join, modify, and leave. After establishing the device ring, a mediator can generate its key and use it to *join* in the mediators ring and create the corresponding similarity table. In case of a new resource showing up at a mediator, a new key is the generated and another round of mediator advertisement takes place to *modify* the previous key. When a mediator *leaves* its cluster, we follow the same lazy approach as devices to discover the failure through failed communication (Section 10.3.1.2). Then, a new mediator is elected and joins the mediators ring.

10.3.2   Resource allocation

On an established ring, *Kinaara* is ready to receive resource requests. To initiate resource allocation, *Kinaara* goes through two steps, *resource request* and *lookup*. On *mediators*, the former generates a request out of the application's required resources, while the latter performs the resource lookup.

10.3.2.1   Resource request

Mediators intercept incoming requests to create a resource query for discovery. The request is an application that includes a manifest file with detailed resource and feature requirements, like android app's structure, which *Kinaara* uses to generate a *search query* with the same format as *keys* (Section 10.3.1.1), except for a prefix. Tables 10.2 and 10.3 show features of the prefix: *Count*, required amount per resource; *Priority*, whether the resource is mandatory or optional; and *Diversity*, says which resources must be discovered on the same device.

Range queries target a range of features per resource. *Kinaara* codes its features in small ranges, if the query range is wider than the feature ranges, it is split among them generating multiple requests corresponding to the main request's feature ranges.

Request language
Discovery Script (*DiScript*), pronounced as "dee script," is an XML-based language to express the need for a set of resources, and all details around their features[‡]. It has three

Table 10.2   Search query prefix

Feature	Value
Count	4 bits, 4 devices per increment
Priority	1 bit showing optional or mandatory
Diversity	1 bit, "1" = resources on a single device

Table 10.3   Search key prefix

Feature	Value
Count	4 bits, 4 devices per increment
Priority	2 bits dividing task to four levels
Distribution	4 bits each representing a direction (N, S, E, W), with 0000 as uniform
Device	1 bit, "1" means resources on a 1 device

[‡]In the future, we will provide a user-friendly graphical user interface to generate *DiScripts*.

parts: *DiScript Initialization, Resource Specifications,* and *Resource Aggregation* as shown in Figure 10.7.

DiScript Initialization is the set of attributes defining the request (i.e., user, lifetime, operation range, count, and resource distribution). *User* holds *Kinaara's* ID for the user creating the script. *Lifetime* holds the expiry date of the discovery process. The start date is not included as a parameter as we assume that sending the script is the kickoff date. Although, the script can be composed any time, but once dispatched it will be in action. The dynamic nature of edge networks would impose needles overhead keeping a script on mobile nodes if dispatched before its designated execution time. *Location* is the GPS location of the origin where discovery should be performed. Then *range* to declare an area of operation in miles starting from the origin. *Distribution* is the distribution of devices to discover in this region. For example, we can request to locate samples from the North West area from origin as shown in Figure 10.7, line 4. *Count* mentions the required number of each upcoming resource unless overridden in the resource tag. Finally, *memo* (line 49), a message sent to device owners, in case a verbal message is required.

Resource Specification is the core part delivered by *DiScripts,* and it details the required resources with their features. Each script should hold at least one resource, otherwise discarded. Each resource has two types of features: *Basic* that include common features by any resource type (i.e., name, count, priority, and distribution) and *Complimentary* that are resource-specific features (e.g., only camera has frame rate feature). *Basic features* are included in every resource. It consists of *name, count* of the units to look for, and *priority,* which states if the resource in question is mandatory to find or optional, and the *distribution* if a specific sensor has to override the selected option in initialization. *Complementary features* are resource-specific features that differ from a resource to the other, for example, Camera (video, pictures) having encoding bit rate, orientation, size, frame rate, focus area, focus mode, face detection, snapshot, flash mode, light exposure, etc.; Sensors with type (e.g., accelerometer), frequency, accuracy, range, delay, direction (three-axis sensors) or all three axes, etc.; Audio (bit rate, channels, sampling rate, etc.); Network Status with interface to monitor (e.g., Wi-Fi, Cellular, or Bluetooth), bandwidth, etc.; and GPS reporting frequency and provider [13].

Resource Aggregation tag is used to inform the mediator what resources are required to be collocated on a single device. Later in this section, we will explain how this will reflect on actual device lookup process.

Figure 10.7 shows a sample *DiScript* used to recruit 150 resources of 4 types to monitor an earthquake in action. It starts by initializing the *DiScript* (lines 3–8 and 49), and then requesting four resources: Accelerometer (lines 9–15), GPS (lines 16–18), Camera (lines 19–29), and Audio (lines 30–36), respectively. Within each of them different complementary configuration applies. For example, the camera is required to provide a minimum of 10 Mb resolution, 30 fps, flash feature working, and face detection capabilities. Finally, two aggregation features, lines 37–42 and 43–48, to specify subsets of the request are needed on one device.

```
1   <xml>
2     <dscript>
3       <user>WillSmith</user>
4       <lifetime>18:00 7/15/16</lifetime>
5       <location>36.886, -76.304021</location>
6       <range>5mile</range>
7       <distribution>uniform</distribution>
8       <count>150</count>
9       <resource>
10        <name>Accelerometer</name>
11        <complimentary>
12          <freq>20</freq>
13          <direction>gravity</direction>
14        </complimentary>
15      </resource>
16      <resource>
17        <name>GPS</name>
18      </resource>
19      <resource>
20        <name>Camera</name>
21        <priority>optional</priority>
22        <count>50</count>
23        <complimentary>
24          <resolution>10M</resolution>
25          <framerate>30</framerate>
26          <flash>1</flash>
27          <c_1>facedetection</c_1>
28        </complimentary>
29      </resource>
30      <resource>
31        <name>Audio</name>
32        <complimentary>
33          <channel>mono signal</channel>
34          <sample_rate>44100Hz</sample_rate>
35        </complimentary>
36      </resource>
37      <aggregation>
38        <r>GPS</r>
39        <r>Accelerometer</r>
40        <count>40</count>
41        <distribution>NW</distribution>
42      </aggregation>
43      <aggregation>
44        <r>Audio</r>
45        <r>Accelerometer</r>
46        <count>50</count>
47        <distribution>uniform</distribution>
48      </aggregation>
49      <memo>capture faces as possible</memo>
50    </dscript>
51  </xml>
```

Figure 10.7   DiScript sample

10.3.2.2   Resource lookup

Figure 10.8 depicts *Kinaara*'s resource lookup algorithm. The *mediators* initiate lookup comparing chunks from the search query against its similarity entries, then hop to the most resource similar device (line 3). On each hop, *Kinaara* checks the resource availability and searches the similarity entries for similar devices to visit (lines 4–7). Available resources are held for a *Holding Period*, waiting for an application to execute, otherwise they are free for other resource requests.

In case of finding all or subset of the request on a device, the following operations are preformed: *First*, the resources found by the request are removed by eliminating their portion of the search query. *Second*, the selected resources are temporarily marked as *on-hold* until the mediator decides on whether to recruit or not. During the holding time, these resources are viewed as busy by other resource requests. If these resources are not utilized by the mediator, they become available after a *Holding period* time-out. *Finally*, this procedure is repeated with the upcoming similarities until forming a path of devices to fulfill the resource request (lines 2–9). The lookup algorithm has two outputs: *Path Length*, the number of devices visited to match the resource request; and *Discovered Devices*, whose resources are *on-hold* waiting for recruitment.

In designing the lookup operation, we had to consider two aspects, the similarity function and lookup style. *Similarity function* compares search strings with device keys as shown in the lookup algorithm in Figure 10.8—we compared multiple token comparison algorithms and chose Hamming distance for consistency and low latency. *Lookup style* defines how to select the next hop between proximal cluster devices. It can be either looking through the current node's similarity entries one by one or the closest entry in each visited node till establishing the path. The former is a breadth-first search (BFS), while the latter is depth-first search (DFS). As the similarity

```
1: function lookup(Node n, SearchKey s, Path p)
2:   loop r = s.resources [1 to m]
3:     if (n.checkAvailability(r))
4:        s.remove(r)
5:        n.remove(r)
6:        p.add(n,r)
7:        r.hold(t)
8:     end if
9:   end loop
10:  if (not empty (s.resouces))
11:     lookup (n.successor, s, p)
12:  else
13:     return p
14:  end if
15: end lookup
```

Figure 10.8   Kinaara lookup algorithm. The pseudocode is written like DFS for readability purposes; however, the actual implementation is BFS

between devices and number of hops are inversely proportional, *Kinaara* favors the BFS approach, as it utilizes the spatial locality created on the *similarity table*.

Mediator allocation
In case an application needs borrowing resources from other mediators, the current mediator searches its mediator similarity table for the corresponding resources and selects a target. The target mediator receives a request similar cloud server's resource request, except the source is another mediator. Mediators comply with such requests as explained earlier and reports their resources back to the requesting mediator. The requesting mediator appends the returned results to the list of *Discovered Devices* to be used by the edge application.

10.4   Implementation and evaluation

In this section, we evaluate *Kinaara* through simulation using two kinds of experiments: First, evaluating *Kinaara* against similar approaches and validating design choices (e.g., similarity function and lookup techniques); second, focus on *Kinaara*'s performance under various conditions including varying the percentage of available network resources, changing the number of service requests received per minute, impact of real mobility scenarios, testing *Kinaara* under intensive mobility patterns, and monitoring the impact of holding a resource on the following service requests.

In our experiments, we used the following set of parameters: *Network Size*, total number of devices in the network; *Path Length*, total number of devices visited till fulfilling a service request; *Discovered devices*, subset of *Path Length* sufficient to fulfill the service request; *Request Success*, number of discovered resources as a percentage of the requested ones; *Request Rate (RR)*, number of received service requests per minute; *Holding Time*, period used to label a resource unavailable to other service requests; *Mobility Rate*, percentage of available resource joining or leaving the experiment.

Throughout our experiments, we simulated devices carrying 4 resources each, given that we support 16 types of resources. Also, our simulated service requests ask for 2% of network resource per request. Note that all results presented are the average of 100 operations, each simulating 1 day long (1,440 min). Our key findings include the following:

- *Kinaara* is as efficient as Chord in discovery with 70% shorter path length.
- *Kinaara*'s distributed design results in $\approx$50% smaller path length compared to *Centralized* scheme.
- The impact of resources scarceness decreases as the network size increases.
- An increased RR per minute can significantly affect the *Request Success*.
- Mobility affects discovering the first resource holding device, and then the similarity table smoothly finds others.

10.4.1 Simulation platform

10.4.1.1 *Kinaara* simulator

A Java-based simulator consisting of ≈2,500 lines of codes with no external dependencies to carry all the features explained earlier in the text. The implementation was designed in a modular way (27 classes) for future extensions. We executed our simulator on two machines: first, i7 2.6 GHz quad core, 4 GB RAM running Ubuntu 14.04; second, an i7 2.2 GHz quad core, 8 GB RAM running OSX 10.9.

10.4.1.2 Data set

We used WiFiDog, an extensive 6-year data set of user mobility traces from public Wi-Fi APs [14]. It contains 2,177,835 records of data with 149,861 users moving between 345 Wi-Fi APs. An average of 5,732 users visited each AP, each spending an average of 78 min/AP. Also, on average each user visited 14 different APs. In our simulations, we assume the WiFiDog users are *Kinaara* edge devices and the mediators are deployed at the Wi-Fi APs.

10.4.1.3 Referenced approaches

We compared *Kinaara* to two alternative approaches *Centralized* and Chord [15]. In *Centralized*, *mediators* maintain a data set of all edge devices in a cluster, on a single table, without using the ring structure. *Mediator* can look up his data set to locate devices, but must query them sequentially for availability. Assuming *mediators* up-to-date knowledge of resource availability would fit the purpose of discovery, but it's impractical in predicting the application's execution time. This is required to determine the resource availability for hosting edge applications. *Chord*, a Peer-2-Peer (P2P) approach used for locating files over a large number of nodes. A node in Chord looks up a query through hopping to one of its known nodes, with no knowledge of inter-node similarity. Since Chord has a similar strategy to *Kinaara*, we compared them to evaluate the similarity table and resource-based keying design.

10.4.2 Kinaara clusters in WiFiDog

To understand the need for *Kinaara*, we analyzed the WiFiDog data set, for real-time device coexistence. In *Kinaara*, resources are related to the number of available devices, hence we needed to explore the device availability. In WiFiDog, users spend an average of 78 min/AP, hence we split the data set to time intervals nearly half of this time, i.e., 40 min, and studied those carefully. Our findings showed ≈12K time intervals where *Kinaara*'s ring holds at least 1,000 distinct devices (8,000 resources) from collocated APs, either through single or multiple mediator scenarios. This means that for those time intervals *Kinaara* ring would experience join and leave operations but at least 1,000 devices stayed for the whole period. Investigating APs in the corresponding intervals, we collected those resources from as low as 9 APs, which is a low number in enterprise networks, e.g., mall. Results from real traces as WiFiDog shows the feasibility and need for a distributed approach to manage those resources.

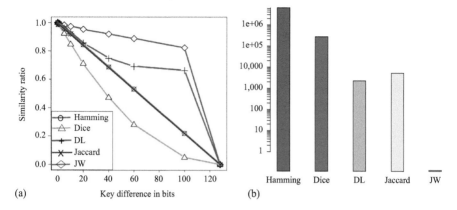

Figure 10.9 Comparing five similarity functions to identify the one suitable for Kinaara (a) Similarity ratio (b) Throughput (ops/s)

10.4.3 Similarity function

We examined five token-based similarity functions: Hamming Distance [16], Dice's Coefficient [17], Damerau-Levenshtein (DL) [18], Jaccard [18], and Jaro-Winkler [18].

In this experiment, we started with two identical 128-bit strings. We had 128 iterations to alter one of them, each flipping one random bit that was not previously flipped. At the end of each iteration, we compared the two strings using the functions mentioned above. Figure 10.9(a) depicts the string comparison at each iteration. Although Hamming distance and Jaccard were consistent with key changes, we chose Hamming distance for its throughput superiority as shown in Figure 10.9(b).

10.4.4 Centralized vs. distributed resource discovery

In this experiment, we compared *Kinaara* to the Centralized approach explained earlier. Centralized places all the logic on the mediator without using rings or similarity tables. When receiving a resource request, mediator shortlists devices with the required resources and contacts them one by one to check their resource availability. In this experiment, we mimic real-life scenarios where mediators have no control on application execution, hence no way to predict if a resource is busy or finished executing its application. In this experiment, we modeled a busy resource as the summation of two parameters: (a) *holding time* of 2 min and (b) *App execution time*, a random period between 1 and 10 min.

Figure 10.10 shows *Kinaara* to visit fewer number of devices, as *Centralized* has higher failure rate from visiting devices with busy resource. Figure 10.10 shows *Kinaara* to visit fewer devices, e.g., 40% in 2K resource cluster, with 90% *request success*.

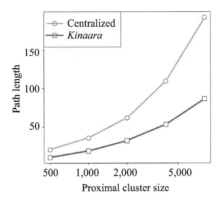

Figure 10.10   Centralized vs. Kinaara resource discovery

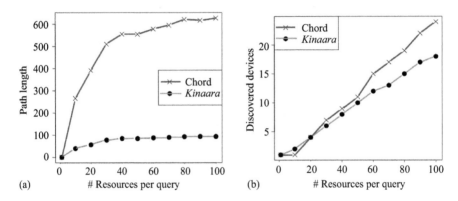

Figure 10.11   Kinaara's selective lookup vs. Chord (a) Path length (b) Discovered devices

10.4.5   Efficient path length

In this experiment, we investigate the number of device hops needed to fulfill a search query. We compare *Kinaara* to Chord's open-source code [15] with both subject to the same input. *Kinaara* selects its next device to look for resources through resource similarity comparison with the search query, while Chord hops sequentially between devices till finding its target. Using randomly generated queries, we performed this experiment on a 1K device cluster (8,000 resources, a practical number from Section 10.4.2).

Figure 10.11(b) shows Chord and *Kinaara* to discover almost the same number of devices. *Kinaara*, however, visits fewer devices, which results in a customized resource lookup that can reach 70% fewer device visits as shown in Figure 10.11(a).

This experiment shows that the similarity table significantly decreases the number of device hops per search query.

10.4.6 Cluster allocation

In this experiment, we measured the impact of a congested cluster over *Kinaara*. This occurs when resources are either scarce or pre-allocated to other applications. In this experiment, we used variable cluster sizes; each was subject to an assumption that a portion of its resources was pre-allocated.

Figure 10.12 shows an increase in the path length to fulfill the same search query as the initial assumption decreased available resources. We monitored a decreasing rate of the path length increase as shown in Figure 10.13, while achieving the same *request success*. This shows another benefit of using a key that conveys available

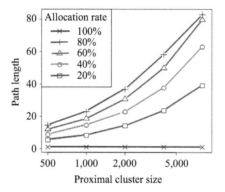

Figure 10.12   Cluster allocation, impact of increasing resource usage ratio on discovery

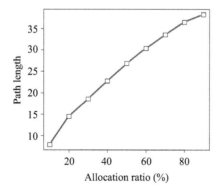

Figure 10.13   Path length under different cluster allocations on a 2K resource cluster

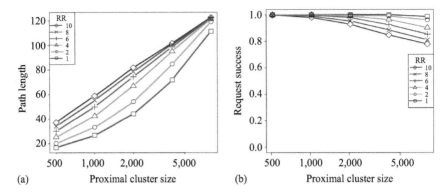

Figure 10.14   Impact of RR on resource discovery (a) Path length (b) Request success

resources and a similarity table that rectifies the scope of lookup to the most similar peer, not just any peer.

10.4.7   Resource request rate

In this experiment, we monitored the impact of multiple RR on path length and request success.

Figure 10.14(a) shows the path length to increase as the *RR* increases; however, the spaces between the curves decrease implying a controlled *path length* increase. The *path length* behavior came along with a decrease *request success* due to discovery failure under intensive requests as shown in Figure 10.14(b). Increasing the *RR* holds large number of resources; for example, $RR = 10$ on a 2,000 resource network results in 400 resource request per minute, which leads to requesting the whole network resources in 20 min. Therefore a *mediator* has to control *Kinaara RR* while considering the number of resources available in the cluster. Also, they have to report to *cloud server* that a *proximal cluster* is receiving many requests asking to target other clusters.

10.4.8   Mobility rate

In this experiment, we measured the impact of variable mobility patterns on *Kinaara*. Mobility pattern does not belong to WiFiDog dataset. This means that within each time interval, i.e., 1 min, a percentage of the cluster devices move in or out. This scenario shows the impact on discovery by *Kinaara*'s device leave strategy (Sections 10.3.1.2) that does not remove entries in similarity tables for devices that left the cluster.

We investigated multiple mobility patterns, i.e., 10%–80%, and all had similar impact on *Kinaara*. Figure 10.15 depicts the 0% and 20% patterns. We witnessed low impact on clusters up to 3,000 resources, while path length increased between 20% and 45% in larger clusters. Hence, mediators should consider mobility prior to expanding the cluster size from neighboring APs.

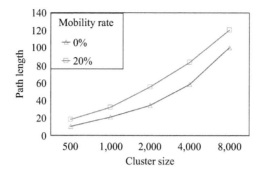

Figure 10.15   Mobility rate and its impact on discovery

10.5   Open issues and challenges

In this chapter, we presented how edge devices and their resources can be orchestrated towards executing applications. However, this approach has other research aspects to be covered. In this section, we will go through some of those.

10.5.1   Mediator

10.5.1.1   Recruitment

Extracting a subset of discovered devices to fulfill the request. In this chapter, we presented the fundamentals of the *recruiter* module. Once a group of resources are discovered, *mediator* should decide which nodes to appoint according to the following features: *Shortest Path*, *Expected Time Departure*, and *History*.

Shortest Path elects the minimum number of devices to fulfill the resource request. For example, if the discovery request was looking for three camera, and three accelerometers, and one GPS, the discovery path came back with five devices all with accelerometer, three with cameras, and three with GPS as follows: A: Accelerometer, GPS; B: Accelerometer, Camera, GPS; C: Accelerometer, Camera; D: Accelerometer, GPS; and E: Accelerometer, Camera. In this case, we need an algorithm to fulfill the request only through devices A, B, and E.

Expected Time Departure. Proximal clusters have to maintain track of its mobility pattern and it's estimated average time spent by a device within its range. The recruitment module tracks that time and generates a continuously updated local average. Once a device joins a proximal cluster, the time is recorded; and when it leaves, the time spent is calculated to update the local average. This approach can be expanded towards a smarter estimation incorporating all features in a machine learning algorithm.

History is the cumulative ranking received per device upon executing a service. Seeking the best candidates, we maintain history of devices in terms of latency, service completion, and accuracy. *Latency* measures the time spent on execution, and whether the device usually performs other concurrent Apps delaying the execution. *Service*

Completion, is the percentage of completed services. For example, if got 10 requests and completed 5 of them that is 50% service completion. Finally, *Accuracy*, how is the returned result from a device is compared to peers in the proximal cluster, and percentage of generating outliers. This is another aspect of that needs to be addressed.

10.5.2 Orchestrator

In Section 10.2.1.2, the Orchestrator can be enhanced to further facilitate applications. Proximal applications are cached at mediators that have limited memory. Users place their requests that run through the cache first. Providing this efficient caching would alleviate plenty of networking overhead from edge networking. Aggregators should be used to disambiguate the results retrieved from edge devices. Otherwise, devices are likely to send back similar results, which decreases the amount of information per byte sent over the network.

In summary, the *orchestrator*, with its position in the *LAMEN* architecture, presents an opportunity to introduce smartness to the edge. We have presented two samples but this is wide open for other smart edge solutions.

10.5.3 Rewards

Unless rewarded, users will be reluctant to using *LAMEN*. Hence, we proposed a *Rewards* component on *LAMEN*. The idea is providing an approach to reach a mutual and fair agreement between both requesting user and recruited devices. Now *LAMEN* uses flat rate values that are static in the mediator. However, a dynamic algorithm that considers resource availability, quality, demand, and supply among other features is expected to help the adoption of *LAMEN*.

10.5.4 Mobility management

Edge devices are mobile, hence continuous relocation between clusters needs to be addressed. Mediators detect device departures using heartbeat and network time-out techniques. Similarly, the device itself detects loss of connection to a cluster and starts discovering other clusters via standard service discovery protocols [19]. However, this is likely to cause data and computational loss that needs to be addressed.

10.6 Conclusion

This chapter presented a framework to leverage distributed edge resources in executing applications. We started by a three-tier architecture explaining how to manage the large number devices at the edge of the network, *LAMEN*. Then we introduced *Kinaara* on top of it to provide indexing, discovery, and allocation. We presented performance evaluation metrics to support the presented work and identify areas of improvement. Finally, we presented some areas that we think are good points for future research on top of this work.

In this chapter, we presented, in deep details, *Kinaara* an edge architecture along with a distributed resource discovery solution for mobile edge networks. First, we proposed the concept of keys to encode resources on each device, and then designed and implemented *Resource Encoder* that maps resources to keys. Second, we used keys to sort devices on a logical ring, each with a data structure, i.e., similarity table, pointing to devices with similar keys. Third, we leveraged previous modules for an optimized resource lookup. Finally, we evaluated *Kinaara* against other approaches and under stress testing conditions. Our evaluation showed *Kinaara* to efficiently discover resources per incoming request, showing *Kinaara* 70% better than Chord and 40% than Centralized. In terms of mobility, *Kinaara* had low overhead at high mobility rates in clusters up to 3K resource compared to stationary modes.

On the other hand, our results showed lessons to be learned. First, it showed the need for a smart load balancing system at the cloud to avoid overwhelming a specific mediator with a high RRs, more than the cluster can accommodate, which degrades the request success rate. Second, we learned from the mobility experiments that *Kinaara* could scale up to 3,000 resource per cluster. While creating proximal clusters and sharing resources between mediators, we need to keep the resources within a cluster below the threshold that would lead to a degraded performance.

References

[1] ABI Research. Data Captured by IoT Connections to Top 1.6 Zettabytes in 2020, As Analytics Evolve from Cloud to Edge; 2015. https://www. abiresearch.com/press/data-captured-by-iot-connections-to-top-16-zettaby/.

[2] EMC Digital Universe. The Digital Universe of Opportunities: Rich Data and the Increasing Value of the Internet of Things; April 2014. http://www. emc.com/leadership/digital-universe/2014iview/executive-summary.htm.

[3] Salem A. Leveraging Resources on Anonymous Mobile Edge Nodes [dissertation]. Old Dominion University. Norfolk (VA); 2018.

[4] Salem A, and Nadeem T. LAMEN: Leveraging resources on anonymous mobile edge nodes. Proc of the Eighth ACM Wireless of the Students, by the Students, and for the Students Workshop. 2016; pp. 15–17.

[5] Salem A, and Nadeem T. LAMEN: Towards orchestrating the growing intelligence on the edge. 3rd IEEE World Forum on Internet of Things (WF-IoT). 2016; pp. 508–513.

[6] Gaonkar S, Li J, Choudhury RR, *et al.* Micro-blog: Sharing and querying content through mobile phones and social participation. Proc of the 6th ACM Int'l Conference on Mobile Systems, Applications, and Services. 2008; pp. 174–186.

[7] Open Connectivity Foundation. AllJoyn Open Source Project. 2019. https:// openconnectivity.org/developer/reference-implementation/alljoyn.

[8] Raychoudhury V, Cao J, Niyogi R, *et al.* Top K-leader election in mobile ad hoc networks. Pervasive and Mobile Computing. 2014;13:181–202.

[9] Kosba A, Miller A, Shi E, *et al.* Hawk: The blockchain model of cryptography and privacy-preserving smart contracts. IEEE Symposium on Security and Privacy (SP). 2016; pp. 839–858.

[10] Salem A, Salonidis T, and Desai N. Kinaara: Distributed discovery and allocation of mobile edge resources. Proc of the 13th IEEE Int'l Conference on Mobile Ad Hoc and Sensor Systems (MASS). 2017.

[11] Kevik. Camera in Android, How to Get Best Size, Preview Size, Picture Size, View Size, Image Distorted? 2014. https://tinyurl.com/jfxl4su.

[12] Audacity Team. Audio Sampling Rates. 2019. https://tinyurl.com/q7x9msm.

[13] Android Developers Guide. Introduction to Android, Resource features. 2018. http://developer.android.com/guide/index.html.

[14] Lenczner M, and Hoen AG. CRAWDAD ilesansfil/wifidog (v. 2015-11-06); 2015. Traceset: session. 2015. http://crawdad.org/ilesansfil/wifidog/20151106/session.

[15] Stoica I, Morris R, Karger D, *et al.* Chord: A scalable peer-to-peer lookup service for internet applications. ACM SIGCOMM Computer Communication Review. 2001;31(4):149–160.

[16] Norouzi M, Fleet DJ, and Salakhutdinov RR. Hamming distance metric learning. Advances in Neural Information Processing Systems. 2012; pp. 1061–1069.

[17] Lin D. Citeseer. An information-theoretic definition of similarity. International Conference on Machine Learning (ICML). 1998;98(1998):296–304.

[18] Sun Y, Ma L, and Wang S. A comparative evaluation of string similarity metrics for ontology alignment. Journal of Information & Computational Science. 2015;12(3):957–964.

[19] Baccelli F, Khude N, Laroia R, *et al.* On the design of device-to-device autonomous discovery. Proc of the Fourth IEEE Int'l Conference on Communication Systems and Networks (COMSNETS). 2012; pp. 1–9.

Chapter 11
Collaborative platforms and technologies for edge computing

Yongli Zhao[1], Wei Wang[1], Qingcheng Zhu[1], Yajie Li[1] and Jie Zhang[1]

The increasing number of Internet-based applications and users is driving the continuous growth of cloud computing, and the emergence of interactive applications is posing new challenges to cloud computing. In this case, the performance of many applications is hardly to be guaranteed by the centralized cloud data centers (DCs) which are usually far away from most end users (EUs). To address these challenges, edge computing is emerging as a promising solution to provide ultralow latency and bandwidth-hungry services by extending cloud computing capabilities to the network edge. However, the network edge is a highly distributed concept, and the edge DCs are usually much more compact than cloud DCs. With limited capacity, edge DCs typically do not work independently, and they collaborate with other edge/cloud DCs when necessary to provide cloud-like services. This chapter focuses on collaborative edge computing, and tries to figure out how collaborations are achieved in edge computing from the following aspects: (1) edge computing: ecosystem and players; (2) computing and networking collaborations in edge computing; (3) use cases and applications in collaborative edge computing; and (4) platforms and prototypes of collaborative edge computing.

11.1 Edge computing: ecosystem and players

11.1.1 Introduction of edge computing

The success and rapid adoption of cloud computing are creating new business opportunities; meanwhile, it is also posing complex technical challenges to the information technology (IT) industry. It is expected that the global cloud computing market by 2024 will reach $1 Trillion [1]. New cloud computing applications are emerging, among which several of them are requiring low-latency and high bandwidth service. Thus, the traditional cloud computing architecture, which is usually composed of only

---

[1] State Key Laboratory of Information Photonics and Optical Communications, Beijing University of Posts and Telecommunications

a few large DCs interconnected by long distance networks, is being challenged by these new emerging applications, as these centralized DCs are usually far away from EUs and cannot provide ultralow latency and high bandwidth connectivity. To deal with these challenges, edge computing was introduced as a supplemental paradigm for cloud computing, in which data, computing/storage capacity and applications are distributed in network edge (typically in metro segment of the network). Located at the place that is closer to users, edge computing provides an intermediate anchor between the users and cloud and thus extends cloud computing capabilities to the network edge.

Besides cloud and edge computing, there are some similar definitions about other computing paradigms: (1) Mobile cloud computing (MCC) emerged as an extension of cloud computing in mobile networks, which is a network-scenario-specific name. MCC aims at offloading the processing tasks and the storage tasks of mobile devices to computational powerhouses. (2) Multi-access edge computing (MEC), a performance-motivated definition, aims to provide IT and cloud computing capabilities within the radio access network (RAN). MEC is able to offer ultralow latency and direct access to real-time radio network information. MEC has overlaps with other concepts, especially with edge computing. (3) Fog computing, an application-specific name, is an extension of cloud computing to meet the requirements of emerging applications in Internet of things (IoT). Compared to traditional cloud computing, fog computing can support delay-sensitive service requests from EUs with reduced energy consumption and low traffic congestion. Technically, fog computing has many overlaps with edge computing, and it shares some of the technical problems with it. These computing paradigms need both IT resource in DCs and network resources, and these resources should be capable of being virtualized, integrated and orchestrated by set techniques (e.g., software-defined networking (SDN) and network function virtualization). In general, edge computing, MEC and fog computing are similar, but they target on different scenarios/applications. In the following parts, we will NOT focus on the difference of the edge-related concepts; instead, we will take the term "edge computing" as a representative of them to discuss their common collaborative platforms and technologies at the network edge.

In summary, edge computing is not only a technology about computing, but also an architectural concept that has many impacts on the related ecosystem. First, the presence of distributed IT resources at network edge will introduce transformations to the infrastructures in traditional cloud computing DCs. Second, the computing capability that is provided by edge DCs can enable more edge-based service paradigms. Thus, with edge computing, the Internet will be no longer a centralized service paradigm, because edge DCs will take care of some traffic directly.

11.1.2   Ecosystem of edge computing

Edge computing is in fact a distributed and collaborative ecosystem that requires infrastructure transformation, resource orchestration and service provisioning. Figure 11.1 shows a general architecture of edge computing, in which edge DCs reside between the large scale of users and the centralized cloud DCs. To provide cloud-like service to EUs, edge DCs must be connected to the cloud DC and EUs through network

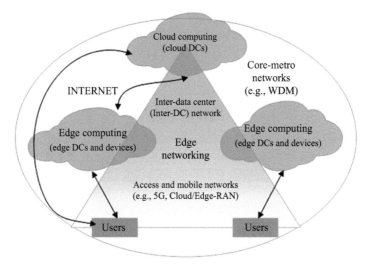

Figure 11.1   Edge computing and networking

infrastructures (we will refer such edge-DC-related networking issues as "edge networking"). At the DC side, edge DCs are connected to the cloud DC through the core/metro networks; at the user side, edge DCs are connected to users through the access networks. Moreover, the distributed edge DCs with networking infrastructures between users and the cloud DC, along with the corresponding resources they can provide, must be managed and orchestrated properly for cloud-like service provisioning. The following subsections will introduce the overall ecosystem of edge computing from two aspects: (1) the infrastructure components and (2) the service framework.

11.1.2.1   Infrastructure components in edge computing

From the infrastructure perspective, we categorize the edge computing ecosystem into two domains: (i) for computing, physical processor components that support heterogeneous and distributed processing and storage; (ii) for networking, physical network components that support communication between distributed computing elements.

Processor infrastructure

In the sense that edge computing is a kind of extension of cloud computing, cloud processor infrastructures are still parts of the edge computing system. In addition, edge computing also has its processor infrastructures that are distributed network edge. In particular, the edge-side infrastructures are heterogeneous in different derivations of edge computing. Considering these infrastructures together, this section forms the processor infrastructure in edge computing as three types, which are (1) cloud side; (2) edge side and (3) user side.

1. Cloud side

Cloud DC: It provides large amounts of centralized devices or servers for data processing and content placement in the core of the network. There are usually tens of thousands, even hundreds of thousands of servers in a single-cloud DC, and they can serve millions of users in a client/server manner. Cloud DC in edge does not have much difference with that in cloud computing, and we will not comment much on it.

2. Edge side

Edge DC: It is smaller than a cloud DC (i.e., between tenths to hundreds servers), and it is usually placed close to the EU devices, typically in the metro network or in the edge of metro network, e.g., network providers' central offices. In the derivations concepts of edge computing, edge DC might be named as other terms, as follows:

Cloudlet: In the context of MCC, the IT infrastructure is called cloudlet, and it refers to a local computing node that comprised several multicore computers with connectivity to the remote cloud servers [2]. With Cloudlet, mobile devices' workloads can be executed locally

Fog DCs/Servers: In fog computing, the IT infrastructure is usually called fog DC/servers, which are geo-distributed and are deployed at very common places, e.g., bus terminals, shopping centers, roads and parks [3].

MEC Server: Edge DC is also called MEC servers in the context of MEC. MEC servers at the edge of the RAN usually have some insights to the real-time radio and network information (such as subscriber location and cell load) that can be leveraged by applications and services to offer context-related services. Such services are capable of differentiating the mobile broadband experience [4].

3. User side

User side device: Compared with edge DCs, they are nearer to users and can be part of a router, a gateway of IoT, a personal computer, a laptop or a smart phone, in which there are processing, memory and storage resources. In some cases, the user side devices are formed as a micro/nano DC to work in a collaborative manner [5]. Note that these devices are usually from individual users, and their availability depends on users' permission for sharing their personal computing and storage resources with others.

Network infrastructure

The other part of infrastructure in edge computing is the network components which provide connectivity between the cloud DCs, edge DCs and users' devices. We categorize them into two layers: (1) access networks that connect user devices with edge DCs and (2) transport networks that connect the edge DCs with cloud DCs.

1. Access networks

According to the specific location of edge DCs, EUs could be connected to edge DCs through one of the three different access technologies, i.e., cellular wireless networks, passive optical networks (PONs) and fiber-wireless access networks. In case where edge DCs are placed at the wireless access point, users can access edge DCs directly through the radio channels. Cooperative communications ability of wireless channels can help to optimize task offloading in the form of relaying via the nearer mobile device [6]. In cloud-based RAN (C-RAN), when edge DC is deployed in the central office that hosts the baseband processing unit, users' traffic is aggregated to the edge DC through the cellular channels and PON [7]. In addition, in the same case of edge computing in C-RAN, the wireless access party might be the typical RAN technologies (i.e., wireless local area network (WLAN)) instead of the cellular channels [8]. In this case, the connectivity between users and edge DC will be the typical RAN and PON, which is also referred to as the fiber-wireless network.

2. Transport networks
In general, transport networks do not have much difference with that in cloud computing, as it is not aware of the traffic flows for specific services. However, from the end-to-end view, transport networks, including the packet and optical domains, need to be orchestrated with cloud/edge DCs and user devices to provide connectivity for edge–cloud resource sharing and synchronization [9].

11.1.2.2 Service framework for edge computing system

The physical edge computing infrastructures can provide computing, storage and networking resources, but they are not capable of serving users' traffic directly, unless corresponding service-oriented functional and operational service entities are equipped. Figure 11.2 shows an example framework from the perspective of functionality components, and it has three layers, i.e., mobile device layer, cloudlet layer and cloud layer. In mobile device layer, there is a sub-layer edge application-programming interface which provides a set of predefined functions, such as task offloading, application monitoring, cloudlet discovery and synchronization, and application migration. Cloudlet layer offers edge-based entities and services, i.e., virtual machines (VMs) or containers that can host applications and data. Cloud layer focuses on orchestration functions, such as replication and load balancing.

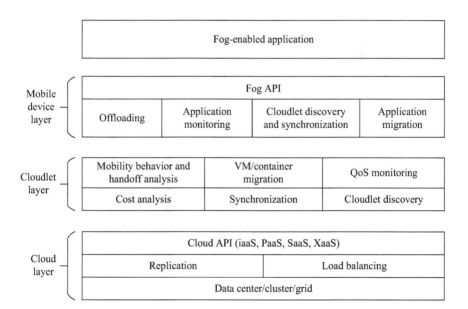

Figure 11.2   Layered architecture of edge computing

11.1.3 Players in edge computing ecosystem

Edge computing is an ecosystem that includes applications, platforms and networks. On the one hand, some of the biggest players in technology—including Amazon, Microsoft and Google—are exploring edge computing, potentially giving rise to the next big computing race. While Amazon Web Services (AWS) remains dominant in the public cloud landscape, it remains to be seen who will emerge as the leader in this nascent edge computing space. On the other hand, it is necessary for an edge computing industry alliance, for example, OpenFog Consortium, to fully explore industry service scenarios, integrate industry resources through operators and combine application requirements with edge computing platform standards, to promote the development of the edge computing industry together.

As shown in Figure 11.3, the players in edge computing ecosystem include infrastructure equipment vendors, telecom equipment manufacturers, telecom operators, third-party application developers, content providers and EUs [10]. Telecom operators are the core of the whole industrial ecological chain, and are also the foundation of industrial collaboration. Telecom operators are successively beginning network reconstruction and transformation and changing from traditional pipeline connectors to industrial integrators, aiming to become service providers. By relying on the establishment of edge computing platforms, telecom operators can provide their platform capabilities to third-party application developers, rapidly launch user-oriented innovative services and shorten the time to market.

In addition, operators can make the storage, computing, network and security capabilities of the platform open up to third-party application developers and content providers, and provide over-the-top (OTT) applications with unified edge deployment and management. Further, the edge computing platform can abstract telecom network capability information into a variety of services (e.g., Road Network Inventory System (RNIS), location services, bandwidth management and Transmission Control Protocol (TCP) optimization) and make them open up to third-party applications and vertical industries to improve their service performance and competitiveness among their peers.

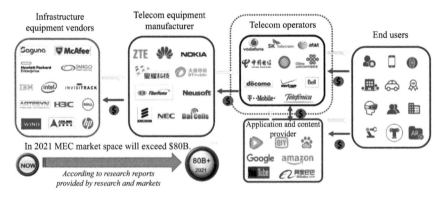

Figure 11.3 Landscape of most players in edge computing ecosystem

The players in edge computing can accomplish more tasks, thanks to the benefits provided by edge computing. Edge computing concept focuses on important metrics, such as delay and high bandwidth that are accomplished by limiting data movement to edge servers than to centralized servers with severe latency cost. Moreover, power consumption is also one of the main concerns. Computational tasks are migrated to external resource-rich systems to increase the battery lifetime of user equipment (UE). With respect to the players (telecom operators, application and content providers, EUs), edge computing benefits include the following [11]:

1. Telecom operators could enable RAN access to third-party vendors to deploy their applications and services in a more flexible and agile manner. These enabling services could generate revenue by charging based on the services used, such as storage, bandwidth and other IT resources. OTT services and digital video recorder services offered by cable operators may likely be faster since their services could reside in edge servers.
2. Application and content providers could gain profit by an edge computing platform at the network edge, which makes services scalable along with high bandwidth and low latency. Application and content providers could also get real-time access to the radio activity that may develop more capable applications. RAN is revamped into service-aware RAN which provides the location information of the subscriber, cell load and network congestion.
3. EUs could experience fast computational applications through offloading techniques that are handled by MEC servers within RAN. In addition, tight RAN assimilation and physical close servers could improve the user quality of experience (QoE), such as high throughput browsing, video caching and better Domain Name Server (DNS).

11.2 Computing and networking collaborations for edge computing

Edge DCs are typically close to users and can provide low-latency and high-QoE services. However, to manage infrastructure cost, the capacity of edge DCs is usually limited. Thus, one individual edge DC is not able to work independently, and it may need cloud's support when necessary. There are two types of collaboration in edge computing: horizontal and vertical collaboration [12], which refer to the collaboration among elements within one layer (e.g., among user devices or edge DCs), and the collaboration across user devices, edge DCs and clouds DCs, respectively. The following sections will discuss (1) collaborative resource management in edge computing; (2) collaborative task offloading and scheduling in edge computing; and (3) collaboration between edge computing and networks.

11.2.1 Collaborative resource management in edge computing

In order to improve the QoE, as well as application deployment and delivery efficiency, the collaborative resource allocation in edge computing plays an important role. The resources in edge computing include physical resources and virtual resources. On the one hand, the physical IT resources in edge computing are typically formed by three types: cloud-DCs, edge DCs and micro-DCs. The physical network resources that support edge networking are a subset of network components that provide connectivity between the cloud DCs, edge DCs, micro DCs and EUs. On the other hand, thanks to the virtualization technology, we are able to provide IT and network resources in a more flexible manner through aggregation, partition and migration of sliced resources. Over the physical IT resources, there are virtualization hypervisors for abstracting a physical computing device into one or more virtual devices (e.g., VMs). Similar to IT-resource virtualization, network-resource virtualization is important for edge networking, as edge infrastructure can largely benefit from elastic network-resource provisioning.

Due to the geographically distributed nature of edge computing, the resource management is an important issue for edge computing and networking, as it directly decides the efficiency and performance of edge computing systems. Several works have been done on this topic.

11.2.1.1   Horizontal collaboration for resource management in edge computing

Horizontal collaboration in edge computing refers to the collaboration among elements within one layer (e.g., among user devices or edge DCs). Regarding horizontal collaboration, a few works have studied the collaboration in user device layer and edge DC layer.

Horizontal collaboration can be used to achieve load balancing and failure recovery. Ref. [16] warns from the fact that overloaded or failure edge DC will significantly degrade the QoE and negate the advantages of edge computing. In case of overloaded or failed edge DC, two recovery schemes are proposed. One recovery scheme focuses on the collaboration in edge DC layer. Once overload or failure happens to an edge DC, the users, who are originally served by it, will try to offload its workload to another available edge DC within transfer range. Focusing on the collaboration among user devices, the other recovery scheme is designed for the situations when there is no available neighboring edge DC within transfer range. In this case, some nearby user devices will be chosen as *ad hoc* relay nodes, and be used to bridge the affected user devices with unreachable edge DCs.

Ref. [13] focuses on the horizontal collaboration at MEC server layer. It investigates VM placement and workload assignment for a collaborative MEC system to minimize hardware consumption under the latency constraint. In the process of deciding the number of VMs for each application at each DC (VM placement) and allocating VM capacity to each given flow (workload assignment), since each request flow is aggregated from a certain amount of users, some flows might be too large for local existing VMs to process. In this case, one request flow will be split into several sub-flows for collaborative processing as shown in Figure 11.4(a). On the other hand, when the capacity required by a sub-flow is less than the capacity of a single VM, the sub-flow might be assigned to a VM which is shared with other sub-flows, as shown in Figure 11.4(b). Hence, in the collaborative edge computing system, multiple

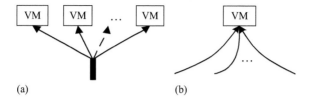

(a)   (b)

Figure 11.4 Sub-flow assignment scenarios (a) One big flow (b) Multiple small flows

edge DCs are jointly orchestrated, and hardware resources inside them are managed properly. Numerical results show that MEC server utilization can be optimized by leveraging remote VM placing and workload aggregating.

11.2.1.2 Vertical collaboration for resource management in edge computing

Vertical collaboration in edge computing is an approach that can coordinate user devices and edge and cloud DCs for performance optimization. Many works have studied the vertical collaboration, especially the collaboration between edge and cloud DCs.

In the system perspective, Ref. [14] proposed a solution to extend the existing cloud computing software stacks to edge DCs to enable seamless service collaboration and orchestration. By using the so-called "external drivers," any organization can develop their own drivers to support new, specific networking equipment in edge computing system. With the system-level support for vertical collaboration, application-level vertical collaboration can also be achieved.

Ref. [15] developed a vertical collaboration infrastructure which aims to achieve high user QoE. As shown in Figure 11.5, the infrastructure is constructed by a set of supernodes that are responsible for rendering results to nearby users. In this case, cloud only helps edge to handle intensive computation and sends update information to supernodes, and this paradigm can reduce processing latency and bandwidth consumption significantly.

11.2.2 Collaborative task offloading and scheduling in edge computing

As the resources in the individual edge DCs or the user devices are limited, the task offloading of large-scale task needs the collaboration between the infrastructure components of the edge computing ecosystem, so as to satisfy the application in need of low latency and high quality of service (QoS). Several works have been done on the topic of collaborative task offloading and scheduling in edge computing.

11.2.2.1 Horizontal collaboration for task offloading and scheduling in edge computing

When it comes to the task offloading and scheduling, the horizontal collaboration in the edge DC layer guarantees the trade-offs between the system costs and the task

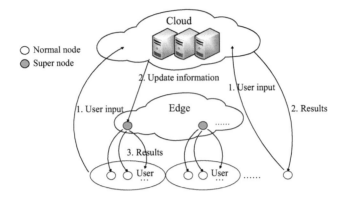

Figure 11.5   Vertical collaboration infrastructure

completed latency. However, the limited computing capacity of edge DCs needs to be considered. Ref. [16] clarified that the computation task offloading process includes three parts: offloading, calculation and computation result feedback. To reduce the task completed latency, the paper proposed a recommended solution: if the excessive workloads are outsourced, the tasks will further be offloaded to other edge DCs deployed at the adjacent access point.

Considering edge computing as a novel paradigm that brings computing applications, data and services closer to the edge of the network, Ref. [17] proposed a cooperative scheme between two DCs installed at the edge of the network that exchanges each other generic computation requests when one of them is temporarily overloaded. If a service request arrives at one DC with its request buffer full, then the request is forwarded to the other cooperating DC and served by that DC, consuming its CPU cycles. The cooperative load-balancing scheme minimizes the blocking states at each DC while reducing the execution delay of the tasks.

To solve the problem that the presence of neighboring node is highly uncertain, Ref. [18] proposed an effective way to select the suitable edge nodes to complete the task offloading. Based on the online k-secretary framework, in exploration stage, an edge node decides how to offload the computation tasks between other edge nodes and the cloud server. Basically, the edge node selects the most suitable neighboring edge node to construct the network. Afterward, an optimization algorithm is formulated to minimize the overall computation delay of all edge nodes by suitably selecting the set of edge nodes.

11.2.2.2   Vertical collaboration for task offloading and scheduling in edge computing

In edge computing system, task offloading is a critical point which enables mobile devices to support resource-intensive applications. Ref. [19] proposed a novel collaborative task offloading model, as is shown in Figure 11.6. The agent decides that the tasks are running on the mobile device, offloading to the local cloud or offloading to the remote cloud. Once a new task is generated by a user, it can be executed on

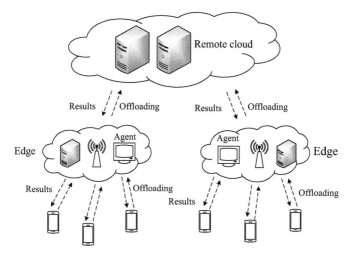

Figure 11.6   Collaborative task offloading model

the mobile device. If the mobile device is not able to perform this task or take too long, the manager would decide that the task should be offloaded to the local cloud through the wireless link. If the local cloud is not able to perform this task or take too long, the manager would decide that the task should be offloaded to the remote cloud through the Internet. The vertical collaboration in edge computing effectively brings the edge computing power closer to the mobile user.

11.2.3   Collaboration between edge computing and networks

This section will discuss the collaboration between edge computing and two types of networks—RANs and passive optical access networks. In addition, Section 11.2.3.3 will dig into the cooperative relationship between edge computing and the popular software-defined technology.

11.2.3.1   Edge computing and RAN

In the RAN, the collaboration between edge computing and radio has the significant advantages of local radio signal processing, cooperative radio resource management and distributed storage capability to tackle the massive users' demands at the edge. However, due to constrained fronthaul capacity, achieving ultralow latency for emerging cellular networks is still challenging. Some work has been done to solve the problem. The core idea is to take full advantage of local radio signal processing, cooperative radio resource management and distributed storing capabilities in edge devices, which can decrease the heavy burden on fronthaul and avoid large-scale radio signal processing in the centralized baseband unit pool.

Ref. [20] proposed an edge computing model in the RAN which utilizes the existing infrastructure, e.g., small cells and macro base stations, to achieve the ultralow latency by joint computing across multiple RAN nodes and near-range communications at the edge. Then, it proposed a latency-driven cooperative task computing algorithm with one-for-all concept for simultaneous selection of the RAN nodes to serve with proper heterogeneous resource allocation for multiuser services. The numerical results show that the low-latency services can be achieved via latency-driven cooperative task computing. Ref. [21] focuses on alleviating the heavy burden on fronthaul and achieving ultralow latency by proposing a loosely coupled architecture with the collaboration between edge computing and RAN, where a large number of RAN nodes are able to participate in joint distributed computing and content sharing regardless of nearness communication by satisfying the minimum latency demand. Numerical results reveal that the ultralow latency can be achieved by properly utilizing the loosely coupled architecture.

Ref. [22] presented a novel edge computing architecture in RAN shown in Figure 11.7. Compared with the traditional RANs (globe centralized mode), it is notable that the novel architecture (local centralized mode) has the radio signal processing and radio resource management unit adaptively implemented at network edge, where is closer to the EUs. In [23], another architecture was proposed with three candidate transmission modes: device-to-device, local distributed coordination and global C-RAN. A related resource allocation algorithm is proposed in the architecture.

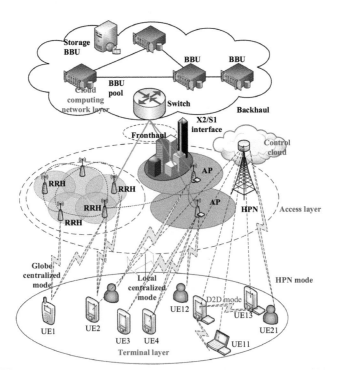

Figure 11.7   System model for collaboration between edge computing and RAN

11.2.4 Edge computing and PON

The huge bandwidth capacities and low costs of PONs combined with their high data rates have made them strong candidates for wireless backhauls. Edge computing is referred to as decentralized computing at the network access segment so as to facilitate computation capability closer to EUs. PON is seen to be one of the key players in expansion of communication networks. Many designs have therefore been proposed to integrate PONs with edge computing paradigms, which are essential for many emerging applications and have paved the way in realizing high-speed broadband Internet access to the EUs.

Ref. [24] presents an architecture which is the first effort toward presenting an integrated architecture of edge computation facilities and PON. Placing edge computation facilities close to an optical line terminal (OLT) can have several advantages, including locally content caching, number of packet loss reduction, providing computational support to the EUs (code offloading) and meeting QoS requirements of EUs' applications. Ref. [25] studies the performance of edge computing in long-reach PONs (LR-PONs), where long propagation delays pose challenges to the bandwidth allocation performance. It compared centralized multithread polling against a modified decentralized scheme. From the simulation results, the paper concluded that only the latter can support true edge computing in LR-PONs since it requires no OLT involvement and achieves lower delays for edge traffic.

11.2.4.1 Edge computing and software-defined technology

SDN is a popular control technique for managing and virtualizing distributed network devices. It is also suitable for managing an edge computing system, in which edge DCs are also distributed. Some works have already proposed possible control architecture for SDN-based edge computing.

Ref. [26] proposed a location-aware VM designation scheme in edge computing using hierarchical control architecture of SDN, in which VMs are designated for different requests with different latency requirements. Ref. [27] considered an IoT scenario, for which an SDN-based control platform for edge computing was implemented. Internet of Vehicles is a special use case of edge computing, and Ref. [28] has described an SDN-based control plane for vehicular *ad hoc* network. The proposed control plane can manage various heterogeneous characteristics (e.g., physical medium, mobility, topology and capability) of cloud computing. As an important enabling technology for networking, there are many potential application scenarios for edge computing and SDN.

Software-defined systems (SDS) inherit the properties of network softwarization and generalize them to other systems. In the past few years, researchers have been experimenting with SDS such as software-defined storage [29] and software-defined security [30]. Ref. [31] introduced wireless-based software-defined storage simulation framework for edge computing, where storage services are served collaboratively and provided by the closest edge node to the EUs, consisting of data layer (storage infrastructure), control layer and the application layer. At the stage of performing the storage request, the cooperation among edge nodes takes place. The controller sorts edge nodes according to their distance from the local edge (the closest first). The controller then loops over edge nodes, to see who is going to handle the request either partially or completely. The remaining chunks are handled that same way they were handled by the local edge. If the number of tapped MEC nodes exceeds a predefined threshold, the cooperative search strategy is suspended as it is going to be infeasible in terms of time required to store the data, thus, preserving the QoS.

11.3 Use cases and applications in collaborative edge computing

Edge computing can reduce the service latency and decrease bandwidth consumption in the backbone networks. With these advantages, edge computing can serve many latency-critical and bandwidth-intensive applications. This section discusses several popular use cases and applications for collaborative edge computing, such as video processing, caching, social sensing and big data.

11.3.1 Video processing

Edge computing is an emerging technique of enabling distributed computing for the preprocessing of video chunks which reduces the transmission delay [32]. By leveraging the edge computing technique, redundant computation and communication capabilities of multiple mobile devices in the proximal can be utilized to handle delay-sensitive video processing through short-range wireless communications.

Ref. [33] studies a cooperative video processing scheme in an edge computing framework to tackle the challenges of optimally forming mobile devices into video processing groups and dispatching video chunks to proper video processing groups, which achieves suboptimal performance on the human detection accuracy. In Ref. [34], the authors envision a collaborative joint caching and processing strategy for on-demand video streaming in MEC networks, utilizing both caching and processing capabilities at the MEC servers to serve users' requests for videos with different bitrates. Collaboration among the MEC servers balances processing load in the network.

11.3.2 Caching

Caching aims to balance the trade-off between the transmission rate and storage. If the transmission rate is high, the requirement for storage is low. In fog-computing based RANs, although the scale of content acquired by service providers is growing significantly, it is unnecessary to cache all content in the cloud DCs, which increases the end-to-end delay. Edge caching has emerged as a promising approach to alleviate the heavy burden on data transmission through caching and forwarding contents at the edge of networks. Some local traffic is stored in edge devices, which can significantly decrease burden on the constrained fronthaul [35].

It is significant to pose intelligent caching resource allocation strategies and cooperative caching policies among edge devices. Meanwhile, to exploit the edge caching benefits, some key factors should be considered and jointly optimized, such as the cache load, cache hit ratio, number of content requests, cost of caching hardware and cost of radio resource usage. And the caching policies, deciding what to cache and when to release caches in different edge devices, are crucial for improving the overall caching performance [36].

In edge caching networks, by utilizing the storage resources at the edge nodes, popular contents can be cached close to EUs. As effective cooperation of edge caching nodes needs to be strategically managed, a hybrid architecture that harnesses the benefits of edge caching and cloud access networks was proposed in [37]. To further utilize C-RANs and provide a more flexible caching service in 5G mobile systems, a caching scheme with a virtualization-evolved packet core concept was introduced in [38], where third-party service providers can be adaptively empowered. Ref. [39] proposes a new cooperative edge caching architecture for 5G networks, where mobile edge computing resources are utilized for enhancing edge caching capability. Numerical results indicate that the proposed scheme minimizes content access latency and improves caching resource utilization.

11.3.3 Social sensing

Social sensing has received a significant amount of attention due to the proliferation of low-cost mobile sensors and the ubiquitous Internet connectivity. A large set of social sensing applications are sensitive to delay, i.e., have real-time requirements. Examples of such applications include intelligent transportation systems [40], video crowdsourcing from mobile devices [41], urban sensing [42] and disaster and emergency response [43].

Edge computing systems (encompassing sensors, edge devices and servers in the cloud) are a natural platform for social sensing applications. For today's social sensing applications, heavy data analytic tasks are transferred, i.e., offloaded, to external servers or devices. Pushing all the computation tasks to the remote servers can be rather ineffective particularly for delay-sensitive applications due to the limited network bandwidth and high communication latency. Hence, collaborative edge computing makes a difference.

Ref. [44] developed a cooperative-competitive game-theoretic task allocation framework for delay-sensitive social sensing applications in edge computing systems. An overview of the framework is given in Figure 11.8. The framework consists of three major components: (i) a novel cooperative–competitive game that models the competing objectives between edge devices and applications; (ii) a decentralized fictitious play with negotiation scheme followed by edge devices to make local decisions and autonomously form collaborations to maximize individual payoffs while obeying the task dependency and trust constraints; and (iii) a dynamic incentive adjustment scheme that dynamically tunes the incentives to address the dynamic availability of EUs while ensuring QoS of the application. The framework addresses three fundamental challenges in solving the task allocation problem for delay-sensitive social sensing applications in edge computing systems, namely competing objectives, constrained cooperativeness and dynamic availability.

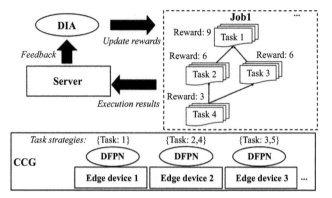

Figure 11.8   Overview of the cooperative–competitive game-theoretic task allocation framework

11.3.4 Big data

In the era of IoT, the demand of distributed big data sharing and processing applications will dramatically increase since the data producing and consuming are pushed to the edge of the network. Data processing in collaborative edge environment needs to fuse data owned by multiple players, while keeping the computation within players' data facilities. To attack this challenge, Ref. [45] proposed a new computing paradigm which is designed for big data processing in collaborative edge environment. The paradigm fuses geographically distributed data by creating virtual shared data views that are exposed to EUs via predefined interfaces by data owners. By pushing the data processing as close as to data sources, it avoids data movement from the edge of the network to the cloud and improves the response latency.

Ref. [46] designed a self-organizing platform, in which part of data processing capacity and service delivery operations are processed locally in "small servers," i.e., close to where data are collected. This platform deals with protocols to facilitate the local computing processing and relies on more complex operations running on virtual entities avoiding the traditional approach of centralized cloud computing.

11.4   Platforms and prototypes of collaborative edge computing

The section researches the design and implementation of a collaborative edge computing platform which can serve as a standard development environment for prototyping. Then several examples of platforms and prototypes of collaborative edge computing are given.

11.4.1   Design goals of a collaborative edge computing platform

There are several designing goals for a collaborative edge computing platform [47].

- *Latency*: It is fundamental for edge computing platform to offer EU low-latency-guaranteed applications and services. The latency comes from the execution time of a task, the task offloading time, the time for cyber foraging and speed of decisions making, etc.
- *Efficiency*: While at first glance the efficiency may have its own impact on latency, it is more related to the efficient utilization of resources and energy. The reasons are obvious and quite different from counterparts in cloud computing scenarios: (1) not all edge nodes are resource rich–some of them have limited computation power, memory and storage; (2) most of edge nodes and UE are battery-powered, such as handhold devices, wearables, and wireless sensor units.
- *Generality*: Due to the heterogeneity of edge node and UE, we need to provide the same abstract to top layer applications and services for UE. General application programming interfaces (APIs) should be provided to cope with existing protocols and APIs (e.g., machine-to-machine protocols and smart vehicle/smart appliance APIs).

11.4.2   Components of a collaborative edge computing platform

Ref. [47] suggests a collaborative edge computing platform be composed of the following components, as shown in Figure 11.9. We briefly explain several important components.

- *Authentication and authorization*: The access of edge computing services and resources needs to be authenticated and authorized. Edge computing opens the door for new authentication and authorization schemes since it is close to EUs and can identify user using access pattern, mobility pattern and trusted secure devices.
- *Offloading management*: Offloading is an important component that has impact on all design goals. There are extensive existing research on this topic. The offloading in edge computing needs to solve several problems: (1) what kinds of information are needed in offloading decisions, (2) how to partition application for offloading and (3) how to design optimal offloading scheme.
- *Location services*: Location services need to maintain a location list of neighbor nodes (mobile and non-mobile node), track mobile EUs and share location information among involved edge nodes. It maps network locations with physical locations, and adopts mobility model provided by EU or learns the mobility model if possible. The tracking and mapping on mobile nodes will need information from multiple layers (physical (ultrasound, wireless signal and signature, GPS, IMU sensor), network (IP address) and application (social activities)), which will call for new design for this component.
- *System monitor*: System monitor is a standard component in cloud infrastructures, which can provide useful information such as workload, usage, energy to help lots

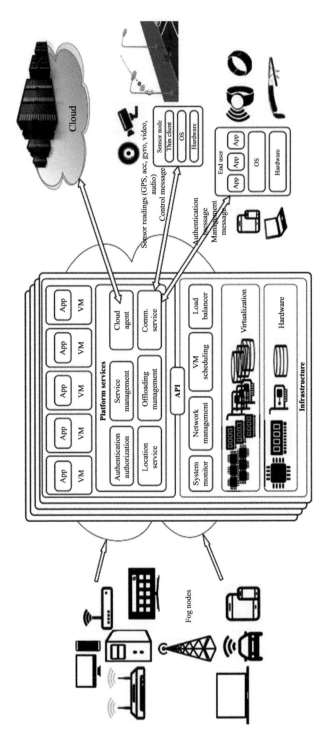

Figure 11.9   Components for a collaborative edge computing platform

of decision-making and pricing. We highlight this component in edge computing platform since it provides crucial information for other components.

- *Resource management*: The resource management will be responsible for most tasks related to resource discover, resource allocation, the dynamic joining and leaving of edge node, and provisioning and maintaining the resource pool in a distributed manner.
- *VM scheduling*: The VM scheduling needs a brand new design due to fused input of system usage, workload stats, location information and mobility model. New scheduling strategies are needed to provide optimal solution for scheduling VMs.

11.4.3 Implementation of collaborative edge computing platforms and prototypes

With the rapidly growing requirements for edge-based applications such as IoT, artificial intelligence and stream data analytics, edge computing becomes more and more important for cloud computing. To make application development in edge computing easier, several cloud providers have put forward their own edge computing platforms. These platforms provide the ability to deploy and orchestrate applications, such as machine learning models, on edge devices in the form of stateless serverless functions or user code in containers. In 2018, Seattle Cloud Lab, Huawei R&D, USA, has implemented a collaborative edge computing platform called KubeEdge [48]. As shown in Figure 11.10, KubeEdge is a multi-tenant infrastructure platform for edge computing. The platform includes the followings, excluding Kubernetes:

1. KubeBus: A virtual network layer connecting edge nodes and cloud VMs as one addressable network space in a multi-tenant environment.
2. EdgeController: A Kubernetes controller plug-in to enable KubeEdge (and Kubernetes) to remotely manage edge nodes as the cluster nodes, and allow applications or services to be deployed on the edge from the cloud through Kubernetes API.
3. MetadataSyncService: A bidirectional metadata sync services between edge and cloud for the platform itself and user applications.
4. EdgeCore: A lightweight agent running on the edge nodes to start up and manage container-based applications as well as serverless functions.

In addition, the Infrastructure of KubeEdge leverages Kubernetes container platform to provide remote procedure call-based communication channel between edge and cloud, the runtime execution environment of containers and serverless functions, as well as a mechanism to sync and store metadata to support self-management of an application running on the edge in an offline scenario.

Apart from the edge computing platform KubeEdge, there are two of the most popular edge computing platforms currently available, AWS Greengrass [49] and Microsoft Azure IoT Edge [50]. The Greengrass pipeline is shown in Figure 11.11. Greengrass edge devices run the Greengrass core software. The core software allows users to run Lambda functions locally on the edge devices and manage, modify or update them through the AWS console website or deployment API. Developers can

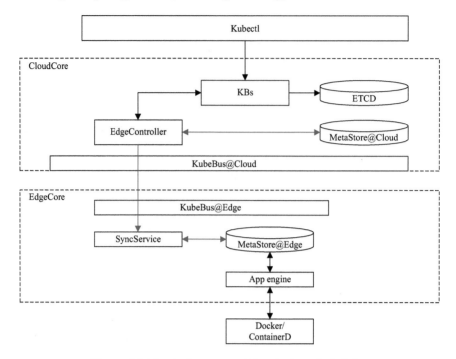

Figure 11.10   Architecture of the platform KubeEdge

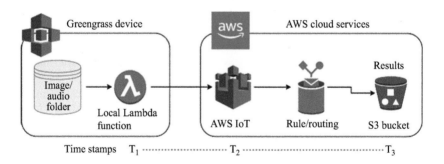

Figure 11.11   Architecture of the platform AWS Greengrass

constrain the maximum memory usage of the local Lambda functions. The Greengrass core software also takes care of the authentication, authorization and secure message routing, through the Message Queuing Telemetry Transport (MQTT) protocol [51], between the devices, Lambda functions and the cloud. Azure Edge uses lightweight virtualization, specifically, Docker compatible containers, to deploy computation on edge devices. The Docker containers run as "edge modules" in the Azure Edge platform, as shown in Figure 11.12. The modules can contain Azure Functions, user code and libraries [52].

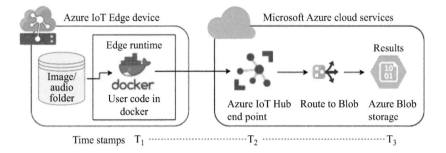

Figure 11.12   Architecture of the platform Microsoft Azure IoT Edge

11.5   Conclusion

Edge computing extends cloud computing capability to the network edge by providing computing and storage resources at the close proximity to Internet users. Based on the fact that the distributed edge infrastructures usually works collaboratively for cloud-like service provisioning, this chapter introduces the collaborative platforms and technologies for edge computing in four aspects: (1) edge computing: ecosystem and players; (2) computing and networking collaborations in edge computing; (3) use cases and applications in collaborative edge computing; and (4) platforms and prototypes of collaborative edge computing. In collaborative edge computing system, the existence of edge infrastructures offers chances for providing low-latency and high-QoE services. However, the distribution nature of edge infrastructures determines that collaboration must be performed for cloud-like and efficient service provisioning. That is to say, to achieve the low latency and high QoE in edge computing, more complex and intelligent strategies must be used to enable collaboration of edge-related infrastructures. With computing and storage at network edge, collaborative platforms and technologies for edge computing can help to build more application scenarios, where users' activities are sensitive to the latency caused by computing and network transmission. However, the technical challenges of edge computing do not only consist in the distributed deployment of edge DCs, but also in infrastructure transformation, resource orchestration and service provisioning. Hence, for each specific use case, there is much space to facilitate edge computing by developing various types of collaboration strategies.

References

[1]   Global Cloud Computing Market Forecast 2019–2024, Tabular Analysis, https://marketresearchmedia.com/global-cloud-computing-market/,2018, [Online; Accessed January 2018].
[2]   M. Satyanarayanan, P. Bahl, R. Cáceres and N. Davies, "The case for VM-based cloudlets in mobile computing," IEEE Pervasive Computing, vol. 8, no. 4, pp. 14–23, 2009.

[3] R. Mahmud and R. Buyya, "Fog computing: A taxonomy, survey and future directions," Distributed, Parallel, and Cluster Computing, 2017, pp. 1–28.

[4] ETSI, "Mobile edge computing (MEC); technical requirements," Etsi Gs Mec 002 – V1.1.1, 2016.

[5] D. Satria, D. Park and M. Jo, "Recovery for overloaded mobile edge computing," Future Generation Computer Systems (FCGS), vol. 70, pp. 138–147, 2017.

[6] X. Hu, K. Wong and K. Yang, "Wireless Powered Cooperation-Assisted Mobile Edge Computing," IEEE Transactions on Wireless Communications, vol. 17, no. 4, pp. 2375–2388, 2018.

[7] W. Wang, Y. Zhao, M. Tornatore, H. Li, J. Zhang and B. Mukherjee, "Coordinating Multi-access Edge Computing with Mobile Fronthaul for Optimizing 5G End-to-End Latency," 2018 Optical Fiber Communications Conference and Exposition (OFC), San Diego, CA, 2018.

[8] B. P. Rimal, D. P. Van and M. Maier, "Mobile edge computing empowered fiber-wireless access networks in the 5G era," IEEE Communications Magazine, vol. 55, no. 2, pp. 192–200, 2017.

[9] R. Muñoz, R. Vilalta, N. Yoshikane, *et al.*, "Integration of IoT, transport SDN, and edge/cloud computing for dynamic distribution of IoT analytics and efficient use of network resources," Journal of Lightwave Technology, vol. 36, no. 7, pp. 1420–1428, 2018.

[10] China Unicom. White Paper for China Unicom's Edge-Cloud Service Platform Architecture and Industrial Eco-System, February 2018.

[11] N. Abbas, Y. Zhang, A. Taherkordi, *et al.*, "Mobile edge computing: A survey," IEEE Internet of Things Journal, vol. 5, no. 1, pp. 450–465, 2018.

[12] T. X. Tran, A. Hajisami, P. Pandey, and D. Pompili, "Collaborative mobile edge computing in 5G networks: New paradigms, scenarios, and challenges," IEEE Communications Magazine, vol. 55, no. 4, pp. 54–61, 2017.

[13] W. Wang, Y. Zhao, M. Tornatore, *et al.*, "Virtual machine placement and workload assignment for mobile edge computing," Cloud Networking (CloudNet), 2017 IEEE 6th International Conference on, Prague, Czech Republic, 2017.

[14] I. Cardoso, J. Barraca, C. Goncalves, *et al.*, "Seamless integration of cloud and fog networks," International Journal of Network Management, vol. 26, no. 6, pp. 435–460, 2016.

[15] Y. Lin and H. Shen, "Cloud fog: Towards high quality of experience in cloud gaming," Proceedings of the International Conference on Parallel Processing, 2015.

[16] C. Yang, Y. Liu, X. Chen, W. Zhong and S. Xie, "Efficient mobility-aware task offloading for vehicular edge computing networks," IEEE Access, vol. 7, pp. 26652–26664, 2019.

[17] R. Beraldi, A. Mtibaa and H. Alnuweiri, "Cooperative load balancing scheme for edge computing resources," 2017 Second International Conference on Fog and Mobile Edge Computing (FMEC), Valencia, 2017, pp. 94–100.

[18] G. Lee, W. Saad and M. Bennis, "An online secretary framework for fog network formation with minimal latency," Proc. IEEE ICC, May 2017, pp. 1–6.

[19] Q. Zhu, B. Si, F. Yang, *et al.*, "Task offloading decision in fog computing system," China Communications, vol. 14, no. 11, pp. 59–68, 2017.

[20] A. Pang, W. Chung, T. Chiu and J. Zhang, "Latency-driven cooperative task computing in multi-user fog-radio access networks," 2017 IEEE 37th International Conference on Distributed Computing Systems (ICDCS), Atlanta, GA, 2017, pp. 615–624.

[21] G. M. S. Rahman, M. Peng, K. Zhang and S. Chen, "Radio resource allocation for achieving ultra-low latency in fog radio access networks," IEEE Access, vol. 6, pp. 17442–17454, 2018.

[22] M. Peng, S. Yan, K. Zhang and C. Wang, "Fog computing based radio access networks: issues and challenges," IEEE Networks, vol. 30, no. 4, pp. 46–53, 2016.

[23] H. Xiang, M. Peng, Y. Cheng, *et al.*, "Joint mode selection and resource allocation for downlink fog radio access networks supported D2D," 11th EAI International Conference on Heterogeneous Networking for Quality, Reliability, Security and Robustness (QSHINE 2015), Taipei, Taiwan, August 2015.

[24] S. H. S. Newaz, W. Susanty Binti Haji Suhaili, G. M. Lee, *et al.*, "Towards realizing the importance of placing fog computing facilities at the central office of a PON," 2017 19th International Conference on Advanced Communication Technology (ICACT), Bongpyeong, 2017, pp. 152–157.

[25] A. Helmy and A. Nayak, "Toward parallel edge computing in long-reach PONs," IEEE/OSA Journal of Optical Communications and Networking, vol. 10, no. 9, pp. 736–748, 2018.

[26] Y. Zhao, Y. Li, W. Wang, *et al.*, "Experimental demonstration of VM designation in hybrid cloud-fog computing with software-defined optical networking," ACP2016, Wuhan, China, November 2016.

[27] I. Abdullahi, S. Arif and S. Hassan, "Ubiquitous shift with information centric network caching using fog computing," Computational Intelligence in Information Systems, Brunei, Darussalam, pp. 327–335, 2014.

[28] X. Hou, Y. Li, M. Chen, *et al.*, "Vehicular fog computing: A viewpoint of vehicles as the infrastructures," IEEE Transactions on Vehicular Technology, vol. 65, no. 6, pp. 3860–3873, 2016.

[29] A. Darabseh, M. Al-Ayyoub, Y. Jararweh, *et al.*, "SDStorage: A software defined storage experimental framework," IEEE IC2E, March 2015, pp. 341–346.

[30] A. Darabseh, M. Al-Ayyoub, Y. Jararweh, *et al.*, "SDSecurity: A software defined security experimental framework," 2015 IEEE International Conference on Communication Workshop (ICCW), June 2015, pp. 1871–1876.

[31] J. Al-Badarneh, Y. Jararweh, M. Al-Ayyoub, *et al.*, "Software defined storage for cooperative mobile edge computing systems," 2017 Fourth International Conference on Software Defined Systems (SDS), Valencia, 2017, pp. 174–179.

[32] G. Pedro, M. Alberto, E. Dick, *et al.*, "Edge-centric computing: Vision and challenges," ACM SIGCOMM Computer Communication Review, vol. 45, no. 5, pp. 37–42, 2015.

[33] C. Long, Y. Cao, T. Jiang and Q. Zhang, "Edge computing framework for cooperative video processing in multimedia IoT systems," IEEE Transactions on Multimedia, vol. 20, no. 5, pp. 1126–1139, 2018.

[34] T. X. Tran, P. Pandey, A. Hajisami and D. Pompili, "Collaborative multi-bitrate video caching and processing in mobile-edge computing networks," 2017 13th Annual Conference on Wireless On-demand Network Systems and Services (WONS), Jackson, WY, 2017, pp. 165–172.

[35] Q. Li, H. Niu, A. Papathanassiou and G. Wu, "Edge cloud and underlay networks: Empowering 5G cell-less wireless architecture," Proceedings of European Wireless 2014, Berlin, Germany, May 2014, pp. 676–681.

[36] M. Peng, S. Yan, K. Zhang and C. Wang, "Fog-computing-based radio access networks: Issues and challenges," IEEE Networks, vol. 30, no. 4, pp. 46–53, 2016.

[37] R. Tandon and O. Simeone, "Harnessing cloud and edge synergies: Toward an information theory of fog radio access networks," IEEE Communications Magazine, vol. 54, no. 8, pp. 44–50, 2016.

[38] X. Li, X. Wang, K. Li and V. C. M. Leung, "CaaS: Caching as a service for 5G networks," IEEE Access, vol. 5, pp. 5982–5993, 2017.

[39] K. Zhang, S. Leng, Y. He, S. Maharjan and Y. Zhang, "Cooperative content caching in 5G networks with mobile edge computing," IEEE Wireless Communications, vol. 25, no. 3, pp. 80–87, 2018.

[40] Z. Xu, H. Gupta and U. Ramachandran, "STTR: A system for tracking all vehicles all the time at the edge of the network," Proceedings of the 12th ACM International Conference on Distributed and Event-based Systems. ACM, 2018, pp. 124–135.

[41] D. Y. Zhang, Q. Li, H. Tong, J. Badilla, Y. Zhang and D. Wang, "Crowdsourcing-based copyright infringement detection in live video streams," Proceedings of the 2018 IEEE/ACM International Conference on Advances in Social Networks Analysis and Mining 2018, 2018.

[42] Y. Zhang, N. Vance, D. Zhang and D. Wang, "Optimizing online task allocation for multi-attribute social sensing," The 27th International Conference on Computer Communications and Networks (ICCCN 2018). IEEE, 2018.

[43] C. Huang and D. Wang, "Topic-aware social sensing with arbitrary source dependency graphs," Proceedings of the 15th International Conference on Information Processing in Sensor Networks. IEEE Press, 2016, p. 7.

[44] D. Zhang, Y. Ma, C. Zheng, et al., "Cooperative-competitive task allocation in edge computing for delay-sensitive social sensing," 2018 IEEE/ACM Symposium on Edge Computing (SEC), Seattle, WA, 2018, pp. 243–259.

[45] Q. Zhang, X. Zhang, Q. Zhang, et al., "Firework: Big data sharing and processing in collaborative edge environment," 2016 Fourth IEEE Workshop on Hot Topics in Web Systems and Technologies (HotWeb), Washington, DC, 2016, pp. 20–25.

[46] C. Prazeres and M. Serrano, "SOFT-IoT: Self-organizing fog of things," 30th International Conference on Advanced Information Networking and

Applications Workshops (WAINA), Crans-Montana, Switzerland, March 2016.

[47] S. Yi, Z. Hao, Z. Qin and Q. Li, "Fog Computing: Platform and Applications," 2015 Third IEEE Workshop on Hot Topics in Web Systems and Technologies (HotWeb), 2015, pp. 73–78.

[48] Y. Xiong, Y. Sun, L. Xing and Y. Huang, "Extend Cloud to Edge with KubeEdge," 2018 IEEE/ACM Symposium on Edge Computing (SEC), Seattle, WA, 2018, pp. 373–377.

[49] Amazon Web Services, "AWS Greengrass Developer Guide," https://docs. aws.amazon.com/greengrass/latest/developerguide/gg-dg.pdf, 2018. [Online; Accessed July 2018].

[50] Microsoft Azure, "Azure IoT Edge Documentation," https://docs.microsoft. com/en-us/azure/iot-edge/, 2018. [Online; Accessed July 2018].

[51] "Message Queuing Telemetry Transport," http://mqtt.org/, 2018. [Online; Accessed July 2018].

[52] A. Das, S. Patterson and M. Wittie, "EdgeBench: Benchmarking edge computing platforms," 2018 IEEE/ACM International Conference on Utility and Cloud Computing Companion (UCC Companion), Zurich, 2018, pp. 175–180.

Chapter 12
Serverless architecture for edge computing
Bahman Javadi[1], Jingtao Sun[2] and Rajiv Ranjan[3]

12.1 Introduction

Growth in adoption of various technologies including smartphones and Internet of things (IoT) [1] has been unprecedented in recent years, and as a result, a vast amount of public and private data sources are available for organizations, which leverage them in the form of smart applications [2, 3]. These applications incorporate data-driven, actionable insights into the user experience and gradually are becoming part of daily life [4]. For example, smart cities' applications enable efficient management of a number of urban aspects such as real-time monitoring of loads on the bridges, which affect the bridge lifetime and maintenance costs and noise monitoring providing evidence of illegal works being carried out or public order disturbances that should demand immediate action from authorities [5, 6]. In another example, autonomous vehicles carry many IoT sensors to enable safe navigation without human intervention [7]. What all these applications have in common is the need for advanced data analytics and machine learning algorithms which are normally hosted in cloud computing infrastructures. The drawback of the cloud is high communication latency between the points where data are generated and the location where the analysis is needed to be done [8]. To address this challenge and provide better quality of experience for users, *Edge Computing* has emerged [9], in which computing and storage nodes are placed at the network's edge in close proximity to users.

Gartner estimated that, by 2022, about 75% of data will be created and processed outside traditional, centralized data centers or cloud computing systems, up from currently less than 10% [10]. This is the main driver for enterprises and organizations to integrate edge computing into their projects in the next few years. The global edge computing market size is projected to reach USD3.24 billion by 2025 where the Asia-Pacific is estimated to have the highest growth during the forecast period, according to a study conducted by Grand View Research, Inc. [11].

There is a hard line between the edge and the cloud parts of smart applications in terms of responsibilities, design and runtime considerations. Contemporary solutions

[1]School of Computer, Data and Mathematical Sciences, Western Sydney University, Sydney, Australia
[2]National Institute of Informatics, Tokyo, Japan
[3]School of Computing Science, Newcastle University, UK

for cloud-supported real-time data analytics mostly apply analytics techniques in a rigid bottom-up approach regardless of the data's origin. Having data analytics on the edge forces developers to resort to *ad hoc* solutions specifically tailored to the available infrastructure. The process is largely manual, task-specific and error-prone and usually requires good knowledge of the underlying infrastructure [12]. Consequently, when faced with large-scale, heterogeneous resource pools, performing effective data analytics is difficult. Moreover, the inherent decentralization in edge computing raises the complexity in traceability and integrity of user data [13]. So, while users are getting better experience in terms of response time and scalability in smart applications, there is less control for users to audit and trace the data in distributed edge computing environments and more challenges to meet any required regulatory compliance (e.g., European General Data Protection Regulation (GDPR) [14]). This opens up a new challenge regarding programming models for edge-cloud computing.

In order to address the challenge of complexity in the new edge-cloud computing, *Serverless Computing* [15] could be a potential solution. Serverless computing emerged as a solution for the complexity of cloud platforms and consists of services where users only provide the computing code that needs to be executed and cloud providers manage all the infrastructure and platforms that enable code execution [15]. So, having serverless model to develop smart applications for edge-cloud computing environments could improve the productivity of the application developers.

In this chapter, we will review various aspects of edge computing and serverless computing and present a new framework to integrate them. The rest of this chapter is organized as follows. In Section 12.2, we will review the architecture and characterization of edge computing. The detailed specifications and architecture of serverless computing are presented in Section 12.3. We will propose a conceptual architecture for serverless edge computing with a sample case study in Section 12.4. The future research and open problems are discussed in Section 12.5, followed by conclusions in Section 12.6.

12.2   Edge computing

The proven economic benefits of cloud computing led to its widespread adoption and presence in the current and foreseeable future in the computing landscape [16]. To circumvent the latency limitation for smart applications in clouds and to enable better data privacy, the concept of *edge computing* [9] has emerged. This technology promises to deliver responsive computing services, scalability, privacy enforcement and the ability to mask transient cloud outages [17]. Examples of edge devices are small servers hosted by clients on-premises, network routers and single-board computers (e.g., Raspberry Pis). As a beneficial side effect, this extra layer of computation helps to hide cloud outages from the user applications. This concept is illustrated in Figure 12.1.

The edge has some distinctive characteristics that make it more appropriate for applications requiring low latency, mobility support, real-time interactions, online

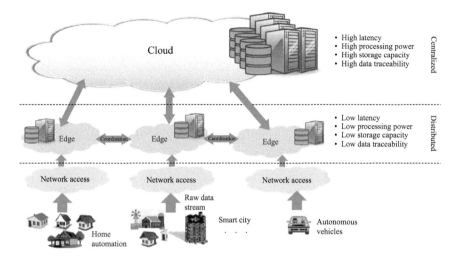

Figure 12.1   Edge and cloud computing platform for smart applications

analytics and interplay with the cloud [18]. Instead of sending all data to the cloud, an edge device or software solution may perform a preliminary analysis and send a summary of the data (or metadata) to the cloud. The benefits of edge computing are countered by the rise of new challenges regarding the need for coordination between edge and cloud, its underlying resources and capabilities. Furthermore, as now the data can be distributed and moved across edge devices, issues arise with data integrity and traceability of changes.

12.2.1   Characteristics of edge computing

Edge computing can be considered as an extension of older technologies such as peer-to-peer networking, distributed data, self-healing network technology and remote cloud services. It can provide several advantages over traditional centralized cloud architectures such as optimizing resource usage in a cloud computing system and reducing network traffic, which reduces the risk of a data bottleneck. Edge computing also improves security and privacy by encrypting data closer to the network core and keeps the private data away from shared cloud environments [19].

In order to have a better view, Table 12.1 compares edge computing with cloud computing for various characteristic. As the data are collected and pre-processed, in the edge prior to offloading to the cloud, the amount of transmitted data is much less than the data collected by IoT devices. Also, the data analytics on the edge can be real time while the analytics on the cloud is normally offline. Edge generally has limited computing power and storage, with lower network latency in contrast to the cloud. The edge offers a high level of fault tolerance as the jobs can be migrated to the other edge in the vicinity in the event of a failure which is an important factor for smart applications as the reliability is one of the main requirements.

Table 12.1   Edge computing vs. cloud computing

Characteristic	Edge	Cloud
Processing hierarchy	Local data analytics	Global data analytics
Processing fashion	In-stream processing	Batch processing
Computing power	GFLOPS	TFLOPS
Network latency	Milliseconds	Seconds
Data storage	Gigabytes	Infinite
Data lifetime	Hours/days	Infinite
Fault tolerance	High	High
Processing resources	Heterogeneous (e.g., CPU, GPU and TPU)	Homogeneous (data center)
Versatility	Only exists on demand	Intangible servers
Provisioning	Limited by the number of edges in the vicinity	Infinite, with latency
Mobility of nodes	Maybe mobile	None
Cost model	Pay once	Pay-as-you-go
Power model	Battery-powered/electricity	Electricity

Edge nodes may employ various types of hardware such as computing boards (e.g., Raspberry Pis), multicore processor, GPU or TPU* with fine granularity versus a cluster of homogenous nodes in the cloud [20]. Each edge device employs fixed hardware resources that can be configured by the user for each application, whereas the allocated resources are mainly intangible and out of user's control in the cloud. An advantage of edge is the ability of integration to mobile IoT nodes which is essential for many smart applications [21]. In this case, multiple edge devices in close proximity dynamically build a subsystem in which edge devices can communicate and exchange data. Cloud offers a proven economic model of pay-as-you-go while edge is a property of the user. There are some cloud providers that also provide edge services as well such as AWS Greengrass [22] and Azure IoT Edge [23]. Edge devices can possibly be battery operated, so they need to be energy-efficient while the cloud needs electrical power supply with energy-efficient resource management.

12.3   Serverless computing

Serverless computing or Function as a Service (FaaS) [15] is a computing model where clients can specify fragments of computing code (or functions) that need to be executed in response to a request from applications or IoT sensors. What makes the FaaS model particularly attractive is that the underlying hardware and software stack is completely hidden to cloud clients, freeing them from the burden of managing virtual machines, containers, web servers and programming frameworks.

---

*https://cloud.google.com/tpu/

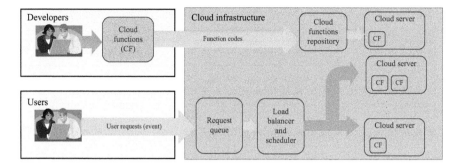

Figure 12.2   Serverless computing architecture

There is a lot of misunderstandings and ambiguities about the serverless especially with the name. Servers are still required for data processing and execution of functions, the only difference here is that the developers are not particularly concerned regarding the management of those servers and their related hardware [24]. Decisions regarding the number of servers count and their respective capacity is handled by the serverless platform, where the capacity of the server is automatically adjusted as per the need of the workload. Due to this flexibility, the computation is in the form of a function which is stateless, hence it in not known from where it is going to execute [24]. In order to distinguish serverless computing from the traditional cloud computing model, we refer to the latter as *server-aware* computing.

Event processing system is one of the core functionalities of a serverless platform, as shown in Figure 12.2. User requests in the form of events trigger the process to execute a cloud function (CF). These functions are already implemented by the developers and ready to be executed. There is a request queue where a load balancer can take each request one by one and provide a cloud server to execute the specific function. Each cloud server executes the CF in a sandbox to provide function isolation [25]. For the first execution, cloud server needs to fetch the CF from a function repository and keeps it for future execution. As can be seen in Figure 12.2, there is a scheduler which can work with the load balancer to allocate the functions to each cloud server and mange stopping and releasing resources for idle functions.

There are a number of serverless platforms available on commercial cloud providers as listed in Table 12.2. They support majority of the programming languages for function developments as well as several methods to handle the events to trigger the functions. All cloud providers have a similar pricing to charge for serverless computing. The model has three main components, namely the number of function requests or invocations; how long the function runs for; and the size of used memory. This pricing model is more complex than server-aware services as this is only charged for the execution of the functions. This could potentially save the application costs as there will be no charge for the idle time. However, there is a charge for the number of invocations that might increase the total cost for serverless applications [26].

Table 12.2   Commercial serverless platforms

Provider	Languages	Execution model
AWS Lambda	Node.js, Java, Python, C#, Ruby, PowerShell, Go	Maximum of 15 minutes, 1,000 executions at a time
Google Cloud Functions	Node.js, Python, Go	Maximum of 1 minute, 1,000 executions at a time
Azure Functions	Node.js, Java, Python, C#, PHP, F#	Maximum of 5 minutes, unlimited executions
IBM Cloud Functions	Node.js, Java, Python, Ruby, Swift	Maximum of 10 minutes, 1,000 executions at a time
Alibaba Function Compute	Node.js, Java, Python, C#, PHP, Go	Maximum of 10 minutes, 100 executions at a time

In contract to server-aware services, serverless functions can only run for a limited duration. As listed in Table 12.2, each function execution for commercial cloud providers varied between 1 and 15 minutes. Moreover, the number of concurrent executions of the same function is limited [27].

12.3.1   Characteristics of serverless computing

There are number of profound and distinguishing characteristics about serverless platforms that developers need to be aware about them before choosing it as a platform for deploying the code or applications. We will review the most important ones in the following:

- **Performance and limits:** There are various limits implied on the serverless code executed, including the number of requests at a single unit of time, maximum limit of CPU usage and memory available for the function. Some limits can be increased as per the requirement of the users, such as increment in the number of requests threshold. Moreover, in some commercial cloud platforms such as Google Cloud Functions, there is possibility of increasing the execution time up to 9 minutes (see Table 12.2).
- **Monetary cost:** In traditional cloud computing platform, servers are always ready to process the requests. The constant server availability leads to high money costs in the monthly bill, irrespective to the amount of usage of memory and CPU time. In contrast, when serverless functions are executed then the users have to pay only for the resources, which is a key aspect of the serverless platform. The resources which are generally metered are CPU, memory based on the pricing models as determined by the cloud providers.
- **Programming model:** Since the serverless platforms are built for automatic scaling, they have a tailored programming model. To enhance the scaling, the function state is not maintained by the serverless functions between the executions. In fact, the developer can update and retrieve any state as per the requirement by writing the code in the function. As per the current scenario, serverless

platform execute only a single main function with a number of inputs and outputs.

- **Programming languages:** Serverless platform supports major programming languages such as Python, C#, Java, JavaScript, Swift, Pearl, Ruby and Go (see Table 12.2). Moreover, most of available platforms can support integration of any programming languages using Docker containers.
- **Composability:** The serverless platform generally supports invocations of one serverless function from another serverless one (nested functions). Moreover, there is demand for new tools to compose a large number of serverless functions in a bigger application [28]. AWS Step Functions [29] is one of the available services which can help to coordinate multiple serverless functions to create a workflow for smart applications.
- **Accounting and security:** Since the serverless platforms are multi-tenant, there is a need to isolate the function executions for different users. The current approach is to use containers to run each function [25]. As the functions are completely isolated, accounting details can be provided to the users so that it becomes easy for them to understand how much they are required to pay for each service.

12.4 Combining serverless and edge computing

While serverless architecture is becoming popular in cloud computing, this model introduces certain constraints in the functions that make them impractical to be adopted for edge computing [30]. Among these limitations, there is provider-imposed time-outs for function execution, lack of support for stateful applications and limits on the amount of computation and memory that a given function can consume [15].

There is very limited work about extending serverless capabilities to edge computing and early attempts were developed in the form of conceptual models [31, 32], but without demonstration of the viability of the concepts. There are also some research related to the mobile edge computing [33] and using serverless functions for computation offloading on edge [34, 35].

One key aspect still to be addressed is the *complexity* required to manage and operate existing edge platforms. For example, StreamSight, one of the simplest platforms that has been developed with ease of use as a core concept, still requires two highly skilled professionals (one DevOps and one software developer) for its operation [36]. Recent work in this area revealed that providing a programming model to reduce the complexity for the application developers is essential, especially for data-centric applications [37].

Figure 12.3 depicts a conceptual framework which forms a layer between end users and the infrastructure (i.e., edge nodes and cloud servers). It performs a number of tasks on behalf of end users, as listed in the figure. Users only interact with the user workbench and the rest of the architecture is transparent, so the whole framework is presented as a serverless architecture for users. In this architecture, user workbench is a studio-like interface that facilitates the development and execution

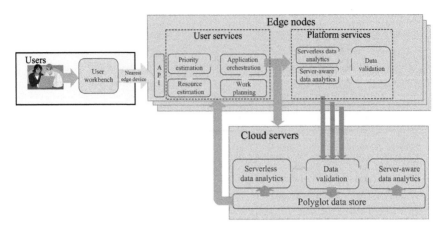

Figure 12.3   Serverless edge computing platform

of smart applications. Here, users express the application(s) to be executed, their relationship (such as dependency in computation and data) and their requirements. This is converted in a complete execution plan containing what needs to be executed, where (cloud or edge and within each in which resource), and what data protection mechanisms will apply. In the following, we will explain each component in detail.

12.4.1   User services

This is a component of edge nodes and will be an interface to users and the server functionalities. We explain each module in the following:

- **Priority estimation:** In this task, the functional structure of smart applications to create an application profile will be identified. The functions applied to data for each process will be determined using various methods including static code analysis or profiling previous runs. As a result, a blueprint of commonly used functions will be archived for use and the "building blocks" of such functions will be cataloged. The catalog will contain information about the function (its effect, input and output) and the applications that use them. Once these functions are known, they will be profiled so there is a good understanding of how they perform across different types of cloud and edge resources. With these data in hand, statistical characterization of such functions will be developed to support optimization and heuristic algorithms of other tasks.
- **Resource estimation:** Edge devices are heterogeneous by nature. They can go from fully computing servers under control of the user to network routers and even smart devices that have limited memory capacity. The amount of work that can be carried out in the edge depends on the capacity of available devices, and it can vary over time. Therefore, in this part, there will be methods to determine the capability of available edge devices. This will involve cataloging these devices, determining what characteristics (metrics) are relevant for each type of edge device and how

this information can be obtained. Techniques for aggregation, and potentially normalization, of this information will also be needed in this component.

- **Work planning:** In this component, algorithms that make selection of cloud resources will be developed. These algorithms will analyze the capabilities of different cloud and edge resources (the latter enabled by resource estimation module) and the resource requirements of the functions that users want to carry out and will select the number, size and type of machines according to user-defined criteria, including cost, energy consumption on the edge, network latency and execution time. This is a multi-objective optimization problem, and solutions could be developed using techniques such as Mixed Integer Linear Programming.

- **Application orchestration:** The objective of this component is to enable functions to be combined to form new smart applications. Applications will then be stored as graphs whose vertices represent the functions and the edges represent dependencies between them. Notice that they differ from traditional scientific workflows because, the latter are represented as *acyclic graphs*, whereas many smart applications require functions to be repeated until specific conditions are reached. Service composition techniques and ontologies (for function description) should be utilized to enable the system to make sense of the objectives of processes so they are cataloged for future use and to establish the control structures that need to be executed alongside the functions (such as loops, branching and conditional execution). As part of this component, the most commonly used functions identified in Priority Estimation will be optimized to leverage edge capabilities. In particular, we will analyze how data are acquired and computed and how the patterns of computation and data transfer are affected by the existence of resources in the edge or in the cloud. It means looking for manners in which data transfer is minimized and data are likely to be available in the preferred resource type for the function. The main objective of this task is to reduce the latency and consequently processing time of individual functions.

12.4.2 Platform services

This is the second component of edge nodes and will be an interface to cloud services. In order to do that, we need new methods to remove the main barriers of serverless computing to compose the application execution into two parts of serverless and server-aware. Selecting and offloading of different modules and functions of smart applications will be done in the User Service component for both edge and cloud resources. In another words, Platform Services will be given a set of functions to be executed using the following modules:

- **Serverless data analytics:** This module is responsible to execute serverless functions which have been identified in the User Service component. These functions are stateless and require short execution time. However, they are part of a bigger application which might need other functions to be executed with longer execution time and stateful, so we need another module to handle that.

- **Server-aware data analytics:** This module is responsible to execute server-aware functions which have been identified in the User Service component. These functions are stateful and require long execution time. This module is particularly useful if the application is latency-sensitive to execute the functions to process data and send it back to users.

- **Data validation:** Combining serverless and server-aware functions require synchronizations and state storages which will be handled in this module. The main challenge for this module is to have a high-performance storage to store and retrieve the application states which could be updated by serverless and server-aware functions.

12.4.3   Cloud service

As mentioned earlier, due to resource limitations in the edge nodes we need to use cloud servers to execute most components of smart applications. As can be seen in Figure 12.3, Cloud Servers also has the same components as the Platform Services in the edge nodes. This is mainly to run serverless and server-aware functions which cannot be handled by the edge modes or they need more resources which are not available on the edge. For instance, training of machine learning models with large data sets cannot be run on edge nodes, so it could be executed as a server-aware component on the Cloud. Also, Data Validation module is responsible to manage the data synchronizations between serverless and server-aware functions in Cloud Servers. Another important aspect of the framework is the way data is handled. The cloud storage is polyglot, by which we mean that the platform will support both traditional relational databases and no-SQL databases which are relevant for many smart applications. While the edge nodes also have some storage capabilities, the data storage is mainly located on the Cloud due to better scalability, reliability and security.

12.4.4   Case study

In this section, we will provide a sample smart application to reveal how serverless edge computing can be used in practice. This application is about smart nutrition monitoring system to enable users to measure and analyze their food intake [38]. Healthy eating habits are considered a major factor for people to maintain a healthy life. Unawareness of what constitutes healthy eating can cause health problems, obesity or overweight. Because of this, there is a need for nutrition monitoring systems that maintain and improve people's health by monitoring what types of foods they are eating daily or in a fixed period. In order to improve public health, these systems need not only to monitor and analyze different types of foods, but also provide necessary advice to users about their meals. While there are several solutions to use various technologies for diet management, most of them are impractical for self-monitoring, largely due to participant burden and low scalability, and rely heavily on user memory and recall [39, 40].

Considering an open challenge to design a noninvasive solution to monitor nutrition intake in real-life scenarios with a high degree of accuracy, we developed a

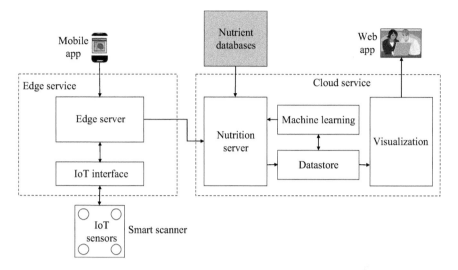

Figure 12.4 Serverless edge computing architecture for smart nutrition system

prototype of smart nutrition monitoring system [38]. The start point of this approach is a *Smart Scanner* where users deposit their dish with the food. The smart scanner contains a number of IoT sensors including smart scale, molecular sensors and an array of cameras. It recorded the weight of the dish and uploaded the photos and a time stamp to a cloud server for processing and analysis.

The proposed serverless edge computing architecture for smart nutrition monitoring system is depicted in Figure 12.4. The system architecture has interface to the end users through different services. The main interface is a mobile application enabling registration and access to the smart scanner. The user authentication will be handled using edge service's API through the mobile app. The other component of the system interface is a web application which provides data visualization to users.

The Edge Service is the central component of the architecture and will be implemented as serverless functions. It interfaces with mobile devices, smart scanner and the cloud services. Internally, this service contains two components. The first is the IoT Interface module whose role is to interface with the sensors in a number of existing interfaces (e.g., MQTT and Bluetooth). The IoT devices interact with the second component, the edge server. The edge server is responsible for authorizing users to scan and aggregate input from sensors, submit the data to the cloud for storage, and trigger the food recognition and analysis. The edge server compromises a set of serverless functions where they will be triggered by the smart scanner in the event of new scan requests by users. In the current implementation, there are two serverless functions, one for user authentication and another one for data collection from the sensors. The user authentication function will call another serverless function in the Cloud Service to complete the user verification.

The Cloud Service supports two types of activities. The first is the activities that are computationally demanding to be executed on mobile devices or on the edge, but at the same time are not latency-sensitive, such as the machine learning for food detection. The second type of activities is related to data storage and visualization. The nutrition server is responsible to communicate to the edge service and store the data in the database. This will be using a serverless function which will be executed on cloud platform. Machine learning component is a model for food recognition where it uses the food image as an input and provides the list of ingredients as the output to the nutrition server. These ingredients will be translated to the nutritional information using API calls to external nutrient databases (e.g., FatSecret). Since, machine learning training needs long execution time and must be stateful, we use server-aware service to implement that.

Adoption of edge computing in this architecture will enable users to have more flexibility and scalability in terms of applications and services. For the smart food scanner, we adopted several sensors which interfacing them with a mobile phone is challenging, or even impossible due to unavailability of technologies. Edge computing enables us to create a loosely coupled architecture and improve and modify the food scanner system with no impact on user devices and their capabilities. Moreover, offloading the computations and communications to the edge will help to decrease the power consumption and storage usage on the mobile phones and improve the usability of the proposed system.

12.5   Future research and open problems

There are several research works that can be done to complete a full serverless architecture for edge computing. We will review some of the important open problems in the following.

12.5.1   Resource model

One of the main limitations of the current serverless frameworks is to limit applications to specific execution time and memory size [30]. This hinders extending the framework to other type of resources on edge and cloud. The challenge is to make a trade-off of simplicity for developers to be able to have more options in resource selection while keeping the spirit of serverless intact so that they can run applications with less resource overhead. As mentioned in previous section, one approach to solve this challenge is to profile the application and log the requirements of the basic blocks for future execution on other resources.

12.5.2   Function orchestration

While applications are running on edge-cloud systems, all serverless functions will be executed independently which possibly need data storage and data communication to complete their tasks within the applications [15]. This challenge could be solved by having an orchestration unit to provide data dependencies for applications while they are running on edge and cloud resources. There will be a number of open researches to investigate the efficiency and performance of such orchestrations with various centralized and decentralized architectures on different type of data-intensive and computation-intensive applications.

12.5.3 State storage

One of the main features of the serverless frameworks is to have stateless functions. To overcome with this issue, we need to save the state of each function for the next function. This requires a fast and low-latency storage system [28]. Since applications could have a large number of functions, this storage should be relatively cheap to keep the execution cost as low as possible. One approach could be in-memory service which can be allocated and deallocated automatically during the application execution.

12.5.4 Communication model

In the edge-cloud computing environments, we have some functions running on edge and some of them running of the cloud. Given these functions need to communicate during the execution, we might have a large number of messages on the local and interconnection networks. Since we are not able to select the location of severs to run the functions, these communication patterns might impose significant overhead on the communication network, especially between edge and cloud. The possible approach for this challenge is to propose a communication optimization model to use the application profile to do dynamic resource allocation to reduce the network overhead.

12.5.5 Pricing model

One of the issues for serverless applications is the current pricing model which is based on the duration and amount of resources that each function consumed [25]. This could lead to a very expensive execution compared with server-aware applications [26]. Having a better pricing model for applications to combine both serverless and server-aware functions is essential. One approach could be using profiling to see the behavior of each function and use the more appropriate resource in the next runs.

12.5.6 Security

While there are a number of security challenges in serverless and edge computing environments, the main security issue to be addressed is to make sure that both serverless and server-aware components are able to be executed in edge servers or cloud servers with no data leakage [28]. Edge nodes can be managed and maintained by users or third parties, which makes it more challenging to control the security requirements. Moreover, since we need to compose the application from a number of small functions and these functions could be executed in any server on edge or cloud, the application security analysis will be quite complex.

12.6 Conclusions

In this chapter, we present a review over two emerging technologies, namely edge computing and serverless computing. Both technologies have great potential to be extended and adopted in next few years for development of smart applications. In addition, there are many cloud providers working toward enabling users to get benefit from these services. We strongly believe that combining these two technologies provides a number of benefits for developers to be able to use the edge-cloud computing systems with less complexity and effort. We presented a conceptual framework along with a case study to show how the serverless edge computing architecture can help to develop smart applications. There are several technical challenges that should be investigated in this area, which we have presented as the open questions for future work.

References

[1] J. Gubbi, R. Buyya, S. Marusic, and M. Palaniswami, "Internet of Things (IoT): A vision, architectural elements, and future directions," *Future Generation Computer Systems*, vol. 29, no. 7, pp. 1645–1660, 2013.

[2] K. Liu, A. Gurudutt, T. Kamaal, C. Divakara, and P. Prabhakaran, "Edge computing framework for distributed smart applications," in *2017 IEEE SmartWorld, Ubiquitous Intelligence & Computing, Advanced & Trusted Computed, Scalable Computing & Communications, Cloud & Big Data Computing, Internet of People and Smart City Innovation (SmartWorld/ SCALCOM/UIC/ATC/CBDCom/IOP/SCI)*, 2017, pp. 1–8.

[3] N. Bessis and C. Dobre, *Big Data and Internet of Things: A Roadmap for Smart Environments*. Basel, Switzerland, Springer, 2014.

[4] *Smart Applications: Deliver Insights in Context*. Available: https://pivotal. io/smart-applications

[5] A. Zanella, N. Bui, A. Castellani, L. Vangelista, and M. Zorzi, "Internet of Things for smart cities," *IEEE Internet of Things Journal*, vol. 1, no. 1, pp. 22–32, 2014.

[6] H. Arasteh, V. Hosseinnezhad, V. Loia, and A. Tommasetti, "IoT-based smart cities: A survey," in *2016 IEEE 16th International Conference on Environment and Electrical Engineering (EEEIC)*, Florence, Italy, 2016, pp. 1–6: IEEE.

[7] H. Khayyam, B. Javadi, M. Jalili, and R.N. Jazar, "Artificial intelligence and Internet of things for autonomous vehicles," in *Nonlinear Approaches in Engineering Applications*. Basel, Switzerland, Springer, 2020, pp. 39–68.

[8] B. Zhang, N. Mor, J. Kolb, *et al.*, "The cloud is not enough: Saving IoT from the cloud," in *7th {USENIX} Workshop on Hot Topics in Cloud Computing (HotCloud 15)*, 2015.

[9] M. Satyanarayanan, "The emergence of edge computing," *Computer*, vol. 50, no. 1, pp. 30–39, 2017.

[10] R. Meulen, "What edge computing means for infrastructure and operations leaders," Gartner, October 2018.

[11] "Edge computing market size, share: Global Industry Report 2016–2025," Grand View Research, March 2018.

[12] F. Mehdipour, B. Javadi, and A. Mahanti, "FOG-Engine: Towards big data analytics in the fog," in *2016 IEEE 14th Intl Conf on Dependable, Autonomic and Secure Computing, 14th Intl Conf on Pervasive Intelligence and Computing, 2nd Intl Conf on Big Data Intelligence and Computing and Cyber Science and Technology Congress (DASC/PiCom/DataCom/CyberSciTech)*, 2016, pp. 640–646.

[13] B. Varghese, M. Villari, O. Rana, *et al.*, "Realizing edge marketplaces: challenges and opportunities," *IEEE Cloud Computing*, vol. 5, no. 6, pp. 9–20, 2018.

[14] *General Data Protection Regulation (GDPR)*. Available: https://gdpr-info.eu/

[15] I. Baldini, P. C. Castro, K. Shih-Ping Chang, *et al.*, "Serverless computing: Current trends and open problems," in *Research Advances in Cloud Computing*, S. Chaudhary, G. Somani, and R. Buyya, Eds. Singapore: Springer Singapore, 2017, pp. 1–20.

[16] F. Etro, "The economics of cloud computing," in *Cloud Technology: Concepts, Methodologies, Tools, and Applications*. IGI Global, USA, 2015, pp. 2135–2148.

[17] P. Hu, S. Dhelim, H. Ning, and T. Qiu, "Survey on fog computing: Architecture, key technologies, applications and open issues," *Journal of Network and Computer Applications*, vol. 98, pp. 27–42, 2017.

[18] M. Satyanarayanan, P. Simoens, Yu Xiao, *et al.*, "Edge analytics in the Internet of things," *IEEE Pervasive Computing*, vol. 14, no. 2, pp. 24–31, 2015.

[19] M.M. Kwame-Lante Wright, U. Chadha, and B. Krishnamachari, "SmartEdge: A smart contract for edge computing," presented at the 1st International Workshop on Blockchain for the Internet of Things, 2018.

[20] F. Mehdipour, B. Javadi, A. Mahanti, and G. Ramirez-Prado, "Fog Computing Realization for Big Data Analytics," in *Fog and Edge Computing: Principles and Paradigms*. John Wiley & Sons, USA, 2019, pp. 259–290.

[21] C. Pereira, A. Pinto, D. Ferreira, and A. Aguiar, "Experimental characterization of mobile IoT application latency," *IEEE Internet of Things Journal*, vol. 4, no. 4, pp. 1082–1094, 2017.

[22] *AWS IoT Greengrass*. Available: https://aws.amazon.com/greengrass/

[23] *Azure IoT Edge*. Available: https://docs.microsoft.com/en-us/azure/iot-edge/

[24] S. Hendrickson, S. Sturdevant, T. Harter, V. Venkataramani, A.C. Arpaci-Dusseau, and R.H. Arpaci-Dusseau, "Serverless computation with openlambda," in *8th {USENIX} Workshop on Hot Topics in Cloud Computing (HotCloud 16)*, 2016.

[25] L. Wang, M. Li, Y. Zhang, T. Ristenpart, and M. Swift, "Peeking behind the curtains of serverless platforms," in *2018 {USENIX} Annual Technical Conference ({USENIX}{ATC} 18)*, 2018, pp. 133–146.

[26] Q. Pu, S. Venkataraman, and I. Stoica, "Shuffling, fast and slow: Scalable analytics on serverless infrastructure," in *16th {USENIX} Symposium on Networked Systems Design and Implementation ({NSDI} 19)*, 2019, pp. 193–206.

[27] G. McGrath and P.R. Brenner, "Serverless computing: Design, implementation, and performance," in *2017 IEEE 37th International Conference on Distributed Computing Systems Workshops (ICDCSW)*, 2017, pp. 405–410: IEEE.

[28] E. Jonas, J. Schleier-Smith, V. Sreekanti, *et al.*, "Cloud programming simplified: A Berkeley view on serverless computing," *arXiv preprint arXiv:1902.03383*, 2019.

[29] *AWS Step Functions*. Available: https://aws.amazon.com/step-functions/

[30] J.M. Hellerstein, J. Faleiro, J. E. Gonzalez, and J. Schleier-Smith, "Serverless computing: One step forward, two steps back," *arXiv preprint arXiv:1812.03651*, 2018.

[31] S. Nastic and S. Dustdar, "Towards deviceless edge computing: Challenges, design aspects, and models for serverless paradigm at the edge," in *The Essence of Software Engineering*. Basel, Switzerland, Springer, 2018, pp. 121–136.

[32] S. Nastic, T. Rausch, O. Scekic, *et al.*, "A serverless real-time data analytics platform for edge computing," *IEEE Internet Computing*, vol. 21, no. 4, pp. 64–71, 2017.

[33] P. Mach and Z. Becvar, "Mobile edge computing: A survey on architecture and computation offloading," *IEEE Communications Surveys & Tutorials*, vol. 19, no. 3, pp. 1628–1656, 2017.

[34] L. Baresi, D.F. Mendonça, and M. Garriga, "Empowering low-latency applications through a serverless edge computing architecture," in *European Conference on Service-Oriented and Cloud Computing*, 2017, pp. 196–210: Springer.

[35] X. Chen, L. Jiao, W. Li, and X. Fu, "Efficient multi-user computation offloading for mobile-edge cloud computing," *IEEE/ACM Transactions on Networking*, vol. 24, no. 5, pp. 2795–2808, 2015.

[36] Z. Georgiou, M. Symeonides, D. Trihinas, G. Pallis, and M.D. Dikaiakos, "StreamSight: A query-driven framework for streaming analytics in edge computing," in *2018 IEEE/ACM 11th International Conference on Utility and Cloud Computing (UCC)*, 2018, pp. 143–152.

[37] B. Cheng, J. Fürst, G. Solmaz, and T. Sanada, "Fog function: serverless fog computing for data intensive IoT services," *arXiv preprint arXiv:1907.08278*, 2019.

[38] B. Javadi, R.N. Calheiros, K.M. Matawie, A. Ginige, and A. Cook, "Smart nutrition monitoring system using heterogeneous Internet of Things platform," in *Internet and Distributed Computing Systems*. Fiji: Springer International Publishing, 2018, pp. 63–74.

[39] G. Rateni, P. Dario, and F. Cavallo, "Smartphone-based food diagnostic technologies: A review," *Sensors*, vol. 17, no. 6, p. 1453, 2017.

[40] T. Vu, F. Lin, N. Alshurafa, and W. Xu, "Wearable food intake monitoring technologies: A comprehensive review," *Computers*, vol. 6, no. 1, p. 4, 2017.

Chapter 13

Open-source projects for edge computing

Michel Gokan Khan[1], Auday Al-Dulaimy[1],
Mohammad Ali Khoshkholghi[1] and Javid Taheri[1]

13.1 Introduction

Edge computing (EC) is one of the emerging paradigms that promises the integration of computing, storage, and network, and it gains a vast popularity both in academia and industry. It's one of the key enablers of Internet of Things (IoT) as it allows data to be processed at the edge of network. In recent years, a sheer number of publications, open-source projects, and standardization consortiums as well as industrial firms focused on its theoretical and infrastructural challenges as well as the architecture recommendations, deployments, and tools.

The EC technology (Figure 13.1) has been driven by the futuristic vision of IoT, and it aims to integrate computations, storage, network, and even custom user-specific resources (i.e. graphical processing unit (GPU)) at the edge of the network [1]. This enables robust communication and extremely low delay for critical applications, and significantly increases the availability [2].

As mentioned in previous chapters, the implementations of Fog Computing (FC) along with its related EC paradigm (bringing computation near the edge of the network) can be classified into four different categories [3,4]: FC, Multi-access Edge Computing (MEC), Cloudlet Computing or Cloud Computing (CC), and Mist Computing. In FC [5], nodes can be placed at "any point of the architecture between the end device and the cloud"; therefore, it may be considered as a superset to entire EC paradigm implementations [6]. EC, itself, may be categorized in two parts: MEC and cloudlets. In MEC [7], nodes are "within the Radio Access Network (RAN) (or macro base-stations) to reduce latency and improve context awareness" [3]. A cloudlet [8], on the other hand, is a new architectural element and referred to "data centers in the box" capable of running CC resources (i.e. Virtual Machine (VMs) or containers) physically close to edge devices. Mist Computing, the term first introduced by Cisco [9], brings the computation power even more closer at the extreme edge of the network fabric using microcomputers and microcontrollers to feed into FC nodes and potentially onward toward the CC platforms. Mobile Computing (MC) and Mobile

[1]Department of Mathematics and Computer Science, Karlstad University, Karlstad, Sweden

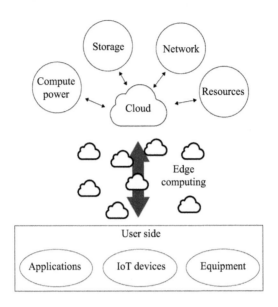

Figure 13.1   An abstract overview to EC

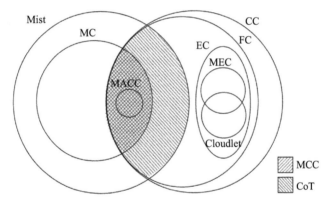

Figure 13.2   Scope classification of FC and related computing paradigms.
Source: Yousefpour et al. [4]

ad hoc Cloud Computing (MACC) can be categorized as subsets of Mist Computing, and the intersection of CC, FC, and Mist Computing forms Cloud of Things (CoT) where IoT devices establish a virtual cloud infrastructure. Figure 13.2 represents a scope classification of FC and related computing paradigms.

Depending on the type of use case, one may require a specific type of implementations. In this chapter, we aim to investigate available open-source projects as well as

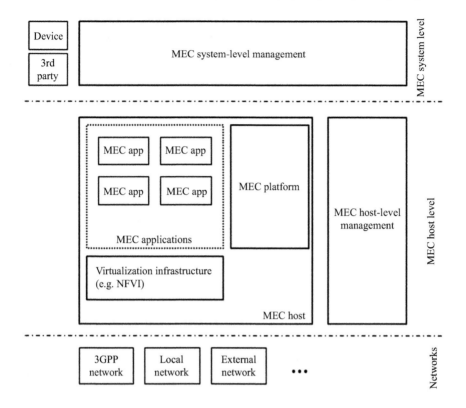

Figure 13.3   ETSI MEC framework. Source: ETSI GS MEC 003 v.2.1.1 (2019-01)

reference architectures related to different implementations of EC and discuss them in detail.

13.2   State-of-the-art architectures

In this section, we aim to review available reference architectures as well as open-source communities and companies who are actively contributing and working in EC paradigm.

13.2.1   European Telecommunications Standards Institute

European Telecommunications Standards Institute (ETSI) [10] is an independent standardization organization that aims to produce globally applicable standards across different areas of telecommunication industry.

Within this organization, there is an Industry Specification Group on MEC that aims to help all vendors, service providers, and developers to smoothly integrate their application across an MEC platforms. While EC is a concept, MEC basically referred to a widely accepted standard architecture and ETSI aims to standardize the way MEC applications get implemented on different infrastructures (mainly virtualized) as individual software. They proposed an MEC framework [11] (Figure 13.4) that illustrates general entities as well as their categorizations.

One of the key principles behind ETSI MEC standardizations is virtualization. ETSI uses network function virtualization architecture in its standardization; therefore, the Edge Technology should necessarily support virtualized or containerized environments. Moreover, according to this standard, an MEC application should be relocatable from cloud to edge hosts while guarantying application-level criteria. An MEC application can be deployed in a wide range of location in the edge: in New Radio nodes, aggregation points, hardware accelerators, or anywhere at the edge of the core network.

The *MEC platform* is one of the key elements in ETSI edge architecture that contains all the required functionalists for running edge applications on top of a particular infrastructure (mostly virtualized) to enable them provide or use MEC services to others. The *MEC Host* is responsible for hosting the *MEC platform* as well as the virtualization infrastructure that *MEC applications* are running on it. Moreover, the *multi-access edge orchestrator* is the core component to manage system-level configurations and has an overview of the entire MEC system. The *MEC platform manager* and the *virtualization infrastructure manager* are handling MEC-specific functionalities as well MEC host and its applications.

13.2.2 Edge Computing Consortium

Edge Computing Consortium (ECC) [12] consists of six industry partners* and they "aim to foster industry coordination in an open and innovative way, and promote prosperity and development for all parties." Figure 13.5 represents their proposed reference architecture [13] on EC.

The *Smart Services* layer consists of software development interfaces framework as well as automatic deployment and operations services (DevOps). It also defines the edge-to-edge (E2E) service flow through the *Service Fabric* (SF) layer. The *Connectivity and Computing Fabric* is responsible for automatic deployment and operations of services on infrastructure. Finally, the *Edge Computing Node or Edge Compute Network* (ECN) is defined the compute node that is compatible with "a variety of heterogeneous connections, support real-time processing and response, and deliver integrated hardware and software security" [12].

13.2.3 The 3rd Generation Partnership Project

The 3rd Generation Partnership Project (3GPP) [14] is an international standardization organization specifically for LTE, 5G and anything related to protocols for mobile telephony.

---

*Huawei Technologies Co., Ltd., Shenyang Institute of Automation of the Chinese Academy of Sciences, China Academy of Information and Communications Technology (CAICT), Intel Corporation, ARM Holdings, and iSoftStone Information Technology (Group) Co., Ltd.

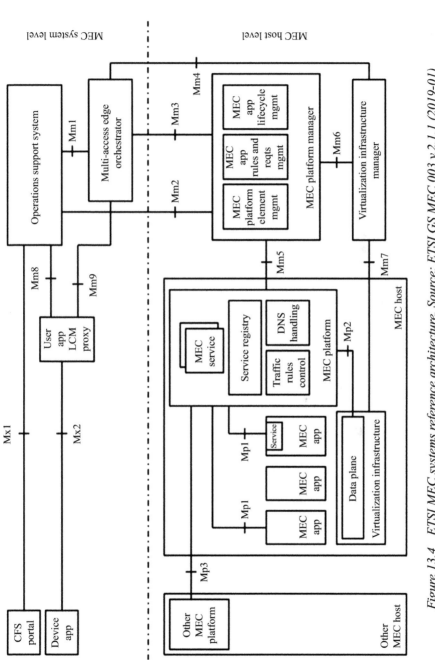

Figure 13.4   ETSI MEC systems reference architecture. Source: ETSI GS MEC 003 v.2.1.1 (2019-01)

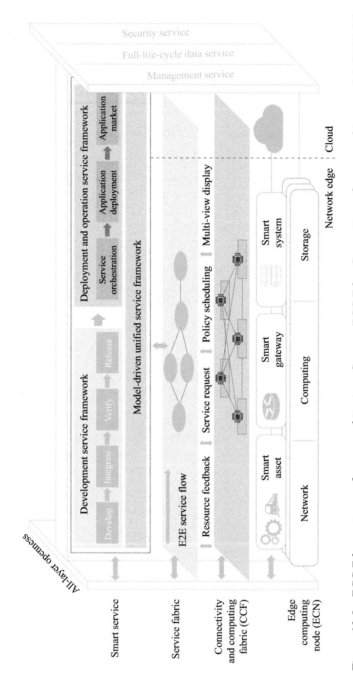

Figure 13.5   ECC Edge systems reference architecture. Source: ECC Edge Computing reference architecture 2.0 (2017-11)

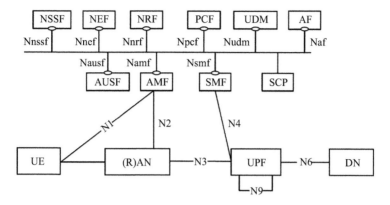

Figure 13.6 3GPP 5G reference architecture. Source: 3GPP TS 23.501 v16.1.0 (2019-06)

Similar to other aforementioned standardization organization, they also had a direct attention to MEC. In their recent technical specification on system architecture for the 5G system [15] (Figure 13.6), they mentioned, "the 5G Core Network selects a User Place Function (UPF) to the User Equipment (UE) and executes the traffic steering from the UPF to the local Data Network (DN) via an N6 interface."

13.3   Open-source projects, communities, consortium, and companies active in the field of EC

In addition to aforementioned standardization institutes, there are numerous independent or collaborative open-source efforts happening in the field of EC [16]. In this section, we review a few famous communities in this field as well as their key contributions in this field.

13.3.1   The Linux Foundation's EdgeX Foundry

The Linux Foundation [17], the nonprofit organization supporting several open-source projects today, launches an umbrella organization *LF Edge* [18], to find an EC framework that is "independent of hardware, silicon, cloud, or operating system." One of the main projects that is supported by LF Edge, called The EdgeX Foundry [19], is a "vendor-neutral open source project hosted by The Linux Foundation building a common open framework for IoT edge computing." Figure 13.7 represents its platform architecture.

EdgeX Foundry follows a microservice-based architecture, and apart from its underlying System Services (Security and System Management), it's been organized into four service layers: Core Services (CS), Supporting Services (SS), Export Services (ES), and Device Services (DS).

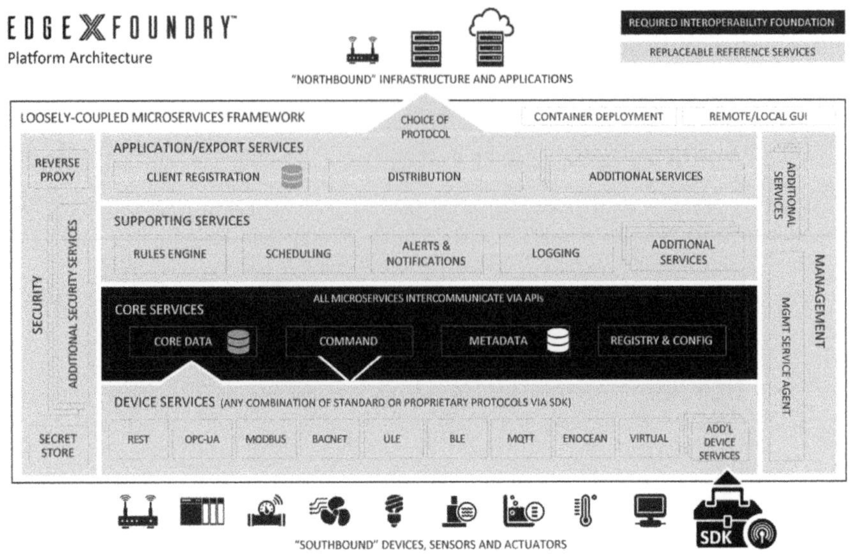

Figure 13.7   EdgeX Foundry platform architecture. Source: EdgeX Foundry documentation (as of 2019-09)

Regarding EdgeX Foundry's terminology, the entire edge spectrum is divided into two parts: the *South Side* and the *North Side*. The *South Side* is referred to "all IoT objects, within the physical realm, and the edge of the network that communicates directly with those devices, sensors, actuators, and other IoT objects, and collects the data from them." The *North Side* in the other hand is referred to "the Cloud (or Enterprise system) where data is collected, stored, aggregated, analyzed, and turned into information, and the part of the network that communicates with the Cloud, is referred to as the 'north side' of the network."

As shown in Figure 13.7, the CS layer is separating the *South Side* and the *North Side* layers at the edge. It consists of *Core Data* component (persistence storage of *South Side*), *Command* (actuation control from the *North Side* to the *South Side*, *Metadata* (metadata repository), and *Registry and Configuration* (microservices information, configuration properties, and initialization values).

Microservices in SS layer are responsible for providing the "edge analytics and intelligence." Moreover, common duties such as logging, scheduling, and data cleanup (scrubbing) are performed in this layer.

EdgeX Foundy's ES layer enables the system to independently operate with other systems depending on the situation. Microservices in this layer are responsible for enabling off-gateway clients to register for data that they require, coming from the *South Side* objects and knows the time, location, format, and shape of data delivery.

The DS layer is dealing with the connectors interacting with the Devices or IoT objects. The EdgeX Foundry provides a Software Development Kit (SDK) in different languages (such as Go and C) for generating the shell of a DS.

Even though we can access EdgeX Foundry microservices through a common Application Programming Interface (API), there are also efforts on providing a web-based graphical user interface (GUI) to manage local gateway devices, microservices, and view console logs (Figure 13.8).

EdgeX Foundry is released under Apache 2.0 open-source licensing model and it's a collection of several microservices. Developers need to download required source code, SDKs, and tools to deploy, run, and develop EdgeX Foundry microservices, but normal users can take advantage of pre-compiled Docker containers that can easily be installed using Docker compose. As EdgeX Foundry is both OS-agnostic and HW-agnostic, it supports many operating system, including Ubuntu, Windows, and Mac OS.

13.3.2 The Linux Foundation's Akraino Edge Stack

Akraino Edge Stack [20] is another project of LF Edge organization supported by the Linux Foundation and initiated by AT&T and Intel. It intends to develop a "fully integrated edge infrastructure solution" and aims to support almost all layers that a provider requires to provide an Edge solution as well as supporting workloads in any form (VM, container, and bare metal). It is a complementary open-source project and interfaces with the existing open-source projects such as Acumos AI [21] (a platform to deploy AI apps), Airship [22] (cloud provisioning automation), Ceph [23] (object/block storage service), DANOS [24] (the Disaggregated Network Operating System), EdgeX Foundry [19], Kubernetes [25], LF Networking [26], ONAP [27] (a platform for orchestration and automation of physical and virtual network functions), OpenStack [28], and StarlingX [29].

Figure 13.9 represents Akraino Edge Stack building blocks.

The Akraino Edge Stack is "a collection of multiple blueprints." A blueprint is a configuration of entire stack (i.e. cloud platform, API, and applications). The Akraino community receives the blueprints and validates them in the Akraino community lab and validation lab set up by the users.

There are several open-source blueprints approved by Akraino so far (11 blueprints as of 2019-09), and here we enlisted just a few of them:

- *Integrated Edge Cloud* (IEC) is an approved blueprint family of Akraino Edge Stack sponsored by Arm, Huawei, and Ene. It intends "to develop a fully integrated edge infrastructure solution" toward EC. It comes in two types: Small Edge and Medium Edge.
- *Kubernetes-Native Infrastructure (KNI) Blueprint Family* is a family of blueprint sponsored by RedHat. It aims to "declaratively manage EC stacks at scale and with a consistent, uniform user experience from the infrastructure up to the services and from developer environments to production environments on bare metal or on public cloud."
- *Connected Vehicle Blueprint* aims to form an MEC platform as a backbone for vehicle-to-everything (V2X) applications and sponsored by Tencent, Arm, Intel, and Nokia.

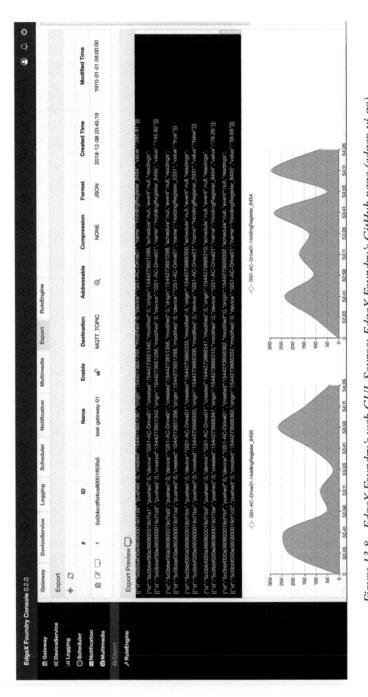

Figure 13.8 EdgeX Foundry's web GUI. Source: EdgeX Foundry's GitHub page (edgex-ui-go)

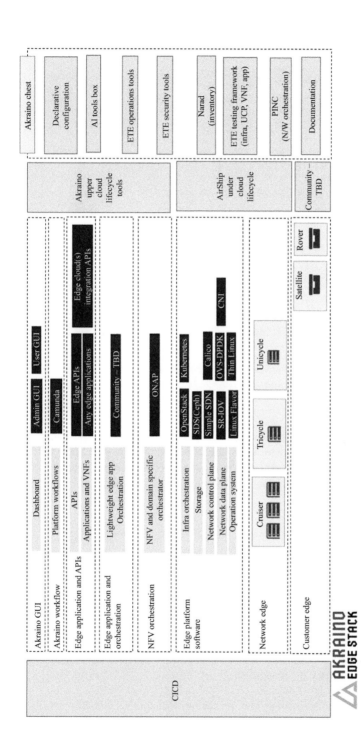

Figure 13.9 Akraino Edge Stack building blocks. Source: AT&T

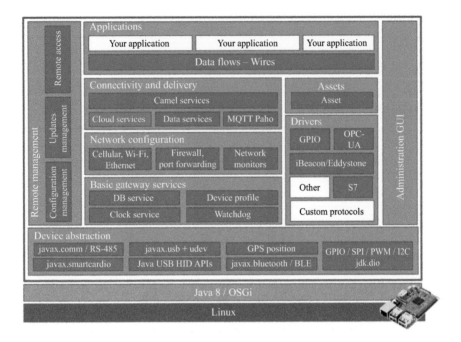

Figure 13.10   Eclipse Kura™ framework architecture. Source: Eclipse Kura™ V. 4.1.0 documentation (as of 2019-09)

- *Telco Appliance Blueprint Family* is "a collection of deployment automation tooling and tuning designed to allow the creation of purpose-built Open Source 'appliances' which will be tested through extensive automated testing in order to certify a specific level of performance of a specific application or combination of applications."

13.3.3   Eclipse Kura™

Eclipse Kura™ [30] is a Java-based and open-source IoT Edge framework for building IoT gateways. It leverages Open Services Gateway initiative (OSGi) framework as a dynamic component system for developing and deploying its various types of modules. Eclipse Kura™ allows its users to write their own IoT applications on top of it by providing various types of APIs and enabling remote management of IoT gateways. Figure 13.10 represents Eclipse Kura™ high-level architecture.

According to its documentation, Eclipse Kura™ categorizes its wide range of services into the following categories:

- *I/O services*: For accessing I/O ports such as Bluetooth, USB, Serial, GPS, etc.
- *Data Services*: Stores telemetry data and provide a policy-driven publishing system.

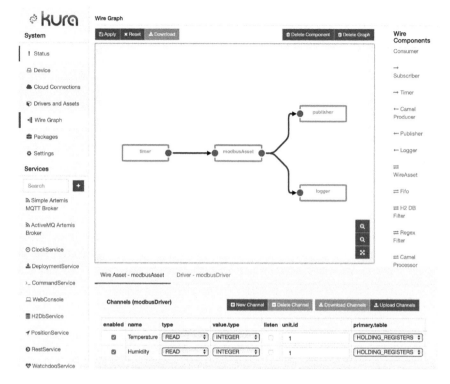

Figure 13.11 Eclipse Kura™ administration GUI. Source: Eclipse Kura™ V. 4.1.0 documentation (as of 2019-09)

- *Cloud services*: An API layer for IoT applications that provides a simple request/response, publish/subscribe, and resource management mechanism.
- *Configuration Service*: Provides configuration snapshot of all registered services in the container, as well as importing necessary configurations.
- *Remote management services*: Enables remote upgrades, managing deployment and configuration of IoT applications (dependent to the *Configuration Service*).
- *Networking*: Provides API for managing network interfaces available in the gateway like (Ethernet, Wi-Fi, Cellular, etc.).
- *Watchdog service*: Forces system reset when detects a problem in a registered component.
- *Web administration interface*: A web-based GUI to manage gateways (Figure 13.11).
- *Drivers and assets*: To provide a unified-model that simplifies the communication with the attached devices.
- *Wires*: A visual dataflow programming tool to design data collection and processing pipelines as well as providing a repository of available and common workflows (Figure 13.11).

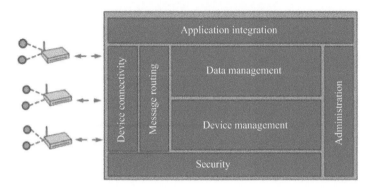

*Figure 13.12   Eclipse Kapua™ functional architecture. Source: Eclipse Kapua™
          overview page (as of 2019-09)*

Eclipse Kura™ is released under Eclipse Public License and can be installed on
Raspberry Pi 2-3, Intel UP2, Rock960 or a custom workspace. It is also available in
a containerized form and can be installed as a Docker container.

13.3.4   Eclipse Kapua™

Eclipse Kapua™ [31] is an open-source project sponsored by Eclipse and an IoT
platform on the cloud side that integrates devices and their data. It can also get
integrated with the Eclipse Kura™, and together they can form an entire end-to-end
foundation for any kind of IoT projects and applications. Figure 13.12 represents
Eclipse Kapua™'s functional architecture.

The function architecture of Eclipse Kapua™ consists of the following modules:

- The *Device Connectivity* module is responsible to provide the connectivity of
  devices through a message broker that supports various types of protocols such
  as MQTT, AMQP, and WebSockets for application integration. This module also
  authenticates connections, enforces the appropriate authorization, and maintains
  a Device Registry.
- The *Message Routing* module is responsible for handling data stream that is
  published by devices through configurable message routes.
- The *Device Management* module enables remote management of the connected
  devices.
- The *Data Management* module archives telemetry data sent by the devices in a
  NoSQL database.
- The *Security* layer is responsible for providing the management of users, accounts,
  and tenants through a role-based access control.
- The *Application Integration* layer is responsible for exposing all platform func-
  tionalists for integration with existing applications by providing Representational
  State Transfer (REST) web APIs.
- The *Administration Console* (Figure 13.13) is web-based GUI for managing all
  devices and performing administrative operations.

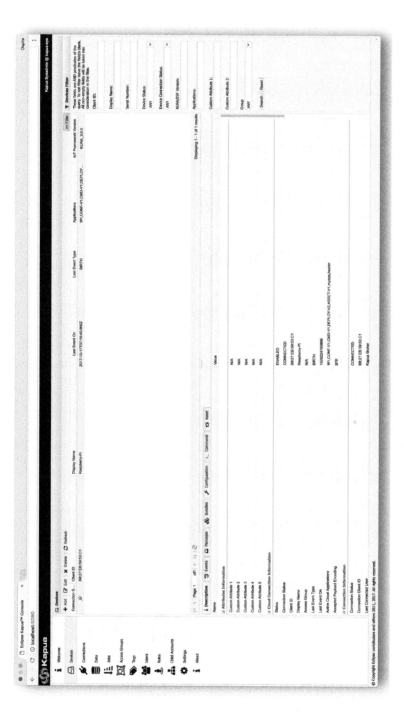

Figure 13.13   A screenshot of the Eclipse Kapua™ Administration Console. Source: Eclipse Kapua™ documentation (as of 2019-09)

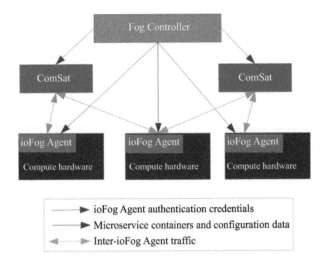

Figure 13.14 ioFog architecture. Source: Eclipse Newsletter (2017)

13.3.5 Eclipse ioFog™

Eclipse ioFog™ [32] is another open-source project sponsored by Eclipse. It's providing an EC platform for deploying and running microservices in the form of Linux kernel containers at the edge. It aims to facilitate the development of software for edge devices; in other words, it lets you develop microservices and distribute them at the Edge. Figure 13.14 represents Eclipse ioFog™ architecture.

ECN is responsible for running ioFog and may consist of several nodes. Inside each node, an ioFog Agent is running and responsible for active microservices in the node and the ioFog Controller is responsible for orchestrating these microservice across the network. Microservices may communicate with each other via a daemon called ioFog Connector, which is also responsible for automatic discovery and NAT traversal.

Eclipse ioFog™ has been released under the terms of Eclipse Public License v. 2.0, and all source codes are available at GitHub. The installation is very straightforward and can be installed on Linux, Windows, and Mac OS operating systems. It also supports Raspberry Pi as workers on the edge.

13.3.6 StarlingX (stewarded by the OpenStack Foundation)

StarlingX [29] is an open-source and integrated multi-server Edge Cloud software stack. They claimed to have integration with the OpenStack [28], Kubernetes [25], Ceph [23], and OVS-DPDK, and according to their documentation, one of their main goals is to "fill in the gaps in the open-source ecosystem to enhance deployment, maintainability and operation of the software components."

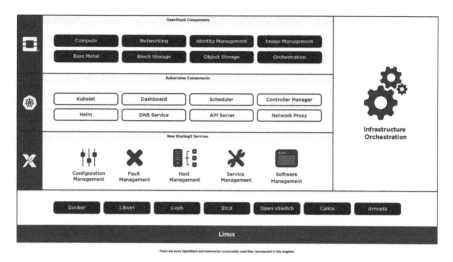

Figure 13.15   StarlingX platform architecture. Source: StarlingX Homepage (as of 2019-09)

Figure 13.15 represents StarlingX framework architecture and it consists of the following main services:

- *Configuration Management service*: Provides node configuration and inventory management services and supports autodiscovery and configuration of new nodes.
- *Fault Management*: Manages alarms and logs for registered events in compute nodes and virtual resources.
- *Host Management*: Manages host machines via a REST API interface and instantiates automatic node recovery in case of failures. It also provides out-of-band remote reset, power-on/off, and H/W sensor monitoring.
- *Service Management*: Allows remote updates and rolling upgrades.

StarlingX is stewarded by the OpenStack Foundation, released under Apache 2 license, and hosted on OpenDev.org. It can be installed in both bare-metal and virtual environments (support Libvirt/QEMU and VirtualBox). The installation scripts as well as ISO images are available in their Git repository.

13.3.7   Microsoft Azure IoT Edge

Microsoft Azure IoT Edge [33] is a service that provides an easy way to move workloads (analytics, custom business logics, etc.) from the cloud to the edge by enabling its users to package and move any kind of services in a standard containerized format to the IoT devices. In other words, users will be able to deploy various types of services on any kind of IoT edge device that support containers (i.e. Raspberry Pi). These services can be either Azure standard services, third-party services, or even users own custom scripts. It also helps IoT devices to spend less time communicating with the cloud and react faster to changes by offloading some workloads to the edge.

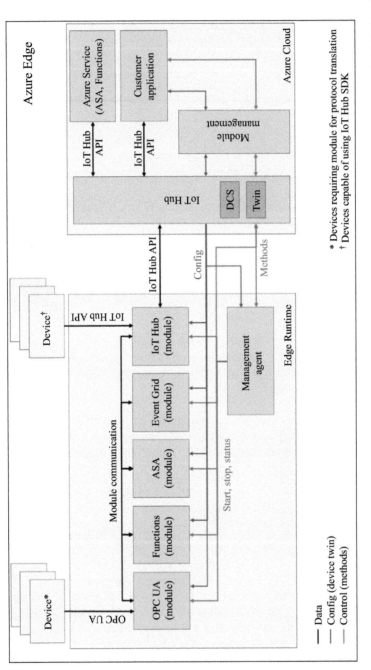

Figure 13.16 Microsoft Azure IoT Edge platform architecture. Source: Microsoft Azure IoT Edge Documentation in GitHub (as of 2019-09)

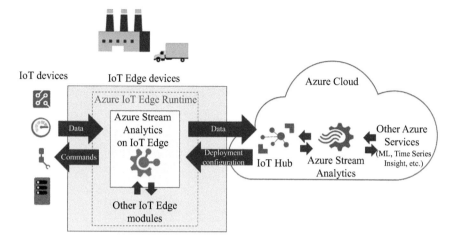

Figure 13.17   Microsoft Azure IoT Edge high-level overview. Source: Microsoft Azure IoT Edge Documentation (as of 2019-09)

Figure 13.16 represents Microsoft Azure IoT Edge platform architecture and it consists of three main components:

- *IoT Edge Modules*: Containers that run different services (third party or Azure official). These modules are deployed to IoT edge devices and get executed locally there.
- *IoT Edge Runtime*: It runs inside each IoT edge device to manage modules that run there.
- *Cloud-based Interface (Azure Cloud)*: Remote monitoring and management of IoT Edge devices.

Even though Microsoft Azure IoT Edge is a free and open-source package released under the MIT license, but it's been built on top of Azure IoT Hub which is a part of Microsoft Azure IoT cloud service. Figure 13.17 presents the high-level overview of Microsoft Azure IoT Edge.

13.3.8   KubeEdge project

KubeEdge [34] is an open-source platform that brings Kubernetes power to the edge devices by extending native containerized application orchestration to the edge devices. It enables key infrastructural support for network, deployments, and application synchronizations between the cloud and the edge.

It's been released under the Apache 2.0 license and the project hosted on GitHub. Figure 13.18 represents its architecture and it consists of the following components:

- *CloudHub*: On the cloud side, *CloudHub* acts as a web socket server responsible for watching changes, caching, and sending messages to the *EdgeHub*.

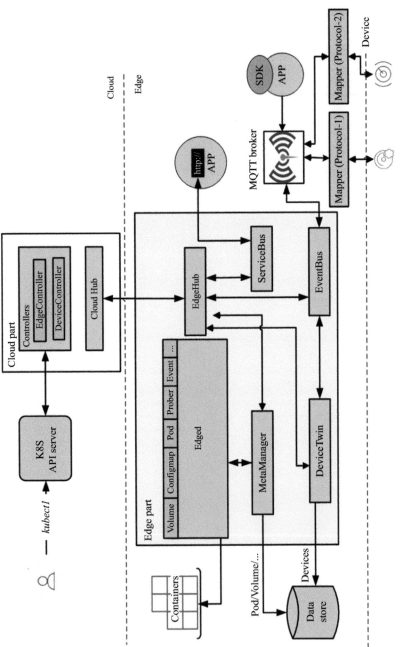

Figure 13.18 Kube platform architecture. Source: Kube Edge Documentation in GitHub (as of 2019-09)

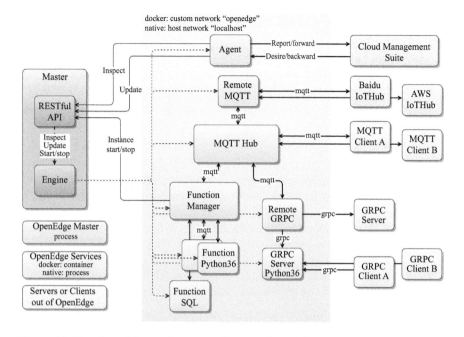

Figure 13.19   OpenEdge architecture. Source: OpenEdge Documentation in GitHub (as of 2019-09)

- *EdgeController*: It's an extended Kubernetes controller and acts as a bridge between Kubernetes API server and the *EdgeCore* which run on the edge side.
- *DeviceController*: Similar to *EdgeController*, DeviceController is also an extended controller to manage devices on the edge side.
- *EdgeHub*: Similar to *CloudHub* on the cloud side, *EdgeHub* acts as web socket client to interact with the *CloudHub*.
- *Edged*: A daemon runs inside the edge nodes to manage containers.
- *EventBus*: Offering publish and subscribe capabilities to other components.
- *ServiceBus*: Providing HTTP client capabilities to components of cloud to reach HTTP servers running at edge.
- *DeviceTwin*: Responsible for syncing device status with the cloud.
- *MetaManager*: Metadata manager and responsible for processing messages between *Edged* and *EdgeHub*.

13.3.9   Baidu's OpenEdge

OpenEdge [35] is an open-source EC framework announced by Baidu, Inc. that extends the CC service to the edge. It is a set of containers written in the Go programming language and it's heavily dependent on the Baidu cloud platform. Figure 13.19 represents OpenEdge architecture.

OpenEdge consists of the three main components: *Master*, *Services*, and *Volume*:

- *Master*: The core component of OpenEdge and responsible for managing all storage volumes and services via a REST API or Command Line Interface.
- *Service*: A set of running applications that provides specific functions.
- *Volume*: Refers to "the directory used by the Service, can be a read-only directory, such as a directory for placing resources such as configuration, certificates, scripts, etc., or a writable directory to persist data, such as logs and database."

As shown in Figure 13.19, in each building block OpenEdge has several official modules: openedge-agent for communicating with the Baidu IntelliEdge (BIE) Cloud Management Suite, openedge-hub for providing reliable messaging services in low-bandwidth and unreliable networks, openedge-function-manager for providing the computing power based on the MQTT message mechanism, openedge-*function-** providing a way for developers to handle messages by writing their own functions (in Python, Node.js, etc.), and openedge-remote-mqtt for bridging two MQTT Servers for message synchronization.

Even though OpenEdge is released under Apache 2.0 license, it's heavily dependent to Baidu cloud and it's not clear whether it can be used independently.

13.3.10   Elijah: cloudlet-based EC

Elijah project is initiated by the Carnegie Mellon University to enable the implementation of cloudlet-based environments. The main part of Elijah project is OpenStack++ [36,37] which is a set of extensions to OpenStack that makes it capable of deploying cloudlets. Another part of Elijah is a set of MC applications that build upon OpenStack++, such as GigaSight [38], QuiltView [39], and Gabriel [40].

13.4   Open issues and challenges

The open-source model enables rapid advancement in scientific computing, and edge is not an exception. Many open-source projects have been introduced in the past few years to help both researchers and industry partners to take advantage of the state-of-the-art edge technologies as well as coordinately collaborate on different aspects of edge infrastructure problems and overcome its current challenges. In this chapter, we discussed about the state-of-the-art edge technologies and standardizations, open-source communities (both in industry and academia), as well as some of the most influential open-source projects in this area. But in between all these technologies and advancements in the area of EC, there are still a few open issues and challenges [41,42] that need to be considered.

13.4.1   Data security and privacy

One of the key challenges to IoT and EC platforms today is the data security and preserving the privacy of edge users [43,44]. Important factors in data security, including security mechanisms in edge, integrity of information (ensuring that messages are securely conveyed without external modifications), and privacy-preserving approaches in data transmission, are still not fully considered in most of state-of-the-art edge platforms.

13.4.2 Quality of service and quality of experience

One of the most classic challenges in the age of CC is the service-level agreement awareness of quality of service and quality of experience in resource allocation, placement, and configuration of compute nodes and applications. In the EC era, this problem gets even more complicated by getting more dimensions, such as physical space and precise location of edge devices. This problem is still an open research challenge in EC.

13.4.3 Support and maintenance

EC is fairly new and emerging technology; therefore, still there are not many professional technicians available in the market to provide high quality and affordable support for deploying and maintaining available open-source edge platforms. In short term, for organizations that are planning for an edge strategy, this shortage of professional experts in the market from the one hand and lack of necessary internal skill set from the other hand will lead them to spend high deployment and maintenance cost. Moreover, in many locations, there are not enough skilled personal to deploy edge devices; therefore, in many cases a very simple instruction is essential to deployed edge devices.

13.4.4 Scalability

The enormous bandwidth demand for cloud applications today makes them not scalable in long run. One of the key motivations behind EC is to spread this bandwidth among several edge nodes. However, in city-scale and heavy use cases [45] (such as video analytics, Augmented Reality (AR) and Virtual Reality (VR)), there are still open challenges in managing and placing edge nodes.

13.5 Conclusions

In this chapter, we covered an overview to the EC technologies as well as a scope classification to its entire paradigm. We also reviewed the state-of-the-art reference architectures and standardization, as well as top ten open-source projects and platforms in EC. Moreover, we mentioned open issues and challenges in the EC paradigm and discussed them in detail.

References

[1] Li C, Xue Y, Wang J, *et al.* Edge-oriented computing paradigms: A survey on architecture design and system management. ACM Comput Surv. 2018;51(2):39:1–39:34. Available from: http://doi.acm.org/10.1145/3154815.

[2]   Khan WZ, Ahmed E, Hakak S, *et al.* Edge computing: A survey. Future Generation Computer Systems. 2019;97:219–235. Available from: http://www.sciencedirect.com/science/article/pii/S0167739X18319903.

[3]   Dolui K, and Datta SK. Comparison of edge computing implementations: Fog computing, cloudlet and mobile edge computing. In: 2017 Global Internet of Things Summit (GIoTS); 2017. pp. 1–6.

[4]   Yousefpour A, Fung C, Nguyen T, *et al.* All one needs to know about fog computing and related edge computing paradigms: A complete survey. Journal of Systems Architecture. 2019;98:289–330. Available from: http://www.sciencedirect.com/science/article/pii/S1383762118306349.

[5]   Mahmud R, Kotagiri R, and Buyya R. Fog computing: A taxonomy, survey and future directions. In: Di Martino B, Li KC, Yang LT, Esposito A, editors. Internet of Everything. Internet of Things (Technology, Communications and Computing). Springer, Singapore: Springer Singapore; 2018. pp. 103–130. Available from: https://doi.org/10.1007/978-981-10-5861-5_5.

[6]   Naha RK, Garg SK, Georgekopolous D, *et al.* Fog computing: Survey of trends, architectures, requirements, and research directions. CoRR. 2018;abs/1807.00976. Available from: http://arxiv.org/abs/1807.00976.

[7]   Tanaka H, Yoshida M, Mori K, *et al.* Multi-access Edge Computing: A Survey. Journal of Information Processing. 2018 01;26:87–97.

[8]   Satyanarayanan M, Bahl P, Caceres R, *et al.* The case for VM-based cloudlets in mobile computing. IEEE Pervasive Computing. 2009;8(4):14–23.

[9]   Cisco pushes IoT analytics to the extreme edge with mist computing; 2014. Available from: https://rethinkresearch.biz/articles/cisco-pushes-iot-analytics-extreme-edge-mist-computing-2/.

[10] The European Telecommunications Standards Institute (ETSI). 2019. Available from: https://www.etsi.org.

[11] Multi-access Edge Computing (MEC); Framework and Reference Architecture; ETSI GS MEC 003 V2.1.1 (2019-01). The European Telecommunications Standards Institute (ETSI); 2019.

[12] Edge Computing Consortium (ECC). 2019. Available from: http://en.ecconsortium.org/.

[13] Edge Computing Reference Architecture 2.0. Edge Computing Consortium (ECC) and Alliance of Industrial Internet (AII); 2017.

[14] 3rd Generation Partnership Project (3GPP). 2019. Available from: https://www.3gpp.org.

[15] 3rd Generation Partnership Project Technical Specification 23.501 (V16.1.0); Technical Specification Group Services and System Aspects; System Architecture for the 5G System; Stage 2 (Release 16). 3rd Generation Partnership Project (3GPP); 2019.

[16] Liu F, Tang G, Li Y, *et al.* A survey on edge computing systems and tools. Proceedings of the IEEE. 2019; pp. 1–26.

[17] The Linux Foundation. 2019. Available from: https://www.linuxfoundation.org.

[18] LF Edge Organization. 2019. Available from: https://lfedge.org.
[19] Edgex Foundry. 2019. Available from: https://www.edgexfoundry.org.
[20] Akraino Edge Stack. 2019. Available from: https://www.lfedge.org/projects/akraino/.
[21] Acumos AI. 2019. Available from: https://acumos.org.
[22] Airship. 2019. Available from: https://airshipit.org.
[23] Ceph Project. 2019. Available from: https://ceph.io.
[24] Danos Project. 2019. Available from: https://danosproject.org.
[25] Kubernetes (K8s). 2019. Available from: https://kubernetes.io.
[26] LF Networking Project. 2019. Available from: https://lfnetworking.org.
[27] Onap Project. 2019. Available from: https://onap.org.
[28] OpenStack Project. 2019. Available from: https://openstack.org.
[29] StarlingX Project. 2019. Available from: https://starlingx.io.
[30] Eclipse Kura™. 2019. Available from: https://www.eclipse.org/kura/.
[31] Eclipse Kapua™. 2019. Available from: https://www.eclipse.org/kapua/.
[32] Eclipse ioFog™. 2019. Available from: https://iofog.org.
[33] Microsoft Azure IoT Edge. 2019. Available from: https://github.com/Azure/iotedge.
[34] KubeEdge. 2019. Available from: https://www.kubeedge.io.
[35] OpenEdge. 2019. Available from: https://openedge.tech.
[36] Ha K, Satyanarayanan M. OpenStack++ for Cloudlet Deployment; 2015.
[37] OpenStack++ Project. 2019. Available from: https://github.com/OpenEdge Computing/elijah-openstack.
[38] Simoens P, Xiao Y, Pillai P, *et al.* Scalable crowd-sourcing of video from mobile devices. In: Proceeding of the 11th Annual International Conference on Mobile Systems, Applications, and Services. MobiSys'13. New York, NY, USA: ACM; 2013. pp. 139–152. Available from: http://doi.acm.org/10.1145/2462456.2464440.
[39] Chen Z, Hu W, Ha K, *et al.* QuiltView: A crowd-sourced video response system. In: Proceedings of the 15th Workshop on Mobile Computing Systems and Applications. HotMobile'14. New York, NY, USA: ACM; 2014. pp. 13:1–13:6. Available from: http://doi.acm.org/10.1145/2565585.2565589.
[40] Ha K, Chen Z, Hu W, *et al.* Towards wearable cognitive assistance. In: Proceedings of the 12th Annual International Conference on Mobile Systems, Applications, and Services. MobiSys'14. New York, NY, USA: ACM; 2014. pp. 68–81. Available from: http://doi.acm.org/10.1145/2594368.2594383.
[41] Shi W, Cao J, Zhang Q, *et al.* Edge computing: Vision and challenges. IEEE Internet of Things Journal. 2016 10;3:1–1.
[42] Mao Y, You C, Zhang J, *et al.* A survey on mobile edge computing: The communication perspective. IEEE Communications Surveys Tutorials. 2017;19(4):2322–2358.
[43] Zhang J, Chen B, Zhao Y, *et al.* Data security and privacy-preserving in edge computing paradigm: Survey and open issues. IEEE Access. 2018 03;PP:1–1.

[44]   Roman R, Lopez J, and Mambo M. Mobile edge computing, Fog *et al.*: A survey and analysis of security threats and challenges. Future Generation Computer Systems. 2018;78:680–698. Available from: http://www.sciencedirect.com/science/article/pii/S0167739X16305635.

[45]   Maheshwari S, Raychaudhuri D, Seskar I, *et al.* Scalability and performance evaluation of edge cloud systems for latency constrained applications; 2018.

Chapter 14

Simulators and emulators for edge computing

Atakan Aral[1] and Vincenzo De Maio[1]

In this chapter, we perform a study of the existing tools for the evaluation of Fog/Edge infrastructures. First, we analyze the state of the art in the simulation of Fog/Edge infrastructures and determine the main challenges in simulation and modeling such infrastructures. Then, we use a scientific methodology to identify the most important simulation and emulation tools, identifying their main characteristics, and define a classification. Each tool is then described in detail, and compared with the others. Finally, we conclude the chapter with a discussion about future research directions in the area.

14.1 Introduction

Modeling and simulation of Cloud computing infrastructures have attracted significant interest in the distributed computing research community. The reason for this has to be found not only in the commercial interest and widespread diffusion of such infrastructures but also in the fact that testing and validation of resource management strategies for Cloud computing is very challenging for researchers. This is due to three main factors: (1) the use of commercial infrastructures, such as Amazon, Azure or Google Cloud, or private experimental test beds, affects the reproducibility of experiments; (2) some measurements might not be available on commercial infrastructures, due to privacy issues; and (3) deployment and management of a real-world Cloud infrastructure to perform experiments is either costly or time-consuming. The use of simulation and emulation tools for Cloud infrastructures allows testing of provisioning and resource management strategies before deploying them on a real Cloud infrastructure, minimizing risks for researchers and Cloud providers. For these reasons, the development of accurate simulation and emulation tools is of paramount importance for the advancement of research in this field.

Considering the recent affirmation of Fog/Edge computing, modeling and simulation of Fog/Edge computational resources become even more complex. This is because in comparison with Cloud computing, the application areas of Fog/Edge

---

[1]Institute of Information Systems Engineering, Vienna University of Technology, Vienna, Austria

computing vary by the extent of (1) geographical distribution, (2) scale, (3) hetero-geneity, (4) processing type (batch or near real-time), (5) mobility, and (6) the interplay between the Edge, the Fog, and the Cloud [1]. These challenges are described in the following sections.

14.1.1   Geographical distribution

While Cloud data centers are distributed around the globe, and often very far from the source of the data, Fog/Edge nodes are deployed in close proximity to the data sources. This geographical proximity to the data sources has effects on latency and the time required for data transfer and processing, which has to be considered in the modeling of Fog/Edge nodes.

14.1.2   Scale

Due to the higher number of devices that can be present in a Fog/Edge infrastructures (e.g. Cloud data centers, Fog micro data centers, Edge devices, Mobile devices, and Internet of things (IoT) devices), and the consequently larger scale of systems to be modeled, there is the need for providing models and simulators/emulators that can deal with the greater scale of such systems. Another issue in this sense is related to the evaluation: while there is a plethora of real-world data sets for the execution of Cloud applications, at the moment we can notice a lack of real-world data and difficulty of measurements for systems of such scale.

14.1.3   Heterogeneity

While Cloud infrastructures rely on centralized data centers and relatively homoge-neous commodity hardware, Fog/Edge infrastructures move computation closer to the source of data, relying on heterogeneous computing facilities (e.g. mobile devices, IoT devices, and micro data centers). Moreover, some of these computing facilities are not designed to perform the processing required by typical Fog/Edge applications, demanding for different modeling approaches, more advanced than the one used for typical computing facilities.

14.1.4   Processing type

Typical Fog/Edge applications range from batch processing applications to near real-time applications. Each of these applications has different objectives and charac-teristics, requiring different modeling strategies. For this reason, the simulation and the modeling of Fog/Edge application should provide ways to model a wide range of applications.

14.1.5   Mobility

Modeling the mobility of mobile computing devices becomes of paramount impor-tance in the context of Fog/Edge applications. In fact, many works such as [2,3] investigate the benefits of offloading mobile application to Fog/Edge infrastructure.

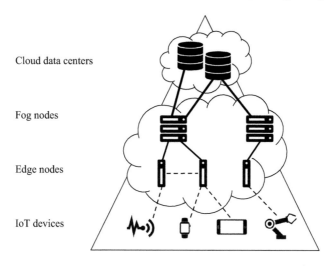

Cloud data centers

Fog nodes

Edge nodes

IoT devices

Figure 14.1   Fog and Edge computing architecture

In addition, mobile devices can also be seen as Edge devices, due to their computational capabilities [4]. In order to accurately model Fog/Edge infrastructures, then, it is necessary to provide accurate modeling of different mobility patterns, ranging from pedestrian to vehicular mobility, and the influence of mobility over computations and network communications.

14.1.6   The interplay between Edge, Fog, and Cloud

According to [5], Fog/Edge computing is not supposed to replace Cloud computing, but mostly to interoperate with it: for example, large-scale batch computation could be executed on the Cloud, while near real-time applications could perform low-latency data processing on the Fog/Edge layers (as demonstrated in Figure 14.1). To this end, there is the need to model the different types of processing at different layers of the infrastructure, as well as orchestration and network connections available at different layers.

Such challenges cannot be addressed by typical Cloud simulators and require specifically tailored solutions for simulating such infrastructures. To the best of our knowledge, there exists only a single literature survey on simulating Fog and Edge computing [1]. Our work extends this study in the following ways:

• We provide a detailed classification of the simulators, identifying six key criteria regarding the modeling capability. Among these, only mobility is considered in previous work [1].
• We widen the scope of the reviewed simulators/emulators by considering newer tools. The total number of tools increased from 7 to 11. Particularly, FogExplorer, YAFS, RECAP, and Sleipnir simulators, as well as Cloud4IoT emulator, are missing in previous work. On the other hand, we exclude IOTSim [6]

because it models IoT applications that are hosted on centralized Cloud and not in Fog/Edge infrastructures.

- We explicitly describe the research methodology of our systematic literature review and classification.
- We redraw the high-level architecture diagrams of the simulators and emulators (where available) in a uniform format for quick comparison.

The rest of the chapter is structured as follows. In Section 14.2, we introduce our proposed classification and the methodology behind it. Then we proceed to describe existing solutions for deterministic simulators (Section 14.3), stochastic simulators (Section 14.4), and emulators (Section 14.5). Finally, we compare the simulators, discuss future research directions, and draw conclusions in Section 14.6.

14.2 Classification of simulators

14.2.1 Research methodology

A systematic literature review follows precisely defined steps and reduces bias. It also increases the reproducibility of the results. In this section, we describe the methodology used for discovering simulators and emulators, as well as for classification. We utilized Google Scholar digital library to discover candidate works for our study. The following query is executed to match only the titles of the works.

```
("edge" OR "fog")("simulator" OR "simulation"
OR "emulator" OR "emulation" OR "evaluation")
```

Additionally, we limited the publication year from 2017 onward. After several trials, no relevant work is discovered before that year. The query is first executed in December 2018 to obtain the initial set of work. It is repeated in July 2019 to account for works that are more recent. Indeed, YAFS is included in our study only after the second query. This procedure returned 406 results in total, which are then subjected to a selection procedure based on the following exclusion criteria inspired by [7].

- Works that are not published in a peer-reviewed venue.
- Works that do not specifically address Fog/Edge computing infrastructures.
- Works that do not propose a general-purpose simulator or emulator.

Consequently, we obtained 11 relevant works to include in our study. Then we proceeded to extract main contributions and highlighted features from each work and the descriptions in the corresponding source code repository. This procedure yielded 29 features. After combining redundant features and excluding generic features that are supported by all simulators, six classification features remained. Excluded generic features include high-level network model (e.g. topology definition) and resource management.

14.2.2 *Features*

In this section, we describe the main features of the simulation and emulation tools considered in our classification. Our classification is presented in Table 14.1. Emulators are excluded from this classification because they refer to a specific platform and are used mostly to test the deployment of applications on this specific environment. In each column, "**Y**" indicates a supported feature, "**N**" a missing feature, and "**N***" a feature that is currently not supported but indicated as a future work either in the paper or source code repository. This table also contains general information about each simulator including underlying simulation platform, license for the source code availability, the programming language used, and recent activity of the project. We assume that the projects with a git commit within the last six months are active (**Y**) as of July 2019.

Behavior

We propose the deterministic or stochastic behavior of the simulator as the main distinctive feature. As described in the following two sections, this feature may completely change the way the simulator is utilized. The top six simulators in Table 14.1 are deterministic, whereas bottom two (separated by a bar) are stochastic.

Energy model

This feature indicates whether the energy consumption of the Fog/Edge nodes or user devices is simulated or emulated.

Cost model

A cost model accounts for the monetary aspects of the computation based on different pricing schemes.

Low-level network model

All simulators support high-level network topology design. This feature is about whether packet-level granularity is available.

Mobility model

Mobility indicates the possibility of the user and/or compute node movement during the simulation runtime.

Failure model

This feature indicates whether it is supported to simulate the failure and unavailability of certain nodes or links.

14.3 Deterministic simulators

Simulators introduced in this section do not contain random variables; hence, they produce always the same output given a particular input. Deterministic models are known to be easier to build and implement than stochastic ones. We review following

Table 14.1 *Comparison of Fog/Edge computing simulators (N* indicates a planned but not yet implemented feature)*

Edge/Fog simulator	General information				Classification				
	Underlying platform	Source availability	Prog. language	Currently active	Energy model	Cost model	Low-level network	Mobility model	Failure model
iFogSim	CloudSim	Apache v2.0	Java	N	Y	Y	N	N*	N*
EdgeCloudSim	CloudSim	GPL v3.0	Java	Y	N*	N	N	Y	N*
FogNetSim++	OMNeT++	GPL v3.0	C++	N	Y	Y	Y	Y	N
FogExplorer	N/A	MIT License	JavaScript	N	N	Y	N	N	N
YAFS	SimPy	MIT License	Python	Y	N*	Y	N	Y	Y
RECAP	N/A	N/A	N/A	N/A	N/A	N/A	N/A	N/A	N/A
FogTorchPi	N/A	MIT License	Java	N	Y	Y	N	N	Y
Sleipnir	FogTorchPi	MIT License	Java	Y	Y	Y	N	Y	Y

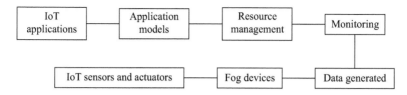

Figure 14.2   High-level architecture of iFogSim

six deterministic simulators: iFogSim, EdgeCloudSim, FogNetSim++, FogExplorer, YAFS, and RECAP.

14.3.1   iFogSim

To the best of our knowledge, iFogSim* is the first simulator specifically addressing Fog/Edge computing infrastructures. At the time of writing, it is also the most cited work that is discussed here and arguably the most widely used one. iFogSim is developed for IoT and Fog environments and considers the impact of resource management techniques in latency, network congestion, energy consumption, and operational costs [8].

The simulator supports the Sense–Process–Actuate model—that is, data are produced by the sensors, processed by the Fog nodes, and consumed by the actuators. Alternatively, the stream-processing model is also allowed. In this model, streaming data from the sensors are processed online at the Fog nodes and then forwarded to cloud data centers for long-term analytics. The Fog computing environment is modeled as a layered architecture shown in Figure 14.2, which includes the following elements from the bottom to the top.

1. **IoT sensors/actuators** are the sources and the sinks of the data, respectively. They both interact with the environment or an external physical system.
2. **Fog devices** are the main computation sources. They host application modules and can be located anywhere between the cloud and the network edge.
3. **Data streams** are either IoT data emitted from the sensors or log data generated by the Fog devices.
4. **Infrastructure monitoring** collects log data from Fog devices, sensors, and actuators. It keeps track of resource use, power consumption, and availability.
5. **Resource management** is where placement and scheduling decisions are made. They are responsible for confirming quality-of-service (QoS) constraints. Complex resource management mechanisms such as migration can be implemented by the user.
6. **Application model** represents the IoT application as a directed graph based on the distributed data flow (DDF) model.

---

*https://github.com/Cloudslab/iFogSim

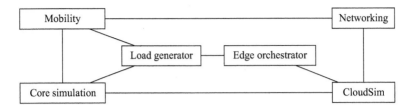

Figure 14.3   High-level architecture of EdgeCloudSim

ifogSim is implemented as an extension to the widely used event-based cloud computing simulator, CloudSim[†] [9]. Two application placement strategies, namely cloud-only and edge-ward placement, are already implemented as reference. Additionally, a graphical user interface is available to describe the physical network topology intuitively. Instructions to build the simulation of a Fog/Edge environment are provided in [10].

An extension to ifogSim that supports data placement strategies is also available[‡]. This extension also supports the formulation of the data placement problem as a mixed-integer linear program and includes a parallel solver in order to decrease the simulation time [11].

14.3.2   EdgeCloudSim

EdgeCloudSim[§] is another extension to CloudSim with edge computing support. Based on our literature review, it is the only deterministic simulator that targets the edge computing systems specifically, instead of the whole Fog computing continuum. The focal points of the simulator in addition to the general features of CloudSim include edge-specific applications, mobility, and wide-area or wireless network. The five main modules of EdgeCloudSim are shown in Figure 14.3 and described as follows [12].

1. **Core simulation** supports the XML-based configuration of simulation scenarios and detailed logging to facilitate the analysis of results.
2. **Edge orchestrator** manages the available resources, particularly taking offloading, placement, and replication decisions. In EdgeCloudSim, there is a single centralized orchestrator.
3. **Networking** module deals mainly with wireless networks and wide-area networks (WANs), which are missing in CloudSim. Both WLAN and cellular networks are supported for the communication between the edge servers and the users. WAN design follows the single server queue model.

[†]http://www.cloudbus.org/cloudsim/
[‡]https://github.com/medislam/iFogSimWithDataPlacement
[§]https://github.com/CagataySonmez/EdgeCloudSim

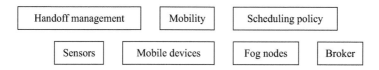

Figure 14.4   High-level architecture of FogNetSim++

4. **Mobility** of the users is simulated in EdgeCloudSim via a nomadic mobility model. It is possible to extend this model for other mobility strategies such as vehicular mobility.

5. **Load generator** provides the capability of defining different application types and generates application tasks according to a Poisson arrival process, by default.

EdgeCloudSim is designed flexibly through the factory pattern that facilitates extensions. Indeed, in a recent study [13], it is extended with a point-of-interest-based mobility model and a node availability model that is based on the failure–repair process.

14.3.3   FogNetSim++

FogNetSim++[||] [14] is a simulator that focuses on the network aspects of the Fog/Edge computing infrastructure rather than data generation and consumption. This results in the consideration of packet drop/error rate, network congestion, and channel collision. It allows the creation of a network system with static and dynamic nodes and supports various Fog/Edge protocols for communication, including MQTT, CoAP, and AMQP. Another focus of the simulator is the realistic mobility of the users. It supports various mobility models as well as handover mechanisms. The simulation kernel library is provided by the widely used discrete event library, OMNeT++[¶]. FogNetSim++ modules are developed as an extension to the INET framework[**], which is an OMNeT++ model suite for wired, wireless and mobile networks. Design architecture of the simulator is given in Figure 14.4. Three main modules are described as follows.

1. **Broker** is the centralized resource manager which is responsible for task scheduling, execution, and handover. Handovers are carried out due to either user mobility or load balancing. The broker also manages the communication between Fog nodes, Cloud data center, and end users.

2. **Fog node** is the provider of the computation. It is a static node located on a network gateway. They communicate with users and sensors through wireless access points.

3. **User and sensor** are the sources of the data and requests. Different from sensors, which only generate data, users can also receive data. Random waypoints as well

---

[||] https://github.com/rtqayyum/fognetsimpp
[¶] https://omnetpp.org/
[**] https://inet.omnetpp.org/

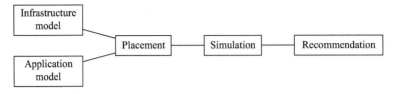

Figure 14.5   High-level architecture of FogExplorer

as Mass, Gauss Markov, Chaing, Circle, Linear, and vehicle mobility models are available.

The simulator also includes a graphical user interface as well as ready-to-use pricing models and an energy model. Pricing models include pay-as-you-go, subscription, pay-for-resources, and a hybrid one; whereas the energy model considers the consumption of both the device and Fog node. The scheduling policy is left to the programmer to implement.

14.3.4   FogExplorer

FogExlorer[††] is an interactive simulator intended for the design phase of Fog/Edge infrastructures, and particularly for the definition of the application architecture, the runtime infrastructure, and the mapping between these two [15]. It is based on iterative modeling and simulation shown in Figure 14.5 with the following steps.

1. High-level modeling of the application (modules and intermodule data streams) and the infrastructure (machines and interconnections).
2. Manual placement of the application modules on Fog machines.
3. Simulation and calculation of QoS and cost.
4. Recommendations for optimizing the placement by highlighting under-provisioned resources and missing connections.

Since FogExplorer targets the application design phase, both application and infrastructure models are quite abstract [16]. Application modules can be of three types: sources which produce the data; services which process them; and sinks which consume them. Sources are defined by an output rate and services by processing time as well as the ratio of output size. Outputs of the sources and services are either duplicated or equally distributed to all subsequent services or sinks. Required bandwidth between the modules is derived from these data. All three types of modules also have predefined memory requirements. Infrastructure nodes are defined by a processing performance indicator, available memory, and unit memory price. Connections, on the other hand, have available latency and bandwidth, as well as bandwidth cost properties.

[††]https://github.com/OpenFogStack/FogExplorer

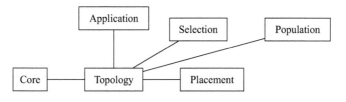

Figure 14.6   High-level architecture of YAFS

After the user defines the environment and suggests a module placement, the simulator calculates four metrics: processing cost, processing time, transmission cost, and transmission time. Additionally, it highlights under-provisioned machines and connections as well as the cases that a data stream cannot flow due to missing connections between the machines. Based on this feedback, the user can update the models or placement and a new simulation is triggered. FogExplorer is implemented as a front-end only web-based tool with JavaScript.

14.3.5   YAFS

Yet Another Fog Simulator[‡‡] focuses on network topology aspects of Fog/Edge computing. It is developed on top of the SimPy discrete-event simulator framework[§§]. Similar to EdgeCloudSim, YAFS supports text-based (JSON) configuration and ready to analyze CSV results. Authors list the network, workload sources, customized placement, custom processes, post-simulation data analysis, and scenario definition as the highlights of the YAFS [17]. The following are the main modules of the simulator that provide these features.

1. **Topology and entity modeling** implements the complex network theory (e.g. scale-free networks) and represents the Fog devices and the intercommunication links as a graph. It is possible to import CAIDA and BRITE topology models in different file formats.
2. **Application model** follows the DDF model similar to iFogSim. Here, an application is defined as a directed acyclic graph (DAG) where the nodes represent the tasks and the links their interoperability.
3. **Dynamic policies** deal with resource selection, task placement, and resource allocation. It is also possible to define custom processes that model user mobility and resource unavailability (due to failures).
4. **Results** include two types of events, task execution and network transmissions, which are logged to CSV files. It is then possible to visualize these events as graph animations.

The high-level architecture of YAFS is presented in Figure 14.6. Among all simulators, it seems to be most actively developed and maintained one with recent

---

[‡‡]https://github.com/acsicuib/YAFS
[§§]https://simpy.readthedocs.io/

improvements. For instance, the latest version allows importing GPX traces for the user and device mobility.

14.3.6 RECAP simulator

The RECAP simulator [18] is currently under development within the scope of the Horizon 2020 project *Reliable Capacity Provisioning and Enhanced Remediation for Distributed Cloud Applications* (RECAP).[ǁǁ] The project promises autonomous and optimal strategies for reliable and predictable capacity provisioning, application placement, and infrastructure management [19]. The scale of the considered systems hinders full-scale deployment for experimentation. Correspondingly, the RECAP simulator will cooperate with the RECAP optimizer component to simulate distributed cloud applications as well as the underlying infrastructure for a reproducible and controllable evaluation. The simulator will consist of (1) Experiment Manager, which gathers all models and experimental system information; (2) Simulation Manager, which controls the simulation; (3) Event Coordinator, which serializes simulation results and manages optimization and failure events; and (4) Event Generator, which injects events such as new tasks or failures to the simulation. At the time of writing, further details regarding the implementation and features of the simulators are not published, to the best of our knowledge. This refrains us from providing a fair comparison to other simulators. Hence, the RECAP simulator is excluded from our proposed classification.

14.4 Stochastic simulators

In this section, we describe simulations based on stochastic models of Fog/Edge infrastructures. The main advantage of using stochastic simulators is that in contexts with high mobility (e.g. VANETs and mobile computing) or with highly unreliable resources (e.g. IoT), the availability of resources can be easily modeled as a stochastic process, as done in works like [20,21]. In the following, we describe two state-of-the-art simulators: FogTorchPi and Sleipnir.

14.4.1 FogTorchPI

FogTorchPi[¶¶] [5] is an open-source Java simulator of Fog/Edge infrastructures with the high-level architecture depicted in Figure 14.7. FogTorchPi input consists of the following:

- A description of a Fog/Edge infrastructure *i*. In this description, it is needed to specify the (1) IoT devices (a.k.a. "Thing" in the simulator terminology); (2) Fog/Edge and Cloud data centers available for application deployment. (For each one of these data centers, it is needed to specify the hardware capabilities

ǁǁ https://recap-project.eu/
¶¶ https://github.com/di-unipi-socc/FogTorchPI

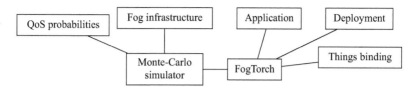

Figure 14.7   High-level architecture of FogTorchPI

(number of cores, amount of RAM and storage).); (3) network infrastructure, along with the probability distributions of the QoS (latency, bandwidth) available on the communication links (Cloud-to-Fog, Fog-to-Fog and Fog-to-Things); (4) cost for purchasing Cloud/Fog virtual instances.

- An application description a. Each application is composed of different components. For each component, it is needed to specify (1) hardware (CPU, RAM, storage), software (OS, libraries, frameworks), and IoT device binding; (2) the QoS (e.g. latency and bandwidth) needed to adequately support component–component and component–Thing interactions after application's deployment.
- An IoT mapping τ, describing the requirements of each connection between each application component and IoT device (Thing).
- A deployment policy δ that describes on which nodes components can be deployed to respect security or business-related constraints.

Starting from the input (i, a, τ, δ), FogTorchPi determines admissible deployments for a over infrastructure i, given the QoS requirements of a, the IoT mapping τ, and the deployment policy δ. QoS requirements of a are determined by the user, while QoS available on the infrastructure is determined by sampling the probability distribution for latency and bandwidth specified in the simulator setup. FogTorchPi follows a Monte-Carlo approach to identify the admissible deployments. First, it performs a sampling of the QoS available on each communication link, according to the probability distribution specified. At the end of the sampling phase, the simulator performs a random admissible deployment of each application component, such that it respects (1) the QoS requirement of application a, (2) the IoT mapping τ, and (3) the deployment policy δ. These two phases are repeated for a given number of iterations. At the end of the iterations, the resulting deployments are collected in a histogram, in order to calculate the frequency of each admissible deployment. For each deployment in the histogram, FogTorchPi also calculates the QoS measures and its cost, according to the cost model specified in the infrastructure description i.

14.4.2   Sleipnir

SLEIPNIR[***] (Spark-enabled mobiLe Edge offloadIng Platform moNte-carlo sImulatoR) is an extended version of FogTorchPi, described in [20]. The main improvement

---

[***]https://github.com/vindem/sleipnir

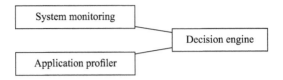

Figure 14.8   High-level architecture of Sleipnir

of SLEIPNIR with respect to its predecessor is the fact that it runs on the Apache Spark platform [22] that allows it to easily scale according to the underlying computational resources. In addition to its predecessor, it also provides simulation support for mobile devices and for mobility traces coming from SUMO. At the time we write, simulator architecture is as given in Figure 14.8 and its input consists of the following:

- A description of an Edge infrastructure $\mathcal{I}$. This description includes the number and specification of Cloud, Edge, and mobile nodes that describes the sets $\mathcal{C}$, $\mathcal{E}$ and $\mathcal{D}$, respectively, and a directed graph $\mathcal{N}$ modeling the network connections between the nodes, as in FogTorchPi.
- A map $\mathcal{M}$ of a geographical area where to place the Edge nodes, according to a placement algorithm. At the moment, the simulator offers only the possibility of deploying Edge over three areas of the city of Vienna.
- An optional mobility trace, coming from SUMO, modeling the mobility of mobile devices over the selected map.
- A workflow $\mathcal{W}$, composed of different mobile application description $\mathcal{A}$. Each application is described as a DAG. At this moment, the simulator offers five different types of applications: NAVIGATOR, modeling a navigation app; CHESS, modeling a chess game on a smartphone; FACEBOOK, modeling the posting of a picture on Facebook; FACERECOGNIZER, modeling a photo-processing app; and ANTIVIRUS, modeling a virus scan. In the workflow, it is also possible to specify the frequency at which each application occurs.

Starting from $\mathcal{I}$, $\mathcal{M}$, and $\mathcal{W}$, the simulator identifies admissible deployments of tasks in $\mathcal{W}$ over infrastructure $\mathcal{I}$. The user specifies the QoS requirement for the workflow, based on which it tries to determine an admissible deployment of tasks on the infrastructure. QoS available on the infrastructure is determined by sampling the probability distribution for latency and bandwidth specified in the simulator setup. The sampling of infrastructure and workflow is repeated for a given number of iterations. At the end of the iterations, the resulting deployments are collected in a histogram, in order to calculate the frequency of each admissible deployment.

Applications and offloading policies are defined in [20], while in [21] it has also been used for comparing different Edge provisioning methods.

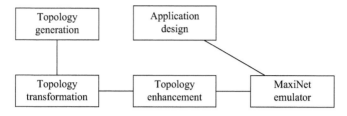

Figure 14.9   High-level architecture of EmuFog

14.5   Emulators

14.5.1   EmuFog

EmuFog[†††] provides a test environment for Fog computing, built on top of MaxiNet [23] (an extension of Mininet [24] that allows the emulation of data center network spanning over multiple network nodes). The main design objectives of EmuFog are (1) scalability, allowing the emulation of large-scale Fog/Edge computing scenarios; (2) emulation of real application/workloads, allowing the developer to package real-world application and run them in the emulated environment; (3) extensibility, to allow each framework's component to be replaced by custom-built components, suiting the scenario to be emulated. The emulation workflow consists of four main steps depicted in Figure 14.9.

1. **Topology generation.** In this phase, the developer generates a network topology using tools like BRITE [25]. EmuFog also allows to load network topology from a topology database, which ensures reproducibility of experiments on real-world network topology.
2. **Topology transformation.** In this phase, the network topology generated in the topology generation phase is converted in the EmuFog network model, which is seen as an undirected graph where each network device is an autonomous system.
3. **Topology enhancement.** In this phase, the network topology is enhanced by adding the Fog/Edge nodes. To this end, first, the edge of the network topology is determined, and then Fog/Edge nodes are placed in the network according to a placement policy. Placement policy is specified in a Fog/Edge configuration file.
4. **Deployment and execution.** In this phase, the enhanced topology is deployed in the emulation environment. Fog/Edge nodes are placed in the emulated network, while the applications are deployed on them in form of Docker containers.

In [26], the emulator is described in detail, including also the performance evaluation.

[†††] https://github.com/emufog/emufog

Figure 14.10　High-level architecture of Cloud4IoT

At the time we write, EmuFog does not provide emulation of mobility and, therefore, does not allow the evaluation of mobile devices (e.g. drones, vehicles, and mobile phones). Also, no emulation of hierarchical Fog/Edge environments is provided.

14.5.2　Cloud4IoT

Cloud4IoT [27] is a lightweight PaaS platform specialized for Edge/Cloud applications, designed for the native support of IoT. Its logical model (Figure 14.10) is composed of three layers: (1) The *Central Cloud platform*, which hosts the central controller functionality and offers additional scalability when needed. This layer works as an orchestrator and a scheduler for the workload running on the platform, and it is implemented on a private OpenStack-based Cloud. (2) The *Edge Cloud Modules*, which are designed to let the data-intensive applications run close to the source of data (in this case, the IoT devices, also defined as IoT gateways). Such modules are small-sized servers with limited storage and computational power. Such servers can be used to offload the workload from the edges to the cloud and vice versa. Moreover, they also improve resilience, providing additional resources to the IoT gateways. (3) The *IoT gateways*, representing the hardware interface with objects and the acquisition of data from IoT sensor objects. Cloud4IoT mainly supports two types of applications: IoT support applications and data logic/processing.

IoT-specific applications support the deployment and the maintenance of new objects/sensors in the field. Such applications offer the following services: (1) *discovery* of new objects attached to an IoT gateway; (2) *retrieval* of the firmware version suitable with OS and model of the needed object; (3) *dispatch* of the data collected on the Edge modules connected to the IoT gateway; (4) *installation* of new applications to support and manage newly acquired and/or updated objects.

The latter type of applications instead is deployed, scheduled, and orchestrated from the central cloud onto the Edge modules, according to the current platform condition. The deployment is performed according to the users' latency requirements: applications with high latency requirements can be deployed on the cloud, while an application with short latency requirements can be deployed on the Edge modules. In the current version of Cloud4IoT, orchestration is performed by employing a simple threshold-based mechanism.

14.5.3　Fogbed

Fogbed is described in [28] with the simplified architecture in Figure 14.11. It is described as a framework and integration toolset for rapid prototyping of Fog components in a virtualized environment. The simulator is based on Mininet [24] and Docker. It extends the Mininet emulator by allowing the use of Docker containers

Figure 14.11   High-level architecture of Fogbed

as virtual nodes. Fogbed emulation works through the deployment of pre-configured container images, such as the following:

1. *Cloud container image*: Containers of this type emulate virtual resources for IoT applications. They can also act as a virtual cloud instance or act as proxies for cloud services located in remote data centers.
2. *Fog container image*: Containers of this type emulate Fog nodes that perform processing and storage of data coming from the IoT gateways. It also performs analytics and filtering of raw data.
3. *Edge container image*: Containers of this type emulate IoT gateways or smart IoT devices. It is also possible to simulate sensors and send data to a virtual Fog instance.

The emulation workflow goes as follows: First, the developer provides the images that he/she wants to instantiate to perform the emulation. Second, the developer defines a network topology for application testing. In contrast with EmuFog (see Section 14.5.1), Fogbed employs its own language for the definition of topology. Afterward, Fogbed executes the emulator with the described topology. Once the emulator starts its execution, the developer starts the management system that connects to the emulated environment using the instance API. The management system then deploys the application on the platform and starts the required services in the virtual nodes. Afterward, the application can run in the platform, and network flow statistics are collected and stored for future analysis. In [28], the authors describe a use case of Fogbed for the development of a health monitoring application using Cloud/Fog infrastructures and data coming from simulated wearable sensors. At the current stage, the emulator does not offer emulation of features like mobile offloading, fault tolerance, and reliable management and security. This might be improved by developing new functionalities that allow injecting failures and simulating security attacks. In addition, a deeper study of the emulation scalability would be required.

14.6   Discussion

In this chapter, we discussed the main issues about modeling and simulation of Fog/Edge infrastructures. Based on these issues, we identified the main characteristics of the most used solutions in the literature for the simulation and emulation of Fog/Edge infrastructures and designed a classification for these tools. Finally, we described the most used solutions in the literature. According to our analysis, we notice that there is no perfect solution for simulation of Fog/Edge infrastructure since each of the existing tools is specifically tailored for the given characteristics. Moreover, at the time we write, some research challenges are left open. We describe them in the rest of this section.

14.6.1   Reliability

Fog/Edge computing hardware is prone to failures due to geographical dispersion, limited resources, and the absence of advanced support systems as in cloud data centers [29]. The reliability of the resources has a direct impact on other QoS parameters such as latency and energy efficiency. However, this aspect of Edge computing is mostly overlooked in existing simulators. It is left as future work in two most widely used simulators, namely iFogSim and EdgeCloudSim. Other works such as YAFS and FogTorchPi support dynamic availability of compute nodes and network links due to failures. More detailed failure models (e.g. correlated failures or Byzantine faults) are needed for the realistic simulation of the Fog/Edge environment.

14.6.2   Network simulation

The advent of distributed services rapidly removes the borders between computing and networking systems and demands their joint consideration. Reflecting this circumstance, all Fog/Edge simulators and emulators support network modeling to a certain extent. However, network models are limited to high-level topology design in almost all cases. Only FogNetSim++ supports low-level details such as packet routing and switching. This is because it is developed as an extension to an existing network simulator, OMNeT++.

14.6.3   Validation

At the time we write, most of the simulation and emulation frameworks lack an extensive and rigorous evaluation of results. This is because of the lack of real-world implementations of large-scale Fog/Edge infrastructures. Also, the only commercial providers delivering Edge services are Amazon, with Lambda@Edge[‡‡‡] and Azure IoT Edge.[§§§] However, commercial platforms do not allow to measure all the parameters that are needed by researchers, which poses several issues in collecting the data that are necessary for validation of the simulations. In papers like [30], validation is performed on data coming from a smart building use case. However, such data sets are used only as an example of the workload of typical Fog/Edge infrastructures. In many works, validation is performed using Cloud or IoT data sets, which are not suitable to simulate near real-time applications typical of Fog/Edge infrastructures. In the future, there is the need for developing data sets representing real-world Fog/Edge infrastructures or deploying more real-world infrastructures that allow to perform measurements or to deploy applications for validation of simulations.

[‡‡‡] https://aws.amazon.com/en/lambda/edge/
[§§§] https://azure.microsoft.com/en-us/services/iot-edge/

14.6.4 Missing general-purpose solution

As our classification in Table 14.1 demonstrates, there currently exists no general-purpose solution for all simulation and emulation needs. ifogSim is the most widely used simulation tool despite the absence of low-level network, mobility, and failure modeling support. In problems, where the network plays the most important role, one may prefer FogNetSim++. Alternatively, if reliability is the main focus, YAFS, FogTorchPi, or Sleipnir might be chosen. However, these solutions are not yet as mature or stable as iFogSim.

14.7 Conclusion

In this chapter, we propose a classification of all existing simulators and emulators for Fog/Edge computing. First, we describe the main challenges in simulation and modeling for Fog/Edge infrastructures. Then, we describe the research methodology that we use to identify the main characteristics of Fog/Edge simulators and emulators and classify existing tools for simulation and emulation of Fog/Edge infrastructures. Afterward, we describe Fog/Edge simulators and emulators, identifying their pros and cons. Finally, we describe the possible future research directions and identify issues that should be solved to deliver an accurate simulation of Fog/Edge infrastructures. In the future, we expect increased interest in the simulation and modeling of such infrastructures. Such interest will be even more encouraged by the increasing diffusion of Fog/Edge infrastructures that will help to produce data set that can be used to perform validation and give more insights on the shape of real-world Fog/Edge infrastructures.

Acknowledgments

This work has been funded through the Rucon project (Runtime Control in Multi Clouds), FWF Y 904 START-Programm 2015.

References

[1] Sergej Svorobej, Patricia Takako Endo, Malika Bendechache, *et al.* Simulating fog and edge computing scenarios: An overview and research challenges. *Future Internet*, 11(3):55, 2019.

[2] Qiliang Zhu, Baojiang Si, Feifan Yang, and You Ma. Task offloading decision in fog computing system. *China Communications*, 14(11):59–68, 2017.

[3] Long Chen, Jigang Wu, Xin Long, and Zikai Zhang. ENGINE: Cost-effective offloading in mobile edge computing with fog-cloud cooperation. *CoRR*, abs/1711.01683, 2017.

[4] Andreas Reiter, Bernd Pünster, and Thomas Zefferer. Hybrid mobile edge computing: Unleashing the full potential of edge computing in mobile device

use cases. In *2017 17th IEEE/ACM International Symposium on Cluster, Cloud and Grid Computing (CCGRID)*, pages 935–944, 2017.

[5]   Antonio Brogi, Stefano Forti, and Ahmad Ibrahim. How to best deploy your fog applications, probably. In *2017 IEEE 1st International Conference on Fog and Edge Computing (ICFEC)*, pages 105–114, May 2017.

[6]   Xuezhi Zeng, Saurabh Kumar Garg, Peter Strazdins, Prem Prakash Jayaraman, Dimitrios Georgakopoulos, and Rajiv Ranjan. IOTSim: A simulator for analysing IoT applications. *Journal of Systems Architecture*, 72:93–107, 2017.

[7]   Pooyan Jamshidi, Aakash Ahmad, and Claus Pahl. Cloud migration research: A systematic review. *IEEE Transactions on Cloud Computing*, 1(2):142–157, 2013.

[8]   Harshit Gupta, Amir Vahid Dastjerdi, Soumya K. Ghosh, and Rajkumar Buyya. iFogSim: A toolkit for modeling and simulation of resource management techniques in the Internet of things, edge and fog computing environments. *Software: Practice and Experience*, 47(9):1275–1296, 2017.

[9]   Rodrigo N. Calheiros, Rajiv Ranjan, Anton Beloglazov, César A.F. De Rose, and Rajkumar Buyya. CloudSim: A toolkit for modeling and simulation of cloud computing environments and evaluation of resource provisioning algorithms. *Software: Practice and Experience*, 41(1):23–50, 2011.

[10]   Redowan Mahmud and Rajkumar Buyya. Modelling and simulation of fog and edge computing environments using iFogSim toolkit. *Fog and Edge Computing: Principles and Paradigms*, pages 1–35, 2019.

[11]   Mohammed Islam Naas, Jalil Boukhobza, Philippe Raipin Parvedy, and Laurent Lemarchand. An extension to iFogSim to enable the design of data placement strategies. In *IEEE 2nd International Conference on Fog and Edge Computing (ICFEC)*, pages 1–8. IEEE, 2018.

[12]   Cagatay Sonmez, Atay Ozgovde, and Cem Ersoy. EdgeCloudSim: An environment for performance evaluation of edge computing systems. *Transactions on Emerging Telecommunications Technologies*, 29(11):e3493, 2018.

[13]   Atakan Aral, Ivona Brandic, Rafael Brundo Uriarte, Rocco De Nicola, and Vincenzo Scoca. Addressing application latency requirements through edge scheduling. *Journal of Grid Computing*, 17(4):677–698, 2019.

[14]   Tariq Qayyum, Asad Waqar Malik, Muazzam A. Khan Khattak, Osman Khalid, and Samee U. Khan. FogNetSim++: A toolkit for modeling and simulation of distributed fog environment. *IEEE Access*, 6:63570–63583, 2018.

[15]   Jonathan Hasenburg, Sebastian Werner, and David Bermbach. FogExplorer. In *Proceedings of the 19th International Middleware Conference (Posters)*, pages 1–2. ACM, 2018.

[16]   Jonathan Hasenburg, Sebastian Werner, and David Bermbach. Supporting the evaluation of fog-based IoT applications during the design phase. In *Proceedings of the 5th Workshop on Middleware and Applications for the Internet of Things*, pages 1–6. ACM, 2018.

[17]   Isaac Lera, Carlos Guerrero, and Carlos Juiz. YAFS: A simulator for IoT scenarios in fog computing. *IEEE Access*, 7:91745–91758, 2019.

[18] James Byrne, Sergej Svorobej, Anna Gourinovitch, *et al.* RECAP simulator: Simulation of cloud/edge/fog computing scenarios. In *2017 Winter Simulation Conference (WSC)*, pages 4568–4569. IEEE, 2017.

[19] Per-Olov Östberg, James Byrne, Paolo Casari, *et al.* Reliable capacity provisioning for distributed cloud/edge/fog computing applications. In *2017 European Conference on Networks and Communications (EuCNC)*, pages 1–6. IEEE, 2017.

[20] Vincenzo De Maio and Ivona Brandic. First hop mobile offloading of DAG computations. In *2018 18th IEEE/ACM International Symposium on Cluster, Cloud and Grid Computing (CCGRID)*, pages 83–92, 2018.

[21] Vincenzo De Maio and Ivona Brandic. Multi-objective mobile edge provisioning in small cell clouds. In *Proceedings of the 2019 ACM/SPEC International Conference on Performance Engineering*, ICPE'19, pages 127–138. ACM, 2019.

[22] Matei Zaharia, Reynold S. Xin, Patrick Wendell, *et al.* Apache Spark: A unified engine for big data processing. *Commun. ACM*, 59(11):56–65, 2016.

[23] Philip Wette, Martin Dräxler, Arne Schwabe, Felix Wallaschek, Mohammad Hassan Zahraee, and Holger Karl. Maxinet: Distributed emulation of software-defined networks. In *2014 IFIP Networking Conference*, pages 1–9, 2014.

[24] Bob Lantz, Brandon Heller, and Nick McKeown. A network in a laptop: Rapid prototyping for software-defined networks. In *Proceedings of the 9th ACM SIGCOMM Workshop on Hot Topics in Networks*, Hotnets-IX, pages 19:1–19:6, New York, NY, USA, 2010. ACM.

[25] Alberto Medina, Anukool Lakhina, Ibrahim Matta, and John Byers. BRITE: An approach to universal topology generation. In *MASCOTS 2001, Proceedings Ninth International Symposium on Modeling, Analysis and Simulation of Computer and Telecommunication Systems*, pages 346–353, Aug 2001.

[26] Ruben Mayer, Leon Graser, Harshit Gupta, Enrique Saurez, and Umakishore Ramachandran. EmuFog: Extensible and scalable emulation of large-scale fog computing infrastructures. *CoRR*, abs/1709.07563, 2017.

[27] Daniele Pizzolli, Giuseppe Cossu, Daniele Santoro, *et al.* Cloud4IoT: A heterogeneous, distributed and autonomic cloud platform for the IoT. In *2016 IEEE International Conference on Cloud Computing Technology and Science (CloudCom)*, pages 476–479, 2016.

[28] Antonio Coutinho, Fabiola Greve, Cassio Prazeres, and Joao Cardoso. Fogbed: A rapid-prototyping emulation environment for fog computing. In *2018 IEEE International Conference on Communications (ICC)*, pages 1–7, May 2018.

[29] Atakan Aral and Ivona Brandic. Dependency mining for service resilience at the edge. In *2018 IEEE/ACM Symposium on Edge Computing (SEC)*, pages 228–242. IEEE, 2018.

[30] Ivan Lujic, Vincenzo De Maio, and Ivona Brandic. Adaptive recovery of incomplete datasets for edge analytics. In *2018 IEEE 2nd International Conference on Fog and Edge Computing (ICFEC)*, pages 1–10, 2018.

Part III

Applications

Chapter 15

Smart cities enabled by edge computing

Wuhui Chen[1], Zhen Zhang[1], and Baichuan Liu[1]

Recently, smart city is a very hot topic, which uses a variety of information technologies to integrate the constituent systems and services of cities to improve the efficiency of resource usage, optimize urban management and services, and improve citizens' quality of life. The popularity of smart cities cannot be separated from the rapid development of the Internet of Things (IoT), and the IoT infrastructure plays an important role in smart cities. With the increase in urbanization scale, more and more IoT devices are integrated into cities. Therefore, the amount of urban data is increasing rapidly, and the data are becoming more diversified and heterogeneous, posing great challenges for the operation of smart cities. Fortunately, the rise of edge computing has provided very good solutions for the development and construction of smart cities. The integration of edge computing model on the basis of cloud computing can ensure more real-time processing and accurate decision-making of large-scale data in the context of smart cities. Nowadays, many practical applications based on the edge computing model have been implemented, such as video monitoring system, smart home, intelligent manufacturing and intelligent traffic. To sum up, edge computing model is an ideal platform for smart city.

15.1 Smart city makes life better

15.1.1 Why to build a smart city?

Urbanization is getting faster and faster. According to UN statistics, by 2050, there are over 6 billion people living in cities around the world. At the same time, the city consumes about 70% of the world's energy [1]. As the number of cities increases, the size of the city becomes larger and the city becomes more and more crowded, it is more and more challenging to solve the problem of transportation, medical care, education, food supply, culture and entertainment in cities.

Smart cities apply techniques such as IoT, communication and information management to use resources more efficiently and intelligently, so that the quality of

[1]School of Data and Computer Science, Sun Yat-Sen University, Guangzhou, China and National Engineering Research Center of Digital Life, Sun Yat-Sen University, Guangzhou, China

urban social and economic services is improved. The purpose of building smart cities is to solve various problems brought about by urban population growth through technologies and to achieve sustainable development of cities.

15.1.2 Definition of a smart city

Currently, there is still no clear definition of what smart city is about precisely yet. IBM defines a smart city as "one that makes optimal use of all the interconnected information available today to better understand and control its operations and optimize the use of limited resources" [2].

With the development of communication technologies such as 5G, the infrastructure construction of smart cities in the future will further show the characteristics of the IoT. In the city, numerous sensor devices will be installed to collect data involving urban security, transportation, energy utilization, medical health and other aspects. These sensors will generate a large amount of data that needs to be processed, which cannot avoid the 3V's characteristics of big data, namely volume, variety and velocity. In the era of 5G, the number of IoT devices accessing the network will be far more than the one of personal devices. These IoT devices make contribution to smart cities by offering data for urban decision-makers to analysis, calculation, prediction and detection, so that cities can provide citizens with better services. In conventional cloud computing model, if a large amount of data generated by sensors is transmitted to the cloud computing center for processing, although the computing capacity and storage of the cloud data center is affordable, the problem of high latency of data transmission cannot be solved. Moreover, the conventional cloud computing models may fail to work in complex network environments (such as network disconnection and power outage). In addition, it is also difficult to solve the problem of user data privacy leakage when keeping user's data in the public cloud. Therefore, building a smart city need to use edge computing to help solve the above problems. However, edge devices have limited computing power and storage capacity and are not capable of computing-intensive tasks. In the context of a smart city, a single computing model cannot solve all the problems. Therefore, the integration of multiple computing models is required, and edge computing plays an important role in smart cities.

15.1.3 Architecture of smart cities enabled by edge computing

Today, many organizations have proposed solutions for building smart cities. These solutions have some common features, such as layered model, in which different layers are responsible for implementing different functions. According to [3], a general architecture of smart city is shown in Figure 15.1.

As shown in Figure 15.1, the system architecture for smart cities mainly includes four parts: sensing layer, network layer, data layer and application layer.

- *Sensing layer.* Including a variety of sensors and devices that provide data for smart city applications such as unmanned ground vehicles (UGVs), unmanned aerial vehicles (UAVs), cameras, meteorological instruments, smoke alarms and

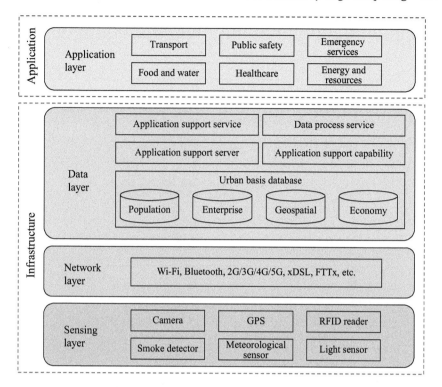

Figure 15.1   General layer smart city architecture

personal electronic devices, and other devices that have the ability to sense the city's natural environment. These devices can be deployed outside towers, bridges, etc., or integrated into public facilities such as street lights, power grids, and water supply facilities, and can be installed in the home. They have limited processing power and storage capacity.

- *Network layer.* Responsible for providing network connectivity for devices in sensing layer and data layer. The network layer is responsible for transmitting the data collected by the sensor to the cloud computing center and the edge servers. Due to the heterogeneity of data generated by sensors, the communication standards of the network layer are various, which can be 4G, 5G mobile networks, Wi-Fi, Bluetooth, wired networks, etc., so the implementation of the network layer is complex. However, it does not need to build a network layer from scratch, and we can implement it based on the existing communication network.

- *Data layer.* Including hardware facilities such as servers, databases and data ware-houses to implement data storage and processing. This layer analyzes organizes various data collected by the sensor and turn them into knowledge which can be used as a reference for the decision-makers. At the same time, the data layer also provides reliable and robust hardware and software services for smart city applications.

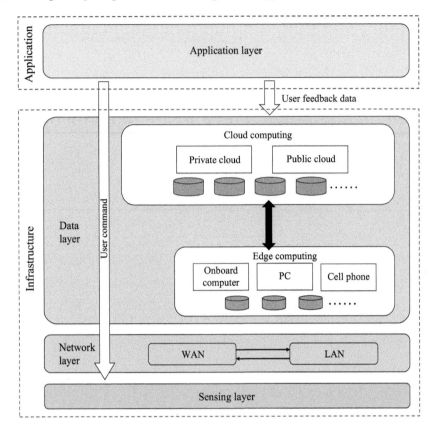

Figure 15.2   Smart city architecture enabled by edge computing

- *Application layer.* Including various applications, such as apps on smart phones and web applications. These applications use the valuable data and software and hardware services provided by the data layer to serve the citizens in all aspects of daily life, including cultural entertainment, medical health, transportation and other services. On the other hand, the citizens can feed back to the data layer through the applications, generate and upload user data, and interact with the devices in the sensing layer.

However, this generalized model does not emphasize the role of edge computing in smart cities. The basic purpose of the edge computing system platform is to provide a solution for edge computing applications with low latency and improved real-time data processing ability. Therefore, a solution that combines edge computing technology with a smart city is shown as Figure 15.2.

At the network layer, network can be divided into local area network (LAN) and wide area network (WAN). The LAN is responsible for providing high reliability, high bandwidth and low-latency network services for communication devices in the sensing layer and data layer. The WAN is responsible for providing network services for the cloud data center in data layer and the sensors in the sensing layer. Also, some edge devices can access the cloud data center through WAN.

At the data layer, the edge servers are geographically closer to the sensors of the sensing layer, so they connect to the sensors through the LAN and directly provide computing, storage and other services to the sensing layer devices, such as UAVs and UGVs. With the help of edge servers, IoT devices can speed up some low-complexity task and mitigate the transmission pressure of massive data in the network. Connecting through the WAN, the cloud server can support the edge devices to tackle the compute-intensive tasks. On the other hand, in some scenarios where the application is not time-sensitive, the cloud servers communicate with the sensing layer devices through the WAN to provide powerful computing power and mass storage.

15.1.4 Combination of IoT and edge computing in smart city

According to the definition in Wikipedia, IoT is a system of interrelated computing devices, mechanical and digital machines, objects, animals or people that are provided with unique identifiers (UIDs) and the ability to transfer data over a network without requiring human-to-human or human-to-computer interaction [4]. Various technologies are involved implementing the idea of IoT, such as radio-frequency identification (RFID), near-field communication, machine-to-machine communication and vehicle-to-vehicle communication [5]. With these technologies, tens of thousands of devices are connected and share information with each other.

In the last few years, IoT applications usually implement with cloud platform. Sensor devices collect information just like sensory organs in a human body. To make best use of the these IoT devices, it still needs a smart brain to organize, process and analyze the collected data. So, the cloud data center plays the role as the "smart brain." However, security and privacy issues of these cloud-based IoT application are intractable, and overdependence of the stable network connection is also the major issues. Fortunately, the combination of IoT and edge computing becomes a good solution to the above issues. To make task computing take place as close as possible to the data source, edge-based IoT applications don't have to upload the data through Internet, so it can effectively avoid hacker attacks and privacy leaks. Nowadays, many edge-based IoT applications have been deployed in the city to make our life better:

- ThyssenKrupp, a German manufacturer, has more than one million elevators worldwide, and they are already using the edge computing and IoT cloud platform to predict when the elevator will fail and take precautions in advance. To handle the connections and analysis of one million elevators, it needs an adequate computing power to process the massive data. ThyssenKrupp uses edge computing to deal with the immediate feedback tasks while it leaves the complex tasks to the cloud data center.
- Coca-Cola uses edge computing and IoT cloud platform to manage beverage machines located throughout the country. Edge devices allow customers to quickly customize their products from over 100 different beverage combinations and

collect large amounts of information related to consumer preferences, which are then shared with the Coca-Cola central data center via the cloud.

15.1.5   Application of edge computing in smart city

The application of information technology is the most direct and effective way to prove whether a new technology is valuable. Similarly, the value of edge computing technology for smart cities depends on the its applications. Only through the examples of applications can we find the challenges and opportunities encountered in the smart cities enabled by edge computing. Therefore, several practical applications of edge computing technology in smart cities are given next. In these cases, we can find the prospects of edge computing.

15.1.5.1   CCTV system enabled by edge computing

The closed-circuit television (CCTV) system enables system play an important role in dealing with public issues such as crime and social management. By deploying a large number of cameras in public areas, it can not only record the criminal evidence of criminals, but also effectively shock the criminals. CCTV system can also monitor the flow of people in different areas to prevent sudden public safety events. In addition, the CCTV system can also support object recognition functions to track lost vehicles or lost children. In order to achieve the above functions, a smart brain of the camera is indispensable. The camera of the traditional CCTV system has no computing power, and if the video is uploaded to the cloud for processing, it will consume a lot of network bandwidth. Therefore, using edge devices to process and store the video captured by the camera is a good solution. The CCTV system and the edge computing devices are connected through the LAN, and the data can be quickly transmitted. At the same time, the edge device can use a special image processing chip to process the video content more efficiently [6].

15.1.5.2   Smart home enabled by edge computing

At the beginning, smart home mainly relied on the remote control of electrical appliances. With the development of the IoT, the scope of smart home devices has been continuously expanded, including lighting control systems, video surveillance, kitchen and television systems [7]. To make smart homes more automated and energy efficient, and improve the life of citizens, smart home devices must have a smart brain that helps them process and analyze data. In the conventional cloud computing model, a cloud computing center is not enough to meet the needs of smart homes. For the sake of limited bandwidth of data transmission and individual privacy, the processing of these sensitive data should be done within the family. A smart home system platform based on edge computing can not only process the data collected by the home equipment in the family, avoid the problem of privacy leakage, but also reduce the delay of data transmission, making feedback to the users more timely, which leads to a better user experience.

15.1.5.3 Intelligent manufacturing enabled by edge computing

Since the German government proposed the concept of Industry 4.0, intelligent manufacturing has become more and more concerned. Intelligent manufacturing is a human–machine integrated intelligent system composed of robots and human experts. It can carry out intelligent activities such as analysis, reasoning, judgment and decision-making in the manufacturing process. The key of Industry 4.0 is to build a highly flexible intelligent and digital intelligent manufacturing model through the cyber–physical system [8], which belongs to the domain of edge computing.

15.1.6 Specific applications of edge computing in urban traffic

With the growth of urban population and the vehicles held by citizens, urban traffic is facing increasingly severe challenges. The larger the scale of city, the more serious the traffic congestion. The impact of road traffic congestion on the economy is significant. A report from the Texas Transportation Institute estimated that, in 2014, the economic loss caused by road traffic congestion in terms of extra travel delay and fuel consumption was 160 billion dollars [9].

A remarkable result on dealing with urban congestion has been achieved in Guangzhou, China. Government shares real-time information on the bus (such as speed and position) with developers, and the bus arrival time at different stations can be viewed on the map apps in real time. At the same time, the map apps can calculate the congestion status of each road segment by processing the user-generated content data [10] and predict the commute time and plan the optimal path. With the help of map apps, citizens can plan ahead in advance to shorter their time wasted on road.

Although Guangzhou has made great efforts in traffic management, there will still be congestion at the rush hour. Looking to the future, unmanned driving [11] is one of the best solutions to traffic congestion, but it puts extremely high demands on delay. For the well-known reasons, offloading data or computation to the cloud introduces inevitable delays. It is impossible to apply a pure cloud computing model for driverless vehicle, because the road information obtained from the cloud will be biased compared with the ever-changing road conditions. So, the unmanned driving cannot be achieved without the help of edge computing. A schematic diagram of a smart transportation system based on edge computing is shown in Figure 15.3. The sensor layer mainly includes various devices to obtain traffic information, such as cameras, GPS, speedometers, etc., which are installed in places such as vehicles, UAVs and traffic lights. The edge devices include various computing devices, such as onboard computers on vehicles, roadside base stations and personal computers. These devices form a vehicular *ad hoc* network (VANET) [12] where information is shared with each other. Devices can join or leave the VANET at any time. The cloud service includes public and private clouds, which can make up for the lack of computing power of the edge devices.

The operation of the entire smart transportation system is the result of close collaboration between the devices. As shown in Figure 15.3, when a traffic jam occurs in a road section, the sensors on the vehicles near the accident site first senses the change of the road condition and communicates with the nearby vehicle through

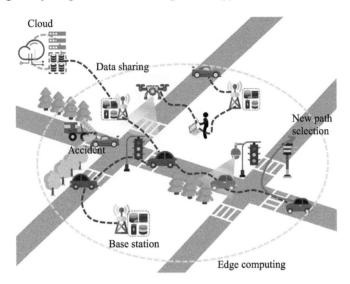

Figure 15.3   Example of edge computing applied in urban traffic: sensors and edge devices in ad hoc network work synergistically to avoid traffic congestion

the *ad hoc* network to inform the accident. After the vehicles get the information, they continue to disseminate it to the adjacent vehicle and plan a new path to avoid the congested road. The traffic information can also be provided by a CCTV system or UAVs [13]. The roadside surveillance camera can sense changes in traffic and pass the data to the edge computing device which stores and sends the data to the vehicle entering the area. In areas where surveillance cameras are not deployed or additional monitoring is required, UAVs can be deployed. The UAV transmits the road condition information to the ground station, and the latter analyzes it and then uploads it to the cloud computing center.

As a typical application of edge computing in smart cities, smart transportation system combined with edge computing can not only provide real-time traffic conditions to help citizens to shorter their commuting time, but also enable city managers to make optimal decisions when deploying public transportation resources.

15.2   Computation offloading, resource allocation and task scheduling in smart city

With the rapid development of smart city, the data processed by smart city system are becoming more and more diversified, and the amount of data is also increasing. Moreover, the data should be processed as quickly as possible. Because some of the emerging applications in the smart city are time-sensitive, such as the real-time application used for public safety and so on. In fact, the intelligent city system is full of information complexes composed of various applications and heterogeneous resources in urban space. Therefore, adopting what kind of data management and processing method is the key to the smart city system, which also poses a major challenge to the urban data processing center. Based on existing cloud computing technology, the data center of smart city can put data on cloud servers with powerful computing capabilities for processing, and the emerging edge computing technology can effectively preprocess the data at the network edge and reduce the transmission delay from edge nodes to cloud servers, thus meeting the delay requirements of many applications and improving the efficiency of data processing. In some dynamic scenarios, the smart city system needs to dynamically allocate computing resources, and offload and schedule computation tasks so as to ensure low latency and high efficiency of data processing in the system.

The core idea of edge computing is making task computing take place as close as possible to the data source. Such a task computing method can reduce the amount of task transmission, thereby reducing the transmission delay. For example, Wang *et al.* proposed an edge cloud-assisted cyber–physical–social systems framework for the smart city to process the data generated base on the factors of cyber, physical and society, which integrates edge computing and cloud computing to guarantee real-time service delivery for smart city applications [14]. A case study of an intelligent transportation system illustrates their framework. This edge cloud-based framework demonstrates that offloading computation tasks to the edge clouds is necessary to reduce the latency of service delivery. In edge computing system, it needs time and energy consumption to migrate the computation task from the data source to the edge. The edge computing system determines whether a task is offloaded or not by running a computation offloading algorithm. Therefore, the performance of edge computing system is directly related to the performance of the computation offloading algorithm. In addition, in order to balance the computing load on the edge servers, the edge computing system needs to dynamically allocate and release computing resources according to the resource requirements of the applications, which is also one of the major problems that need to be solved in the future implementations of smart city. In the following, we will carefully introduce the technologies of computation offloading, computing resources assignment and task scheduling for smart city.

15.2.1 Computation offloading

Edge computing claims that computation should happen as close as possible to the data source. Therefore, in smart city, edge computing places resource-rich nodes near smart devices to provide low-latency computing service. For meeting the requirements of the smart devices in terms of time and energy, the resource-limited devices need to offload their respective computation tasks to the resource-rich edge nodes which play an import role in edge computing. Compared with the traditional central cloud-based architecture, the edge cloud-based smart city implementation scheme has better

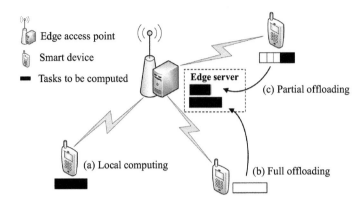

Figure 15.4   Offloading decisions

applicability and feasibility. In theory, the manners of computation offloading can be divided into binary offloading and partial offloading according to whether the computing tasks are separable. In implementation, the manners of computation offloading can be divided into virtual machine (VM)-based computation offloading [15] and Docker container-based computation offloading [16].

15.2.1.1   In theory

General speaking, a critical problem with respect to computation offloading is to determine the offloading decisions of each device. In the manner of binary offloading, the task can be entirely executed either at the corresponding device or at the edge node. While in the manner of partial offloading, the task can be divided into two parts, one part is executed locally, and the other part is executed at the edge node. In the latter case, what and how much should be offloaded to reduce consumption is also a question. Basically, the offloading decision of a device may be [17] the following:

- *Local computing.* The entire computation task is executed at the device (see Figure 15.4). This reason may be because that the computing resources at the edge nodes are unavailable or offloading will result in more overhead in terms of time and energy.
- *Partial offloading.* A part of the task is executed locally and the rest is offloaded to the edge node for performing. This offloading decision occurs when the task is separable, and can process the task more effective.
- *Full offloading.* The task is entirely offloaded and processed at the edge node. This is usually because the edge nodes have a large amount of computing resources.

In the offloading decisions mentioned above, the partial offloading is most difficult to implement. The partial offloading is a complex process affected by many factors such as the quality of wireless link, the computational capabilities of devices, the availability and computational capabilities of edge nodes, the performances of applications and so on. Therefore, we determine whether binary or partial offloading

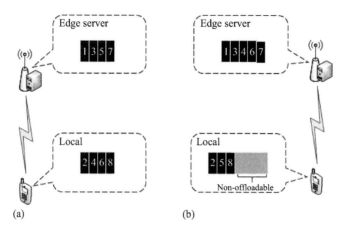

Figure 15.5   *The illustration of the partial offloading of a task without*
non-offloadable part (a) and with non-offloadable part (b)

is feasible based on the type of application. Meanwhile, what and how can be offloaded is also an important part. Mach *et al.* proposed that we can classify the applications based on the following criteria [17]:

- *Offloadability of application.* The application that is separable and parallelizable in data or code can be divided into two types. The first type is the applications which can be divided into N parts that all can be offloaded (see Figure 15.5). These parts may be divided by considering several factors such as data and code independence, causing that the input-data size and required computation of each part are different. Therefore, when designing the computation offloading algorithm, we need to carefully consider which parts will be offloaded to maximize the system performance. As shown in Figure 15.5(a), the 1st, 3rd, 5th and 7th parts are offloaded to process in the edge node, and the rest are performed locally. The second type of the applications is composed of the non-offloadable part and offloadable part. In Figure 15.5(b), the device computes the non-offloadable part together with the 2nd, 5th and 8th parts locally, while the rest of the computation task is offloaded to the edge node.
- *Knowledge on the amount of data to be processed.* The type of the applications can also be classified based on the knowledge on the amount of data to be processed. The first type of the applications (e.g., face and voice recognition, and natural language processing) is that the input-data size can be known in advance. The second type of the applications are the applications whose processing data cannot be known beforehand. These applications (such as the real-time traffic detection application in smart city) usually perform tasks with continuous data flow, so we cannot predict their execution time. Therefore, in edge computing, offloading these continuous-execution applications is intractable.
- *Dependency of the offloadable parts.* The last criterion for determining which computing offloading decisions an application can take is the interdependencies

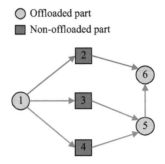

Figure 15.6   Dependency of divided parts

among the divided parts of the application. The relationship among the parts of the application can be either independent or dependent. If the parts are independent, they can be offloaded simultaneously and processed in parallel at the edge nodes. If the parts are dependent, which means that the output of one part may be the input of another, it's obvious that the partial offloading may be inapplicable. Without loss of generality, we use directed graph to represent the dependency between each individual part. The dependency relation among the individual parts is described in Figure 15.6, in which the computation task is divided into M (1st, 5th- and 6th parts in Figure 15.6) offloadable parts and N (2nd, 3rd and 4th parts in Figure 15.6) non-offloaded parts. For the case in Figure 15.6, 2nd, 3rd and 4th parts can only be offloaded after 1st part was offloaded, and 5th part can be offloaded only after 3rd and 4th parts were offloaded.

In conclusion, the computation offloading decisions that an application can make are determined by the type of the application. In addition, the computation offloading process should be carefully managed, which is also a quite important aspect. The device can predict the consumption of computation offloading by monitoring wireless connection conditions and computing resources of the edge nodes so as to decide whether to offload and what to offload.

15.2.1.2   In implementation
Edge computing involves the execution of computation task on the computing platforms, usually considered as cloudlets, which are located close to many smart devices. In the implementation of edge computing, the manners of VM migration or lightweight container migration are usually used to offload the computation tasks of the devices to the edge nodes. Ha *et al.* proposed a VM handoff technology to achieve the VM-based computation offloading [15]. In edge computing use cases where the safety and management attributes of VM encapsulation are important, VM handoff enables rapid and transparent placement changes to executing code in the edge nodes. This versatile primitive offers the functionality of classic live migration but is highly optimized for the edge.

As edge computing gains enormous attention, there is growing debate on the form of encapsulation used for application code that is executed on cloudlets. Consideration of small memory footprint, rapid launch and low Input/Output (I/O) overhead suggest that lightweight encapsulations such as Docker are a natural fit for edge computing. However, these are not the only attributes of importance in edge computing. Safety and management attributes such as platform integrity, multi-tenant isolation, software compatibility and ease of software provisioning can also be important in many edge computing use cases. When those concerns are dominant, classic VM encapsulation is superior. Therefore, Ha *et al.* proposed a mechanism called VM handoff that supports agility when operating conditions change, thereby rendering suboptimal the current choice of a cloudlet. There are many edge computing cases in which agility is important and valuable. For example, an unexpected flash crowd may overload a small cloudlet and make it necessary to temporarily move some parts of the current workload to another cloudlet or cloud. A second example is when advance knowledge is received of impending cloudlet failure due to a site catastrophe such as rising flood water: the currently executing applications can be moved to safer cloudlet without disrupting service. Site failures are more likely at a vulnerable edge location than in a cloud data center. A third example arises in the context of a mobile user offloading a stateful latency-sensitive application such as wearable cognitive assistance. The physical movement of the device may increase end-to-end latency to an unacceptable level. Offloading to a closer cloudlet could fix this, provided application-specific volatile state is preserved.

VM handoff bears superficial resemblance to live migration in data centers. However, the turbulent operational environment of VM handoff is far more challenging than the benign and stable environment assumed for live migration. VM handoff preserves many attractive properties of classic live migration for data centers while optimizing for the turbulent operational environment of edge computing. It needs low bandwidths through preferential substitution of cloudlet computation for data transmission volume. It dynamically retunes this balance in the face of frequent bottleneck shifts between cloudlet processing and network transmission. It uses a parallelized computational pipeline to achieve maximal throughput while leveraging a variety of data reduction mechanisms. As the research of Ha *et al.* [15], the following three principles should be followed in VM handoff:

- Avoid data transmission as much as possible. Using deduplication, compression and delta-encoding to ruthlessly eliminate avoidable transfers.
- Improve network bandwidth utilization as much as possible. When the network is busy, network bandwidth is a precious resource, and should be kept at the highest possible level of utilization.
- Go with the flow. Adapting at fine time granularity to network bandwidth and cloudlet compute resources.

Connectivity between cloudlets is subject to widely varying WAN latency, bandwidth and jitter. VM handoff also differs from live migration in the primary performance metric of interest. Downtime, which refers to the brief period toward the end when the VM is unresponsive, is the primary metric in live migration. In contrast, it is total completion time rather than downtime that matters for VM handoff. In most use cases, prolonged total completion time defeats the original motivation for triggering the operation. Abe *et al.* have shown that a narrow focus on downtime can lead to excessive total completion time [18]. The essence of VM handoff is preferential substitution of cloudlet computation for data transmission volume. VM handoff dynamically retunes this balance in the face of frequent bottleneck shifts between cloudlet processing and network transmission. Using a parallelized computational pipeline to maximize throughput, it leverages a variety of data reduction mechanisms. Comparing with live migration, VM handoff is agile and reduces total completion time by one to two orders of magnitude.

In edge computing environment, offloading computation tasks to the nearest edge server is key to reducing network delay, and improving the user experience. However, when a mobile device moves away from its current offloading server, network delay will increase, affecting the performance of offloading service significantly. Ideally, when the user moves, the edge server offloading service also should adapt, and move to the nearest so as to keep highly responsive service. Therefore, migration of the offloading service from the current edge server to an edge server nearer to the user is an important activity in the edge computing infrastructure. Ma *et al.* proposed to build an efficient service handoff system based on Docker container migration [16]. The system leverages the Docker container's layered file system to support high-speed migration of offloading service within the edge computing environment. By only encapsulating and transferring the thin writable container layer and its incremental runtime status, we reduce total handoff time significantly. There are several approaches to migrating offloading services. VM handoff has been proposed to accelerate service handoff across offloading edge servers. It divided VM images into two stacked overlays based on VM synthesis techniques [19]. The result is that the mobile device only needs to transfer the VM top application overlay to the target server instead of the whole VM image volume. However, considering that the total transferred size is usually on order of tens or hundreds of megabytes, total handoff time is still relatively long for latency-sensitive mobile applications. In addition, VM image overlays are hard to maintain, and not widely available due to limited support and deployment in the real world.

In contrast, the wide deployment of Docker platforms raises the possibility of high-speed offloading service handoff. As a container engine, Docker [16] has gained increasing popularity in industrial cloud platforms. It serves as a composing engine for Linux containers, where an application runs in an isolated environment based on OS-level virtualization. Docker's storage driver employs layered images inside containers, enabling fast packaging and shipping of any application as a container. The framework proposed by Ma *et al.* enhances service handoff across edge offloading served by leveraging the layered storage system of Docker containers to improve migration performance. The system enables the edge computing platform to continuously provide offloading services with low end-to-end latency while supporting high client mobility. By leveraging the layered file system of Docker containers, they eliminate transfers of a redundant and significant portion of the application file system.

By transferring the base memory image ahead of the handoff, and transferring only the incremental memory difference when migration starts, the total transfer size is further reduced. Finally, their experiments show that the time of handoffing is reduced significantly compared to the start-of-the-art VM handoff for the edge computing platform.

15.2.2 Resource allocation

Edge computing helps meet the strict requirements of future smart city IoT applications. Edge computing extends the cloud computing paradigm by bringing computing services closer to the end devices, thus reducing the communication latency and saving energy. However, there is still a large number of research challenges with regard to this paradigm because edge computing is in its early stages and needs more attention to evolve. One of the main challenges is the efficient resource allocation, since service can be placed at highly congested locations, or quite far from the users, which causes high communication delay because of the limited onboard resources of current user devices. Therefore, efficient resource allocation approaches should be studied to minimize resource costs and achieve high quality of service.

Smart city aims to enhancing the quality of living by providing its citizens with high-quality service for life. These services are varied and realized by integration of technologies, e.g., smart transportation, time-sensitive and cost-effective street lighting and smart home. There is no doubt that these applications involve the optimal allocation of various resources. With respect to resource allocation problem, Santos *et al.* [20] presented a resource provisioning integer linear programming (ILP) model that takes into account not only cloud requirements but also the constraints of wireless resource. In the model, end devices send requests for these IoT applications through wireless gateways. These gateways communicate with the edge–cloud infrastructure, managing a set of computational resources. Each service must be allocated and instantiated on a given set of computational resources, subject to multiple constraints:

- Computing resources have limited CPU and memory.
- Communication links between computing resources have limited bandwidth.
- Gateways have limited association identifiers, so end devices can associate and send requests for IoT application.
- IoT application services cannot be instantiated on every computing resource, due to specific hardware or software requirements.

The above constraints are factors that we need to consider in the real-world scenarios. In addition, the work in [21] involves multiple optimization objectives that have been extended to address the IoT application placement problem identified in [20]. In the model of [21], each iteration has an optimization objective, and each iteration adds a new constraint. Hence, the resource allocation problem in the model is addressed iteratively. This way, the solution space continuously decreases since iterations must satisfy the previous optimal solutions. Every iteration refines the previous obtained solution by improving the model with an additional optimization objective. The optimization objectives considered in the model are the following:

- maximization of accepted IoT application requests;
- maximization of service bandwidth;
- minimization of service migrations between iterations;
- minimization of number of active computing nodes;
- minimization of the number of active gateways;
- minimization of hop count between comp. nodes and end devices;
- minimization of path loss.

Obviously, except the above optimization objectives, there are many other optimization objectives that need to be determined according to the actual application scenario. Except for the optimization method of ILP, there are many other optimization methods such as welfare maximization, maxmin fairness, auction, game theory and market theory. The welfare maximization solution, which is also often the design goal of many auction models, typically allocates most of the resources to agents with high marginal utilities while giving very little to agents with low marginal gains; the maxmin fairness allocation often gives too many more resources to the agents with low marginal utilities; the allocation method based on game theory needs to prove the existence of Nash equilibrium; the optimization method based on market theory (i.e., the Fisher market) needs to prove the existence of market equilibrium. In addition, computation offloading and resource allocation are highly correlated. Hence, in the actual application scenarios, we need to jointly optimize computation offloading decision and resource allocation.

15.2.3　Task scheduling

For the edge computing system oriented to smart city, it needs not only efficient computing offloading algorithm, but also efficient task scheduling algorithm to make reasonable use of computing resources in edge nodes and cloud computing center, and to achieve load balance of edge computing system. Task scheduling is a critical issue due to the limited computational power, storage and energy of mobile devices in the smart city. It can improve computing efficiency, reduce task completion time and utilize idle resources from other device in edge computing system for smart city. Deng *et al.* focus on the problem that how to schedule tasks for these computation-intensive and time-sensitive smart city application with the assistance of Internet of Vehicle (IoV) based on multi-server. To handle tasks from the aforementioned applications in the shortest time, they introduced a cooperative strategy for IoV and formulate an optimization problem to minimize the completion time with a specified cost, which can be solved by the alternating direction method of multipliers [22].

For the ability to provide low-latency video analytic service, Yi *et al.* presented Latency-aware Video Analytics on Edge Computing Platform (LAVEA) [23], a system built on top of an edge computing platform, which places computation from clients to edge nodes, and collaborates nearby edge nodes, to provide low-latency video analytics at places closer to the users. The system utilizes an edge-first design and formulated an optimization problem for offloading task selection and prioritized offloading requests received at the edge node to minimize the response time. In addition, they have designed the following three placement schemes for inter-edge collaboration [23].

- Shortest transmission time first (STTF). The STTF task placement scheme tends to place tasks on the edge node that has the shortest estimated latency for the edge-front node to transfer the tasks. The edge-front node maintains a table to record the latency of transmitting data to each available edge node. The periodical re-calibration is necessary because the network condition between the edge-front node and other edge nodes may vary from time to time.
- Shortest queue length first (SQLF). The SQLF task placement scheme, on the other hand, tends to transfer tasks from the edge-front node to the edge node which has the least number of tasks queued upon the time of query. When the edge-front node is saturated with requests, it will first query all the available edge nodes about their current task queue length, and then transfer tasks to the edge node that has the shortest value reported.
- Shortest scheduling latency first (SSLF). The SSLF task placement scheme tends to transmit tasks from the edge-front node to the edge node that is predicted to have the shortest response time. The response time is the time interval between the time when the edge-front node submits a task to an available edge node and the time when it receives the result of the task from that edge node. Unlike the SQLF task placement scheme, the edge-front node keeps querying the edge nodes about the queue length, which may have performance issue when the number of nodes scales up and results in a large volume of queries. We have designed a novel method for the edge-front node to measure the scheduling latency efficiently. During the measurement phase before edge-front node chooses task placement target, edge-front node sends a request message to each available edge node, which appends a special task to the tail of the task queue. When the special task is executed, the edge node simply sends a response message to the edge-front node. The edge-front node receives the response message and records the response time. Periodically, the edge-front node maintains a series of response times for each available edge node. When the edge-front node is saturated, it will start to reassign tasks to the edge node having the shortest response time. Unlike the STTF and SQLF task assignment schemes, which choose the target edge node based on the current or most recent measurements, the SSLF scheme predicts the current response time for each edge node by applying regression analysis to the response time series recorded so far. The reason is that the edge nodes are also receiving task requests from client nodes, and their local workload may vary from time to time, so the most recent response time cannot serve as a good predictor of the current response time for the edge nodes. As the local workload in the real world on each edge node usually follows certain pattern or trend, applying regression analysis to the recorded response times is a good way to estimate the current response time. To this end, we recorded measurements of response times from each edge node, and offloads tasks to the edge node that is predicted to have

the least current response time. Once the edge-front node starts to place task to a certain edge node, the estimation will be updated using piggybacking of the redirected tasks, which lowers the overhead of measuring.

Each task allocation scheme described above has some advantages and disadvantages. For example, STTF scheme can quickly reduce the workload of edge-front nodes. However, because the STTF scheme does not collect workload information on target nodes, it is possible to place tasks on edge nodes that already have intensive workloads. When the network delay and bandwidth between all available edge nodes are stable, the SQLF scheme works well. When the network overhead varies greatly, the scheme does not consider the network condition and always chooses the edge node with the smallest workload. When a dense workload is placed under high network overhead, this scheme may degrade performance because it requires frequent workload measurements. SSLF task placement scheme estimates the response time of each edge node by tracking the task offloading process. Response time is a good indicator, which edge node can be selected as the target of task placement according to the load and network overhead. SSLF scheme is a good compromise between the first two schemes. However, if an inappropriate model is chosen, the regression analysis may bring great errors to the predicted response time. We believe that in order to achieve good system performance, the decision of which task allocation scheme should be adopted should always take into account the workload and network conditions.

15.3   Security and privacy protection in smart city

As cities become smarter, people may suffer from a series of security and privacy threats due to the vulnerability of smart city applications. For example, malicious attackers may generate false data to manipulate perception results, which may affect the "intelligence" of services, decision-making and control in intelligent cities. In addition, these malicious attackers may launch denial-of-service attacks to destroy perception, transmission and control, thereby deteriorating the quality of intelligent services in smart cities. In addition, the ubiquitous video surveillance in smart cities captures a large number of images and video clips which can be used to infer the trajectory of local residents and inherently endanger their privacy. Smart home applications collect and manage information about the home area, which may pave the way for revealing the highly privacy-sensitive lifestyle of the house, and even cause economic losses. Although some ready-made technologies (encryption, authentication, anonymity, etc.) and strategies can be directly applied to avoid these problems, emerging "smart" attackers can still infer and invade privacy in many other ways, such as side-channel attacks and cold-start attacks. If there is not enough security and privacy protection, users may not accept smart city, which will remain a distant future idea.

Alrawais *et al.* [24] proposed a mechanism that employs edge computing to improve the distribution of certificate revocation information among IoT devices for security enhancement. In their scheme, they use a bloom filter to create a short list that can effectively reduce the revocation list size with acceptable overhead. A boom filter is a space-efficient data structure to store a group of elements in a bit-vector $(0, \ldots, m - 1)$ that can be used to check whether an element is the member of the group. Initially, an empty bloom filter vector is set to 0. To store certificate revocation information, they use the certificate's serial number, which is considered to be its UID within a certificate authority. The serial number should be hashed with k independent hash functions mapping it to a group of bit locations that should be set to 1.

In addition, they also proposed some open issues on edge computing, security and privacy in IoT environments [24], for example, the following:

- Privacy. Edge computing can protect the data privacy of users, because it can put the sensitive data of users in the edge for processing rather than transferring to the cloud center for analysis. The way of making computation happen close to IoT devices (or data sources) can really help to process and analyze the data at the edge of the network. Meanwhile, this method also brings some challenges to the data privacy of users, because privacy protection technology needs certain resources (e.g., CPU and storage). In the collaborative model of edge and cloud, it's feasible to apply privacy protection technology between edge and cloud to protect data privacy because both edge and cloud have rich resources. However, it is very difficult to run privacy technology between edge and IoT devices because IoT devices are usually limited in resources. One possible solution is a privacy preservation technique based on homomorphic functions, which can be used to maintain the privacy of transmitted data [25]. Differential privacy is another technique to ensure that privacy in data sets is not disclosed. However, the computational overhead of this method will cause great concern.

- Access control. With the assistance of edge computing, it is necessary to design a new access control method to overcome the limitation of IoT devices. In edge computing, a policy-based user access authorization management is proposed. Edge computing will help to adopt many standard access control models, such as access control list or property-based access control in the IoT environment. In distributed architecture, we regard edge computing as an ideal candidate for granting access tokens to the authorizers who use them to perform a given operation. In addition, we can use the edge computing platform in the centralized architecture to authorize the access and relay data between the authorizers and the IoT devices.

- Attack detection. Some abnormal behaviors and malicious attacks can be checked by edge computing. The signature-based or anomaly-based detection systems check attacks with existing possible models. On the one hand, the developed cloud detection system can be reused in edge platform because edge is the extension of cloud at the edge of network. Shi *et al.* [26] proposed a cloudlet mesh architecture based on cloudlet member collaboration to observe and detect malware, malicious attacks and other threats. This type of collaborative intrusion detection technology can be used between edge nodes to monitor the IoT environment and their surroundings. On the other hand, the existing data security protection methods are not fully applicable to edge computing because the resources of the edge are also limited compared with the central cloud. Moreover, the highly dynamic environment at the edge of the network will make the network more vulnerable to attack. Therefore, in order to effectively utilize the limited resources of the IoT devices and protect the data security of the users, it is necessary to build a defense model adapted to the edge computing environment. Although edge computing has many advantages, the research of edge computing security is still n the development stage and there are many places to be improved.

15.4 Conclusion

The development of smart cities is inseparable from the application of edge computing technology. The value of edge computing in smart cities is reflected in specific application scenarios. So, this chapter mainly introduces the definition of smart cities and their architecture, and enumerates some applications with edge computing technology. It also introduces how edge computing technology is applied in dealing with urban traffic congestion. Next, the computation offloading, resource allocation and task scheduling problems in edge computing-enabled smart city are discussed according to the academic research. Finally, we discuss the security and privacy problem in edge computing-based smart city. The application of edge computing in smart cities is much more than that mentioned in this chapter. With experts and scholars in different domain investing in edge computing research, the role of edge computing in smart cities will be further enhanced.

References

[1] World Urbanization Prospects: The 2018 Revision [homepage on the Internet]. New York: United Nations. Available from: https://population.un.org/wup/Publications/.

[2] Cosgrove M, Harthoorn W, Hogan J, *et al.* Smarter cities series: Introducing the IBM city operations and management solution. IBM Corporation. 2011.

[3] I.-T.F.G. on Smart Sustainable Cities. Master plan for smart sustainable cities. International Telecommunication Union, Focus Group Technical Report; 2015.

[4] Internet of Things—Wikipedia; 2019. Available from: https://en.wikipedia.org/wiki/Internet_of_things.

[5] Shah SH, and Yaqoob I. A survey: Internet of Things (IOT) technologies, applications and challenges. In: 2016 IEEE Smart Energy Grid Engineering (SEGE). IEEE; 2016. pp. 381–385.

[6] Fredj AH, and Malek J. Real time ultrasound image denoising using NVIDIA CUDA. In: 2016 2nd International Conference on Advanced Technologies for Signal and Image Processing (ATSIP). IEEE; 2016. pp. 136–140.

[7] Stojkoska BLR, and Trivodaliev KV. A review of Internet of Things for smart home: Challenges and solutions. Journal of Cleaner Production. 2017;140:1454–1464.

[8] Baheti R, and Gill H. The impact of control technology. Cyber-Physical Systems. 2011;12(1):161–166.

[9] David S, Bill E, Tim L, and Jim B. 2015 Urban Mobility Scorecard. 500 Fifth Street, NW Washington, DC 20001: The Transportation Research Board, The National Academies of Sciences, Engineering, and Medicine; 2015.

[10] Prihatmanto AS, and Zafir MR. Integration of traffic camera network & user generated content for traffic load balancing system. In: 2013 Joint International Conference on Rural Information & Communication Technology and Electric-Vehicle Technology (rICT & ICeV-T). IEEE; 2013. pp. 1–5.

[11] Zhang X, Gao H, Guo M, *et al.* A study on key technologies of unmanned driving. CAAI Transactions on Intelligence Technology. 2016;1(1):4–13.

[12] Yousefi S, Mousavi MS, and Fathy M. Vehicular ad hoc networks (VANETs): challenges and perspectives. In: 2006 6th International Conference on ITS Telecommunications. IEEE; 2006. pp. 761–766.

[13] Jian L, Li Z, Yang X, *et al.* Combining unmanned aerial vehicles with artificial-intelligence technology for traffic-congestion recognition: Electronic eyes in the skies to spot clogged roads. IEEE Consumer Electronics Magazine. 2019;8(3):81–86.

[14] Wang P, Yang LT, and Li J. An edge cloud-assisted CPSS framework for smart city. IEEE Cloud Computing. 2018;5(5):37–46.

[15] Ha K, Abe Y, Eiszler T, *et al.* You can teach elephants to dance: Agile VM hand-off for edge computing. In: Proceedings of the Second ACM/IEEE Symposium on Edge Computing. ACM; 2017. pp. 12.

[16] Ma L, Yi S, and Li Q. Efficient service handoff across edge servers via Docker container migration. In: Proceedings of the Second ACM/IEEE Symposium on Edge Computing. ACM; 2017. pp. 11.

[17] Mach P, and Becvar Z. Mobile edge computing: A survey on architecture and computation offloading. IEEE Communications Surveys & Tutorials. 2017;19(3):1628–1656.

[18] Abe Y, Geambasu R, Joshi K, *et al.* Urgent virtual machine eviction with enlightened post-copy. In: ACM SIGPLAN Notices. vol. 51. ACM; 2016. pp. 51–64.

[19] Satyanarayanan M, Bahl V, Caceres R, *et al.* The case for VM-based cloudlets in mobile computing. IEEE Pervasive Computing. 2009.

[20] Santos J, Wauters T, Volckaert B, *et al.* Resource provisioning for IoT application services in smart cities. In: 2017 13th International Conference on Network and Service Management (CNSM). IEEE; 2017. pp. 1–9.

[21] Moens H, Hanssens B, Dhoedt B, *et al.* Hierarchical network-aware placement of service oriented applications in clouds. In: 2014 IEEE Network Operations and Management Symposium (NOMS). IEEE; 2014. pp. 1–8.

[22] Deng Y, Chen Z, Yao X, *et al.* Task scheduling for smart city applications based on multi-server mobile edge computing. IEEE Access. 2019;7:14410–14421.

[23] Yi S, Hao Z, Zhang Q, *et al.* LAVEA: Latency-aware video analytics on edge computing platform. In: Proceedings of the Second ACM/IEEE Symposium on Edge Computing. ACM; 2017. pp. 15.

[24]   Alrawais A, Alhothaily A, Hu C, *et al.* Fog computing for the internet of things: Security and privacy issues. IEEE Internet Computing. 2017;21(2):34–42.

[25]   Yi S, Qin Z, and Li Q. Security and privacy issues of fog computing: A survey. In: International Conference on Wireless Algorithms, Systems, and Applications. Springer; 2015. pp. 685–695.

[26]   Shi Y, Abhilash S, and Hwang K. Cloudlet mesh for securing mobile clouds from intrusions and network attacks. In: 2015 3rd IEEE International Conference on Mobile Cloud Computing, Services, and Engineering. IEEE; 2015. pp. 109–118.

Chapter 16

Smart healthcare systems enabled by edge computing

Yucen Nan[1], Wei Li[1], Shuiguang Deng[2], and Albert Y. Zomaya[1]

As we know, the tremendous upsurge in size of data sets has started gaining momentum since a decade ago in science, finance and every slice of our everyday life. The same scenario of the data volume explosion also arose in the realm of medical healthcare due to the advance of medical equipment technology. An elaborate management and exhaustive exploration of these heterogeneous data play important roles in medical care services. We must admit that traditional healthcare system (e.g. paper-based healthcare system) are too weak to cope with such complex situations nowadays. After the popularity of digitized medical records, data storing in a hospital physically may not be possible in some cases. The evolution of the worldwide network interconnection has prompted the cloud computing to be proposed and successfully applied in the field of healthcare by considering its advantages in competitive edge, information sharing and dynamic resources. Meanwhile, along with the growing aspiration of patients, it is inevitable to gradually reform the structure of healthcare system from hospital-oriented centralized healthcare system to patient-oriented distributed mobile health or mobile healthcare (also termed as mHealth) systems. Moreover, accompanied with the improvement of data acquisition capability of wearable devices and the widespread adoption of mobile communication, Internet of Things (IoT) provides an efficient and structured way to implement distributed patient-oriented mHealth system. For example, mHealth systems embedded with IoT wearable devices are able to fully supplement the out-of-hospital data and provide 24/7 daily monitoring for people who need special care at home. However, numbers of IoT devices are generating medical data exponentially. In order to better adapt to the requirements (like time and energy consuming) of mHealth, edge computing has emerged as an effective implementation to complement and improve mHealth systems supported by cloud computing. It is a big step to make healthcare systems more sensitive and flexible. The establishment of the edge-based smart healthcare system is one of the best methods to alleviate the gigantic press on public medical care.

[1]Centre of Distributed and High Performance Computing, The University of Sydney, Sydney, NSW, Australia
[2]College of Computer Science, Zhejiang University, Hangzhou, Zhejiang, China

In this chapter, we first give a synopsis of the routing of global healthcare systems' reformations. And then, we describe the circumstances of the current phase of medical reform comprehensively. In this part, we tend to depict three essential parts in a complete healthcare system: data collection, data transmission and data processing. First, we introduce the architecture of medical IoT (mIoT) through presenting several novel medical sensors and explain how they collect data. Second, we give a description of the wireless body sensor network (WBSN) which is derived by the development of mobile medical sensors and mIoT devices. Followed by that, we propose an edge-based healthcare system and show several popular applications on daily health monitoring and disease early warning. After this, we look ahead to the future directions about the reform and amelioration of healthcare systems that are generally recognized currently. Obviously, due to the rapid development of mIoT devices and sharp increment on the demand of time-dependent requests, edge-based healthcare systems will inevitably emerge. Finally, we illustrate the open issues and challenges in edge-enabled smart healthcare system and conclude this chapter.

16.1 Introduction

The most pressing issues facing countries across the world, such as poverty, climate change and population health, are very important and consume a lot of national resources. Specifically, the increasing demand of healthcare is derived from the aging populations, prevalence of chronic disease and the growing aspiration of patients. And the global healthcare expenditures are expected to keep rising from USD $7.724 trillion to USD $10.059 trillion from 2017 to 2022 with an annual increasing rate of 5.4% [1]. This will definitely have a long-lasting impact on the sustainability of the global healthcare ecosystem. In order to better utilize medical data and expand medical big data industry, a sound healthcare system is obligatory.

The traditional form of healthcare systems, like paper-based medical records, might have negative consequences on business efficiency and patient safety [2]. A structured and unified healthcare system is indispensable. One of the operative approaches to build up a credible system is to apply the information and communications technology (ICT) to healthcare, which is acknowledged as health information technology (HIT) [3]. That is to say, modern healthcare is a dynamic complex integrated system with many participants including patients, nurses, lab technicians, researchers, receptionists as well as IT professionals. Digital transformation through the broad and in-depth use of HIT across the healthcare system, while in conjunction with other complementary changes, can reduce the cost and improve the quality of medical healthcare. The first electronic health record (EHR) system was designed and deployed starting in the late 1960s [4]. Then, the digitization of all clinical exams and medical records has become the standard for hospitals these days [5,6], and emerged as a key dimension of contemporary healthcare policy delivered in many countries, although there are significant challenges in achieving the benefits [7]. In short, preventive medicine and public health were driven by the use of digital medical technology. And this transformation is variously termed as digital health, E-health, Medicine 2.0 or Health 2.0.

The volume of EHRs is expected to grow significantly in the coming years as more departments adopt electronic records, and the development of medical technology brings more measurable bio-indicators. In other words, the rapid and continued expansion of digital healthcare systems will bring medical data to exploding unavoidable. Therefore, in some cases, local storage and processing may not meet the actual application needs. Moreover, obtaining wide range of medical-related information from other similar patients through data sharing also benefits to personalized diagnosis and treatments. As an upgrade to local processing, the cloud computing paradigm enriches capabilities by migrating compute and storage resources from multiple individual servers to the cloud for consolidation. This makes it a well-deserved preferred platform for ever-expanding digital healthcare systems which can provide information flows between multiple entities, such as hospital clinics, pharmacies and laboratories [8].

Furthermore, in view of the characteristics of the cloud computing, it is not only the basic computing platform for artificial intelligence (AI), but also one of the convenient ways to integrate AI into millions of applications. Conversely, AI can not only enrich the characteristics of cloud computing services, but also make cloud computing services more in line with the needs of business scenarios and further liberate human resources. Interestingly, AI is likened to the twenty-first-century stethoscope, which is expected to become a powerful coadjutor besides classic medical providers and institutions currently. First, intelligence services have been widely used for hospital management, automating administrative and repetitive work to improve hospital operational efficiency. Then, AI can also be used to predict, prevent and control major epidemics, and achieve precise medical treatment. There are many mature and successful applications of AI technology in both clinical diagnosis [9–15] and new drug development [16]. Overall, AI can expressively improve the efficiency and quality of medical healthcare services, and help save medical expenses simultaneously. Besides, it is obvious that the emergence, application and popularization of cloud-based smart healthcare systems are undisputed.

The amelioration of the healthcare system cannot stop here. Along with the development of medical technologies and the improvement of patient expectations, onefold in-hospital data cannot satisfy the demand of both doctors and patients. Meanwhile, many experts believe that the future model of efficient healthcare systems should not only provide more rights for medical practitioners, but also give patients a sense of participation. The medical industry urgently needs to shift the core of the healthcare system from hospital-oriented to location-insensitive and patient-oriented model [4], in order to reduce the hospitals' workload and improve patients' initiative. Specifically, with the widespread adoption of mobile communications, IoT technology provides an efficient and structured way to implement distributed mHealth system [17], which is actually a subsegment of digital health. One of attractive advantages is that mobile medical system can not only fully supplement the out-of-hospital data and achieve 24/7 continuous monitoring to the prevent accidental sudden occurrence, but also provide uninterrupted and detailed data to hospital doctors to help them make a more accurate diagnose. This is critical for some chronic patients and elders those who live in out-of-the-way areas. In this sense, the IoT-based system will reshape the healthcare industry in terms of social benefits, penetration and cost-efficiency. It has been predicted that in the following decades, the way healthcare is currently provided will be transformed from hospital-centered, first to hospital-home-balanced in 2020th, and then ultimately to home-centered in 2030th [18].

However, the rise of the IoT and mobile computing has put a lot of pressure on network bandwidth, all of which have led to the need for computational migration. In addition to that, some major deficiencies [19] in cloud computing may diminish the performance of digital healthcare systems. For example, current prominent cloud providers (e.g. Amazon EC2/S3 [20] and Microsoft Azure [21]) are still not providing full transparency and capabilities for tracking and auditing of file access history and data provenance of the physical and virtual servers utilized [8]. On top of that, in some real-time cases, the long-distance round-trip transmission of data should be avoided to save resources and time. Therefore, edge computing came into being. The edge computing is a new paradigm for data processing that adds extra computing power between the devices and the cloud, as well as close to the data source. This architecture can reduce the amount of data that was planned to send to remote cloud servers, and perform them on the edge of the network immediately. In other words, the edge computing improves performances and reliability of applications and services by dropping data transfer distance, saving operating cost and easing bandwidth and latency. According to [22], they predicted that in terms of market share, the three most leading verticals for edge computing in 2022 will be utilities, transportation and healthcare. Wearable devices provide the basic form of edge computing applications in the medical field. In the past, watches and fitness bands monitor the wearers' health condition and then send the data to the cloud sharing service for processing and storage. With the increase in computing capability of edge devices, we can collect daily health data through various medical sensors, and then process these data and compute results timely at the edge of the network, instead of sending data to the cloud.

Through daily health monitoring, the disease can be effectively prevented and predicted. Compared with taking a series of complicated, consuming and no-guarantee treatments after a clear diagnosis, daily health monitor can not only reduce the medical cost, but also improve the patient's comfort. It is critical to people who need special care and continuous monitoring, like chronic disease patients, elderly people with disabilities. Another scenario of edge-based healthcare system application is in the emergency medical services. Ambulances are primarily used as transportation for local hospitals today, but due to the impact of edge computing and the IoT, ambulances will soon become a mobile emergency room. The next generation of practitioners will be able to have high-definition two-way video conversations with emergency room staff and doctors. This real-time messaging will enable hospital staff to predict the information coming from the scene.

In general, at the era of Healthcare 2.0, a large quantity of clinical data, collected through various clinical observations and medical tests in hospitals, was recorded as EHRs and served as the main source of user's medical data. Aligned with the progress of Web 3.0*, we came into the age of Healthcare 3.0. Followed by that, it is sure that

---

*Web 3.0 is slated to be the new paradigm in web interaction, and explained as connective intelligence, connecting data, concepts, applications and ultimately people [23].

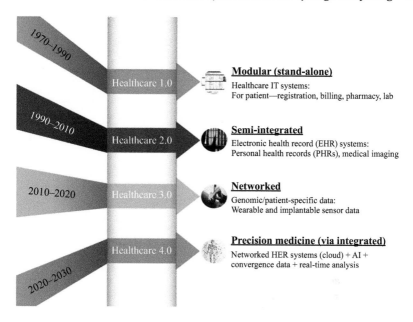

Figure 16.1   The evolution of digital health

we are moving into a new decade called Healthcare 4.0, which imagines a world where everyone is connected through smart and energy-efficient wearable devices, and every point of patients is getting recorded no matter where they are. All of these innovations show that the implementation of AI on the edge computing is the general trend of future healthcare. Just as the edge is a complement to the cloud, clinical practice with smart technologies will not replace clinicians, but provide them with more time to accompany patients, allowing them to focus more on the prioritized people and work. Overall, the evolution of the healthcare system is shown in Figure 16.1 chronologically.

16.2   Medical IoT

Current technology typically involves downloading patient data from the doctors' dedicated devices for further use, but this is far away enough. The modern healthcare industry is adopting to the bloomed IoT, and the emergence of mIoT improves healthcare equipment and services by monitoring and transmitting more accurate, real-time data for patients. The mIoT will make healthcare more participatory, personalized, predictive and preventive [24].

Primarily, the healthcare is a data-intensive industry, especially the modern healthcare in the Internet epoch relies more on data. Combining new materials, nanotechnology, biotechnology and peripheral technologies (such as power supply technology and new communication technologies), it spawned many medical

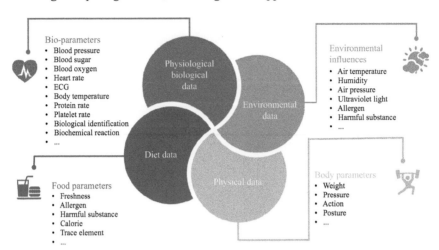

Figure 16.2   Mobile sensors' data collection type

products with innovative sensor technology as the core, like wearable devices, to collect patients' real-time health data in a high rate of accuracy. Patients can use these devices to continuously collect their daily health indicators on their own without time and location restriction. These data can act as the effective complement and further explanation of the in-hospital data sets, thus breaking the deadlock of the single data source. With the rapid development of the functional diversity of personal wearable devices and the continued improvement of their communication modules, a new network paradigm, WBSN, is designed. WBSN is used to gather and communicate the collected personal health information and communicate among mobile/edge devices (usually smartphones) within the same WBSN via Bluetooth or other low-frequency communication channel. Additionally, WBSNs send out information to remote end via 3G/4G or Wi-Fi. This allows patients to share information between users and other stakeholders and form a medical social network.

16.2.1   Medical sensors

The medical sensors (transducers) are the entrance of the entire mHealth system and play an important role in it. They are able to convert the physiological information of the human body into an electrical signal or other signal conversion device having a determined function relationship. Medical sensors collect a wide variety of data in the healthcare field. We can roughly divide these data into physiological/biological data, environmental data, physical data and data about food ingredients. All these can be seen in Figure 16.2. Among them, the most commonly used field of medical sensors is the collection of physiological/biological data, including human body vital signs, physiological signs and biological reactions, etc. In recent years, with the wide application of the mobile Internet and the effective combination of data acquisition and wireless transmission, people's capability of monitoring data changes has been greatly improved. Instantly, the value brought by medical sensors is further amplified. Novel medical sensors are more sensitive, and with other characteristics like small in size, easy to use, low in cost, noninvasive or minimally invasive. Additionally, some of them have communication modules. All these advantages make medical sensors unprecedented in value and can be widely used in mHealth for fitness management, food testing, chronic disease management and auxiliary medical treatment. We will briefly introduce the state-of-the-art and well-utilized types of medical sensors in the market.

1. **Biosensors** are stand-alone integrated devices that use biometric components to provide qualitative or semiquantitative analysis of information. More precisely, corresponding reactions occur after contact of the analyst with the receptor, which alters the biochemical properties of the receptor surface, further causing changes in the optical or electrical properties of the receptor surface. Then, these changes are converted by the converters into measurable electrical signals and transmitted to the detectors. This kind of sensor is highly specific, including with characters like high speed and accuracy [25]. Glucose meters [26], one of the most familiar portable medical monitors, are established on glucose biosensors interacted with one of the following three enzymes: hexokinase, glucose oxidase (GOx) or glucose-1 dehydrogenase (GDH). Currently, the glucose biosensor technology including point-of-care devices, continuous glucose monitoring systems and noninvasive glucose monitoring systems has been successfully applied in our daily life.

2. **Flexible sensors** are based on flexible materials and flexible circuit technology. A flexible sensor is typically an analog resistor, and the inside is a flexible substrate with a carbon-resistive element. When the sensor is bent, the resistance changes, and the degree of bending varies with the degree of resistance, causing a change in the output of the entire circuit. This kind of sensor is thin, soft, flexible and suitable for fiber carriers. Flexible sensors are the ideal wearable device sensor because they are very comfortable to touch with human skin and does not cause any discomfort or even feel its presence [27]. WiSP, for example, an ultrathin and highly flexible epidermal wearable cardiac sensor proposed by [28], can effectively measure cardiac signals like ECG and heart rate.

3. **Implantable sensors or embedded sensors** are invasive sensors that need to be implanted in the body, so they are often new materials which are compatible with the human body. Typically, the power required is extremely small and can be self-powered while transmitting information using wireless technology. This kind of sensor is small in size, light in weight and biocompatible [29], and is able to reduce the burden on users to wear, without having to develop wearing habits. Currently, implantable sensors are mainly used in brain control, heart failure monitoring and blood glucose monitoring.

4. **Ingestible sensors** are miniature sensors made from biodegradable electronic materials. The entire sensor working system consists of the smartphone, smart pills and other accessory items, and the ingestible sensor is attached to the inside

of the smart pill [30]. Naturally, the sensor uses the interaction between the pill itself and the digestive tract liquid to supply energy, and then transmits the detected relevant data to the smartphones or other terminals through the communication module. Compared with traditional methods such as gastroscope and colonoscopy, the cost is greatly reduced, the use is convenient and the pain of the patient is alleviated. It is mainly used for drug compliance, disease diagnosis and other aspects.

5. **Nanosensors** are sensors with ranging in size from 10 to 100 nanometers [31]. They can detect the presence of nanoscale or even smaller substances, such as molecules, atoms, etc.. In terms of working principles, nanosensors can be classified into optical nanosensors, physical nanosensors, chemical nanosensors and bio-nanosensors. From the perspective of its materials, the nanosensors can be classified as nanoparticles, nanotubes and nanowires. The nanosensors can be applied in various areas of medical-related research, like creating fluorescent biomarkers in research and diseases diagnose [32], protein detection and cancer treatment.

From wearable, flexible materials, to long-term implantable, 3D printing, and digestible sensors, data acquisition technologies are being tried to better integrate the human body in order to better capture real-time human data. Despite huge innovations of medical sensors, they also face several critical challenges at the same time, like energy supplying, network connecting and data processing. In addition, in order to collect comprehensive health data while ensuring user comfort, sensor integration is another challenge for mHealth.

16.2.2 *Wireless body sensor network*

Besides daily health data collection, WBSN technologies are considered as another key research areas in the mHealth applications. It is a wireless network consisting of spatially distributed autonomous devices [33]. By utilizing WBSN, a ubiquitous computing platform with integrated hardware, software and wireless communication technologies can be structured. And this platform is able to achieve the integrated functions about disease monitoring and prevention. In detail, every medical sensor is installed in the WBSN, and each sensor acts as a body sensor unit to collect data. Then relevant sensors can transmit and merge data to one node known as terminal devices. The existing measurement device access network mainly realizes the wireless communication connection through a built-in wireless communication module. From these terminal devices, the data are passed on further to a network access point by using existing wireless standards such as Bluetooth and ZigBee. From here, the data are passed on to the gateway (such as smart mobile phones, tablets or laptops) which is used to connect to a wide range of networks [34]. In WBSN, the main obstacles of each sensor node are power consumption problems of both data transmission and storage. Increasing storage capacity and the battery is unrealistic because it will affect the size and cost of the sensor node. That is to say, one of the best ways is to reduce the transmission volume of data while ensuring the validity. The characteristics of the edge make it a suitable platform to support both energy-constrained WBSN.

16.2.3 Intelligence service with mIoT

Accompanied with the wide spread of mIoT, we are entering the age of Health-care 4.0. The primary objective of Healthcare 4.0 is focusing on consumer-patient prototypes, which means it synthesizes the patient-centered care approaches and consumer-directed commercial models. This novel healthcare system would be a combination of AI, IoT, genomics and big data, where AI to help us make the right decisions about treatment, genomic analysis to warn us about future risks and big data to make sense of the tons of data from wearable devices. Through using this completed and advanced system, the medical industry may improve the quality of healthcare services to individuals and gradually move to Personalized Precision Medicine in the future. However, the highest yield of the achievement transformation of this healthcare system is in the section of data analysis.

Initially, we look at the application of data analysis and machine learning in mHealth. In general, data analytics and learning is a process of transforming the raw data into useful information, and in the field of healthcare, it is classified into descriptive, diagnostic, predictive and prescriptive analytics [35]. For big data analysis in medicine and healthcare, it covers integration and analysis of mass amount of heterogeneous data such as omics data, biomedical data, EHR data and so on. Data mining as one of data analysis approaches, for specific, is the process of grouping similar objects into large data sets and then allowing for patterns to be identified in these data. This process can be carried out through the use of AI, as well as machine and deep learning. Data mining a lot of patients for different treatment options and their outcomes can help determine which treatment will have the best result. Comparisons can be made to similar clinical conditions and treatment profiles to lead to shared decision-making (both patients and physicians can actively discuss which interventions are appropriate for the specific case). In short, great data mining can help to determine more appropriate selections of treatment.

Unsurprisingly, applying AI technology in medical healthcare will increase the accuracy and efficiency for the clinical diagnosis result. AI aims to create computer systems with human-like intelligence, while machine learning is a subset of AI where large amounts of data are fed into an algorithm and the machine learns how to perform a task. Deep learning is an additional subset, where certain information has different weights in the algorithm, in order to model high-level abstractions in the data. There are many mature and successful applications of AI technology in healthcare currently. For example, higher accuracy medical image recognition can assist doctors in cancer diagnosis [9,10]; intelligent medical tools can help doctors improve diagnosis based on medical records and symptoms and a large amount of medical data and knowledge [11–13], and develop personalized and accurate treatment plan [14,15]; AI applied in new drug development can significantly reduce the monetary cost, shorten the development cycle and assist in the discovery of new drugs [16]; robot-assisted surgery can improve the accuracy and success probability of the operation [36]; virtual nurses [37] and wearable devices can achieve self-management. In the field of medical care, there are two aspects of advantages by using AI technology: for patients (stratification of medical ability or stratification of patient needs) and for medical staff (provide decision-making advice for prescription reviews, clinical decisions, etc.).

Furthermore, along with the diversification of clinical tests, medical data are often collected from different methods, such as various feature extraction or sensors. This is because the single particular measuring method cannot comprehensively describe all relevant symptoms and information of the condition which results in weakening of the final diagnostic results. Although these individual views might sometimes be sufficient on their own for a given learning task, it is obvious that, by exploiting, the consistency and complementary proprieties of different views can effectively improve the performances on the learning task. In this case, the features from different sources belonging to the same sample can be naturally divided, and data from each source can be considered as a view. For example, a complete consideration of blood test digital data, semantic electronic medical records data, medical imaging data, etc., can help doctors to get better understanding of the patient's medical condition and guide further treatments. However, the existing works on multi-sources data simply concatenate all features into one space. This approach brings two nonnegligible shortcomings: (1) it breaks the balance between the size and the dimension of data and causes overfitting [38], and (2) ignores the physical interpretation differences between different views. Multi-view learning, one of burgeoning directions in machine learning, is now being used to deal with homogeneous and heterogeneous medical data to achieve highly accurate diagnostic results. It is the branch of machine learning concerned with the analysis of multi-model data, i.e. patterns represented by different sets of features extracted from multiple data sources [39]. Recent years, multi-view learning methodology has become increasing popular, and a high number of medical applications based on multi-view data have been recorded in literature. The reason for its popularity is that for the same sample, different kinds of measurements provide sufficient and complementary information with each other to enrich the expression of the underlying relationship between them. Its ultimate challenge consists in building an integrated base of knowledge derived from heterogeneous sources. Moreover, the reason for the rapid spreading of this learning approach is the constant increase of real-world problem where heterogeneous data are available to describe the same phenomenon.

Nevertheless, all mentioned smart applications in medical healthcare do not fulfill the need of the Healthcare 4.0 because of long time response. To overcome the challenges of today's healthcare (Healthcare 3.0) such as delay in patients care, the cloud computing is not the best solution even with excellent processing ability. The cloud-based healthcare system owns serious drawbacks such as poor real-time response and delay, while a little delay can cost a patient's life. Therefore, to enhance services and applications, edge computing has come into picture. Edge computing empowers on-time service delivery with high consistency while overcoming difficulties such as delays, jitters or cost overheads while transmitting information to the cloud. It is a distributed flat architecture that enhances the storage, computational and networking resources along the cloud computing. Edge computing offers three major benefits such as low latency, privacy and resiliency against cloud computing [40]. Additionally, since we do data processing on the edge, we can further advance the

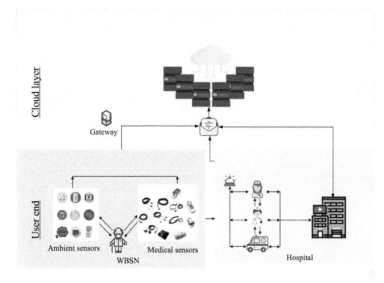

Figure 16.3   Cloud-based healthcare system

development of mobile medical care. The future medical care can focus on precision medicine, combining clinical in-hospital data, and out-of hospital data including mobile medical data and home healthcare data.

16.3   Edge-based smart healthcare system

16.3.1   Healthcare system architecture

In the past, people always sent all of medical data to cloud for unified management and high performance processing. Applying the cloud computing, medical data collected from sensors and actuators can be stored and analyzed remotely by the strong server. The results can then be delivered back to the user end via the Internet (see Figure 16.3). As more and more sensor nodes are joining in the WBSN, the network bandwidth connected to the cloud model for data storage and analysis is increasingly unable to bear the data avalanche. One of the best approaches is to push data processing out to the edge of the network where closer to the data generating devices. Then, we try to process the real-time data at the edge of the networks to save time and energy while ensuring the processing performances. Edge computing is an architecture for data handling that can offload part of medical data from the cloud, process it nearby the patient and transmit information from edge devices to edge devices or users in milliseconds or seconds [41]. Compared to cloud computing, edge computing have four significant advantages:

- faster transmission speed,
- less bandwidths dependence,

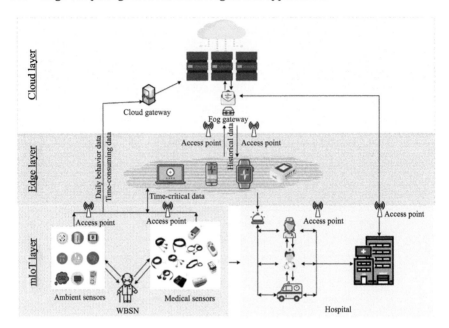

Figure 16.4   Edge-based healthcare system

- better user privacy and security and
- lower costs because more sensor-derived data are processed locally and less data are transmitted remotely [42].

The evaluations of edge-based healthcare system are presented in Figure 16.4.

16.3.2   Things layer

As can be seen in the bottom-most part of the Figure 16.4, the Things layer (also termed as physical and virtualization layer, or mIoT layer) comprises of different medical devices embedded with innovative sensors. In the Things layer, a number of IoT-based mobile medial devices, such as smart watches, smart bands and other medical measurement devices, empower the patient-oriented healthcare system to monitor the patients' real-time body status and collect health data continuously. Then, a group of medical devices (usually all medical devices belong to a patient) form a WBSN, and the data transmit to the next layer via a edge gateway with appropriate communication protocols.

16.3.3   Edge layer

Once the data are generated from the mIoT layer (Things layer), it is sent to the middle layer of the proposed healthcare system, the edge layer. The data are either analyzed and processed in the edge layer, or sent to the next layer for further analysis.

In these layers, there are many low-power and high-performance computing nodes called edge nodes. Each edge node is positioned closely to the medical smart devices and assigned to a group of local medical devices to perform relevant data analysis in real time. Undoubtedly, the basic advantage of the edge-based healthcare system is response time-critical medical data. The edge nodes need to decide which part of medical data is filtered and to be offloaded to the next layer for processing or storage, and which part of data can be processed in edge layer for time saving and energy efficiency.

16.3.4 Cloud layer

The highest level of Figure 16.4 is the cloud layer, which contains a high-performance data center that provides centralized control. Within the cloud layer, there are three sub-layers named connection layer, data management layer and application layer. In the cloud layer, data can be stored and retrieved permanently. In addition, the cloud server is responsible for the additional storage and aggregation of patient data sent from the edge layer.

16.3.5 Implementation for edge-based smart healthcare system

Considering to the requirements of modern healthcare systems, such as communication delay, scalability, transmission capacity and data privacy, such an edge-based mHealth system comes from the P4 medicine, and accurate analysis is more and more important. For example, in order to prevent fetus antenatal and intrapartum intrauterine injury or death, fetal health status evaluation and monitoring is now transforming from periodic in-hospital auscultation to timely remote fetal monitoring systems. This remote fetal monitoring system consists of a wearable maternal device and an edge device. The mobile sensors can detect signals and make real-time sampling. The edge device can be any device that is compatible with the wearable maternal device, such as smartphones, tablets, desktops or laptops. These devices can receive sensor readings through wireless connection such as Bluetooth BLE. And then, some signal extraction and data pre-processing are executed on data sets to clean and normalize the signals for further processing and diagnosis results retrieve. After that, historical data, diagnosis results and parts of time-noncritical data will be sent to remote powerful end or storage. On top of this system, various E-health applications can be envisaged, such as obstetrics assistant and popular knowledge of pregnancy.

16.4 Case study

Daily monitoring and early warning of diseases play an important role in timely taking effective prevention and treatment measures which greatly reduce the damage caused by it. Instead of using clinical symptoms to draw a definite diagnosis in the advanced stage of disease, detecting subtle and decentralized changes occurred in the early stage through daily monitoring is more meaningful for chronic disease patients. In term of medical sensors and mHealth, the applications for diabetes, cardiovascular, respiratory and other chronic diseases still dominate. But from 2018, the products of brain and nerve diseases such as stroke, epilepsy and autism are gradually increasing. Patient-oriented self-management programs are increasingly appearing on the market, and the main direction is chronic disease products, not only because of the accessibility of medical services, but also because chronic diseases are conditional and suitable for self-management and continuous monitoring. Here we list several well-applied edge-enabled mHealth systems in different types of diseases.

1. **For diabetes:** Some older blood glucose meters are essentially asynchronous telemedicine systems; they don't upload data automatically and require a cable to connect with a hub device or a computer. Currently, more and more wearable and portable wireless diabetes devices are offering Bluetooth communication capability. They can pass the collected data to a smartphone or tablet, which serves as an edge node by performing some basic analytic processes. Moreover, the monitored information can be sent out further to the cloud. These devices include blood glucose monitors, continuous glucose monitors, insulin pens, insulin pumps and closed-loop artificial pancreas systems.

   - *Eversense CGM system:* This system contains a blood glucose sensor implanted in the upper arm of a diabetic patient, and a mobile device. It can continuously monitor blood glucose through an implantable sensor [43]. The device contains a fluorescent polymer that is sensitive to blood glucose levels. When the blood glucose concentration changes, the signal transmitted by the material changes and is transmitted to the mobile device worn by the patient in real time. Upon simple discrimination on edge devices, the device will alarm when the concentration is too high or too low. Moreover, the transmitter can also connect to the user's computer to review personal blood glucose historical data.

   - *IDx-DR:* The IDX's AI Sugar Screen Screening System [44] analyzes the images taken with the Topcon NW400 retinal camera and uploads them to the cloud server. Within a few minutes, the software provides a flat result for the doctor to detect if the patient has diabetic retinopathy. It is worth noting that since the results of the system do not require the interpretation of a clinician, they can be provided to a clinic that does not have an ophthalmic service.

2. **For cardiovascular diseases:** With the fast development of mobile technologies, efficient portable and body-worn devices and systems to follow-up and monitoring out-of-hospital cardiac patients' physiological parameters have been successfully proposed. Patients belonged to arterial hypertension, malignant arrhythmia, heart failure or post-infarction rehabilitation are highly encouraged to use this portable recording equipment and a mobile phone that supported ECG data transmission and wireless application protocol.

   - *KardiaMobile 6L monitoring system:* KardiaMobile 6L is a portable device for remote monitoring of individual vital signs and six-lead electrocardiograms, by tapping fingers on the electrodes [45]. This system can be applied in several scenarios, including remote monitoring from doctors, monitoring of patients during the transition from hospital to home after discharge and monitoring patients during clinic visit. Clinical professionals can quickly diagnose, classify and formulate the patient's treatment plan based on these data.

3. **For neurological disease**
   - *RAPID CTA 3D imaging platform:* RAPID CTA [46], a 3D imaging platform for computed tomography angiography (CTA). Based on clinically validated machine learning algorithms, RAPID ASPECTS automatically generates standardized scores that allow doctors to easily understand the extent of ischemic changes in patients and determine the feasibility of thrombectomy (clot removal). In addition, RAPID ASPECTS provides clear brain visualization so clinicians can better examine each area and confirm automatic scoring. This technology allows doctors to fully understand the blood vessels in the brain, and doctors can rotate images at different angles on the platform. The CT map also has four colored overlays so doctors and caregivers can see which areas of the brain have reduced blood vessel density. RAPID CTA image maps are available to physicians via e-mail for viewing on any device, PACS system and web browser. These images provide an intuitive and easy-to-interpret cerebrovascular view that helps doctors make clinical decisions regarding triages, community hospitals and specialists, and patient referrals.

16.5 Open issues and challenges

With the edge-based smart healthcare system, all kinds of multimedia medical information can be collected and gathered to the patients' personal smart devices such as smartphones or laptops. Patients can control their own tests and questionnaires using their smart device habitually, while doctors can observe patients' status regularly. However, there are still several research issues and challenges associated with edge-enabled smart healthcare systems.

16.5.1 Data management

Modern healthcare systems obtain a huge amount of patients medical data, which encounters big data 5 V's data value, volume, veracity, variety and velocity. It is unavoidable to receive heterogeneous data like image and text. Not only that, data may come from different sources such as glucose meters and ECG monitor. In order to handle these complex data, the smart gateway in this edge-based system must be aware of appropriate protocol for different types of data.

16.5.2 Offloading strategy

Considering the different priority of data and tasks, a suitable data offloading strategy between edge layer and cloud layer is important. A proper offloading strategy can save both time and energy and achieve better efficiency. Moreover, in view of processing location (either edge or cloud), right partition of processing resources is another key challenge related to resource management.

16.5.3　Scalability

Data collection is taking place either from wearable or portable medical devices with innovative medical sensors. In order to well deploy and structure the environment of smart healthcare system, various kinds of medical devices need to cover the entire clinic or hospital, so that every patient can collect and check their health indicators through smart devices. Further, the smart healthcare system can be scaled up to the entire community or city. In addition, the scalability benefit to a smart city can provide efficiency improvement, reduce the misdiagnosis and build trust among patients, doctors and other stakeholders.

16.5.4　Medical privacy protection

In the edge-based healthcare system, medical privacy protection is considered as one of the most important issues requiring more attention. First of all, personal information and medical data of patients cannot be accessed without corresponding authorization. This is the basic step for guaranteeing data security under the environment of data sharing. And then, after the healthcare system empowered by edge computing, there are complex structures established and intricate relationships allocated among different kinds of system nodes. From the one hand, the more system nodes we have, the easier data can be stolen and misused. The misused data will result in huge loss, and especially in medical care it might threat to life. From the other hand, the transmission process needs some form of trust management model between these devices. Even some trust models have been applied successfully, but they still need to work with the given complexity and dynamics of edge computing in healthcare.

16.5.5　Network connectivity

Since the devices connected to the edge-based healthcare system are different, the standardization of protocols and interfaces is indispensable, including device interfaces, data aggregation interfaces, communication protocol and gateway interfaces. These should be seamless between different devices. Additionally, there are a wide variety of protocols for communication such as Wi-Fi.

16.5.6　Medical multi-view learning

The complementary information from different views can effectively improve the performance of medical auxiliary diagnosis system. How to better utilize the relationships between views and integrate views is still one of the important aspects of multi-view medical learning. Ritchie *et al.* [47] present several data integration methods, but a good integration method is not enough, and an excellent data representation is another aspect to explore. In short, medical multi-view learning is a promising direction in healthcare system which can not only combine different symptom features to derive better diagnostic results, but also can encourage cooperation between different departments in hospital.

16.6   Conclusion

Proliferation of mIoT devices and mobile communication technology along with intelligence services prompt the emergence of edge-based smart healthcare system. This innovation results in the reformation of the healthcare system from hospital oriented to patient oriented. Edge computing makes modern healthcare system more time-critical and sensitive through reducing the time waste in data transmission compared to the stand-alone cloud-based system. And coupled with the intelligence services, it can help doctors to make smart decision during emergency cases. In this chapter, we first look back to the evolution process of modern healthcare systems and give a detailed introduction about the mIoT. After that, a three-layer modern healthcare system enabled by edge computing was proposed in this paper, and it is a good approach to deploy and implement patient-oriented distributed healthcare system to improve precision medicine services. And then, we present some successful applications of daily health monitor system in the market. Finally, we highlight several open issues and challenges associated with the implementation of the edge-based healthcare system. In future, we can integrate this smart healthcare system into the application of smart city, and figure out how to cooperate with other parts in smart city, such as smart transportation and smart building to make our life more convenient.

References

[1]   Allen S. 2019 Global Health Care Outlook; 2019. Available from: https://www2.deloitte.com/global/en/pages/life-sciences-and-healthcare/articles/global-health-care-sector-outlook.html.

[2]   Stausberg J, Koch D, Ingenerf J, and Betzler M. Comparing paper-based with electronic patient records: lessons learned during a study on diagnosis and procedure codes. Journal of the American Medical Informatics Association. 2003;10(5):470–477.

[3]   Shaw T, Kielly-Carroll C, and Hines M. Impact of Digital Health on the Safety and Quality of Health Care. Level 5, 255 Elizabeth Street, Sydney NSW 2000: Australian Commission on Safety and Quality in Health Care; 2018.

[4]   Goldschmidt PG. HIT and MIS: implications of health information technology and medical information systems. Communications of the ACM. 2005;48(10):68–74.

[5]   Adler-Milstein J, Holmgren AJ, Kralovec P, Worzala C, Searcy T, and Patel V. Electronic health record adoption in US hospitals: the emergence of a digital "advanced use" divide. Journal of the American Medical Informatics Association. 2017;24(6):1142–1148.

[6] Curtis JR, Sathitratanacheewin S, Starks H, *et al.* Using electronic health records for quality measurement and accountability in care of the seriously ill: opportunities and challenges. Journal of Palliative Medicine. 2018;21(S2):S–52.

[7] Agarwal R, Gao G, DesRoches C, and Ashish KJ, [Research Commentary] The digital transformation of healthcare: current status and the road ahead. Information Systems Research. 2010;21(4):796–809.

[8] Sato M. Personal data in the cloud: a global survey of consumer attitudes. Minato-u, To yo. 2010; pp. 105–7123.

[9] Rawat RR, Ruderman D, Agus DB, and Macklin P. Deep learning to determine breast cancer estrogen receptor status from nuclear morphometric features in H&E images. AACR; 2017.

[10] Esteva A, Kuprel B, Novoa RA, *et al.* Dermatologist-level classification of skin cancer with deep neural networks. Nature. 2017;542(7639):115.

[11] Manogaran G, Vijayakumar V, Varatharajan R, *et al.* Machine learning based big data processing framework for cancer diagnosis using hidden Markov model and GM clustering. Wireless Personal Communications. 2018;102(3):2099–2116.

[12] Bax JJ, van der Bijl P, and Delgado V. Machine Learning for Electrocardiographic Diagnosis of Left Ventricular Early Diastolic Dysfunction. Elsevier; 2018. Journal of the American College of Cardiology, Vol.71(15), pp.1661–1662.

[13] Yamamoto Y, Saito A, Tateishi A, *et al.* Quantitative diagnosis of breast tumors by morphometric classification of microenvironmental myoepithelial cells using a machine learning approach. Scientific Reports. 2017;7:46732.

[14] Nicolae A, Morton G, Chung H, *et al.* Evaluation of a machine-learning algorithm for treatment planning in prostate low-dose-rate brachytherapy. International Journal of Radiation Oncology, Biology, Physics. 2017;97(4):822–829.

[15] Valdes G, Simone II CB, Chen J, Lin, Alexander Yom, Sue S Pattison, and Adam J. Clinical decision support of radiotherapy treatment planning: a data-driven machine learning strategy for patient-specific dosimetric decision making. Radiotherapy and Oncology. 2017;125(3):392–397.

[16] Zhang L, Tan J, Han D, and Zhu H. From machine learning to deep learning: progress in machine intelligence for rational drug discovery. Drug Discovery Today. November 2017;22(11):1680–1685.

[17] Germanakos P, Mourlas C, and Samaras G. A mobile agent approach for ubiquitous and personalized eHealth information systems. In: Proceedings of the Workshop on "Personalization for e-Health" of the 10th International Conference on User Modeling (UM'05). Edinburgh; 2005. pp. 67–70.

[18] Thota C, Sundarasekar R, Manogaran G, and Varatharajan R. Centralized fog computing security platform for IoT and cloud in healthcare system. In: Exploring the Convergence of Big Data and the Internet of Things. IGI Global; 2018. pp. 141–154.

[19] Kofahi NA, and Al-Rabadi AR. Identifying the top threats in cloud computing and its suggested solutions: a survey. Networks. 2018;6(1):1–13.

[20] Amazon AWS Greengrass. Available from: https://aws.amazon.com/greengrass/.

[21] Microsoft Azure IoT Edge. Available from: https://azure.microsoft.com/en-in/campaigns/iot-edge/.

[22] Research. Size and Impact of Fog Computing Market. OpenFog; 2017. Available from: https://www.openfogconsortium.org/wp-content/uploads/451-Research-report-on-5-year-Market-Sizing-of-Fog-Oct-2017.pdf.

[23] Giustini D. Web 3.0 and medicine. The British Medical Journal. December 2007;335(7633):1273.

[24] Dimitrov DV. Medical Internet of things and big data in healthcare. Healthcare Informatics Research. 2016;22(3):156–163.

[25] Gui Q, Lawson T, Shan S, Yan L, and Liu Y. The application of whole cell-based biosensors for use in environmental analysis and in medical diagnostics. Sensors. 2017;17(7):1623.

[26] Yoo EH, and Lee SY. Glucose biosensors: an overview of use in clinical practice. Sensors. 2010;10(5):4558–4576.

[27] Khan Y, Ostfeld AE, Lochner CM, Pierre A, and Arias AC. Monitoring of vital signs with flexible and wearable medical devices. Advanced Materials. 2016;28(22):4373–4395.

[28] Lee SP, Ha G, Wright DE, Ma Y, Sen-Gupta E, Haubrich NR, *et al.* Highly flexible, wearable, and disposable cardiac biosensors for remote and ambulatory monitoring. npj Digital Medicine. 2018;1(1):2.

[29] Lucisano JY, Routh TL, Lin JT, Gough, and David A. Glucose monitoring in individuals with diabetes using a long-term implanted sensor/telemetry system and model. IEEE Transactions on Biomedical Engineering. 2017;64(9):1982–1993.

[30] Kiourti A, and Shubair RM. Implantable and ingestible sensors for wireless physiological monitoring: a review. In: Antennas and Propagation & USNC/URSI National Radio Science Meeting, 2017 IEEE International Symposium on. IEEE; 2017. pp. 1677–1678.

[31] Meixner H, and Jones R. Micro- and nano-sensor technology trends in sensor markets. Sensors: A comprehensive survey, vol. 8. Weinheim, Germany: Wiley-VCH Verlag GmbH.

[32] Mousavi S, Hashemi S, Zarei M, Ali MA, and Aziz B. Nanosensors for chemical and biological and medical applications. Med Chem (Los Angeles). 2018;8:205–217.

[33] Yick J, Mukherjee B, and Ghosal D. Wireless sensor network survey. Computer Networks. 2008;52(12):2292–2330.

[34] Sangwan A, and Bhattacharya PP. Wireless body sensor networks: a review. International Journal of Hybrid Information Technology. 2015;8(9):105–120.

[35] Senthilkumar S, Rai BK, Meshram AA, Angappa G and Chandrakumarmangalam S. Big data in healthcare management: a review of literature. American Journal of Theoretical and Applied Business. 2018;4(2):57–69.

[36] Sarikaya D, Corso JJ, and Guru KA. Detection and localization of robotic tools in robot-assisted surgery videos using deep neural networks for region

proposal and detection. IEEE Transactions on Medical Imaging. 2017;36(7): 1542–1549.

[37] Kalis B, Collier M, and Fu R. 10 Promising AI applications in health care. Harvard Business Review. 2018.

[38] Xu C, Tao D, and Xu C. A survey on multi-view learning. arXiv preprint arXiv:13045634. 2013.

[39] Serra A, Galdi P, and Tagliaferri R. Multiview learning in biomedical applications. In: Artificial Intelligence in the Age of Neural Networks and Brain Computing. Elsevier; 2019. pp. 265–280.

[40] Kumari A, Tanwar S, Tyagi S, and Kumar, N. Fog computing for Healthcare 4.0 environment: opportunities and challenges. Computers & Electrical Engineering. 2018;72:1–13.

[41] Li W, Santos I, Delicato FC, *et al.* System modelling and performance evaluation of a three-tier Cloud of Things. Future Generation Computer Systems. 2017;70:104–125.

[42] Klonoff DC. Fog computing and edge computing architectures for processing data from diabetes devices connected to the medical Internet of Things. Journal of Diabetes Science and Technology. 2017;11(4):647–652.

[43] eversense. The Eversense Long-Term CGM System. 2019. Available from: https://www.eversensediabetes.com/.

[44] IDx. IDx-DR. 2019. Available from: https://www.eyediagnosis.co/.

[45] alivecor. KardiaMobile 6L Monitoring System. 2019. Available from: https://www.alivecor.com/kardiamobile6l/.

[46] iSchemaView. RAPID CTA. 2019. Available from: http://www.ischemaview.com/cta.

[47] Ritchie MD, Holzinger ER, Li R, Pendergrass SA, and Kim D. Methods of integrating data to uncover genotype–phenotype interactions. Nature Reviews Genetics. 2015;16(2):85.

Chapter 17
Smart hospitals enabled by edge computing

Antonino Galletta[1], Alina Buzachis[1], Maria Fazio[1],
Antonio Celesti[1], Javid Taheri[2] and Massimo Villari[1]

In last few years, achievements in information and communications technologies (ICTs), such as the electronic health record (EHR), have improved the healthcare system. However to be effective, paramedics and doctors have to consult the most recent version of EHRs anytime and anywhere. A possible solution is to store EHRs on remote storage services. However, the EU General Data Protection Regulation (GDPR) does not allow to store plain files containing personal data in services accessible remotely. To solve this challenge, a possible solution is to use Edge computing devices running Secret Sharing algorithms to split and merge EHRs on demand; however, these techniques have not been evaluated before for these purposes. To address this issue, in this work we analyse the redundant residue number system (RRNS). In particular, considering different EHR sizes (from 10 kB to 1 MB), we evaluated computation time (split and recomposition), transfer time (upload and download) from/to public Cloud storage providers (Google Drive, Mega and Dropbox) and storage requirement. Results showed that, in configuration with seven levels of redundancy, the RRNS uses only 50% of the storage required for the simple file replication. We also discovered that Google Drive, due to synchronization overhead, is slower than other Cloud service providers for the upload of chunks but faster for the download.

17.1 Introduction

Nowadays computer-assisted tools are becoming much more popular in all fields from cities to farm, to industries, etc. Even hospitals, in recent years, are interested in this phenomenon. That is, old medical devices are replaced by new computer-assisted ones, or new achievements in ICTs are adopted. Among these, the EHR is becoming much more popular. It contains the whole clinical life of patients. Therefore, if managed properly, it can help to reduce clinical errors inside and outside

[1]MIFT Department, University of Messina, Messina, Italy
[2]Department of Mathematics and Computer Science, Karlstad University, Karlstad, Sweden

the hospital. The management of EHRs is a very hard task, because paramedics and doctors have to consult the most recent version of EHRs anytime and anywhere. A possible solution is to store EHRs on remote public or private Cloud storage services. However, they can arise several privacy and security threats such as the following:

1. Hackers could violate the privacy of people by attacking these servers. In fact, this has been a real concern during the last few years; for example, Google revealed that more than 1 million of Google accounts were hacked by Gooligan in three months [1]; Yahoo disclosed that hackers breached between 1 billion and 1.5 billion accounts [2], and Dropbox denounced that more than 68 million account details were disclosed [3].
2. Cloud service providers can be discontinued as it happened to Copy-Cloud [4], Ubuntu One [5], DELL Data Safe [6], etc.
3. Hospitals can be affected by the vendor lock-in, and thus their data cannot be easily migrated among Cloud service providers [7].
4. Servers can be affected by the ransomware (e.g. WannaCry [8]) and become the subject of ransom payments. In fact, during the last few years several cases have been announced; for example, in UK roughly 200,000 computers have been affected costing for the National Health Service (NHS) about 92 million pounds [9].

Furthermore, the new EU GDPR [10] came into force on 25 May 2018. It does not allow that plain files containing personal information can be stored in public or private services accessible remotely. A possible solution is to use Edge computing devices for splitting and add redundancy to EHRs. In literature, several approaches have been proposed, and among them, algorithms belonging to Secret Sharing family better fit these requirements. However, these techniques have not been evaluated before for splitting EHRs. To address this issue, in this work we analyse the RRNS. In particular, considering different EHR sizes (from 10 kB to 1 MB), we evaluated computation time (split and recomposition), transfer time (upload and download) from/to public Cloud storage providers (Google Drive, Mega and Dropbox) and storage requirement. Results showed that, in configuration with seven levels of redundancy, the RRNS uses only 50% of the storage required for the simple file replication. We also discovered that Google Drive, due to synchronization overhead, is slower than other Cloud service providers for uploading chunks of EHR but faster in downloading.

The chapter is organized as follows: Section 17.2 analyses the state of the art. In Section 17.3, we discuss the EHR. Motivation and use cases are described in Section 17.4. The proposed approach is discussed in Section 17.5. The performance assessment of the proposed approach is discussed in Section 17.6. Open issues and challenges are described in Section 17.7. The Section 17.8 concludes the work and provides directions of the future.

17.2 State of the art

Edge computing is a very hot topic within the scientific community. Recently, the advent of Internet of things (IoT) and Industry 4.0 is increasing the interest on such a topic. However, currently there are not so many works available in literature focusing on Edge-based services for hospitals.

In [11], the authors present RASPRO (Rapid Active Summarization for effective PROgnosis), an IoT-Edge based system for telemedicine. The proposed system is composed of wearable sensors that send data to RASPRO which summarizes row data into severity symbols called PHMs (personalized health motifs).

A similar approach is discussed in [12]. The authors presented a telemedicine visualization tool for patients' clinical big data. The system is composed of Edge devices that acquire and transmit data to the Cloud engine that create markers in coloured circles representing the health status of patients.

In [13], the authors proposed an architecture based on narrowband IoT devices to interconnect objects inside and outside hospitals. The proposed system, by using Edge devices, is able to fulfil latency requirements of medical processes.

In [14], the authors focused their attention on DICOM (Digital Imaging and Communications in Medicine), a standard for storing and managing medical imaging. They proposed a hybrid model for Cloud-based Hospital Information System (HIS) focusing about public and private Clouds. The last one was able to manage and store computer-based patient's records and other important information, while public Cloud was able to handle management and business data. In order to share information among different hospitals, the authors adopted VPN (virtual private network).

In [15], the authors analysed the possibility to adopt the electronic patient clinical record (ePCR) in pre-hospital emergencies. In particular, they survey different UK ambulance services. More than 50% of them, 7 over 13, were using ePCR. Instead, four of the six remaining companies in the past adopted the ePCR but reverted to the paper records.

In [16], the authors proposed an Edge computing-based gateway for the interoperability of healthcare systems. In particular, they mapped heterogeneous and geographically distributed medical centres and pharmacies as nodes of their system. Each node is able to interact with others by means of restful application program interfaces (APIs).

In [17], the authors analysed the indoor localization problem for visitors of hospitals. In order to solve this challenge, they proposed a navigation and localization system based on low-cost Edge devices. The devices composing the system, by using Bluetooth low-energy and ultra-wideband sensors, are able to identify the position of visitors and to send them back localization information.

In [18], the authors discuss the placement problem in the era of single-board computers. In particular, they analysed two use cases related to smart train and smart hospital, respectively. They proposed solutions that rely on Edge devices. However, the proposed solutions are suitable for small and medium environments (such as a train or a small hospital). Considering a big hospital with high number of rooms, the proposed approach does not scale properly; therefore, it is necessary to realize a hybrid approach based on Edge and Cloud devices.

17.3   The electronic health record

The EHR encapsulates and represents patient's life in a digital way. It can be seen as an extended collection of electronic medical records (EMRs that we will discuss in Section 17.3.1); indeed it could include the following types of data:

- medical history;
- demographics;
- allergies;
- laboratory test results;
- radiology images;
- medication;
- personal statistics such as the weight and the age;
- immunization status;
- vital signs;
- billing information.

Furthermore, the EHR allows to create specific private views managed by patients, the electronic patient record (EPR), that we will discuss in Section 17.3.2. The EHR is not a new concept; indeed, some works such as [19] in the early 2000s discussed the need of a National Electronic Health Record Architecture. In particular, the authors described the Australian and the American models. The Australian model, called HealthConnect, extracts and aggregates patients' medical data in order to create centralized HealthConnect records. These records can be shared among authorized actors. The HealthConnect is based on a 'push' approach; this means that patients decide which part of the health record can be pushed to the HealthConnect record. In the USA, instead local governments launched several local initiatives. The result was a proliferation of different EHRs. In order to harmonize EHR information, a US national model has been developed. This model is based on a 'pull' approach; this means that semantically similar data are imported from local EHRs into the national one. In the last few years, each European country developed its own EHR, based on local rules and laws, and the objective is to have a centralized European health record system before the 2020. The EHR from a clinical point of view is very useful; indeed, it allows to have a clear vision of each treatment that the patient followed allergies and medicines that s/he took. As the reader can see, in Figure 17.1 is shown an example of EHR. It can be divided in two parts: on the left side, personal and historical data such as appointments, diagnoses and meetings are shown, and on the right part is shown an EMR.

Furthermore, the EHR allows to reduce duplication of effort and clinical errors. By means of HealthConnect, the Australian government estimated to save AUD $300

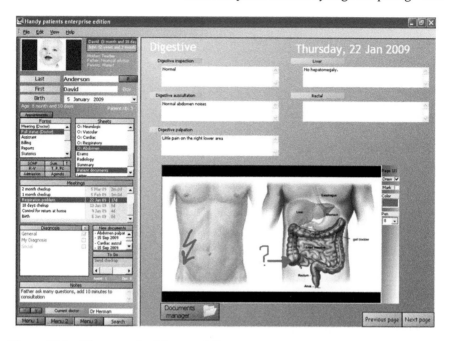

Figure 17.1   Electronic health record. Source: Oguntoye patient's electronic medical record (free open source version)

million per year [20]. However, EHR presented security issues in terms of data privacy protection that blocked its proliferation. In Europe, in order to protect the processing of personal data, including that for purposes of healthcare, the European Parliament in 2016 approved the GDPR [10].

A well-known family of standards for exchanging EHR is the Health Level Seven (HL7) [21]. It defines how information must be packaged and transmitted among parties. The HL7 provides seven reference categories:

1. **Primary.** Standards for compliance and inter-operability.
2. **Foundational.** Standards that define infrastructure and fundamental blocks.
3. **Clinical and administrative domains.** Standards that define messaging and document.
4. **EHR profiles.** Standard for the definition of models and profiles of the EHR.
5. **Implementation guides.** Supplemental material of parent standards. This section contains the documentation for the interaction with existing standards.
6. **Rules and references.** This section contains developer manuals and technical guides.
7. **Education and awareness.** Projects and standards for trial use.

17.3.1 Electronic medical record

The EMR, instead, represents the digital version of the clinical paper documents. It allows to eliminate handwritten medical records, reducing interpretation errors. The EMR can contain notes, treatments, medical tests and diagnoses.

In Figure 17.2, an example of EMR is shown, and in particular it's shown a DICOM. DICOM is the standard used in medicine in order to represent medical images. The extension of DICOM files is dcm. It is composed of the header that contains metadata (such as personal patient information, software version and number of frames) and the image data set acquired as single image, cine loop or multiple frames of a study.

17.3.2 Electronic patient record

The EPR, like the EHR, contains information about medical history, demographics, allergies, etc. The difference between EHR and EPR is in the management of the medical records. Indeed, in the first case it's managed by hospital employees such as doctors, practitioners and nurses; instead, the EPR is managed by the patients who can decide which kind of their health information have to stay in a private zone [22].

Patients' access and management rights on EPRs depend on the country's legislations. The authors, in [23], considering ten countries (the United States,

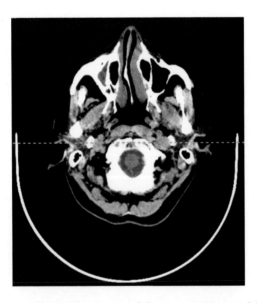

Figure 17.2   Digital Imaging and Communications in Medicine

New Zealand, Australia, Netherlands, France, Estonia, Sweden, Denmark, Norway and Finland) all around the world, made a comparison in terms of login procedures, management of the EPR of the underage patients and available data sets. In particular, they considered two kinds of regulations: 'soft' and 'hard'. Soft laws refer to voluntary rules, instead of hard to mandatory ones. The study revealed that access and management rights depend on the country in which the patients live. Furthermore, they highlight the absence of a cross-national system that can give the same access and management rights in order to solve common problems.

17.4   Motivation and use case definition

As we discussed in previous sections, the EHR can help to reduce clinical errors inside and outside the hospital.

For example, considering the first aid in the emergency room of the hospital or in ambulance, knowing the patient's allergies, can avoid the administration of wrong drugs. Instead, considering a patient hospitalized, an exchange of medical records could lead to unnecessary surgery [24] or the patient's death [25,26].

Considering these as use cases, in this chapter, we define a possible system based on Edge devices able to manage efficiently the EHR.

17.4.1   UC 1: Hospitalized patients

This use case (UC 1) is focused on hospitalized patients. In Italy, in last few years, the rate of hospitalization was 132.5 out of 1,000 citizens [27]. As we discussed in Section 17.4, exchange medical records of two patients could be very dangerous. Also in this case, the use of the EHR can help to avoid such problems. In particular, we propose a system that allows patients to be moved among ambulatories with their EHR. The proposed system exploits the same technologies of use case 2 (UC 2). That is, an Edge device, installed on the bed of the patient, can split and recompose EHRs stored as chunks on the public Cloud.

17.4.2   UC 2: smart ambulances

This use case is focused on first aid done by ambulances. In Italy, in the last few years, roughly the 47% of medical emergency calls required the intervention of ambulances [28]. During the first aid, one of the possible medical problems concerns the administration of drugs to which the patient is allergic. The use of the EHR can avoid this because it contains allergies and the whole clinical history of the patient. However, to be effective, the last recent version of EHRs has to be accessible from ambulances by nurses and paramedics. Storing EHRs on local hard disk drives or network attached storages installed on ambulances could make

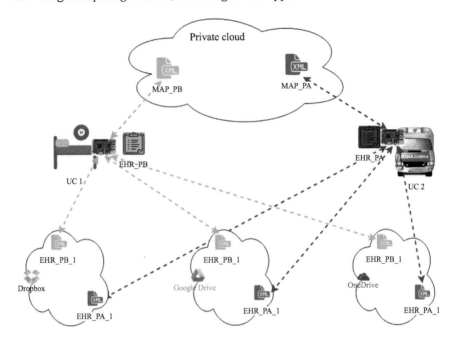

Figure 17.3   Overall architecture

difficult the synchronization among ambulances and hospitals. A possible solution is represented by the use of remote Cloud storage services for storing EHRs and Edge devices installed on ambulances for retrieving and showing EHRs to practitioners.

17.5   The Edge-based HIS

In this section, we discuss the design of the proposed system. The enabling technologies are Edge devices. That is, the computation of split and recomposition algorithms is done by these devices. Figure 17.3 shows a high-level representation of the architectural diagram. As the reader can observe, for both use cases the architecture is the same. It is composed of the following:

1. the private Cloud storage service of the hospital for storing 'map files' (special files containing information about the location of chunks);
2. public Cloud services for storing chunks of EHRs;
3. Edge devices running the RRNS installed on the bed (UC 1) or ambulances (UC 2).

17.5.1 *The redundant residue number system*

The RRNS is a cryptographic technique belonging to Secret Sharing algorithms. The basic idea of Secret Sharing techniques is to split a secret in chunks called shares and recompose it by using all chunks, (n, n) schema, or a subset, (k, n) schema. The RRNS is based on the residue number system (RNS). RNS choose p prime, positive integers $m_1, m_2, \ldots, m_p$ called *moduli* such as $M = \prod_{i=1}^{p} m_i$ and $m_i > m_{i-1}$ for each $i \in [2, p]$. Given $W \geq 0$, we can define $w_i = W \mod m_i$, the residue of W modulus m_i. The p-tuple $(w_1, w_2, \ldots, w_p)$ is named the *Residue Representation* of W with the given moduli and each tuple element w_i is known as the ith residue digit of the representation. For every p-tuple $(w_1, w_2, \ldots, w_p)$, the corresponding W can be reconstructed by means of the Chinese remainder theorem:

$$W = \left(\sum_{i=1}^{p} w_i \frac{M}{m_i} b_i \right) \mod M \tag{17.1}$$

where $b_i, i \in [1, p]$, is such that $\left(b_i \frac{M}{m_i} \right) \mod m_i = 1$ (i.e. the multiplicative inverse of $\frac{M}{m_i}$ modulus m_i). We call *RNS*, with residue moduli $m_1, m_2, \ldots, m_p$, the number system representing integers in $[0, M)$ through the p-tuple $(w_1, w_2, \ldots, w_p)$. Considering $p + r$ modules $m_1, \ldots, m_p, m_{p+1}, \ldots, m_{p+r}$, we have

$$M = \prod_{i=1}^{p} m_i \tag{17.2}$$

and

$$M_R = \prod_{i=p+1}^{r} m_i \tag{17.3}$$

without loss of generality $m_i > m_{i-1}$ for each $i \in [2, p+r]$. We define *RRNS* of moduli $m_1, \ldots, m_{p+r}$, range M and redundancy M_R, the number system representing integers in $[0, M)$ by means of the $(p + r)$-tuple of their residues modulus $m_1, \ldots, m_{p+r}$. Although the above-mentioned *RRNS* can provide representations to all integers in the range $[0, M \cdot M_R)$, the legitimate range of representation is limited to $[0, M)$, and the corresponding $(p + r)$-tuples are called *legitimate*. Integers in $[M, M \cdot M_R)$ together with the corresponding $(p + r)$-tuples are instead called *illegitimate*. Let now consider an *RRNS* whose range is M and redundancy M_R, where $(m_1, m_2, \ldots, m_p, m_{p+1}, \ldots, m_{p+r})$ is the $(p + r)$-tuple of moduli and $(w_1, w_2, \ldots, w_p, w_{p+1}, \ldots, w_{p+r})$ is the legitimate representation on a W integer in $[0, M)$. If an event making unavailable d arbitrary digits in the representation occurs, we have two new sets of elements $\{w'_1, w'_2, \ldots, w'_{p+r-d}\} \subseteq \{w_1, \ldots, w_{p+r}\}$ with the corresponding

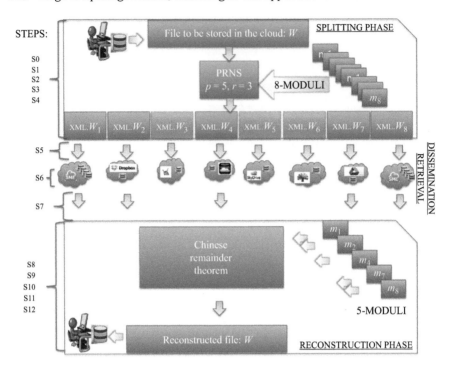

Figure 17.4   RRNS split and recomposition

moduli $\{m'_1, m'_2, \ldots, m'_{p+r-d}\} \subseteq \{m_1, \ldots, m_{p+r}\}$. This status is also known as *erasures* of multiplicity d. If the condition $d \leq r$ in true, the *RNS* of modules $\{m'_1, m'_2, \ldots, m'_{p+r-d}\}$ has range

$$M' = \prod_{i=1}^{p+r-d} m'_i \leq M \tag{17.4}$$

since $W < M$, $(w_1, w_2, \ldots, w_p, w_{p+1}, \ldots, w_{p+r})$ is the unique representation of W in the latter *RNS*. Integer W can be reconstructed from the $p + r - d$-tuple $(w'_1, w'_2, \ldots, w'_p, w'_{p+1}, \ldots, w'_{p+r-d})$ by means of the Chinese remainder theorem (as in the case of (17.1)):

$$W = \left(\sum_{i=1}^{p+r-d} w'_i \frac{M'}{m'_i} b'_i \right) \bmod M' \tag{17.5}$$

where b_i is such that $\left(b'_i \frac{M'}{m'_i} \right) \bmod m'_i = 1$ and $i \in [1, p+r-d]$. As a consequence, the above-mentioned *RRNS* can tolerate erasures up to multiplicity r.

Figure 17.4 shows a practical example on how RRNS can be applied for data replication. Let us assume W is a file, with $p = 5$ and $r = 3$. W is split in eight residue segments, i.e. $W_1, W_2, W_3, W_4, W_5, W_6, W_7$ and W_8. Supposing that a fail occurs and

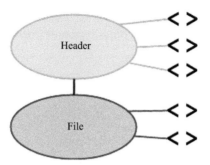

Figure 17.5   Map-file structure

Listing 17.1   An example of map file considering five chunks

```
<id>
  <Header>
    <Hospital>Hospital X</Hospital>
    <Patient>Patient Y</Patient>
    <SizeType>noBig</SizeType>
    <Padding>4</Padding>
  </Header>
  <File>
    <Chunk num="2">url_chunk_2</Chunk>
    <Chunk num="10">url_chunk_10</Chunk>
    <Chunk num="9">url_chunk_9</Chunk>
    <Chunk num="4">url_chunk_4</Chunk>
    <Chunk num="6">url_chunk_6</Chunk>
  </File>
</id>
```

that W_3, W_5 and W_6 are not available anymore, W can be reconstructed considering residue segments W_1, W_2, W_4, W_7 and W_8 and corresponding moduli using the Chinese remainder theorem.

17.5.2   Map files

The map file is a special XML file that contains both metadata of the EHR and the mapping of chunks. Its structure can be divided in two parts: the 'header' section (containing metadata such as the hospital and the patient) and the 'file' section containing URLs of chunks. A graphical representation of the structure is shown in Figure 17.5, and an example is provided in Listing 17.1.

To each EHR multiple map, files can be associated. In order to have a valid map file, the 'file' section has to fulfil the following requirements:

- it has to contain the minimum number of chunks needed for the recomposition;
- any two different sections belonging to different files have to differ at least for one element.

In order to better understand how the map file is made, for simplicity we consider a (3, 2) RRNS schema. This means that RRNS creates three shares (S_1, S_2, S_3) but, for the recomposition, needs only two of them. In this case, it is possible to build three valid map files: mf_1 which contains in the 'file' section the couple (S_1, S_2); mf_2 which contains in the 'file' section the couple (S_2, S_3); and mf_3 containing in the 'file' section the couple (S_1, S_3). The order of chunks is not significant. That is, the couple (S_1, S_2) is equal to (S_2, S_1).

Considering the (4, 2) RRNS schema, six valid map files can be built: (S_1, S_2), (S_1, S_3), (S_1, S_4), (S_3, S_2), (S_4, S_2) and (S_3, S_4).

In general, considering the (k, n) RRNS schema, it is possible to build

$$C(k, n) = \frac{k \times k - 1 \times \cdots \times k - n + 1}{n!} \tag{17.6}$$

different valid map files, where $C(k, n)$ is the combination of k elements by n.

17.6 Performance assessment

In this section, we discuss the performances of the proposed system. In particular, we analysed three different aspects:

1. EHR split and recomposition;
2. upload and download;
3. storage required.

We made a scalability analysis in several considering three different EHR sizes: 10 kB, 100 kB and 1 MB. and increasing levels of redundancy: 1, 4, 7. In order to have accurate results, we executed the same operations 30 times and considered the mean time.

Table 17.1 summarizes the performed experiments.

For storing chunks, we considered three public Cloud storage providers (Google Drive, Mega and Dropbox). Instead, the Edge device, in which the RRNS was executed, is a Raspberry Pi for which hardware (HW) and software (SW) characteristics are shown in Table 17.2.

17.6.1 EHR split and recomposition

In this section, we discuss the RRNS split and recomposition performance.

As the reader can observe in Figure 17.6(a), the time needed for the split of EHRs grows up with the increase in both EHR size and redundancy. In particular, the behaviour is linear, and the time spent for the split starts from 1.4 seconds considering

Table 17.1 *Summary of experiments performed*

Parameters	Values
Analyses	Execution time, transfer time, storage required
Environments	IoT (Table 17.2)
Secret Sharing algorithms	RRNS
Functions	Split, merge
Primaries (p)	5
Redundancy (r for split)	1, 4, 7
EHR size	10 kB, 100 kB, 1 MB
Number of iterations	30
Public Cloud providers	Google Drive, Mega, Dropbox

Table 17.2 *Hardware and software characteristics of test beds*

Parameters	Values
Model	Raspberry Pi 3
RAM	1 GB LPDDR2-900 SDRAM
CPU	1.2 GHz quad-core ARM Cortex A53
Storage	MicroSD 8 GB (write throughput: 12.7 MB/s; read throughput: 20.8 MB/s)
Networking	10/100 Ethernet, 2.4 GHz 802.11n wireless
Operating system (OS)	Raspbian
GFLOPS	5

EHRs of 10 kB in configuration with a single level of redundancy growing up until roughly 3 seconds to split EHRs of 1 MB.

In Figure 17.6(b), the behaviour of the recomposition task is shown. In this case analysis, it is not necessary to consider different degrees of redundancy. This because, as we discuss in Section 17.5, the RRNS for the EHR recomposition needs a fixed number of chunks.

As the reader can see, also in this case the behaviour is linear. The time needed for the recomposition is 0.7 seconds for EHRs of 10 kB, and it grows up until 3.5 seconds for EHRs of 1 MB.

17.6.2 EHR upload and download

In this section, we discuss the time needed for the upload and download of EHR chunks into the public Cloud storage providers.

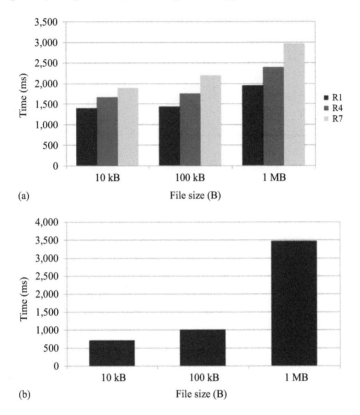

Figure 17.6   RRNS split on IoT (a) RRNS split (b) RRNS merge

The upload behaviour is shown in Figure 17.7(a)–(c). In particular, Figure 17.7(a) refers to 10 kB EHR, Figure 17.7(b) to 100 kB whereas Figure 17.7(c) to 1 MB. The *y*-axis of the chart represents the time needed for the upload expressed in milliseconds, whereas the *x*-axis the number of chunks stored in each Cloud service provider. We remark that, in our performance evaluation, we considered the degree of redundancy equal to 1 (2 chunks per each Cloud service provider), 4 (3 chunks per each Cloud service provider) and 7 (4 chunks per each Cloud service provider). As can be observed in Figure 17.7(a) and (b), the time required for the upload of chunks is constant with increase in the number of chunks. This behaviour is justified by the fact that chunks are very small; therefore, the time required for internal synchronization is greater than the effective time needed for the upload. A different behaviour can be seen in Figure 17.7(c). In this case, the time required for the upload is not negligible; therefore, the total time required for the upload depends on the number of chunks. As the reader can observe, in all presented scenarios Google Drive (the blue bar) presents the worst performance because it requires more time to start the synchronization. Furthermore, in Figure 17.7(c) we can see that the time required from Dropbox (the yellow bar) increases faster than Mega (red bar) because this

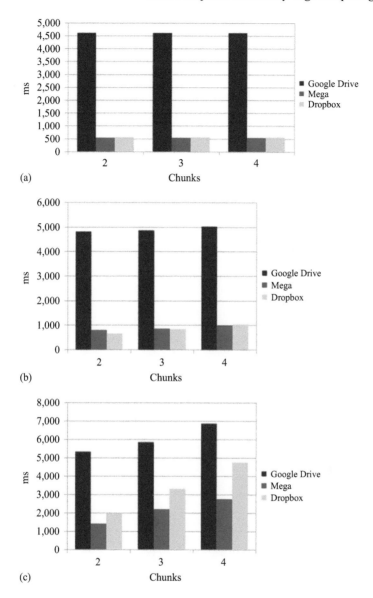

*Figure 17.7   Upload of chunks of EHR in public Clouds (a) Size = 10 kB
(b) Size = 100 kB (c) Size = 1 MB*

Dropbox, in order to optimize the storage, divides files in chunks of 100 kB before the transmission.

Figure 17.8(a)–(c) shows the behaviour for the download of HERs of 10 kB, 100 kB and 1 MB, respectively. In these figures, the y-axis represents the time needed for downloading chunks expressed in milliseconds, whereas, the x-axis the number

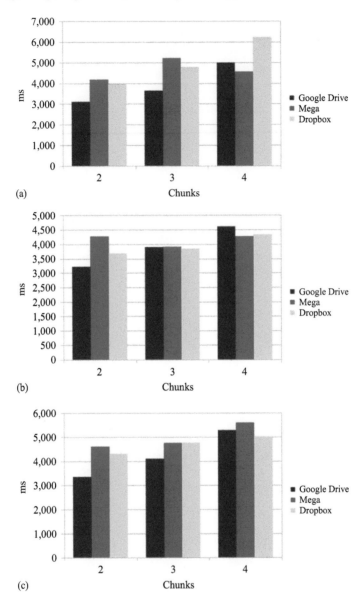

*Figure 17.8   Download of chunks of EHR from public Clouds (a) Size = 10 kB
(b) Size = 100 kB (c) Size = 1 MB*

of chunks stored in each Cloud service provider. As we have done for the upload, in
this case we also considered 2, 3 and 4 chunks in each Cloud storage provider. As
the reader can observe, in all scenarios, differently from the upload phase, the time
required from all Cloud service providers are comparable and Google Drive has better
performances that others.

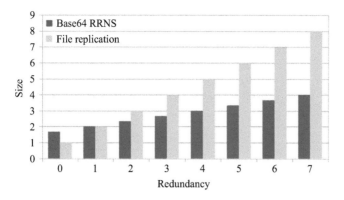

Figure 17.9   Storage required for Base64 RRNS and replication approaches

17.6.3   Storage required

In this section, we discuss the storage required for the proposed approach considering different degrees of redundancy. In particular, we compared the RRNS with the file replication. For seven levels of redundancy, the RRNS requires roughly the 50% of the capacity required from file replication. This because each fragment in RRNS is the result of the modulo operation between the secret and a modulo. This means that each fragment will be smaller of both the secret and the modulo. In our implementation, we codified as 'integers (32 bits)' the secret and 'bytes (8 bits)' modules and fragments. Therefore, the size of each fragment is one-fourth of the size of the EHR. For compatibility reasons, we codified each chunks as Base64 that introduces the 33% of overhead. The mathematical formula that expresses the storage required is the following:

$$S = \frac{p + r}{4} \times 1.33 S_{\text{EHR}} \tag{17.7}$$

where p is the number of primaries (fixed to 5 in our case), r the level of redundancy and S_{EHR} the size of the EHR. Figure 17.9 shows the behaviour of two approaches.

17.7   Open issues and challenges

In this section, we discuss the security issues related to the system we proposed in Section 17.5 in both use cases presented in Section 17.4.

Generally, in the healthcare sector, the main obstacle to effective EHR systems to ensure ongoing continuity of healthcare is the lack of interoperability of EHR systems used by patients, healthcare providers and security of patient's data. The lack of data integration makes it difficult to offer accurate and timely treatments. Therefore, the proposed EHR system requires the collaborations outside the organizational boundaries in order to promote effective delivery of healthcare for individuals and companies, as well as allowing savings and efficiencies. During the medical assistance service, a large amount of data are created which must be securely stored.

Data transfer and consent management in use cases presented in Section 17.4 can become complex and inconvenient: the patient may need to get in touch with the caregiver and sign consent in the hospital from which s/he is not receiving care any longer. Transfer of data can take time, and on receiving the hard copy of the patient data, a clinician will have to introduce them into the system again. Furthermore, with this approach, it is very difficult for the patients to maintain any access control or log of their data and to have a complete view of the data. Furthermore, the lack of integration makes it difficult to maintain the privacy and security of the patient's confidential information. Patient's EHR security is a cause for concern especially when patient's data are transmitted over a network. On the other hand, however, sharing EHR can benefit patients and medical organizations in various ways. First, data sharing can facilitate medical research, such as bringing together multiple medical studies for better knowledge and scientific discoveries. Second, collaboration between different health organizations (including cross-border cases) will be easier, such as doctors accessing patient records, reimbursement of medical care in a foreign country, and so on. Third, regulations and standards will be developed and strengthened to facilitate secure sharing of data centres, which in turn will increase trust between different medical organizations and can therefore offer patients better service and further improve medical research. The main security issues related to EHR sharing are confidentiality, privacy, access control, integrity, data authenticity, user authentication, audibility and transparency. It is urgent to resolve these problems to enable secure sharing of EHRs.

During recent years, blockchain technology has been advocated as a promising solution to solving EHR interoperability and security issues. A blockchain is a decentralized, trustless protocol that combines transparency, immutability and consensus properties to enable secure, pseudo-anonymous transactions stored in a digital ledger. Blockchain enables a potentially evolving and open set of parties to maintain a safe, permanent and tamper-proof digital ledger of transactions, without a central authority. It consists of consecutive chained blocks, replicated and stored by the nodes of a peer-to-peer network, where blocks are created in a distributed fashion by means of a consensus algorithm. Such algorithm, together with the use of crypto-mechanisms, provides two properties of blockchain: (1) decentralization and (2) democratic control of data. This ensures that data on the chain cannot be tampered maliciously, operations on the chain are non-repudiable and their origin is fully tracked. Blockchains are then typically classified in two main categories:

1. Permissionless: A block can be added to the blockchain by any process, but only if a cryptographic puzzle is solved (Proof-of-Work). Examples are Bitcoin, Zerocash and Ethereum.
2. Permissioned: Closed group of processes execute a (traditional) Byzantine consensus algorithm to add a block to the blockchain. Consensus decisions are either taken unilaterally by this central entity, or by a preselected group (so-called 'consortium blockchains'). Permissioned blockchains can be further categorized into public and private. Examples include Hyperledger.

Unlike Bitcoin, new types of blockchains such as Ethereum and Hyperledger Fabric have recently appeared with featuring smart contracts: programs deployed and executed on blockchain. Smart contract allows the creation of the so-called decentralized applications, i.e. applications that operate autonomously and without any control by a system entity and whose logic is immutably stored on a blockchain. We discuss each of the above-mentioned security issues and how blockchain technology can solve each one in the following:

Confidentiality. It is one of the major concerns in sharing patient's EHRs between multiple organizations over the network. Using the blockchain, the patient can have full access to the data and control how the data are shared maintaining privacy and security. For example, patients who are part of the blockchain would be able to approve or deny any sharing or modification of their data, helping to ensure a greater level of privacy and greater consumer control. Furthermore, the blockchain is based on consolidated cryptographic techniques to allow each participant in a network to interact without the pre-existing trust between the parties. Due to the encryption of blockchain information, patient EHR's confidentiality is preserved when it is shared between the parties involved.

Privacy. Ensuring the safety of the EHR and the underlying components of the ecosystem is crucial but difficult due to the interaction and complexity between systems and components. Furthermore, the privacy and integrity of the extremely sensitive healthcare data must be ensured not only from outside attackers, but also from unauthorized access attempts within the network (e.g. health service provider employee or cloud service provider) [29]. Intentional and unintentional attacks (e.g., data loss or data alteration) can be criminally liable, for example, under the Health Insurance Portability and Accountability Act. Therefore, data protection and traceability are the fundamental principles of the chain of trust. Smart contracts allow to encrypt patient data, and permissions are sometimes taken to access this content. The data will be digitally signed, and caregivers will need access grants to access it.

Access control. There are mainly two aspects related to EHR access, namely a patient accessing their EHRs and a medical personnel accessing the patient's EHRs. For instance, the patients should be able to grant who can access their EHRs and should also maintain and track any change of their medical history. By applying blockchain for the permissions management, we enable the exchange of patient-controlled data between medical organizations and an interoperable content management system for physicians who supervise these records. Moreover, in the future, this verifiable history of medical interactions between patients and suppliers technology can be relevant for regulators and payers (e.g. insurance).

Integrity. Another concern in patient's EHRs sharing is the integrity; EHRs integrity is crucial to prescribing the correct treatment. Any modification can produce potential patient's death. Furthermore, data integrity is guaranteed by blockchain. This is mainly achieved by using the consent protocol and cryptographic primitives such as hashing and digital signatures. The use of hashing and digital signatures makes the manipulation, verification and accessibility of patient data or data with public and private keys almost impossible, and in essence, security is fully guaranteed. In fact, it is computationally difficult to tamper with the contents of a block without changing the hash value stored in the next block. Furthermore, the distributed blockchain architecture is integrated into fault tolerance and disaster recovery.

Data authenticity. Any entity involved (e.g., patients and medical personnel) who created an EHR should guarantee its authenticity, i.e., prove that he/she is the original creator of the EHR. In order to ensure this, patients and medical personnel must sign their EHR before being added to the blockchain. With these signatures, blockchain provides the authenticity of the data.

Audibility and transparency. Given that a patient can be treated from different doctors belonging to different healthcare organizations and therefore each one generates a different EHR for each treatment, patients should be able to track their medical history. Blockchain technology is the most suitable solution. As all changes in patient data will be recorded and then added to the blockchain, an integrated, clear and transparent audit trail of EHR changes can be maintained, and patients can have access to these paths as long as they have access to the blockchain network.

Interoperability. The patients can be treated by different medical organizations also belonging to different jurisdictions. The current medical system consists of a complex network of healthcare organizations; each organization uses its own method for storing and accessing medical data (e.g. offline architecture with centralized and local databases); cooperation and sharing among the various organizations is almost inexistent. In general, data exchange in a coherent manner requires a shared network, as well as a solid platform for sharing and cooperation, enabling easy understanding and operation. Unlike a centralized network where different healthcare organizations have their own systems, the decentralization of the blockchain is designed to be convenient for each entity to communicate with each other, which means that all the blockchain entities will use the same standard for EHRs' sharing and management.

17.8 Conclusions and future works

In this chapter, we discussed the use of Edge devices for the management of EHR. In particular, we considered two use cases: hospitalized patients and ambulances. We described a possible architecture consisting of private and public Cloud storage services and Edge devices running the RRNS. In order to evaluate the proposed approach, we made three different types of analyses: (i) execution time for the EHR split and recomposition; (ii) time required for upload and download of EHR chunks; and (iii) storage required. We considered three different EHR sizes from 10 kB to 1 MB and three different public Cloud storage providers (Google Drive, Mega and Dropbox). With regards to EHR split and recomposition, we made the scalability analysis. We have seen that, contrary to the RRNS merge, the execution time of the RRNS split depends on the level of redundancy. Whereas, regarding upload and download of chunks, we have seen that Google Drive, due to synchronization overhead, is slower than other Cloud service providers for the upload of chunks but faster for the download. In future works, in order to monitor the accesses to EHRs and discover attackers, we plan to design and implement a logger system based on blockchain.

References

[1]   More than 1 million Google accounts breached by Gooligan. Last access: March 2019. Available from: http://blog.checkpoint.com/2016/11/30/1-million-google-accounts-breached-gooligan/.

[2]   Yahoo hack: 1bn accounts compromised by biggest data breach in history. Last access: March 2019. Available from: https://www.theguardian.com/tech nology/2016/dec/14/yahoo-hack-security-of-one-billion-accounts-breached.

[3]   Stolen Dropbox passwords are circulating online. Here's how to check if your account's compromised. Last access: March 2019. Available from: http://qz.com/771196/stolen-dropbox-passwords-are-circulating-online-heres-how-to-check-if%2Dyour-accounts-compromised/.

[4]   Copy Cloud Storage service's life ends on May 1, 2016. Last access: March 2019. Available from: https://www.ghacks.net/2016/02/02/copy-cloud-storage-services-life-ends-on-may-1-2016/.

[5]   Shutting down Ubuntu One file services. Last access: March 2019. Available from: https://blog.ubuntu.com/2014/04/02/shutting-down-ubuntu-one-file-services.

[6]   Dell DataSafe Online. Last access: March 2019. Available from: https://web.archive.org/web/20140625035604/, https://www.delldatasafe.com/.

[7]   Opara-Martins J, Sahandi R, and Tian F. Critical analysis of vendor lock-in and its impact on cloud computing migration: a business perspective. Journal of Cloud Computing. 2016;5(1):4. Available from: https://doi.org/10.1186/s13677-016-0054-z.

[8]   Hsiao S, and Kao D. The static analysis of WannaCry ransomware. In: 2018 20th International Conference on Advanced Communication Technology (ICACT); 2018. pp. 153–158.

[9]   WannaCry cyber attack cost the NHS 92m as 19,000 appointments cancelled. Last access: April 2019. Available from: https://www.telegraph.co.uk/technology/2018/10/11/wannacry-cyber-attack-cost-nhs-92m-19000-appoint ments-cancelled/.

[10] 2018 reform of EU data protection rules. Last access: April 2019. Available from: https://ec.europa.eu/commission/priorities/justice-and-fundamental-rights/data-protection/2018-reform-eu-data-protection-rules_en.

[11] Pathinarupothi RK, Durga P, and Rangan ES. IoT-based smart edge for global health: remote monitoring with severity detection and alerts transmission. IEEE Internet of Things Journal. 2019;6(2):2449–2462.

[12] Galletta A, Carnevale L, Bramanti A, and Fazio M. An innovative methodology for big data visualization for telemedicine. IEEE Transactions on Industrial Informatics. 2019;15(1):490–497.

[13] Zhang H, Li J, Wen B, Xun Y, and Liu J. Connecting intelligent things in smart hospitals using NB-IoT. IEEE Internet of Things Journal. 2018;5(3):1550–1560.

[14] He C, Jin X, Zhao Z, and Xiang T. A cloud computing solution for Hospital Information System. In: 2010 IEEE International Conference on Intelligent Computing and Intelligent Systems. vol. 2; 2010. pp. 517–520.

[15] Porter A, Potts H, Mason S, *et al.* 70 The digital ambulance: electronic patient clinical records in prehospital emergency care. British Medical Journal; 2018;8(Suppl 1).

[16] Sigwele T, Hu YF, Ali M, Hou J, Susanto M, and Fitriawan H. An intelligent edge computing-based semantic gateway for healthcare systems interoperability and collaboration. In: 2018 IEEE 6th International Conference on Future Internet of Things and Cloud (FiCloud); 2018. pp. 370–376.

[17] Khare SP, Sallai J, Dubey A, and Gokhale A. Short Paper: Towards low-cost indoor localization using edge computing resources. In: 2017 IEEE 20th International Symposium on Real-Time Distributed Computing (ISORC); 2017. pp. 28–31.

[18] Tata S, Jain R, Ludwig H, and Gopisetty S. Living in the cloud or on the edge: opportunities and challenges of IOT application architecture. In: 2017 IEEE International Conference on Services Computing (SCC); 2017. pp. 220–224.

[19] Gunter TD, and Terry NP. The emergence of National Electronic Health Record Architectures in the United States and Australia: models, costs, and questions. J Med Internet Res. 2005 Mar;7(1):e3. Available from: http://www.jmir.org/2005/1/e3/.

[20] Australian Government Department of Health and Ageing. Last access: January 2019. Available from: http://www.healthconnect.gov.au/pdf/bav1.pdf.

[21] Introduction to HL7 Standards. Last access: January 2019. Available from: http://www.hl7.org/implement/standards/.

[22] What are the differences between electronic medical records, electronic health records, and personal health records? Last access: January 2019. Available from: https://www.healthit.gov/faq/what-are-differences-between-electronic-medical-records-electronic-health%2Drecords-and-personal.

[23] Essén A, Scandurra I, Gerrits R, *et al.* Patient access to electronic health records: differences across ten countries. Health Policy and Technology. 2018;7(1):44–56. Available from: http://www.sciencedirect.com/science/article/pii/S2211883717300722.

[24] Scambio di cartelle cliniche, donna rischia l'intervento chirurgico. Last access: January 2019. Available from: https://www.agro24.it/2016/03/scambio-di-cartelle-cliniche-donna-rischia-lintervento-chirurgico/.

[25] Scambio di cartelle cliniche in ospedale: morto un 62enne. Last access: January 2019. Available from: http://www.responsabilecivile.it/scambio-di-cartelle-cliniche-ospedale-morto-un-62enne/.

[26] Scambio di cartelle cliniche: 70enne subisce un ciclo di chemioterapia, ma non ha un tumore e muore. Last access: January 2019. Available from: https://retenews24.it/scambio-di-cartelle-cliniche-70enne-subisce-un-ciclo-di-chemioterapia%2Dma-non-ha-un-tumore/.

[27] Rapporto annuale sull'attività di ricovero ospedaliero. Last access: January 2019. Available from: http://www.salute.gov.it/imgs/C_17_pubblicazioni_2651_allegato.pdf.

[28] Sistema di emergenza sanitaria territoriale "118". Rilevazione nazionale. Last access: January 2019. Available from: http://www.salute.gov.it/imgs/C_17_pubblicazioni_845_allegato.pdf.

[29] Esposito C, Santis AD, Tortora G, Chang H, and Raymond Choo K-W. Blockchain: a panacea for healthcare cloud-based data security and privacy? IEEE Cloud Computing. 2018;5(1):31–37.

Chapter 18
Smart grids enabled by edge computing
Alem Fitwi[1], Zekun Yang[1], Yu Chen[1] and Xuheng Lin[1]

A smart grid is the nervous system of the power generation, transmission, and distribution systems that makes a great use of the information and communications technologies (ICTs). The ICT enables the smart grid to timely detect, monitor, and react to local changes in usage and in the event of electrical faults of various types. The smart grid is the nexus of distributed electrical sensors, smart energy meters, smart appliances often deployed in customer premises, transducers, network interfaces, remote terminals, servers, and a multiplexed communication system which transmits data and commands between parts installed across the entire power grid system components. The main power grid components include the power generation station, high-voltage transmission system, distribution systems, and customer premises. The sensors that can be interconnected to one another using various network architectures and computing paradigms are the eyes and ears of the smart grid which provide information vital for efficient and timely fault detection, monitoring, and controlling the entire power grid system. Hence, the smart grid is derived from the general-purpose network architecture and computing models in a manner as to fit the purposes of the electrical grid system.

The main thing that distinguishes a smart grid from the general-purpose computer network is that it is one specific application of it. The most striking characteristic of computer networks is their generality. They are not optimized for a specific application like the smart grid. They are built principally from general-purpose programmable hardware capable of carrying and supporting many different types of data, and a wide spectrum of ever growing applications. Just like the general-purpose computer network, the smart grid could be deployed in client-server, peer-to-peer, or distributed architecture. In a similar fashion, the computational paradigm of the smart grid could be cloud, fog, or edge based. But the smart grid is typically the embodiment of the Internet of Things (IoT) or cyber-physical systems; hence, the most suitable computing paradigm is one that brings the computation and data storage closer to the point where data are created and garnered.

[1]Binghamton University, Binghamton, New York, USA

Thus, this chapter looks at the typical ways how the edge computing paradigm is applied to improve reliability, the load forecasting capability, security and privacy of the smart grid. To put it another way, this chapter focuses on four things. It, first, lays down the foundations and background knowledge about the power grid, smart grid, and edge computing paradigm. Second, it explains the factors that affect the reliability of the smart grid and explains the ways how the edge computing techniques can improve the reliability of the smart grid. Third, it explores the requirements and ways how power consumption prediction could be accurately performed at the edge using artificial intelligence (AI), machine learning (ML), and deep learning (DL) methods coupled with advanced electrical signal processing techniques. Finally, it presents how the security and privacy issues of a smart grid enabled by edge computing could be addressed.

18.1   Introduction to edge computing-enabled smart grids

Electrical grid is one of the leading and greatest technological inventions of the twentieth century. The genesis of early power systems and electric power grids during the past 130 years was enabled by automation and control of electromechanical machinery and power delivery networks. It has delivered the life blood for the technological innovations and advancements in the computing and communication arenas. The demand and economic, technical, environmental, and political challenges have pressingly called for radical changes on how electricity is generated, transmitted, distributed, controlled, monitored, consumed, and managed ending the times the grid could be taken for granted. As the concepts and techniques energy is generated make continuous advancements, it has become a necessity to employ a modernized grid system capable of meeting the ever-increasing needs of the customers by efficiently addressing the problems associated with power outages and thefts. As a result, today's end-to-end power and energy systems fundamentally depend on embedded and often overlaid systems of sensors, computation, communication, control, and optimization. There are even more opportunities and challenges in today's devices and systems, as well as in the emerging modern power systems ranging from watts, emissions, standards, and more at nearly every scale of sensing and control. Recent policies combined with potential for technological innovations and business opportunities have attracted a high level of interest in the electric grids [1–3]. Hence, the apropos employment of an intelligent grid management system called a smart grid [4] is of astronomical importance. Smart grid is an electricity network that can efficiently integrate the behavior and actions of all generators, consumers, and prosumers so as to guarantee economically efficient, sustainable power system with low losses, and high levels of quality and security of supply and safety. The smart grid is introduced in a bit more detailed manner in Section 18.1.1. Besides, an introduction to edge computing paradigm and how it can help improve the load forecasting capability, reliability, resilience, availability, and intelligence of smart grid is briefly presented in Section 18.1.2.

18.1.1 The smart grid

The potential for a highly distributed system with a high penetration of intermittent sources poses opportunities and challenges. Any complex dynamic infrastructure network typically has many layers and decision-making units, and is vulnerable to various types of disturbances. Effective, intelligent, and distributed control is required to enable parts of the networks to remain operational and to even automatically reconfigure in the event of local failures or threats of failures. Here is where the smart grid becomes so handy. That is, it is one of the major areas of applications of the IoT that plays roles of paramount importance in improving the generation, transmission, distribution, and consumption of electricity in terms of reliability, resilience, availability, and cost [3–5].

The traditional electric grid has been engulfed with a plethora of problems including outages, lower availability due to elongated fixing times in the event of component failures, unpredictable power disturbances, unattractively fixed prices of electricity, and failures to detect fraudulent consumers. These drawbacks, in one way or another, contribute to the increasing consumption of fossil fuels and subsequent increase in utility costs. Correct estimation of demands and peak load duration plays very pronounced role in the wise utilization of resources while meeting customer demands. The smart grid addresses the inefficiencies and unreliability of the grid. It efficiently delivers electricity from suppliers or utilities to consumers and prosumers using two-way digital communications to control appliances at consumers' homes. This could save energy, reduce costs, and increase reliability and transparency if the risks inherent in executing massive information are avoided. It overlays the ordinary electrical grid with an information and net metering system that includes smart meters [3,4]. Smart grids are being promoted by many governments as a way of addressing energy independence, global warming, and emergency resilience issues. The grid usually encompasses myriads of local area networks (LANs) that use distributed energy resources to several loads to meet specific application requirements for remote power, municipal or district power, premium power, and critical loads protection. It has infinitely many benefits like performing dynamic pricing, enabling real-time exchange of information between providers and consumers through the use of smart meters, and interconnecting green energy sources (like micro-grid, solar panels, and biofuels) to the grid that increases the reliability of electricity distribution.

However, the many benefits of the smart grid come along with some costs. As stated in the previous paragraphs, it employs a myriad of computing and communications technologies; as a result, most of the security issues faced in the information technology (IT) networks still exist in the smart grid as well. What is more, the smart grid invades the privacy of consumers as it collects massive data via its smart sensors deployed in the customers' building area network (BAN) [6] and suffers from some reliability and availability issues as well. Hence, these limitations necessitate improvements. That is, the employment of contemporary technologies like AI, ML, or DL coupled with edge computing paradigm can help solve some of the problems faced by the cloud-centric smart grid deployment.

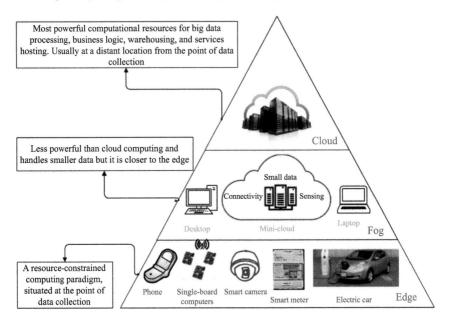

Figure 18.1   Hierarchical computing paradigm: cloud, fog, and edge

18.1.2   Edge computing paradigm

Big organizations or IT services providers make use of hierarchical computing paradigms similar to the one depicted in Figure 18.1, depending on data size, computational needs, and applications they run. That is, this architecture of computing infrastructures enables organizations or applications like the Industrial IoT to take advantage of a variety of computing and data storage resources. Cloud computing paradigm frees organizations from the requirement to keep expensive data center infrastructure on-site. It allows data to be collected from multiple *distant* sites and devices. It is accessible from anywhere around the globe. Fog computing and edge computing look similar for they both bring the intelligence and processing power closer to the point of data creation and collection. However, a fog environment places intelligence at the enterprise campus area network where data are transmitted from end points to a gateway for processing. The edge computing places intelligence and processing power in devices such as embedded automation controllers and smart meters. That is, it allows the processing of data to be performed locally at multiple decision points for the purpose of enabling real-time communication and decision-making by reducing network traffic, response time, and risk of security and privacy breaches.

The cloud-centric smart grids get data processed in distant cloud centers and suffer from network congestion, unpredictable response time, and security and privacy issues. These shortcomings have the potential to undercut the reliability, availability, and resilience of the smart grid [5,7]. In lieu of sending data from IoT devices to the cloud inefficiently, fog nodes analyze the data on the network relatively closer to the edge avoiding the need to transfer data back to the distant center of the network. But the edge computing paradigm directly addresses most of these issues by pushing computing power and intelligence away from centralized clouds to sites closer to consumers, producers, and prosumers [8]. In such a way, it drastically reduces the volumes of data transported to cloud centers, thereby cutting down on the latency and the transmission costs. As a result, edge computing-enabled smart grids outperform the cloud-centric smart grids.

18.2 Availability and reliability of edge-enabled smart grids

The fast and continued advancement in IT networks and computing paradigms like distributed, cloud, fog, and edge computing have drastically revolutionized the way electrical power is generated, transmitted, distributed, controlled, and billed. The electrical grid that takes full advantage of these technologies and methods is called a "smart grid" [2,4]. They play very pronounced roles in making the smart grid more reliable, more available, more efficient, and more secure. However, smart grids are capable of breaking down that could cause power blackout due to the fact that they comprise a great deal of components. Hence, analyzing factors and designs that affect the availability and reliability of smart grids is of paramount importance. The availability and reliability are required to be as higher as possible at all stages including the electricity generation stations, electric power transmissions, electricity distributions, and control and monitoring systems. This section presents how availability and reliability of smart grids are affected and how edge computing could help improve these important attributes of the smart grid. The respective details are provided in Sections 18.2.1, 18.2.2, and 18.2.3.

18.2.1 The availability of smart grids

Given a specified observation period which could be in hours, days, weeks, months, or years, the availability is the ratio of the uptime (time during which it is in operation) of the smart grid to the observation period as stated in (18.1). In other words, it can be defined as the ratio of observation period minus its downtime to the observation period, stated in (18.2).

$$Availability\ (\%) = \left(\frac{Uptime}{Observation\_Period} \right) * 100 \tag{18.1}$$

$$Availability\ (\%) = \left(\frac{Observation\_Period - Downtime}{Observation\_Period} \right) * 100 \tag{18.2}$$

In a more realistic way, availability can be expressed using exponential distribution so as to provide a good measure for identifying the prospect that the grid is operational. This is modeled using the time until a component of the smart grid breaks down and the time taken to fix it. Equation (18.3) gives the time until the component of a smart grid breaks which is modeled using exponentially distributed function. Given the failure rate λ, the mean time of failure (MTF) is $1/\lambda$. In a similar fashion, the average downtime or the time required to fix the broken component can be modeled with parameter μ using the exponential distribution. Hence, the mean time to repair (MTR) is equal to $1/\mu$.

$$f(t) = \begin{cases} \lambda e^{-\lambda t} & \text{if } \lambda > 0 \text{ and } t > 0 \\ 0 & \text{else} \end{cases} \tag{18.3}$$

The availability of the smart grid is therefore computed in terms of mean uptime (MTF) and mean downtime (MTR) as depicted in (18.4). In principle, there is no difference among (18.1), (18.2), and (18.4), but (18.4) is more realistic for it takes the probabilistic nature of failures into account.

$$Availability\ (\%) = \left(\frac{MTF}{MTF + MTR} \right) * 100 \tag{18.4}$$

The smart grid often comprises components connected in both series and parallel. Assuming that there are n redundant components that are in parallel in the smart grid, the overall availability can be computed using (18.6), which gives a better result than (18.4) when n is at least greater than one. As the degree of redundancy, n, increases, the exponential term decays to zero giving an availability of 100%. Hence, the major takeaway here is that availability is improved when there are more redundant devices and communication links in the smart grid. The total availability of components connected in tandem, given in (18.5), is much smaller than the availability of a single device given in (18.4), clearly indicating that the probability of failure is much higher. We know that a smart grid comprising a single series connection component is prone to a single point failure that substantially affects the availability of electricity. Simply, all the mathematical models emphasize how much pronounced roles the distributed and edge computing architectures can play in improving the availability of a smart grid [9].

$$\prod_{i=1}^{n} Availability_i \tag{18.5}$$

$$\prod_{i=1}^{n} (1 - (1 - Availability_i)^i) \tag{18.6}$$

For instance, as portrayed in Figure 18.1, the computational power and distance from the point of data creation increase as we move up along the pyramid. However, the number of devices (of smaller computational power) and communication links increase as we move downwards. The former affects the redundancy which in turn impacts the availability as stated in (18.6). That is, in the event of a failure, it takes relatively increased MTR affecting the MTF. This lowers the availability. On the other hand, the edge computing comprises many devices with some computational power and intelligence installed at least per BAN basis. This approach cuts off the reliance on few distant cloud centers. That is, the failure of an edge device at one point of data collection does not affect others. The downtime is much smaller that keeps the MTF higher, which in turn gives higher service availability. Let us consider a BAN connected to three sources of energy making use of the edge devices computational power and intelligence where the observation period is assumed to be a day and the downtime is about 0.0101 day. The availability is computed to be about 99%. But in the absence of edge computing where the connection is one way series, the availability goes down to 97%. The calculations were performed according to (18.1)–(18.6).

18.2.2 The reliability of smart grids

One of the noble goals of the electric power industry is creating a reliable and resilient grid operations. The reliability and resilience refer to the ability of the smart grid to recover as quickly as possible in the face of failures that might be caused by both man-made and natural disasters [10,11]. The natural weather events are liable for the lion share of power outages in the USA and their frequency has been rising for long. But the impact of cyberattacks cannot be underestimated as well [12]. It is worth noting. Hence, it is important to invest in technologies that can empower the smart grid to have the ability to respond to power outages inflicted by natural disasters and to proactively deter potential cyberattacks. The underpinning concept of reliability is that even when stricken or attacked, the grid should be able to reroute power flows quickly and automatically, thereby reducing the number of affected customers from downed power lines or from parts of the grid disabled by cyberattacks [10–13].

Just like the availability, the reliability of electronic components of the smart grid can be modeled using the exponential distribution which is scaled up to compute the overall reliability of the smart grid. Given the hazard rate of a component to be λ and the mean time between failures to $1/\lambda$, the reliability at a specific point in time (t) can be computed using (18.7).

$$\int_t^\infty f(t)dt = e^{-\lambda t} \tag{18.7}$$

Reliability, another important attribute of smart grids, is the probability of a failure occurring at some component of it or whole part of it as stated in (18.7). It refers to the ability of the smart grid to continuously and consistently operate as designed. As (18.7) shows, the smart grid components wear out with time. A reliable smart grid is completely free from any technical errors theoretically. In practice, that is not the case; it is expressed as a percentage and it is the capacity of the smart grid to continuously offer the same services amid component failure or partial failures. It should be designed in such a way that a single failure wouldn't bring it down on its knees. A perfectly reliable smart grid relishes 100% availability; however, when failures occur at any part of the grid, the availability might be affected in various ways depending on the nature of the problem and whether the smart grid has redundant design. A centralized smart grid is less reliable and liable to single point failure and the availability could be severely affected whenever a failure takes place. But an edge-enabled smart grid, where there are distributed edge devices and fog servers, has a better reliability and availability than the one that relies on fewer cloud servers. That is, reliability of the smart grid affects its availability. But if the smart grid no matter how redundant is severely affected by cyberattack, its reliability and efficiency are diminished, which, in turn, affects its availability. Details about how the availability of smart grids is affected by cyberattacks are provided in Sections 18.4 and 18.4.1.1 methodically and profoundly.

18.2.3   Edge computing-enabled solutions for smart grids

Grids designed based on a centralized architecture (client-server) and cloud computing paradigms have a number of limitations. Hence, an improvement is needed in the way the smart grid carries out such tasks as measurement, data processing, communication, and controlling. The smart grid has a huge number of devices and sensors capable of continuously creating and garnering massive data. The centralized and cloud computing paradigms, which are often placed in distant locations from the points where data are collected, incur a lot of latency, bandwidth congestion, and privacy problems [5,7,8,13]. That is, the server-client and cloud computing architecture have powerful computational powers at distant locations, but the tremendous amount of data produced by the many sensors that constitute the smart-grid has the potential to cause some unpredictability in the response time. They consume a lot of bandwidth [14,15]. Besides, they are prone to a number of cyberattacks including interruption, eavesdropping, and tampering. These limitations make such computing architectures less reliable and greatly affect the availability of the grid to both consumers and prosumers. Here is where edge computing paradigm becomes so handy. In other words, the smart grid needs to have mini-brains at the edge of its networks on top of its ears and eyes (the sensors) to improve its reliability and availability by reducing latency, by avoiding traffic congestion, by dropping the probability of cyberattacks, and by addressing the privacy concerns of customers and prosumers alike.

The edge computing keeps the computing tasks at the edge of the smart grid, in the BAN, where the smart sensors equipped with edge computing capabilities reside. That is to say, the data processing tasks, the data analytics, and the partial storage of the data generated by the smart sensors are performed within closer proximity of the points where data are generated and collected. The majority of the tasks that used to be processed by clouds or central data centers after data have been sent by the edge sensors are now being acted upon locally at the edge nodes of the grid's network. As a result, edge computing provides a number of benefits to smart grids. First, it greatly cuts down on the latency by reducing the network traffic. That is, the edge computing performs the data processing and storage closer to where the data are collected that eschews unnecessarily bandwidth congestion, processing queues, and risk of privacy breaches. The reduction in latency creates an auspicious situation for real-time data exchange, monitoring, and control. Furthermore, it provides a better platform for addressing the privacy problems by enforcing privacy conserving measures closer to the point of data collection. The central and cloud computing architectures endanger the privacy of customers. A huge amount of data is transported over communication networks, which are prone to several cyberattacks, to distant central locations for processing and storage. These heaps of data could help easily deduce the behavior and patterns of customers [16].

The edge computing has also the potential to bring intelligence closer to the consumers and prosumers, which empowers BANs to implement energy management, supply prediction, and demand management methods locally using both supervised and unsupervised learning methods [17]. It enables data analysis and decisions to be made at the edge of the network, where significant impacts could be made, in lieu of exclusively doing those tasks in the servers sitting in the back office of the utilities that incurs latency on top of being vulnerable interceptions. The ML-based methods added to the edge can perform many a task including data mining, information processing, regression for supply prediction from green energy sources like solar panels, classification for determining operating and nonoperating appliances or for identifying individual power consumption of appliances, clustering for putting data into different groups, conserving privacy, and decision-making. Besides, it creates markets for prosumers who both consume and produce electricity. The edge computing enables customers, who produce excess green energy from solar panels, biofuels, and micro-dams, to sell their excessive energies to other customer back through the smart grid [5,8].

In summary, edge computing aims to deliver compute, storage, intelligence, and bandwidth much closer to the data input points and end costumers of the smart grid. This computing paradigm has a great potential to improve the reliability, resilience, and availability of the smart grid in many ways. Some of the benefits it provides are precisely outlined in what ensues.

- It allows the *bidirectional* flow of energy allowing customers to be both consumers and producers of energy. That is, customers can produce environmentally friendly energy from solar, biofuels, or micro-grids and sell back their excessive production to other consumers in the easy market created by the edge computing-enabled smart grid. Increasing the energy generation stations enhances the reliability and availability of the electric power grid. Besides, it promotes the production of clean energy.
- It lowers the *latency*, brought about due to reliance on distant cloud computing, by avoiding the back and forth transportation of massive data collected by the sensors between the edge and cloud computing centers.
- It enables *real-time* processing and communication of refined information, not bulky raw data.
- It provides intelligent energy management, consumption and supply prediction, appliance classification based on their power consumption, and clustering of data based on their sensitivities or other criteria.
- It greatly enhances *reliability and availability*. The world of electrical grid includes some pretty remote rural territories with less optimal environments concerning Internet connectivity. Hence, the fact that edge devices can locally store and process ensuing data improves the reliability. That is, temporary disruptions in intermittent connectivity will not impact the operation of the edge device merely due loss connection to the cloud.
- It improves the *quality of power* delivered to consumers. The power quality at customers' premises or places of business can have a tremendous effect on their

daily works. Hence, the edge devices installed nearer to the customer premises make sure the power coming in is of the right quality that can meet the settings of the customers' machines and appliances. That is, the edge computing creates an enabling situation for fast and proactive handling of issues that affect the power quality. The factors that affect the quality of power include momentary power interruptions, electrical noises, grounding loops, voltage sags and surges, extended power interruptions, harmonic distortion, lightning damage, and high-speed transients.

- It improves the *security and privacy breaches* by enforcing pertinent measures right at the point of data collection. The chance of cyberattacks being realized while massive raw data are being exchanged between sensors and clouds without good security measures in place is higher. And the same is true with the privacy. The edge computing creates an enabling environment for enforcing security and privacy conserving mechanisms at the point of data creation where the details are explained in Section 18.4.

18.3   Edge-enabled power consumption forecasting

The smart grid technologies coupled with the edge computing paradigm improve the traditional power grids in many ways. One way, on top of the many ways mentioned in the previous sections, is improving the efficiency of the grid system by performing in-advance prediction of load. In the premises of customers who own households or industrial companies/factories, there are a number of appliances and machines that have varying power consumption rates at different times of the day. They are connected one another by means of the smart grid. That is, the smart grid has become one of the major components of smart cities by exploiting the fast advancing IT and IoT technologies for reliably interweaving the cities' buildings and factories. It, therefore, needs to be equipped with the capabilities of intelligent scheduling and planning of electricity delivery based on robust and efficient power consumption forecasting and analysis.

Having appropriate methods for accurate power consumption prediction and customer demand management at the edge of an electrical grid is very vital. It creates an enabling environment for carrying out a comprehensive analysis and evaluation of the power consumption of every BAN by continuously monitoring both noncommercial and commercial buildings connected to that network for their respective energy consumptions. The data continuously garnered from the electric meters are used for monitoring and analyzing energy consumption. The result is, then, employed to formulate strategies vital for improving energy efficiency by reducing wastage, answering future demands with no more ado, and performing real-time pricing. Besides, good techniques for power consumption prediction enable utility companies to plan their future well on short-, medium-, and long-term basis with minimized risks, thereby increasing their revenues.

These days, the accurate prediction of power consumption is done through the application of computational intelligence techniques like artificial neural networks,

ML, or DL in conjunction with the right choice of computing paradigms like centralized, cloud or edge. Regression and clustering methods, for instance, can be employed to perform the prediction of power consumption continuously as a function of time and environmental factors like temperature in real time using data from the BANs of many commercial and noncommercial buildings. In Sections 18.3.1 and 18.3.2, the different methods of energy disaggregation and load monitoring and ML-based power consumption prediction methods are discussed, respectively.

18.3.1   Intrusive and nonintrusive analysis of load monitoring

Nowadays, electricity load monitoring of customer appliances has a very important task of utility companies in an effort to study the power consumption behaviors of customers. For long, the operational status of the appliances in customer buildings has been traditionally addressed either by installing sensors on every appliance, or through the use of an intermediate monitoring system in order to record the appliance's operational dynamics and power consumption histories. That is to say, the power consumption by consumers can be traced intrusively or nonintrusively using automated methods. The intrusive load monitoring (ILM) is a distributed method of sensing loads that requires the installation of a sensor or meter for every appliance in a customer premises [18], whereas nonintrusive load monitoring (NILM) techniques require only a single smart meter per BAN or per customer. As a result, the ILM method provides a better accuracy in measuring energy consumption of every appliance in the customer BAN in comparison to the NILM where a single smart meter capable of performing sophisticated signal processing is employed per BAN and the accuracy is relatively lower. The ILM method, however, suffers from some critical practical issues including high costs due to its requirement for higher number of sensors and accessories, multiple sensor setup, and higher complexity of sensor installations unlike the NILM where a single smart meter is employed per BAN that drastically reduces both initial and operation costs. Besides, NILM has less installation complexity and is convenient for large-scale deployments where scalability is a key factor. For that matter, the inception of the NILM can be traced back to the late 1980s at MIT in the US. By then George Hart proposed a method to automatically track the operation of individual home appliances based on changes in real and reactive power consumption measured at the utility meter [19].

In other words, the NILM entirely relies on a unique point of measurement called the smart meter whereas the ILM relies on low-end electricity meter devices spread inside the customer premises [20,21]. In both approaches, feature extraction and ML algorithms can be employed at edge, closer to the points where data are created and collected. The NILM equipped with feature extraction and ML algorithms is capable of analyzing the changes in electrical quantities (the voltage and current) going into a customer BAN and deducing what types of appliances are deployed in the customer premises and their individual energy consumption. The utility companies integrate NILM technology into their electric meters so as to survey the specific uses of electric power in different customer homes which is vital for better future scheduling and planning. The NILM is considered to be a low-cost alternative to intrusively attaching individual monitors on each appliance which increases the complexity of installation that impacts the cost and maintenance process. That is, the NILM method is much more economical than the ILM method in terms of initial and running costs, and network complexity. Furthermore, it can enhance smart meters save energy and money by reducing waste. The NILM requires only a single meter and disaggregates the measured power consumption of the customer BAN into individual contributing loads of the appliances based on some peculiar features using advanced signal processing coupled with ML algorithms. That is, it determines how much energy is being consumed by each connected appliance in the customer premises. For instance, NILM does a good job for smart home applications which are based on the concept of monitoring and control of the low-voltage (LV) loads. They require the knowledge of the operational status of each LV appliance within an installation of the home. This information can therefore be used in the context of demand side management programs towards energy savings and efficiency through the implementation of personalized incentives for overall consumed energy reduction and peak shaving.

Even though the NILM approach leads to a lower implementation cost, there has been a challenge of correctly disaggregating the load from aggregated voltage and current signals measured at a single point. The NILM algorithms often rely on the utilization of the electrical and functional characteristics of the loads towards the formulation of distinct and robust data fingerprints, also known as Load Signatures (LS). The higher the uniqueness of these LS, the easier the identification procedure. This eventually led to the development of nonintrusive appliance load monitoring (NIALM) technique by Hart, George Williamled [19]. Nowadays, thanks to the advancement of the AI, ML, and DL fields, the load disaggregation task has become more simplified. Some of the trending ML-based methods employed for power consumption prediction at the edge are presented in Section 18.3.2. However, the NILM, ILM, and the methods discussed in Section 18.3.2 are not the perfect solutions yet. Their uses pose privacy concerns. The personal data processed at the NILM point in the BAN and exchanged with the utility servers can potentially be accessed by unauthorized parties causing a lot of information about the behavior of customers and other sensitive personal information to be divulged into the wider cyberspace. The security and privacy challenges, along with their proposed solutions, are discussed in Section 18.4.

18.3.2   Power consumption prediction

As a result of the evergrowing energy consumption and technological advancement, there are various concomitant critical economic and environmental challenges like maintenance and planning costs, and carbon emissions from energy generation. A multitude of research works have been carried out since the early 1990s in the design of nonintrusive algorithms capable of extracting useful information about the individual power consumption of electrical devices in a domestic environment only from an aggregated load measured at single point in order to significantly improve the efficacy of energy usage and accurately predict future consumption and peak load times [18, 20,21]. The energy disaggregation process, as described in Section 18.3.1, refers to

NILM. Through the employment of a set of techniques based on advanced signal processing and ML, it can be used to estimate the electrical power consumption of individual appliances from measurements of voltage and/or current taken at a fewer locations in the power distribution system of a BAN. It often requires only a single smart energy meter which is installed at the main feeding panel of a BAN so as to effectively monitor and identify the status of every appliance within the BAN. As a result, this approach coupled with the state-of-the-art ML algorithms and the edge computing paradigm has gained tremendous attention from the electrical utilities. It meets the interest of electrical utilities and systems by providing load profile details at nodes of electrical grid and commercial buildings. Given these characteristics, the computing paradigm that fits well to it is the edge computing, described in Section 18.1.2, which pushes most of the computational processes closer to the customer premises relieving the network from unnecessarily higher and chatty traffics.

One of the premises and bases for the design of a contemporary, more robust, and efficient smart grid is the capability to obtain an accurate evaluation of the power consumed by customers of all kinds. Besides, it must have a reliable forecasting model integrated into it that can inform utility owners about the power consumption change effectively and timely. Predicting the electricity consumption based on ML or lightweight convolutional neural networks has been a hot research topic during the last decade that considers a number of factors like weather conditions, holidays, weekdays, and the weekend. They are designed with the capability to assess the impact of every factor for more profound insight. The edge computing architecture drastically reduces the delays, latencies, and traffic congestions incurred during the processing of data in a centralized and cloud computing architectures, thereby improving the timeliness and quality of communication. Performing the power consumption evaluation and prediction at the edge creates an auspicious environment for enforcing security and privacy measures closer to the source where data are created and collected. Some of the upsides of performing load forecasting at the edge are enumerated in what ensues:

- It improves the computational times by reducing the latencies. In the cloud- or centralized data center-based smart grids, the data collected from the distributed sensors must be sent over the network to the servers for processing which has a lot of problems like higher latency, traffic congestion, security and privacy issues, and reliability problem. But performing the computational processes nearer to the points where data are generated and collected drastically improves the response time.
- The accurate prediction of power consumption improves the return of investment through the maximum utilization of power generating plants with minimum wastage. That is, the prediction creates an enabling environment for the plant owners and/or utilities to produce and distribute only the required amount of energy at the right times by avoiding both under and over generation.
- It has paramount importance in determining the amount of logistics and resources required to smoothly run the power generation plant in advance. It equips

the power grid with the ability to determine the fuels, mobilization of human resources, and other resources that are needed to ensure economical and uninterrupted generation and distribution of the power to the consumers in time. Moreover, forecasting provides utilities better information to craft sound short-, medium-, and long-term plans to improve their operation and management of the supply to their customers.

- It plays very pronounced roles in helping decide and plan the right times for performing preventive maintenance of the power grid systems. In other words, prior knowledge of the demands enables the utilities to decide the right time during which the maintenance must be carried out with minimum impact on the consumers. It is advisable to do the maintenance during the part of the day when most customers are out of their homes (or at work) and the demand is very low. And the low-demand period is determined by the load prediction system in use.

- Electrical power consumption prediction techniques increase the efficiency and revenues of companies engaged in the generating and distribution of electrical power. It enables them to plan on their capacity and operations well ahead so as to sustainably supply all consumers with the right amount of energy at the right time.

- It important in planning the size, location, and type of a generating plant that must be built in the future to meet the growing demands of customers. The predictions collected from different edges or BANs can be used to determine the customer regions with higher and growing demands, thereby enabling the utilities to build a power generation station nearer to the area with higher demand to minimize transmission and distribution infrastructures and associated losses. As a result, energy can be availed to customers at reasonable prices.

- It helps minimize the risks for the utility companies. Putting it another way, knowledge of the future long-term load creates an enabling situation for the companies to plan and make economically viable decisions with respect to their future investments.

- It enables the implementation of new reconfigurable security framework based on edge computing to fix the security and privacy issues of smart grids. It includes measures against availability, integrity, and confidentiality attacks. Besides, the BANs equipped with edge devices tantamount to Raspberry Pi 3, Tinker Board, or Jetson Nano, are capable of performing cryptographic functions and simplified key managements.

Summing it up, good power-consumption prediction enables electric utility owners to make insightful and data-driven decisions on the generation and purchasing of electrical power, the switching of loads from region to region, the planning of maintenance, and the development of new power plant infrastructure. Depending on the duration of the period over which the prediction is made, load forecasting can be short term, medium term, or long term. The short-term load forecasting is usually done over a period of one hour to one week. It helps to estimate the power flows that provide insightful information to make decisions that prevent overloading. The medium load forecasting spans over a period of a week to a year while the long-term load prediction spans over a period longer than a year. In a number of research outputs including research articles and textbooks, and other literature, many load forecasting techniques have been presented and implemented. Some of them are multiple regressions, knowledge-based expert systems, stochastic time series, iterative reweighted least squares, exponential smoothing, Fuzzy logic, neural network, ML, ML, and the ARMAX model based on genetic algorithm. However, load forecasting is yet a challenging task. That is to say, it is sometimes challenging to exhaustively consider and accurately fit the great deal of complex factors that affect the demand for electricity into the forecasting models. In addition, it may not be easy to obtain an accurate demand forecast based on parameters such as change in temperature, humidity, and other factors that influence the power consumption. As a result, the tendency to employ a deep neural network capable of taking all the factors that impact the power consumption has been growing.

18.4 Security of smart grids enabled by edge computing

A smart grid that employs the state-of-the-art technologies promotes energy and cost efficacy. An edge computing-enabled smart energy network automatically reads and reacts to supply and demand changes without waiting for computational support from a central server. This offers the potential for much improved security of supply through efficiency. When this is coupled with the deployment of edge-enabled smart meters capable of performing NIALM, it encourages consumers to adjust their own real-time demands and facilitate the integration of renewable energy like private wind turbines into the grid. This has a great potential to improve efficiency of the power grid system. That is, the NIALM is the technique for analyzing changes in electrical quantities like voltage, current, and operating frequencies when energy is consumed in customer houses. It is capable of deducing what kind of appliances are used in a customer premises and the individual energy consumption of every appliance. Furthermore, edge-enabled electric meters are fitted with ML-based algorithms and technologies for precise survey and prediction of the specific uses of electric power in different customer premises or houses. This is less prone to failure and low-cost solution to detect and monitor the power consumption of each customer appliances and alert them so as to take corrective measures. However, on top of the chronic security problems of the old and centralized smart grid, this enhanced smart grid presents privacy concerns [6,16]. It has the potential to divulge a lot of personal information of customers to the wider cyberspace.

In general, the smart grid is a subset of the vast cyber-physical system and inherits many of the security problems that the cyber-physical system suffers. In other words, to effectively control and monitor the power plant along with its transmission and distribution systems, as portrayed in Figure 18.2, the smart grid combines the powers of three vital components, namely communication network, computational systems, and control systems. As a result, it is vulnerable to a multitude of attacks described in Section 18.4.1.

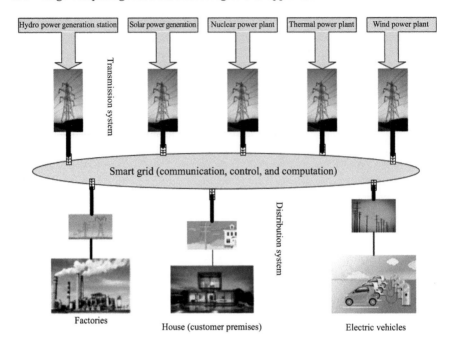

Figure 18.2   Major components of a smart grid

18.4.1   Security challenges of smart grids

Distributed sensors and edge devices are the eyes, ears, and brains of a smart grid which provide information and computational power vital for fault detection, analyzing the individual power consumption of home appliances, monitoring and controlling the entire power generation, transmission, and distribution systems. Therefore, secure exchange of information among the sensing and decision-making entities is essential as security breaches may bring the entire system on its knees [22]. Smart grid technologies are designed to take advantage of the benefits of the ICTs and incorporate them into the old and traditional physical networks of electrical power grid for efficient and smart operation, and accurate billing of energy. In other words, the smart grid is a digital technology, like IT networks, that allows a bidirectional or duplex traffic flows between the utility and its customers equipped with smart sensing capability along the transmission and distribution lines, and various substations. More like the IT networks or the Internet, it comprises important components such as computers, automation, controls, protocols, and new technologies and equipment working in unison. It is known that the transmission control protocol/Internet protocol (TCP/IP) has become the most widely used network interconnection protocol; there was insufficient security concerns at the beginning of the design, though. Since then, IT engineers and researchers have been dealing successfully with enterprise network securities. Today there are many security products in daily use in enterprises which are never the cases in the operational networks where the smart grid is extensively employed. Networks like industrial control system and supervisory control and data acquisition (SCADA) have a lot of security problems. In general, cybersecurity has been a challenge on control networks for the same techniques and tools used to secure IT networks cannot be directly applied. That is to say, smart grid networks have unique requirements. They have different operational, security focus, vulnerability management, and interoperability requirements. Besides, highly sophisticated attacks, probably the first of their kinds, have been perpetrated on SCADA networks during the last two decades that have a potential of causing power network disruption and total power blackout.

Furthermore, in the case of the smart grid, the technologies are proprietary and specifically designed to work with the electrical grid with the ability to digitally respond to the quickly and dynamically changing demand of electricity. It is more of a cyber-physical nature that makes is more vulnerable to tones of attacks that could be perpetrated at various levels including the physical layer or communication links, media access layer, and networking. Eavesdropping, jamming, and replay attacks are the typical examples of attacks often launched on the smart grid. The security of IT networks primarily focuses on the protection/privacy of information whereas that of the smart grid focuses on the protection/safety of the plant or process. Hence, the security goals of smart grid are availability, integrity, and confidentiality, the priority of availability being the highest and that of confidentiality being the lowest. The converse is true in the case of the IT networks in that the highest priority is affixed to confidentiality/privacy and the lowest one is affixed to availability. All efforts to remedy the security problems of smart grids are, therefore, tuned this way. Hence, notwithstanding the fact that there are a lot of security products and solutions for IT networks on the market and a number of researches pertinent to smart grid security have been conducted especially following the discovery of the most threatening SCADA network attack perpetrated on the Iranian Nuclear Facilities where control and monitoring center crews were faked by replay attacks, there still exists a gaping hole begging for bridging. Hence, the subsections that ensue discuss the security and privacy issues of a smart grid system. The various types of security challenges and attacks directed on smart grid which include availability, integrity, and confidentiality attacks, and privacy issues are discussed in Sections 18.4.1.1 through 18.4.1.3, and the privacy issues of the smart grid are explained in Section 18.4.1.4. Adversaries manage to realize these attacks often by exploiting the vulnerabilities in the generation system, transmission system, distribution system, and telemetry infrastructures.

18.4.1.1 Availability attacks on smart grids

Availability attack is often realized when authorized personnel or an adversary manages to gain an access or a control of the grid system. It also involves interruption caused by physical damage or electrocution of smart grid components. Following such type of attack, authorized personnel are denied of access to the smart grid; hence, it is also known as a denial-of-service (DoS) attack. When the DoS attack is escalated and applied in a distributed manner using botnets, it is known as distributed DoS (DDoS) attack. Both the DoS and DDoS attacks have the potential to interrupt, delay, or corrupt data and command information flow causing unavailability of information exchange in the smart grid or power. On top of a service interruption in a smart grid system where billing is computed centrally based on meter readings received via the smart grid network, the availability attack could cause substantial loss of revenues. Jamming is a type of availability attack. It is an active attack that can disruptively interrupt the transmission of data often achieved by transmitting simultaneously whenever the target transmits or receives data. This overwhelms the target and causes an availability attack or DoS. It occurs at the media access control (MAC) layer, and the adversary can deliberately corrupt the control packets or exhaust the whole available channel causing DoS. That is, the legitimate nodes will not be able to access the channel or medium as a result of which their throughput goes down and eventually becomes zero. MAC and address resolution protocol (ARP) flooding are, for instance, DoS attacks directed on the medium access layer [6,22].

The most devastating availability attack recently launched on a smart grid is the cyberattack on Ukraine's power grid in December 2015. It caused extensive power supply interruptions. The attack temporarily cuts off electricity supply from three energy distribution companies to a number of consumers' premises in Ukraine. The exploited security loopholes have been made public yet, but the adversaries managed to gain access to the control and information systems of these suppliers. Then, they successfully compromised the power grids and brought down 30 substations across the nation that had left more than 230 thousand people without electricity for a quarter of a day [12].

18.4.1.2 Integrity attacks on smart grids

It is the unauthorized and malicious modification of data and critical information of the control and command center, the sensory devices, computers, smart meters, and software [6,22]. This could result in the provision of wrong information or command to the decision-making components of the smart grid; that is, the exchange of corrupted data starts to take place in the smart grid following an integrity attack that could potentially impair its decision-making capability. One way of compromising the integrity of the smart grid is through the injection of bad data during state estimation that could inflict power mismanagement. Besides, unless the integrity of whatever software running in the smart integrity is maintained at all times, it could open a door for an adversary who can employ compromised software to gain access to the critical sections of the smart grid. In today's smart grid system, SCADA is the heart of any load dispatching centers. In the old days, the SCADA system used to be a LAN or wide area network (WAN) on its own isolated from the Internet. However, today many a company who transmits and distributes power has integrated its SCADA communication network into the Internet for cost-effectiveness, improved efficiency, and reliability. But this approach has its own cost. It gives the opportunity for any adversary, who has access to the Internet, to look for loopholes in the SCADA system which increases the risk of infiltration and compromise of data and control information that can bring down the entire system on its knees.

The intercommunication systems of the major components of the SCADA system like master terminal units, remote terminal units and programmable logic controllers

(PLCs) are said to have vulnerabilities that could be exploited to compromise the integrity of data and information. Most of the attacks perpetrated on the IT network can also be launched on the smart grid. Due to its proprietary nature, the smart grid has not many available solutions unlike the IT networks. For instance, a malicious cross-site request forgery (CSRF) could be launched. That is, uniform resource locator (URL) scripts could be broadcast to the SCADA network and when they happen to be opened at any of the human–machine interfaces (HMIs), they can detect and invade the PLCs and other components. This attack can be launched on both types of smart grids, the cloud-centric and edge-enabled one. But the effect is less in case of the edge-enabled smart grid.

18.4.1.3   Confidentiality attacks on smart grids

An attack on the confidentiality of data and control commands is a hazardous intrusion into the smart grid network. It refers to the unauthorized access of sensitive power usage data, price information, and control commands that have the potential to invade the security of the power grid and the privacy of customers. It could also expose a lot of proprietary information about the power utilities. Intercepting the data and control commands exchanged between the various smart grid components is so easy for adversaries. For instance, it is next to impossible to prevent adversaries from eavesdropping the smart grid network. Eavesdropping is a passive attack where the adversary stealthily listens to the private communications of the smart grid communicating parties without their knowledge and consent. Putting it another way, unauthorized parties listen to the smart grid network with the help of wiretapping without any traceable or detectable interactions. Then, they conduct analysis on the captured data to uncover the data and commands being communicated. Hence, the success of the confidentiality attack lies on whether the information is exchanged in strongly encrypted-text form or clear-text form. Hence, the smart grid should be able support end-to-end encryption and germane key exchange protocols for secured exchange of information.

As part of the smart grid systems, the SCADA system is installed and deployed in almost all power generation plants for continuous monitoring and controlling of the complex processes of the plant. The HMIs of the SCADA system serve as a dashboard that visually tracks, analyzes, and displays measures, feedbacks, statuses, and alerts to monitor the health of the plant in which thousands of processes are concurrently running. One common problem that had repeatedly compromised the confidentiality of generation plants is the use of default manufacturer passwords after first log-in. Exploiting this weakness, an adversary could gain access to the plant SCADA system LAN and tamper with some parameters. For example, they could change the frequency measurements provided to the automatic governor control and destabilize the plant. This is the case of a confidentiality attack leading to availability attack. That is, once the adversary gains an access to confidential data, keys, passwords, or commands, they can perpetrate any kind of attack on the system. The Stuxnet is the most popular example of a sophisticated attack that combines confidentiality, replay, and availability attacks [23]. This attack is believed to have been perpetrated on the Natanz uranium enrichment plant in Iran. It is believed to have managed to destroy more about one thousand centrifuges in the Iranian Nuclear facilities, thereby causing a delay in the uranium enrichment process. Once it somehow gained access to one of the SCADA computers in the nuclear facility, it is believed to have gained access to the SCADA server using the default/factory password of the server exploiting the IT experts negligence to change the password after first log-in following the commissioning of the network. Using relatively big-size most complicated ever computer virus or malware (Stuxnet), the adversaries had adeptly recorded the system dynamics for quite some time and later replayed it to deceive human operators or programs while covertly perpetrating damage on the centrifuges by changing the operating frequencies.

The smart grid advanced metering infrastructure may employ such communication technologies as power line communication (PoLC), wireless LAN (WLAN), ZigBee, Worldwide Interoperability for Microwave Access (WiMax), Ethernet Passive Optical Networks (EPON), and Mobile radio frequency (RF) mesh. All of these technologies do not have default security and authentication mechanisms [6,16,24]. The PoLC is an open-wire communication technology that supports the sending of data over existing power cables. However, it is prone to misguiding. The WLAN which follows the IEEE 802.11 standards is also susceptible to such attacks as eavesdropping, traffic analysis, and session hijacking. The ZigBee (IEEE 802.15.4 standards) can be jammed easily and it suffers from delays caused by the cluster-tree-based routing strategy. What is more, the WiMax, which works based on the IEEE 802.16 standard, is liable to replay and scrambling attacks. Similarly, the EPON is susceptible to eavesdropping, DoS, and spoofing attacks. The mobile communication system could also be employed but it is unprotected medium that could potentially cause the invasion of customers' privacy through the disclosure of their energy consumption data. Hence, unless additional measures are enforced into the grid system, the communication technologies employed in grid system don't have default means for ensuring confidentiality.

18.4.1.4   Privacy concerns in smart grids

The smart grid represents a new era in the electrical sector and has a spectrum of advantages including efficient energy generation, transmission and distribution, accurate bill calculation, balancing cost, and support of green energies. Notably, it can keep customers apprised of their daily energy consumption, the individual consumption of their appliances, and measures they should take to keep their bills lower. However, it has remarkable impact on the privacy of customers' data. It has the capability to garner a lot of detailed information on individual energy consumption usage and the patterns within consumers' premises. If all these data are divulged into the wider cyberspace, they have the potential to disclose about what kind of appliances the customer has, which appliance they frequently use, from which providers they have tapped electricity, personal information like names and addresses, and their billing information. Hence, unless smart grid technologies are designed to inherently incorporate a robust customer privacy conserving mechanism by design, they can potentially sacrifice the privacy of consumers.

Privacy is the number one concern of consumers and distribution utilities. A smart grid that increases the confidence of distribution utilities and customer alike is badly in need. But why are customers so concerned about their personal data ending up in the hands of third parties or in the wider cyberspace? Why are the customers so paranoid about privacy? Well, we could look into the potential threats that could be posed to answer these questions. It is known that the smart meters installed at the consumers' premises exchange customer energy usage data and control signals with the respective customers' BAN gateway which is connected to the smart grid WAN in turn. But the networks could have exploitable flaws in that they could cause data leakage when eavesdropped. This could reveal a lot information about customers including account numbers, plug-in electric vehicles information, personal behavior as inferred from social networking activities, whether a residence or facility is occupied, what people are doing, technologies used, manufacturing output, sale events, etc. For customers who own factories or manufacturing industries, this could amount to technological espionage that could be transferred to foes or competitors. Hence, this calls for a serious endeavor to address the issues of privacy caused by smart grids. Edge computing technologies provide better opportunities to address the privacy concerns at the customer premises. The possible edge-enabled solutions are presented in Section 18.4.2.

18.4.2 *Edge-enabled solutions to the smart grid security problems*

Following the most sophisticated Stuxnet malware attack on SCADA system, many utilities have started to look for better security solutions for their power grids. In addition to preventing potential security attacks, there are stringent requirements for the cybersecurity mechanisms of smart grids to be robust and resilient enough to address natural disasters, inadvertent compromises of the information infrastructure due to user errors, and equipment failures. The state-of-the-art security solutions of enterprise IT networks like intrusion detection systems, firewall, antivirus, virtual private networks, and public key infrastructure cannot be employed as they are in the smart grid. This is because the two networks have intrinsic differences as explained at the outset of Section 18.4.1. Hence, enhancement is required to bridge the differences. But the security objectives are the same in both cases; the priorities of their importance are conversely related, though. That is, the prime focus is plant availability in the smart grid, whereas privacy of information is the top priority in IT networks.

In general, any network including the smart grid is said to be secure only if it can ensure the three basic cybersecurity goals: availability, integrity, and confidentiality (AIC). As depicted in Figure 18.3, only the intersection of the three security objectives is said to be secure, which implies that all objectives must be achieved to have a secure network. Any failure to do so has a negative impact on the generation, transmission, and delivery of electricity. In other words, the three cybersecurity objectives form an AIC triad which is the foundation for all security models. The triad serves as the basic guide in formulating policies for information security within the premises of an organization. For data exchanged over a certain network to be completely secure, all of these security goals must be ensured inseparably. Besides, Figure 18.4 depicts specific security requirements that must be met to achieve the three security goals. Having a mechanism for identity and security authentication and access control, resource

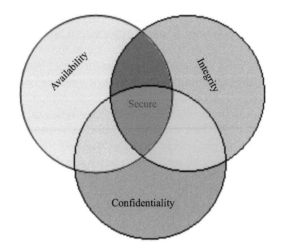

Figure 18.3   Security goals

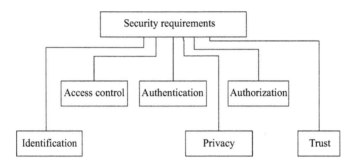

Figure 18.4   Security requirements

access authorization, conserving privacy, and establishing trusted system are vital for preventing the availability, integrity, and confidentiality attacks.

The edge-enabled smart grid allows the dynamic bidirectional flow of power and sharing of information among nodes. Unlike the conventional power grid where power flows in one direction from main generation stations to customer premises, the edge computing-enabled smart grid supports two-way flow of energy. That is to say, the smart edge devices installed at customer premises have the capability to smoothly connect electricity generated by green sources like micro-dams, solar panels, and wind station at customer sites back to the main grid. This gives the power grid a good energy mix and balance. To put it another way, customers are not only consumers in an edge computing-enabled smart grid but also producers of energy. They produce environmentally friendly green energy and contribute to the wider power grid system. In a similar fashion, the edge computing contributes a lot in providing better security and privacy solutions as compared to the conventional grid system. For instance, it enables us to enforce intrusion detection and prevention systems, and many other security and privacy measures at the edge of the smart grid network to thwart attacks or potential threats before they can cause substantial damages to the grid system. Consistent scanning and monitoring of the security statuses is made at the edge not at a central location; that is, computing and security enforcement are performed right at the part of the network, where the data are generated. Hence, all security measures and policies enforced to prevent and detect any potential attack directed on the smart grid are enumerated in this subsection in what ensues. The edge computing-enabled security measures principally focus on mechanisms that can prevent potential availability, integrity, and confidentiality attacks and privacy invasion from being realized. Attacks are warded off at the edge, at every customer's premises and other major nodes.

- *Preventing availability attacks.* Availability is one of the three major objectives of a sound security service or mechanism. In cyber-physical systems like the smart grid, availability of a plant is the top priority that makes sure that the plant is available 24/7 and information or services is accessible to authorized parties at the right time [22]. In other words, service or information is invaluable only if it can be accessed by the right/authorized people at the right times. But cyber-physical systems like power plants and information websites are attacked by adversaries. They are often taken down by DoS or DDoS attacks. Physical damage or interruption, ping flood, smurf attack, SYN attack, jamming, and buffer overflow are some of the common methods of attack that might render the smart grid, information, or services unavailable to legitimate users. They have the potential to deny the legitimate users access to the smart grid by degrading the performance of the system to the point of complete service disruption. That is, physically damaging some components of the smart grid or by hitting the target machine with simultaneous superfluous requests disrupts the normal functionality of the system. Hence, the solutions enforced to deter such attacks must have the capability of analyzing and authenticating incoming requests to identify whether the source is legitimate or not. Besides, it should be smart enough to detect superfluous requests coming from a single or multiple sources and be able to stop them before they could exhaust resources.

    The best strategy for security enforcement in an edge-enabled environment is to equip the edge devices in every BAN with lightweight identity and security authentication mechanism with pre-configured but dynamic access control list (ACL) [22]. That is, an ACL, initially created by the utility owner, is stored in every edge device connected to every BAN to ensure authentic and secure access to the BAN components. It contains details about authorized users, unique node identifications, MAC addresses, system program attributes, and application program attributes which can be securely updated whenever change takes place. Hence, using the mini-ACL, the edge device can make identity and security authentication of request sources and share any presumed security risks with peers in the same or different neighboring BAN and the server. It can stop any unauthorized access or superfluous requests before potentially resulting into DoS attack. The edge devices periodically report the incidents they have experienced to the nearest utility server. Hence, threats or attacks are thwarted at the entry point in an edge computing-enabled smart grid without much support from a central powerful server or firewall.

• *Preserving integrity of data and control commands.* Phasor measurement units (PMUs), phasor data concentrators (PDCs), and control centers (CC) of a smart grid can be compromised [6,25]. That is, adversaries can inject and send forged PMU frames with manufactured data to a PDC or CC which can cause a potential havoc in the system. Hence, preserving the integrity of data and software is of paramount importance. Integrity of information refers to the mechanism of conserving information from being tampered or altered by unauthorized parties. It ensures that that information or command signal is exchanged over the communication channel between authorized parties intact; it can be altered only by legitimate users. Besides, the integrity of all sorts of software running in the smart grid must be maintained at all times by means of check-sums or equivalent methods to make sure that no compromised software is in the system that could serve as a gateway to adversaries. The fundamental thing here is that information or a software has value if and only if it is not tampered by illicit users.

The integrity of data and software can be checked using hash functions where the integrity of data is authenticated before every decision to use or access that data. Besides, the edge device in every BAN is equipped with a software integrity checker that reports manipulations or changes on any software running on the BAN. The attributes of the system programs and applications are compared against a database of initially generated hashes and check-sums residing in every edge device. Hash or check-sum mismatches imply that software was probably tampered and appropriate actions must be enforced with no more ado. The edge devices with computational power equivalent to tiny single-board computers like Tinker Board, Raspberry Pi 3, or NVIDIA Jetson Nano can perform any of the hashing functions with great ease. In addition, the edge devices support such mitigation scheme as dynamic state estimation (DSE) to dynamically deduce the state of the smart grid components based on measurements collected BAN-wise to guard against replay attack by injection of recorded states. The DSE covers the progressive development of the state over a series of measurement instants so as to produce an accurate dynamic state of the system [6]. Summing it up, the edge computing enables the smart grid to have a platform for collaborative prevention against integrity attacks and injection of forged frames.

• *Ensuring confidentiality of smart grids.* The confidentiality here refers to the secrecy of the information exchanged over the smart grid communication network or the information stored in every utility server and BAN edge device. In the eyes of confidentiality, information is the most valued asset. Hence, all confidentiality assurance methods are therefore designed with this in consideration. Confidentiality ensures that a robust mechanism is in place to prevent the information from any disclosure to unauthorized parties; often cryptographic methods are used. Unlike the conventional grid where enforcing encryption mechanisms is not possible due to the fact that the end devices lack the computation power required to perform decryption and the inverse process, the edge computing-enabled smart grids can enforce cryptographic methods to ensure secure exchange of data. That is, in a setting where the smart grid has edge devices at every BAN, standard cryptographic methods like advanced encryption standards (AES)-128, AES-192, AES-256, or other signal processing-based schemes [24] can be employed to create encrypted duplex communication. For key management, the Diffie–Hellman key exchange protocol or other public key methods could be employed.

- *Conserving customer privacy at the edge.* The many upsides of smart grid systems come with huge privacy risks. In other words, even though the smart grids components like smart meters and edge devices installed in customer premises or BANs have positively impacted the way power is generated, transmitted, and distributed, and the way revenues are collected, they have the potential to invade the privacy of customers. The privacy concerns of the power grid customers include identity theft, determination of personal behavior patterns, deducing the specific appliances used, and carrying out real-time surveillance. The smart grid garners such sensitive private data and could end up in the bad hands of adversaries when its weaknesses are exploited and attacked. The smart grid industry still lacks transparently defined privacy principles and mechanisms. Government agencies may enact laws and impose regulations on utility owners but they lack the means to reflect the realities of a smart grid where consumers actively contributes sensitive personal data on daily basis. That is, instructing or requiring distribution utilities by law alone lacks the means to prevent privacy breaches. The utilities may strive hard to obey the laws and regulations to protect customers' privacy; however, the edge devices, smart meters, sensors, communication networks, or storage devices can be compromised and intruded resulting in the private data ending up in the hands of hackers or adversaries.

Edge computing provides convenience for enforcing privacy-conserving mechanisms at the point of customer data collection unlike the cloud-based smart grid where account information, billing amount, appliance types, energy meter reading, frequency meter reading, etc., are transported to the cloud location for computational processing and decision-making, which likely increases the chance of privacy breaches. Hence, the most feasible solution is to design and manufacture smart grid edge devices which are privacy aware. That is, privacy by design is the best solution for the smart grid enabled by edge computing. The edge devices can compute the bills based on the meter readings and they can only send the amount of bill to the utility server attached to unique customer ID via an encrypted channel. All other customer-specific data like the individual power consumption of appliances are solely provided to the customer for future decisions. Hence, the edge device can be further made more intelligent to perform robust classification of data into sensitive and nonsensitive through the incorporation of lightweight machine learning algorithms (LWMLAs) that can effectively run in a resource-constrained environment. That is, edge devices equipped with LWMLA are capable of anonymizing and aggregating customer data required for research and analysis uses to improve services and the technologies. They can effectively identify sensitive personal data and household identity and obscure them to prevent the exposure of customers' privacy.

18.5   Summary

This chapter has covered the major problems in the electrical grid and explained how the smart grid addresses many of the issues. Besides, it discusses the impact of the computing architectures on the reliability, resilience, security, and privacy of the grid and details the upsides of employing edge computing-enabled smart grids. The electrical grid is the greatest technological inventions of the twentieth century that has paved the ways for the advancement of other technologies like computing and communication systems. However, it lacks smart means for efficient generation, transmission, distribution, and management of electricity. This has served as a push factor for the invention of an intelligent grid management system called a smart grid. It efficiently integrates the behavior and actions of all generators, consumers, and prosumers in ways that guarantee economically efficient and sustainable power system with low losses, and high levels of quality and security of supply and safety. It solves most of the problems that had been beleaguering the traditional electric grid. That is, the smart grid addresses the inefficiencies and unreliability of the grid. It can efficiently deliver electricity from suppliers or utilities to consumers and prosumers using two-way digital communications to control appliances at consumers' homes and enable the interconnection of green energies produced by prosumers. It is, however, not an impeccable solution. It has a number of issues including reliability, resilience, availability, security, and privacy issues. These problems can be solved by employing contemporary technologies and appropriate computing paradigms. The edge computing is one that stands out as the best computing paradigm for smart grid. It processes the data at the edge of the IoT network closer to the embedded devices where the data are created and collected. It cuts down on the volumes of data transported to cloud centers for processing by handling it at the point of creation, and pushes intelligence to smart devices of the smart grid installed in the customers' premises. Hence, it improves the response time, enables real-time communication and decision-making, creates a facilitated environment for effective enforcement of security- and privacy-preserving measures, and promotes green energy production by prosumers.

References

[1]   Gungor VC, Sahin D, Kocak T, *et al.* A survey on smart grid potential applications and communication requirements. IEEE Transactions on Industrial Informatics. 2012;9(1):28–42.

[2]   Momoh JA. Smart Grid: Fundamentals of Design and Analysis. vol. 63. Piscataway, NJ: IEEE Press; 2012.

[3]   Yan Y, Qian Y, Sharif H, and David T. A survey on smart grid communication infrastructures: Motivations, requirements and challenges. IEEE Communications Surveys & Tutorials. 2012;15(1):5–20.

[4]   Ipakchi A, and Albuyeh F. Grid of the future. IEEE Power and Energy Magazine. 2009;7(2):52–62.

[5] Samie F, Bauer L, and Henkel J. Edge computing for smart grid: An overview on architectures and solutions. In: IoT for Smart Grids. Springer; 2019. pp. 21–42.

[6] Pandey RK, and Misra M. Cybersecurity threats smart grid infrastructure. In: 2016 National Power Systems Conference (NPSC). IEEE; 2016. pp. 1–6.

[7] Varghese B, and Buyya R. Next generation cloud computing: New trends and research directions. Future Generation Computer Systems. 2018;79: 849–861.

[8] Boccadoro P. Smart grids empowerment with edge computing: An overview. arXiv preprint arXiv:180910060. 2018.

[9] Van Roy J, Leemput N, De Breucker S, *et al.* An availability analysis and energy consumption model for a Flemish fleet of electric vehicles. In: European Electric Vehicle Congress (EEVC), October 26–28, 2011, Brussels, Belgium; 2011.

[10] Niyato D, Wang P, and Hossain E. Reliability analysis and redundancy design of smart grid wireless communications system for demand side management. IEEE Wireless Communications. 2012;19(3):38–46.

[11] Islam A, Domijan A, and Damnjanovic A. Assessment of the reliability of a dynamic smart grid system. International Journal of Power and Energy Systems. 2011;31(4):198.

[12] Zetter K. Inside the cunning, unprecedented hack of Ukraine's power grid. Wired. March 3, 2016; 2017.

[13] Wang W, Xu Y, and Khanna M. A survey on the communication architectures in smart grid. Computer Networks. 2011;55(15):3604–3629.

[14] Fitwi A, Chen Y, and Zhu S. No peeking through my windows: Conserving privacy in personal drones. arXiv preprint arXiv:190809935. 2019.

[15] Fitwi A, Chen Y, and Zhu S. A lightweight blockchain-based privacy protection for smart surveillance at the edge. 1st International Workshop on Lightweight Blockchain for Edge Intelligence and Security (LightChain, colocated with IEEE BlockChain Conference). 2019.

[16] El Mrabet Z, Kaabouch N, El Ghazi H, *et al.* Cyber-security in smart grid: Survey and challenges. Computers & Electrical Engineering. 2018;67: 469–482.

[17] Khan S, Paul D, Momtahan P, *et al.* Artificial intelligence framework for smart city microgrids: State of the art, challenges, and opportunities. In: 2018 Third International Conference on Fog and Mobile Edge Computing (FMEC). IEEE; 2018. pp. 283–288.

[18] Ridi A, Gisler C, and Hennebert J. A survey on intrusive load monitoring for appliance recognition. In: 2014 22nd International Conference on Pattern Recognition. IEEE; 2014. pp. 3702–3707.

[19] Hart GW. Nonintrusive appliance load monitoring. Proceedings of the IEEE. 1992;80(12):1870–1891.

[20] Chang HH. Non-intrusive demand monitoring and load identification for energy management systems based on transient feature analyses. Energies. 2012;5(11):4569–4589.

[21]   Norford LK, and Leeb SB. Non-intrusive electrical load monitoring in commercial buildings based on steady-state and transient load-detection algorithms. Energy and Buildings. 1996;24(1):51–64.

[22]   Fitwi A, Chen Y, and Zhou N. An agent-administrator-based security mechanism for distributed sensors and drones for smart grid monitoring. In: Signal Processing, Sensor/Information Fusion, and Target Recognition XXVIII. vol. 11018. International Society for Optics and Photonics; 2019. pp. 110180L.

[23]   Langner R. Stuxnet: Dissecting a cyberwarfare weapon. IEEE Security & Privacy. 2011;9(3):49–51.

[24]   Fitwi AH, and Nouh S. Performance analysis of chaotic encryption using a shared image as a key. Zede Journal. 2011;28:17–29.

[25]   Paudel S, Smith P, and Zseby T. Data integrity attacks in smart grid wide area monitoring. In: ICS-CSR; 2016.

Chapter 19

Smart surveillance for public safety enabled by edge computing

Deeraj Nagothu[1], Ronghua Xu[1], Seyed Yahya Nikouei[1], Xuan Zhao[1] and Yu Chen[1]

19.1 Introduction to smart surveillance security

The traditional surveillance system comprises a system where a visual feed is collected and stored remotely for a later inspection. Alarms are raised in case of a security breach after inspecting remotely stored surveillance feed, which generally incurs an extra delay. The surveillance community is aware of this issue and has been presenting new models to make the detection automated faster.

The cloud computing approach that offloads data to the cloud for further processing makes many applications feasible and more accessible because of the widespread Internet connection. However, in case of the surveillance system, cloud computing has additional overhead due to transferring high-resolution video streams to a remote cloud center. The data transfer results in bandwidth consumption, which may cause network congestion, or increases the risk of data leak due to higher probability of being attacked by hackers.

On the other hand, the edge computing paradigm with advanced computing hardware at the edge improves the capability of instant, on-site data processing. Video streams can be processed at the edge for any decision-making algorithms, reducing the reliance on the cloud. Based on this hierarchy, a smart safety system can detect the abnormal behavior of a person in the frame and raise the alarm to the authorities in less than a second. The system leverages the edge processor along with a fog device connected for process outsourcing, and the cloud node is used for analytical and historical studies. In contrast to the conventional data processing methods used in most cases today, the proposed smart safety system introduces a layered architecture. Each layer controls individual calculation before the results are reported.

19.1.1 Decision-making process

Deep learning models [1] are used to detect humans in the real-time video frame and track the subject for extracting features. Decision-making algorithm processes the

[1]Electrical and Computer Engineering, Department at Binghamton University, Binghamton, NY, USA

features extracted from the active tracking of human subjects. Based on the detection method employed, the frames per second (FPS) can be changed, where the number of FPS processed can be selected based on human speed.

We added a unique identifier as a tracker so that when the person is detected, the data belonging to the subject are isolated from other moving subjects in the frame. The reason lays in the detection algorithm that is applied to each frame with no history of the previous ones. Thus, a pedestrian that is detected in frame n and marked as the number one detection can be detected and remarked as number 2 in the frame $n + 1$. The detection algorithm controls the tracker, so as soon as the detection loses the object, the object is deleted from the tracker queue.

The tracker can be picked from the several faster models that are based on the CPU [2] unit which provides a generally acceptable performance [3]. Based on the experimental results, this hybrid two-step algorithm to process each frame is managed by the edge hardware with acceptable processing speed. The decision-making algorithm then makes the decision based on the movement of the object of interest and in the context of location and time.

Recently, the concept of microservices was introduced which breaks down code into smaller services that can function independently of each other and makes distributed computing easier and manageable as only one service can be changed or updated at a time [4]. Docker containers are excellent examples of such a structure. Each container can run separately and use the resources of the host without having issues regarding the security of the hardware and unwanted access [5]. Figure 19.1 shows the edge-level process from the frame receipt to the packet stream to the network. To preserve the computing resources, the video frame stream is halted in case of no listeners who acknowledge the frame on the other side.

At the fog device, several edge devices are handled at the same time. Depending on the location of the camera and other parameters that can be important to the surveillance system such as the building shutdown time, the features that are streamed from the edge are contextualized. Based on this architecture, the edge device provides the specific object of interest's features [6], and at the fog, context is added to the features and sent for the decision-making.

Figure 19.2 represents the steps taken by the fog node for each of the edge devices that are connected to it. With the frames processed by the edge device, at least one object of interest (which in our case, the object is a human) is detected. The fuzzy logic was introduced by Prof. Zadeh [7] to help decide based on the same principles that humans use for decision-making. The features are converted into linguistic variables in the process of fuzzification. Based on the results obtained, defuzzification helps to have a number in percent form to show the activity.

By monitoring the activity of a person of interest, the activity-tracking algorithm raises the alarm in case of suspicious activity. Authorities receive an e-mail alert, where the operator accesses the real-time footage of the cause of alarm along with the subject features. Developments in the surveillance systems and its capability of decision-making have improved public safety. Improved response time for suspicious activity with edge processing has eliminated the need for relying on cloud services, but network attacks are still a concern such as visual layer attacks. The analysis and

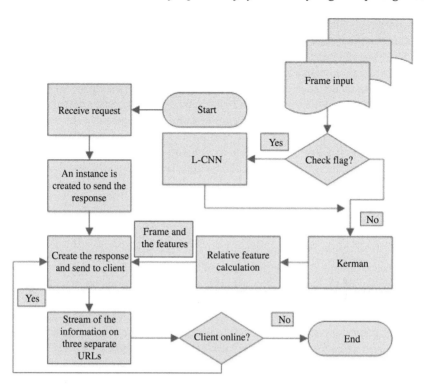

Figure 19.1   Frame pathway in the edge-level node

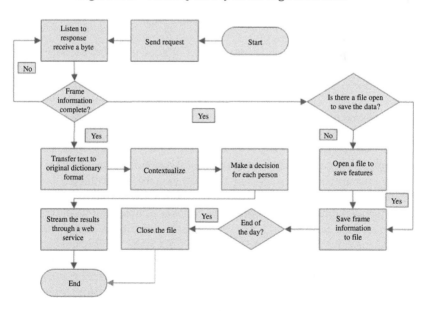

Figure 19.2   Frame pathway in the fog-level node

decision-making depends on the visual feed received by the edge-processing system, and hence authenticating the feed received is of crucial importance.

The remaining of this chapter is as follows. Section 19.2 demonstrates a security threat on surveillance system in the form of visual layer attacks. Section 19.3 proposes an authentication system for attacks on the system using an environmental fingerprinting technique, and Section 19.4 discusses a blockchain-enabled edge computing architecture to improve the security of the surveillance system compared to traditional central monitoring system. Section 19.5 presents a case study of deploying a secure smart surveillance system as microservices in blockchain architecture. Section 19.6 gives some discussions and Section 19.7 concludes this chapter.

19.2   Visual layer attacks on surveillance system

The advancements in smart surveillance have increased the security of large infrastructures with minimal human intervention; this has also proportionally increased the reliability of the system. The network communications make it vulnerable to network-based attacks like man in the middle or distributed denial-of-service (DDoS) attacks. The attacks could originate on a firmware level through a backdoor exploit on manufacturer's system, or by directly gaining physical access. Either way without a proper authentication system of the visual feed, processing and making a decision based on the received feed could be ineffective. While the other attacks discussed earlier can be noticed once compromised, but visual layer-based attacks can cause more harm. These attacks remain undetected and continue to deceive the decision-making or monitoring system, making frame duplication attacks one of the most common attacks.

19.2.1   Smart online frame duplication attack

Many detection techniques on frame duplication attacks were proposed, and leveraging these detection techniques, we developed a smart frame forging an attack on the surveillance system with remote triggering capabilities [8]. This attack is to advocate more focus on the security of the surveillance system and develop authentication for the visual feed received.

Figure 19.3 represents the flow of the attack algorithm. It consists of two modules named monitoring audio/video module and deploying the attack module. Monitoring the surveillance feed includes both audio and video content since any mismatch in either of the recording can raise suspicions. Module 1 consists of monitoring visual and audio feed for any changes in the environment. A motion detection algorithm is used to detect movement in the video; it waits for a static background and records the latest recording of the surveillance visual feed. Thereon, the recorded feed is updated with the latest recording whenever there is no motion detected. This allows the replay recording to be most recent, reflecting any changes in the environment like object displacement or difference in environmental light intensities. Simultaneously, the audio monitoring system uses fast Fourier transform (FFT) to detect background

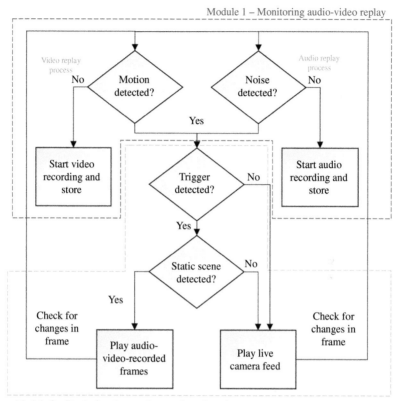

Figure 19.3 Flow diagram of the frame duplication algorithm

noise in frequency domain representation of input audio stream and start a replay recording when there is no noise in the vicinity. Overall, module 1 is responsible for gathering replay recordings of both video and audio by tracking changes in the surrounding and updating it with any changes.

Deploying the attack module consists of a trigger mechanism, and upon triggering, the live feed is masked with the pre-recorded replay audio/video stream. The triggering mechanism consists of detecting a cue to start the replay recording, and this cue could be of any form like quick response (QR) code on someone's T-shirt, subjects face or even voice-activated. Here, we used face detection as a trigger mechanism. Modern surveillance camera produces high-resolution video streams, and FPS of high-resolution video processing is lower. Even with lower FPS, a single frame with a target face is sufficient to trigger, which makes lower FPS irrelevant. As part of the face recognition module, a histogram of oriented gradients (HOG) descriptor is used for human/face detection. The gradient for human faces is trained using a machine learning (ML) algorithm, and each face has its unique encoding. The encoding vector

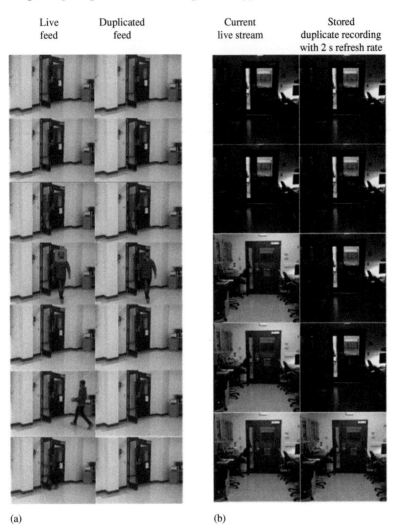

Live feed   Duplicated feed   Current live stream   Stored duplicate recording with 2 s refresh rate

(a)   (b)

Figure 19.4   Face detection trigger and frame duplication attack deployed

is used later for detecting the appropriate face. In our attack, the face encoding vector of the intruder is generated in advance. When the intruder is detected in the frame, the algorithm waits for static background and deploys the replay recording. The static background is preferred to avoid suspicion of the sudden disappearance of human from the frame.

Figure 19.4 represents the attack algorithm with its triggering mechanism and adaptability to the environment. Figure 19.4(a) shows the live feed and the duplicated feed, where once the intruder is detected, the attack algorithm waits for a static scene and deploys the replay audio/video module. Figure 19.5 shows the original audio

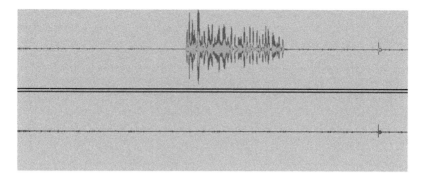

Figure 19.5   Original audio recording masked with replay recording

recording with some noise. Upon trigger, the static noise is used to mask the live audio stream. Figure 19.4(b) demonstrates the capability of the algorithm to adapt to the changes in the environment with a refresh rate of 2 s. Here the lights are turned on, and this change is detected, recorded, and replayed. Along with frame duplication attacks, another prominent threat to surveillance system includes attacks on the face recognition module.

19.2.2   Face spoofing attacks on face recognition module

Detecting and recognizing a human face in the surveillance video, these image processing technologies and applications play an increasingly important role in today's technological development. For example, in the public safety field, many monitoring devices have been deployed in public areas with high population density, which enables fully automatic identification and retrieval of targets and their motion collection in the video. The content after this section mainly introduces the flow and implementation of face recognition technology.

In the face recognition process, the application scenarios are generally divided into 1:1 recognition and 1:N recognition. 1:1 face recognition is to determine whether two photos are the same person. It is usually applied to the matching of people, such as whether the ID card and the real-time photo are the same people. In the 1:N face recognition application scenario, the registration process is performed first, and the N input includes the face photo and its ID identifier, and then the identification link is performed. Given a face photo as input, the output is an ID in the registration link or not in the database. Figure 19.6 represents the face recognition flow, which consists of image acquisition, pre-processing, face feature extraction, and classification modules.

Despite the advantages of the face recognition system, the use of deceptive facial evidence to deceive the system by some unauthorized attackers and intruders poses significant challenges to biometric systems. Attackers can find ways to spoof the face data in biometric systems. People who have easy access to facial images or facial video social networks may inhale intruders to exploit facial spoofing in biometric systems.

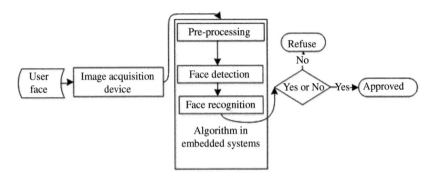

Figure 19.6   Face recognition pipeline

Facial spoofing is a serious threat to the security of face recognition systems. Facial spoofing is a means by which an illegal person attempts to spoof a facial biometric system by accessing a user's facial image, video, or mask on the face of the camera to gain access to secure resources. Face spoofing can also be divided into two groups: two-dimensional (2D) face spoofing and three-dimensional (3D) face spoofing. 2D facial spoofing can print photo attacks and replay video attacks. This type of fraud is easy to use and low cost. Therefore, this method is more common, and our usual anti-spoofing method is also aimed at this type of attack. On the other hand, 3D facial spoofing may be a 3D mask attack and a plastic surgery attack. This method requires a high cost, but the anti-spoofing method for this case is also very challenging. Figure 19.7 represents the spoofing attacks on face recognition module [9].

Many detection techniques have been proposed to detect frame duplication attacks, but most of these detection techniques are performed on previously stored media files that can be delayed from event occurrence. To eliminate the delay caused, from the moment of attack to detection, we propose an online frame forgery detection technique using electrical network frequency as a reference authentication signal. An anti-spoofing module is also proposed in the face recognition system to detect the face spoofing attacks discussed.

19.3   Surveillance authentication system using ENF signature

Authentication at the edge is an integral part for a secure networked interconnected grid like smart surveillance system. In this section, we introduce electric network frequency (ENF) signals and its applications in authenticating or detecting false frame forgery attacks [10].

19.3.1   ENF signal presence and applications

The ENF is an instantaneous frequency in power distribution networks, which varies across its nominal frequency 50/60 Hz based on the power supply demand. The

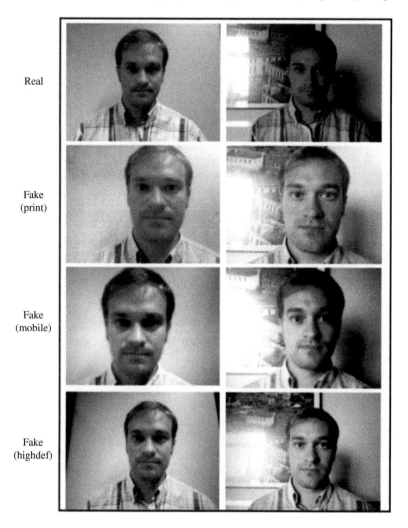

Figure 19.7   2D and 3D face spoofing attacks

fluctuations in ENF are typically very close to the nominal frequency; in the United States, the fluctuation range is $[-0.02, 0.02]$, whereas in Asian and European countries the fluctuation varies in the order of $[-0.05, 0.03)$ from its nominal value. Multimedia recordings were found to have traces of ENF fluctuations depending on the type of source. In case of audio recording for a device directly connected to the power grid, the ENF is embedded due to electromagnetic interference. For a battery-powered audio recording device, the source of ENF is the audible hum generated by electrical devices connected to power grid [11,12]. Video recordings also carry ENF instantaneous signatures through varying light intensity, where the source of light is connected to the

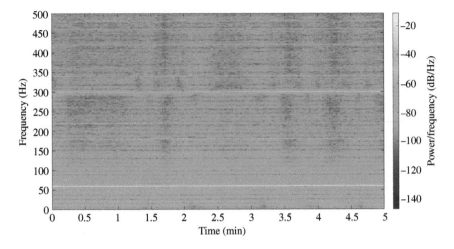

Figure 19.8   Spectrogram of a power recording

power grid, and ENF is stored in the form of illumination frequency. Figure 19.8 represents the spectrogram of an audio recording of the power grid with 1,000 Hz sampling frequency; the presence of ENF is confirmed through this along with its harmonics.

ENF signal was first introduced in multimedia forensic to authenticate media recordings as proof for legal jurisdiction to verify that the evidence has not tampered [13]. Many extraction algorithms have been introduced to extract ENF from media recordings [14–17], which as a result detected forgeries as false evidences. Applications of ENF signal include geographical location estimation, multimedia synchronization, and time-stamp verification. These studies show the usefulness of ENF, so we adopted this technique to extract ENF signals from our surveillance recording. Due to its instantaneous behavior of fluctuations which is similar everywhere in a power grid, this makes the forgery of ENF signal even harder. Figure 19.9 represents the ENF signal extracted from an adjacent building in one surveillance grid, and it can be seen that the fluctuations in the ENF signal are similar. We used the measure of correlation coefficient to judge the similarity between two signals, which varies from 0 to 1, where 1 is the highest similarity factor.

ENF is also present in video recordings, and algorithms have been proposed to extract ENF signal using illumination frequency [14,18,19] using rolling shutter technique, super-pixel-based approach, or pixel-averaging technique. The selection of the algorithm depends on the type of sensor using complimentary metal-oxide-semiconductor (CMOS) or charge-coupled device (CCD).

For our application in surveillance grid at the edge, the video frame rate is lower compared to audio sampling frequency violating Nyquist criterion for proper signal extraction. The lower frame rate problem can be overcome using the rolling shutter technique where each row of the frame is exposed to light at different time

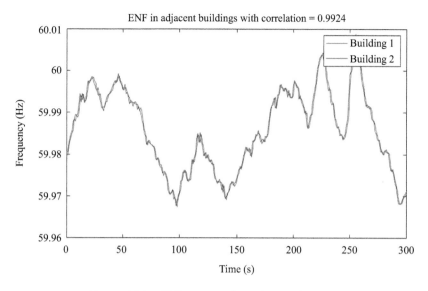

Figure 19.9 ENF captured in adjacent building

instant, hence increasing the samples. However, the idle period associated with each camera manufacturer varies, and it makes it difficult to standardize the algorithm to all cameras in the surveillance grid. The edge-processing power is also limited to process high-resolution video frame. Instead, a super-pixel-based technique can be used to select the part of the frame where ENF signal is strong using signal-to-noise ratio (SNR). In this section, we have discussed audio-based ENF extraction and authentication algorithm.

19.3.2 Applied model

For a reliable authentication of the recording made, a correlation coefficient threshold-based method is introduced using a standard reference database of ENF and extracted ENF from the multimedia recording at real time. Any mismatch between the two signals can help identify inserted or deleted media recording. To reduce the configuration and processing complexity, we opt to use audio recording as the source compared to light-based video recordings.

ENF traces occur around the nominal frequency range 50/60 Hz as $f_{ENF} = f_o + f_\Delta$, where f_o is the nominal frequency and f_Δ is the instantaneous frequency fluctuations from the nominal value. The nominal frequency in audio recording usually varies based on the type of microphone used, but in most cases it is 120 Hz.

For the spectrogram calculation of the recorded signal, we used a frame size of 1 s and nFFT = 8,192, which gives a frequency resolution of 0.122 Hz for a signal with a sampling rate of 1,000 Hz. The length of recorded signal used for each instance is 6 s. The power spectral density (PSD) of the ENF carrying signal is used to extract certain spectral bands $s(f)$, where the PSD $S(\omega)$ is computed from the FFT of the signal and $f \in k[f_o - f_v, f_o + f_v]$. f_v is the variation width of the ENF signal, f_o is the nominal frequency, and k represents the harmonic frequency band. The PSD $S_{N_{XX}}(f)$ is

$$S_{N_{XX}}(f) = \frac{1}{N}|X_N(f)|^2$$

where $X_N(f)$ is the Fourier transform of the signal

$$X_N(f) = \sum_{n=-\infty}^{\infty} x_n e^{-j\omega nT}$$

where $w = 2\pi f$, T is the period of the signal duration, and n is the number of samples $1 \le n \le N$. Sampling at discrete times $x_n = x(n\Delta t)$ for a period $T = N\Delta t$, the PSD is

$$\overline{S}_{XX}(\omega) = \frac{(\Delta t)^2}{T} \left| \sum_{n=1}^{N} x_n e^{-j\omega n \Delta t} \right|^2$$

The spectral band obtained gives the instantaneous frequency for each frame window estimated by the maximum value in each power density vector for that time instant. Quadratic interpolation is used to obtain its dominant frequency from the maximum value in each vector. In quadratic interpolation of the spectral peak, the peak location is given as

$$\Delta = \frac{1}{2} * \frac{\alpha - \gamma}{\alpha - 2*\beta + \gamma}$$

where α is the previous bin of the max spectral bin, β is the max spectral peak, and γ is the next bin. If k^* is the bin number of the largest spectral sample at the peak, where $1 \le k^* \le K$ for K bins, then $k^* + \Delta$ is the interpolated peak location of the bins and the final interpolated frequency estimate is

$$f_\Delta = (k^* + \Delta)\frac{f_s}{N}$$

here f_s is the sampling frequency and N is the number of FFT bins used. The instantaneous frequency estimate of the ENF signal is then given as $f_{ENF} = f_o + f_\Delta$.

19.3.3   Detecting malicious frame injection attacks

Obtaining the power recordings and the audio recording simultaneously, a correlation factor is used to test the similarity between two signals. The ENF signal from power P_{ENF} and audio A_{ENF} is given as

$$\rho(l) = \frac{\sum_{n=1}^{N} [f_{P_{ENF}}(n) - \mu_{P_{ENF}}][f_{A_{ENF}}(n-l) - \mu_{A_{ENF}}]}{var(P_{ENF}) * var(A_{ENF})}$$

where $f_{P_{ENF}}$ and $f_{A_{ENF}}$ are the frequency estimation of the ENF signal from power and audio recordings, respectively. μ and var are the mean and variance of the frequency signal. l is the lag between the two signals. Even though the recordings are made at the same time; due to the oscillator error between the two devices, the signals

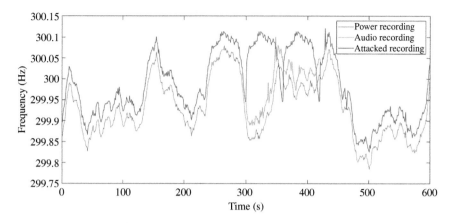

Figure 19.10   ENF estimated from power, audio, and attacked audio recording

are not in sync. The lag is used to match the signals and a threshold decides the similarity between the two signals. If the difference between the reference and the current detection goes beyond a certain threshold, the system considers that a false frame injection attack is detected.

Figure 19.10 represents the ENF signals extracted from the power recording and the audio recording. We simultaneously collected original audio recording to represent the change in ENF signal. The ENF is captured from fifth harmonic due to strong SNR computed using ENF PSD. This shows that ENF can be used to detect any tampering; to detect the signal inconsistency, a sliding window-based approach is adopted. We tested various window sizes and step sizes. Figure 19.11 represents the correlation coefficient between power-attacked recording and power-original recording. The window size used is 60 s, which means an initial delay of 60 s is required to start the signal comparison. The step size is 5 s, which means the signals are compared every 5 s, and any drop-in correlation can be detected in 5 s. The threshold for correlation used is 0.8. It is clear that the drop-in correlation coefficient represents a mismatch in the reference power ENF and extracted ENF, detecting a forgery attack. For a more detailed analysis and test bed setup, readers are encouraged for further reading [8,10].

19.3.4   Face anti-spoofing module for face recognition

Face spoofing is a means by which an illegitimate person tries to spoof a biometric face system by presenting a face image, video, or a face mask of a legitimate user at the face of a camera to gain access to the secured resources.

In the face recognition system, a face is accepted at the sensor level, and then it is passed to the face anti-spoofing module. If the input face is found to be a real face, then it goes to the next phase of the system, or it exits if it is found to be a fake face. The objective of face anti-spoofing system is to protect the biometric face system

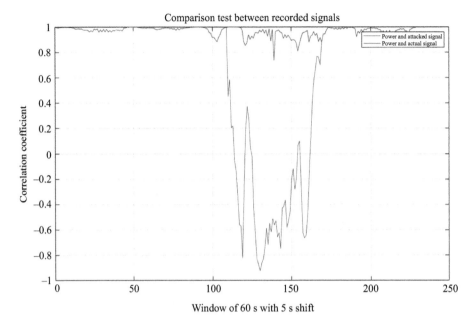

Figure 19.11   Correlation coefficient comparison

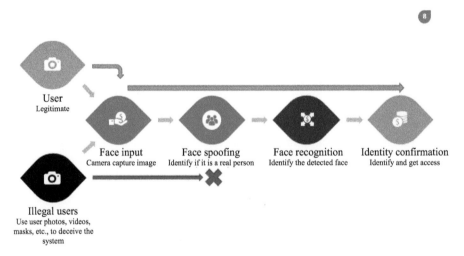

Figure 19.12   Face anti-spoofing module in face recognition pipeline

from unauthorized access. The position of the face anti-spoofing module in the face recognition system is as shown in Figure 19.12.

Face anti-spoofing is mainly divided into two categories: the image based and the living detection based. Image-based face anti-spoofing is a method of comparing the face image collected by the camera with the database face image by using the inherent features of the image, such as image quality or image texture. Face anti-spoofing-based living detection can be categorized in two groups:

- *Active living face detection*: The user is required to randomly perform blinking, left-turning, and right-turning movements, and complete the required action within the specified time to pass the face anti-spoofing module.
- *Silent living face detection*: Detecting a person using facial structure extracted from a single frame (or multi-frame fusion) image.

With the addition of anti-spoofing module to the existing surveillance system, attacks on face recognition module can be minimized. Beginning with the advantages of smart surveillance system in increasing the security of infrastructure and the simultaneous increase in attacks on the surveillance system to compromise a highly reliable system, we have introduced an authentication system to detect frame forgery attacks and addition of face anti-spoofing module. These attacks could be minimized with a more distributed computing paradigm compared to centralized computing. Further, we discuss the implementation of the surveillance system network grid in a blockchain-enabled data access control (AC) system to prevent unauthorized access to the surveillance feed.

19.4   Blockchain-enabled data AC

Edge/fog computing has been recognized as a promising approach to address new requirements incurred by the smart surveillance networks, such as scalability, heterogeneity, and flexibility. Migrating computational tasks and intelligence from the centralized cloud server to the distributed edge of network allows smart things to perform edge computing-driven intelligence locally. However, highly connected smart Internet of things (IoT) devices with heterogeneous platforms and insufficient security enforcement incur more concerns on security and privacy. Therefore, a data AC mechanism is necessary to protect the data shared among distributed computing nodes. Owing to key features, such as decentralization, anonymity, and automation, the blockchain and smart contract provide a promising solution to provide manageable and efficient security mechanism to meet the requirements raised by fog/edge computing systems.

19.4.1   Blockchain and smart contract

As a fundamental technology of Bitcoin [20], *blockchain* initially was used to promote a new cryptocurrency that performs commercial transactions among independent entities without relying on a centralized authority, like banks or government agencies. Essentially, the blockchain is a public ledger based on consensus rules to provide a verifiable, append-only chained data structure of transactions. Thanks to the decentralized architecture that does not rely on a centralized authority, blockchain allows the data to be stored and updated distributively. The transactions are approved by miners and recorded in the time-stamped blocks, where each block is identified by a cryptographic hash and chained to preceding blocks in a chronological order.

In a blockchain network, a *consensus mechanism* is enforced on a large amount of distributed nodes called miners to maintain the sanctity of the data recorded on the blocks. Thanks to the "trustless" proof mechanism running on miners across the network, users can trust the system of the public ledger stored worldwide on many different decentralized nodes maintained by "miner-accountants," as opposed to having to establish and maintain trust with a transaction counter-party or a third-party intermediary [21]. Thus, blockchain is an ideal decentralized architecture to ensure distributed transactions among all participants in a trustless environment, like edge-based IoT networks.

Emerging from the intelligent property, a *smart contract* allows users to achieve agreements among parties through a blockchain network. By using cryptographic and security mechanisms, a smart contract combines protocols with user interfaces to formalize and secure relationships over computer networks [22]. A smart contract includes a collection of predefined instructions and data that have been saved at a specific address of blockchain as a Merkle hash tree, which is a constructed bottom-to-up binary tree data structure. Through exposing public functions or application binary interfaces (ABIs), a smart contract interacts with users to offer the predefined business logic or contract agreement.

The blockchain- and smart contract-enabled security mechanism for applications has been a hot topic, and some efforts have been reported recently in the field of, for example, smart surveillance system [23–25], social credit system [26], space situation awareness [27], biomedical imaging data processing [28], identification authentication [29] and AC [30,31]. Blockchain and smart contract together are promising to provide a solution to enable a secured data sharing and access authorization in decentralized IoT systems.

19.4.2 A blockchain-enabled decentralized data AC mechanism

To address above security issues in Smart Public Safety (SPS) system, blockchain is a very promising solution to provide a decentralized trust network and data sharing service, where data and its history are reliable, immutable, and auditable. The virtualization technology, like virtual machines (VMs) or containers, is an independent platform and could provide resource abstraction and isolation features; they are ideal for system architecture design to address the heterogeneity challenge in IoT-based SPS system. Compared to VMs, containers are more lightweight and flexible with OS-level isolation, so that is an ideal selection for resource-limited edge computing.

Inspired by the blockchain and container technologies, a blockchain-enabled data accessing control mechanism, called BlendDAC, is proposed as a microservice-based architecture. It's aimed to enable a scalable, flexible, and lightweight data sharing and AC services that are fit in the IoT-based smart surveillance system. Figure 19.13 illustrates the architecture of BlendDAC. Following the divide-and-conquer principle, the BlendDAC is divided into two main components: permissioned blockchain network and blockchain-enabled security services. A permissioned blockchain infrastructure

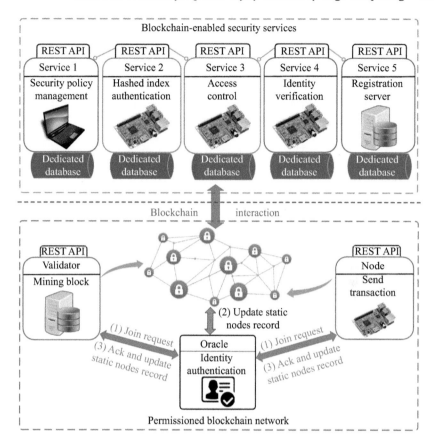

Figure 19.13   Illustration of BlendDAC architecture

running on a decentralized peer-to-peer network is managed by administrators, and it could provide a reliable, traceable, and immutable distributed ledger for trusted data exchanges and smart contract-based DApps in SPS system. Utilizing the containerized microservices architecture, the security functions of BlendDAC system are decoupled into multiple microservices and deployed on distributed computing hosts. Those decentralized microservices work as a blockchain-enabled services pool to offer a scalable, flexible, and lightweight security and privacy protection mechanism for public safety system.

19.4.2.1   Permissioned blockchain network

The permissioned blockchain network requires that only registered entities are authorized access to the network, so that they can interact with the blockchain and perform blockchain-based services, such as mining block, sending transactions, and deploying smart contracts. The bottom of Figure 19.13 shows the identity authentication process to enroll a new participant in the permissioned blockchain network. The administrator of SPS system could work as an oracle, and maintains a global identity profile and authorization policies for the permissioned blockchain network management. Given computation capacity of host devices and management policy, all participants are categorized as validator (miner) or node (non-miner). The validators are able to cooperatively executing consensus algorithm to maintain the integrity and immutability of distributed ledger. While nodes are only capable of launching transactions to synchronize data with the blockchain.

Unlike a centralized database, the oracle just manages the entities who want to join the permissioned blockchain network rather than control the data source. For participants, validators could add data via consensus protocols and nodes could access data in distributed ledger, but they all cannot change the network configuration. Compared to a public blockchain network that suffers from performance and security issues, such as low throughput, poor privacy, and lack of governance, the permissioned blockchain can enforce a more efficient but lightweight consensus mechanism to improve the transaction rate and data storage capacity. Furthermore, through limiting participants with clearly defined privacy policies, the sensitive data could be only visible to the authorized participants but not to the public. Therefore, the permissioned blockchain network also enables a more strict privacy policy than a public blockchain network does.

19.4.2.2 Security policy service

The blockchain-enabled security services layer, as shown in upper part of Figure 19.13, acts as a fundamental microservices-oriented infrastructure to support security mechanism for SPS system. Those microservices-based providers work as nodes in permissioned blockchain network, and interact with smart contracts to provided decentralized security functions. The key elements and operations are described in the following:

- *Identity authentication*: Since each account uniquely indexed by its address derives from his/her own public key, a blockchain account address is ideal for identity authentication that is needed by other security services, such as hashed index recording and AC. Through exposing public RESTful API, identity authentication service could serve other service providers who apply for referring identity verification results. Once an authentication service request is received, the identity authentication decision-making process queries the requester identity profile from the registration service, and returns the identity verification results according to the predefined policies.
- *Security management*: The security management is mainly responsible for data and security policy, which are associated with smart contracts to support hashed index authentication and the AC strategies. After the smart contracts have been deployed successfully on the blockchain network, they become visible to the entire network owing to the transparency and publicity properties of the blockchain protocol.
- *Hashed index authentication*: This service uses data integrity technologies to ensure data access at the same time avoid storing a huge amount of data in the

blockchain. To avoid saving large data on blockchain and improve transaction rate, only hashed index values of feature data files are saved on blockchain. Therefore, the feature data owners (edge devices) transcode hashed index recording and verification functions as smart contracts and deploy them on blockchain. This microservice provides the dynamic data synchronization and efficient verification through simply called ABIs of smart contract.

- *Access control*: The data owners could transcode AC models and policies into a smart contract-based AC microservice. The AC microservices allow those service providers to control their data and resource without relying on a centralized third-party authority, and it provides a decentralized AC solution to the SPS system.

Though implementing each security model or policy as a single service provider that works independently from each other, the security policy services cluster could address scalability and heterogeneity in IoT-based smart surveillance systems by offering more flexible, interoperable, and lightweight security solutions. After discussing the applicability of the blockchain architecture in the smart surveillance network, we present a case study using microservices to handle the raw processing data in a blockchain architecture.

19.5 Secure smart surveillance as microservices in blockchain architecture: case study

To address the challenges in a smart surveillance system running on cloud-based architecture, we introduced the fog-edge computing paradigm as a promising approach that migrates computing tasks to the edge of the network. The edge computing enables the smart surveillance to meet the delay-sensitive, mission-critical requirements by locally processing raw video streams and extracting, recognizing, and labeling useful features [24]. To support the challenges in building large-scale, distributed smart applications, we adopted a microservices architecture. The microservice architecture divides an application into multiple atomic services where each service performs only one task and requires lightweight communication with other services. For the integration of smart decision-making algorithm, authentication system with ENF, and anti-face spoofing module with blockchain architecture, we used microservices to deploy each algorithm [23].

Secure communication between the microservices is also an essential requirement to avoid network-based intrusion or sniffing attacks. Integrating a hybrid encryption mechanism leveraging both the symmetric and asymmetric key encryption reduces the risk of network sniffing. Finally, a blockchain-enabled index authentication scheme is integrated to enhance the security of smart surveillance system. Figure 19.14 represents the overall system architecture introduced. Microservices in smart surveillance like facial recognition, license plate recognition, and behavior/gesture analysis process of video feed after the ENF-based authentication microservice approve the authenticity (see Figure 19.15). Any malicious frame injected into the video stream is

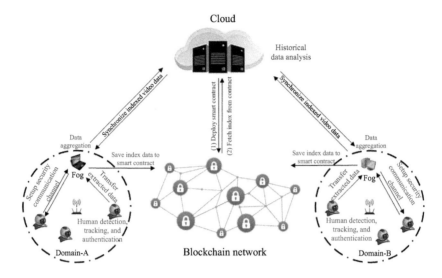

Figure 19.14   Illustration of system architecture

detected prior to running any decision-making algorithm. Authenticating the visual feed is the first step in processing the raw footage.

After the authentication of the live surveillance feed, the microservices like Facial recognition or Behavioral Analysis algorithm are responsible for extracting features from the subject of interest. This reduces the payload to transfer and to reduce the redundant data from processing the live feed. Storage of raw footage is also a challenging issue, so extracting and storing features from the subject of interest reduces both processing load and network traffic to avoid congestion, along with increased storage efficiency.

Figure 19.16 represents a sample feature set collected from subject moving in the frame. This also leaves room for additional features to be concatenated in the future if required. A hash of the feature set is calculated and stored in the blockchain network, so any tampering to the stored footage would have a mismatch with the feature set in the blockchain. Tampering a blockchain or gaining full access to blockchain is very difficult due to its distributed database network protected by smart contracts.

To evaluate the performance of the blockchain-enabled security mechanism, a service access experiment is carried out on a physical network environment which includes Raspberry Pis (edge) and desktops (fog). The general cost incurred by the proposed scheme both on the edge and fog device is measured in terms of processing time and network communication delay, and 50 test runs have been conducted based on the proposed test scenario, where the client sends a data query request to server side for an access permission.

The computational overhead is evaluated according to execution time of running data integrity microservices on both edge and fog sides. Since the fog nodes have more computation capacity than the edge nodes do, while the execution time of querying

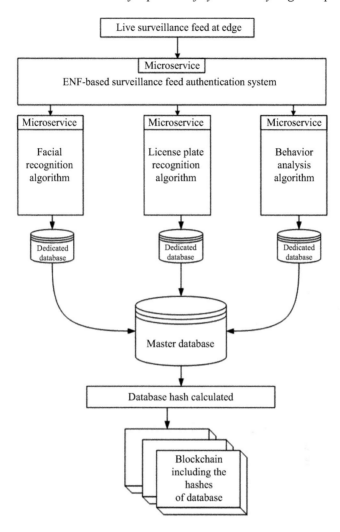

Figure 19.15   Interconnected microservices and surveillance feed processing

```
'2018-12-10 12:07:06.004615':  10    595    1    (273, 249)    West        2.02484567313
'2018-12-10 12:07:06.004615':  10    596    1    (254, 254)    South-West  3.98497176903
'2018-12-10 12:07:06.004615':  10    597    1    (244, 255)    South-West  4.97292670366
'2018-12-10 12:07:06.004615':  10    598    1    (230, 255)    South-West  6.33482438588
'2018-12-10 12:07:06.004615':  10    599    1    (214, 254)    South-West  7.89176786278
'2018-12-10 12:07:06.004615':  10    600    1    (205, 254)    West        6.81835757349
```

Figure 19.16   Feature set extracted in form of a library that has the time of detection as key, camera ID, frame sequence, number of people detected, object's current position, direction, and speed (pixel/second)

hashed index token on Raspberry Pi is about 56.4 ms, the same operation takes only 6.9 ms on the desktop.

For network latency evaluation, we compare the execution time of the AC service and a benchmark without any AC enforcement. At the Raspberry Pi, the AC service request takes on average 122.2 ms for fetching requested data versus service request without AC takes on average 28.5 ms. At the desktop, the benchmark without AC enforcement takes an average 20.4 ms for fetching requested data versus that the AC service request consumes on average 31.3 ms.

19.6   Discussion

For human detection and tracking, with the introduction of new models and faster processing boards, we hope to achieve the real time of 30 FPS. On the other hand, in the decision-making process, we have a couple of things that are worthy of further investigation. Introduction of new deep learning models to predict human behavior can improve the gesture-based decision-making algorithm predictions.

Along with the improvement in the decision-making algorithms, the authentication system also needs more reliable input along with the audio feed. ENF artifacts are also embedded in video recordings as illumination frequency, and for indoor-based surveillance system, the camera feed has higher chances of the presence of light source in its recording. Developing a lightweight algorithm to extract ENF for authentication from video recording can reinforce the security of the surveillance feed.

Lastly, the blockchain-enabled security solution is built on PoW-based blockchain network which offers good node scalability. However, it is inevitable to introduce trade-off with poor performance, such as low transaction rate and high energy consumption. Although Byzantine Fault Tolerant (BFT) based blockchain improves throughput performance with small numbers of replicas, it has intuitively very limited scalability in a distributed environment with large volumes of participants. Also, the ever-increasing blockchain data imposes significant storage overhead on the blockchain client. To address scalability-performance trade-off issues in existing standard blockchain technologies, we propose to design a hybrid blockchain consensus protocol that provides security, scalable, efficient, and lightweight distributed ledger for IoT systems.

19.7   Conclusion

With the evolution of the smart surveillance system, the reliability on the system has exponentially increased. The growing dependence resulted in creating a potential target for perpetrators and hijacking the visual feed for malicious benefits. The visual layer attacks on the surveillance system where the decision-making process relies on the authenticity of video feed obtained can be a potential threat to the safety and security of the infrastructure. A fingerprint-based authentication system using electrical network frequency is applied to detect any maliciously injected frames and raise the alarm.

To address issues in traditional security solutions relying on centralized third-party authority, a blockchain-enabled decentralized security services framework is proposed, and it provides a secure data sharing and AC mechanism for heterogeneous, distributed smart surveillance system. Leveraging the fine-granularity and loose-coupling features of the microservices architecture, the security functionalities are decoupled into multiple containerized microservices that are computationally affordable to each individual device. The brief experimental results validated that the blockchain-enabled microservices solution is able to efficiently and effectively enforce security in a distributed IoT system.

References

[1]   Li H, Ota K, and Dong M. Learning IoT in edge: Deep learning for the Internet of Things with edge computing. IEEE Network. 2018;32(1):96–101.

[2]   Kiani Galoogahi H, Fagg A, Huang C, Ramanan D, and Lucey S. Need for speed: A benchmark for higher frame rate object tracking. In: Proceedings of the IEEE International Conference on Computer Vision; 2017. pp. 1125–1134.

[3]   Henriques JF, Caseiro R, Martins P, and Batista J. High-speed tracking with kernelized correlation filters. IEEE Transactions on Pattern Analysis and Machine Intelligence. 2014;37(3):583–596.

[4]   Boettiger C. An introduction to Docker for reproducible research. ACM SIGOPS Operating Systems Review. 2015;49(1):71–79.

[5]   Bui T. Analysis of Docker security. arXiv preprint arXiv:150102967. 2015.

[6]   Nikouei SY, Chen Y, Song S, and Faughnan TR. Kerman: A hybrid lightweight tracking algorithm to enable smart surveillance as an edge service. In: 2019 16th IEEE Annual Consumer Communications & Networking Conference (CCNC). IEEE; 2019. pp. 1–6.

[7]   Zadeh LA. Fuzzy logic. Computer. 1988;21(4):83–93.

[8]   Nagothu D, Schwell J, Chen Y, Blasch E, and Zhu S. A study on smart online frame forging attacks against video surveillance system. In: Sensors and Systems for Space Applications XII. vol. 11017. International Society for Optics and Photonics; 2019. p. 110170L.

[9]   Galbally J, Marcel S, and Fierrez J. Biometric antispoofing methods: A survey in face recognition. IEEE Access. 2014;2:1530–1552.

[10] Nagothu D, Chen Y, Blasch E, Aved A, and Zhu S. Detecting malicious false frame injection attacks on surveillance systems at the edge using electrical network frequency signals. Sensors. 2019;19(11):2424.

[11] Fechner N, and Kirchner M. The humming hum: Background noise as a carrier of ENF artifacts in mobile device audio recordings. In: IT Security Incident Management & IT Forensics (IMF), 2014 Eighth International Conference on. IEEE; 2014. pp. 3–13.

[12] Chai J, Liu F, Yuan Z, Conners RW, and Liu Y. Source of ENF in battery-powered digital recordings. In: Audio Engineering Society Convention 135. Audio Engineering Society; 2013.

[13]   Grigoras C, Smith J, and Jenkins C. Advances in ENF database configuration for forensic authentication of digital media. In: Audio Engineering Society Convention 131. Audio Engineering Society; 2011.

[14]   Garg R, Varna AL, Hajj-Ahmad A, and Wu M. "Seeing" ENF: Power-signature-based timestamp for digital multimedia via optical sensing and signal processing. IEEE Transactions on Information Forensics and Security. 2013;8(9): 1417–1432.

[15]   Hajj-Ahmad A, Garg R, and Wu M. Spectrum combining for ENF signal estimation. IEEE Signal Processing Letters. 2013;20(9):885–888.

[16]   Ojowu O, Karlsson J, Li J, and Liu Y. ENF extraction from digital recordings using adaptive techniques and frequency tracking. IEEE Transactions on Information Forensics and Security. 2012;7(4):1330–1338.

[17]   Rodríguez DPN, Apolinário JA, and Biscainho LWP. Audio authenticity: Detecting ENF discontinuity with high precision phase analysis. IEEE Transactions on Information Forensics and Security. 2010;5(3):534–543.

[18]   Su H, Hajj-Ahmad A, Garg R, and Wu M. Exploiting rolling shutter for ENF signal extraction from video. In: Image Processing (ICIP), 2014 IEEE International Conference on. Citeseer; 2014. pp. 5367–5371.

[19]   Vatansever S, Dirik AE, and Memon N. Detecting the presence of ENF signal in digital videos: A superpixel-based approach. IEEE Signal Processing Letters. 2017;24(10):1463–1467.

[20]   Nakamoto S. Bitcoin: A peer-to-peer electronic cash system. 2008.

[21]   Swan M. Blockchain: Blueprint for a new economy. O'Reilly Media, Inc.; 2015.

[22]   Szabo N. Formalizing and securing relationships on public networks. First Monday. 1997;2(9):1–21.

[23]   Nagothu D, Xu R, Nikouei SY, and Chen YA. A microservice-enabled architecture for smart surveillance using blockchain technology. In: 2018 IEEE International Smart Cities Conference (ISC2). IEEE; 2018. p. 1–4.

[24]   Nikouei SY, Xu R, Nagothu D, *et al.* Real-time index authentication for event-oriented surveillance video query using blockchain. arXiv preprint arXiv:180706179. 2018.

[25]   Xu R, Nikouei SY, Chen Y, Blasch E, and Aved A. BlendMAS: A blockchain-enabled decentralized microservices architecture for smart public safety. In: 2019 IEEE International Conference on Blockchain (Blockchain). IEEE; 2019. p. 564–571.

[26]   Xu R, Lin X, Dong Q, and Chen Y. Constructing trustworthy and safe communities on a blockchain-enabled social credits system. In: Proceedings of the 15th EAI International Conference on Mobile and Ubiquitous Systems: Computing, Networking and Services. ACM; 2018. pp. 449–453.

[27]   Xu R, Chen Y, Blasch E, and Chen G. An exploration of blockchain enabled decentralized capability based access control strategy for space situation awareness. Optical Engineering. 2019; 58(4): 041609.

[28]   Xu R, Chen S, Yang L, Chen Y, and Chen G. Decentralized autonomous imaging data processing using blockchain. In: Multimodal Biomedical Imaging XIV. vol. 10871. International Society for Optics and Photonics; 2019. pp. 108710U.

[29]   Hammi MT, Hammi B, Bellot P, and Serhrouchni A. Bubbles of trust: A decentralized blockchain-based authentication system for IoT. Computers & Security. 2018;78:126–142.

[30]   Xu R, Chen Y, Blasch E, Chen G. and Blend CAC. BlendCAC: A blockchain-enabled decentralized capability-based access control for IoTs. In: The 2018 IEEE International Conference on Blockchain (Blockchain-2018). IEEE; 2018. pp. 1–8.

[31]   Xu R, Chen Y, Blasch E, Chen G. and Blend CAC. BlendCAC: A smart contract enabled decentralized capability-based access control mechanism for the IoT. Computers 2018;7(3):39. Access on: http://wwwmdpicom/2073-431X/7/3/39. 2018.

Index